The Bloomsbury
Companion to Kant

The *Bloomsbury Companions* series is a major series of single volume companions to key research fields in the humanities aimed at postgraduate students, scholars and libraries. Each companion offers a comprehensive reference resource giving an overview of key topics, research areas, new directions and a manageable guide to beginning or developing research in the field. A distinctive feature of the series is that each companion provides practical guidance on advanced study and research in the field, including research methods and subject-specific resources.

Aesthetics, edited by Anna Christina Ribeiro

Aristotle, edited by Claudia Baracchi

Continental Philosophy, edited by John Mullarkey and Beth Lord

Epistemology, edited by Andrew Cullison

Ethics, edited by Christian Miller

Existentialism, edited by Jack Reynolds, Felicity Joseph and Ashley Woodward

Hegel, edited by Allegra de Laurentiis and Jeffrey Edwards

Heidegger, edited by Francois Raffoul and Eric Sean Nelson

Hobbes, edited by S.A. Lloyd

Hume, edited by Alan Bailey and Dan O'Brien

Kant, edited by Gary Banham, Dennis Schulting and Nigel Hems

Leibniz, edited by Brandon Look

Locke, edited by S.-J. Savonius-Wroth, Paul Schuurman and Jonathan Walmsley

Metaphysics, edited by Robert W. Barnard and Neil A. Manson

Philosophy of Language, edited by Manuel Garcia-Carpintero and Max Kolbel

Philosophy of Mind, edited by James Garvey

Philosophy of Science, edited by Steven French and Juha Saatsi

Plato, edited by Gerald A. Press

Pragmatism, edited by Sami Pihlström

Philosophical Logic, edited by Leon Horsten and Richard Pettigrew

Socrates, edited by John Bussanich and Nicholas D. Smith

Spinoza, edited by Wiep van Bunge

THE BLOOMSBURY
COMPANION TO KANT

EDITED BY

Gary Banham[†]
Dennis Schulting
and Nigel Hems

B L O O M S B U R Y
LONDON · NEW DELHI · NEW YORK · SYDNEY

Bloomsbury Academic

An imprint of Bloomsbury Publishing Plc

50 Bedford Square	1385 Broadway
London	New York
WC1B 3DP	NY 10018
UK	USA

www.bloomsbury.com

Bloomsbury is a registered trade mark of Bloomsbury Publishing Plc

First published as The Continuum Companion to Kant 2012

British Library Cataloguing-in-Publication Data
A catalogue record for this book is available from the British Library.

ISBN: PB: 978-1-47258-678-0
ePDF: 978-1-47258-680-3
ePub: 978-1-47258-679-7

Library of Congress Cataloging-in-Publication Data
Continuum companion to Kant

The Bloomsbury companion to Kant / edited by Gary Banham,
Dennis Schulting and Nigel Hems.—Second edition.

pages cm

"First published as The Continuum Companion to Kant, 2012."
Includes bibliographical references.
ISBN 978-1-4725-8678-0 (paperback)

1. Kant, Immanuel, 1724–1804. I. Gary Banham, 1965–2013– editor.
II. Dennis Schulting, 1969–, editor. III. Nigel Hems, 1966–, editor. IV. Title.
B2798.C753 2015
193—dc23
2014033851

Typeset by Newgen Knowledge Works (P) Ltd., Chennai, India
Printed and bound in Great Britain

CONTENTS

CONTENTS

Aesthetic Judgment / Amphiboly / Analogy / Analogies of Experience /
Analysis / Anthropology / Anticipations of Perception / Antinomies / Appearance
/ Apperception (Self-Consciousness) / A Priori, A Posteriori / Art (Genius) /
Axioms of Intuition / Categorical Imperative (Moral Law) / Cosmopolitan(ism)
/ Critique / Deduction (Categories) / Dialectic / Duty, Duties / Enlightenment
/ Enthusiasm / Experience (Sensibility) / Form, Formal / Freedom / Geometry
/ Idea, Ideas / Identity / Imagination / Inner and Outer Sense / Interest /
Intuition / Judgment (Understanding) / Kingdom of Ends / Knowledge / Laws
(of Nature), Lawfulness / Logic (Concept, Thought, Syllogism) / Mathematics
/ Metaphysics / Method / Morality / Natural Science / Necessity / Object,
Objectivity / Paralogisms / Postulates of Empirical Thinking / Principle of

(Non-)Contradiction / Principle of Sufficient Reason / Proof / Proofs of the Existence of God / Psychology / Pure / Radical Evil / Reality (Objective Reality) / Reason / Refutation of Idealism / Regulative Principles / Religion (Highest Good) / Representation / Right / Schematism / Spontaneity / Sublime / Synthesis (Synthetic A Priori) / System / Teleology (Purposiveness, End) / Thing in Itself / Transcendental / Transcendental Aesthetic / Transcendental Ideal / Transcendental Idealism / Truth / Virtue, Virtues / Will (Choice)

PREFACE

There are few philosophers whose influence is more widely felt across the range of the subject in the contemporary world than is the case with Immanuel Kant (1724–1804). Despite the breadth of Kant's influence on contemporary philosophy, it can be extremely difficult to get a grip on the nature of Kant's own work. One of the central reasons why this can be so difficult is precisely because of the range of Kant's own philosophical contributions. To make a major impact on the understanding of metaphysics would be sufficient reason for a thinker to be regarded as a 'major' philosopher. But Kant's ethics are surely as central to debates in contemporary moral philosophy as the *Critique of Pure Reason* is in contemporary metaphysics and epistemology. Nor does Kant's importance end there since, as is widely recognized, the *Critique of Judgment* is foundational for the modern discipline of aesthetics (in addition to raising questions about teleology that have, if anything, gained in resonance in recent years). Finally, the comprehension of the status of scientific laws and the way science itself is philosophically understood are topics that often lead thinkers to read or re-read *The Metaphysical Foundations of Natural Science*. When these points are put together, it becomes evident that Kant' s influence is not only broad in range on contemporary philosophy but comprehending the nature of this influence is itself something that requires extended reflection and for such reflection to be effective, there is a need for guidebooks that clearly map all the central elements of Kant's philosophy.

It is the point of this *Companion* to fill this need, something that many guides to Kant's philosophy only partially do. In order to meet this requirement we have assembled a wideranging, international team that can together help general readers to find their way around both the specific parts of Kant's philosophy and the inter-relations between them. Whilst the work of each of us as editors of this volume has been considerable, the effect of the *Companion* would be without doubt that much less were it not for the many contributions we solicited and received. For the work provided here, we would like to thank Lucy Allais, Tom Bailey, Steven M. Bayne, Karin de Boer, Kees Jan Brons, John Callanan, Luigi Caranti, Howard Caygill, Martin Davies, Katerina Deligiorgi, Corey Dyck, Wolfgang Ertl, Richard Fincham, Samuel Fleischacker, Brett Fulkerson-Smith, Ido Geiger, Gregory Johnson, Johan de Jong, Christian Krijnen, Beth Lord, Michela Massimi, Giuseppe Motta, Ernst-Otto Onnasch, Christian Onof, Marcel Quarfood, Aviv Reiter, Yaron Senderowicz, Marco Sgarbi, Scott Stapleford, Rudi te Velde, Jacco Verburgt, Falk Wunderlich and Job Zinkstok.

PREFACE

Dennis Schulting also wants to thank both Daniel Lopatin of Oneohtrix Point Never and Mark McGuire for delivering the viscerally stirring goods in the form of their respective 'kosmische' music albums *Rifts* and *A Young Person's Guide to Mark McGuire*, which alongside copious amounts of Bruckner he played on repeat whilst copy-editing this *Companion*.

The Editors
Gary Banham
Dennis Schulting
Nigel Hems

PREFACE TO THE SECOND EDITION

For this paperback edition, revisions were carried out and several more entries were added. In the Section 'Philosophical and Historical Context' there is now also an essay on Herder, an important erstwhile student and later tough opponent of Kant, and an article on School Philosophy, which provides more insight into the philosophical background of Kant's thought. The lemma on Rousseau, in the Section 'Sources and Influences', has been rewritten and expanded. In the Section 'Key Themes and Topics', four more entries on 'Appearance', 'Intuition', 'Postulates of Empirical Thought in General', and 'Thing in Itself' have been added, which, although dealt with in other entries in the first edition, merited a separate treatment. In the Section 'Reception and Influence', an essay on Schopenhauer's interpretation of Kant adds to the topic of the reception of Kant's work in post-Kantian philosophy. Lastly, the bibliography has been improved and updated with the newest literature. I am very pleased that Robert Clewis, Wolfgang Ertl, Christian Onof, Sandra Shapshay and John Zammito have contributed to the new edition of the Companion.

Sadly, slightly over a year after the publication of the first edition of the Companion, Gary Banham, the originator of the project for this Companion, died suddenly when on holiday in Rome in March 2013. This expanded edition is dedicated to his memory. The Section 'Key Works', which was singlehandedly written by Gary, is left largely unchanged.

The Editor
Dennis Schulting

LIST OF ABBREVIATIONS
OF KANT'S WORKS

Throughout the Companion the following abbreviations are used followed by the page numbers only of the respective volume in the Academic edition of Kant's work (AA) (*Kant's gesammelte Schriften*, Berlin: de Gruyter, 1900–). So, for example, a reference to the *Critique of Judgment*, say, is provided thus: **CJ** 284. The *Reflexionen* are cited by means of the abbreviation **Refl** followed by the *Akademie* Adickes number.

For the first *Critique* the standard way of referring to the original pagination is adhered to, by means of the A/B citation, where A stands for the first or so-called A-edition, published in 1781, and B for the second or B-edition, published in 1787.

Quotations are in almost all cases from *The Cambridge Edition of the Works of Immanuel Kant* (Cambridge: Cambridge University Press, 1992ff.), which contains English translations of almost all of Kant's published works and many of the lectures, correspondence, unpublished manuscripts and so-called Reflections.

Where available, for each specific work in translation the volume number of *The Cambridge Edition* (CE) is given after the AA volume number according to the following list of volumes already published:

1. *Theoretical Philosophy 1755–1770*
2. *Critique of Pure Reason*
3. *Theoretical Philosophy after 1781*
4. *Practical Philosophy*
5. *Critique of the Power of Judgment*
6. *Religion and Rational Theology*
7. *Anthropology, History, and Education*
9. *Lectures on Logic*
10. *Lectures on Metaphysics*
11. *Lectures on Ethics*
12. *Opus postumum*
13. *Notes and Fragments*
14. *Correspondence*
15. *Natural Science*
16. *Lectures on Anthropology*

LIST OF ABBREVIATIONS OF KANT'S WORKS

A   = *Critique of Pure Reason*, A-edition (CE 2)
AL   = *M. Immanuel Kant's Announcement of the programme of his Lectures for the winter semester 1765–1766* (AA 2; CE 1)
Anthr   = *Anthropology from a pragmatic point of view* (AA 7; CE 7)
B   = *Critique of Pure Reason*, B-edition (CE 2)
CBH   = *Conjectural Beginning of human History* (AA 8; CE 7)
CF   = *Conflict of the Faculties* (AA 7; CE 6)
CJ   = *Critique of (the power of) Judgment* (AA 5; CE 5)
Corr-I/II/III = Correspondence (AA 10-13; CE 14)
CPrR   = *Critique of Practical Reason* (AA 5; CE 4)
Disc   = *On a Discovery whereby any new critique of pure reason is to be made superfluous by an older one* (AA 8; CE 3)
DR   = *Of the Different Races of human beings* (AA 2; CE 7)
DRTBaum   = *Danziger Rationaltheologie Baumbach* (Mrongovius) (AA 28)
DS   = *Concerning the ultimate ground of the differentiation of Directions in Space* (AA 2; CE 1)
DSS   = *Dreams of a Spirit-Seer elucidated by dreams of metaphysics* (AA 2, CE 1)
E   = *What is Enlightenment?* (AA 8; CE 4)
EAR   = *Untersuchung der Frage ob die Erde in ihrer Umdrehung um die Achse [. . .] einige Veränderung seit den ersten Zeiten ihres Ursprungs erlitten habe* [Earth's Axial Rotation] (AA 1; CE 15)
EMH   = *Essay on the Maladies of the Head* (AA 2; CE 7)
End   = *The End of all things* (AA 8; CE 6)
EPh   = *Essays regarding the Philantropinum* (AA 2; CE 7)
F   = *Succinct exposition of some meditations on Fire* (AA 1; CE 15)
FI   = *Critique of (the power of) judgment, First Introduction* (AA 20; CE 5)
FS   = *The False Subtlety of the four syllogistic figures* (AA 2; CE 1)
G   = *Groundwork of metaphysics of morals* (AA 4; CE 4)
HR   = *Determination of the concept of a Human Race* (AA 8; CE 7)
ID   = *On the form and principles of the sensible and the intelligible world* [Inaugural Dissertation] (AA 2; CE 1)
Inq   = *Inquiry concerning the distinctness of the principles of natural theology and morality* (AA 2; CE 1)
JL   = Jäsche Logic (AA 9; CE 9)
LA   = Lectures on Anthropology (AA 25; CE 16)
LE   = Lectures on Ethics (AA 27; CE 11)
LE-M   = Lectures on Ethics; Mrongovius (AA 29; CE 11)
LenFr   = Leningrad Fragment I 'Vom inneren Sinn', in R. Brandt & W. Stark (eds), *Kant-Forschungen*, Bd. 1 (Hamburg: Meiner, 1987), pp. 18–27 (CE 13)
LF   = *Thoughts on the true estimation of Living Forces* (AA 1; CE 15)
LL   = Lectures on Logic (AA 24; CE 9)
LM   = Lectures on Metaphysics (AA 28; CE 10)
LM-M/V   = Lectures on Metaphysics; Mrongovius/Vigilantius (AA 29; CE 10)

LP	= Lectures on Pedagogy (AA 9; CE 7)
LPöl	= Lectures on the Philosophical Doctrine of Religion; Pölitz (AA 28; CE 6)
MFNS	= *Metaphysical Foundations of Natural Science* (AA 4; CE 3)
MM	= *Metaphysics of Morals* (AA 6; CE 4)
MR	= *Neuer Lehrbegriff der Bewegung und Ruhe* [Motion and Rest] (AA 2; CE 15)
MT	= *On the Miscarriage of philosophical trials in Theodicy* (AA 8; CE 6)
ND	= *A new elucidation of the first principles of metaphysical cognition* [Nova Dilucidatio] (AA 1; CE 1)
NH	= *Universal Natural History and theory of the heavens* (AA 1; CE 15)
NM	= *Attempt to introduce the concept of Negative Magnitudes into philosophy* (AA 2; CE 1)
Obs	= *Observations on the feeling of the beautiful and sublime* (AA 2; CE 7)
Obs-R	= Remarks on *Observations on the feeling of the beautiful and sublime* (AA 20; CE 13)
OP-I/II	= *Opus postumum* (AA 21-22; CE 12)
OPD	= *The Only Possible argument in support of a Demonstration of the existence of God* (AA 2; CE 1)
Opt	= *An attempt at some reflections on Optimism* (AA 2; CE 1)
OT	= *What does it mean to Orient oneself in Thinking?* (AA 8; CE 6)
P	= *Prolegomena to any future metaphysics* (AA 4; CE 3)
PE	= *What real progress has metaphysics made in Germany since the time of Leibniz and Wolff?* [Prize Essay] (AA 20; CE 3)
PG	= *Physical Geography* (AA 9; CE 15)
PhM	= *Physical Monadology* (AA 1; CE 1)
PP	= *Toward Perpetual Peace* (AA 8; CE 4)
PTS	= *On a recently Prominent Tone of Superiority in philosophy* (AA 8; CE 3)
R	= *Religion within the boundaries of mere reason* (AA 6; CE 6)
Refl	= Reflections (*Reflexionen*) (AA 14-19; CE 13)
SRL	= *On a Supposed Right to Lie from philanthropy* (AA 8; CE 4)
TP	= *On the common saying: that may be correct in Theory, but it is of no use in Practice* (AA 8; CE 4)
UH	= *Idea for a Universal History with a cosmopolitan aim* (AA 8; CE 7)
UTP	= *On the Use of Teleological Principles* (AA 8; CE 7)

LIST OF CONTRIBUTORS

Professor Dr Lucy Allais
University of California San Diego,
USA / Wits University, South Africa

Dr Tom Bailey
John Cabot University
Italy

Dr Gary Banham[†]
Manchester
UK

Dr Steven Bayne
Fairfield University
USA

Professor Dr Karin de Boer
Leuven University
Belgium

Dr Kees Jan Brons
University of Amsterdam
The Netherlands

Dr John Callanan
King's College London
UK

Dr Luigi Caranti
University of Catania
Italy

Professor Dr Howard Caygill
Kingston University
UK

Dr Robert Clewis
Gwynedd-Mercy University
USA

Martin Davies
University of Leicester
UK

Dr Katerina Deligiorgi
University of Sussex
UK

Dr Corey Dyck
University of Western Ontario
Canada

Professor Dr Wolfgang Ertl
Keio University
Japan

Dr Richard Fincham
The American University in Cairo
Egypt

Professor Dr Samuel Fleischacker
University of Illinois at Chicago
USA

Dr Brett Fulkerson-Smith
Harper College
USA

Dr Ido Geiger
Ben-Gurion University
Israel

LIST OF CONTRIBUTORS

Dr Nigel Hems
Manchester Metropolitan University
UK

Dr Gregory Johnson
San Francisco
USA

Johan de Jong
University of Amsterdam
The Netherlands

Dr Christian Krijnen
VU University Amsterdam
The Netherlands

Dr Beth Lord
University of Aberdeen
UK

Dr Michela Massimi
University of Edinburgh
UK

Dr Giuseppe Motta
University of Graz
Austria

Dr Ernst-Otto Onnasch
University of Utrecht
The Netherlands

Dr Christian Onof
Imperial College London
UK

Dr Marcel Quarfood
Stockholm University
Sweden

Aviv Reiter
Tel Aviv University
Israel

Dr Dennis Schulting
Munich
Germany

Dr Yaron Senderowicz
Tel Aviv University
Israel

Dr Marco Sgarbi
University of Venice
Italy

Dr Sandra Shapshay
Indiana University
USA

Dr Scott Stapleford
St Thomas University
Canada

Professor Dr Rudi te Velde
University of Amsterdam
The Netherlands

Dr Jacco Verburgt
Amsterdam
The Netherlands

Dr Falk Wunderlich
University of Mainz
Germany

Professor Dr John Zammito
Rice University
USA

Dr Job Zinkstok
Amsterdam
The Netherlands

INTRODUCTION

In 1970, at the conclusion of his presidential address to the Eastern meeting of the American Philosophical Association, Wilfrid Sellars wrote that there was not an earlier time at which Kant had been taken so seriously as today, particularly in the English-speaking world as 'a whole new generation of commentators is coming into existence'.[1] Sellars' words ring, if anything, even more true today and, as always, there is 'a whole new generation of commentators' who are presenting new vantage-points upon the work of Kant. As a result, one of the objectives of this *Companion* is to help introduce to a wider philosophical public some sense of the debates and currents within contemporary Kantian philosophy in addition to providing resources enabling an introduction to the broad themes of Kant's philosophy and the reasons why it remains such a fertile area for philosophical research.

Before setting out some reasons for viewing this companion as a useful addition to the reference literature that exists on Kant, it is first worth taking some time to mention the important existent texts of similar type, partly in order also to make clearer to the general reader the geography of the work that exists in connection with Kant and how it intersects with broader philosophical concerns. One of the ways in which Kant's philosophy has to be approached is clearly in relation to the historical context of the Enlightenment and eighteenth-century Germany in particular. Foremost among the responses to this kind of historical concern with Kant's philosophy is work of a biographical character.[2] However, while a biographical focus gives important information concerning the formation of Kant's ideas and helps us to comprehend something of the way the Critical philosophy emerged, it is of less help in comprehending the manner of the reception of Kant's philosophy and how that reception may in turn have prompted Kant to revise and rearticulate his philosophy.[3] The relationship between the context from which Kant arose and the context of his reception is one that raises a number of philosophical and historiographical questions which have received extensive treatment in recent years.[4]

There has been a noted turn toward such historical studies of Kant, particularly in relation to his reception of and relationship to the subsequent movement of German Idealism, in recent years.[5] A number of recent companions to Kant are also influenced by this 'historical turn' including, invariably, essay-length pieces that focus on either Kant's original context of writing,

1

tracking his development, or, conversely, on the reception of his work.[6] However, the essay-length pieces featured in these companions are quite different from the kinds of contributions that are featured in this companion. What is standard in the current run of companions to Kant is the provision of largely single-author essay-length pieces that provide overviews to the areas in question. By contrast, *this* companion is intended to be a genuine handbook, including sections devoted to both the historical background of Kant's work and to the reception of it. These sections are written by many hands and are presented here as short guides to the areas in question, often including reviews of areas complete with bibliography for further reading. Thus, by contrast to the model of 'companions' now current, this one is aimed at providing information that provides an easy guide to both areas and sub-areas and presents a plurality of voices with regard to the questions covered. The fact that such an approach is possible within this handbook is a tribute to the work previously done but it also enables a divergence from that work by providing shorter, more succinct entries that cover more discrete topics.[7]

Philosophical work on Kant has tended, for obvious reasons, to split between its three clear poles. Some, that is, has focused exclusively on Kant's theoretical philosophy and its relationship to the previous history of metaphysics, other works just on Kant's practical philosophy and its relationship to predominant schools of ethics and political philosophy, while, finally, a third group has focused more or less exclusively upon Kant's aesthetics.[8] These distinct foci have provided much work of value and stimulated a series of important debates.

The key topics of Kant's theoretical philosophy include the status of the synthetic a priori, the nature and extent of his reply to Hume's scepticism, particularly in relation to causation, the justification of the categories, the understanding of transcendental idealism and the problematic 'defence' of free will. This list is one that arises purely from thinking through the topics of the *Critique of Pure Reason*, undoubtedly the work of Kant's that has had widest philosophical influence despite its evident difficulty. The *Critique* is generally understood to have changed the landscape of modern philosophy, as it helped both to bring a certain style of philosophy to an end in addition to promoting the formation of new styles of philosophy. The importance of the former has been widely recognized with the conception of Kant as 'all-destroying' in relation to traditional arguments for the existence of God and, indeed, the general role of philosophy that was promoted at least since Descartes, challenged and overturned.[9]

However, this image of Kant as an 'all-destroyer' is itself capable of promoting a view of his achievement that makes it harder to comprehend him as having contributed to the reformation of metaphysics, rather than to its destruction. Among earlier generations of Kant interpreters, for example, a broadly deflationary view of Kant's own metaphysical views had the effect of popularising an image of Kant as being a philosopher who was 'opposed' to metaphysics.[10] More recent commentators have, in response, sought to restore the notion that Kant is indeed a contributor to metaphysics and not merely a critic of it.[11] This 'turn' in the interpretation of Kant's theoretical philosophy has been accompanied by a much greater degree of attention to Kant's lectures on metaphysics and to the interplay between the *Critique* and Kant's subsequent works on theoretical philosophy.[12] I don't mean to suggest here that a new 'consensus' view has thereby emerged in relation to Kant's metaphysics as it remains an area of lively contention. But what such contention involves, increasingly, is a sense that the resources of metaphysics in Kant are broader than was previously suggested and that techniques of research that have had success in relation to other figures in early modern philosophy also have pertinence with regard to Kant.

If the area of Kant's theoretical philosophy has been the site of much controversy concerning the relation this philosophy has to the general area of metaphysics, the interpretation of his practical philosophy, by contrast, has been determined largely by an overly reductive response to his intervention in this area. Until comparatively recently, the response to Kant's practical philosophy was overwhelmingly oriented by a view of it based on a reading of his initial Critical work in the area, the *Groundwork for the Metaphysics of Morals*. However, such a view of Kant's ethics has been strongly challenged in recent years. On the one hand, the upsurge of interest in Kantian ethics that flowed from Rawlsian work in the area has given rise to the general conception of 'Kantian constructivism'.[13] This reading of Kant promoted an understanding of the 'categorical imperative procedure' that highlighted the importance of Kant's appeal to the universal law of nature and aimed to show that consistency of willing is a more substantive conception than some critics of Kant have tended to think.

In contrast to the 'constructivist' reading of Kant's ethics, there has been a resurgence of interest in the wider setting of Kant's writings, going beyond the *Groundwork* and looking in addition at Kant's wider writings on practical philosophy. This has included assessing his work on religion, both *Religion within the Limits of Reason Alone* and the

Conflict of the Faculties.[14] This general tendency has, however, been a main focus in new concentration on the work the *Groundwork* was intended to prepare the way for: *The Metaphysics of Morals*.[15] In addition to providing such a broader vista, this concentration has suggested that the attempt to deny Kant a 'comprehensive' conception in the area of practical philosophy is doomed to failure and that such a failure is likely to be a good thing in promoting an integrated reading of Kant's practical philosophy. Part of the point of such an integrated reading would further be to suggest that the understanding of the 'unity of reason' requires relating Kant's practical philosophy more carefully to his theoretical philosophy.

If both the theoretical and practical philosophy of Kant are areas in which there is considerable debate concerning the nature of his legacy, this is likewise true in response to the work that has come to seem to some the most important part of his Critical philosophy, namely, the *Critique of Judgment*. Concentration on this has traditionally been concerned with the first half of the book, the 'Critique of Aesthetic Judgment', a concentration that has, however, tended to have the effect of ensuring that it has become obscure to contemporary readers why it is that Kant also treated the topic of teleology in the same book. This has not been helped by treatments of the Third *Critique* that downplay the topic of 'reflective judgment'.[16] The effect of such readings of the Third *Critique* has been wide-ranging, not least in the areas of art criticism and art theory.[17] The arrival of challenges to such a conception of the Third *Critique* has taken a number of forms. One element of the arrival of new readings of the work has been the increased attention given in recent years to Kant's view of the sublime, something long marginalized by works that concentrated largely on his account of the beautiful.[18] This shift in focus has helped to complicate the understanding of Kant's philosophical aesthetics although the integration of his treatment of aesthetics in the Third *Critique* with that provided elsewhere in his Critical philosophy is a broader challenge.[19] A broad reading of the whole of the Third *Critique* bringing out both the relationship between the logic and the aesthetic of reflective judgment and the rationale for Kant's discussion of teleology has been a focus of the most important recent works on the area.[20] There has also been a resurgence of historical work on the Third *Critique* that has argued for revisionist conceptions of its composition[21] and for revisions of understanding of his view of teleology.[22] As is the case with the new work being undertaken in other areas of Kantian philosophy, so also with the new work on the Third *Critique* the result has been both a challenge to the received image of the work and a resulting greater complexity in the idea of Kant's contributions both to the areas investigated in the work and his relationship to the history of both aesthetics and teleology.

Across the areas of Kantian philosophy, there has thus arisen in recent years a series of challenges to the received conceptions both of the import of Kant's own principles and methodology and of the relationship between Kant's works and contemporary philosophy. It was, for a time, easy to view Kant as being a major figure in the history of philosophy without necessarily assenting to the idea that his work was of importance to ongoing philosophical work. The challenge to this complacent view has come about through a combination of scholarly attention to the range of Kant's works, something that has been assisted by a range of translations of works into English that were not previously available and the rise of an historical sense that was often lacking in previous generations of Anglo-American philosophers. Alongside this scholarly challenge has come a philosophical one as the interplay between philosophers in different countries has grown wider and a result of this has been the undermining of the conception that there is only one philosophical method that is respectable. The rise of such philosophical pluralism has led to the revival of Kantian studies as it has promoted new insights into areas of Kant's works that were previously unexplored or underexplored.[23] This has included attention being finally given both to Kant's final torso of a work, the *Opus Postumum*[24] and to his early, so-called, 'pre-Critical' works.[25]

Putting together the result of these challenges is to make clear the need for a survey of Kant's work in a form that is accessible to the general philosophical public and yet which includes a sense of the transition through which the reception of this work is undergoing. The 'Key Works' section of this companion is intended to provide part of this service, giving, as it does, an account of each of the major works Kant wrote and rendering, in the process, a comprehensible and yet succinct treatment of the major points of these works. Alongside this treatment, the 'Themes and Topics' section is meant further to orient the reader to the key areas in Kant's works. It is also important that a general bibliography be made available which enables works on each of the major areas of Kant's philosophy to be brought together and the companion concludes with this.

The importance of Kant's philosophy for contemporary philosophers does indeed, as Wilfrid Sellars wrote 40 years ago, continue to grow. It is the hope of the editors of this companion that we have provided a map to navigate the terrain of Kant's philosophy, including an account of the context of its production, its reception, its themes and a guide to its major works. The companion is oriented to the needs of general philosophers and aims to introduce them to the resources that Kantians are aware of and think others need to also be cognizant of. If it furthers engagement with Kant's philosophy by a wider public it will have served its purpose admirably. – GB

NOTES

1. W. Sellars, "'. . .this I or he or it (the thing) which thinks. . . .'", in J. F. Sicha (ed.), *Kant's Transcendental Metaphysics: Sellars' Cassirer Lecture Notes and Other Essays* (Atascadero: Ridgeview, 2002), p. 362.

2. Perhaps the most important recent work in this vein is M. Kuehn, *Kant: A Biography* (Cambridge: Cambridge University Press, 2001). A more general attempt to relate Kant to his German philosophical context is provided in L. W. Beck, *Early German Philosophy: Kant and His Predecessors* (Chicago: University of Chicago Press, 1969), which, despite its age, is still a vital guide to the background of Kant's work but which is also well complemented by M. Kuehn, *Scottish Common Sense in Germany, 1768–1800: A Contribution to the History of Critical Philosophy* (Kingston/Montreal: McGill-Queen's University Press, 1987) and H. Caygill, *The Art of Judgment* (Oxford/New York: Blackwell, 1989). For historical background to Kant's practical philosophy see J. B. Schneewind, *The Invention of Autonomy: A History of Modern Moral Philosophy* (Cambridge: Cambridge University Press, 1989) and J. B. Schneewind, *Essays on the History of Moral Philosophy* (Oxford/New York: Oxford University Press, 2009).

3. In fact, works that attempt to investigate this are rarer than general surveys of the type referred to in the previous note. For a collection of important texts of early respondents to Kant see B. Sassen (ed.), *Kant's Early Critics: The Empiricist Critique of the Theoretical Philosophy* (Cambridge: Cambridge University Press, 2000). For more general attempts to situate Kant in relation to his contemporaries see K. Ameriks, *Kant and the Fate of Autonomy: Problems in the Appropriation of the Critical Philosophy* (Cambridge: Cambridge University Press, 2000) and F. C. Beiser, *German Idealism: The Struggle Against Subjectivism 1781–1801* (Cambridge, MA: Harvard University Press, 2002).

4. Scholarship in Germany, in particular, has focused on some of these questions, not least in the work of Manfred Frank and Dieter Henrich although only a small portion of their work is as yet available in English translation. See D. Henrich, *Between Kant and Hegel: Lectures on German Idealism*, trans. D. S. Pacini, (Cambridge, MA: Harvard University Press, 2003), D. Henrich, *The Unity of Reason: Essays on Kant's Philosophy*, trans. R. L. Velkley (Cambridge, MA: Harvard University Press, 1994), and M. Frank, *The Philosophical Foundations of Early German Romanticism*, trans. Elizabeth Millan-Zaibert (Albany, NY: SUNY Press, 2004). There have been some important compilations of translations relating to Kant's reception such as the aforementioned work by Sassen and G. Di Giovanni, H. S. Harris (eds), *Between Kant and Hegel: Texts in the Development of Post-Kantian Idealism* (Indianapolis and Cambridge: Hackett Publishing Company, 1985). See also the important translation by K. Ameriks of Reinhold's *Letters on the Kantian Philosophy* (Cambridge: Cambridge University Press, 2005).

5. This has taken a number of forms from works such as B. Lord, *Kant and Spinozism: Transcendental Idealism and Immanence From Jacobi to Deleuze* (Basingstoke/New York: Palgrave Macmillan, 2011) and P. Franks, *All or Nothing: Systematicity, Transcendental Arguments, and Skepticism in German Idealism* (Cambridge, MA: Harvard University Press, 2005) to K. Ameriks (ed.), *The Cambridge Companion to German Idealism* (Cambridge: Cambridge University Press, 2001) and F. C. Beiser, *The Fate of Reason: German Philosophy From Kant to Fichte* (Cambridge, MA: Harvard University Press, 1987). Focus on the relationship between Kant and early modern philosophy is something that is less developed though it was part of Wilfrid

Sellars' interest as is evidenced in P. Amaral (ed.), *Kant and Pre-Kantian Themes: Lectures by Wilfrid Sellars* (Atascadero: Ridgeview, 2002) and see for a sustained attempt to connect scholarship on Kant with that on early modern philosophy, B. Longuenesse, D. Garber (eds), *Kant and the Early Moderns* (Princeton: Princeton University Press, 2008).

[6] For some companions that feature such essays see G. Bird (ed.), *A Companion to Kant* (Oxford/New York: Wiley-Blackwell, 2006, 2010), P. Guyer (ed.), *The Cambridge Companion to Kant and Modern Philosophy* (Cambridge: Cambridge University Press, 2006) and P. Guyer (ed.), *The Cambridge Companion to Kant's Critique of Pure Reason* (Cambridge: Cambridge University Press, 2010).

[7] It should be added that it is also the case that understanding the context from which Kant emerged has become easier of late for the English language reader due to the provision of many more of the materials in question in translation. For a selection of texts that influenced Kant and that have previously not been available to the English-language student of Kant, see E. Watkins (ed.), *Kant's Critique of Pure Reason: Background Source Materials* (Cambridge: Cambridge University Press, 2009).

[8] There are also some, albeit fewer, works that focus predominately on Kant's relationship to natural science and some that are based mainly on accounting for his understanding of teleology. For an example of the former see M. Friedman, *Kant and the Exact Sciences* (Cambridge, MA: Harvard University Press, 1992) while, on the latter, J. D. McFarland, *Kant's Concept of Teleology* (Edinburgh: Edinburgh University Press, 1970) and P. McLaughlin, *Kant's Critique of Teleology in Biological Explanation: Antinomy and Teleology* (Lewiston: Edwin Mellen Press, 1990) are both important.

[9] Despite the wide recognition of this role of Kant's Critical philosophy there is, nonetheless, a marked paucity of English-language work on the Transcendental Dialectic, the side of Kant's *Critique* that was devoted above all to this task. Evidence of this is that J. Bennett, *Kant's Dialectic* (Cambridge: Cambridge University Press, 1974) is still one of the few major works exclusively devoted to the subject matter of Kant's dialectic. But see also more recently

M. Grier, *Kant's Doctrine of Transcendental Illusion* (Cambridge: Cambridge University Press, 2001).

[10] G. Bird, *Kant's Theory of Knowledge* (London/New York: Routledge and Kegan Paul, 1962) and H. Allison, *Kant's Transcendental Idealism. An Interpretation and Defense* (New Haven: Yale University Press, 1983), and its second enlarged edition from 2004, are the key works that present this deflationary approach to transcendental idealism, an approach that was absorbed in the wider culture as indicating a Kantian 'opposition' to metaphysics, though the works of Bird and Allison themselves are not consonant with such a view.

[11] Among such newly metaphysical readings of Kant can be listed the works of Ameriks, *Kant's Theory of Mind* (Oxford: Clarendon Press, 1982), R. Langton, *Kantian Humility* (Oxford: Oxford University Press, 1998) and R. Hanna, *Kant, Science, and Human Nature* (Oxford: Clarendon Press, 2006). See, for a more general overview of work on Kant's idealism in relation to even more recent scholarship, D. Schulting, J. Verburgt (eds), *Kant's Idealism: New Interpretations of a Controversial Doctrine* (Dordrecht: Springer Science, 2011).

[12] Translation of Kant's lectures on metaphysics is now part of the Cambridge edition of Kant's works as have been such later works as his final piece on 'progress' in metaphysics.

[13] This notion found its most influential advocacy in J. Rawls, 'Kantian constructivism in moral theory', in *The Journal of Philosophy*, LXXVII, 9 (1980): pp. 515–573, though the view itself was later rejected by Rawls in favour of a 'purely political' constructivism. For an overview of the relationship between Rawls' understanding of it and Kant's own 'constructivism' see O. O'Neill, 'Constructivism in Rawls and Kant', in S. Freeman (ed.), *The Cambridge Companion to Rawls* (Cambridge: Cambridge University Press, 2003), pp. 347–367. For a forceful rejection of 'constructivist' readings of Kant see A. Hills, 'Kantian value realism', in *Ratio* 21, 2 (2008): 182–200.

[14] Among recent work focusing on this area see J. DiCenso, *Kant, Religion and Politics* (Cambridge: Cambridge University Press, 2011), C. L. Firestone, N. Jacobs (eds), *In Defense of Kant's Religion* (Bloomington,

IN: Indiana University Press, 2009) and A. W. Moore, *Noble in Reason, Infinite in Faculty: Themes and Variations in Kant's Moral and Religious Philosophy* (London/New York: Routledge, 2003).

15 For a selection of work on such topics, see M. Timmons (ed.), *Kant's Metaphysics of Morals: Interpretative Essays* (Oxford: Oxford University Press, 2002) and L. Denis (ed.), *Kant's 'Metaphysics of Morals': A Critical Guide* (Cambridge: Cambridge University Press, 2010). For work specifically on the Doctrine of Right, see A. Ripstein, *Force and Freedom: Kant's Legal and Political Philosophy* (Cambridge, MA: Harvard University Press, 2009), B. Sharon Byrd, J. Hruschka, *Kant's Doctrine of Right: A Commentary* (Cambridge: Cambridge University Press, 2010), and O. Höffe, K. Ameriks (eds), *Kant's Moral and Legal Philosophy* (Cambridge: Cambridge University Press, 2009).

16 For classic examples of work on the Third *Critique* that focuses exclusively on the treatment of aesthetics and further cannot clearly accommodate the emphasis on reflective judgment, see H. Allison, *Kant's Theory of Taste: A Reading of the Critique of Aesthetic Judgment* (Cambridge: Cambridge University Press, 2001) and P. Guyer, *Kant and the Claims of Taste* (Cambridge: Cambridge University Press, 1979) though Guyer revises the response to reflective judgment in his *Kant's System of Nature and Freedom* (Cambridge: Cambridge University Press, 2005).

17 For a critical response to the traditional view of Kantian aesthetics promoted within art theory, see T. De Duve, *Kant After Duchamp* (Cambridge, MA: MIT Press, 1996).

18 A key work in this shift is certainly the commentary of J.-F. Lyotard, *Lessons on the Analytic of the Sublime* (Stanford: Stanford University Press, 1994).

19 It is attempted in G. Banham, *Kant and the Ends of Aesthetics* (London: Macmillan, 2000).

20 This includes A. Nuzzo, *Kant and the Unity of Reason* (West Lafayette: Purdue University Press, 2005) and R. Zuckert, *Kant on Beauty and Biology* (Cambridge: Cambridge University Press, 2007).

21 J. H. Zammito, *The Genesis of Kant's Critique of Judgment* (Chicago: University of Chicago Press, 1992).

22 Two types of response to Kantian teleology in recent philosophy are provided by Lord, *Kant and Spinozism* and by A. Toscano, *The Theatre of Production: Philosophy and Individuation between Kant and Deleuze* (Basingstoke/New York: Palgrave Macmillan, 2006).

23 One of many examples of this has been the way that Kant's anthropology has become a respectable object of study that is now often mined for insights of a wider sort than were previously thought available given its 'pragmatic' orientation. For examples of how different types of philosophers have begun to utilize this resource see M. Foucault, *Introduction to Kant's Anthropology* (Cambridge, MA/London: Semiotext(e), 2008), P. R. Frierson, *Freedom and Anthropology in Kant's Moral Philosophy* (Cambridge: Cambridge University Press, 2003) and J. H. Zammito, *Kant, Herder and the Birth of Anthropology* (Chicago: University of Chicago Press, 2002). Also H. Wilson, *Kant's Pragmatic Anthropology. Its Origin, Meaning, and Critical Significance* (Albany, NY: SUNY Press, 2006); and the publication of the *Anthropology, History and Education* volume (2007) in the Cambridge Edition of Kant's works.

24 This work has been only partially translated into English to date and has not received as yet a great deal of attention though Lord, *Kant and Spinozism*, Friedman, *Kant and the Exact Sciences* and E. Förster, *Kant's Final Synthesis: An Essay on the Opus Postumum* (Cambridge, MA: Harvard University Press, 2000) have addressed it. Given the problems associated with this work, problems including the difficulty of assessing the way the parts of it should be ordered, it has to be said it is, as yet, not a work that can be seen as having joined the ranks of Kant's 'major works', which is why it has not been treated in the 'Key Works' section of this companion.

25 A. Laywine, *Kant's Early Metaphysics & the Origins of the Critical Philosophy* (Atascadero: Ridgeview, 1990) gave one response to this area though M. Schönfeld, *The Philosophy of the Young Kant: The Precritical Project* (New York: Oxford University Press, 2000) is much more comprehensive in focus. The discussion of this area in English-language treatment is, however, surely still in its infancy.

PART I:
KEY WRITINGS

1

KEY WORKS

The objective of this chapter is to set out an analysis of the contents of all of Kant's major works. The works are assessed in a way that enables the reader to gain a general overview of Kant's arguments in specific sections and the chronological order in which they are presented should further help the reader to see the means by which Kant's work developed. In the process of seeing the general rationale of the works examined, the reader will also discover something about the types of controversies that exist with regard to the interpretations of the works in question though it is not intended that these entries should do more than indicate these controversies. The views expressed on the works in this chapter will not always coincide with those found elsewhere in this *Companion* as is to be expected with a work that incorporates a commitment to pluralism. Unlike the other sections of this *Companion*, the present chapter is entirely composed by one hand, so as to facilitate the formation of an overall view of Kant's philosophical achievement. – GB

THE ONLY POSSIBLE ARGUMENT IN SUPPORT OF A DEMONSTRATION OF THE EXISTENCE OF GOD (OPD)

This piece was first published in December 1762 and was given a substantial and favourable review by Moses Mendelssohn, a review that began the process of establishing Kant's reputation as a major philosopher. In some respects, this work gathered together thoughts Kant had published in earlier writings. For example, the piece includes the claim that existence is not a predicate, which, in its reiterated form in **CPR**, was influential as a response to the Cartesian ontological argument.

However, it is not here that Kant first published this criticism as it appeared earlier in **ND** in 1755 (**ND** 394). Similarly, in this work Kant publishes a detailed statement of a mechanistic account of the origins of the solar system though in so doing he essentially presents a digest of the account given in his earlier **NH**, published in 1755. Despite these points, there are some substantial reasons why this piece attracted the attention of Mendelssohn although to explain what they are requires a detailed description of the contents of the piece.

The 'Preface' indicates that the intention of the piece had been to provide a rough outline of a main draft and that some of the arguments considered have not been demonstrated to have a distinct connection with the conclusion. The work contains three main sections, which are uneven in terms of length and importance.

The first section is devoted to providing the argument promised in the title of the piece. Here Kant demonstrates why existence is not a real predicate, in the process arguing against positions of Wolff and Baumgarten. We are asked to conceive of a subject and draw up all the predicates that may be thought to belong to it and, once we have done this, we should be able to see that the subject in question could either exist with these determinations or not exist. When we are considering any ordinary subject, it is evident that God could know all the attributes that belong to it without it following that the being in question existed. Since this is so it follows that existence is not a predicate of the thing.

Kant's explanation is that when we use the term 'existence', we are predicating something not of a thing but only of our thought of it. Ordinary language appears to possess the surface characteristic of treating existence as a kind of predicate but this is not what is really taking place when we use the term 'existence'. Existence is itself, when considered in an absolute sense, a concept whose characteristic marks are only marginally more simple than the concept itself. Hence it is hardly possible to analyse the concept of 'existence'.

After stating this point, Kant moves on to showing that the internal possibility of all things presupposes that there must exist something as without this there would be no grounds for anything. This leads to a connection between possibility and actuality and the point of this is to show that there is a notion of possibility that is 'real'.

Kant moves next to absolutely necessary existence as the ground of the possibility of anything actual as without there being something necessary there would be no grounds for there being something at all. The real importance of the argument consists not so much in its being a ground for thinking that

there exists a God as in demonstrating that the notion of possibility has to be understood in a different sense to the logical one if it is to relate to actuality.

The second main section purports to show how the mode of proof of the first section is useful but does not really do this. Instead, in this section, Kant surveys a posteriori arguments for the existence of God, which he purports to take seriously but in which instead other matters are manifested. For example, the unity in the manifold of the essence of things is shown by reference to the properties of space and this shows the extent to which space is already pictured by Kant as an intuitive construction.

Similarly, the discussion of demonstrating the unity of the manifold by reference to laws of motion shows a commitment to seeing these laws as having something necessary in them. Kant here also discusses Maupertuis' principle of the greatest economy of action, a principle he takes here to demonstrate the need to link the laws of motion to the very thought of matter.

Subsequent discussions include the propensity of adaptation in nature, the need to understand events in nature in a way that removes references to miracles and the reformulation of 'physico-theology' to ensure that universal laws of nature are always sought behind each phenomenon. A short digest of the mechanistic account of the solar system is also provided.

The concluding third section shows that the a posteriori arguments apparently taken seriously in the second section are none of them possible grounds for an argument showing the existence of God. Kant here concludes the point concerning existence and predication raised in the first section, demonstrating from it the impossibility of the Cartesian ontological proof. Kant now treats the argument of the first section as the basis of a revised ontological proof and shows that a posteriori arguments, by contrast, can attain only probability at best and are insufficient to establish the existence of a supreme being even probabilistically.

The final section also includes a wry comment that suggests that Kant does not take the proof of the first section even that seriously. The real weight of the piece concerns the need to see possibility differently from the way it is approached in logic, on the one hand, and the right way for philosophy to approach the investigation of nature on the other.

THE INAUGURAL DISSERTATION (ID)

This work, officially titled *De mundi sensibilis atque intelligibilis forma et principiis*, was originally written in Latin to inaugurate Kant's professorship and was the subject of a public disputation. It was probably written between March and August 1770, in some haste, according to Kant's own account, and initially published for the 1771 book fair in Königsberg in a limited edition but also distributed by Kant to Marcus Herz, Johann Lambert, Johann Sulzer and Moses Mendelssohn. This distribution produced, in response, some important objections to the work.

ID is sometimes characterized as belonging to Kant's 'Critical' period and has even been described as his first 'Critical' work though, as we shall see, there are problems with seeing it that way and it is perhaps better understood as a transitional work. It is divided into five sections. The first section is concerned with the concept of a world in general. In discussing the notion of a world, Kant first describes it in mereological terms

as a whole which is not a part as opposed to a simple which is a part that is not a whole. Subsequently, however, he moves from this analysis to a concern with the genesis of the concepts in question describing the difference between 'ideas of the understanding' and the 'laws of intuition'. The former are governed by processes of analysis, and the latter by synthesis. The introduction of this difference requires reference to time in the latter case and to the point that it is possible for the mind to entertain ideas which cannot be made concrete in intuition.

The Concept of the World

After these opening moves have been made, Kant goes on to give a definition of the concept of a world through the distinction of three factors. The first is matter, the parts of which are understood here to be substances. The second is form which co-ordinates the substances together (in accord with Kant's notion of synthesis) and involves mutual determination in this case. For a world to be given as a unity, it is required that the substances are capable of influence upon each other as otherwise one is left with a plurality of worlds that have no connection (an argument with some ancestry in Kant's work going back to **ND** and even his initial piece **LF**). So a connection between the possible influences of the substances is essential to the form of the world and the form has to remain constant and invariable.

The third element is entirety or absolute totality of component parts. With this notion, Kant describes certain antinomies involved in thinking the notion of absolute totality if we think of substances as given either successively or simultaneously and thus requires in the latter case discussion of the conditions of intuition.

THE SENSIBLE AND THE INTELLIGIBLE

The second section concerns the distinction between sensible and intelligible things in general, a distinction which certainly appears to require further discussion given the conclusion of the first section. This section begins with a description of sensibility as involving the receptivity of a subject, namely, their capacity to be affected by some object. By contrast, intelligibility is the capacity to represent something that cannot come before the senses. The object of sensibility is classed as phenomenon, that of intelligibility, the noumenon. We *appear* here to have arrived at a cardinal Critical distinction but *that it is not this yet* becomes clear when Kant glosses this difference further. In so doing, Kant presents the thinking that is involved with phenomena as a representation of how things appear, while that of representations of noumena is how things *are*.

In sensory cognition, there is a distinction between form and matter where the latter refers to sensation as evidence for the presence of something whereas the former provides a law that is inherent in the mind by means of which it co-ordinates together, or synthesizes, that which has been sensed. After making this distinction, Kant follows up with a different one, concerning this time the use of the understanding. Concepts of the understanding are now divided in terms of their use between 'real use' and 'logical use' (a distinction reminiscent of both the earlier **Inq** and **OPD**). The 'real' use gives the concepts of the things or relations 'themselves' while the 'logical' use defines the means by which concepts are presented in relation to each other (through hierarchical combinations). So if we are dealing with sensible concepts, these are combined together and their combination is distinct from that of intelligible

concepts and it is never possible to move, by combination alone, from the sensible to the intelligible. So the most universal empirical laws are still sensory concepts as are the most exact rules of geometry. Kant sketches a process of concept formation that shows that sensible concepts become more general by a process of comparison and combination. As these concepts increase in generality so we arrive at a sense of 'experience' while Kant contends that prior to this stage we only have 'appearances'.

The concepts that have a 'real' use arise from the nature of the understanding itself and do not include any form of sensitive element. For this reason, Kant refers to them as 'pure ideas' and distinguishes them from the abstract concepts that arise in experience. Having made these distinctions, Kant can now explain his opposition to the rationalist conception that the sensible is a 'confused' form of the intelligible by pointing out that while geometry is sensible in genesis it is exact and distinct whereas metaphysics, which is in principle the pure science, is often characterized by confusion. Kant uses the term 'metaphysics' here to stand for an enquiry into the first principles of the use of pure understanding. What is carried out in **ID** is distinguished from 'metaphysics' so understood, as what this work does is merely a propaedeutic for metaphysics.

The concepts of the understanding have two basic uses, the first of which is negative, namely to keep the distinction between the sensible and the intelligible clear. The second use is to describe the pure concepts of understanding in pure sciences. In our cognition, we can only relate to the understanding by symbols and not through singular concepts. The common principle of what belongs to the sensible, by contrast, is its representation by means of singular concepts, those of

14

space and time. Through these singular concepts, we can attain to a science that is based only on quantity, namely pure mathematics including under this heading geometry, pure mechanics and arithmetic.

PRINCIPLES OF THE SENSIBLE WORLD

The third section discusses the principles of the form of the sensible world. This section importantly anticipates the Transcendental Aesthetic of **CPR** though there are some differences. A minor one is that time is treated prior to space, a more important difference being the lack of distinction between metaphysical and transcendental expositions. Seven arguments are presented with regard to time and only five with regard to space. Common to both are the arguments aiming to show that they are not notions derived from the senses, that they are singular and not general, that they are intuitions, that they are not 'objective and real' and yet that they are indisputably true conditions of sensitive cognition. Additionally with regard to time, Kant here seeks to show that it is a continuous magnitude and connects this argument to a discussion of Leibniz's principle of continuity. Further, Kant asserts that time is an absolutely first formal principle of the sensible world, something not stated of space. Although very similar arguments are presented in **CPR** Kant does not, in **ID**, explicitly argue that space and time are a priori cognitions.

PRINCIPLES OF THE INTELLIGIBLE WORLD

The fourth section concerns the principle of the form of the intelligible world. Here Kant points out that since we have only thus far concerned ourselves with the subjective conditions of sensitive cognition, we still have to determine how it is that the principle of relations between substances, which we understand as their mutual interaction, holds. Kant immediately rejects any suggestion that this can be grounded in the mere existence of the substances, thereby distinguishing his view from 'vulgar' forms of physical influx theory. Since the world also cannot consist of necessary beings as no one necessary being would have any relation of dependence on anything else it follows that the world is composed of contingent beings. These contingent beings are also suggested to depend upon a being which is necessary and a unique cause, a version of the cosmological argument already discussed in **OPD**. The dependence of the substances on the necessary being is described as a universal interaction by means of a true physical influence or real (rather than merely ideal) whole.

METAPHYSICS

The fifth and final section concerns method in metaphysics and returns to the distinction between what is sensitive and what belongs to the understanding. This section is a rudimentary form of the Transcendental Dialectic in which Kant argues for the importance of marking this distinction and the inevitable problems that will arise if we do not. The general character of the illusions that will ensue if this distinction is not followed are characterized by Kant as the metaphysical fallacy of subreption and the reduction of all such is provided by keeping concepts of the understanding distinct from relations of space and time. After outlining the illusions that emerge from contravening the distinction in question, Kant concludes the work by laying out two principles of harmony which are required as without them we would hardly be able to make any judgments about objects at all. The first such principle is that the naturalist one that all things in the universe take place in accord with the order of nature. The second is Occam's Razor, that we ought not to multiply principles beyond necessity and the third is that nothing material comes into being or passes away. In concluding with these principles, Kant again anticipates part of the argument of the Dialectic, namely, that touching upon regulative ideas of pure reason.

It can be seen when the work is examined with care that there are important differences between the views expressed in it and what is to come in **CPR**. The suggestion that intelligible principles describe what really is, as opposed to what appears, indicates a residue of rationalism here that **CPR** later renounced. However, the arguments concerning sensible cognition are the principal part of the work and already contain much that is to become cardinal in the Critical philosophy.

CRITIQUE OF PURE REASON (CPR)

After completion of **ID**, Kant passed a decade without publishing, which is often referred to as his 'silent decade'. During this period he reflected on **ID** in his correspondence and raised a question concerning it in a letter to Marcus Herz that has often been taken to be significant in relation to the formation of the horizon that led to the publication of **CPR**. This was in a letter dated 21 February 1772 in which Kant refers to the 'key to the whole secret of metaphysics' as residing in the question: 'What is the ground of the relation of that in us which we call "representation" to the object?' (**Corr-I** 130) This question, generally known as the question of the 'Herz letter' (although Kant also wrote many other significant letters to Herz) does mark a

movement away from the stance of **ID** since it includes a reflective question that requires an investigation of 'representation'.

Stress on this notion also formed part of the horizon of the first generation of interpretations of **CPR** following the precedent of Reinhold. Allied with the question raised in the so-called Herz letter is Kant's remark in **P** that it was considering 'Hume's problem' that awoke him from his previous 'dogmatic slumber'. As with the question in the letter to Herz so also the nature of what Kant took 'Hume's problem' to consist in has been variously interpreted. In the passage in **P** in which Kant refers to this 'problem', however, he gives a clear statement of what he took it to reside in when he remarks: 'We cannot at all see why, in consequence of the existence of one thing, another must necessarily exist, or how the concept of such a combination can arise *a priori*.' (**P** 257; trans. Ellington) Despite Kant's stress on this question in **P**, there is considerable debate as to whether **CPR** offers any kind of sustained response to it and responses to **CPR**, from as early as Salomon Maimon, have denied that it does present a serious reply to Hume. The combination of the question Kant arrived at in the so-called 'Herz letter' with 'Hume's problem' will be suggested here to provide the basis for interpreting Kant's most famous work.

CPR was initially published in 1781 and, despite the length of its germination, there is some suggestion it was written hastily. One of the recurrent themes of interpretation of it has concerned whether there are various strata contained within its text. Norman Kemp Smith and Hans Vaihinger both promoted the conception of a 'patch-work' view of **CPR** based on the suggestion that it contained 'pre-Critical' elements that Kant never got around to excising. This suggestion was presented initially on the basis of the claim that different passages refer to different periods of Kant's development but contemporary adherents of the 'patchwork' view no longer present it in this way. Following the lead of Dieter Henrich, both Howard Caygill and Paul Guyer have argued that the 'patchwork' notion is a way of presenting a certain kind of hermeneutic approach that stresses problems and tensions in the text rather than resolutions.[1] H. J. Paton's commentary is often presented as opposed to the principle of this reading but careful reading of Paton shows that he also often manifests it (for example, in his account of the Transcendental Deduction).[2] The 'patchwork' reading is, nonetheless, rightly controversial and many contemporary writers reject both early and late versions of it in favour of stress on a unitary conception of the work.

A further element that produces difficulty in interpreting the work is the history of its publication. After first being published in 1781, CPR was subjected to a hostile reception in the shape of the notorious Garve-Feder review, which treated the central doctrines of the work as essentially of a piece with those of George Berkeley, a view that incensed Kant. In response, Kant worked at revising CPR and he rewrote substantial parts of it, especially the Transcendental Deduction and the Paralogisms. Elsewhere in CPR he added important sections, changed titles and formulations of principles and deleted much. The fact that two distinct editions hence exist has further divided critics who have tended to stress one edition rather than another. Schopenhauer famously argued that the idealism of the first edition was compromised in the second and hence favoured the first edition. Conversely, twentieth-century philosophers from the phenomenological tradition have favoured the first edition, following the lead of Husserl and Heidegger, due to a preference for the views on time allegedly expressed there. Analytic philosophers, by contrast, have followed the lead of the neo-Kantians, in stressing the alleged 'objectivity' of the second edition. While these disputes are not without importance it is not obvious that they have contributed to greater clarity concerning either the central views expressed in CPR or much understanding of the rationale for the changes Kant made in its structure.

THE STRUCTURE AND CONTENT OF THE 'CRITIQUE OF PURE REASON'

The organization of CPR elaborates and reflects Kant's growing passion for ordered exposition. The penultimate chapter of the whole work discusses 'architectonic' and the work exhibits continuous concern with it. Many critics allege that this concern is to the detriment of Kant's discussion but without attention being paid to it much that is important gets lost. The work is formally divided into two large and asymmetrical parts, the first of which, the Transcendental Doctrine of Elements, being much the largest and being itself subdivided. The other part of the work concerns the Doctrine of Method and has been rarely accorded the emphasis it deserves. The Doctrine of Elements is again divided into two asymmetrical parts, the first part of which, the Transcendental Aesthetic, is much briefer than the second, the Transcendental Logic. The Transcendental Logic is the major part both of the Doctrine of Elements and of the whole work, incorporating both the Transcendental Analytic and the Transcendental Dialectic.

THE PREFACES TO THE 'CRITIQUE'

Prior to encountering this intensive pattern of divisions, the reader first comes to the prefaces to the two editions of the work and its 'Introduction'. All of these are important in manifesting stresses on key elements of the work as a whole. The 'Preface' to the second edition is more than twice the length of the 'Preface' to the first and it is in the second edition 'Preface' that some of the most famous formulations of **CPR**'s general point, method and problem are given. However, the 'Preface' to the first edition opens with a general claim concerning human reason and its predilection for asking questions that it is unable to answer but feels compelled to ask (Avii).

This already foreshadows the general task of the Transcendental Dialectic and leads Kant to bemoaning the state that metaphysics has fallen into. In response, Kant announces the need for reason to come to a reflective awareness of itself, much as he appeared to be articulating in the so-called 'Herz letter' (**Corr-I** 132–139). This call is now presented as requiring a critique of pure reason in the sense that it is necessary to discover what can be asserted that is independent of experience: '[B]ecause the chief question always remains: "What and how much can understanding and reason cognize free of all experience?"' (Axvii). At the same time as raising this as the key question, Kant also does admit that there is a second side to his enquiry that concerns the possibility of pure understanding itself but which he indicates is of less importance to its outcome, an assertion of questionable status. Kant also uses the vocabulary of the 'tribunal of reason' in terms of assessing the claims of parties in disputes, a metaphor that returns subsequently both in the Transcendental Deduction and in the Antinomies.

The 'Preface' to the second edition opens with a lamentation over the state of metaphysics and a suggestion of a need for its reformation, something that the work being presented is evidently intended to help bring about. In this 'Preface', however, the stress of the problem with 'metaphysics' is more sharply defined since now it is alleged that this problem concerns its lack of 'scientific' status, a point not raised in the 'Preface' to the first edition. Concomitant with this stress on 'science' is an extended analysis of how various other disciplines have attained a 'scientific' status.

The first 'science' so investigated is mathematics and the conception of its formation that Kant presents is significant in terms of how he will later present the task for philosophy. The 'true method' that put mathematics on the path of a science, Kant alleges, was demonstrated with regard to how to determine the properties of an isosceles triangle and this consisted in attending to the 'construction' of the object (Bxii). Similarly, 'natural science' generally is said to have been capable of its breakthroughs by following the clue that 'reason has insight only into that which it produces after a plan of its own' (Bxiii). Given that these are the ways that these other disciplines have attained the status of a 'science', it is less surprising than many have been inclined to think that Kant presents the requisite procedure for metaphysics to reside in a mimetic relation to these other 'sciences'. This again involves relating to the need for reason to have a plan of its own and to determine what is given to it in relation to this plan. As Kant puts this, in relation to the problem announced in the 'Preface' to the first edition, 'we can know *a priori* of things only what we ourselves put into them' (Bxviii). This is often referred to as Kant's 'Copernican revolution' though this is not a phrase used by Kant who instead refers to operating in accord with Copernicus' 'primary hypothesis'. This consists in altering the perspective concerning what we regard as stable and what as moving with the result that 'objects' (the concern of the 'Herz letter') be now treated as required to conform to our 'intuition'.

That the change in point of view that enables science and mathematics to have attained their altered status is not only due to Copernicus is, however, later stated in a footnote in which Kant refers to Copernicus' change as only having been a hypothetical one by contrast to the discovery of the central laws of motion of the heavenly bodies carried out by Newton who demonstrated by means of such laws what binds the universe together. So it is not that there was a once-and-for-all Copernican 'revolution' that Kant wishes to follow but rather that the primary thought-experiment or hypothesis that Copernicus advocated of turning the perspective around is similarly taken in the 'Preface' to the second edition of **CPR** to draw attention in this prefatory statement to the need for a transformation to first get adopted as a hypothesis though **CPR** itself, Kant states, will show 'apodictically', not hypothetically, the point of viewing space and time in a different way than has been done by philosophers hitherto. Hence the Copernicus reference, when seen in general context, is meant to show that the Critical philosophy carries out not a 'Copernican revolution' but rather a 'Newtonian' one.

Kant's aim of altering the procedure of metaphysics is now said to be the basis of metaphysics subsequently becoming scientific so that **CPR** itself is not taken to present a system of metaphysics but only a treatise on its method (Bxxii), which accords with the insertion at the front of the second edition of an epigraph from Bacon. From this point about method Kant derives a first discussion of the need for the distinction between appearances and things in themselves, the distinction between the possibilities of pure speculative reason and practical reason and also a discussion of the difference between thinking and knowing, none of which are, from the standpoint of the reader of the 'Preface', as yet very clear. Kant also here alludes to the need for metaphysics to address problems concerning the existence of God, the nature of the soul and the status of freedom. Kant refers to the changes in the text from the first edition while denying that any of his key views have been. It should be added that a footnote included towards the close of the 'Preface' to this second edition also includes changes to the 'proof' of the Refutation of Idealism (Bxxxix–Bxli), which a number of commentators have judged to be very important.

THE 'INTRODUCTION' TO THE 'CRITIQUE'

The 'Introduction' to **CPR** is the place where Kant defines a number of key terms. Firstly, the point is made that to determine the 'a priori' we have to uncover whether there is knowledge that is independent of the senses and the second edition even refers to cognition that is 'absolutely independent of all experience' (B3). Two criteria are determined for something's being a priori: that it is *necessary* (and if it is derived only from something else that is necessary then it is *absolutely a priori* [B3]) and, secondly, that it has 'strict' universality. Having determined the a priori in this way, Kant moves to distinguishing between analytic and synthetic judgments – with the key criteria concerning the principle of contradiction (B12) – in order to arrive at his revolutionary notion of the synthetic a priori.

The claim is subsequently made (again an innovation of the second edition) that all theoretical sciences of reason include synthetic a priori judgments as principles. This is illustrated with discussion of mathematics, physics and metaphysics with the argument emerging that until the possibility of synthetic a priori judgments has been shown the general status of metaphysics cannot be solved. This point is also explicitly connected to 'Hume's problem' with causation (B19). Kant concludes the 'Introduction' with a description of the notion of the 'critique of pure reason' as a special type of 'science' that is the propaedeutic to true transcendental philosophy. Kant describes that which is transcendental as all cognition occupied not so much with objects directly as with the possibility of relating to them a priori (A12=B25). But the full idea of the 'science' of transcendental philosophy cannot be carried out in **CPR** as it is not an exhaustive account of human cognition as 'it carries the analysis only so far as is requisite for the complete examination of knowledge which is *a priori* and synthetic' (A14=B28).

The Transcendental Aesthetic

The Transcendental Aesthetic is the first major division of the Doctrine of Elements and, while relatively brief, contains much that is important. The purpose of this section is to discern what must belong to sensibility a priori (as opposed to what has to belong to conceptuality a priori). The argument of it has a careful character though one that is not always respected. Kant explicitly points out that here he specifically isolates sensibility from understanding despite having the general purpose of showing their synthetic combination. In isolating sensibility, he seeks both to show what has to belong to it empirically and what has to belong to it entirely purely. In the course of examining these questions, Kant first introduces the specific term of art 'intuition' (*Anschauung*).

'Intuition' describes an immediate relation that cognition has with 'objects' in the sense that all thought has to involve it. Such an 'immediate' relation arises, however, from cognition generally being affected and such affection occurs, for us, through sensibility. What has to belong to the empirical element of sensibility is sensation whereas what has to belong to 'intuition' purely is that which orders sensation and is not derived from it. The latter includes the Cartesian elements of 'body', namely 'extension and figure' (A21=B35) though not the Leibnizian addition, 'force', which will be revealed rather to require a connection of pure intuition to pure concepts.

The subsequent work of the Transcendental Aesthetic concerns the forms of pure sensible intuition, which are argued to be twofold, namely, the forms of space and time. Representation of objects is argued to require space as it is only through space that we have a sense of shape and magnitude while time enables a sense of having inner states. The discussions of space and time that follow are largely parallel and the account of space, for most commentators, is the one that receives most attention since Kant treats it first. These accounts also relate to the parallel ones in **ID**. The general arguments first establish that neither space nor time can be said to be 'empirical concepts' since all empirical descriptions presuppose them and that they are both 'necessary' representations since we can represent nothing without them. The first arguments have two foci: one positive and one negative. The negative point is that space and time are a priori as no particular experience could lead us to the conception of them. Hence this lack of particularity is indirectly thought to show that they are universal. The positive element of the argument, by contrast, is that space and time are *necessary* conceptions. So the two distinct criteria of the a priori are argued to attach to space and time, albeit by means of different types of argument.

Kant next provides claims for the intuitive nature of space and time. Whereas the initial account of intuition stressed immediacy and receptivity however, Kant now introduces a different understanding of intuition that allows for seeing it as distinct from conceptuality. This second determination of intuition requires describing it as 'singular' in contrast to the universality of concepts. Interestingly, since the universality of intuition itself has only been accounted for negatively (through showing lack of particularity), Kant here mainly seeks to show that intuition cannot be described through the forms of universality that are appropriate for concepts thus maintaining the sense that, while singular, intuitions are also, in a peculiar sense of their own, 'universal'.

The two arguments for the intuitive status of space and time follow the arguments for their a priori status in being both negative and positive in form. The negative arguments present reasons for rejecting attribution to them of conceptual status while the positive arguments are meant to provide a more direct rationale for thinking of them as intuitive. The first argument is to the effect that the representations of space and time are unitary in themselves, not formations from component elements. With regard to space, this is supported by a proposition from geometry. The second argument concerns the claim that representation of space and time presuppose an infinite given magnitude, the infinitude of the givenness in question being the ground of all finite determinations. In the case of time, there is only a single dimension and Kant argues that the representation of this shows the necessary character of

time. The formation of concepts is taken to require a hierarchical relation between parts and wholes while intuitions, by contrast, are taken to involve a connection between parts and wholes that is of a holistic not an aggregative character.

These arguments, when combined with the first set for the a priori status of space and time, are intended to convince us that with space and time we have a priori intuitions that supply the a priori basis of sensibility. The success of the arguments is controversial but the point of them is at least clear. Certain synthetic a priori judgments are also suggested to be grounded on space and time being conceived in this way and not to be explained otherwise with the examples given being (Euclidean) geometry and 'the concept of motion' (B48). The discussion of geometry has taxed much later commentary given the rise of non-Euclidean geometries in the course of the nineteenth century though the question of how the latter relate to 'space' is less clear than many critics allege. The account of 'motion' is less commonly discussed though, in some respects, more fruitful for Kant's general philosophy.

Regardless of the success of the arguments of the Transcendental Aesthetic up to this point, they are restricted in scope. However, Kant now turns to what he describes as a set of 'conclusions' from the concepts of space and time given but which are, in fact, distinguishable as claims from such concepts and introduce us for the first time to arguments in favour of a version of transcendental idealism, a version specifically concerned, as is natural given their place in the Transcendental Aesthetic, with sensibility.

Two 'conclusions' are given with regard to space, but three with regard to time. The first 'conclusion' concerns the subjectivity of space and time and the argument is parallel in the two cases. Essentially Kant here claims that space and time are not 'properties' of things in general or of 'relations' of such things (thus denying the specific claims of both Newton and Leibniz). The reason why they are not such 'properties' or 'relations' is that abstraction from the conditions of intuition, conditions that apply to our sensibility, will leave no determinations of space or time. These determinations have been shown to condition our sensibility's a priori form and are not appropriate to anything distinct from this. This negative claim is then re-stated in a positive form as Kant goes on to claim that space is only the form of outer sense, time the form of inner sense. These points are said to establish the *empirical reality* of space and time and their *transcendental ideality*. Time is argued to be more universal than space as it is the immediate form of inner sense and the mediate form of outer sense. Kant also includes a specific section added to the discussion of time meant to reply to the objections to the theory given when it was first stated in **ID** in correspondence.

Finally, Kant adds four 'general observations' on the whole argument of the Aesthetic (three of which are added in the second edition). The first restates the point that intuition only represents appearances and that such have no existence in themselves and that what 'objects' may be, apart from the conditions of our sensibility, is something we cannot know. Having re-stated this point, Kant goes on to distinguish this view from the Leibniz-Wolff conception that sensibility gives a confused representation of things describing the latter view as giving a 'completely wrong' direction to investigations into cognition (A44=B61).

Kant also argues for the exhaustiveness of the distinctions between intuitions and concepts, a priori and a posteriori. The second claim asserts that everything connected to intuition concerns relations and that 'a thing in itself cannot be known through mere relations' (B67) (a significant claim for Schopenhauer). Thirdly, Kant denies that the result of his discussion is the view that 'objects' are only illusions but rather asserts that we only reach this result if we treat space and time as properties of things in themselves (an anticipation of the argument of the Refutation of Idealism). Fourthly, Kant argues that if space and time were conditions of things in general, they would also be conditions of God (an anticipation of Kant's characterization of 'Spinozism' in **CJ**). The general result of the argument of the Aesthetic is proposed by Kant to be that synthetic a priori judgments 'can never extend beyond objects of the senses; they are valid only for objects of possible experience' (B73).

The position of the Transcendental Aesthetic in **CPR** and its conclusions are both controversial. Its conclusions are controversial principally due to the survival of the alleged 'neglected alternative' objection. Initially stated by F. A. Trendelenburg in his nineteenth-century controversy with Kuno Fischer, this objection has proved surprisingly durable. The claim is to the effect that Kant has neglected to investigate the view that space and time might be *both* conditions of our sensibility and *also* have an independent reality. The assertion that Kant 'neglected' this alternative is correct in the sense that it is not one he explicitly considers. It is not 'neglected' if what is meant is that Kant has no conceptual resources with which to deal with it. The basic response Kant can make here is that for space and time to be independently 'real' in addition to being the forms of sensibility would require some means to be available for us to make sense of it. This would have to either be through intuition or concepts given the exhaustiveness of this division of our cognition. But since he has shown that the forms of intuition are distinct from anything conceptual and that these forms are essential to sensibility no such further means of knowledge is available to us. Paul Guyer presents a slight variation on this position when he claims that Kant does not merely deny knowledge of things in themselves but makes positive dogmatic assertions concerning the nature of the latter but there is no evidence, within the argument of the Aesthetic, for the latter claim being made by Kant.[3]

THE TRANSCENDENTAL LOGIC

The second and much longer part of the Doctrine of Elements is taken up by the treatment of Transcendental Logic, a treatment itself divided into two substantial parts – the Transcendental Analytic and the Transcendental Dialectic. Given that the Transcendental Aesthetic concerned the a priori elements of sensibility, it would be natural to expect the Transcendental Logic to discuss the a priori elements of thought. However, only a very small portion of the Transcendental Analytic is directly devoted to this although the result of the whole of the argument of the Analytic does enable a return to the discussion of the limits of conceptuality.

The specific account of a priori concepts is provided through the claim, made in the context of the Metaphysical Deduction, that the function of concepts is to formulate judgments. Given this claim, Kant proceeds to describe a Table of Judgment that gives, on his view, a description of the different types of functions of unity available for judgment. The table does depend on a response to Aristotelian logic but creatively amplifies some of its elements including moments that are novel (such as

the distinction of 'infinite' judgment from affirmative and negative or the separate consideration of 'singular' from universal and particular). There is some confusion concerning whether the 'table' is part of ordinary or, as Kant terms it, 'general' logic or is part of transcendental logic though the justification given for 'infinite' judgments makes plain that these are part of 'transcendental' logic (A71–72=B97).

However, it is only after describing the parts of the table that Kant introduces the key notion of 'synthesis', the central term of 'transcendental logic', and thus it is at this point that logic appears to become transcendental. Synthesis involves combination of different representations such that they are capable of being grasped in a single manifold and it is the origin of 'real' cognition (A77=B103). It is first stated that pure synthesis is the work of imagination here though Kant immediately adds that for cognition to attain unity we require concepts, a point that leads him to distinguish between the logical forms of judgments, already given, and the transcendental content of representations. The latter are described by the pure concepts of the understanding and Kant provides a list of them in a Table of Categories that corresponds to the earlier Table of Judgment though there is some controversy over how the second table has been derived from the first.

Once the Table of Categories has described the pure a priori concepts the rest of the work of the Transcendental Analytic is intended to show, firstly the justification for assuming these concepts are at work in our experience, and, secondly the procedure whereby they articulate this experience for us. The latter occurs in the Analytic of Principles where a series of synthetic a priori judgments are articulated and argued for.

The Transcendental Deduction

The task of the first part is the work of the Transcendental Deduction. The Transcendental Deduction is one of the major parts of **CPR** and was subjected to serious revision in its second edition. This has produced a series of divergences in the interpretation of the Transcendental Deduction, particularly between phenomenologically oriented readers who have emphasized the argument of the first edition and analytical readers who have tended to follow neo-Kantian precedent in favouring the second edition. This is only part of the problem of interpreting the Transcendental Deduction, however, since both versions of the argument include distinguishable elements with the first edition presenting a 'preliminary' argument prior to the main argument and the second edition including two apparently distinct conclusions. Kant himself also gave the basis for a further type of division by describing the discussion of the argument concerning the categories as an 'objective' deduction by contrast to the 'subjective' deduction that emphasized considerations relating to cognition. Finally, the second edition version incorporates a sustained account of judgment that ties the argument of the Transcendental Deduction more closely to the Metaphysical Deduction.

There are two main aims of the argument of the Transcendental Deduction, aims that are stressed in both versions of the text. On the one hand, there is a generic argument justifying the view that we require the use of the categories in experience and on the other hand there is an investigation of the means by which cognition takes place in terms of what is often described as a 'transcendental psychology' (although this is not an expression used by Kant it does seem appropriate to describe the investigations in question thus). However, in practice, it proves virtually impossible to really distinguish these strands from each other in the detail of Kant's argument as the appeal to 'transcendental psychology' is made throughout the discussion of the need for the categories.

While it is impossible to summarize this section in a manner that is not controversial, it is standard to accept that Kant, in both versions of this argument, presents a strong claim for transcendental synthesis being required for experience to be possible. This claim involves a connection between the possession of a priori concepts and the source of there being anything like conceptuality at all. Kant describes the latter as 'transcendental apperception' and while the details of the arguments vary in the two editions of the work there is, in both versions, a connection between this capacity and the ability to bring together the manifold of sense by means of 'transcendental imagination'.

The first edition version of the argument places great stress on all cognition being subject to time (A99) in accordance with the argument of the Transcendental Aesthetic and this is the key to its synthetic emphasis. The second edition version, by contrast, emphasizes the dependence of representation on 'spontaneity' and uses this emphasis to connect the capacity to form judgments to the ultimate source of conceptuality in 'transcendental apperception'. This much would be conceded by most interpreters but the details of how the arguments go and the success of them have proved deeply controversial. The suggestion of a deep difference between the two versions of the argument is, however, difficult to sustain when the appearance of the same aims and the same central notions is noted.

The Analytic of Principles

Assuming that the argument of the Transcendental Deduction succeeds in justifying the need for a priori concepts in the articulation of experience, Kant next turns to the procedure by means of which they are connected to intuition. That such connection takes place was the burden of the emphasis on synthesis in the argument of the Transcendental Deduction but the mechanics of how this connection happens was not explicated there. In the chapter 'On the Schematism', Kant accounts for this in general terms by stressing a relationship between a priori concepts and a priori intuition through the form of time. Time is as universal as the concepts and yet, also, as part of the conditions of sensibility, is meant to mediate the connection of concepts to sensibility. In some respects, the absence of discussion of space in the account of transcendental schematism is surprising (particularly given that Kant does, independently, describe a 'pure sensible' schema that does involve space) and, indeed, this want later has to be made good when Kant goes on to 'apply' the schema in the subsequent argument of the Analytic.

Placing the categories under the conditions of a priori intuition essentially produces the specific principles of the rest of the Analytic, which is organized in accordance with the Table of Categories. Schematizing the categories produces Kant's Principles. From the schematization of the categories of quantity we arrive at the Axioms of Intuition, schematizing the categories of quality produces the Anticipations of Perception, schematizing the categories of relation produces the Analogies of Experience and, finally, schematizing the categories of modality produces the Postulates of Empirical Thought. All of these parts are worth examining in detail as

is the division between the first two set of principles and the second set.

Kant describes the principles of the Axioms and the Anticipations as 'mathematical' in nature while those of the Analogies and Postulates are, by contrast, termed 'dynamical'. This distinction is meant to indicate the diverse things made possible by the principles as the 'mathematical' principles are not principles *of* mathematics but are rather principles that make mathematics (in a certain sense) possible (and similarly with the dynamical principles). So the division between them is essentially that the mathematical principles are principles *of* intuition while the dynamical ones are rather principles that relate to the existence of things for us.

The Analogies of Experience

By far the lion's share of commentary on these principles has, however, been taken up responding to the principles of the Analogies of Experience and there are a number of reasons why this is so. The most obvious one is that it is here that Kant formulates a view of causality which has been often presented as his 'reply' to 'Hume's problem' and it is also with the 'analogies' that we get something like a clear view of 'objects' and their relation to 'representations' (thus a response to the question of the so-called Herz letter).

There is a general principle of all the analogies in addition to there being principles for each of the three specific analogies. The second edition version of the general principle states that experience is possible only through 'the representation of a necessary connection of perceptions' (B218) and this makes more precise the first edition formulation that referred to a priori rules of time (A177). The specific argument for the general principle includes an attempt to disambiguate distinct senses of 'experience' in order to justify the specifically Kantian notion announced in the second edition formula. The argument also relates the necessary unity of apperception to the empirical consciousness of perception by means of connecting it to the three modes of time. Kant here also indicates the reason for talking of 'analogies' by discussing qualitative relations and how, from them, we gain a priori cognition of a relation without it being the case that we have the determinate sense of what this is a relation with (A179–180=B222).

The three analogies are schemas of the categories of relation with the first relating the category of substance to time. The unschematized notion of substance is as a subject of predication while the schematized form of it gives us the notion of sempiternality or 'permanence'. While the first edition formula describes the permanent as the 'object itself' (A182), the second edition, controversially, states a conservation principle (B224). This analogy, like the other two, includes as part of its argument the assertion that time itself cannot be perceived and that, in the absence of time, something analogous to it has to be given which, in this case, is substance in the field of appearance (B225). The general argument that there must be something persistent that enables the recognition of change is at least as old as Aristotle but is here applied only to the sphere of appearances. Alteration is, by this means, indicated to be something that only affects the determinations of substances and not these substances themselves. Kant refers to an 'empirical criterion' of necessary permanence in his conclusion of the argument (A189=B232) but does not supply it within the argument itself, a first signal that the arguments for the three analogies are interdependent.

The Second Analogy is by the far most famous of the three and has attracted some of the most extensive treatment in the secondary literature (only the Transcendental Deduction being ahead in this regard). The formulation of the principle changes somewhat between the two editions with the first edition emphasizing that what happens begins to be according to a rule (A189) while the second, much more explicitly, states that alteration takes place in conformity with cause and effect (B232). Since the argument of the First Analogy had treated the notion of 'alteration', the second edition treatment effectively begins from where the First Analogy left off.

While the argument of the Second Analogy is, by the standards of **CPR**, fairly long, and appears to involve a number of elements, most contemporary commentary focuses on trying to unravel the general argument rather than, like the classic commentaries of Kemp Smith and Paton, subdividing into sets of sub-arguments. The major dispute concerning the Second Analogy is between 'weak' and 'strong' readings of its claim. The 'strong' reading focuses on claiming that the argument must commit Kant to showing that if we have the same cause we will have the same effect (SCSE), the 'weak' reading, by contrast, suggests that all Kant need show is that for every effect there is some cause (EESC). The dispute between these readings, despite having the character of a local textual argument, has some large implications for how the Critical philosophy is viewed.

Alongside the contention over which principle Kant is aiming to prove in the Second Analogy, there are also disputes over which argument is the one which will have to sustain the main premise. For reasons which are somewhat obscure, since at least the reading of Peter Strawson[4] there has been a tendency to emphasize the first of the arguments Kant considers in the text of the Second Analogy, the so-called 'irreversibility argument'. The consensus on this is surprising, not least since Strawson's own emphasis on it was intended to show the failure of the argument.

However, what few other than Paul Guyer and Gary Banham[5] have attempted to emphasize is that the argument must not only be about the notion of causality but also be connected to the sense that Kant is generally giving to the 'object of representation' (or, otherwise put, to an intentional sense of objectivity). Kant does, however, raise this point explicitly early in the argument (A189–190=B234–235). After restating the point that we need the distinction between appearances and things-in-themselves, Kant goes on to point out that this raises a specific question: 'What, then, am I to understand by the question: how the manifold may be connected in the appearance itself, which yet is nothing in itself?' (A191=B236).

Assuming that the manifold united in the representation gives us what we term an 'object', then there is required a rule which enables us to distinguish any given such particular one from every other one. 'The object is *that* in the appearance which contains the condition of this necessary rule of apprehension.' (A191=B236) The discussion of this point, directly relevant to the problem of the 'Herz letter', immediately precedes the 'irreversibility argument'. In this, Kant stresses the need for appearances to be presented in continuity as, without this, there would be times that were empty of content. This point is meant to show that it is a necessary requirement that perceptions are related to each other.

Kant subsequently introduces a contrast between a 'house' and a 'ship', a contrast widely misinterpreted. Kant here uses these empirical examples to reach the point that we need a distinction between 'subjective'

and 'objective' succession and that the former must be parasitic upon the latter as without the sense of 'objective succession' being primary there would be no settled permanence for 'subjective succession' (whose manifold is only that of 'inner sense') to attach to. This leads to the provisional conclusion that the rule referred to in the principle of the Second Analogy is one that asserts that events have a necessary order of appearance (A194=B239). '[T]he occurrence, as the conditioned, yields a secure indication of some condition, but it is the latter that determines the occurrence.' (A194=B239) This view is contrasted with the Humean one that sees the notion of causation arising genetically from perception and comparison, as on Kant's view no such perception and comparison of particulars could take place without a pre-existing rule which distinguished them from one another. Kant is explicit in viewing this point as requiring a sense of 'continuity' (A199=B244 and A209=B254), a point that 'weak' readings of the principle generally do not refer to.

The Third Analogy schematizes the category of community or coexistence in order to connect mutual interaction with the notion of simultaneity. The second edition version of the principle is, again, sharper than the first edition version including, as it does, a reference to space. As in the other two analogies, Kant makes much of the point that time itself cannot be perceived and thus for a temporal notion such as simultaneity to make sense for us, something in our experience has to 'stand in' for time. Since simultaneity could not be revealed by reference to the synthesis of imagination, as this would be insufficient to establish when things were co-existent, we require a pure concept and this is the one of mutual interaction of substances.

Subsequent to the treatment of the three analogies, Kant discusses first the Postulates, which schematize the principle of modality and then the distinction between phenomena and noumena, in which latter Kant articulates a difference between positive and negative references to noumena in preparation for the Transcendental Dialectic. Finally, the 'Appendix' to the Transcendental Analytic explicitly introduces the notion of 'concepts of reflection' although there is a good case for thinking they were implicitly being referred to earlier in the work. These concepts are four paired groups that effectively describe conditions for formulation of how other concepts are possible (which must surely include the categories). The explicit purpose for their introduction is to provide a Critical riposte to the debate between Locke and Leibniz showing ways in which both failed to respect the transcendental distinction but the discussion of the concepts of reflection is one that has large potential implications for understanding the argument of the Transcendental Deduction.

THE TRANSCENDENTAL DIALECTIC

The second part of the Transcendental Logic is taken up by the Transcendental Dialectic. This concerns, as Kant states at the outset, a 'logic of illusion' (A293=B349) which traces the destructive effect of crossing the transcendental distinction and is hence termed 'transcendental illusion'. One of the difficulties of discussing transcendental illusion is that detection of it is not sufficient to cease its operation (as would be the case with logical illusion). In order to explain this, Kant finally arrives at his discussion of 'reason', something that comes relatively late in a book apparently concerned with its critique! Reason is initially described as concerned with 'principles', and 'principles' are then defined as involving cognition 'in

which I cognize the particular in the universal through concepts' (A300=B357). This definition leads to viewing the procedure of reason as typically taking place by means of syllogisms.

The next key point is that reason, unlike understanding, is not concerned with the unification of appearances by means of rules but rather with the unification of the rules of understanding under principles (A302=B358). Pure reason, by contrast to a limited empirical reason, is concerned with relating all conditioned claims to cognition to something that is unconditioned. On the basis of this general account of reason, Kant determines the 'concepts' of reason to be 'ideas' and describes these as concepts that transcend the possibility of experience and thus as not being capable of being given in intuition (A327=B383). The subsequent discussion of specific problems and illusions is all guided by this general account.

THE PARALOGISMS

The first part of Kant's discussion of illusions is the account of the Paralogisms of pure reason, a section elaborately reconstructed in the second edition of **CPR**. A 'paralogism' is a pseudo-syllogism, which is, however, grounded in the nature of human reason, as follows from the general account of the procedure of the Dialectic. The paralogisms discussed concern the pretensions to a purely 'rational' psychology, that is, one not based on empirical data. As such, it is built, states Kant, 'on the single proposition *I think*' (A342=B400).

There are four paralogisms, which are related to the Table of Categories, though the table is not approached in its normal order, since the First Paralogism concerns substance. Each Paralogism connects the category to a view about mind so the First Paralogism states that the mind is a substance. The other three discuss the quality of the soul (that it is simple), its quantity (unified) and its relation (to possible objects in space). The first edition discusses each of the paralogisms in great detail while, in the second edition, Kant compresses his treatment greatly and moves much of the discussion of the fourth Paralogism to an appendix to the Postulates (in the form of a Refutation of Idealism). Despite the fascination of this alteration there is remarkably little discussion of this transformation in the secondary literature (with the singular exception of Karl Ameriks[6]).

In treating the Paralogisms, Kant first gives them their form as presented in standard treatments and later indicates the reason why the argument is given as well as detecting a fallacious move within them by which the supporter of the argument hopes to pass off a formal point as a substantive one. So the First Paralogism presents the soul as substance on the basis of the predicative criterion of substance and then pretends this establishes the permanence of substance. The Second Paralogism treats the soul as simple and hopes thereby to establish that it is incorporeal. The Third Paralogism is a variation on the first as here it is hoped to show that since there is numerical identity at each point of a mind's self-consciousness that it must therefore be permanent. Finally, and most controversially, the Fourth Paralogism aims to show that since there is required an inference to move from the mind to external objects that the latter are thereby doubtful.

While few commentators have attended in great detail to the responses Kant makes to the first three paralogisms, the fourth, which involves Kant in distinguishing his own transcendental idealism from the 'dogmatic'

idealism of Berkeley and the 'problematic' idealism of Descartes, has attracted considerable commentary. The revision of this argument in the second edition has substantially added to this debate, although there are few who have pointed to the wealth of Kant's earlier and later discussions of idealism.[7]

The basic distinction Kant seeks to make here is to the effect that both the forms of idealism he wishes to distance himself from are 'empirical' while his view of idealism is 'transcendental'. The thrust of this is that while Berkeley and Descartes arrive at a problem with 'empirical' objects by testing them against standards that would be appropriate for things in themselves (and thus in accord with a postulate of transcendental realism), Kant, by contrast, takes empirical objects to be 'real' in their own terms once we have affirmed a postulate of ignorance with regard to things in themselves.

The language of the first edition version of **CPR** casts this argument in terms of 'representations' and this has often been viewed as creating a problem for Kant's argument, one that is suggested by some to have been removed in the re-cast argument of the second edition though others are sceptical as to whether the argument succeeds at all. There is considerable misunderstanding of the argument as is evidenced by Heidegger, for example, who assumes that Kant here is attempting to 'prove' the existence of the external world while he is rather aiming to show instead that we cannot adopt a postulate of being 'beyond' it and always find ourselves within it.

THE ANTINOMIES

After the Paralogisms, Kant turns to the Antinomies. As the former were concerned with a supposed 'rational' psychology, the latter are interested in the claims of a sup-posed 'rational' cosmology. However, while paralogisms were merely faulty syllogisms, antinomies involve competing claims of argu-ments, both of which appear compelling but which are mutually incompatible. As with the Paralogisms, Kant sets these out in rela-tion to the Table of Categories and, indeed, the antinomies could be elaborately related to the discussion of the schematized catego-ries in the Transcendental Analytic.

All the antinomies are concerned with a problem about how to complete a series with two forms of completion competing with each other. The first kind of completion involves an infinite regress so that the series is, in principle, incapable of being completed while the second, by contrast, finishes with a first member taken to complete the whole series. This distinction between two kinds of completion is then run through each of the categories so that we see the basis of certain impossible conflicts. The first, concerning quantity, is whether the world has a begin-ning in time or is limited in space, with the thesis being in favour, the antithesis argu-ing against. The second, concerning quality, concerns whether the world is made up of simple parts, again, with the thesis arguing in favour, the antithesis against. These first two antinomies, concerning the world, are 'math-ematical' antinomies as they correspond to the mathematical principles of the Analytic. The second two antinomies are 'dynamical' with the third concerning relation in terms of origin with the thesis arguing for an origin of natural causality in a different causality of freedom and the antithesis denying this. Finally, the Fourth Antinomy is an antinomy of modality and discusses whether nature depends on something that is a necessary cause with the thesis arguing in favour and the antithesis against.

There are a number of debates about the Antinomies, not least the relation they possess to the principles of the Analytic. Recently, some writers have suggested,[8] in contradiction of established readings, that the argument of the Third Antinomy bears no specific connection to the Second Analogy, a view that depends in its turn on how the latter is viewed. The Antinomies have also received uneven treatment as the Third Antinomy has received much greater attention than the others. Kant's general 'solution' to the antinomies involves invoca-tion of the transcendental distinction. Kant basically suggests that in the cases of the first two antinomies there is no ground at all for determining a solution and that the problem arises by treating appearances as things in themselves. By contrast, the Third Antinomy does have a solution since freedom turns out to be negatively available as something that is not inconceivable and need not be in con-flict with the operation of nature. The Fourth Antinomy reference is, similarly, a possible one though no determinateness could be given to any such 'necessary' referent.

KANT'S CRITIQUE OF THEOLOGY

The discussion of the Fourth Antinomy is a preliminary to the following account of the 'ideal' of pure reason, which is a reference to the individuation of an idea (A568=B596). The transcendental ideal describes some-thing that is the 'sum total of all possibility' (A573=B601) and Kant goes on to discuss the speculative proofs that have been given of the existence of this being. This discussion is one of the most famous parts of **CPR** and is certainly one of its most influential. Kant argues that there are three such proofs: the ontological, the cosmological and the phys-ico-theological (or argument from design).

Kant's objection to the ontological argument repeats the point already made in **OPD** that existence is not a predicate and it is now added that the argument appears to involve a *petitio principii* since it assumes all along the being whose existence is apparently only hypothetical. Kant also objects to the view that there is some special status attached to propositions concerning the existence of God, referring to his cardinal distinction between synthetic and analytic judgments, showing thereby that the former cannot be true by definition and that the latter can introduce no new information.

The cosmological proof apparently appeals to experience but only in terms of the most general predications (existence and causation) but then seeks to ground these on something necessary where the concept of the latter is, in fact, surreptitiously borrowed from the ontological argument. Since causation cannot be used beyond the level of experience there is already a different problem with the argument, an argument that also confuses logical and transcendental possibility. Finally, the physico-theological argument is one that appeals to the notion of purposiveness, a procedure that renders this the most popular of all the arguments. Unlike the previous two, it would not, even if successful, prove a supreme being but only an artificer of products. Like the cosmological argument it pretends to rest on empirical grounds but secretly smuggles in the supreme being as defined by the ontological argument.

THE REGULATIVE USE OF IDEAS OF REASON

After dispatching 'rational' theology, Kant concludes the treatment of the dialectic with an 'appendix' that discusses the positive use ideas of pure reason can be put to. This argument was for long much neglected but

has been the source of some debate in recent years. The basic point concerning it is that here Kant denies constitutive employment of ideas but then introduces a regulative use of them. This latter is complicated in its deployment since Kant distinguishes here between the hypothetical employment of reason and the transcendental regulative principles of reason. This distinction is often overlooked with the effect that considerable confusion ensues. The former principles describe a generic form of unity but do not introduce the criteria for empirical truth that emerges from the latter and which are essentially related to a series of principles, foremost among which are the principles of parsimony, continuity and specification that had a first appearance in the 'principles of harmony' of **ID**. These principles appear to be as necessary for experience as the more famous ones of the Transcendental Analytic.[9]

THE DOCTRINE OF METHOD

The final section of **CPR**, after the closure of the Doctrine of Elements is the Doctrine of Method. This part of **CPR** has been much overlooked although it contains 'the formal conditions of a complete system of pure reason' (A708=B736). It is divided into four chapters of very uneven length with the majority of pages devoted to the 'discipline' of pure reason where this concerns not the content of pure reason, which has already been dealt with, but only its 'method'. In the course of this discussion, Kant elaborates further his distinction between philosophical and mathematical method, the distinction first clearly introduced by him in **Inq**. Kant here shows that the exactness of mathematics is not attainable by the philosopher through an examination of definitions, axioms and demonstrations. The necessity for the procedure of critique is further discussed with Kant making a claim concerning the 'legal' status of it that helps to clarify the legal metaphors with which the work abounds. In this chapter, Kant also discusses the role of hypotheses and proofs in philosophy.

The second chapter, on the 'canon' of pure reason, introduces the truncated practical philosophy of **CPR**. Here Kant discusses the ends of reason, in particular in connection with the questions about the existence of God, the immortality of the soul and the possibility of freedom, that he had described, as early as the introduction, as central to metaphysics. The discussion of morality that follows is clearly preparatory but already indicates that its measure cannot be by means of happiness. The nature of belief is also investigated with the specific status of it in practical philosophy emphasized.

In the third chapter, Kant discusses the 'architectonic' of reason or the need of it to form a system. This discussion is a remarkable one as it compares the activity of systematization to the growth of an animal body and Kant introduces here a form of schema which has received little commentary but which I would term a 'final end schema'. In the course of expounding it, Kant indicates the basis of the historicity of science which must begin with an idea to organize all its enquiry but which that enquiry will alter in the course of its execution. This alteration in the course of exposition for science is related to the need of philosophical systematization. Philosophy is now described as 'the science of the relation of all cognition to the essential ends of human reason' (A839=B867), which ensures that it has to be understood as something that has never been realized (to be an idea). Metaphysics is subsequently determined as that part of philosophy which 'is to present that cognition in this systematic unity' (A845=B873). It has the end of wisdom and it seeks it by the means of science. Kant here promises a metaphysics of morals and metaphysics of nature on the basis of **CPR**.

The final chapter of this section and of the whole work concerns the 'history' of pure reason and Kant here distinguishes between three types of history, one concerned with the 'object' of previous philosophical enquiry, one with its mode of cognizing and one in respect of method. In the first sense, the key contrast in philosophy has been between 'sensualists' such as Epicurus and 'intellectualists' such as Plato. In the second sense, the key contrast has been between those who derive cognition from experience, such as Aristotle or those who derive cognition from intelligible principles, such as Plato. The third contrast is drawn between 'naturalists' and 'scientists' with the former condemned as naïve in their attempt to proceed without the method of science from the senses alone and the latter divided between dogmatists (such as Wolff), sceptics (such as Hume) and critics (Kant himself).

PROLEGOMENA TO ANY FUTURE METAPHYSICS THAT WILL BE ABLE TO COME FORWARD AS SCIENCE (P)

This work was published in 1783, two years after the publication of the first edition of **CPR** and very much as a consequence of it. The initial reception of **CPR** was not favourable with the notorious Garve-Feder review particularly outraging Kant and effectively leading to him writing **P**. This is made clear by the 'Appendix' to this work where Kant attacks the review at some length making especially clear his displeasure at the comparison of the *Critique* to the work of Berkeley (P 372–380). The other element of the review and the general reception of **CPR** that annoyed and surprised Kant was the attack on its style and lack of popularity. In response, in the 'Preface' to this work, Kant attacks the 'common sense' philosophy but proceeds to present **P** as a popular presentation of the main doctrines of **CPR**. Also in this 'Preface', Kant makes the famous remark about having been awoken from his 'dogmatic slumbers' by remembering Hume's 'problem' with the notion of causality, a 'problem' Kant here specifically states to concern the *origin* of the concept.

THE METHOD OF THE 'PROLEGOMENA'

The 'Preamble' that follows the 'Preface' is where Kant makes clearer both the specific method of **P** and the difficulties of metaphysics that have occasioned his general Critical work. It is here that Kant first makes manifest his emphasis on metaphysics attaining a 'scientific' form as becomes key to the treatment of the second edition of **CPR**. Kant proceeds to distinguish between analytic and synthetic judgments and to make the principle of contradiction key to the former though, in his discussion of the syntheticity of mathematics, he has to point out that synthetic judgments might accord with the principle of contradiction without being generated by it.

Kant goes on to present the method of **P** to be an 'analytic' one in contrast to the 'synthetic' method of **CPR** but, again, distinguishes this method from the sense of 'analytic' at work in analytic judgments. In the case of the 'analytic' method, we begin by treating something as given and then work out the conditions under which it is possible for it to be given. So the general question of synthetic a priori judgments is now treated in relation to certain cognitions of pure reason that are already given. The subsequent division of the work is four-fold in accordance with the four elements treated as so given which concern pure mathematics, pure natural science and a two-fold inquiry into metaphysics, namely, first 'in general' and, secondly, 'as a science'.

PURE MATHEMATICS

The treatment of 'pure mathematics' aims to show that its possibility depends on its reliance on pure intuitions which concern only the form of sensibility. So, pure mathematics depends on the pre-given intuitions of space and time. In responding to the general objection that space and time are qualities of things in themselves, Kant introduces the argument from incongruent counterparts, an argument not used in **CPR** but which he had previously used, to very different effect in his early essay on regions of space (**DS**). Kant also points out that treating geometry as dependent on the pure intuition of space resolves the 'problem' of its application *to* space and rejects the confusion of his transcendental idealism with the idealism of Berkeley, even suggesting a new title for his own idealism, namely, 'critical' idealism.

PURE NATURAL SCIENCE

The treatment of pure natural science identifies 'pure natural science' as concerned with universal laws of nature, which are completely a priori. So, in this section, Kant treats the universal conditions of the possibility of experience, or, put another way, rehearses several of the central doctrines of the Transcendental Analytic of **CPR**. In the course of doing so, Kant introduces a novel and controversial distinction between judgments of perception and judgments of experience. The distinction is intended to correspond to the positive and negative uses of 'experience' in **CPR** itself with judgments of perception being the kind of judgments that arise purely from a relation to the sensory manifold in contradistinction to the principles that enable cognizance of the manifold, which latter are termed judgments of experience.

The distinction has caused some controversy and confusion[10] since Kant includes the notion that there are some judgments of perception that are intrinsically incapable of becoming judgments of experience due to their ineliminable subjectivity. However the distinction in general is less novel than many have claimed and is preliminary to a restatement of the derivation of the Table of Categories from the Table of Judgment as in **CPR**. The main point of it appears to be a critical one, to the effect that judgments of perception are incapable, by themselves alone, of leading to justification of the universal laws that are necessary if there is to be a 'pure natural science'. Kant proceeds to give, in very summary form, a statement of the central principles of **CPR** including his response to Hume's doubt concerning causality, which is treated as arising by trying to find something *in* experience that is in fact a necessary condition *for* experience (**P** 313).

METAPHYSICS

The treatment of the general possibility of metaphysics reprises many of the key arguments of the Transcendental Dialectic of **CPR**. In discussing the pure rational concepts or ideas, Kant refers to the treatment of them as constituting the 'essential end' of metaphysics and again discusses the ideas as arising from a need for completeness. Treatments of the Paralogisms, the Antinomies and the Transcendental Ideal all follow with the first of these given in a compressed form that anticipates the briefer account of the second edition of **CPR**. The antinomies are also

described as a device for rousing philosophy 'from its dogmatic slumber', a less famous use of this phrase. Kant's treatment of the positive regulative use of ideas is here very compressed.

At this point, the divisions in the treatment of the material become more confusing since a 'conclusion' is inserted prior to the discussion of the possibility of metaphysics as a science and this 'conclusion' concerns the 'bounds' of pure reason. Here Kant includes remarks on Hume's *Dialogues Concerning Natural Religion* as part of his distinction between 'limits' and 'bounds'. Mathematics and natural science are said to have 'limits' but not bounds where limit indicates that there is something beyond their inquiries but 'bounds' would be something internal to them that curtailed their means of operation. If mathematics and natural science have such limits but not bounds, the case is different with metaphysics as the latter does have 'bounds' and these are revealed in the Antinomies. In the course of making this argument, Kant suggests ways in which Hume's scepticism could be avoided without making dogmatic assertions through an appeal to an analogical use of reason. In the course of making this point, Kant suggests that the transcendental ideas help to lead us past pure naturalism but he here really points forwards to practical philosophy. The 'solution' of the question concerning the possibility of metaphysics as a science is revealed to be that it must first be subjected to critique.

THE GROUNDWORK FOR THE METAPHYSICS OF MORALS (G)

Published in 1785, this is the first work exclusively devoted to practical philosophy in the Critical period. It is also the single most influential contribution Kant made to moral philosophy. The point of it is clearly demarcated in the 'Preface' where Kant makes clear the need for a pure moral philosophy that is cleansed of all reference to the empirical and hence does not depend on anthropological data. The argument supporting the need for such an enquiry consists in the claim that all moral philosophy generally rests upon the pure element. The reason supporting this view is that there exists a moral law and the nature of this moral law will itself be demonstrated by means of a pure enquiry. This work is, however, specifically and clearly stated by Kant, not merely in its title but also in the argument of the 'Preface' to provide only a preliminary work on the foundations of the metaphysics of morals and not to give the metaphysics in question itself. In order to provide this foundation, there is only one task the work is devoted to and this is seeking out and establishing the supreme principle of morality (G 392). The application of this principle to a system of ethics is deferred though this has not prevented many readers of this work from trying to discern it here.

PHILOSOPHICAL METHOD IN THE 'GROUNDWORK'

The work is divided into three parts, each of which signals a 'transition' from one type of claim to another and Kant indicates that the work has a double type of method since initially he will proceed 'analytically' from ordinary moral claims to a determination of the supreme principle of morality and then work back 'synthetically' from an examination both of the principle itself and its sources to ordinary moral claims 'in which we find it used' (G 392). Surprisingly little has been made of this dual methodology, and where it has been commented on it has tended to be assumed that Kant is using the terms 'analytic' and 'synthetic' in the manner in which they work with regard to judgments, rather than methods of exposition as suggested in P.

There is, in fact, something of a combination of uses in Kant's reference here to 'analytic' and 'synthetic' since, on the one hand, he will show how certain kinds of connections are 'analytic' in the meaning of 'analytic judgments' while, on the other, he will develop his exposition after first an 'analytic' and then a 'synthetic' method. The distinction between these methods, as made in P, is that an 'analytic' method assumes something as given and then demonstrates the conditions under which it is given while a 'synthetic' method, by contrast, attempts to build something up by means of reference to its first conditions. As will become apparent, the first two sections of G operate according to an 'analytic' method, in addition to demonstrating 'analytic' types of connection in judgments while the third section operates in a 'synthetic' way to show the basis of a 'synthetic' judgment.

THE FIRST PART OF THE 'GROUNDWORK'

The first part of the work heralds a 'transition' from ordinary rational moral claims to philosophical ones. It begins with a famous discussion of the 'good will', which is hailed as that which is good without qualification or is an unconditional good. It is suggested that ordinary reason admits this notion, a point that Kant derives from his analysis of this ordinary reason (thus operating analytically with regard to ordinary reason). This is done by connecting the 'good will' to duty where it is shown that acting in accord with the good will requires no reference to inclination, and it is later suggested that actions done from duty have their work in the maxim according to which they are determined. Reference to the 'necessity' of acting out of respect for the law is also introduced but this notion is not here clearly defined since 'moral worth' is clearly stated not to follow from any effect expected from an action.

Kant does here arrive at an initial statement of the categorical imperative (**G** 402) as the law that arises when reference to expected effects is removed from the will. An initial example is also introduced to illustrate what it means to act in accord with such a law with the case of promising introduced (**G** 402–403). Kant admits, however, that while he takes himself to have analytically derived this law from ordinary rational moral claims, ordinary reason does not think this law abstractly in its universal form. Further, Kant suggests that the problem for ordinary moral claims is that it is possible to be led astray from this implicit universality as it is led into a 'natural dialectic' with the demands of inclination. In order to escape this dialectic, such reason is led to practical philosophy, not on speculative grounds, but on practical ones.

The Argument of 'Groundwork II'

The second section begins from the type of philosophy that ordinary practical claims are led to, namely 'popular' moral philosophy, and seeks to show how, analytically, there is a need to move from such grounds towards a metaphysics of morals. In opening this section, Kant states that while the purpose of the first part had been to show that ordinary use of practical reason was sufficient to demonstrate that there is a moral law, that it does not thereby follow that this law was derived from 'experience'. In showing that this is the case, Kant points out that there are many complaints to the effect that there is no basis, in reference to experience, for thinking

that there even exists such a moral law as he discovered in the first section. In addition, if there is a moral law, such a law could not, in any case, apply only to human beings but must, instead, apply to all rational beings. Kant also adds a word of caution concerning examples since he points out that morality cannot be derived *from* them.

In discussing 'popular moral philosophy', Kant clearly has in view the claims of 'common sense' as articulated by philosophers of the day as he similarly did when arguing against it in **P**. Such 'common sense' it is now suggested cannot arrive at purity of insight in moral matters but must eclectically ground its principles on a number of sources. In opposition to this tendency, Kant affirms again the need for *a method of isolation* that will permit the exposition of a metaphysics of morals unmixed with anthropology (or theology or anything else). After making this declaration, Kant proceeds to make the argument for moving towards such a pure enquiry. In doing so, Kant examines the structure of moral claims and describes them as imperatives that describe something as good to do. Having made this point, Kant proceeds to distinguish between hypothetical and categorical imperatives where the first sort indicates that something is good for a purpose that is either possible or actual. Such imperatives are distinct from categorical ones as the latter claim something to be necessary without reference to any further end.

The discussion of hypothetical imperatives is divided into two kinds with the point made that everything technical is accomplished by describing something as possible with regard to the adoption of certain ends. These types of hypothetical imperatives are termed by Kant 'imperatives of skill' and have a problematic modality according to the Table of Categories of **CPR**. By contrast, if we assume happiness as an actual end (even if we do not know in what this consists), then the adoption of means to it gives us imperatives of prudence which have an assertoric modality. Finally, the categorical imperative commands something without reference to any further purpose and is the imperative of morality whose modality is one of necessity.

After describing these kinds of imperative, Kant enquires after their possibility and describes the two forms of hypothetical imperative as involving analytical connections between means and end. By contrast, the categorical imperative involves a synthetic connection as the willing of action is connected immediately with the will of a rational being even though there is no analytic relation between the two elements. Hence, the problem of the possibility of the categorical imperative concerns how a practical imperative can take the form of a synthetic a priori connection. Having raised this problem, Kant proceeds to defer its solution and to concentrate instead on the question of whether there is not a different kind of analytic connection in the categorical imperative. This is a connection between the mere concept of the categorical imperative and the formula of such an imperative. This cannot exist for a hypothetical imperative as the end must be given before we know in what it consists. But since the categorical imperative contains no reference to an end other than the one involved in its own formulation there is, Kant suggests, an 'immediate' connection between thinking it and cognizing what it must state. In the thought of the law stated in such an imperative we have the conception that maxims must accord with it necessarily and no restriction on the condition of the law. If the law is unrestricted, however, this is as much as to say that it must be given as universal. This leads Kant to formulate the

categorical imperative quite simply as a formula of universal law (G 421).

Despite Kant's claim for the formula of universal law there is considerable controversy in the interpretation of this section concerning formulas of the categorical imperative with Herbert Paton classically claiming that Kant gives five formulas of it while others have been content to find only three.[11] The solution to this question is found by looking at Kant's method of procedure after stating the categorical imperative as a formula of universal law. After stating this Kant adds that all imperatives of duty (specific moral claims) can be derived from the categorical imperative as this will tell us the principle of all such duties. However, prior to giving his first set of 'examples' of application of the law, Kant first follows the procedure of CPR and treats the formula of universal law as he there treated the categories. That is, Kant proceeds to schematize the categorical imperative by connecting it to the conditions under which causal connections are generally given. These were determined in CPR as essential for arriving at the conception of 'nature' or a whole of universal laws and Kant now takes this conception of 'nature' and reformulates the formula of the categorical imperative in order to arrive at what he terms a 'universal imperative of duty'. This latter is stated as the view that we should act *as if* the maxim of our action were to become through our will a universal law of nature (an interestingly regulative statement of law). It is only after so re-formulating the categorical imperative that examples are then given in order to test it.

The examples are said to be taken from the 'usual division' of duties into duties to ourselves and others and perfect and imperfect duties though these divisions are not here explained or accounted for. The examples are divided into two classes as the first two, concerned with suicide and (once again) promising involve cases where to take a certain maxim as giving the rule to 'a system of nature' would produce a direct contradiction into such a system.

The second two examples, concerned with the cultivation of talents and beneficence, do not produce such a direct contradiction into the 'system of nature' but the reasons for not adopting certain maxims now are stated to instead reside in a contradiction in willing certain types of end universally. This division is complex and controversial though Kant's general point is stated simply as requiring consistency in willing with reference to the standpoint of reason.

After having examined these points, Kant confesses that he has not as yet shown that the categorical imperative really exists. In order to press further on with his enquiry, Kant now assesses the question of whether it is necessary for all rational beings to judge actions according to maxims in such a way that the maxims in question serve as universal laws. Such a law, if it exists, would have to have an a priori connection with the concept of the will of rational beings. In order to discover the connection between the law and the will, however, Kant moves decisively into the terrain of the metaphysics of morals.

As with his earlier discussion of types of imperatives, Kant now discusses types of motivation of the will, discarding empirical motivations and looking for objective laws and describing ends as either 'subjective' in being based on inclination or 'objective' in being based on something that would be valid for all rational beings. Having made this distinction, Kant also points to the ground of subjective principles as requiring a matter of a certain kind (just as hypothetical imperatives required a certain pre-given end). By contrast, objective principles would be formal only, not requiring a pre-given matter to be given to them. Similarly, ends which require a certain matter to be given are relative to those ends and take their worth only from the worth of the ends in question. By contrast, if there is something whose worth is not relative but absolute then it would provide the ground of the categorical rather than merely hypothetical imperative.

That which is taken to have such an absolute worth by Kant is the existence of rational beings themselves precisely because, in their possession of reason, they possess something which does not have a merely relative worth but is rather the ground of all else having worth. So the rational being is an end-in-itself and not merely a means to something else. This leads to Kant formulating what he terms the 'practical imperative', which is generally known as the formula of humanity and from which he states all laws of the will must be able to be derived. It follows from this claim that it should coincide in application with the schematized formula of universal law and the same four examples are used as were given for the previous formula. One difference in the application of this formula is that while the first two examples are treated as conflicting with the end of humanity directly, the second two forms are argued only 'not to harmonize' with it. This distinction has, somewhat surprisingly, drawn significantly less attention than the division in the treatment of duties arising from the schematized formula of universal law.

After stating the formula of humanity and describing the examples in relation to it, Kant goes on to discuss the distinction between them is that the first formula gave the rule according to universality and then describe the means of rendering it as a law (through reference to the type of nature) while the second, by contrast, describes the subject of all ends in the form of an end-in-itself. The third principle is then described as a combination of the first two, namely, a rational being that wills universal law and by this means Kant arrives at the notion of the autonomy of the will, which is contrasted with principles of heteronomy. The total vision of beings generally acting in accord with the law provides us with the image of a 'kingdom of ends' where each rational being is sovereign and all laws derive from the same single source of reason.

Kant schematically presents maxims as having a form, which is universal, a matter, which is an end and a complete determination in the notion of the kingdom of ends where this latter is clearly an analogue to the transcendental ideas discussed in **CPR**. Having reached this point, Kant can now descend back to the notion with which he began the first section, the notion of the 'good will' and describe the good will as that which takes maxims whose universality are willable as the ground of its laws. However, this section closes with the question arising again of how the synthetic practical a priori proposition whose content has been thus uncovered is itself possible.

THE ARGUMENT OF 'GROUNDWORK III'

The third and final section of the work has been one of the most controversial parts with wide misunderstanding of its argument and rejection of its results. Here Kant makes the last 'transition', this time from a metaphysics of morals to a critique of pure practical reason. The section opens where the previous section closed, with the notion of the will but examines it now in terms of its causality. In accord with **CPR**, Kant describes freedom as a spontaneous causality and connects such a notion to the categorical imperative.

Kant confesses a certain circularity of reasoning in getting the categorical imperative supported by freedom as freedom is a reciprocal idea with autonomy and thus not able to support it. In response, Kant develops the notion that we look at ourselves from two different points of view on the basis of the distinction between appearances and things in themselves. Reason, as a pure form of spontaneity, as is expressed in its formation of ideas, appears to go well beyond anything offered to the mind by sensibility. In looking at our power of reason, we view ourselves from the standpoint of intelligence rather than that of sensibility. So when we think of ourselves as free we look at ourselves on the pattern of our reason and it is also from this that we arrive at the notion of autonomy.

The synthetic a priori proposition that is the categorical imperative is based on connecting the will, viewed as something capable of being affected, with the idea of the will as something intelligible with the sense that the latter can determine the former through reason. The law is hence something like a category of reason which may well explain the process of schematization of it in accord with the general idea of unity taken from understanding (nature). The world into which we move when we think reason, the intelligible world, is not one that can be thought in any way except through the nature of its formal adherence to law, so we cannot explain how it is possible that pure reason can be practical. The intelligible world is rather only what remains when we have excluded from motivation all that comes from the law of sense. Kant closes the work with a confession of the impossibility of seeking further for the ground of possibility of morality.

METAPHYSICAL FOUNDATIONS OF NATURAL SCIENCE (MFNS)

This work was published in 1786, a year prior to the second edition of **CPR** and there are many respects in which its writing appears related to the re-drafting of the Analytic of Principles of **CPR** and also to indicate, along with **P**, the emphasis that emerges in the second edition of **CPR** on the notion of metaphysics as a 'science'. Of all the key works of the Critical period, it has received least attention though the attention it has been paid has tended to be lively with Gerd Buchdahl and Michael Friedman presenting sharply different interpretations of the import of the principles provided in this book.[12] It is divided into four parts, each of which accords both with the Table of Categories of **CPR** and with the Analytic of Principles that schematized the table.

In the 'Preface', Kant begins by discussing the term 'nature', distinguishing between the sense of it applied when we speak of the 'nature' of a thing, which he describes as its 'internal principle' or essence and the term when it is used to describe the totality of objects of experience. The latter could further be sub-divided between 'body' and 'soul'. After making these points concerning 'nature', Kant turns next to the discussion of 'science', describing it as 'a whole of cognition ordered according to principles' (**MFNS** 467). For there to be a 'science' of nature it would have to be the case that cognition of it would be a rational one concerned with coherence. However, and more importantly, the notion of natural science is also presented by Kant as having two possible forms, one concerned with a priori principles and the other with 'laws of experience' and he is firm in declaring that only the former is truly 'science' as only it can attain apodeictic certainty.

On the basis of this point concerning a priori principles, Kant denies that chemistry is a 'true' science. 'Nature' is also understood to involve a reference to necessary laws, which relates the notion to the sense of 'science' given. The work is an extended investigation into 'pure natural science', the possibility of which had been a subject of investigation in the second part of **P**. Unlike in **CPR** where Kant looked at the laws that make possible nature in general, here we are focused on a 'special' nature. In order to look at this 'special' nature, we require an empirical concept to be given to us, which, in this case, is the concept of 'matter'. In order to undertake a 'special' doctrine of nature, however, we must grasp the concept of the 'science' of this nature in terms of mathematics. The reason for this is that we are dealing, in the case of this 'special' science, with determinate natural things and to do that we cannot proceed with concepts alone but also require a priori intuitions (as was detailed in the discussion of pure natural science in **P**). These latter, to give us a sense of something determinate, have to be rendered in the form of mathematics. It is precisely the impossibility of rendering the claims of chemistry in such mathematical form that leads Kant to disqualify its attempt to be termed a 'science' (**P** 471) though it is arguable that chemistry attained this status around the time Kant published this work. More importantly than the status of chemistry is the inability of discussions of the mind being viewed by Kant as 'scientific' since, with the mind, there is no necessary reference to external intuition. So Kant's view of what counts as a 'science' is certainly more restrictive than standards that have since tended to be applied though its significance as a standard is that it allows a clear sense to be given of what is meant by a division of 'science' between 'pure' and 'applied', a division that other accounts often cannot meet so well.

The investigation of a pure doctrine of body thus emerges as the province of the work with this notion based on an analysis of 'the concept of a matter in general' (**MFNS** 472). This notion of 'matter' is itself taken from experience but it is now isolated in relation to pure intuition and this method of isolation enables Kant to produce a metaphysics of corporeal nature. In referring to the dependence of his exposition on the Table of Categories, Kant also adds a famous footnote promising a recasting of the Transcendental Deduction on the basis of 'a single conclusion from the precisely determined definition of a judgment in general' (**MFNS** 475–476n.), which points again to the second edition of **CPR**. However, in relation to the application of this table to the concept of matter, Kant next argues that matter must be seen in motion as only thereby are the senses affected. So natural science is now concisely defined as 'either a pure or an applied doctrine of motion' (**MFNS** 477) with this work providing the former. Effectively, in introducing the notion of motion in this way, Kant immediately schematizes the bare concept of matter and does so in accord with the programme of mechanist philosophers at least as early as Descartes. The four headings of the work relate matter in motion to the four titles of the Table of the Categories.

THE FOUNDATIONS OF PHORONOMY

The first part, phoronomy, relates motion to pure quantity without consideration of quality and corresponds to the treatment of the Axioms of Intuition in **CPR**. Matter, understood as movable, requires reference to space as space is the intuitive basis of the claim of movement. Kant opens the discussion, however, by distinguishing between the space in which such movement can be grasped and the basis of thinking movement as such which requires a distinction between relative and absolute space. The space in which all movement is given requires reference to a space that can be thought as enabling movement to be given and this latter would not itself be movable but would be absolute and hence an object of thought, not of intuition.

Movement, understood in abstraction from quality, is something purely external and is hence equivalent to a point which can have velocity and direction. Space in which there is movement must itself be capable also of movement in order to be sensed as otherwise our senses would not be affected by it. Further, there is the distinction of levels of movement where something is seen moving in relation to something else of similar scale but to be at rest relative to something of a different scale and this requires a distinction of spaces that are given in movement. So we assume absolute space as a fixed reference point for all the movable spaces though such absolute space is not itself an 'object' but only a 'logical' universal (**MFNS** 482).

Motion involves changes of external relations though, Kant suggests, it is only with points that we can truly say that motion is always a change of place as larger bodies can move without changing place or change place without moving. Kant also uses the discussion of incongruent counterparts that was mentioned in **P** to illustrate what is meant by the claim that with some different motions the only distinction is 'internal' without having recourse to any concepts of quality. In the case of two circular motions that differ only in direction we have incongruent counterparts and the difference here is not conceptual but only intuitive.

Kant next provides a purely phoronomic sense of permanence as rest or endurance

41

(**MFNS** 485). As with the discussion of move-ment, so also the account of rest has to typi-cally revise the naïve sense given to the term since rest, if interpreted as lack of motion, will not be capable of being intuitively constructed and so, in place of it, Kant substitutes the sense of a motion 'with infinitely small speed throughout a finite time' (**MFNS** 486).

After making these points, which do not immediately require a sense of motion being produced by relations between points, Kant turns to the more difficult case, which he terms 'composite motion' (**MFNS** 486), where we intuitively present a movement as arising from the effect of two conjoint movements being united. Since we are only dealing with movement as quantitative alone we cannot, in consideration of this conception, include as yet any reference to forces. So motion, in a general sense, when we are at the level of phoronomy, is equivalent to the description of a space. However, this is distinct from a merely geo-metrical consideration as we refer not merely to the space but also to the time and velocity with which the point describes the space.

Cartesian investigation of motion was hence entirely carried out at the level of phoronomy. In accounting for composition of motions at this level, we merely reduce them to condi-tions under which a motion is compounded from two others and built up from there. Two motions can be considered in one of three pos-sibilities: either as in the same direction; in opposite directions; or in an angle. These three possibilities are subsequently constructed in intuition by Kant and then related to the three moments of quantity from the Table of Judgment of **CPR**.

THE FOUNDATIONS OF DYNAMICS

The second chapter of the work concerns dynamics where Kant considers the movable insofar as it *fills* a space, that is, in relation to quality, which corresponds to the treatment of sensation in the Anticipations of Perception of **CPR**. Filling a space involves resistance to other parts of matter that 'strive' to fill the space in which the current matter is present. This dynamical sense of matter is based upon the phoronomic one but, in its reference to a capacity of resistance, builds in a further feature that could not be considered at the level of pho-ronomy alone. The 'resistance' in question at the level of dynamics is still restricted since we work here not with the notion of a resistance persisting after movement has taken place but rather only the resistance that would prevent diminution of the extension of matter in space.

The filling of space does not take place just due to the existence of matter since, on that basis alone, we would only have phoronomic considerations. Rather, what is required for such filling to take place is a special moving force. If matter enters a space, it does so by moving but resistance to such entry dimin-ishes movement or even requires rest. But the only thing capable of resisting movement would itself be movement and this requires that such latter movement must itself be forc-ing the first movement. So matter fills space by means of moving force. In making this claim, Kant opposes the view of Lambert (and Locke) that the principle by which space is filled is solidity. The problem with viewing the property of filling space as being merely solidity is that it seems to imply that there is something conceptually involved in matter being resistant, a view Kant ridicules by say-ing that the concept of contradiction does not force matter back. In other words, we have to include in the conception of matter something that enables repulsion to take place before we could claim that there was a contradiction involved in non-resistant matter. We cannot just postulate this force in matter: we have to intuitively demonstrate its existence, not simply attempt to derive it from a concept.

Having opened with this point, Kant goes on to distinguish between attractive and repulsive force, with the former being a moving force of matter that leads other matter to be drawn towards it. The latter force, by contrast, leads other matter to retreat from the vicinity. All extension into space has a degree, however, and can be envisioned as greater or smaller to an infinite degree.

The filling of space occurs through the expansion of matter and such expansion is also termed by Kant 'elasticity' and is an original property of matter that cannot be derived from anything else. Although matter can be compressed to infinity, therefore, it cannot be penetrated by any other matter as this would require an infinitely compressive force which is impossible. The sense of impenetrability involved is relative to the degree of compression while an absolute notion of impenetrability would not permit compression at all without positing empty space within matter. The mathematical notion of impenetrability does not reach the notion of physical properties while the dynamical one determines the possibility of extension existing at all and the means by which it can be diminished.

The dynamical conception of substance is that it is that in space which, without reference to anything existing outside it in space, is nonetheless movable. Kant also postulates the infinite divisibility of matter with all the parts of matter being themselves forms of matter and not of something else. In making this claim, Kant repudiates the position he adopted in **PhM** where he had denied the infinite divisibility of matter and he here replies to his own earlier argument (**MFNS** 504–508). Kant now points out that infinite divisibility of matter, while not following from the infinite divisibility of space, does follow if we assume all parts of

space are filled with matter and adopt the additional assumption that matter cannot be broken down into something that is not matter. We can see this in the following way. If space is filled with matter and matter cannot be broken down into something that is not matter then, in filling all the parts of space, it has to fill all the parts of its division. In filling all the parts of the division it also indicates that a force of resistance belongs to each part of matter. However, due to the transcendental distinction between appearances and things in themselves, we cannot say that it therefore follows that there is *actual* divisibility to infinity since we deal only with appearances and do not have an actual division to work with. Further division is indefinite and possible only and belongs only to appearances without in itself being able to lead us to reject the notion of monads. However, the monads are not available physically but only intelligibly.

Kant moves on to argue specifically for the need of the notion of attractive force as part of matter. Impenetrability has been shown to make extension possible but not only does it do this but it also allows the continued expansion of matter. If impenetrability were matter's only force, then there would be no bounds to the extension of any given part of matter so we would be unable to assign any particular quantity of it to any assignable space. Due to this, we require the notion of a force that is opposed to the extensive one, a force that compresses matter and hence operates against repulsion, which would be to operate in a way that was attractive. However, attractive force likewise could not exist alone as its effect is only to compress and if it existed alone the universe would shrink to a single point. The nature of attraction in matter is that it acts as an immediate action 'through empty space' of one matter upon another.

In addressing this point, Kant attempts to answer the basis of attractive force by means of metaphysics, a basis Newton sought to avoid addressing by an allegedly instrumentalist use of mathematical notions. The means by which Kant addresses this is through reference to the original conditions of attraction. Attraction must precede any given specific contact of matter and be independent of such contact since it renders it possible. But if it is independent of such contact in its original operation then it is independent of the filling of space between the two moved matters so it must take place originally without the spaces all needing to be filled and hence by means of empty space. So attraction is originally action at a distance. Attractive force can be no further explained than this since it is an original force that cannot be derived from anything else. However, Kant's argument shows a basis for contact and further demonstrates that contact alone is merely a cessation of motion and so cannot be the basis of attraction. The original attractive force is also argued to extend itself through the whole universe to infinity.

In his 'general observation' on dynamics, Kant adds a basis for thinking of space as now filled throughout in opposition to the contemporary deployment of 'empty space', repeating here an argument first used in **CPR** (A173–175=B215–217), here adding that 'empty space' is now only a hypothesis and not a principle. After making this point, Kant moves on to contrast two ways of responding to nature, the 'mathematico-mechanical' and the 'metaphysical-dynamical', pointing out that the former requires the notion of absolute impenetrability, which he has shown to be false and that with its interpolation of empty space into the interior of matter it allows the imagination inordinate freedom.

The Foundation of Mechanics

The third chapter concerns mechanics and here we arrive at the notion of 'moving force' or the communication of motion from one part of matter to another. For this to be thought requires that the teachings of dynamics have first been given. It is at this point that Kant can introduce, for the first time, the grounded determinate notion of 'body' as a mass of determinate shape. The first point made here is that the quantity of matter can be estimated only by a quantity of motion at a given velocity, a view that leads him to officially repudiate the conception of 'living forces' with which he began his philosophical career, adopting now the view that the forces of dynamics are 'dead' forces and that if 'living' forces are to be spoken of this can only be by means of mechanics.

Kant next goes on to state the three laws of mechanics in turn, starting with the conservation principle that the quantity of matter stays constant (which affects the restatement of the First Analogy in the second edition formulation in **CPR**). The substance dealt with in mechanics is that of matter and the conservation principle gives us the mechanical formula for substance. In remarking on this point, Kant points to the difference between speaking of substance in spatial terms as opposed to attempting to apply it to non-spatial ones, as in the latter case there is no contradiction in something fading away (a point used against Moses Mendelssohn at B414–415).

The second law of mechanics is the principle of inertia that each body stays in the same state unless something external brings about a change in it, which is rendered in general as the claim that we require external causes for matter to change, the first specific and direct reference to 'causes' in the whole work. Kant here refers to the proof of the Second Analogy and determines its generic principle in relation to matter which brings in external relations of space. Kant denies that the claim concerning actions having equal and opposite reactions states a genuine law of inertia as it does not tell us what matter is prevented from doing, and to posit the law of inertia in a positive form suggests that matter is endowed with positive striving to conserve its state. To do the latter is to move towards the view that matter contains life, the view Kant calls 'hylozoism' and which he terms 'the death of all natural philosophy' (**MFNS** 544).

The third law of mechanics is then stated as the rule concerning action and reaction being always equal in communication of motion. As with the previous two laws so with this one Kant refers first to the generic principle taken from **CPR**, namely, in this case, the Third Analogy. The main point now is to show that reciprocal action is best understood as reaction. This is shown by building on the arguments given so far in mechanics, namely, by referring to the claim that all changes of matter are changes of motion and that all changes of motion are reciprocal and equal (based on the conservation of motion). If we add to this the point that every change of matter has an external cause as just shown in the second law, then the cause of the change of motion of one body entails an equal and opposite change of the other, which is sufficient to show that action must be equal to reaction. In his remarks on this law, Kant refers to Newton as failing to bring this law out of a priori concepts and Kepler's viewing it as based on a force of inertia (of the sort ruled out in the discussion of the second law). In his 'general observation' on mechanics, Kant refers also to the mechanical law of continuity as based on the inertia of matter.

THE FOUNDATIONS OF PHENOMENOLOGY

The fourth and final chapter is concerned with phenomenology or the modal experience of the motion of matter. The general notion that is here explicated is matter in motion as an object of experience. Motion is given as an appearance like everything represented through sense and thus here Kant merely draws together the doctrines of the work, finally indicating a modal status to some determinations of matter. This is done in three propositions. In the first, Kant describes rectilinear motion as merely possible and shows that even as possible it can only be relative. This possible motion is equivalent to that analysed in phoronomy. Circular motion, by contrast to rectilinear, is an actual predicate of matter and is equivalent to what was expressed in dynamics. Finally, the equal and opposite motion of a body in regard to another body, is a necessary predicate of matter in experience, equivalent to the notion analysed in mechanics. In the 'general remark' on phenomenology, Kant also discusses absolute space and shows that it is an idea of reason, connecting it thereby to the regulative ideas of pure reason discussed in the Transcendental Dialectic of **CPR**.

CRITIQUE OF PRACTICAL REASON (CPrR)

Published in 1788, a year after the second edition of **CPR**, this work is often simply termed the 'second *Critique*' though Kant himself only used the name '*Critique*' to refer to **CPR**. This work appears three years after **G** and many commentators have been confused about the relationship between these two works. It has also confused some with its title since the contrast with that of **CPR** suggests to them that practical reason is not pure. Kant's view, however, as stated explicitly in the first sentence of the 'Preface', is quite the opposite. The reason for writing the book is to show, on the basis of a criticism of practical reason in general, that there is such a thing as pure practical reason. On the basis of this demonstration, Kant seeks to show, further, the reality of transcendental freedom. The relation between freedom and the moral law is somewhat complicated since, on the one hand, freedom is the condition of the moral law and, on the other hand, the relationship is also the reverse. The essence of the moral law is explicated as consisting fundamentally in freedom and so in this sense freedom is the condition of the moral law. On the other hand, the way in which one comes to know about freedom is through the moral law and so in this sense the moral law is the condition of freedom.

In this work, Kant also finally cashes out his claim that metaphysics ultimately deals, in a positive way, with the immortality of the soul and the existence of God though these notions, unlike freedom, despite being said to have 'practical-objective reality', do not have the same type of 'reality' as freedom. In making these claims, Kant also here presents his claim for the primacy of practical reason, a claim that was of some significance to the German Idealists. Of further significance is the way this work corroborates the argument of **CPR** that there is a dual aspect to the self and, indeed, further provides its own argument for the importance of the ideality of space and time. These specific points are stressed by Kant himself as reasons why this work had to be written (**CPrR** 6–7) and do relate it closely to **CPR** (something that is not the case for **G**). The specific relationship to **G** that Kant states is that this work relates to the formula of the principle of duty provided by the earlier work but that it is otherwise independent

of it (in the sense of not relying upon the earlier work's demonstrations). Kant also states that in this work he has responded to an objection raised against **G** by showing a reason why the notion of the 'good' arises from the consideration of the law and not the other way around (often referred to in contemporary philosophy as the priority of the right over the good).

The organization of this work is partially modelled on that of **CPR** but with some important changes, only some of which Kant is explicit about. It is divided, as was the earlier *Critique*, into a doctrine of elements and a doctrine of method though the latter is very short and is less significant than was the case with **CPR**. The Doctrine of Elements includes a division between an analytic and a dialectic but there is no separate 'aesthetic' though there are reasons for thinking that there is a chapter on an 'aesthetic' of practical reason within the Analytic (as is partially admitted by Kant). Kant himself is clear about the changes in the organization of the Analytic as with this work we have an analytic of principles prior to an analytic of concepts with the reason given that we have, in the area of practical reason, to deal with the will and its causality. So we have to start with the conditions of general causality of the will and purify them to reach the form fit for our enquiry prior to applying this will first to objects and secondly to the subject (in terms of the conditions of the 'aesthetic' of practical reason).

The Analytic opens with a definition of practical principles as 'propositions that contain a general determination of the will' (**CPrR** 19). If we have principles that would hold for any rational being then they will be 'laws' (as opposed to 'maxims' which are merely subjective). Practical rules generally involve prescription of means to given ends.

Practical Theorems

Three 'theorems' follow this definition, the first stating that practical principles that presuppose an object or matter are, in virtue of this presupposition, empirical only and hence not fit to produce 'laws'. The second theorem then classifies all material practical principles as being of the same kind and listing them under the general heading of principles of happiness (which amounts to treating them as 'prudential' as **G** would state). Since these material rules require the sense of inclinations that are aimed at some sense of gratification, the corollary is that they are all part of the 'lower faculty of desire' and if there were not also purely formal laws of the will, there would be no higher faculty of desire. This prompts two further 'remarks' added to the discussion of the second theorem with the first pre-empting John Stuart Mill in arguing against the view that the distinction between 'lower' and 'higher' could be explicated by taking different 'objects' of pleasure. The second remark points out that principles of self-love can include universal rules of skill but that such rules are theoretical and not practical principles. The third theorem then draws the reverse implication of the second to the effect that to think practical universal laws these must be determined only in terms of form. Kant again adds a 'remark' to this point giving the example of determining maxims by their form with the example of lying in relation to deposits.

Two 'problems' are next stated, the first of which concerns finding the constitution of a will that is determinable by law alone and the second asking how we find the law that could determine a free will necessarily. The answer to the first 'problem' is that a will that is free is so determinable by law alone and the answer to the second is that only a

formal law could determine a free will necessarily. So we have already reached an argument for seeing a free will and a formal law as closely related to each other.

After showing this Kant first states the 'fundamental law' of pure practical reason in the form of the categorical imperative (**CPrR** 30). Thinking the will merely formally requires thinking it separately from all empirical conditions and to become aware of such a law is now termed by Kant a 'fact of reason' (**CPrR** 31). The fourth theorem claims that the sole principle of all moral laws and of duties in keeping with them is autonomy (which accords with the argument of **G**). This notion is thought just negatively when we consider ourselves as independent of determination from all matter but is thought positively when we think the moral law as itself grounded in reason alone. There is required for any act of willing a matter that is willed but this is not sufficient to reach the conclusion that the determining ground of all volition is itself a matter. To begin with, this does not fit the notion of rational beings as such (which would have to include the way God would will). But, further, this determination by the matter could not give the basis of morality in any case. In demonstrating this second claim Kant considers examples as he had in the second part of **G**. Key among the examples is false testimony (lying), which presents a maximal image of someone determined only by prudential maxims. The point of the examples in this case is only to act as a *reductio* of the view that happiness could serve as a universal basis of moral law.

The Deduction of the Principles of Pure Practical Reason

Kant next turns to a 'Deduction' of the principles of pure practical reason. In the course of presenting this, Kant refers to the difference of procedure of this *Critique* to the first one. Whereas **CPR** proceeded by means of a contrast between concepts and intuitions and then arrived at synthetic a priori principles **CPrR**, on the basis of the moral law, points to a pure world of the understanding that is determined positively.

The point now is to show that the sensible world can be contrasted with a supersensible one and the latter has its basis in terms of the autonomous laws of pure reason. This law is the moral law which transfers us, in thought, into a nature governed by pure reason. Again, the nature of 'testimony' is adduced to demonstrate the way in which such a law can determine us.

The problem of how pure reason can be an immediate determining ground of the will requires no reference to a priori intuition but only to the concept of freedom. This is sufficient to give an *exposition* of the supreme principle of practical reason. The *deduction* concerns the justification of the objective and universal validity of the synthetic a priori that is stated in the law. But there is no 'deduction' of the law itself as it is rather the case that the law is the basis of the deduction of freedom. The moral law is, as has been shown, a law of causality by means of freedom and so it fills in the blank merely problematic possibility of freedom that was bequeathed by **CPR**. This law is a determinate law of causality in an intelligible world.

The Cognition of Pure Practical Reason

To think the moral law is however to relate the form of law of the intelligible world to the sensible world in a causative way and this requires extending cognition beyond the sensible world, something that was denied as possible in **CPR**. The practical use of pure reason thus appears to extend cognition beyond what is possible for theoretical reason. This requires relating practical reason to theoretical reason in order to think again about the boundaries of cognition. Kant reverts back to the case of Hume's doubts concerning causation, first mentioned in **P** as the basis of critique starting work. The result of this, as summarized again here, was the transcendental distinction between appearances and things in themselves and that the problem of causal connection was resolvable if seen as a question of appearances and their condition in temporality. The reason why all this is invoked again here, however, becomes clearer when we recall that the causality of the will is the starting point of **CPrR**. The objective reality of the pure will is given a priori by the moral law and the causality of this will involves freedom. The notion of causation in the most general sense was shown by the ability to think causality as a pure category and we have now connected this thought to that of the moral law.

The 'Objects' of Practical Reason

Kant now turns to the Analytic of Concepts of **CPrR** where 'a concept of an object of practical reason' means 'the representation of an object as an effect possible through freedom' (**CPrR** 57). The type of possibility in question is clearly moral possibility and the only objects of it are 'the *good*' and 'the *evil*'. The 'good' however, if thought as the basis of law, can only mean some form of pleasure and that would be to take the good to be equivalent to the agreeable. The 'paradox of method' of this work is thus explained, namely, the reason why the concepts of good and evil are not determined prior to the notion of the moral law but only as a consequence of the latter. In presenting the priority of the law over the concepts of the good and evil, Kant reverses the procedure of moral philosophy since this has traditionally taken an object of the will as a matter and ground of the law. This left two forms of heteronomous ethics, that grounded in feeling alone (happiness) and that based on a matter derived from concepts (such as the will of God). Having made this point Kant performs next a kind of 'metaphysical deduction' of the categories of freedom (**CPrR** 66).

While the concepts of good and evil give an object for the will, this object is itself based on a practical rule of reason. Now, at this point, Kant returns to the question of the relationship between such a rule of reason and the specific determination of actions. Specific actions are empirical and hence are part of the experience of nature so the question arises of how a law of freedom applies to the particulars of nature. After all, the supersensible world appears completely different in kind to the sensible. So the law relates not to the actions directly but rather to actions by means of a schema, but not one that involves intuition so that what the law is related to is not imagination but rather the understanding. The understanding provides the type of a law of nature and it is by relating to this that the moral law is schematized which gives what Kant terms 'the rule of judgment under laws of pure practical reason' (**CPrR** 69), which is nothing other than the law of nature formula that was set out as the first basis for discussion of examples in **G**. This provides us with a thought experiment by which we can relate to actions as if they were the basis of a law of nature. Kant again invokes the example of lying to show this. The type of the sensible world is used thus to govern the intelligible world.

THE 'AESTHETIC' OF PRACTICAL REASON

The last major chapter of the Analytic is taken up with the provision of an 'aesthetics' in which the question is addressed of how to give the law influence on the will. For the law to be operative, we must relate to our will as free, namely, as independent of material inclinations but this is only a negative account of the law's operation on the will. This negative effect operates when we compare our conduct to that enjoined by the will and find it wanting; there we suffer a feeling of humiliation. But the positive way the law operates on the will is as an object that is itself positive as it is an intellectual causality that is an object of respect. The purely negative effect is pathological but respect is a feeling produced solely by reason itself. The latter is given an example in the conduct of another who demonstrates by their way of acting the possibility of being moral. Duty is that to which we are called by the law. The condition of agreement with the autonomy of the will is the self-direction of reason to act in accord with duty and this shows the inner presence of action in accord with the law to lie within ourselves. Hence the real incentive to act morally is that such action brings out the intelligible nature of personality. The Analytic of **CPrR** closes with a 'critical elucidation' that investigates and justifies the form of the Analytic itself. Here Kant again compares the organization of **CPrR** with that of **CPR** and shows en route that without the ideality of space and time there would be no way to forestall fatalism (**CPrR** 101–102).

THE DIALECTIC OF PURE PRACTICAL REASON

The Dialectic that follows the Analytic relates, as did that of **CPR**, to an unconditioned totality, here in terms of the 'highest good'. Kant distinguishes first between two types of notion of the 'good' distinguishing the 'supreme' good (which is the moral law) from the 'highest' which refers to a world in which all that is desirable is brought together so that there is harmony between the law and happiness. The two elements of the highest good are heterogeneous to each other and yet have to be combined if there is a thought of such a world possible.

Kant refers to the antinomy between ways of relating happiness and the good together through a rendition of the doctrines of the Epicureans and the Stoics. If the Epicurean doctrine is understood as suggesting the good will results from happiness, the Stoic, on the contrary, suggests happiness will result from acting in a way that is good. Neither describes what occurs in the world for us though there is some conditional truth in the Stoic claim since overcoming the inclinations for the sake of the law is capable of producing contentment.

Kant next introduces the thesis of the primacy of practical reason over theoretical using it to show a necessary basis for arriving at a sense of the unity of reason as a whole. It is then possible to introduce the 'postulates' of pure practical reason, freedom, the immortality of the soul and the existence of God. Attainment of the highest good is not possible unless the soul is immortal since it is only viewed as such that the attainment of the state described of a harmony between the law and the will could be achieved. However for nature to correspond with the will in the way pictured in the postulate of the immortality of the soul is for there to be an inner ground of connection between the two. The basis of this thought requires a causality that could be the ground of such connection and this is in the thought of God. Kant's rendition of the possibility of such a virtuous world is

thus presented here in a different way to G as it is now in the form of a kingdom of God (CPrR 128) rather than merely as a kingdom of ends.

After stating the postulates, Kant returns a second time to the question of how an extension of pure reason for practical purposes can be granted without extending this to the cognition of theoretical reason. The point is here made that pure practical cognition requires reference to a priori purposes. The postulates are required in order to think the highest good but this does not give us any intuitions that correspond to the thought given so there is no theoretical cognition supplied here. God is thus adopted as a notion not of physics but only of morals.

The last part of CPrR concerns the Doctrine of Method which is understood here as the way in which the laws of pure practical reason are to be given access to the mind so that they can influence the nature of our maxims. Here Kant provides some elementary remarks on moral education attacking in particular the reference to noble or supererogatory ideas to spur on moral conduct. The general point is that morality is best presented as an incentive in education the more purely it is shown and separated from all feelings.

CRITIQUE OF JUDGMENT (CJ)

This work was published in 1790 and is the third and final work that is titled with the term 'critique'. It is, of the three 'critiques', the most complicated in terms of its textual organization. This is for a couple of reasons. Firstly, it has not one but two 'introductions'. What has become generally referred to as the 'First Introduction' (FI) was the first one Kant wrote but it was not included in the first published edition of **CJ**. Kant officially rejected it because of its length although he appears to have been working on it as late as the early months of 1790 and referred to it in correspondence as a useful entry into the work. It was first published in 1833 and became part of the *Akademie* edition of Kant's writings in the twentieth century.

The second introduction, published in **CJ**, does to an extent parallel the first one but is also different from it. Students of **CJ** do tend to discuss both and there is much controversy about the relationship between them. The second, even more important textual difficulty, concerns the fact that **CJ** contains within its covers two distinct works, which are apparently also united in the book as a whole. The first half of the book is entitled a 'Critique of Aesthetic Judgment' while the second part is titled a 'Critique of Teleological Judgment'. Both the two halves of the work include the division between analytic and dialectic and method that was given in **CPrR** though the discussion of method is very extended in the Critique of Teleological Judgment but only very brief in the case of the Critique of Aesthetic Judgment. The question of why two apparently distinct works are joined together in the cover of one book has often puzzled commentators, though some have neglected the discussion of teleology altogether (this is particularly true for Anglo-American philosophers).

These two complicated textual questions are related as the two introductions both contain detailed discussions of the nature of the Critical system and the reason there is a need for an independent critique focused on the faculty (or 'power') of judgment and so give pointers to how to understand the relationship between the two halves of the book. There is, in addition, a 'Preface' in which Kant points out that **CPR** was concerned

really only with cognition and hence with the faculty of the understanding as only it could provide us with constitutive a priori principles. **CPrR**, by contrast, demonstrated that the constitutive a priori principles of the faculty of reason could only exist in relation to the capacity of desire. **CJ** investigates the question of whether judgment, which mediates between understanding and reason, also has a priori principles of its own and, if it does, whether they are constitutive.

As part of the general 'critique of pure reason' (as opposed to what is carried on under that name in the book of that title) it is necessary to address this question. In order to investigate it, the principle of judgment, if it has one, must be distinguished from the a priori concepts that are the province of understanding and hence it must be something that serves as a rule for the power of judgment itself. Kant indicates a link of this question to the investigation of judgments concerning the beautiful and the sublime as these judgments do not provide us with cognition but still belong to the cognitive power and relate this power to the feelings of pleasure and displeasure. This is different from a logical judgment of nature that relates to a lawfulness that sensible concepts appear unable to reach and which relates in some sense to the supersensible. The latter type of judgment has no direct relation to pleasure and would, alone, just be a kind of appendix to **CPR**. Kant also announces the completion of his Critical enterprise with the publication of this book and indicates he will now proceed to the doctrinal one though this makes little sense of his previous publication of **MFNS**.

THE FIRST INTRODUCTION

FI opens with a discussion of philosophy as a system, which appears to relate back to the discussions of architectonic in **CPR**. Kant here states that the general 'critique of pure reason' does not belong to a system of philosophy but rather examines *the idea* of this system. If philosophy is not merely concerned with logic, then it has material principles that concern the objects we think about. Philosophy is then divided into two parts, theoretical and practical, and this leads Kant to correct the common confusion of 'practical' precepts with 'technical' ones.

Kant next proceeds to look at the higher cognitive powers that lie at the basis of philosophy repeating the distinction between understanding, judgment and reason. The point of this distinction is to show that judgment is a power to subsume concepts that are given to it from somewhere else. So if there is a specific principle of judgment, it has to relate to nature as something that conforms to the special power of judgment. This relation turns out to have to do with how higher and lower laws are connected to each other. In this case, the question is how we are able to treat empirical laws as part of a system of experience, something that is quite different from what is achieved by the understanding. In this case, we appear to have a formal notion of lawfulness (similar to what was discussed in practical philosophy) which relates to specific laws. Such an inquiry belongs to the general 'critique of pure reason' but not to the system of philosophy as a doctrine.

Kant next turns to discussing the system of the powers of the mind, distinguishing between cognition, pleasure and displeasure, and desire. Kant here rejects the intellectualist desire to subsume all these powers under cognition and makes clear the need for an investigation of the feelings of pleasure and displeasure as determined by the power of judgment. Experience as a system for judgment is investigated with Kant suggesting that empirical laws could be so heterogeneous to each other that they might not be able to be brought under a common principle. Since the only way to forestall this is if we have a principle of the unity of such laws we need to presuppose that there is such a principle. The presupposition in question is a principle of judgment and it is on the basis of it that we can adopt formulas that state claims on the economic organization of nature (**FI 210**).

Judgment is now examined as containing two possible abilities, either reflecting on that which is represented in terms of its possibility or determining concepts by means of some given empirical presentation. This distinguishes between reflective and determinant judgment and the reflective power is now described as a specific power of judgment (as opposed to the formation of universal concepts of nature which is a determinative act of judgment). But for judgment to be able to reflect, it must have its own principle, a principle that enables at least the logical organization of empirical laws (**FI 215–216**). Roughly put, it is on this basis that teleological judgment is possible.

Now, in **CPR**, Kant had restricted the sense of the 'aesthetic' in such a way as to deny any scientific status to judgments of taste. Here, however, he makes a change allowing for the notion of aesthetic judgments but doing so as something that refers not to a determination of objects but only to the manner of judging of subjects. Such an aesthetic judgment is not produced directly from sensations of objects but rather from a sensation produced by a relationship between the faculties of the subject in relation to certain objects being given to it. This is termed by Kant a legislation that is heautonomous (not autonomous as with reason) as here judgment does not legislate either to nature or to freedom but only to itself.

In **FI,** Kant describes the division of **CJ** as a distinction between the aesthetic of reflective judgment and its logic (where the latter is provided by teleology). Kant adds to this a distinction between intrinsic and relative purposiveness where the former is based in the presentation of the object and the latter on some kind of use of the object's way of being given. This division relates the sense of intrinsic purposiveness to beauty and the relative sense to sublimity whereas intrinsic teleological purposiveness concerns perfection and relative purposiveness use.

THE SECOND INTRODUCTION

The published second introduction also begins with the division of philosophy, referring to the distinction between theoretical and practical philosophy with the focus of the first on nature and the second on freedom. Following the discussion in **G,** Kant points out that the notion of freedom requires a moral sense of determination that is distinct from anything technical. Subsequently Kant points to understanding as having its realm in nature and reason in that of freedom. In contrast to both notions is the supersensible as something unbounded but the basis of unity between the concepts of nature and freedom appears to have a necessary relationship to the supersensible. Judgment is now introduced as a mediating link between understanding and reason and the independent province of judgment emerges when it is considered reflectively. This reflective use of judgment concerns particular empirical laws which are viewed by it as if an understanding that was distinct from ours had given them a unity. The unity in question is presented as a 'purposive' one. Kant next connects this sense of purposiveness to the feeling of pleasure since the means by which we arrive at

the sense of the purposiveness in question is not due to response to features of objects but rather to our mode of viewing them.

Judgments of taste are judgments in which the pleasure that is expressed is one that claims universal validity. Kant clearly distinguishes these judgments of taste from the other form of aesthetic judgment, the judgment of sublimity as the latter is concerned with 'intellectual feeling' connecting imagination to reason rather than understanding. The second introduction is clearer than the first both in terms of the distinction between the beautiful and the sublime and in terms of the need for reference to the supersensible.

THE ARCHITECTONIC OF THE CRITIQUE OF AESTHETIC JUDGMENT

The Critique of Aesthetic Judgment opens with an analytic of aesthetic judgment, which is sub-divided in ways that has caused confusion. There is a distinction between the Analytic of the Beautiful and the Analytic of the Sublime but, after the closure of the Analytic of the Sublime, there is a return to the beautiful with a section deducing judgments of taste, a section itself followed by an undeclared final section that discusses art. The Analytic of the Beautiful is divided into four headings following the Table of Categories of **CPR** but, in this case, the moment of quality is presented first.

TASTE AND AESTHETICS

This first moment declares a judgment of taste to be an aesthetic one as its determining basis has no ground in the object judged. An important implication of this is then drawn out, to the effect that the kind of liking involved in a judgment of taste is distinct from all 'interest' meaning by this that it has no necessary relationship to the object judged about existing. This distinguishes the judgment of taste from judgments concerning both what is merely agreeable (which refers to the senses) and what is good (which refers to the will's desire for something to exist).

AESTHETIC UNIVERSALITY

The quantity of the judgment of taste is universal as what is presented as beautiful is something that we expect all to like but the liking in question, since it is aesthetic, will have a subjective form of universality. The logical quantity of aesthetic judgments is also, in a sense, singular since it requires connection to feelings of pleasure and displeasure and can only be made once it has been seen to accord with them. So aesthetic universality is also singular, hence is unlike logical universality in having this character. Despite this, statements concerning aesthetic universality have the form of logical universality. Kant at this point resolves this problem, which we will see to recur, through the postulation of a universal voice that lays claim to general agreement.

After invoking this universal voice, Kant turns to the problem that he claims is 'key' to the critique of taste, namely whether the feeling of pleasure precedes the judgment of taste concerning an object or whether the judging precedes the pleasure. Having raised this question, Kant rules out the first answer immediately since, he claims, it would require us to view the pleasure as being the same as what occurs with the agreeable, basically that it would be grounded in sensation. So there must instead be something in the mental state that leads us to express the judgment of taste and is its condition that leads to the pleasure arising later. This something is taken by Kant to be 'universal communicability'

and is argued to be grounded on a relationship between the capacities of imagination and understanding when they connect the presenting of something to the notion of cognition in general. The suggestion is that this connection requires the cognitive powers to be 'in free play'.

Explaining this point requires Kant to revert back to the account of cognition derived from **CPR** as he reminds us now that imagination combines the manifold and the understanding unifies it. In the case of the judgment of taste, these two are brought together without *conceptual* unification, which is why the result is a subjective universality. The unification in question is a form of relationship between the faculties that leads to the 'feeling' of accord between them without this feeling being the result of a sensation that was externally produced.

AESTHETIC PURPOSIVENESS

The relational element of judgments of taste is thought in terms of purposiveness as would be expected after the discussions of the two introductions. Kant now arrives at the notion of purposiveness without a purpose which does not invoke the causes of the purpose in question but rests purely on the form of purposiveness of an object but, given the earlier claim about the absence of interest in judgments of taste, this notion of purposiveness has to be distinguished from the kind of 'charm' that depends on material features of objects. This leads Kant to emphasize instead the notion of 'design' and, later, to formulate his conception of the Ideal of Beauty.

The Ideal refers to the interesting problem of general agreement concerning judgments of taste, an agreement that persists despite the subjective nature of such assessments. Kant at this point invokes the notion that some products of taste are exemplary and grounds this on the view that the models of taste are ideas which have been presented to sensible exhibition. However, the Ideal of beauty is not an object of an entirely pure judgment of taste since it includes a reference to a basis for taste in something intellectual and Kant suggests it only really refers to humanity itself as the appropriate object of such idealization. This Ideal basically expresses something moral and is the first explicit point of connection between taste and morality. The modal status of judgments of taste expresses necessity and refers to another Idea, the Idea of Common Sense. This idea seeks to give a further basis to the normative claims involved in judgments of taste and Kant returns later to this idea.

The Aesthetics of the Sublime

The Analytic of the Sublime opens with a contrast between judgments concerning the beautiful and those expressing sublimity. The former are now suggested to require indeterminate concepts of understanding while the latter, by contrast, require indeterminate concepts of reason. However the two judgments are also distinguished in terms of the fact that while judgments of beauty arise directly and immediately, judgments of sublimity are indirect and mediated. There is some sort of check on us before we assert that we are faced with something sublime, something that holds us back before allowing us to go forward and, due to this, Kant defines the pleasure that accompanies sublimity as a 'negative' form of pleasure. This 'negative' element of sublimity is further accentuated when Kant describes the arising of the feeling that accompanies this judgment as one that is 'violent' and 'incommensurate' with our capacity to exhibit things. The discussion

of the sublime that follows also differs from the account of the beautiful as it is divided between the 'mathematical' and the 'dynamical' sublime (following the division of the Table of Categories in **CPR**).

Kant opens the account of the mathematical sublime by describing the sublime as involving what is absolutely large, a point that ensures that the mathematical sublime is not a quantity as it exceeds all measure. Largeness is a notion that normally involves comparison but in this case we are not operating with a standard that is one of determinate magnitude but only with an aesthetic one. The aesthetic relation to such a notion of largeness involves a kind of liking and since nothing fits the standard of absolute largeness it follows that this is not a standard that describes objects of sense themselves but rather the way our mind expands in relation to such. For this to arise we have a connection to our intuition in terms of whether it is possible to take something in, which requires our apprehension to match an ability of comprehension. This meets limits as when we are faced with something that as we try to measure its extent before us exceeds our ability to combine moments of its presentation together and then we have an aesthetic experience of largeness.

This checking of our power runs up against the endeavour to think the entirety of the exhibited in concepts as is required by reason. In order even to be able to think of something as large to the extent that such notions as the infinite can arise there must be a supersensible power within us and it is to this that the surpassing power of the exhibition must be related (which is a connection of imagination to reason). The feeling that is aroused in us by the sense that there are exhibitions that defeat our measuring power is a feeling of respect. Our inability to determine the absolutely large proves both the inade-quacy of our mind to deal with all phenom-ena and yet also shows a sense of it that is admirable since it aims to meet an ideal that is beyond it. So the feeling of the mathemati-cal sublime is a kind of displeasure arising from our inadequacy combined with a pleas-ure in our possession of rational ideas.

The discussion of the dynamically sub-lime opens with a discussion of the might of nature where 'might' means something supe-rior to all obstacles. Nature, when related to as possessed of dynamic sublimity, is under-stood to contain such power. Kant provides examples of the way nature appears thus to us and then represents us as not directly con-fronted with nature's power but as contem-plating it. It is by this means that we arrive at the dynamically sublime. Again, it is by being raised above nature that we arrive at the sense of sublimity. This does require the sense that we are receptive to ideas, however, and due to the need for this, judgments of dynami-cal sublimity require culture. Kant's discus-sion of the sublime is much briefer than his account of judgment though it has produced some of the most creative commentary.[13]

AESTHETIC DEDUCTION

After the discussion of the Analytic of the Sublime, Kant returns to the question of judg-ments of taste in order to provide a 'deduc-tion' of pure aesthetic judgments. The reason this deduction is provided for pure aesthetic judgments and not for judgments concerned with sublimity is due to the claim that a deduction is needed if the liking in question concerns the form of the object (since judg-ments of sublimity suppose something 'form-less'). Further, the reason for the deduction in question is that the pure aesthetic judgment has a form of necessity despite not being

cognitive. Since it is not cognitive, its univer-sality is not a result of established agreement but rests in some way on the autonomous powers of subjectivity.

Judgments of taste are peculiar in that they make a claim to universal assent as if they were objective and yet are only subjective. However, there is no apparent way of prov-ing a judgment of taste to be correct, despite this claim they possess to universal validity. Kant goes on to argue that judgments of taste are synthetic a priori judgments and thus connects the problem concerning them to the general problem of Critical philosophy. The liking expressed in the judgment of taste is argued to be grounded on the purposiveness of the form of an object for the capacity of judgment. If there is such a connection for us then we have to work on the assumption that it is possible also for others. We simply make this assumption in the deduction as we do not have to show the 'objective' reality of the judgment of taste. Despite this being the case, we can make the assumption due to the point that the capacities assumed as opera-tive were shown in **CPR** to be required for cognition. This leads Kant into the extended discussion of 'common sense' that proved so important for Hannah Arendt[14] and in which Kant discusses the procedure of comparing our judgment with the possible standards of others in order to arrive at a merely formal basis for our statements.

KANT'S ACCOUNT OF ART

At this point, Kant begins the final part of the Analytic of the Beautiful but does so without formally announcing the opening of a new part. In the remainder of the Analytic, he concerns himself with an enquiry that hinges primarily on a discussion of art. It opens, however, with a discussion of something ruled out of account earlier as part of the Analytic of the Beautiful, namely, an investigation of empirical interest in the beautiful. This interest is something that, we are now told, can be considered *after* we have discussed the pure aesthetic judgment. It arises in society where we expect communication of pleasures to take place and where it can become refined. Kant next considers 'intellectual' interest in the beautiful, which he relates to the beauty of nature rather than to the beauty of art. The reason for this claim is then argued to be that in the case of interest in the beautiful in nature we concern ourselves with a connection between the mind and that which in nature seems to accord with it and this is taken by Kant to be grounded on a 'moral' interest. This even leads him to making claims about the connection of the colour spectrum to moral qualities (CJ 302).

Interestingly, it is after these two discussions of different kinds of 'interest' that can be attached to the beautiful that Kant turns to discussing art, a discussion that fills the rest of the Analytic of Aesthetic Judgment. First, Kant gives a generic account of art distinguishing it from nature, science and craft. After this generic description has been given, Kant then turns to a specific discussion of 'fine' art, which intends to arouse feelings of pleasure in relation to cognition and so has a standard in reflective judgment and not sensation. The basis of such art is next shown to reside in 'genius' as this 'gives the rule' (CJ 307) to art. Genius is presented as a talent to produce something that transcends determinate rules and is original but also exemplary. Since genius has, however, no specific 'science' by which it operates it cannot be said to be grounded on a theory but is rather expressive of a 'nature'. Given this account of genius, it is not surprising that Kant concludes that genius is only operative in art and

has no place in science, since science would require precisely the determinate rules that are missing in the productions of genius.

The principle of genius is subsequently argued to be the ability to exhibit aesthetic ideas where these ideas are presentations of imagination to which no concept is adequate (the reverse of rational ideas). So the mental powers that are brought into connection by genius are imagination and understanding. For fine art to exist, both genius and taste are required as genius alone will give something that is inspired but not refined while taste alone would give refinement but not necessarily inspiration. Taste is thus presented as not merely necessary for judging but also for producing aesthetic art even though such art is not judged by pure judgments of taste.

Kant subsequently divides the fine arts into three classes, those of speech (rhetoric and poetry), visual arts (plastic and painting) and beautiful play of sensations (music and the art of colour). Subsequently to this is added an account of how the different arts can be combined together in such mixed forms as drama, dance and opera. Kant concludes his discussion of art by a consideration of the respective aesthetic value of the different fine arts ranking poetry the foremost art and indicating that music has less value than other arts due to its greater dependence on sensation and to its inability to produce more than a transitory impression. The final 'comment' section of the Analytic expands the discussion to include laughter and even an account of jokes.

AESTHETIC DIALECTIC

The second division of the Critique of Aesthetic Judgment concerns the dialectic of it. The Dialectic is carefully stated not to be a dialectic of taste itself but rather of the critique of taste and to be concerned with the principles of this critique. Kant now presents an antinomy that concerns whether or not taste is based on concepts since, on the one hand, it appears there is no disputing concerning taste, while, on the other hand, we can and do quarrel about it. Resolving this antinomy requires showing that the parties to it have different senses of a 'concept' in question. In agreement with those who suggest that taste does depend on a concept, Kant points to the claims of such judgments of taste to necessary validity. However, in agreement with those objecting to the claim that taste is based on concepts, Kant points to the inability to prove claims about taste. In indicating this, Kant points to the difference between concepts of the understanding and concepts of reason where the first are determinate and the second are not. The concept on which a judgment of taste depends is hence not susceptible to proof as it is not a concept of understanding. But there is a concept that enables quarrelling to happen and this is a concept of reason. The indeterminate concept on which taste depends is the supersensible substrate of appearances.

Having stated and 'resolved' this antinomy, Kant proceeds to connect it to the antinomies that were the concern of the dialectics of the two earlier *Critiques* and does so by suggesting that the theoretical antinomies point to the undetermined supersensible of nature, the practical antinomy to the supersensible as the principle of our cognitive power and the antinomy of reflective judgment as the principle of the harmony of the two preceding forms of the supersensible. The Critique of Aesthetic Judgment then reaches a conclusion with a discussion of how beauty can be a symbol of morality in which an analogy is presented between the beautiful and the good. Finally, there is a very brief discussion

of 'methodology' in which Kant argues that there can be no 'science' of the beautiful.

KANT'S CRITIQUE OF TELEOLOGY

The Critique of Teleological Judgment follows immediately after the discussion of why there can be no independent 'method' of pure aesthetic judgment. By far, the lion's share of attention given to CJ has concerned the Critique of Aesthetic Judgment though there are now studies that are beginning to challenge this.[15]

Kant opens this discussion by arguing for the need for an account of 'objective' purposiveness in nature albeit understood as a regulative and not a constitutive principle. Kant begins by distinguishing formal purposiveness from material purposiveness, describing now the former as manifested in geometry and as not requiring teleology. Relative purposiveness is next distinguished from intrinsic where the latter is imputed to the object itself rather than merely something concerning its use. Finally, Kant refers to 'natural purposes', which are the real subject of the rest of his investigation and which possess recursive causality giving the example of a tree (CJ 371–372). Such natural purposes have parts whose possibility depends on the whole due to being reciprocally causes and effects of the form in question, a claim that leads Kant to distinguish the 'force' of organized beings from that of beings that are only 'machines' (CJ 374).

Having given this account of 'natural purposes', Kant discusses next the principle by which nature in general is approached as a system of purposes, which involves an economical approach to nature as an integrated whole (CJ 379). Teleology is next described as having a place in natural science only as providing us with a method of approach and not as justifying the postulate of a separate causality for explanation so the necessity attaching to teleology is not one suggested to be present in the physical character of things.

The Dialectic of Teleological Judgment is unusual in being slightly longer than the Analytic. In introducing the Dialectic, Kant points out that determinant judgment has no concepts of objects and no antinomy of its own but that reflective judgment is different in this regard. However, when he goes on to present this antinomy, he suggests the difference between an antinomy that concerns regulative principles and one which concerns constitutive ones with regard to empirical laws of nature. The antinomy that concerns regulative principles arises naturally from reflective judgment and has to be answered by means of its examination while a constitutive antinomy here is not plausible since reason could not, in this province, prove either of the two possible conflicting maxims. Hence it is false to claim, as is often done, that Kant resolves the antinomy of teleological judgment by merely showing both assertions in it to be regulative. Rather, it is *as* an antinomy of regulative maxims that he examines it. The antinomy broadly concerns the question of whether merely mechanical laws are sufficient to account for nature or whether we also require the invocation of final causes.

Reflectively considered, it is necessary to consider final causes as something distinct from mechanism; that much is also shown by the Analytic of Teleology. Kant goes on to consider the various systems that have been proposed in response to the problem of accounting for teleology and distinguishes them as consisting either in idealistic or realistic interpretations of purposiveness. The former either base nature on laws of motion alone (ancient materialistic systems are mentioned) or on fatalistic principles (where Spinoza is mentioned). Realistic accounts of purposiveness, by contrast, see it either as physically realistic (hylozoism) or as realistic in relation to an intelligent being (theism). Kant proceeds to argue against all these systems stating that the ancient materialisms failed to distinguish the technic of nature from mechanism and had to call in chance as an ultimate basis of law while the fatalistic form of account deprives the world of contingency and makes all necessary. The hylozoistic view is denied since Kant can give no sense to the idea of living matter and the theistic account presupposes an earlier determinative judgment about the need for the intelligent being to explain nature.

This survey of dogmatic solutions to the problem of teleology leads Kant to reassert the point that natural products contain natural necessity while also having contingent form. It is due to this combination that they form a problem for reflective judgment. We are required, in order to address this, to examine our cognitive powers even to the extent of seeing that there is no determinate way (as theism supposes) of proving the existence of God but only of showing the cognitive reasons we are led to suppose such an existence as required in the system of nature. Kant next reverts to the point that understanding and intuition are necessarily heterogeneous for us and that this, combined with the need of reason to reach totality, creates the basis of the antinomy of teleological judgment. But a different understanding to ours would not have the same characteristics and an intuitive understanding is conceivable. Not only is such an understanding conceivable but we have already been led to suppose that nature has a supersensible substrate by earlier inquiries. We can further see how, for such an understanding, there could be a common higher principle of nature's laws beyond both mechanism and teleology. For ourselves we cannot *explain* organized beings in terms of mechanism though this is only a point for reflective judgment on organized beings. This leads to the conclusion that all we can do is subordinate the mechanistic production of organisms to the teleological one without requiring, in so doing, a scientific ground for the use of teleology. The two principles are assumed to be reconciled entirely in the supersensible substrate but in ways we cannot know. All explanation has to follow the mechanistic model although the production of organized beings cannot be so accounted for.

The 'methodology' of teleological judgment is one of the longest methodologies in the *Critique*s. It opens with Kant reiterating that teleology does not belong to natural science but only to critique and indicating that we should use the principle of mechanism as far as we possibly can. Kant also here considers and counters Hume's objections to teleological discussions as Hume fails to understand the extrinsic character of purposes to nature. Kant also flatly rejects Leibnizian pre-established harmony, occasionalism and what he terms 'the theory of evolution' (**CJ** 423), which is a form of theory of pre-formation of matter and which is contrasted with epigenesis. The latter theory, derived in part from Blumenbach, sees organization as original and as having a force separate from that of matter as Kant had argued earlier in the Analytic.

Kant next turns to the 'ultimate purpose' of nature as a teleological system and describes humanity as the 'ultimate purpose' of nature and gives an argument for seeing human culture as more important than human happiness. This discussion marks a turn in the work which from this point on becomes more concerned with practical rather than theoretical questions about teleology.

Kant provides a miniature description of his view of human historical development including the need within it for war as part of this development. After this interlude, Kant returns to the basis for viewing humanity as the 'ultimate purpose' of nature and suggests it is humanity considered as noumenon that is such a purpose. After making this claim, Kant describes the reasons why physical teleology has always tended to be the primary form that is presented and yet discounts the view that moral claims can be founded on it stating that a purely physical teleology could at best be the basis of a demonology. By contrast, an ethical teleology can be presented on the basis of the idea, first broached in **G**, of a 'kingdom of ends'. Kant also provides here a further statement of the 'moral proof' of the existence of God which was first given in **CPrR**. It is given greater vividness here and the status of the postulate of God is more clearly defined as one that can be subjectively understood to be 'constitutive' (**CJ** 457). The properties of God are only presented by means of analogy and God is denied to be a possible object of cognition. Considering God in only such a practical role prevents theology from either soaring too high or sinking too low and leaves God as an object of 'faith' in the sense of being beyond theoretical cognition.

RELIGION WITHIN THE BOUNDARIES OF MERE REASON (R)

The complication in the textual history of this work concerns Kant's engagements with the censorship of his time. Kant originally intended to write a series of essays on religion for the *Berlinische Monatsschrift* and submitted the initial one (on the topic of radical evil) without problem but had the second essay refused the right to publication. Kant therefore took back the second essay and decided he would re-publish the first essay (first published in 1792) with the following three he had intended to accompany that essay in book form. Since the second essay had been rejected by a theology censor, Kant now took the trouble to assess whether the works really merited being considered as belonging under the heading of theology. So it was submitted to the theology faculty at Königsberg who declared it to be outside their remit as it was a philosophical work. It was then submitted to the philosophy faculty at Jena who declared it fit for publication and it was duly published in 1793. However, in October 1794 a royal rescript accused Kant of having abused his philosophy for the purpose of 'distorting and disparaging several principal and fundamental doctrines of Holy Scripture and of Christianity' including within this book. Further, Kant was enjoined not to publish further on this area and, while defending his book from these accusations, Kant agreed to comply with this directive until King Frederick William II died in November 1797 after which Kant deemed himself released from the rescript and published all the details of it in **CF**.

After being published in 1793 this work quickly went through a series of reprints and new editions and Kant adds a series of additional notes to the second edition of 1794 and a new preface. In addition to the two prefaces, it is divided into four parts. In the 'Preface' to the first edition, Kant declares that morality is complete so long as it is based only on freedom and the moral law so that it does not need religion for these purposes. However,

while morality needs nothing further for the ground of its maxims it has a necessary reference to an 'end' in terms of its consequences. What is meant by this is that the result of our conduct is not something indifferent to us and he refers again to the notion of the highest good mentioned in the Dialectic of **CPrR**. This notion of the 'highest good' is referred to as a special point of unification for our ends (or as a 'final end') and related to the question (prominent in the examples in **G**) of the kind of world we would create. These ideas are now connected (as they were in the postulates of practical reason) to 'religion' or 'the idea of a mighty moral lawgiver outside the human being' (**R** 6).

Having introduced the concept of religion, Kant proceeds to distinguish between two kinds of theology, 'biblical' and 'philosophical', though he does little here to make clear the province of the former. The distinction is markedly introduced to discuss the question of censorship and the need for philosophical theology to be based and judged on the criterion of reason alone. The 'Preface' to the second edition discusses the pure religion of reason as something that could be regarded as 'part' of revealed religion and as the 'part' the philosopher (who 'abstracts' from experience) is concerned with. Kant also indicates in the 'Preface' that if we begin with a given historical religion it may well be possible to hold up fragments of it in such a way that we can be led back to the rational system of pure reason. In making this claim, Kant also makes a distinction between 'religion' and 'cult' where the latter has no reference to reason. Kant also claims here that no special reference to his moral system is needed to read the work but only the standpoint of 'common morality' (though this surely means at least position of **G** part I).

Kant's Conception of Evil

The work is then generally presented as concerned with the 'philosophical doctrine of religion' and the first part concerns the radical evil of human nature. This part opens with the observation that the claim that the world lies in evil is a very old complaint and that the view that the world is progressing is a much newer claim. A first determination of evil follows shortly after. It is to the effect that someone is evil in allowing the 'interference' of evil maxims. Kant discusses the inference of an underlying evil maxim as the *ground* of all particular evil conduct. This ground does not lie in anything directly sensible but in a specific kind of decision to allow the sensible sway over the intelligible. The conflict mentioned at the opening of this part is then reduced to a claim concerning whether we are 'by nature' (that is, in terms of the underlying maxim of conduct) disposed to good or evil.

Kant goes on to look at the 'original predisposition' to good in terms of three headings, namely in relation to 'animality', 'rationality' and 'personality'. In relation to 'animality', there is desire for self-preservation, propagation of the species and community with others. Each of these is shown to have vices concomitant to them (gluttony, lust and wild lawlessness, all termed 'bestial' vices). The predispositions to humanity involve a comparison that involves reason (so are distinct from the predispositions to animality). Here Kant discusses a kind of self-love that involves an inclination to gain worth in the opinion of others and describes this as originally being a desire for equal worth that becomes distorted into a striving for ascendancy and produces the 'diabolical' vices of envy, ingratitude and joy in others' misfortune. Finally, the predisposition to personality is the only really purely good one as it requires respect for the moral law as a sole incentive of choice and so is effectively identical to personality itself.

Kant then moves on to talking about the 'propensity' to evil where 'propensity' is taken to mean a subjective ground of the possibility of an inclination and is distinguished from a predisposition in the sense that it can be understood as freely adopted. Kant distinguishes three different levels of a propensity to evil in terms of *frailty*, *impurity* and *depravity* where the last means a determination to adopt evil maxims. After considering this area, Kant reaches the conclusion that the human being is, by nature, evil and further substantiates this by reference to the inductive reference spoken of earlier. The basis of this evil is the subordination of intelligible incentives to sensible ones. Given the deep-rooted nature of this failing, there is a sense to thinking of the propensity to evil as something inherited. The reason for presenting it this way is that the origin of a free movement cannot be explicated. Kant further presents this point as the basis of the view that we were originally tempted by an evil spirit. The first part then closes with a 'general remark' (the first of four) that concerns the restoration of power to the original predisposition to good (or effects of grace). Here Kant discusses the rational basis of the claim that there remains a 'germ' of goodness in our evil nature but that a 'revolution' in our mode of thought is necessary in order to restore the original predisposition to goodness. This requires a 'decision' to reverse the supreme ground of our maxims and examples of good people are a helpful way to achieve this. The 'remark' concludes with another distinction between types of religion with moral religion compared to cult again and the former enjoining that we do all in our power to be good while the latter is depicted as requiring morally unnecessary measures.

The second part of the work concerns the battle between the good and evil principles and focuses on the need to view our moral situation as consisting in such a fight. Kant again points out that natural inclinations are, in themselves, good and, in doing so, contrasts his approach to that of the Stoics. In contrast to them, Kant sides with the Christian view that there is an evil spirit that it is necessary to engage in combat. After mentioning this idea, Kant discusses the personified idea of the good principle and says it is our duty to elevate ourselves to the ideal of moral perfection, an act that amounts, on his view, to a practical faith in the 'Son of God' (**R** 62). The prototype of such a 'Son' resides only in reason and the use of this ideal is defended by means of a discussion of the procedure of formulating a 'schematism of analogy'.

Kant also considers a series of 'difficulties' that stand in the way of us realizing the idea of a humanity that could be well-pleasing to God. The first difficulty concerns the problem of adopting the position of a 'new man' who has become converted to the law when all our maxims appear at root to be corrupted. This difficulty resides in our necessarily temporal means of representing our moral state but can be met by imagining God's representation as viewing not our moment-by-moment state but rather the totality of our disposition. The second difficulty concerns our moral happiness, i.e. what assurance we have of attaining a constant disposition that always advances in goodness. In relation to this problem, Kant sets out a representation of our general conduct in life as a motivation for our ability to either stay constant or to seek to become so. The third, and most important, difficulty concerns how we wipe out the original debt

of having started out from evil for which we surely continue to deserve punishment. In response to this, Kant argues that the conversion to the moral law is not a separate act from the punishment for the evil disposition which previously reigned and that the pure disposition that thus emerges bears as vicarious substitute the debt of the original evil. This idea involves taking the pure disposition to be personified as the 'Son of God' earlier mentioned. The struggle of the good and the evil dispositions is also presented in this part through a symbolic interpretation of the notion of Satan presented in the Scriptures and the struggle of this with Christ, including a symbolic interpretation of the story of the virgin birth (through a notion of pre-formation [**R** 80n.]).

The discussion of Christ involves the presentation of moral religion irrupting in the presence of cults. The 'general remark' that closes the second part concerns miracles which are presented as something with which moral religion is adorned on its first appearance. The point is made that rational human beings do not subscribe to the view that miracles can occur now, even if they do not rule out their possibility as such in theory. The point is also made that any apparent message from God can always be judged in terms of its accord with moral teaching.

A SOCIETY OF VIRTUE

The third part concerns the manner in which the good principle could be victorious over the evil one. This part opens by tracing the presence of what was termed in the first part as 'diabolical vices' and which are now termed 'passions' in human sociality. In response to this, the picture is now drawn of the establishment of a society in accordance with virtue.

The precondition of such a society ever existing is, as Kant is careful to point out, a political community but the society of virtue has a distinct principle of its own. However, there is an analogy between these types of community so that Kant feels he can discuss the 'ethical state of nature' even though he rules out the view that we could leave this by political means. In discussing how to leave this ethical state of nature, Kant introduces a new conception of the 'highest good' that is different from the one that was referred to in the first part of the work (as the earlier conception drew entirely on the view of **CPrR**). This new sense of the 'highest good' is an idea of reason as a common end of humanity and is pictured as the formation of the ethical community. However, the point of origin of the laws of this ethical community is not presented (as was the case with the kingdom of ends of **G**) as arising purely from humanity itself but instead as having, as its law-giver, God as 'moral ruler of the world' (**R** 99). Having made this point, Kant proceeds to convert his conception of a moral community into a form of church and thus gives next a rational ecclesiology.

KANT'S ECCLESIOLOGY

The notion of the church is differentiated between an invisible one and a visible one. The invisible church is the mere idea of the union of all ethical human beings under a divine world-governance while the visible church is the 'actual' union in accord with such an idea. Kant then sets out the marks of such a church in accordance with the Table of Categories of **CPR**, describing it as universal in quantity, pure in quality, having free relations and an unchanging modality of constitution. However, as Kant goes on to discuss, every 'visible' church has its basis in some type of 'revealed' (or, as he now terms it, 'historical') faith rather than simply being grounded on pure religious faith as drawn from reason. In discussing this point, Kant describes again the distinction between religion and cult and now distinguishes the latter as dependent on the forms of historical revelation at the cost of a priori reason. Further, the type of 'church' that can be formed as a cult is here described as one that depends on 'temples' (outward forms of public service) and 'priests' (who practice piety rather than pure moral religion). Kant also argues that the majority of people have no sense of 'religion' but only of statutory faith (and are thus engaged in 'cults').

KANT'S HERMENEUTICS

At this point Kant also explicitly presents his hermeneutic principles for the interpretation of Scripture which has, as he freely admits, a 'forced' character since it always views its text in light of pure moral demands due to the claim that the reading of these texts should always have in view making human beings better. This moral improvement is the true end of the religion of reason and is the key to Kant's exegesis of Scripture.

By contrast to this hermeneutic approach is set the figure of a scriptural scholar whose task is mainly to preserve the authority of a church but who should really have a broad culture at hand. The latter is clearly intended to be guided by the former and both are opposed to the view of one who reads Scripture according to the dictates of 'feeling'.

THE ANTINOMY OF FAITH

Kant next looks at the question of the gradual transition of ecclesiastical faith towards pure religious faith and, in the course of doing so, explores an antinomy. This is between a notion of faith that finds satisfaction by means of reparation for guilt on the one hand and faith in the ability to become well-pleasing to God by future good conduct on the other. The first is presented as including the problem that if reparation depends only on faith then it would appear to make good conduct unnecessary. But the second, by contrast, appears to make the conversion to the moral law something available to someone who is depraved without making clear how this can be possible. So there appears a difficulty either way in reconciling faith and good works (the classic argument between Protestant and Catholic Christians). In responding to this antinomy, Kant points out that faith alone is something only necessary in a theoretical sense while the need for good works is practically required. Ecclesiastical faith begins from historical faith alone but this is only a vehicle for the promotion of rational faith. The faith that resides in such ecclesiastical forms alone tends toward superstition and takes the ideal of humanity as presented in the 'Son of God' as an empirical historical appearance. However, the sense of the 'Son of God' that is religiously required cannot be the reference to an appearance of the senses but must rather be to the prototype of our reason and faith in that it must be the same as the faith in our ability to act in accord with such an ideal (which is good works). So the antinomy is only an apparent one. The point raised from this antinomy is the need to free faith from empirical historical determination so that it can become purely rational.

Kant next gives an historical sketch of the gradual arrival of pure religion which is concentrated only on one religion, namely that which he takes to have always included as

a possibility in itself the reference to pure rational faith, and this is Christianity. Prior to giving his 'history' of Christianity however, Kant first describes the 'Jewish faith', which he states is 'not a religion at all' but a formation of a political community (**R** 125). Even the Ten Commandments are here described as having only been given to help the formation of a political community and the lack of reference of Judaism to a future life is taken as further evidence of its lack of religious character. Christianity is presented as based on a total abandonment of Judaism and as introducing a pure moral religion, which is supported by means of some of Kant's rather 'forced' exegesis of the New Testament.

However, the history of Christianity is admitted to include little that is uplifting with Kant describing in deprecatory terms the Great Schism between East and West and concluding with an epigraph from Lucretius concerning the evil deeds of religion. So it is really the Christian present that Kant uses as a model, not its historical record.

The 'general remark' with which the third part closes concerns mysteries and Kant points out that there is no way of determining objectively whether mysteries exist but even the Trinity is here discussed only in practical terms and not in theoretical ones. However, this practical idea of the Trinity is presented as the basis of a mystery in the sense that it gives us something practically that we can make no sense of theoretically and the practical sense of it is determined in three respects. Firstly, by means of the idea of the 'call' of us to become members of a virtuous community, based on the mystery of how we can have moral powers at all, something that refers us to God as creator. Secondly, in terms of the mystery of satisfaction, namely of how we can find reparation for our evil, something that we earlier saw involved the notion of vicarious substitution or God as 'Son'. Thirdly, the mystery of election, of how we can attain a state of being well-pleasing to God, which refers to the sense of God as Holy Spirit.

ILLUSORY RELIGION

The fourth and final part of the work discusses false religion or 'priestcraft'. In beginning this section, Kant again refers to the distinction between visible and invisible church and speaks about the form of the former as including within it much that is inessential to pure religion. In further presenting this contrast, Kant speaks about 'natural' religion as something that is apparent to reason and suggests that such could also be spoken of as 'revealed' if by this is meant that its formulas appear through the prism of a chosen historical form. Such 'natural' religion is a pure practical concept of reason and Kant presents Christianity as including it, by means, once again, of his peculiar method of biblical hermeneutics.

By contrast to this 'natural' religion, Kant presents a 'learned' religion as one that requires dogmas that are not apparent to reason and which he relates as dependent on a certain history. The 'counterfeit' service of religion is one that requires unconditional faith in such dogmas and is, in its form, 'slavish'. Such religion is full of 'delusion' where a delusion involves mistaking a certain kind of representation of a thing as equivalent to the possession of the thing. Such delusion is discussed in terms of anthropomorphism and distinguished from rational faith as concerned with outward performances rather than with the disposition of the heart towards good works. The view that performance of cult acts is in itself pleasing to God is declared the basis of cults and to be a superstition.

So far does Kant go in this analysis that he renders equivalent the practices of a shaman and the way of life of some contemporary 'Christians' (R 176). Such a service is further described as a form of fetishism and 'priest-craft' to be fetish-service.

The 'general remark' at the end of this section concerns 'means of grace' and Kant maintains the point here that the only means in our power to attain grace is endeavouring to improve our moral nature. Faith in miracles, mysteries and means of grace, considered theoretically, are all forms of delusory faith. Similarly, prayer, viewed just as a ritual, is a superstitious delusion and would, viewed correctly, be only a means to enliven our aim towards acts that would be 'well-pleasing' to God. Church-going, likewise, as an external worship, has no direct use but should only be seen as a means of the community generally working towards moral progress. Kant's general message is summarized by the final sentence in which he argues that we should not attempt to move from grace to virtue but rather from virtue to grace.

TOWARD PERPETUAL PEACE (PP)

This work was first published in 1795, the year Prussia signed the Peace of Basel with France but refers, in its title, to a long-standing debate on the nature of peace. It is one of Kant's most-cited writings outside the area of philosophy, having been used to maintain quite a variety of positions in the area of International Relations theory. It is somewhat elaborately structured, despite its relative brevity. The main parts of the work are presented as a division of two sections but to these Kant added two supplements and an appendix. The work is also formulated in a style that mimics the form of treaties between states.

The work opens with Kant making a reference to the expression 'perpetual peace' that accompanied a picture of a graveyard on a Dutch innkeeper's signboard. Awareness of a censorial climate is also here indicated with Kant stating that the attitude of the worldly-wise statesman towards the philosopher is often one of taking the latter to be irrelevant with Kant adding that, if this view is consistently held, then there can be no occasion for viewing philosophical works as posing a danger to the state.

THE PRELIMINARY ARTICLES

After this sally of an introduction, the first section presents six preliminary articles for perpetual peace among states, each of which is given some justification. They are: firstly, treaties of peace should include no secret reservations preparing for war; no independently existing state can be acquired by another; standing armies should in time be abolished; national debts should not be contracted with regard to states' external affairs; states shall not forcibly intervene in each other's constitutions and government; in cases of war states shall not employ methods that would make mutual trust impossible during a future peace.

Each of the articles includes a paragraph justifying its argument and Kant later divides the preliminary articles indicating that some of them are strict and should be enforced at once while others, by contrast, can be postponed being put into effect. The ones viewed by him as holding strictly are the first, fifth and sixth articles (concerning secret reservations, non-interference in other states' constitutions and not using methods that would make mutual trust possible later).

However, while half of the preliminary articles are not strict, Kant is firm in the view that this does not entail that they could be postponed for good. This leads Kant to also insert a lengthy note on the notion of 'permissive law', which is here directed 'only to the future way of acquiring a right' but which explains his view of the second article (concerning inheritance of another state) more than his views of articles three and four (concerning standing armies and national debt).

THE DEFINITIVE ARTICLES

The second section contains three definitive articles for perpetual peace and is introduced by a statement concerning the need to supersede the state of nature and to establish a state of peace. Another lengthy footnote discusses the notion of a rightful constitution, distinguishing between being in accord with the right of citizens of a state, a right of nations and the right of citizens of the world.

The three definitive articles are discussed at considerably more length than the preliminary ones and are clearly taken by Kant to be much more important. The first article declares that the civil constitution in every state shall be republican. The nature of such a state is then defined through discussion of the freedom of the members of a society as individuals, their dependence on a single common legislation (as citizens) and on the law of their equality (as subjects). A footnote is then introduced that describes rightful freedom in terms of being governed by external laws to which I could have consented.

The connection of the republican constitution to the goal of perpetual peace is argued to be that this constitution ensures that a people will be less willing to start a war of which they would themselves have to bear the hardships. Kant contrasts a republican constitution with a 'democratic' one though he clearly thinks of the latter in terms of ancient models of democracy and not in terms of representative government. Republicanism is identified here with a separation of executive power from legislative power and contrasted with despotism in which the laws are effectively decrees of a private purpose rather than laws of a public will. Non-representative governments are taken by Kant to be wholly material and without form.

The second definitive article declares that the right of nations shall be based on federalism and includes an extended comparison between the formation of a rightful state from the state of nature and the existing antagonistic relations between states. The prosecution of war is something that needs to be overcome and the formation of a pacific league is taken to be the best means to achieve this. The league is distinguished from a state and includes no provision for public laws of its own. Kant appears here to prefer a state of nations to the pacific league but to advocate the latter as more likely to be adopted.

The third definitive article describes cosmopolitan right as limited to conditions of universal hospitality. Hospitality is here defined as the right a foreigner has not to be treated with hostility on landing in a polity not his own. This notion of hospitality is hence treated as a right to visit and to seek commerce. However, this view is contrasted with the colonial behaviour of European powers, which is roundly condemned, with some sympathy evinced for the Japanese exclusion of foreigners. It is in the context of the discussion of this article that Kant makes the key claim that a violation of right anywhere is now felt everywhere and that this ensures that cosmopolitan right is a 'supplement' to

the unwritten code of the rights of states and nations.

After the statement of the third definitive article, Kant introduces the first of two 'supplements' to the treatise, which concerns what he terms a 'guarantee' of perpetual peace. This 'guarantee' focuses on a discussion of providence and is connected to Kant's account of history in **UH**. The sense of 'providence' invoked here is distinguished from the religious one. Kant presents it in naturalistic terms but the reference to 'nature' is itself to be understood in a practical and not a theoretical sense.

Kant focuses on the way that human beings have spread to every corner of the earth, even into inhospitable regions and connects this to the need for lawful relations between peoples in order to prevent war. The suggestion, in anticipation of Hegel, made here is that there are certain ends that are effectively prosecuted even when we have not wished them. So, war forces constraint on public laws even if we would not wish to be governed by them. Even those who act in ways that are exclusively self-seeking require a state in order to organize their affairs so that even a nation of devils would form one (assuming they had understanding). The point here is that it does not require any desire for moral improvement to see the need for a state but that there are mechanisms of action that bring it about regardless of our wishes or ends. Similarly, Kant argues that the distinction of peoples into separate states is preferable to a universal despotism and this separation is enforced by distinction of languages and religion. The spirit of commerce is also upheld as the best means for ensuring that there is peace.

The second 'supplement' contains a 'secret article' for perpetual peace to the effect that the maxims of philosophers concerning the conditions for public peace should be consulted by states that are readying for war. The reason this 'guarantee' is presented as 'secret' is so that states need not feel that they need to take advice from their subjects as a 'public' matter. Kant stresses here the need to give philosophers a hearing in addition to lawyers to whom states have tended to refer.

The 'appendix' that closes the treatise is divided into two sections. The first concerns the grounds for disagreement between morals and politics when it comes to perpetual peace. Politics is here distinguished between the view of it that emerges from consideration of right (which should not conflict with morals) and that which comes from a doctrine of prudence (which may well come into conflict with morals).

Kant goes on to look at the attitude of those who take it that human beings will never be able to adopt ends leading to the goal of perpetual peace. The reason is taken to be that power will not allow laws to be prescribed to it. In response Kant invokes the figure of a moral politician who would try to reform the practices of state in conformity with the concept of right. However, the practice that is adopted by those who oppose the views of the moral politician are then described and the core of them taken to be 'deal[ing] in *machinations*' (**PP** 373). The maxims of such dealings are then summarized as threefold: seize favourable opportunities for taking possession; always deny the guilt is your own; divide and rule. These maxims are identified as those of an immoral doctrine of prudence and as necessarily requiring to be held in secret. In reply to them, Kant distinguishes between basing practical reason on material principles or on formal ones with the latter formulated in accord with the categorical imperative (**PP** 377). The uncertainty attaching to all maxims of prudence is alleged and

basing state conduct on principles of happiness and welfare condemned. Kant argues for the need for politics to be governed by right and to abandon the standpoint of prudence.

The second part of the appendix describes the agreement of politics with morals in accord with the transcendental concept of public right and opens with Kant abstracting from the matter of public right in order to arrive at the form of publicity. By this means, Kant arrives at the transcendental formula of public right which is that all actions relating to the rights of others are wrong if their maxim is incompatible with publicity (**PP** 381). This maxim is also argued to be not merely ethical but also juridical. Any maxim that has to be kept secret to be successful must involve injustice.

The consequences of this formula are then followed through the three areas of the right of a state, the right of nations and cosmopolitan right. In regard to the right of a state, Kant attacks the view that there could be a 'right' to rebellion since, if the maxims in favour of rebellion were publicly formulated, they could not be successful. With regard to the rights of nations, Kant formulates a more intricate account giving three separate examples, which concern international acts of promising, acts of states operating with regard to the divide and rule formula and the attempt of larger states to incorporate smaller states within themselves.

Cosmopolitan right is merely mentioned but not discussed since Kant claims the maxims of it would be easy to formulate and evaluate. Kant compares the spurious politics that would try and avoid the consequences that attach to the formula of publicity to the maxims of Jesuits. A further principle is then added which is stated in an affirmative form as if we adopt only maxims that *require* publicity in order not to fail in their end then we

at such maxims must also
‿‿ with the right of the public.

METAPHYSICS OF MORALS (MM)

This work was published in two separate parts in 1797 as the first part, or Doctrine of Right, was published first with the Doctrine of Virtue following afterwards but the two parts have always subsequently been treated as belonging together in one work. The publication of this work was the culmination of Kant's practical philosophy but it has only recently received any serious attention in English-language scholarship. Until recently, **G** received the majority of attention without looking at the book that **G** was meant to pave the way for. The pioneering work of Mary Gregor took many years to have influence but has recently been supplemented by Mark Timmons and Gary Banham,[16] all of which have helped to create a situation where this work has begun to be seen as key to comprehending a number of features of Kant's view of ethics.

The 'Preface' to the work is really aimed primarily at introducing the Doctrine of Right. Kant here points out that the work presented is not a comprehensive treatment of right as that would have to include a discussion of empirical variety and that what is presented here are the metaphysical first principles. An explicit comparison is also drawn between the method used in the Doctrine of Right and that which guided **MFNS**. Kant also points out that the earlier parts of the Doctrine of Right are worked over much more thoroughly than the later parts and concludes with a table of divisions of the Doctrine of Right.

There next follow two introductions, one to the metaphysics of morals as a whole and one specific to the Doctrine of Right. The general introduction to the metaphysics of morals as a whole distinguishes the method by which metaphysics relates to natural science from how it relates to morals. While natural science mixes a priori principles together with empirical ones the doctrine of morals requires that laws be seen to be a priori, especially in the sense of being necessary.

Kant points out that if the doctrine of morals were essentially an exposition of happiness, it would be absurd to expect to discern a priori principles. With regard to morals, there is no necessary reference to experience due to the fact that there may be no empirical examples to hand and there is no necessary reference to what experience can teach us. Kant also refers to 'principles of application' of the higher universal principles indicating that these involve bringing in references specific to the nature of human beings. Further, the empirical counterpart of the metaphysics of morals is stated to be moral anthropology although this latter could only discuss what conditions of human nature help or hinder the fulfilment of the metaphysics of morals.

The laws with which the work is concerned are moral laws or laws of freedom. When these are considered as directed only to external actions we have juridical laws but if they also require consideration of the determining grounds of action then they are ethical laws. Kant describes a number of concepts that are common to both parts of the work and explicitly includes the categorical imperative in this list. The difference between the two parts of the work is explained by means of the way the law relates to incentives that are considered. When the law that makes an action a duty is the only thing allowed as an incentive then we are dealing purely with ethics. But when another ground additional to the law is taken to be an incentive for action then we are on juridical ground. In fact, when we are considering juridical action, it is not necessary that the law even be taken as part of your motivation in acting in accordance with it. All duties, as duties, are presented as part of ethics but only because all juridical duties are indirectly ethical.

Kant expanded the introduction to the Doctrine of Right when the second edition of the work appeared in 1798. The first part of the introduction is, however, more frequently referred to than the additional material added. Here Kant addresses the question of what right is by describing it as the 'sum of conditions under which the choice of one can be united with the choice of another in accordance with a universal law of freedom' (**MM** 230). After stating this general account of what right consists in Kant proceeds to state the universal (or supreme) principle of right, which says an action is right if it can coexist with everyone's freedom in accordance with the universal law. If something that can so coexist is hindered by another then the one who so hinders it does a wrong. On this basis, Kant presents right as connected with an authorization to use coercion since if whatever hinders that which is right is wrong then the former, in so hindering the latter, creates a state that needs to be remedied and this is an external state since right governs that which is external. So the external state has to be set back into equilibrium and this can be achieved by removing the check. Hence to coerce someone to cease acting wrongly is itself right.

The concept of right is also described as 'the possibility of connecting universal reciprocal coercion with the freedom of everyone' (**MM** 232). Kant describes 'strict' right as that which is not mixed with anything ethical and states that such strict right requires

only external grounds for determining choice and on this ground right and the authorization to use coercion are presented as identical to each other. After making this claim, Kant includes an extended analogical connection of right to mathematics and physics.

Kant presents the second part of the introduction as an 'appendix' though it is much longer than the first part. Here Kant first presents definitions of some terms and then gives a general division of the duties of right. This general division includes some statements from Ulpian that have been deemed significant by both Höffe and Byrd and Hruschka.[17]

Kant next explicates freedom as the only original or 'innate' right belonging to all by virtue of their very humanity. The introduction concludes with a number of elaborate accounts of the division of the work, which explain its division through a distinction of types of duty, types of obligation and in terms of architectonic.

PRIVATE RIGHT

The Doctrine of Right is itself divided into two major parts; one part concerned with 'private' right and the other with 'public' right. The discussion of private right opens with a discussion of what it means to have something external as one's own. This initially concerns the notion of 'possession' and Kant opens by distinguishing between 'intelligible' and 'empirical' possession, which enables him to understand the possibility of possession that does not require holding the thing in question physically. From this slender basis, Kant moves on to distinguishing between types of possession, which requires distinction of different 'external objects' that can be possessed. The three types indicated are corporeal things, another's choice and another's status. Included under the second heading is someone's promise to act in certain ways and in the latter relations to others, such as the relation to a wife, a child or a servant. The general notion of external objects that are possessed involves a sense that one would be wronged by being disturbed in one's possession even though one does not hold it. So it is intelligible possession that poses the key question for Kant and it is only with regard to such that we are dealing with synthetic a priori judgments (empirical possession being merely analytic).

From this start, Kant states a 'postulate' of practical reason with regard to rights that asserts the possibility of intelligible possession on the grounds of the view that it would be contrary to right that objects of choice should belong to no one. The brief argument given for this postulate concerns the consistency of external freedom with itself. The ground for this claim is that we require removal of conditions of intuition with the practical principles. This is required to be able to uncover the basis of claims to possession in a general sense and is in accord with the procedure of the typic in **CPrR**. To relate the notion of intelligible possession to objects of experience, we have to apply it not to the concept of 'holding' but only to that of 'having' and we connect this concept to the sense of externality where something is distinct from us. At this point, Kant introduces an antinomy concerning possession in view of the conflict between those who take it to be possible to have something external as one's own even though it is not held by one and those who deny this possibility. Kant now resolves this antinomy by showing that the claim to validity here is right if we mean intelligible possession and wrong if we mean empirical possession.

Having given this statement of the basis of intelligible possession, Kant goes on to claim that the possibility of this form of possession requires something further to be given reality. This further element is the existence of a rightful condition, which means the existence of a civil society. The reason for this is that without the existence of the civil condition there is lack of assurance of the mutuality of respect for possession. A unilateral will cannot produce this mutuality, only an omnilateral will can do so. Outside the realm of the civil constitution, the rightful claim to possession does still exist, however, and with it comes the authorization to coerce others to respect such a claim even without the existence of the civil power. What we have in such conditions is a 'provisionally rightful' possession while possession in a civil condition is conclusively rightful possession.

Kant's initial argument concerned how to have something external as one's own and the next stage examines how to acquire something external in the first place. In explicating this second point, Kant uses the postulate of practical reason to show that bringing something under one's control in order to use it has to be combined with an act of will where the latter has to conform to the structure of a possible united (or omnilateral) will. Acquiring something as one's own involves a matter, a form and a basis. The matter of the object concerns the kind of thing that can be acquired and this is either the thing as a substance, another's performance of an action (causality) or the status of another person (coexistence), which shows that matter of the object is connected to the categories of relation. The form of what can be acquired divides the rights in question to either right to a thing, right against a person and right to a person similar to a right to a thing. Finally, the basis of the acquisition is given unilaterally, bilaterally or omnilaterally.

After making these divisions, Kant next looks at the three forms of right, beginning with the right to a thing that leads us to the notion of property right. The right to a thing is a right to the private use of something even though the original possession of it would have been common. This basis of the original right is not directly over the thing itself but rather to the possession of the right to claim the thing as distinct from others having such a right. Kant proceeds to give an a priori genesis of such property rights by describing original acquisition as involving land (a claim that, again, invokes the postulate of practical reason). The possibility of such possession is related to the notion of an original community where this notion refers not to a primitive condition but rather to an a priori claim. What Kant really means by this is that the original community is effectively to be understood as the possible civil condition under which the right is conclusively authorized. However, although such actual conclusive authorization requires the civil condition, it is the mere idea of the possibility of such that is sufficient to act as justification of possession and is hence the ground, in private right, for first possession of land. Provisional right to hold property is justified according to a permissive law of reason on which something that will be right if actual can be grounded in terms of its mere possibility. There is much detailed investigation of this opening section of the Doctrine of Right.[18]

The next form of right, the right against a person, is dealt with under the heading of contract right. Unlike property right, this is not an original right and is not acquired by another acting in a way that is wrong. It requires rather an act of united choice of (at least) two whereby something passes from one to the other. Contract requires, in Kant's view, preparatory and constitutive acts of choice. The preparatory rightful acts are the manner of negotiating which refer to means of offering something and means of assenting to the offering. By contrast, the constitutive elements are the means by which the conclusion of the transfer is brought about and involve promising and accepting. Before a promise of transfer can be made, it is first necessary to establish that what is promised is something that is desired. But the act of transfer only takes place through the uniting of the will of both. The problem that has to be addressed in contract concerns how the united will of both is to be manifested when temporally they make distinct and distinguishable acts.

In reply to this problem, Kant introduces a 'transcendental deduction', which again requires the acts involved in the transfer to be seen as intelligible rather than empirical. What is acquired is the causality of another's choice or another's promise and involves tacit acquiescence in a law of continuity (**MM** 274). The contract is only honoured when the thing in question is delivered.

The third kind of right, the right to a person akin to a right to a thing, is divided into three separate parts but governs what Kant generally terms 'domestic right'. This area is not governed just by a deed on one's own initiative as property right was and nor is it just a contract but involves rather the right of humanity in our own person and is governed by what is termed a 'natural permissive law' and concerns 'most personal' rights (**MM** 276–277). The three-fold division of the area is between marriage right, parental right and the right of a head of a household.

In discussing marriage right, Kant distinguishes natural sexual union from such union in accordance with law and in the process dismisses Catholic natural law arguments, which view marriage right as grounded on procreation alone. The connection between the right to a person and the right to a thing is made in the case of marriage right by the way in which sexual union is understood as divided between animal union and lawful union. Merely sensual or 'animal' union is pursued exclusively for the sake of enjoyment and Kant views this as taking the other merely to be a thing for the sake of one's pleasure. This purely sensuous relation is transformed if there is an act of mutual acquisition as this enables recognition of the personality of each to be incorporated into the act of union. On these grounds, Kant somewhat strictly views sexual union as only permissible under the conditions of marriage. Not only is this so but Kant's conception of the sexual union as a lawful transformation of a 'natural' sexual urge rules out extension of marriage beyond heterosexual union although the strict resources of his argument are hardly sufficient to sustain this. The simple leaving of one partner of a marriage is also ruled out by Kant on the basis that, since we are dealing with a right to a person akin to that to a thing, either partner could retrieve the other and bring them back under control, just as they could with a thing. This seems to involve an overextension of his analogy. Formally, the marriage partners are taken to be equal in their possession of each other though this does not prevent Kant from assuming that the husband could be 'master' of the wife on the grounds of a greater capacity to promote the common interest of the household (**MM** 279). Finally, despite parting from the Catholic tradition of assuming procreation to be the essential end of marriage, Kant views a marriage which involves tacit or expressed wish to avoid sexual union as only a simulated marriage.

Parental right follows next as emerging from the procreation allowed for as a 'natural' element of marriage right. Children are related to as other persons over whom there is right that is akin to the right to a thing. This 'right' over the children is not without obligation since the child has the right to be cared for until it is able to care for itself. Since the child is a person who has emerged from acts of the parents to which the child did not consent, the obligation of the parents to the child is part of the condition of production of the child and is hence original. On these grounds, Kant has a simple argument against infanticide.

The obligations of the parents to the child encompass the education of the child both pragmatically and morally and while the child is still in its minority they have no obligation with which they can charge him other than the duty of gratitude, which is not a matter of right. The right held over the child, as a right over a person, is not alienable although, as in the case of marriage right, the parent has the right to retrieve the child should the child run away. Contemporary work on children's rights in a Kantian vein has moved away from the strictly paternalist form Kant himself gave it and can be seen in the work of Onora O'Neill.[19]

The final part of domestic right concerns the right of a head of the household and this is the briefest part of Kant's discussion. It covers the kind of right that is at work in the holding of domestic servants which involves a contract between the head of the household and free persons who may be employed either to help with the children or in the running of the household. Again, as with the examples of marriage right and parental right, Kant assumes that this involves the right to recover the servant if they depart from the possession of the head without the head's permission. However, despite this somewhat alarming provision, Kant is clear that servants are not owned by the head of the household and so he distinguishes the servant's place from that of either a slave or a serf. Contract is required to govern the relation and its frame must be temporally limited. This part of Kant's discussion of domestic right has not received general discussion although, given that the relations discussed persist, albeit altered in certain ways, there are certainly grounds for thinking it needs to be as extensively responded to as the other elements of domestic right have been.

After the discussion of domestic right, Kant returns to the account of contract right and provides a general division of its possibilities in relation to unilateral or gratuitous contracts (which include acts of lending and gifting), mutual acquisition (including such alienation as buying and selling and contracts of letting and hiring) and those which guarantee what belongs to someone (as when we vouch for something). These forms of division of contract right are organized in a table.

Kant next discusses the nature of money distinguishing the nominal definition of it as a means of alienation from the real definition as the means of exchanging industriousness. This account of money assumes that money is something distinct from bank notes and takes it rather to be something that it has taken a great deal of industry to produce. The empirical concept of money is that which determines the price of things but Kant follows Adam Smith in seeing its 'intellectual concept' to involve reference to industry.

After discussing money, Kant looks at the nature of books in order to discuss the question of the authorization of their publication. The question of such authorization arises as the publisher does not present discourses of

his own to the public but discourses of the author and so has to have the authority of the author to present them to the public. On these grounds, Kant indicates a basis in right for authorization of copyright and indicates objections to such right are based on treating the produced object as if it were independent of its producer. Hence those who violate this right are not respecting the personality expressed in the thing.

Kant next treats the topic of 'ideal acquisition' by which he means something that involves no causality in time and states that such forms of acquisition are at issue when we are dealing with prolonged possession, inheritance and merit after one's death (reputation). The first of these involves the claim that is made when someone has long laid undisputed control over something and discovers eventually that another has the status of being its true owner. In response, Kant argues that without continuity of possession being exerted the claim to ownership eventually lapses. Inheritance involves transfer of possession to someone else by virtue of cessation of empirical existence and willing of possession after this has occurred. Since, however, the transfer requires the cessation of the original owner, there is a sense in which this is not a real transfer but is an ideal one and Kant justifies its possibility outside the civil condition on the grounds of tacit consent to the inheritance. The question of reputation after death is treated as an innate external possession although it is ideal since it is independent of the one who holds it. As it is independent of the actuality of the person in question, it is has to be taken to be a right held by the person in their noumenal sense.

The final part of the discussion of private right concerns acquisition that depends on the decision of a public court of justice.

This can still be treated under the heading of private right on the grounds that the distribution of possession must have principles that are in accord with the general grounds of private right. So here Kant treats what would be distributively right of itself in relation to judgment and suggests there are four cases that need to be treated here. These are, cases of contract to make gifts, contracts to lend things, recovery of things and taking oaths. The contract to make gifts is indicated to require that only a reservation expressly made can prevent the gift being given. The contract to lend something discusses risks of damage to what is lent and in the case of the state of nature it is assumed such risk must be borne by the borrower whereas in the civil condition, by contrast, it falls on the lender.

Recovery of something lost concerns what right is held when something I had is discovered by another who does not know of my claim and Kant indicates that the reference to the notion of a court regulates only the means by which something comes to be held. If the new owner took possession according to general conditions of right then I can have no further claim on the thing. Finally, the discussion of oaths effectively rules out requirements that people be taken to believe in religions and tends to rule against oaths as a means of ensuring truthfulness.

Public Right

Kant concludes the discussion of private right by stating a postulate of public right to the effect that since we cannot avoid living in relation to others we ought to leave the state of nature and enter a civil condition. This opens the discussion of public right. The discussion of public right is divided into three parts, discussing the right of a state, the right of nations and cosmopolitan right and also includes a lengthy appendix of second edition revisions and emendations. The three parts are asymmetrical with the discussion of the right of a state much longer and more detailed than the second two parts.

Kant opens the discussion of public right by describing it generally as a system of laws which emerge from an omnilateral will that, in a constitution, has laid down what is right. The general term for this condition is a civil condition and the totality of persons in this condition are said to be in a state. The point Kant makes in introducing this notion is that it is not due to some experience of malevolence that we can say we need the state. Rather, even a state of nature filled with angels would require supersession since, without the formation of a civil condition, we would always be dependent on subjective agreement concerning what is right. A state of nature is a state of dispute concerning right and lacks a conclusive judge.

The state is divided between three distinct authorities: the sovereign (legislator), the executive and the judicial authority. The legislature is taken to be sovereign as based on the omnilateral will of the people and is the source of all right. The citizens of the state have three attributes, they are free and can be governed only by laws to which they could have given their consent, they are possessed of civil equality and they are independent in holding their preservation only to the existence of the civil condition and are thus not dependent on the favour of any particular persons.

Citizens are such by being able to vote but, in explicating this notion, Kant distinguishes between active and passive citizens, including under the latter heading apprentices, domestic servants, minors and women. The general heading is meant to refer to those who need another to protect and defend them (which explains even if it does not exculpate why Kant places women in this category). This discussion is problematic in more than one way as Kant's examples of who falls under which heading are difficult to take seriously.

The majority of Kant's discussion is, however, focused not on the account of citizens but on the nature of the state. The authorities that make the state up are compared to parts of a syllogism and the ruler of the state is the one who possesses executive authority. Kant hence distinguishes the ruler from the sovereign as the latter power is held by the legislature but he does also indicate that the sovereign can depose the ruler.

At this point, the discussion broadens into an account of the effects that follow with regard to rights from the nature of the civil union. The sovereign is stated to have only rights against his subjects and no duties that he can be forced to fulfil. Even if the ruler proceeds in a way that is contrary to law this can only be met with complaints and not resistance. The basic point Kant seems to be making here is that the constitution cannot contain a clause (as in the United States) allowing a ground for revolt and making revolt a kind of 'right' that can be claimed. The reason for this is that such a clause would limit the authority of the state itself, which would undercut the supreme authority of the state and allow an alternative authority to be held against it. This discussion includes a vivid account of Kant's opposition to the revolutionary trials of Charles I and Louis XVI and is part of a general argument for reform rather than revolution in relation to defective political set-ups. Despite this argument, Kant also rules out any legitimist revolt against a successful revolution as well.

After discussing the problems with claims of a right to revolution, Kant turns to the question of whether the sovereign is the supreme proprietor of the land of the state, answering this question in the affirmative. However, the sovereign has to thereby renounce any claim to land as private property and Kant is opposed to hereditary status rights with regard to land as in the claims of a landed aristocracy. In discussing taxes, Kant makes an argument for an indirect right of the sovereign to support organizations providing for the poor. This is very far from anything like a welfare claim for the poor and hence a long way from the type of provision discussed by Rawls.[20]

The rights of the sovereign are also assessed as including distribution of offices or salaried positions, dignities or estates and the right of punishment. The first two have attracted little attention but there is quite a literature on punishment. The central question concerns whether Kant's view of punishment is strictly retributivist. Punishment is described as a categorical imperative and a principle of public equality is referred to as governing its operation. This principle of public equality visits on the punished the evil he wished to inflict on others but it is only explained in a general figurative way. For the quantity and quality of punishment to be determined, Kant refers to the law of retribution. In the course of his discussion Kant makes a number of intriguing points comparing, for example, the status of a prisoner to that of a slave since he now has to endure forced labour for no more than his subsistence. Kant also advocates capital punishment for murder though with allowance for deportation if reasons of state suggest this. In defending capital punishment, Kant replies to the arguments of Beccaria using the claim that the noumenal self of the punished person would himself subject the phenomenal self to the punishment in question. Kant concludes the account of punishment with a discussion of the sovereign's right to grant clemency.

INTERNATIONAL RIGHT

The second part of public right concerns the right of nations which concerns the rights of states in regard to each other. These rights consist partly in rights to go to war, partly in rights during war and partly in rights after war. Kant argues that the external relation of states to each other is a state of nature and always, at least potentially, a state of war. In this discussion, Kant also investigates the basis of the right states claim to use their citizens as soldiers in war and suggests the only ground for such use is the view of the citizens as having granted that right to the state.

The right to go to war includes the need for a balance of power to attempt to prevent any given state becoming too strong. Right during a war is discussed and certain kinds of methods (including extermination and subjugation) ruled out in principle. Right after a war governs the types of peace treaties that are acceptable. However, Kant also includes discussion of the notion of an 'unjust enemy', which is defined as one whose maxims are such as would make peace impossible. The fact that rights of nations are so exclusively concerned with war leads Kant to conclude the discussion with the need to overcome the state of nature between states, arguing for the formation of a permanent congress of states. The final part of public right concerns cosmopolitan right, which governs commercial relations between peoples. This discussion is very brief but typically anti-colonialist in flavour. The conclusion of the Doctrine of Right is made with a stirring invocation of the need to prevent war and a clear statement that establishing universal peace is the 'entire final end' (MM 355) of the work.

The second edition included an appendix on certain areas in response to critics of the first edition. Here Kant justifies the inclusion of the notion of the right to a person that is akin to a right to a thing and, in the process, describes the need to move away from reified sexual relations. Kant also adds to his discussion of punishment including in the account questions about rape and pederasty though the discussion of these is somewhat inconclusive. Right from prolonged possession is also given a further treatment, as is inheritance, and the establishment of foundations that are meant to be perpetual. The latter includes accounts of charities with a claim that the state must be able to relate to their foundation as changing over time.

THE ARCHITECTONIC OF THE DOCTRINE OF VIRTUE

The Doctrine of Virtue has a much more elaborate division than the Doctrine of Right and its introduction is also itself an extended piece of philosophy. As well as containing such an extensive introduction, the work is then divided between a doctrine of elements and a doctrine of method with the former, as is usual, taking up the lion's share of the work. The 'Preface' to the work justifies its existence by making the maxims of virtue follow from the metaphysical principles of morals generally. Kant here rejects attempts to base virtue on happiness.

The 'Introduction' describes the account of virtue as equivalent to ethics and distinct from right as it is concerned with internal laws. Virtue is shown to be concerned with ends that duties have. These ends are one's own perfection and the happiness of others. Included under the former are the cultivation of one's talents and one's will. The account of the happiness of others does not simply take others' view of what would make them happy but does include provision for the means that will make them unlikely to be tempted by vice.

Ethics does not give laws for actions as right does, but only for the maxims of actions. Ethical duties are also stated to be of wide obligation while those of right are narrow. After making these claims, Kant returns to expounding the ends that are duties further. The discussion of perfection is now divided between an account of 'natural' perfection and the cultivation of morality. Kant's most general description of virtue is as 'the strength of a human being's maxims in fulfilling his duty' (MM 394) and the supreme (or universal) principle of virtue consists in acting in accord with a maxim of ends that it can be a universal law for everyone to have. The division of duties of virtue is presented through two different means, firstly through the distinction of formal and material elements, and secondly through 'internal' and 'external' duties. The material parts of virtue concern the ends of myself and others (perfection and happiness) while the formal parts concern the law. Duties I have to myself are 'internal' while those to others are 'external'.

Kant also discusses subjective conditions for virtue, including under the heading moral feeling, conscience and respect for oneself. Under the heading of moral feeling, Kant makes clear the distinction between pathological and moral feeling while conscience is presented as the way practical reason holds the law before one. Benevolence as a form of practical love leads to the duty to act in ways that are beneficent to others while respect arises within each of us due to the connection between personality and the moral law. Virtue is based on a form of self-governing and is said to presuppose 'apathy' meaning by this a tranquil mind that has firm resolve.

DUTIES TO ONESELF

The Doctrine of the Elements of Ethics is divided into two parts, with the first concerning duties to oneself and the second duties towards others. In introducing the notion of duties to oneself, Kant justifies the notion by means of setting up an antinomy and then resolving it. The problem concerns how it is possible to set up a law for oneself and this is resolved by means of the distinction between the self as phenomenon and the self as noumenon.

The division of duties to oneself has two ways of being described. The first and most objective is in terms of the division between formal and material. The formal duties are negative ones while the material ones are positive. Another way of putting that is that the formal duties concern how to maintain one's moral health while the material ones concern how to become more morally healthy. But there is also a second way of dividing these duties between duties to oneself as a moral being and duties to oneself as an animal being. Duties to oneself as an animal being were first mentioned in R and include self-preservation, the preservation of the species and preservation of capacity to enjoy life. Duties to oneself as a moral being concern only the formal consistency of the maxims of the will with one's humanity.

Kant begins with perfect duties to oneself and discusses firstly which duties to oneself as an animal being fall under this heading. Here the example of suicide that was used in G is returned to and the problem with suicide is traced to its manner of using one's own being as a discretionary end. However, Kant then lists a series of casuistical questions, which are repeated hereafter with regard to all the duties discussed and which suggest cases in which the consideration of suicide is less simple.

After the discussion of suicide, Kant considers use of one's sexual capacity with regard to the formulations of humanity. Here Kant considers 'unnatural' use of sexual capacity, meaning by this masturbation which is suggested to involve a kind of surrender of one's personality by giving oneself over to an animal use of oneself. The argument for this view is less than convincing though surprisingly few have responded to it.[21] The last part of the discussion concerns gluttony and drunkenness and leads Kant to discuss dinner parties and their delights.

The account of the perfect duties to oneself as a moral being is stated to be directly opposed to the vices of lying, avarice and false humility. Lying is placed first as it perverts the medium of communication but the discussion also foreshadows Sartre's account of bad faith in including an account of lying to oneself. Avarice is discussed as undue restriction of one's means of enjoyment and helps to balance the account of masturbation in the discussion of perfect duties to oneself as an animal being. Servility is argued to be problematic in lowering the value of humanity in oneself. Duties to oneself are further discussed in relation to one's own 'innate judge' or conscience, which is here presented as the subjective principle of being accountable to God for all one's deeds. The imperfect duties to oneself are described more quickly and involve the development and increase of both natural and moral perfection.

DUTIES TO OTHERS

Duties of virtue to others are treated mainly as duties to them merely as human beings. Again there are duties that are meritorious and those that are simply owed as such. Feelings of love and respect are here mentioned but not as pathological feelings. The discussion of the relationship between love and respect is compared to the action of laws of attraction and repulsion in physics with love drawing us together as respect keeps us apart. In carrying out duties of love I put another under obligation to me while duties of respect create no obligations but only fulfil them. The general practical notion of love is beneficence and follows what Kant terms the 'law of perfection' that is expressed in the Gospel as loving your neighbour as yourself (**MM** 450). Duties of love are explained as duties of beneficence, gratitude and sympathy. The duty of beneficence is what is expressed in taking others' happiness as your own end and was one of the examples in **G**. Gratitude is distinguished as a moral notion from prudential action while sympathetic feeling concludes the account of duties of love. Vices that are contrary to these duties are subsequently discussed which are envy, ingratitude and malice.

Duties of respect are treated after duties of love and mutual respect is a basic demand that arises from the conception of humanity in general. Having contempt for others is hence a basic violation of the respect all have as their due. Respect for the law is identical with consciousness of one's duty and failure to fulfil duties of respect is to fall directly into vice. The vices that are contrary to the duty of respect are arrogance, defamation and ridicule. Arrogance is a kind of ambition that requires others to think less of themselves in relation to us and involves contempt for others. Defamation is the vice of spreading abroad matters that undermine others' honour and ridicule is a form of malice.

The general Doctrine of Elements concludes with an account of friendship as a union of love with respect. Rules of such intimacy involve the need to keep certain limits of it, not least by means of retaining some elements of distance from the other. However, the problems of friendship are also clear since Kant discusses the need to explain faults to a friend as part of the duties of friendship. The love that is in friendship cannot, in an ideal case, be pathological but must rather be practical. So Kant concludes his account with a discussion of moral friendship as an ideal and distinguishes it from pragmatic friendship.

The Doctrine of the Methods of Ethics concludes the Doctrine of Virtue and is divided into two parts, a part concerned with teaching ethics and a part concerned with ethical ascetics. The discussion of teaching ethics describes a moral catechism as the most essential element for beginning training and provides a fragment of such a catechism. Ethical ascetics, by contrast, cultivates the disposition of dealing with misfortune and doing without superfluous pleasures. It is meant to be part of a regime of moral health and is distinguished from 'monkish' ascetics. Kant concludes the work by ruling out consideration of duties to God as lying beyond the limits of pure moral philosophy.

NOTES

1   Important here also is the work of Wolfgang Carl. See a précis in W. Carl, 'Kant's first drafts of the Deduction of the Categories', and also L. W. Beck's response 'Two ways of reading Kant's letter to Herz. Comments on Carl', both in E. Förster (ed.), *Kant's Transcendental Deductions. The Three 'Critiques' and the 'Opus postumum'* (Stanford, 1989), pp. 3–20 and 21–26 respectively.

2   H. Paton, *Metaphysics of Experience* (London, 1936), vol. 1.

3   P. Guyer, *Kant and the Claims of Knowledge* (Cambridge, 1987), ch. 16.

4   P. F. Strawson, *The Bounds of Sense* (London, 1966).

5   P. Guyer, *Kant and the Claims of Knowledge* (Cambridge, 1987) and G. Banham, *Kant's Transcendental Imagination* (Basingstoke/New York, 2006).

6   K. Ameriks, *Kant's Theory of Mind* (Oxford, ²2000 [1982]).

7   P. Guyer, *Kant and the Claims of Knowledge* (Cambridge, 1987) discusses the latter but not the former and R. Langton, *Kantian Humility* (Oxford, 1998) the former but not the latter.

8   See e.g., G. Bird, *The Revolutionary Kant* (Chicago/La Salle, IL, 2006).

9   This is, at any rate, in accord with I. Geiger, 'Is the assumption of a systematic whole of empirical concepts a necessary condition of knowledge', in *Kant-Studien* 94 (2003): 273–298, and P. Abela, *Kant's Empirical Realism* (Oxford, 2002), but it is disputed in G. Bird, *The Revolutionary Kant* (Chicago/La Salle, IL, 2006).

10 See L. W. Beck, 'Does the Sage of Königsberg have no dreams?', in L. W. Beck, *Essays on Hume and Kant* (New Haven, 1978), pp. 38–60 ; H. Allison, *Kant's Transcendental Idealism. An Interpretation and Defense* (New Haven, 1983).

11 H. Paton, *The Categorical Imperative* (Philadelphia, 1947).

12 See G. Buchdahl, *Metaphysics and the Philosophy of Science* (Oxford, 1969) and M. Friedman, *Kant and the Exact Sciences* (Cambridge, MA, 1992).

13 See J.-F. Lyotard, *Lessons on the Analytic of the Sublime* (Stanford, 1994).

14 See H. Arendt, *Lectures on Kant's Political Philosophy* (Chicago, 1982).

15 G. Banham, *Kant and the Ends of Aesthetics* (New York, 2000); P. Guyer, *Kant's System of Nature and Freedom* (Cambridge, 2005); R. Zuckert, *Kant on Beauty and Biology* (Cambridge, 2007); A. Nuzzo, *Kant and the Unity of Reason* (West Lafayette, 2005).

16 See respectively M. Gregor, *Laws of Freedom* (Oxford, 1963); M. Timmons (ed.), *Kant's Metaphysics of Morals: Interpretive Essays* (Oxford, 2002); and G. Banham, *Kant's Practical Philosophy* (Basingstoke/New York, 2003).

17 See respectively O. Höffe, *Kant's Cosmopolitan Theory of Law and Peace* (Cambridge, 2006) and S. Byrd, J. Hruschka, *Kant's Doctrine of Right: A Commentary* (Cambridge, 2010).

18 The reader is referred to A. Ripstein, *Force and Freedom* (Cambridge, MA, 2009); Byrd, Hruschka, *Kant's Doctrine of Right: A*

Commentary; K. Flikschuh, *Kant and Modern Political Philosophy* (Cambridge, 2000); K. Westphal, 'A Kantian justification of possession', in M. Timmons (ed.), *Kant's Metaphysics of Morals: Interpretative Essays*, pp. 89–109; and G. Banham, *Kant's Practical Philosophy*.

19 O. O'Neill, 'Children's right and children's lives', in *Constructions of Reason* (Cambridge, 1988), pp. 187–205.

20 J. Rawls, *A Theory of Justice* (Cambridge, MA, 1971).

21 But see Banham, *Kant's Practical Philosophy*.

PART II:
KANT'S CONTEXTS

2

PHILOSOPHICAL AND HISTORICAL CONTEXT

This chapter includes a selection of short essays concerned with some of the important ideas, theories and events which helped shape Kant's life and thought. The essays are diverse in content and include historical events that Kant encountered (such as the French Revolution), as well as some of the important individuals who stood out as prominent figures in his cultural and philosophical milieu. The chapter conveys the extent to which Kant's world – being almost entirely confined to the place of his birth, Königsberg – was illuminated by a wide and varied amount of interests that ventured beyond the philosophical sphere in which he made his fame. With some of the entries a list of further reading is provided that will enable the reader to undertake further research. – NH/DS

ACADEMY PRIZE ESSAY

The Berlin Royal Academy of Sciences[1] was established in 1744. The prize for the winning entry was 50 ducats. One of the main attractions of these contests was the fact that many of the judges of the contests were Academy members. As well as Kant, some of the other leading figures who put forward essays included Lessing, → **Mendelssohn**, and → **Herder**. On average, there were about 12 entries per question, although some questions attracted a wider number of entries. For instance, the question from 1780 attracted 42 entries. Due to the difficulty of some of the questions, it was necessary for the Academy to repeat the same question until essays of a sufficiently high standard were received.

The Academy Prize attracted the attention of Kant enough for him to construct answers to numerous questions. These were subsequently published as **EAR** (1754), **Opt** (1759), **Inq** (1764) and **PE**, which was published only posthumously in 1804. The Academy question of 1763 was:

> whether the metaphysical truths in general, and the first principles of *Theologiae naturalis* and morality in particular, admit of distinct proofs to the same degree as geometrical truths; and if they are not capable of such proofs, [. . .] what the genuine nature of their certainty is, to what degree the said certainty can be brought, and whether this degree is sufficient for complete conviction.[2]

ed the 1763 essay competi-
set by the Royal Academy in
the previous year. Kant's essay did not win
the contest, but it did get recognized by the
Academy. Kant received a certificate of merit
for his endeavours, as well as getting his work
published alongside Moses Mendelssohn's
essay, which won the prize. Kant's essay,
published as Inq, was designed to oppose the
fundamental tenets of Christian → Wolff's
rationalist system, by claiming that the methods of mathematics and philosophy were
wholly different, a theme that continued to
resonate in Kant's later 'Critical' or 'transcendental' stage of his career. – NH

ARISTOTELIANISM

Representatives of Aristotelianism claim to
be, or just de facto are, in agreement with →
Aristotle at least insofar as some of his core
doctrines in major areas of philosophy including his overall method are concerned, or at
any rate what they take those to be, which
are, more often than not, highly contentious.
Aristotelianism spans more than two mille-
nia, from his immediate successors as lead-
ers of the Lyceum, the school he founded in
Athens, up to the present, for example in the
movement of virtue ethics. Commentaries
on works of the Corpus Aristotelicum
emerged swiftly following its compilation
in the first century BC, with Alexander of
Aphrodisias, Porphyry, John Philoponus and
Simplicius being perhaps the most important
authors, often giving a Neoplatonist tinge to
Aristotle's positions.

Aristotelian doctrines came into contact
with Christian thought in Patristic philosophy, not least through Boethius who translated into Latin and commented on (some of)

Aristotle's logical treatises of the Organon.[3]
Despite the closure of the Athenian schools of
philosophy in 529, and with a longer period
of continuity in the Eastern Roman Empire,
Aristotelianism, especially in the wake of
the Carolingian Renaissance, nevertheless
remained an important force on the Western
European continent.

It did so at first only on the rather slim
textual basis of the so-called logica vetus,
consisting mainly of the Categories, de
Interpretatione, and Porphyry's Isagoge, an
introductory work to the former two. By virtue of translations from Arabic and Greek and
the dissemination of Averroes's commentaries
from the twelfth century onwards, the whole
of the Corpus Aristotelicum entered the stage
of debates in scholastic philosophy, most
notably in Paris where conflicts between, on
the one hand, the integral or neoplatonizing
heterodox school of Aristotelianism and, on
the other, orthodox Aristotelianism developed
quickly.[4]

These conflicts centred around doctrines
taken to be at odds with Christian teachings, such as the infinite temporal extension
of the world, the uniqueness of the active
as well as passive intellect and human freedom in relation to divine foreknowledge.
Different movements and various interpretations of Aristotle spread, such as Averroism,
Thomism and Scotism, all of which nonetheless integrated Aristotelian doctrines into
larger frameworks together with a number of
other theological and philosophical sources
such as Augustine.

During the Renaissance, Aristotelianism
benefited from the dissemination of new
editions of Aristotle's original texts and
those of the Greek commentators. The pro-
pulsive centre of Aristotle's philosophy was
Italy, especially the schools of Padua and
Bologna. Between 1450 and 1550, Thomism,

Averroism and Alexandrism became the three major Aristotelian movements.

Meanwhile, the religious reformers, in particular Luther with regard to ethics,[5] expressed strong hostility to Aristotelianism. More moderate thinkers such as Melanchthon, however, made sure that Aristotle also took centre stage in the early modern Protestant universities after what they considered to be a purification of his writings and doctrines from distortions by some of the medieval Scholastics. At the same time, and in a similar way to the situation in the High and Late Middle Ages, individual Aristotelian doctrines were upheld within all schools of early modern Scholasticism, for example in Suárez's conception of metaphysics, insofar as he took it to be concerned with *ens in quantum ens* (being as being).[6]

In general, both inside and outside the European universities until the seventeenth century, Aristotelianism,[7] including also political Aristotelianism, particularly in Germany, remained a major factor and thus constituted a crucial context for → **Leibniz**, who attempted to reconcile Aristotelian doctrines, such as that of individual forms as substances, with principles of mechanistic physics. → **Königsberg** University is a case in point: here Aristotelianism was present well into the eighteenth century.

Since its foundation in 1544, Königsberg University, the *Albertina*, was characterized by a strong Aristotelian tradition. Melanchthon's interpretation of Aristotle dominated until the beginning of the seventeenth century, when the works of Jacopo Zabarella and Giulio Pace became available. During that century, Königsberg became a stronghold of Aristotelianism, establishing itself as one of the most important schools in Germany with authors such as Abraham

Calov, Christian Dreier, Melchior Zeidler and Andreas Hedio.

The strength of Aristotelianism was tangible in particular in the field of logic: Calov wrote a *Methodologia*, which is a treatise against the philosophy of Francis → **Bacon** and René → **Descartes**, whereas Zeidler published a commentary on Aristotle's *Analytics* following Zabarella, and Hedio wrote a commentary on Aristotle's entire *Organon*.

The last important exponent of Königsberg's Aristotelianism was Paul Rabe.[8] His works were particularly important because they were adopted as official manuals of the *Collegium Fridericianum* and of the *Albertina*, i.e. at both of the institutions at which Kant himself was educated.[9]

All the professors at the *Albertina* in the first four decades of the eighteenth century were Aristotelians or well-read in Aristotelian philosophy. For example, two of the four professors who were very close to Kant, Johann David Kypke and Georg Gottfried Teske, defined themselves as Aristotelians, while the other two professors, Karl Gottlieb Marquardt and Martin Knutzen, were very erudite in Aristotelian doctrines. During the period when Kant was a student, Wolffianism (→ **Wolff**) was never a dominant movement at the *Albertina*. In fact, no professor could declare himself truly a Wolffian and no Wolffian became full professor in the chair of logic and metaphysics.[10]

The nineteenth century saw the emergence of the Berlin Academy edition of the *Corpus Aristotelicum*, which put the scholarship and the philosophical engagement of Aristotelianism on an unprecedented philologically sound footing, which has continued to influence various schools of philosophy throughout the nineteenth and twentieth centuries. – WE/MS

EBERHARD, JOHANN AUGUST

The publication of Kant's **CPR** in 1781 triggered an immediate response within the philosophical world in Germany. The interest in Kant's philosophy was followed by several debates regarding its adequacy and its claim to novelty. Most of Kant's opponents were representatives of the *Popularphilosophie*. Of all the attacks made on Kant's philosophy, that by J. A. Eberhard (1739–1809), a leading Wolffian who held → **Wolff**'s chair at the University of Halle, was the most dangerous.

Eberhard was born in Halberstadt, and studied theology at the University of Halle (1756–1759), where he also studied some philosophy and classical philology. In 1763, he began pursuing a career as a preacher and theologian, first in Halberstadt and subsequently in Berlin. His book *Neue Apologie des Sokrates, oder Untersuchungen der Lehre von der Seligkeit der Heiden* was first published in 1772. The book – which was published in several editions and translations – was widely discussed at the time. The position he developed in this book involved him in a debate with Lessing, who among other things accused him of having misinterpreted → **Leibniz**. Interestingly, Eberhard himself later made the same accusation against Kant. In 1776, Eberhard published his *Allgemeine Theorie des Denkens und Empfindens*, which was awarded the Berlin Academy prize (→**Academy prize essay**). In 1778, he became Professor of Philosophy at the University of Halle. He published several books on various aspects of philosophy, which also included *Vernunftlehre der natürlichen Theologie* (1787), which Kant himself used in his lectures on the philosophy of religion.

In 1788, together with several other Wolffians, Eberhard founded the *Philosophisches Magazin*, the main goal of which was to challenge Kant's Critical philosophy. The publication of the first issue of the *Philosophisches Magazin* – which included several papers that attacked Kant's philosophy – marked the beginning of a long debate between Kant, Eberhard and their allies. The Kantians' first response was Rehberg's and Reinhold's reviews of the first issues of *Philosophisches Magazin* (1789), which appeared in the *Allgemeine Literatur-Zeitung*. Eberhard responded to Reinhold's review in 1790. In that same year, Kant published his polemical essay **Disc**.

The *Philosophisches Magazin* was succeeded by the *Philosophisches Archiv*, which appeared in two volumes in 1793 and 1794. The controversy culminated in a contest of the Royal Academy of Sciences in Berlin (→ **Academy prize essay**) on the question, 'What real progress has metaphysics made in Germany since the time of Leibniz and Wolff?'. The first prize was awarded to Schwab, a Wolffian, and the second prize went to Karl Leonard Reinhold. Kant's prize essay (**PE**), which was not submitted and was published only in 1804, was his last active contribution to this debate.

Kant's controversy with Eberhard and his allies addressed many issues. Eberhard's main contention was that Kant's claim to novelty in metaphysics and epistemology and, in particular, his claim to novelty regarding the category of synthetic a priori judgments was unfounded. The contention that there was nothing really new in Kant's theory was apparently mistaken, yet the arguments presented in the *Philosophisches Magazin* show that they were supported by an ambiguity inherent in Kant's definitions concerning the role of intuition in synthetic judgments, and in particular, in synthetic a priori judgments.

The relation of the concepts involved in synthetic a priori judgments to sensible intuitions conceived of as a 'condition of possibility' for such judgments was required in order to accomplish the two tasks of **CPR** in one unified theory, namely, to ascertain the a priori foundations of empirical knowledge, and to challenge the dogmatic pretensions to knowledge that is based merely on pure reason. According to Kant's definitions, a synthetic a priori judgment is a judgment in which the predicate is not 'contained' or 'thought' in the subject term and also a judgment that involves a relation to intuition.

Nevertheless, according to Kant's own theory, it seems that judgments could also be characterized as synthetic a priori without involving a relation to intuition, at least insofar as the relation 'not being contained or thought in' is concerned. Moreover, it appears that this must be the case, if the pretentions of knowledge that are based merely on pure reason consist in synthetic a priori judgments. On the one hand, the critique of dogmatic metaphysics is based on the contention that *the* condition of possibility of synthetic a priori judgments is the relation between the concepts involved in such judgments and sensible intuitions. On the other hand, where this kind of synthetic a priori judgment is concerned, it is not possible to establish a relation between the a priori concepts involved in them and the relevant kind of intuition. In other words, Kant holds the view that the judgments that express the pretentions to knowledge merely based on pure reason are synthetic a priori, although the concepts involved in them are not and cannot be related to intuitions. Yet, the generic demand for such a relation regarding all synthetic a priori judgments is essential for the feasibility of his critique of dogmatic metaphysics.

These types of concern seem to underlie Eberhard and his allies' response to Kant's philosophy. Moreover, in their view, if one unties the relation between synthetic a priori judgment and sensible intuitions, it can be shown that the type of judgment characterized by Kant as synthetic a priori was in fact known to philosophers and logicians long before Kant. Synthetic a priori judgments are judgments in which the predicate is an *attribute* of the subject of judgment. The predicate of such a judgment is a concept that refers to a property that is necessarily related to the property to which the subject term refers, although it is not a characteristic of the *essence* of the subject. By contrast, judgments in which the predicates are characteristics that *are part of the essence of* the subject are equivalent to Kant's analytic judgments. The meaning of Eberhard's suggestion can, for example, be understood with the help of the theory presented in Arnauld and Nicole's *Logic or the Art of Thinking*,[11] one of the most influential logic textbooks of the seventeenth and eighteenth centuries.

This and related charges were not fatal to the reception of Kant's ontology and theory of knowledge. Nevertheless, they exposed the apparent ambiguity inherent in Kant's official formulations regarding the role of intuitions in syntheticity, as well as the difficulties related to the possibility of accomplishing the two goals of Kant's Critical philosophy mentioned above in one theory. As a result, philosophers who were exposed to this debate and were inspired by the Kantian revolution in metaphysics attempted to reassess the role of intuition in the vindication of reason without abandoning what they conceived to be the main tenets of the Kantian legacy. – YS

FURTHER READING

H. Allison, *The Kant-Eberhard Controversy* (Baltimore: Johns Hopkins University Press, 1973).

M. Y. Senderowicz, 'Facing the bounds of tradition: Kant's controversy with the *Philosophisches Magazin*', *Science in Context* 11,2 (1998): 205–228.

E. Watkins (ed.), *Kant's Critique of Pure Reason. Background Source Materials* (Cambridge: Cambridge University Press, 2009), ch. 8.

EMPIRICISM

The most common variety of empiricism is concept empiricism. This is the view that all of our concepts are derived from experience. This view is perhaps most famously expressed by John → **Locke** who argues that we do not have any innate ideas. Initially, according to Locke, the mind is like 'white Paper void of all Characters, without any *ideas*'. It is experience alone that is the source 'from whence all the ideas we have, or can naturally have, do spring'.[12] David → **Hume** is another modern philosopher who is also a concept empiricist. Hume argues for the conclusion that 'all our ideas or more feeble perceptions are copies of our impressions or more lively ones'.[13]

When writing about empiricism from the modern period, Kant regularly cites Locke[14] but he typically classifies Hume as a sceptic (e.g. A764=B792 and P 262) rather than an empiricist. Of the ancient philosophers, Kant often cites → **Epicurus** as an empiricist,[15] but Kant writes that among all philosophers 'Aristotle can be regarded as the head of the *empiricists*' (A854=B882). This seems to be due to the fact that Kant attributes to → **Aristotle** the belief that 'nothing is in the intellect which was not first in the senses'.[16]

One of Kant's objections to concept empiricism is that he believes most concept empiricists are inconsistent. Kant's point is not that it is impossible to be a consistent concept empiricist, just that most are not. He especially levels this charge against Locke. Kant has in mind the fact that after arguing that all concepts (including the concept of God) are derived from experience, Locke goes on, in book 4, chapter 10, of the *Essay* to argue that we are able to have demonstrative knowledge of the existence of God.[17] On the other hand, Kant expressly mentions that Epicurus is consistent in his empiricism, 'for in his inferences he never exceeded the bounds of experience' (A854=B882).

Of course, the more important problem that Kant has with concept empiricism is that he believes it is false. One of Kant's fundamental assertions is that some of our concepts, such as the pure concepts of understanding, are not derived from the senses, but instead have their source in the understanding itself.

A second, stronger, variety of empiricism is the view that there is no a priori cognition of any kind – that is, there is no cognition that does not logically depend on experience. It is interesting to note that in a student's lecture notes from the mid-1770s, it is reported that Kant attributed this stronger variety of empiricism to Aristotle himself (LM 542).

A philosopher, however, might be a concept empiricist and yet hold that some of our knowledge is grounded in reason and not experience, and hence is a priori. This is the case, for example, with both Locke and Hume. Hume, for example, accepts that there are Relations of Ideas – propositions dealing with 'the sciences of Geometry, Algebra, and Arithmetic; and in short, every affirmation, which is either intuitively or demonstratively certain' (EHU, 4.1). According to Hume, '[p]ropositions of this kind are discoverable by the mere operation of thought, without dependence on what is any where existent in the universe' (EHU, 4.1).

For Locke, this sort of knowledge arises when we can use intuition or demonstration (both of which are traditionally thought to have their roots in Aristotle's *Posterior Analytics*) to immediately or mediately perceive the agreement between two ideas (ECHU, 4.2). As mentioned above, Locke believes that our demonstrative knowledge extends beyond just the mathematical sciences – it can extend to our moral knowledge as well as to our knowledge of the existence of God (ECHU, 4.4.7ff. and 4.10).

Kant, of course, rejects this stronger version of empiricism as well. He holds that 'although all our cognition commences *with* experience, yet it does not on that account all arise *from* experience' (B1). Kant, however, disagrees with the Lockean and Humean position that this a priori cognition is limited to what he would call analytic judgments, whose 'truth must always be able to be cognized sufficiently in accordance with the principle of contradiction' (A151=B190). Instead Kant believes there are also synthetic judgments that can be cognized a priori. In the case of theoretical synthetic a priori judgments, these are grounded, not in experience itself, but in what is required for the possibility of experience. On the other hand, our a priori practical cognition is rooted in freedom and the fact of reason. – SB

Further Reading

W. Waxman, 'Kant's debt to the British Empiricists', in G. Bird (ed.), *A Companion to Kant* (Malden, MA/Oxford: Wiley-Blackwell, 2010), pp. 93–107.

FREDERICK THE GREAT

'If this ruler is not worthy of being a King, I do not know who is', D'Alembert wrote of Frederick the Great.[18] Praise came both from contemporary writers, including Boswell and Voltaire, as well as historians who sought to emphasize his role as a participant in and promoter of the ideas of the European Enlightenment. During his reign, from 1740 to 1786, Frederick the Great oversaw → **Prussia**'s rise to a great power, yet it is his intellectual range that most impressed visitors at his court at Sans-Souci. As his copious writings testify, he took an active role in philosophical debates of the time, including those that touched on politics and religion. On the latter topic, he recommends tolerance and argues that the monarch has no right to dictate the citizen's beliefs. Yet, as Lewis White Beck observes,[19] there is little evidence that religious and political dissent was rife in Germany, compared to France and England. To that extent, Frederick's maxim, quoted with approval by Kant in **E**, '*Argue* as much as you will and about whatever you will, *but obey*!' (E 37) seems aptly descriptive.

Frederick saw himself as embodying the ideal of 'enlightened absolutism'. The core idea is that absolute rule resembles a wise oligarchy with the king at its head executing policies that aim to promote the common interest and forge a bond of loyalty among the citizens. Frederick even envisaged a role for a philosopher to act as a secret counsellor, advising and instructing on policy, but leaving the practical matter of the exercise of power to the king. Thus, the king enhances his role by uniting in his person wisdom as well as power while making few concessions to the socially and politically emancipatory aspirations of Enlightenment thinkers.

The dialectic of freedom and restraint encapsulated in the motto 'argue but obey' shapes the German debate about the meaning and limits of 'enlightenment', to which Kant is a prominent contributor. The beginning of this 'reflective phase' of the German Enlightenment can be dated to the 1778 essay competition organized by the Royal Academy in Berlin (→ **Academy prize essay**) on a topic suggested by Frederick: 'whether it is to the advantage of the common mass of humanity to be deceived, insofar as they are led into new errors or kept within their customary ones'.[20]

Kant's, → **Mendelssohn**'s and Reinhold's essays on the topic appeared towards the end of Frederick's rule, when Enlightenment was on the wane as an intellectual movement. By addressing the potential conflict between intellectual and political authority, the German *Aufklärer* flesh out the tensions of the uneasy union of knowledge and power of enlightened absolutism itself. Johann Georg Hamann (1730–1788), a fierce critic of Kant's account of enlightenment, argues that immaturity is a correlate of the absolute guardianship of Frederick II. By conveniently 'forgetting' Frederick II, Hamann argues, Kant offers a skewed diagnosis, which renders the public use of reason, the remedy to immaturity, unconvincing.[21]

The fundamental issue that Hamann raises concerns the relation between authority and power in Kant's essay E. While it is true that Kant praises the motto 'argue but obey', he does so in a historical context where even the limited, that is, religious, freedoms granted by Frederick were being rescinded and his power was declining. If we add to this that religious intolerance, which Kant describes as the most pernicious form of all, his endorsement of Frederick's motto acquires a different complexion, expressing support for a very limited freedom that was already under threat.

Still, the question remains of how the freedom to make public use of one's reason fits in with the dictum 'argue but obey'. There is a conceptual ambiguity about the authority that has a legitimate claim to our obedience. Where Hamann's criticisms strike home, in other words, is in his claim that, despite his appeal to the authority of reason, Kant still leaves intact the authority of one guardian, the guardian par excellence, namely Frederick II. The authority of the king is not supported by reason, Hamann points out, but rather by a large and well-disciplined army. He then concludes that it is this external power that keeps the immature in their place, and not their laziness or intellectual cowardice.

One may ask to what extent this power itself can be the object of critical debate. In principle, no subject should be out of bounds to rational criticism, to which, as Kant says, 'everything must submit' (Axii n.). Yet, if the external authority of the king is considered independently binding, then, despite Kant's claim that the public use of one's reason should be free in 'all matters' (E 36), the authority of the king would still be placed outside the legitimate boundaries of critical argument. Those who seek to make public use of their reason would still have to negotiate between two competing claims to authority: one issuing from the king, the other from reason.

A hint of how Kant envisages the issue being resolved is contained in the conclusion of E where he vigorously defends the view that man is more than a machine and should be treated in accordance with his dignity (E 40). Only two years before the publication of this essay, Frederick wrote: 'I regard man as a clockwork machine subject to the springs which drive it [. . .] [which] is humiliating for our pride, but unfortunately only too true.'[22] – KD

FURTHER READING

J. Schmidt (ed.), *What is Enlightenment? Eighteenth Century Answers and Twentieth Century Questions* (Berkeley/Los Angeles: University of California Press, 1996).

FRENCH REVOLUTION

According to contemporary reports, Kant followed closely and discussed with great interest political events generally and the French Revolution and its aftermath in particular. He responded to the Revolution with great enthusiasm and remained its staunch supporter even when this position was rather unpopular and might occasion censure. In view of the great hopes he placed in the Revolution and the subsequent political events in France, it is striking that Kant asserts clearly and often that revolutions are categorically forbidden.

The argument against revolutions, repeated in his published works, is simple. There can be no right to revolt, because revolution is the destruction of the state of right. A 'constitution cannot contain any article that would make it possible for there to be some authority in a state to resist the supreme commander in case he should violate the law of the constitution' (**MM** 319) – an authority higher than the highest authority is 'self-contradictory' (**MM** 319).[23] Indeed, it is a 'law that is so holy (inviolable) that it is already a crime even to call it in doubt *in a practical way* [. . .] that the presently existing legislative authority ought to be obeyed, whatever its origin'

(**MM** 319). This principle indeed extends to a power established by a successful revolution (**MM** 323). If a ruler acts against the law, 'subjects may indeed oppose this injustice by *complaints* (*gravamina*) but not by resistance' (**MM** 319). Even in the case of 'the oppressive power of a so-called tyrant [. . .] it is still in the highest degree wrong of the subjects to seek their right in this way' (**PP** 382).

It is remarkable that Kant does not hold even the tyrannical violation of the original contract by a ruler to be the dissolution of the state of right, because no authority could possibly pronounce such a judgment.[24] Necessary changes in a constitution can be 'carried out only through *reform* by the sovereign itself, but not by the people, and therefore not by *revolution*' (**MM** 322).

There is, of course, no logical contradiction between holding revolutions to be categorically forbidden and believing that a revolution might be a step forward, indeed a necessary step, towards the moral and political destiny of humanity. Indeed, it is the central claim of Kant's philosophy of history that human progress is driven by antagonism and violence. There is, however, a deep tension between these positions, especially when both the necessity and the impermissibility of such violence are seen with great clarity. This tension is evident in Kant's writings.

In an intriguing *Reflexion*, Kant suggests that the French Revolution was not, in fact, a revolution. The National Assembly represented the people and possessed the authority to change the constitution, because Louis XVI himself summoned the Estates-General and invested it with indeterminate legislative authority (**Refl** 8055).

In the Doctrine of Right, he offers again this analysis of events and claims that for this reason the 'monarch's sovereignty wholly disappeared (it was not merely suspended) and passed to the people' (**MM** 341). But in the same text, not many pages before, he seems to claim that such so-called abdications are in fact extorted from the monarch and calls such acts crimes (**MM** 320–322n.). Elsewhere, Kant speaks of revolutions that 'nature of itself has brought [. . .] about' (**PP** 373n.), that is, situations in which 'everything has either of itself become ripe for a complete overthrow or has been made almost ripe by peaceful means' (**PP** 373n.). It bears emphasizing that nature here is human nature.

A fascinating passage in the second part of **CF** (**CF** 79–94) seems to express well Kant's personal position in relation to the French Revolution. He discusses a contemporary event that demonstrates, so he claims, the moral disposition of humanity. This event, it is important to emphasize, is not a political act, but the 'mode of thinking of the spectators' (**CF** 85) in view of it. Kant writes: 'The revolution of a gifted people which [we] have seen unfolding in our day may succeed or miscarry; it may be filled with misery and atrocities to the point that a right-thinking human being, were he boldly to hope to execute it successfully the second time, would never resolve to make the experiment at such cost – this revolution, I say, nonetheless finds in the hearts of all spectators (who are not engaged in this game themselves) a wishful *participation* that borders closely on enthusiasm the very expression of which is fraught with danger; this sympathy, therefore, can have no other cause than a moral predisposition in the human race.' (**CF** 85) – IG

GARVE-FEDER REVIEW

Also known as the 'Göttingen Review' as it was published in a journal based out of

Göttingen, this is one of the very first reviews of **CPR**, which appeared in 1781 shortly after the publication of the first edition. It is a composite production since, although it was originally written by Christian Garve (1742–1798), it was subsequently edited by Johann Feder (1740–1821). Feder's editing was pretty drastic since the final published version was two-thirds shorter than the original and a good portion of the published version was in the form of paragraphs inserted by Feder.

The published version of the review provides an overview of the content of **CPR** but opens with a description of the argument of the Transcendental Aesthetic that explicitly compares Kant's view of sensation with Berkeley's form of idealism. This compressed form of the review moves directly from the Transcendental Aesthetic to the Amphiboly with only minimal discussion of most of the argument of the Transcendental Analytic. The focus subsequently shifts to the Dialectic but expresses disbelief in Kant's solution to the problems raised there. The final paragraph repeats the accusation that Kant's idealism, as based on an account of 'representation', has failed to differentiate itself from what has previously been understood as 'idealism'.

The publication of this review angered Kant and he replied to it in the 'Appendix' he wrote for **P**. Kant here pointed out that the published review, in confusing his position with that of Berkeley's, failed to take account of the point that Berkeley's view is Platonic (→ **Plato**) in attributing true reality only to ideas, not to the data of the senses. By contrast, Kant's own view is that cognition by means of pure reason or understanding alone is illusory and it is only in experience that there is truth, the opposite of the Berkeleyan view (**P** 374). Kant follows this point up through reference to the argument in the Transcendental Aesthetic that there are a priori conditions for sensible perception, something Berkeley does not recognize. On the basis of these points, Kant suggests that his own doctrine should be termed 'formal' or 'critical' idealism (**P** 375), even, at one point, retracting the term 'transcendental idealism' (**P** 293).

Kant further accuses the reviewer of adopting a superior tone of alleged insight, an accusation he later repeats in disputes with Platonists (cf. **PTS**) (→ **Plato**). The key point that the review neglects even to mention the problem of the synthetic a priori is supplemented by a suggestion that if the reviewer found Kant's solution of the Antinomies unconvincing perhaps he might offer one instead. Kant concludes by asking the reviewer to shed his anonymity (**P** 379).

Garve, who knew Kant, was embarrassed when he read Kant's response and revealed to Kant, in a letter dated 13 July 1783 (**Corr-I** 328–333), that he had originally composed the review but added that it had been changed out of recognition by the editor of the journal. The original form of Garve's review was subsequently published unedited. In this much longer response, Garve is explicit about translating Kant's thoughts into more popular idiom, which also involves setting the task of the Critical philosophy in empiricist terms.

Garve's version still says little about either the deductions or the schematism but does (albeit very briefly) survey the Analogies and the Postulates. As with the published review, however, it spends much more time dealing with the Dialectic and explicitly argues that the Fourth Paralogism does no more than abolish the Cartesian conception of privileged access to our own consciousness without proving the existence of bodies (→ **Descartes**).

Garve also expresses dissatisfaction with Kant's account of practical reason and demotes a priori intuition to being only 'a sensible image of a concept of understanding'.[25] He also essentially rejects Kant's attempt to recast the understanding of 'idealism' albeit not quite so harshly as in the published review. It must have been evident to Kant, on reading Garve's original, that the basic problems he had with the published review did apply in equal measure to Garve's original, which likewise did not discuss the problem of the synthetic a priori or present its own resolution of the difficulties set out in the Antinomies.

The influence of this review on both Kant himself and the general reception of the Critical philosophy were considerable. The recasting of the Paralogisms chapter in the second edition of **CPR** and the provision of the new Refutation of Idealism as part of the Postulates are clearly responses to the review's attack on Kant's idealism. The stress the review put on the role of representation in Kant's view also influenced some of Kant's advocates, however, since Karl Reinhold makes this stress key to his work *Letters on the Kantian Philosophy*.[26] The suggestion made by the review that Kant's idealism is close to that of Berkeley has been repeated many times since it was published.[27]

Kant's decision to write **P** at all, not just the appendix, may well have been due to his conception that a popular presentation of the doctrine of **CPR** was necessary to counter that contained in the review and this need for a popular presentation also spurred on the work of Reinhold.[28] – GB

FURTHER READING

F. Beiser, *The Fate of Reason: German Philosophy from Kant to Fichte* (Cambridge, MA: Harvard University Press, 1987), ch. 6.

M. Kuehn, 'Kant's critical philosophy and its reception – the first five years (1781–1786)', in P. Guyer (ed.), *The Cambridge Companion to Kant and Modern Philosophy* (Cambridge: Cambridge University Press, 2006), pp. 630–663.

HERDER, JOHANN GOTTFRIED

A Lutheran clergyman, historian of culture, aesthetic theorist, and philosophical anthropologist, Johann Gottfried Herder (1744–1803) was born in the East Prussian town of Mohrungen (→ **Prussia**) to a family with limited means. By the good offices of a medical officer in the occupying Russian army during the Seven Years War (1756–63), he came to study at the University of → **Königsberg** from 1762 to 1764. There he came to the attention, and became the favourite student, of Immanuel Kant. Herder's notes from Kant's courses of this period represent some of the earliest and most important sources we have for the study of the pre-Critical Kant. Even after Herder left the university, Kant stayed in close contact with him, sending him the segments of his new book, **DSS** (published in 1765), as each set left the printer (→ **Swedenborg**). Herder wrote an enthusiastic review of the finished book as one of his earliest publications.

While a student in Königsberg, Herder befriended and came under the influence of Johann Georg Hamann (1730–88), through whom he learned English and was drawn into aesthetic and literary criticism. Kant and Hamann became the two polar forces in Herder's intellectual development, and a great controversy has ensued over which of the two proved dominant. The noted scholar Isaiah Berlin has contended that

Hamann and Herder represented a 'Counter-Enlightenment' utterly opposed to the rationalism and secularism of Kant and the wider European → **Enlightenment**, with long-term consequences for the rise of German right-wing nationalism.[29] While the latter movement did invoke Herder along these lines, the consensus of current scholarship is that this was a misappropriation of Herder's thought, which belongs quite clearly in the Enlightenment context. The best judgment is that of the nineteenth-century scholar Rudolf Haym, who termed Herder 'a Kantian of the year 1765', that is, a disciple of the *pre-Critical* Kant.[30] In particular, this meant that Herder chose to pursue anthropology, as against philosophy, as his guiding framework for understanding cultural experience. His favourite works of Kant were **Obs** and, even more, **NH**, but he never accepted Kant's 'Critical turn'. Herder's most important work would seek a physiological psychology linked to aesthetic form and a cultural history which articulated the unique expressions of the various peoples primarily of Europe. His rubric for this was anthropology or 'the natural history of human consciousness'.

After a journey to France in 1769, Herder returned to Germany and became the friend and mentor of the young Johann Goethe (1749–1832), and together they launched the *Sturm und Drang* movement in the early 1770s. Herder published two works in 1774, *Oldest Documents of the Human Race and Yet Another Philosophy of History*, which gave vent to a brash sense of personal genius characteristic of this *Sturm und Drang* mood. All this alarmed Kant, who expressed his displeasure first in correspondence with Hamann, and then privately in a set of harsh unpublished *Reflexionen* (**Refl**) over the course of the later 1770s. When Herder published *On Knowledge and Feeling in the Human*

Soul in 1778, articulating a critique of faculty psychology along lines that appeared directly hostile to Kant's own philosophical endeavours over the so-called 'silent decade' of the 1770s, Kant's hostility to Herder hardened still further. When his **CPR** appeared in 1781 to poor reception, Kant held Herder personally responsible for changing the intellectual temper of German reception toward a reckless and self-indulgent aestheticism, as against the dry rigour that Kant believed essential for effective thought.

When Herder published the first volumes of his masterwork, *Ideas for a Philosophy of the History of Mankind*, in 1784, Kant took advantage of an invitation to review the work to make public his distaste for Herder's writings. The review, appearing in the *Allgemeine Literatur-Zeitung* in 1785, had a wide public impact and led to far more overt hostilities between the two figures. In subsequent volumes of his work, Herder counterattacked, and in a second review, Kant continued his criticism. Their conflict widened in the context of the concurrent 'Pantheism Controversy', triggered by the revival of Spinoza's philosophy in Germany (→ **Spinoza/Spinozism**). While Herder welcomed this in his *God: Some Conversations* (1787), Kant sharply repudiated the revival. A letter to Friedrich Heinrich Jacobi (1743–1819) in 1789 showed Kant willing to reach out even to those he did not fully respect in order to build alliances against Herder.

One of the defenders of Herder in the context of Kant's reviews of the *Ideas*, Karl Reinhold (1757–1823), converted in 1786 to become Kant's decisive popularizer in Germany. As Kant became the most famous and influential philosopher of the balance of the century, he organized his disciples actively in opposition to Herder. The latter had moved to Weimar in the 1780s at the invitation of

his friend Goethe, who secured him a position there as General Superintendent of the Lutheran clergy. Goethe sided with Herder in the Pantheism Controversy, just as he had been Herder's most eager companion and reader as Herder composed the *Ideas*. But after an interval in Italy in the late 1780s Goethe returned to Weimar with a different orientation, and this climaxed after 1792, in his new and defining friendship with the poet Friedrich Schiller (1759–1805), who had become an enthusiastic Kantian.

Herder lost his strongest alliance and became increasingly isolated and embittered. The upshot was the publication, near the end of his life, of two book-length diatribes against Kant: first, *Metacritique of the Critique of Pure Reason* (1799), against Kant's theoretical philosophy, and then *Kalligone* (1800), against Kant's aesthetics. The dominant Kantian culture of the end of the eighteenth century accepted the master's judgment that these works demonstrated that 'unreason and deliberate deception are Herder's trademark' (**OP-I** 225). However, a just balance in the appraisal of these two major figures of the German Enlightenment has yet to be achieved. – JZa

FURTHER READING

J. Zammito, '"Method" versus "manner"? Kant's critique of Herder's *Ideen* in the light of the epoch of science, 1790–1820', in H. Adler, W. Koepke (eds), *Herder Jahrbuch/Herder Yearbook* 1998 (Stuttgart: Metzler, 1998), pp. 1–25.

J. Zammito, *Kant, Herder, and the Birth of Anthropology* (Chicago/London: University of Chicago Press, 2002).

J. Zammito, E. Menze, K. Menges, 'Johann Gottfried Herder revisited: The revolution in scholarship in the last quarter century',

Journal of the History of Ideas 71,4 (2010): 661–684.

HUTCHESON, FRANCIS

Kant mentions Hutcheson by name but seldom and only twice in his major works in moral philosophy. In these texts and in lectures on ethics in the 1780s (**G** 442n.; **CPrR** 40; **LE** 253; **LE-M** 621; see also **ID** 396), he seems to dismiss Hutcheson rather curtly as an adherent of the theory of moral sense, classified as a misguided attempt to offer an inner empirical grounding of morality. Yet according to contemporary reports, Kant held Hutcheson in high esteem from the middle of the 1750s and recommended his works for intensive study.[31] This interest clearly did not wane in the next decade. In the announcement of his winter lectures for 1765/66, Kant says that his course on ethics will follow → **Baumgarten**, but adds that the 'attempts of *Shaftesbury, Hutcheson* and *Hume*, although incomplete and defective, have nonetheless penetrated furthest in the search for the fundamental principles of all morality' (**AL** 311; see also **Inq** 300).

This survey has led many to the view that Kant's earlier thinking was influenced by Hutcheson and moral sense theories more generally, but that his mature moral philosophy contains hardly a trace of these early lessons. In a seminal paper, Dieter Henrich argues against this view and indeed calls Hutcheson the → **Hume** of Kantian ethics.[32] According to Henrich, Kant came to believe early on that the universality and categorical obligation of moral laws are sure evidence of the fact that their origin is reason. Nevertheless, he remained indebted to Hutcheson's insight that moral consciousness has an essential affective aspect.

Ultimately, this insight shapes the Critical conception of our peculiar interest in or feeling of respect for morality. But Kant was also motivated by Hutcheson's criticism of rationalist ethics to draw his own conclusions about the reigning, theoretically oriented conception of reason. This influence eventually led Kant to his original conception of the will – a notion Hutcheson employs, but can only think of as affective – as pure *practical* reason.[33]

Kant's conception of the feeling of respect for the moral law is a subject of considerable controversy (**CPrR** 71–89). According to one interpretation, we act morally when consciousness of the law incites a sufficiently strong feeling of respect. But this view seems plainly to contradict the claim that reason alone is the objective determining ground of moral action. Kant may well have Hutcheson in mind when he asserts that we do not act morally if the 'determination of the will takes place *conformably* with the moral law but only by means of a feeling, of whatever kind, that has to be presupposed in order for the law to become a sufficient determining ground of the will' (**CPrR** 71). According to other views, the feeling of respect either necessarily accompanies moral action or is its phenomenological effect. On both views, Kant's mature theory remains indebted to the insight that moral consciousness has an essential affective aspect.

Yet another view holds that while the moral law is the objective determining ground of the will, it is the feeling of respect it evokes that is the effective force driving action. According to this view, Kant's mature theory of moral motivation is indebted to Hutcheson's insight that 'affections' alone can serve as 'exciting reasons'.

No investigation of the role of feelings in Kant's theory of moral agency is complete without examining his later and rather neglected discussion of it (**MM** 399–403). Two points are crucial to its assessment: First, in contrast to his earlier claim that respect is the one moral feeling, Kant seems here to name four more: '*moral feeling, conscience, love* of one's neighbor, and *respect* for oneself (*self-esteem*)' (**MM** 399). Second, these feelings are neither mere accompaniments of moral action nor phenomenological responses to it. They are necessary conditions of moral agency: 'every human being has them, and it is by virtue of them that he can be put under obligation' (**MM** 399).

What precisely are these four affective conditions of moral agency, what are the systematic connections between them and how are they related to the feeling of respect, are questions that demand intensive attention. Also important to ask is what accounts for the affective detail that colours the discussion of the system of duties in the Doctrine of Virtue. Answering these questions will allow us to assess the lasting influence of the idea of moral sensibility on Kant's theory of moral agency. – IG

KÖNIGSBERG

Königsberg, today known as Kaliningrad and part of Russia, was the capital of East → **Prussia** from the Late Middle Ages until 1945 and was Kant's birthplace. It was founded by the Teutonic Knights around 1255 during the Northern Crusades. Due to its crucial position on the Baltic Sea, Königsberg became one of the most vital cultural centres of Prussia during the Renaissance. Its main cultural institution was the University *Albertina*, which was founded by Duke Albrecht I in 1554.

Since its foundation, Königsberg University was characterized by a strong Aristotelian tradition. The great success of → **Aristotelianism** was probably partly due to the intimate relationship between the first dean, Georg Sabinus, and Philip Melanchthon: Sabinus was Melanchthon's son-in-law. The early Aristotelianism in Königsberg was therefore characterized by the Philippistic interpretation of → **Aristotle** that also enjoyed the esteem of the political authorities. In the seventeenth century, Königsberg became a stronghold of Aristotelianism and Scholasticism with important figures like Abraham Calov, Christian Dreier, and Melchior Zeidler. Königsberg was one of the first centres to introduce and comment on Jesuit philosophy in Germany in the first two decades of the seventeenth century, even though Aristotelianism extended its legacy also to the first decades of the eighteenth century.

In Königsberg, the period from the end of the seventeenth and the beginning of the eighteenth century was characterized by a number of reversals of philosophical orientation. The *Albertina* was a crucible of fierce disputes among different schools.[34] More in particular, in the period from 1715 to 1740 Aristotelianism, Eclecticism and Wolffianism (→ **Wolff**) competed for the supremacy in both theology and philosophy, during which period each of these schools alternately prevailed.[35]

Indeed, the beginning of the eighteenth century was characterized by a strong conservatism in both theology and philosophy.[36] Aristotelianism and Protestant Scholasticism were the dominant schools, which both rejected the modern philosophies and sciences such as those of → **Bacon** and → **Descartes**. At least until the winter semester of 1719/20, the university courses were the prerogative of Aristotelians such as Johann Jakob Quandt and Johann Jakob Rohde.[37]

From 1717, → **Pietism** and Wolffianism became increasingly important in the academic setting. In particular, Wolffianism gave a decisive blow to the Aristotelian movement since the early 1720s, becoming effectively part of the academic environment as is evidenced by the philosophical activity of Johann Christian Friedrich Baumgarten, Theodor Reinhard That and Johann Heinrich Kreuschner. Some of the Königsberg professors responded favourably to the new Wolffian publications and some instructors were even prompted to immediately accept 'the new creed as a group ideology'.[38] However, full professors of the philosophical faculty like Georg Thegen and Johann David Kypke, the latter a friend of Kant, 'were impervious to the new trend'.[39]

Nevertheless, Wolffians had a brief moment of glory between 1717 and 1723 when they allied themselves with the Pietists against the conservatism of the Aristotelians. Evidence of this is the widespread and extensive use of Wolffian textbooks. The alliance between Wolffians and Pietists lasted only for so long however; already in 1723 the affair 'Wolff' erupted in Halle, stirred up by the Pietists, especially in Königsberg.[40] Acting against the Wolffians, in 1725 King William I appointed to the theological faculty two Pietist professors, Abraham Wolf and Georg Friedrich Rogall.[41] In 1726, together with Heinrich Lysius Rogall introduced a university reform in conformity with Pietism, against Wolffianism, which was effectively banished until 1740, when Frederick II (→ **Frederick the Great**) became king.[42]

The Pietist movement changed the university curricula, removed Wolffians from teaching posts, and favoured Eclectic philosophers. Instead, the textbooks of Christian Thomasius and Johann Franz Budde became a great success among academics. Aristotelianism and Wolffianism, headed by Jakob Quandt, counterattacked against Pietism, and to resolve the acrimonious situation the king appointed Franz Albert Schultz, who was a Pietist and also a student of Wolff in Halle, as mediator.[43]

However, Wolffians never regained the upper hand, also not when the Pietist interdiction against Wolffian philosophy waned with the coronation of Frederick II: no professor could declare himself truly a Wolffian scholar and no Wolffian became full professor.[44] It was different with the condition of the Aristotelians, such as Kypke and Rohde,[45] who were marginalized by Pietism, but were not banished, and whose doctrines were weakened towards Eclecticism.

The Enlightenment in Königsberg was born against the background of these conflicts, which led to a general Eclecticism, which exercised some influence on the young Kant. At least until 1740, Pietists controlled Königsberg University, and even if afterwards their influence was still strong, there was an increasing dissemination of Wolffian philosophy in the courses, through the mediation of → **Leibniz**'s perspective, as the works of Konrad G. Marquardt and Martin Knutzen show. Both Marquardt and Knutzen were teachers of Kant during his university years.

Along with the dissemination of the Wolffian handbooks, the works of the British empiricists became more and more popular in Königsberg, which thanks to its direct contact with the British world was a hub of Lockeanism (→ **Locke**), involving important projects of translation carried out by Knutzen himself and by Georg David Kypke.

In the same period, the philosophy of Christian August → **Crusius** became very widespread in Königsberg with authors such as Friedrich Johann Buck and Daniel

Weymann, who were both opponents of Kant. In the 1760s, Crusius' philosophy prevailed as the philosophy of the Berlin Academy of Sciences, which was led by Pierre-Louis Moureau de Maupertuis, who was against Wolffianism and promoted the ideas of the French Enlightenment. – MS

LAMBERT, JOHANN HEINRICH

Johann Lambert was born on 26 August 1728 in Mulhouse. He died of tuberculosis on 25 September 1777 in Berlin. In his youth, he worked as secretary of Johann Rudolf Iselin, who gave him access to his private library, which contained books by philosophers such as → **Wolff**, Malebranche and → **Locke**, on which Lambert was taught. In 1756, he travelled around Europe, acting as tutor for the son and the nephew of Count von Salis, and all the while meeting philosophers and scientists such as Abraham Gotthelf Kästner, Pieter van Musschenbroeck, Jean Le Rond d'Alembert and Charles Messier, who influenced his mathematical approach to philosophy.

In his first philosophical essay, the *Criterium veritatis* (1761), which was published posthumously in 1915, Lambert sketched out his main philosophical idea according to which the method of geometry must be applied to philosophical investigation to ensure a solid foundation for all philosophical disciplines. Lambert developed this idea in *Über die Methode, die Metaphysik, Theologie und Moral richtiger zu beweisen* (1762), in *Methodus calculandi in logicis* (1763) and in the *Neues Organon* (1764), which is his philosophical masterpiece.

The *Neues Organon*, which is directly reminiscent of → **Aristotle** and → **Bacon's**

works, is divided into four parts, which correspond to the four instruments of the human mind for finding truth: (1) *Dianoiology*, i.e. the doctrine of reasoning; (2) *Alethiology*, i.e. the doctrine of truth; (3) *Semiotics*, i.e. the doctrine of signs and meanings; (4) *Phenomenology*, i.e. the doctrine of appearances. *Dianoiology* deals with the laws of thought, which turn all common knowledge into demonstrative knowledge. According to Lambert, all syllogisms can always be reduced to geometric representations, which make immediately evident whether an argumentation is valid or not.

In the *Alethiology*, Lambert anatomizes the human mind in order to find a priori the first primitive and simple concepts, which constitute the building blocks of knowledge and of reality. Primitive concepts are such concepts as 'will', 'consciousness', 'existence', 'unity', 'duration', 'succession', 'extension', 'movement' and 'force'. According to Lambert, by means of these concepts it would be possible, following → **Leibniz**'s suggestion, to elaborate a priori a *mathesis universalis*, which would lie at the basis of every rigorous science such as ontology, geometry, physics, etc.

In the *Semiotics*, by contrast, Lambert aims to reduce the doctrine of things to a doctrine of signs. This is possible because symbolic cognition is a necessary means for thinking in order to make clear the obscure concepts through signs. In the *Phenomenology*, Lambert explains how from the appearances of the world given by sensation it is possible to find the real laws of nature.

Thanks to the great success of the *Neues Organon* and with the help of Leonhard → **Euler** and Johann Georg Sulzer, Lambert obtained a position in 1764 at the prestigious Berlin Academy of Sciences. In 1764, he wrote another important work, the *Anlage zur Architectonic*, which was however published only in 1771 in Riga with the help of Kant, who valued Lambert's logical project highly. Even as late as 1800, in **JL**, Kant praises Lambert as the greatest innovator in the field of logic after Aristotle (**JL** 21).

Lambert's main project was to apply mathematical logic, i.e. combinatorics, to metaphysics, developing further and improving the failed attempts of logicians such as the brothers Bernoulli and Gottfried Ploucquet. It is from this particular perspective that Kant's relationship with Lambert must be understood, especially in connection with the pre-Critical writings and **CPR**.

In logic, Lambert's main objective was to find an *ars characteristica universalis*, which could describe the ontological constitution of reality by means of the combination of simple and fundamental concepts (*Grundbegriffe*) according to their relations. The effectiveness of the description was grounded in the analysis of simple concepts, because every truth was based on fundamental concepts, whose possibility and correctness were immediately understood as true by the inner sense. Thus, Lambert conflated Locke's and Leibniz's philosophical approaches by integrating the fundamental concepts as the structure of reality itself and the first concepts of knowledge through which everything can be known.

Lambert's project was never completed. In fact, even in the *Anlage zur Architectonic* he examines a number of fundamental concepts only in outline. He fails to demonstrate how the combination of these primitive concepts could describe and constitute the ontological structure of reality comprehensively.

In the 1760s, Kant was engaged in a reform of metaphysics inspired by the reform of mathematics that Lambert had attempted. However, in **Inq**, Kant implicitly denies and refutes Lambert's results for at least three reasons: (1) in metaphysics there cannot be a complete analysis of simple concepts; (2) metaphysics proceeds by analysis, while mathematics proceeds by synthesis; (3) metaphysical concepts are given in experience, while mathematical concepts are 'arbitrary' and constructed by the human mind.

However, Kant does not dismiss Lambert's project of an architectonic and for a methodology of metaphysics. In 1765, Kant announces to Lambert that he was working on a book entitled *Proper Method for Metaphysics* (**Corr-I** 51), which however was never published. Nevertheless, there are good reasons to believe that Kant had Lambert in mind when working on the parts of **CPR** that deal with methodology and the 'Architectonic'. – MS

FURTHER READING

A. Laywine, 'Kant in reply to Lambert on the ancestry of metaphysical concepts', *Kantian Review* 5 (2001): 1–48.

E. Watkins (ed.), *Kant's Critique of Pure Reason. Background Source Materials* (Cambridge: Cambridge University Press, 2009), ch. 6.

MENDELSSOHN, MOSES

They belonged to the same generation: Kant was born in → **Königsberg** on 22 April 1724; Mendelssohn in Dessau on 6 September 1729. They had the same interests, as Kant confirmed to Mendelssohn in a letter dated 7 February 1766. Dispensing with 'fashionable circumlocutions', he welcomes correspondence between 'two persons whose ways of thinking are, because of the similarity of their intellectual concerns and the mutuality of their principles, in such agreement' (**Corr-I** 67–68).[46]

Both Mendelssohn and Kant had responded to the essay topic set by the Berlin Academy of Sciences for 1763 (→ **Academy prize essay**) on the reliability of evidence in metaphysics: Kant's **Inq** had come second to Mendelssohn's prize-winning *Treatise on Evidence in Metaphysical Sciences*. Both exemplify the philosophical culture of the Enlightenment – Kant taking it to its logical conclusion by revealing in its apparently omnipotent rationalism its constitutive anthropomorphic limits and Mendelssohn representing in the life he lived 'a kaleidoscope of the European intellectual scene, Jewish and non-Jewish, in the second half of the 18th century'.[47]

Yet, within two decades, Kant and Mendelssohn faced each other with mutual incomprehension. Kant was disappointed that his correspondents in the Prussian capital (→ **Prussia**), the centre of the German Enlightenment, including Mendelssohn, were apparently confounded by **CPR**, first published in 1781, remarking to Schütz in November 1785 that Mendelssohn's *Morning-Hours* was 'a masterpiece of the self-deception of our reason', 'this final legacy of a dogmatizing metaphysics' (**Corr-I** 428–429), although its perspicacity would always test the principles of the critique of reason. Mendelssohn, on the other hand, claimed in a letter to Kant that his poor health prevented him from engaging with **CPR** lest it consume all his 'nerve-juice' (**Corr-I** 308). He was dismayed, as he noted in the preface to his *Morning Hours or Lectures on the Existence of God* (1785),[48] by Kant's 'total crushing' of metaphysics, and admitted in his last letter to Kant on 16 October 1785 that, though he no longer had the strength to read his profound

works, he realized that their 'basic principles [did] not coincide' (**Corr-I** 413).[49]

The central debates of rationalist metaphysics, the immortality of the soul and the existence of God, resisted resolution. Mendelssohn's convictions were not, therefore, historically superseded by Kant's critique of reason, even if Mendelssohn admitted that his philosophy was 'no longer the philosophy of the times'.[50] Rather their estrangement exposes their different relationship to philosophy: Kant became a state-appointed Professor of Metaphysics; Mendelssohn kept the accounts in Isaak Bernhard's silk factory. Kant enjoyed personal security and official status; Mendelssohn suffered humiliation and oppression. His secular knowledge was largely self-taught. While he had come to Berlin in 1743, he needed special royal permission, granted only in 1763, to reside permanently in the capital. One vignette speaks volumes: the students mocking and jeering at him while, in 1777 on a visit to Königsberg, unrecognized he waited with them for Kant to come and lecture.[51]

Reluctant though he was to discuss it publicly, Mendelssohn's commitment to Judaism sustained his secular activities.[52] The first modern Jew, he intended to exemplify in his person what the late eighteenth century called the Jews' capacity for 'civic improvement'. Through his association with leading German writers, especially Lessing, Abbt, Nicolai and Moritz, his membership of the eminent philosophical discussion-forum the Berlin Wednesday Society, his contributions as a reviewer to prestigious literary and philosophical journals, and not least his writings on metaphysics, psychology, aesthetics and political philosophy, Mendelssohn demonstrated not just his own, pre-eminent intellectual stature. He was also responding to a political dispensation that closely regulated Jews' involvement in their secular environment. By showing that Jews were not inherently destined for an introverted, ghetto-bound existence, his secular achievements exposed the life-chances they were losing.

Conversely, Mendelssohn's works on Judaism and Jewish philosophy like his practical support for Jewish communities sought, despite the disapproval of the orthodox, to encourage Judaism to modernize itself. He focussed on a 'purified' Judaism based on Mosaic Law and on the Pentateuch (which he published in German translation from 1780 to 1783). Crucially this represented for him not only a core of religious belief Judaism ostensibly shared with Christianity (thereby disarming doctrinal prejudice) but also a theological position that, like Christian faith, could be expressed in terms of rationalist metaphysics.[53]

The process of secularization that the Enlightenment endorsed meant that human self-understanding would have to manage with 'less truth', with diminished metaphysical certainty.[54] But, as its refutation of Mendelssohn's psychological theory in **CPR** (in its second edition) shows (B413ff.), Kant's reductive method that left issues such as the immortality of the soul and the actual existence of God undecidable did undermine Mendelssohn's core metaphysical principles. Mendelssohn already realized this in 1781, but, unlike for example the much younger Salomon Maimon (1753–1800) a decade later,[55] he was indisposed to critique Kant's thinking within a Judaic context.

For Mendelssohn – as for later European-Jewish philosophers generally, such as Marx, Rosenzweig, Bloch and Levinas – ethics shapes epistemology. As Mendelssohn affirmed in his best-selling *Phaedo or On the*

Immortality of the Soul (1767), any apparently true precept indispensable for human happiness and social well-being must for that reason be actually true.[56] Under pressure to justify his own metaphysical-theological position, let alone respond to Kant, he powerfully advocated religious tolerance in *Jerusalem or Religious Power and Judaism* (1783) and deduced the sufficient reason for God's existence in *Morning-Hours* (1785). In 'Über die Frage: was heißt aufklären?' (1784), mindful surely of his own actual, vulnerable civic status, Mendelssohn differentiates between the 'culturally polished' citizen and the 'rationally enlightened' human being.[57]

Unlike Kant in **E, UH** and later in his critique of Mendelssohn's *Jerusalem* (**TP** 307–312), Mendelssohn[58] refuses to sacrifice the living individual for the future benefit of the human species – an insight alone worthy of a 'thinker of the highest rank'.[59] Conversely, in **OT** Kant defended him against Jacobi's presumptuous allegations in the 'pantheism controversy' that so distressed Mendelssohn that they arguably hastened his death on 4 January 1786. Taking issue with Jacobi's zealotry, Kant cites Mendelssohn for insisting in *Morning-Hours* on the need for 'healthy reason' (**OT** 133–134) as an epistemological guide in the realm of metaphysics.[60] Though Mendelssohn would have rejected deducing this orientating 'rational belief' analogically from geographical navigation and mathematical modelling, Kant affirms the basic ontological need for at least the concept of a supreme being. It was in his way a fitting tribute. – MD

FURTHER READING

R. Munk (ed.), *Moses Mendelssohn's Metaphysics and Aesthetics* (Dordrecht: Springer, 2011).

PHYSICAL INFLUX

Physical influx was an account of the inter-action of substances that competed with the occasionalist view of Malebranche and → Leibniz's notion of pre-established harmony. Physical influx held that substances carried within them forces or powers to immediately influence other substances. Kant's early teacher, Martin Knutzen (1713–1751), defended physical influx and the theory itself exercised considerable influence upon Kant's pre-Critical philosophical development. The topic of physical influx originally gained centrality as a characterization of the Cartesian model of mental causation and as an account of the possible 'influence' between mental and extended substances. However, the model was pursued more generally within rationalist metaphysics as an account of the interaction between substances generally.

In his earliest writings, Kant appears to work within a physical influx framework. However, as his thought developed his attitude became more clearly critical, and by the time of the arrival of the Critical philosophy, Kant rejects physical influx theory altogether as one belonging to the broad family of transcendental-realist approaches that Kant firmly rejects. Most crucially perhaps, physical influx represents the model of causation that Kant abandons in favour of his own transcendental-idealist account outlined in the Second Analogy.

In **ND**, Kant claims that there is a 'harmonious dependence' (**ND** 413) that generates a community of things interacting with each other. To this extent, Kant holds that those things, as substances, exert influence upon each other. However, Kant also maintains that this relation also ultimately depends on God as 'the universal principle of beings' (**ND** 413). As such, Kant claims that his

position is neither appropriately characterized as an ordinary physical influx theory – he claims it is 'superior to the popular system' (**ND** 416) since it appeals to an external principle of interaction in the divine – nor as pre-established harmony theory, since Kant's own theory demands the reciprocal dependence of substances upon each other, unlike the Leibnizian model.

By the time of **ID**, Kant further distances himself from physical influence theory, describing it as one whereby 'there is an interaction of substances and transeunt forces, which can be cognised by means of their existence alone' (**ID** 407). Here Kant complains that physical influence fails to offer genuine grounds of explanation and that it 'is not so much a system as indifference to all philosophical system' (**ID** 407). However, Kant is arguably still working within a broad model of physical influx, and is merely criticizing the variants of it put forward by those such as Knutzen and → Crusius (1715–1775) whose accounts he deems non-explanatory.

Kant explicitly returns to the topic of physical influx in the Critical period, in order to criticize it as a theory of mind–body interaction. In the first edition of the Paralogisms (A390–396), Kant first defends 'physical influence' theory from the criticisms of pre-established harmony theorists and occasionalists, before submitting the theory to his own transcendental-idealist criticism. Kant claims that those wishing to modify or improve the theory of physical influx could only do so by assuming that matter is not itself an appearance but instead a thing in itself and then only by assuming the falsity of immediate influence between matter as thing in itself and mind from the outset (A391).

Nevertheless, Kant argues that physical influx theory itself suffers from the same 'transcendental dualism' whereby extended substances are mistakenly understood as things in themselves rather than 'mere representations of the thinking subject' (A392). Kant's critical attitude towards attempts (including prior ones of his own) to resolve mind–body interaction through an account of immediate influence is that they founder on the assumption that the topic is one that is properly answerable within a metaphysical programme, whereas the transcendental idealist can provide the explanatory grounds for human beings' ultimate inability to provide an accurate resolution (A393). – JC

FURTHER READING

E. Watkins, *Kant and the Metaphysics of Causality* (Cambridge: Cambridge University Press, 2005), pt. 1.

E. Watkins (ed.), *Kant's Critique of Pure Reason. Background Source Materials* (Cambridge: Cambridge University Press, 2009), ch. 2.

PIETISM

Pietism was a religious Protestant movement within the Lutheran Church in early and mid-eighteenth century Germany, which reacted against Lutheran orthodoxy, doctrinal as well as ecclesiastical, and which gave rise to an eminently individualist and inward approach to the Christian faith.

One of the main sources of inspiration of Pietism was Philipp Jakob Spener's *Pia desideria*, published in 1675, in which among other things Spener argued for earnest Bible study in small groups, the so called *ecclesiolae in ecclesia*, for universal priesthood (participation of the laity in the religious service), thus displaying radical social

egalitarianism, for the necessity of practical Christian life, and most importantly, for sermons to be a source of inspiration, instilling devotion in the inner soul of the Christian, rather than merely being a display of rhetorical accomplishment.

By nature, Pietism was a very diverse movement. One of its more extremely enthusiastic and even psycho-erotic variants was the *Herrnhuter Brüdergemeine*, founded by Nikolaus Ludwig Graf von Zinzendorf (1700–1760) in 1722. But in whatever form it always manifested, to a greater or lesser extent, an undercurrent of exaltation, mysticism and not uncommonly, theosophy and even occultism. A chief characteristic of Pietism, however, is the emphasis on personal experience. Individual 'conversion' and 'awakening' marked out these so-called *Kernchristen*, who congregated in small local groups notwithstanding the fact that, beyond their immediate environment, they felt a universal bond with like-minded fellow truly born-again Christians, the spiritual community of God's elect, which manifested Pietism's strongly anti-institutional ecumenical nature. Other distinguishing features of Pietism, in which it strikingly differed from mainstream Lutheranism, was a certain amount of chiliasm, the almost exclusive focus on Christology, and a *Blut und Wundentheologie* that opposed the perceived seventeenth-century quietistic distortions of the reformational doctrine of justification, and insisted on the supernatural effusion of the divine life within the soul of the believer, thus bringing about a rebirth.

In general – forming the backdrop of Pietism – the eighteenth-century religious person sought to humanize the transcendence of God, to subjectivize that which is outside him and historically distant (e.g. Christ's death and resurrection), implying an emphasis on the centrality of the present, the concrete and the personal ('one's inner voice'), but also that he only recognized his fellow human being insofar as he would recognize himself in the other. All experience and knowledge of transcendent authority, all things heteronomous or external, he considered in terms of an experience of something that is only relatively distinct from the human being, and so must have a place within the purview of the inner authority of the human being, to which God speaks directly. This meant the inclusion of God in the context of sovereign human self-consciousness and conscience, and the sublation of transcendence into what is experienced internally or purely inwardly.

Individuality and inwardness thus become central tenets of what it means to be a human being in general. In this respect, Pietism is intimately connected to the emergence of the Enlightenment in Germany. The development of Pietism must also be seen against the background of the growing power of the absolute state and the secular subjugation of the Church, or at least the more hierarchical-bureaucratic aspects of the Church, e.g. the appointment of clergymen (caesaropapism), while allowing the co-existence of various religious denominations and leaving the content of one's beliefs to each individual's own conscience.[61] Also the growing centrality of the middle class and its sense of morality, and not least the increasing status of science and philosophy, played a significant role in the emergence of the individualism of which Pietism is a clear religious manifestation.

The bourgeoisification and moralization of the Christian religion meant that faith came to be regarded as something that must contribute to an inwardly experienceable, but no less outwardly concretely observable change in the way one conducts one's own life, the *praxis pietatis*. Christian faith was foremost concerned with the way one gives shape to, and improves, one's life, in the here and now. This expressed the general wish to distance oneself from all too theoretical or intellectualist approaches to being a Christian, which, as evidenced in previous ages, resulted all too often in strife and destructive fervour among Christians. The Christian bourgeois of the eighteenth century opposed orthodox theological theory as unfruitful, if not dangerous. Mere Christian doctrine does not amount to Christian faith, without it having relevance for one's own life, without it satisfying one's own personal needs. True faith means changing one's life in accord with doctrine, not adhering to doctrine for the sake of it. It is therefore not just critical of all the dialectical subtleties of theological erudition, but it also amounts to a positive demand for a practical employment of Christian creeds. This, however, often led to a moralistic, even utilitarian hollowing out of those creeds.

The relation in the academic as well as public arena between the Pietists and the Wolffians (rationalists) (→ **Königsberg**) was often strained, and although they had very different outlooks on life and society, this does not mean that they were always, in all respects, working in opposite directions. Both were oriented to changing life practically, focusing on improving one's life by virtue of good works that necessarily ensued from faith, but the Pietists took care more of the inward good works, whereas the rationalist provided more for the outward ones. They were in unison, however, against any form of Christian quietism (though Pietists were sometimes themselves accused of this).

Furthermore, the Pietists felt only relatively bound by the letter of the Bible and theological doctrine, namely only to the extent that they were morally edifying. The moral principle of leading a good life was paramount in all one's religious activities. Every aspect of one's faith revolved around the idea of a natural, rational Christianity, which was opposed not to revelation or even mysticism and exaltation (they were considered perfectly compatible with a rationally interpreted Christian faith), but to failing to develop the human being, failing to subject one's creeds to the will and agency, and needs, of the individual, of oneself. For the eighteenth-century individual, nature was the totality of objects that were at the disposal of the will, feeling, and mind of the individual. For the Pietist, rational Christianity likewise means a Christianity that is in accord with the power of, and affirmed by, the human being himself, who regards the Christian creeds in terms of his own religious needs.

The main centre of Pietism in → **Prussia** was the University of Halle, where A. H. Francke (1663–1727) propagated Pietistic ideas. It was from here that Pietism spread throughout Prussia. The political importance of Pietism increased when Frederick William I began relying on Pietists for his socio-political reforms in opposition to the conservative forces in Prussia, which were allied to the more orthodox elements within Lutheranism. Francke was a fervent social activist. The Halleian, that is, Franckeian, variant of Pietism had a huge impact in Königsberg. The *Collegium Fridericianum*, attended by the young Kant, was first founded as a *collegium pietatis* by Theodor Gehr in the spirit of the Halle *Anstalten*.[62] An important figure in the intellectual and cultural life of Königsberg, and from whom Kant received his 'earliest religious instruction',[63] was F. A. Schultz, who was behind the attempt to reconcile Pietism and Wolffianism, which was effectively banned in Königsberg between 1723 and 1740. One of Kant's teachers, Martin Knutzen (1713–1751), himself a Pietist and defender of the theory of → **physical influx**, was a student of Schultz.

Among Kant scholars, Kant is often portrayed as straightforwardly hostile to Pietism as he was to religious popular culture, religious ceremony, or ecclesiastical authority in general. True, he denounced the often '*slavish* cast of mind' (**R** 184–185n.) of the Pietists, and their enthusiasm in their 'fantastic' belief of the possibility of *experiencing* the supersensible in terms of the supernatural as the cause of one's empirical mystical experience (**R** 174; cf. **CF** 33, 57n.).[64] Nevertheless, as Allen Wood rightly observes, 'much in Kant's conception of true morality and religion amounts to a rationally purified version of pietism'.[65] It is thus not too fanciful to argue that the central tenet of Pietism, the emphasis on moral autonomy and individuality, as well as the centrality in Pietism of morality and moral life conduct, appears to have left an imprint on the young Kant so much so that, in some more rational form, it influenced his mature theory of morality. – DS

FURTHER READING

R. Gawthrop, *Pietism and the Making of Eighteenth-Century Prussia*, new edition (Cambridge: Cambridge University Press, 2006).

PRUSSIA

In 1525, the Protestant Albrecht I of Brandenburg-Ansbach (1490–1568) united the remaining territories of the *Deutschordensstaat* into the Duchy (*Herzogtum*) of Prussia. This Duchy was not recognized by the Emperor of the Holy Roman Empire of which, as a consequence, it would never form a part.

Since 1657, Prussia had become entirely independent from Poland and in 1701 the country had been turned into a kingdom under the former Elector Friedrich III (1657–1713) of the house of Hohenzollern, who in view of the lack of recognition had to name himself Friedrich I, King *in*, and not *of*, Prussia. Drawing upon the combined power of a standing army and a modern administration system his son Friedrich Wilhelm I (1688–1740) expanded the territory and wealth of the kingdom significantly.

Prussia gained international political significance eventually under the enlightened absolute king Friedrich II (1712–1786), better known as → **Frederick the Great**, who considered himself to be the 'first servant of the state'. Frederick the Great carried forward the reforms of his father mainly by modernizing the legal system of the Prussian state. He abolished torture and also introduced a relative freedom of the press.

An essential element of the new atmosphere that Frederick the Great created in Prussia was his tolerance towards other religions. Judaism, however, was more or less excluded from this tolerance. Consequently, under the reign of Frederick the Great Prussia attracted many emigrants from all over Europe and served as an asylum for French Huguenots too. The flood of emigrants had an important positive influence on the enlightened intellectual climate in Prussia as well as on the state's economic growth and prosperity. Many of Europe's leading philosophers and scientists spent some time in Berlin.

Another positive factor was the freedom of the press introduced by Frederick the Great, even though it became temporarily restricted in 1788 as a consequence of the religious edict from the new Justice Minister Johann Christoph Wöllner, which lasted – albeit in different forms – until 1797 and affected

Kant too. The publication of **R** in 1793 resulted in Kant being summoned in October 1794 by Wöllner, who made him promise to refrain in future from publishing and lecturing on matters of religion.[66]

Mid-eighteenth century Berlin, Prussia's powerful political centre, had also developed into the intellectual centre of Prussia. Already in 1700, Friedrich I had appointed the famous Gottfried Wilhelm → **Leibniz** to establish the Berlin Academy, which subsequently was reformed by Frederick the Great in 1744 and renamed as the *Académie Royale des Sciences et Belles Lettres*. From then on, French was the institute's language of communication. Also, the king served as its president in order to further the interests of the state. This is illustrated by the politically significant topic of 1777's essay contest (→ **Academy prize essay**), which the king himself had proclaimed: 'Does it serve any purpose to deceive the people?'[67]

The Prussian educational system reached its peak with the foundation of the Berlin University in 1809, soon to become the standard for the reformation of German universities into institutions offering both teaching and research programmes. Prussia's most important universities were those of Halle and → **Königsberg**. The main assignment of the first was to educate the future civil servants of the state. The University of Halle enjoyed an excellent reputation for its modern law school with among its staff Christian Thomasius and Christian → **Wolff**. Early in the eighteenth century August Hermann Francke had established in Halle a revolutionary new educational institution for educating both boys and girls, called the *Franckesche Stiftungen*.

The University of Königsberg, on the other hand, was one of the first Protestant, i.e. Lutheran universities in Europe, founded in 1544 by Albrecht I. Its intellectual climate was thoroughly influenced by the centrality of Königsberg as Prussia's economic power-house and its status as a trading hub between Western and Eastern Europe. Many English and Scottish traders living in Königsberg were well educated. Joseph Green for instance was an intimate friend of Kant's and introduced him to English literature, philosophy and politics. He also participated intensively in the writing process of Kant's **CPR**.[68] – EOO

SCHOOL PHILOSOPHY

In Kant scholarship, the term 'school philosophy' usually refers to the discipline and the doctrines of philosophy as taught at universities and other places of higher education in the German speaking areas of Europe in the seventeenth and eighteenth centuries. It normally does not include Kant himself, on account of his singular importance in the history of philosophy. Although in a certain technical sense Kant could, of course, be considered to be a school philosopher as well (but see A838–839=B866–867), the relationship of Kant and school philosophy, in particular with regard to his predecessors, has been a topic of considerable debate.

As far as the seventeenth century is concerned,[69] the universities – like almost all other institutions in Germany – were subject to the after-effects of the Reformation and Counter-Reformation, ultimately resulting in a threefold division into Catholic (e.g. Ingolstadt, Cologne), Calvinist or Reformed (e.g. Heidelberg, Marburg) and Lutheran schools (e.g. → **Königsberg**, Altdorf). Despite these confessional ramifications, philosophy managed to establish a fair, but varying degree of independence from theology, and a rather substantial inter-confessional exchange of ideas prevailed. In general, there was not just considerable institutional continuity, but also a continuity of topics discussed and doctrines held with regard to late and high Scholasticism. That said, the now classic figures of early modern philosophy, who often worked outside of the universities, received some reception within school philosophy as well.

While a finer distinction within catholic German school philosophy is indispensable for a comprehensive account of this movement,[70] it may suffice to restrict this brief overview to the Jesuits, who arguably exerted the largest overall influence. Of particular importance was the genre of the *cursus philosophicus*,[71] i.e. the paradigm textbook that, while drawing mainly on Aristotelian sources, provided an outline of the core doctrines of the philosophical disciplines with an emphasis on logic, metaphysics and physics (the relationship between which is itself more often than not a problem). In the Jesuit *cursus* tradition (represented by, among others, Rodrigo de Arriaga [1592–1667]) moral philosophy was of relatively minor importance, the pertinent material being based on the *Nicomachean Ethics*. This tradition extended not only to other orders, e.g. the Franciscans, but also to Protestantism, such as in Paul Rabe (1656–1713) in Königsberg. As far as metaphysics is concerned, the *cursus* took up the crucial transformation this discipline had undergone in Francisco Suárez's (1548–1617) *Disputationes Metaphysicae* (DM), moving away from mere commentary on Aristotle's *Metaphysics* (→ **Aristotle**).

However, only a relatively small portion of the material discussed in DM entered into the respective section of the *cursus*.[72] These were, for example, the topic of metaphysics as *ens qua ens*, the transcendentals, i.e. those features of Being transcending the categories in that they can be found in each category, and the relationship between Being and materiality. Reflecting tensions between Thomist and Scotist paradigms, the question of the analogy vs. the univocity of Being received broad attention as well as the question as to how the object of metaphysics is different from that of logic. Further important representatives of seventeenth century Catholic school philosophy as a whole are Hirnhaim, Babenstuber, Sannig, and Magni.

Calvinist school philosophy[73] underwent significant Western European influences, in particular of French and Dutch provenance, with Petrus Ramus (1515–72) dominating in the first half, and → **Descartes** in the second half of the seventeenth century. A further trait of Calvinist school philosophy was its encyclopedic tendency, which exemplified the consolidating nature of German school philosophy in an almost paradigmatic manner. With the Ramist conceptions of methodology and completeness being crucial, metaphysics – in the sense of examining Being as Being – did not play the role of a foundational discipline. When it came to metaphysics, it was, overall, conceived of rather in terms of a Christian Neoplatonism (in marked contrast to the Jesuit, as it were, ontological approach) and hence basically as natural theology. Representatives of Calvinist School Philosophy are e.g. Goclenius, Keckermann, Timpler, Alsted, and Clauberg.

Conflicts about the relation between philosophy and theology notwithstanding – as evidenced by attempts at establishing a so-called 'Christosophia', based ultimately on revelation – it was the Lutheran German school philosophers[74] of the seventeenth century who returned to the ontological conception of Aristotelian metaphysics as a foundational discipline, with its focus on an account of *ens inquantum ens*. Given Luther's own outspoken hostility towards Aristotle, this came about as a rather surprising development, bringing the Lutherans more or less in line with the Scotist and Suárezian tradition.

A particularly interesting philosopher in this respect is Abraham Calov (1612–86) who introduced Suárez's metaphysics in Königsberg, and who in many ways held views similar to those of Suárez on a number of important metaphysical issues. Moreover, Calov developed philosophical approaches, which, in the opinion of some commentators at least,[75] are a precursor of sorts to Kant's Critical method, for example gnostology and noology. These relate to Aristotle's distinction between the first and second operation of the intellect and try to account for foundational concepts and principles respectively. Other important Lutherans include Scheibler, J. and C. Martini as well as Scherzer.

With regard to the eighteenth century,[76] the distinctions according to confessions remained very much in place. That said, controversies between, on the one hand, a rationalist strand with thinkers such as → **Wolff** and → **Baumgarten** (who as an author of important textbooks for example in metaphysics and ethics must perhaps be considered *the* author of reference for Kant[77]) and an anti-rationalist strand such as Thomasius, Rüdiger, and → **Crusius**, on the other,[78] were running through German school philosophy of the eighteenth century as a whole, sometimes even occurring within these subdivisions themselves, for example within the Lutheran tradition. Again, it is tempting to gloss over many, often subtle differences, but it would certainly be a mistake to regard all rationalists, e.g. Baumgarten, simply as Wolffians and construe too close an association between the non- or anti-rationalists and more downright religious movements, such as → **Pietism**. Moreover, older traditions, such as Eclecticism and → **Aristotelianism**,[79] the latter particularly at Königsberg university, continued to play an important role. In any event, however, this conflict obviously foreshadowed Kantian themes insofar as the anti-rationalists denied what the rationalists maintained, namely the possibility of transcendent metaphysical knowledge. Here, to be sure, remnants of an earlier conflict came into play too, namely that between different conceptions of metaphysics, i.e. metaphysics as an all-encompassing and foundational ontology, on the one hand, and as an essentially transcendent discipline covering a very special realm of entities, on the other.

While it would certainly be an exaggeration to regard the emergence of Kant's Critical philosophy entirely as an internal affair of German school philosophy, the influence from outside the school tradition altogether, such as from → **Hume**, may sometimes be similarly overstated.

As far as practical philosophy – in particular ethics – is concerned, seventeenth century debates were characterized by the tensions emerging from a predominantly secular outlook adopted especially in the Aristotelian (and Stoic) sources, on the one hand, and the radical nature of some of the Christian demands with regard to a proper conduct of human life altogether, on the other. These demands had been re-emphasized by the Reformers after basically the same issue had created similar frictions in academic circles of the High and late Middle Ages. Suggested solutions included a division of labour between those approaches with regard to the civic, or external, dimension of conduct and the inner, as it were 'spiritual' life respectively, while others insisted that Christian principles must be applied comprehensively

to the entire realm of the practical. Further tensions were caused by the fact that lawyers, theologians and philosophers in many cases claimed to be in charge of basically the same issues, for example the doctrine of practical natural law.[80]

In the eighteenth century debates, a number of crucial controversies also deserve close attention as a context for understanding the development and the structure of Kant's moral philosophy. One of those controversies concerned the status and nature of the will and their implications for normative theory. It is fair to say that here too, traditional Thomist and Scotist strategies were in a sense re-run, for example in Wolff's intellectualism and Crusius's voluntarism, with the latter putting particular importance on the freedom of the will as a foundational notion. While this clearly resonates in Kant's own thought, other ideas, such as Baumgarten's emphasis on obligation as the core concept of morality, are obviously also pertinent[81] – depending, of course, on how we wish to understand Kant's approach in the first place. – WE

SMITH, ADAM

Kant's interest in the Scottish moral sense philosophers is well-known. Kant famously says that David → **Hume** woke him from his 'dogmatic slumber' and quotes him often. He also pays tribute at various points to Francis → **Hutcheson**, identifying him at one point in **CPrR** as the prime representative of the moral sentimentalist school (**CPrR** 40). So it is unsurprising to find that Kant also read and respected the third central Scottish moral sense philosopher, Adam Smith, Hutcheson's student and successor, and one of Hume's closest friends. Smith's name rarely appears in the main body of Kant's work, however, and perhaps for that reason there was until recently far less discussion of Kant's relationship to Smith than of his relationship to Hume or Hutcheson.

Kant seems to have first read Smith's *Theory of Moral Sentiments* (TMS) shortly after it was first translated into German by Christian Rautenberg, in 1770. In a 1771 letter to Kant, Marcus → **Herz** writes that he has heard that 'the Englishman Smith' is Kant's 'favorite' (**Corr-I** 126) among the Scottish moral sense theorists, and Kant makes reference to 'sympathy' and the 'impartial spectator' as alternative foundations for moral judgment – thus, presumably, contrasting Hume with Smith – in an unpublished note that may have been written as early as the fall of 1770. Later in the 1770s, Kant's unpublished reflections include one lamenting the fact that no German writers have treated human moral consciousness with the insight that Smith shows, and one that asks of 'Smith's system' why 'the impartial judge' (a phrase Smith sometimes uses as a synonym for 'impartial spectator') would take an interest in the well-being of others. Yet another such reflection employs the notion of the impartial spectator to clarify the theory of taste. To observe an object from the point of view of the impartial spectator, Kant suggests, is the same thing as observing it from a communal point of view.[82] So Kant clearly read Smith's TMS.

That he read Smith's *Wealth of Nations* (WN) is in one sense easier to show. He quotes from the book in two of his published works, viz. at **MM** 289 and **Anthr** 209. But the passages Kant quotes are relatively dull ones (on the nature of money, and on sumptuary laws), and he may have gotten one of them from a review of the book in the *Göttingische gelehrte Anzeigen*, rather than

by reading the whole book himself. Whether or not he read through the book, Kant does seem to have been one of the first major figures in Germany to take an interest in WN. He also quotes from the book in his anthropology lectures of 1785, a point at which it was not widely known in Germany.[83]

Aside from these explicit references to Smith, there are arguably a whole series of allusions to him scattered throughout Kant's work. **G** discusses the advantages of the 'division of labor' in its preface, refers at another point to a 'rational impartial spectator,' and includes a brief but informed discussion of prices (**G** 388; 393; 434–435). In **UH**, written at more or less the same time as **G**, Kant maintains that restrictions on trade will impede economic growth (**UH** 27), and suggests a sort of 'invisible hand' picture of the workings of history, according to which gains in freedom and well-being come about by way of natural processes rather than the conscious efforts of human beings. A similar view of history and endorsement of the importance of freedom to economic growth appear in **CBH**, from 1786, which in addition contains a version of the stadial theory of economic development associated with Smith and his student John Millar.

Later, in **PP**, Kant makes remarks on national debt that look like they may have come from WN, and endorses a position similar to Smith's on the separation of church and state in **MM**. In **CF** the division of labour re-appears, as an extended metaphor for how universities ought to be run.[84]

Exactly what to make of these remarks and allusions is hard to say. Some contemporary philosophers have suggested that Smith's impartial spectator procedure for moral judgment is closer to Kant's ethical system than any other position among the moral sentimentalists.[85] Some also see anticipations of Kant in Smith's conception of, and support for, political liberty.[86] It is not easy to say whether Kant, if he is responding to Smith in these respects, means simply to endorse his views or in part to criticize them. Kant clearly does favour a large role for the free market in economics, but he also thinks governments should make provisions for the poor. This is not dissimilar, however, to the view of political economy most scholars today attribute to Smith. Kant's categorical imperative can be read as an a priori replacement for Smith's impartial spectator procedure, and the absolute, a priori value he assigns to humanity could be similarly read as a critique of Smith's attempt to establish value on an entirely empirical basis.

But again, versions of these thoughts can plausibly be seen in Smith's own work. It is hard to say with any great precision how Kant saw his own writings in relation to Smith: he does not explicitly discuss Smith in any extended way. Instead, we have hints and allusions – enough for a fascinating series of speculations about the influence of the great eighteenth-century Scottish theorist of freedom on the Prussian one, but perhaps not for any definitive account of that relationship. – SF

SPINOZA, BENEDICTUS (BARUCH) DE; SPINOZISM

Kant probably never read Spinoza directly, but the latter was nevertheless a significant influence on his thought due to the variants of Spinozism that rose to popularity following the 'pantheism controversy' of the 1780s. From that time onwards, Spinoza's became the rival position that, through Kant's opposition to it, shaped much of his later philosophy.

Prior to 1785, Spinoza's philosophy was castigated as atheism, materialism and fatalism by most in the intellectual mainstream. For over 100 years, Spinoza's texts had been banned and ostentatiously refuted in the universities, while simultaneously being circulated and celebrated amongst anti-establishment thinkers. The reasons for this were Spinoza's political and religious radicalism, expressed most powerfully in the *Tractatus Theologico-Politicus* (1670) and the seemingly atheistic metaphysics underpinning it, set out in his major work the *Ethics*.

Spinoza argues that all being is a single, infinite substance that is 'God or nature'. Recognizing no ontological distinction between God and the universe, Spinoza denies transcendence, divine creation, teleology, contingency, and free will, arguing that God is 'the immanent cause of all things' which follow necessarily from his nature. Human beings are finite modes, or properties, of God, and are wholly determined by him. Rejecting the God of theism, Spinoza argues for the illusoriness of organized religion, advocating a route to true knowledge of God through rational understanding of nature. He similarly seeks to reveal the imaginary foundations of contemporary politics and to defend democracy and tolerance on rational grounds.

His critiques of established power structures, founded on an apparently atheistic or pantheistic metaphysics, led his work to being suppressed by the authorities and admired by freethinkers. So dangerous was his thought considered to be, that a published denunciation of Spinoza was virtually a requirement of taking up an academic post in the early eighteenth century (that of Christian → **Wolff** being particularly influential).

The view that Spinoza's philosophy is atheistic, fatalistic, dogmatic metaphysics finds expression in some of Kant's lecture courses and pre-Critical essays. In these remarks, Kant dismisses Spinozism as absurd 'enthusiasm' rendered harmless by transcendental critique. What Kant did not foresee, in 1781, was the surge of interest in Spinoza that would follow the publication, in 1785, of Friedrich Jacobi's *Über die Lehre des Spinoza in Briefen an den Herrn Moses Mendelssohn*. This book, which set off the 'pantheism controversy' of the mid-1780s, reinstated Spinoza as an intellectually respectable philosopher, while strongly criticizing his rationalism. For Jacobi, Spinoza's atheism proves that rationalist philosophy – including Kant's – cannot be made consistent with faith. Without faith, Jacobi thinks, philosophy falls into one of two traps: either Spinozism, affirming rational knowledge of a single absolute and necessary substance, or nihilism, denying our knowledge of the absolute. Either way, as he saw it, God, freedom, and morality were lost.

Kant responded in **OT**, stressing that transcendental idealism limits reason and upholds both freedom and faith, thereby distancing himself from both Spinoza and Jacobi. Yet the popularity of Jacobi's book and the turn to Spinoza amongst younger scholars led Kant increasingly to see Spinoza as a rival and a threat. In Kant's later texts, Spinoza takes on the role of the dogmatic enemy previously played by → **Leibniz**; yet it is not the historical Spinoza with which Kant takes issue so much as his late-eighteenth century adherents.

Whereas Jacobi took Spinoza to be paradigmatic of the exaltation of reason over faith, others saw in his thought the potential to heal the rift. Thinkers such as J. G. → **Herder** sought to rehabilitate Spinoza through *Naturphilosophie*, suggesting that his naturalistic pantheism was compatible with the Christian world-view. Herder argued that Spinoza's God was the organic force immanent to all natural beings that organized them providentially and teleologically, thereby reconciling faith with natural science.

Herder's was the variant of Spinozism to which Kant was most vehemently opposed. Kant and Herder had a philosophical problem in common: how could nature be fully determined through natural laws, while also displaying purposiveness in its organization? Herder's response was to argue that God directs nature from within, according to a wise plan. 'Spinozism' came to name the view that nature was caused and directed by divine intelligence within it, a view that Kant found dogmatic and incoherent.

Kant argued that the idea of God could be conceived only as an intelligent creator *separate* from nature, and that nature's purposiveness was a function not of nature's power, but of our power of judgment. These are the key arguments of the second half of CJ, important not only for solving the problem of purposiveness, but moreover for harmonizing Kant's systems of nature and morality. Kant's defence against Spinozism is therefore crucial to the success of the Critique of Teleological Judgment and to that of CJ as a whole.

In §§72–73 of **CJ**, we find Kant's most explicit refutation of Spinoza. Though ostensibly a diagnosis of Spinoza's failure to account for purposiveness in nature, it is clear that Kant's real objection is to Spinoza's doctrine of immanent causality. Kant contends that this does not explain causality at all, but only the inherence of accidents in substance. Spinoza's substance lacks intentional causality, intelligence, and contingency, meaning for Kant that it cannot explain the idea of purposiveness. Yet the real issue for Kant is Spinoza's denial of the idea of God as intentional, external, and transcendent to creation, for Kant relies on this idea to reconcile natural determinism with purposiveness. Kant's aim here is to show that Spinoza's anti-theism is untenable, because, he suggests, the *idea* of the transcendent God is closely related to the purposiveness that is the principle of reflective judgment (§§76–77). Furthermore, only the idea of a transcendent God can ground our conception of nature as an arena suitable for moral action. The 'special character of the human understanding' (**CJ** 405) effectively rules out the notion of Spinoza's God.

Kant's insistence, *contra* the Spinozists, that the idea of God includes transcendence and externality, is also a feature of his final writings in **OP**. Kant refers frequently and puzzlingly to Spinoza in this text, sometimes appearing to align Spinoza with his own transcendental idealism. Though there is no critical consensus on these passages, it seems likely that they reflect the influence of Spinoza on Schelling and the development of idealism in the early 1800s. In this late period, Kant continued to see Spinozism as a rival position to his own, and continued to object to it as a naturalist philosophy that leaves no room for God or morality. – BL

FURTHER READING

F. Beiser, *The Fate of Reason. German Philosophy from Kant to Fichte* (Cambridge, MA: Harvard University Press, 1987), chs 2 and 3.

J. Edwards, 'Spinozism, freedom, and transcendental dynamics in Kant's final system of transcendental idealism', in S. Sedgwick (ed.), *The Reception of Kant's Critical Philosophy: Fichte, Schelling, and*

Hegel (Cambridge: Cambridge University Press, 2000), pp. 54–77.

B. Lord, *Kant and Spinozism: Transcendental Idealism and Immanence from Jacobi to Deleuze* (Basingstoke/New York: Palgrave Macmillan, 2011).

NOTES

1 *Königliche Akademie der Wissenschaften zu Berlin / Académie royale des sciences et belleslettres de Prusse.*
2 As quoted in 'Introductions to the translations' in CE 1, p. lxii.
3 See S. Ebbesen, 'The Aristotelian commentator', in J. Marenbon (ed.), *The Cambridge Companion to Boethius* (Cambridge, 2009), pp. 34–55.
4 See F. van Steenberghen, *La philosophie au XIIIe siècle*, second edition (Louvain/Paris, 1991), pp. 272, 359.
5 See S. Ozment, *The Age of Reform 1250–1550. An Intellectual and Religious History of Late Medieval and Reformation Europe* (New Haven, 1980), pp. 231–239.
6 See his *Disputationes Metaphysicae* I.
7 See A. Speer, G. Frank, *Der Aristotelismus in der frühen Neuzeit – Kontinuität oder Wiederaneignung* (Wiesbaden, 2007), pp. 9–16.
8 Rabe is the author of important textbooks such as *Dialectica et analytica: scientiarum biga utilissima; Commentarius in librum categoriarum Aristotelis sive primitiae professionis logico-metaphysicae; Cursus philosophicus*; and *Methodologia nova atque scientifica sive tractatus de ordine genuino.*
9 See M. Sgarbi, 'Metaphysics in Königsberg prior to Kant (1703–1770)', */Trans/Form/Ação/* 33 (2010): 31–64.
10 See M. Sgarbi, *La Kritik der reinen Vernunft nel contesto della tradizione logica aristotelica* (Hildesheim, 2010).
11 Antoine Arnauld & Pierre Nicole, *Logic or the Art of Thinking*, ed. J. V. Buroker (Cambridge, 1996).
12 Locke, *An Essay Concerning Human Understanding*, ed. P. H. Nidditch (Oxford, 1975), 2.1.2, p. 104; hereafter ECHU.

13 Hume, *An Enquiry Concerning Human Understanding*, ed. T. L. Beauchamp (Oxford, 1999), 2.5; hereafter EHU.

14 E.g. A854=B882 and **LM** 761ff.

15 E.g. A471=B499, A854=B882, and **LM** 763.

16 **LM** 232, **LM-M/V** 763, **LM** 542, and **LM-M/V** 950.

17 See **LM-M/V** 763 and A854–855=B882–883.

18 F. D. Preuss (ed.), *Oeuvres de Frédéric le Grand* (Berlin, 1854), vol. X, p. 415.

19 L. W. Beck, *Early German Philosophy: Kant and his Predecessors* (Bristol, 1996), p. 10.

20 See W. Krauss, *Studien zur deutschen und französischen Aufklärung* (Berlin, 1963), p. 69.

21 J. G. Hamann, 'Metacritique on the Purism of Reason', trans. K. Haynes, in J. Schmidt (ed.), *What is Enlightenment?* (Berkeley/Los Angeles, 1996), p. 166.

22 F. D. Preuss (ed.), *Oeuvres de Frédéric le Grand*, vol. XXV, p. 226.

23 See also **TP** 299–303, **PP** 381–383; cf. **Refl** 8043.

24 See **TP** 299–300; cf. **Refl** 8051.

25 C. Garve, 'review of *Critique of Pure Reason*', in B. Sassen (ed.), *Kant's Early Critics: The Empiricist Critique of the Theoretical Philosophy* (Cambridge, 2000), p. 75.

26 See K. Ameriks, *Kant and the Fate of Autonomy* (Cambridge, 2000), for a lengthy discussion of the effect of this characterization.

27 See F. Beiser, *German Idealism: the Struggle against Subjectivism, 1781–1801* (Cambridge, 2002), ch. 5.

28 See further the essay 'First Responses to the *Critique of Pure Reason*: the 1780s and Later', this volume.

29 I. Berlin, 'Counter-Enlightenment', in I. Berlin, *Against the Current* (Harmondsworth, 1979), 1–24. See also I. Berlin, 'Herder and the Enlightenment', in I. Berlin, *The Proper Study of Mankind*, ed. H. Hardy, R. Hausheer (New York, 1998), pp. 359–434.

30 R. Haym, *Herder nach seinem Leben und seinen Werken*, 2 vols. (Berlin, 1877/1885).

31 Lessing's translation of *A System of Moral Philosophy* (1755) was published in 1756; Kant owned 1760 and 1762 translations of *An Essay on the Nature and Conduct of the Passions and Affections. With Illustrations on the Moral Sense* (1728) and of *An Inquiry into the Original of our Ideas of Beauty and Virtue; In Two Treatises* (1725).

32 D. Henrich, 'Hutcheson und Kant', *Kant-Studien* 49 (1957/1958): 49–69.

33 It is worth emphasizing that Henrich's paper is based almost exclusively on an analysis of posthumously published *Reflexionen* (**Refl**) and remarks (**Obs-R**); Hutcheson is mentioned by name in these only once (**Refl** 6634).

34 See G. Tonelli, 'Conditions in Königsberg and the making of Kant's philosophy', in A. J. Bucher et al. (eds), *Bewusst-sein* (Bonn, 1975), pp. 126–127.

35 See M. Sgarbi, *Logica e metafisica nel Kant precritico. L'ambiente intellettuale di Königsberg e la formazione della filosofia kantiana* (Frankfurt, 2010), pp. 84–91.

36 See R. Pozzo, 'Aristotelismus und Eklektik in Königsberg', in H. Marti, M. Komorowski (eds), *Die Universität Königsberg in frühen Neuzeit* (Cologne/Weimar/Vienna, 2008), pp. 175–178.

37 See G. Tonelli, *The Critique of Pure Reason within the Tradition of Modern Logic* (Hildesheim, 1994); cf. M. Sgarbi, *La Kritik der reinen Vernunft nel contesto della tradizione logica aristotelica* (Hildesheim, 2010).

38 G. Tonelli, 'Conditions in Königsberg', p. 132.

39 Ibid.

40 See A. Ritschl, *Geschichte des Pietismus* (Bonn, 1844), vol. II, p. 290.

41 See E. Riedesel, *Pietismus und Orthodoxie in Ostpreußen. Auf Grund des Briefwechsels G. F. Rogalls und F. A. Schultz' mit den Halleschen Pietisten* (Königsberg, 1937), p. 30.

42 See G. von Selle, *Geschichte der Albertus-Universität zu Königsberg in Preußen* (Würzburg, 1956), pp. 139–140.

43 See J. J. Fehr, *'Ein wunderlicher nexus rerum'. Aufklärung und Pietismus in Königsberg unter Franz Albert Schultz* (Hildesheim, 2005).

44 See R. Pozzo, 'Aristotelismus und Eklektik in Königsberg', in H. Marti, M. Komorowski (eds), *Die Universität Königsberg in der frühen Neuzeit* (Cologne, 2008), p. 182.

45 See W. Stark, 'Wo lehrte Kant? Recherchen zu Kants Wohnungen', in J. Kohnen (ed.), *Königsberg. Beiträge zu einem besonderen Kapitel der deutschen Geistesgeschichte des 18. Jahrhunderts* (Frankfurt, 1994), p. 88.

46 Kant's word for 'agree', *einstimmig*, connotes 'speaking with one voice'.

47 A. Altmann, *Moses Mendelssohn. A Biographical Study* (London, 1973), p. xiii.

[48] Moses Mendelssohn, *Morgenstunden oder Vorlesungen über das Dasein Gottes*, in *Gesammelte Schriften. Jubiläumsausgabe*, ed. F. Bamberger et al. (Stuttgart, 1971ff.), vol. III.2, pp. 1–175, here p. 3; hereafter JA, followed by volume and page numbers.

[49] See M. L. Davies, *Marcus Herz and the End of the Enlightenment* (Detroit, 1995), pp. 36–38.

[50] Mendelssohn, *Morgenstunden*, JA, III.2, p. 4.

[51] Mendelssohn, *Morgenstunden oder Vorlesungen über das Dasein Gottes. Der Briefwechsel Mendelssohn – Kant*, ed. D. Bourel (Stuttgart, 1979), pp. 252–253.

[52] Mendelssohn, *Schreiben an den Herrn Diakonus Lavater* (1770), JA, VII, p. 8.

[53] Mendelssohn, *Jerusalem oder über religiöse Macht und Judentum*, JA, VIII, pp. 156ff., 164–166, 191ff.

[54] H. Blumenberg, *Säkularisierung und Selbstbehauptung* (Frankfurt a/M, 1974), p. 239.

[55] See for more on Maimon the essay 'First Responses to the *Critique of Pure Reason*: the 1780s and Later', this volume.

[56] Mendelssohn, *Phädon oder über die Unsterblichkeit der Seele*, JA, III.1, p. 88.

[57] Mendelssohn, 'Über die Frage: was heißt aufklären?', JA, VI.1, pp. 117–118.

[58] Mendelssohn, *Jerusalem oder über religiöse Macht und Judentum*, JA, VIII, pp. 163–164.

[59] N. Hinske, 'Das stillschweigende Gespräch: Mendelssohn und Kant', in M. Albrecht, E. J. Engel, N. Hinske (eds), *Moses Mendelssohn und die Kreise seiner Wirksamkeit* (Tübingen, 1994), p. 155.

[60] See also Kant's letter to Schütz from November 1785 (Corr-I 428–429).

[61] This forms the background of the notorious religious edicts by J. C. Wöllner (1732–1800) under Frederick William II, in which Kant also became embroiled in the 1790s, which were often regarded as a demonstration of a conservative censure of Enlightenment but were arguably more intended to counteract the proliferating anarchy of often quite radically heterodox religious opinions and beliefs among both the Lutheran laity and clergy. See the excellent account of the history of Wöllner's policies and Kant's relation to it, B. Stangneth, 'Introduction' to I. Kant, *Religion innerhalb der Grenzen der bloßen Vernunft* (Hamburg, 2003), pp. xvii–lix.

[62] M. Kuehn, *Kant. A Biography* (Cambridge, 2001), p. 36.

[63] M. Kuehn, *Kant. A Biography*, p. 37.

[64] See further especially Kant's extremely interesting account of the metaphysical antinomies that mystical theories of moral regeneration lead to at CF 53–60. Kant acknowledged the rational nature of the 'problem' that Pietists threw 'in the path of the orthodox', namely how 'to make us *other* human beings' rather than 'merely better human beings', but he criticized the 'mystical' nature of their solution for a 'moral metamorphosis'.

[65] A. Wood, 'Introduction', I. Kant, *Religion and Rational Theology* (Cambridge, 2001) (CE 6), p. xii. Cf. J. Hare, *The Moral Gap. Kantian Ethics, Human Limits, and God's Assistance* (Oxford, 1997), pp. 48–60. See Kuehn, *Kant. A Biography*, pp. 40ff. for a more pessimistic evaluation of the influence of Pietism on the mature Kant.

[66] See Kant's letter to king Frederick William II of 12 October 1794 (Corr-II 527–530). On the edict see U. Wiggermann, *Woellner und das Religionsedikt: Kirchenpolitik und kirchliche Wirklichkeit im Preußen des späten 18. Jahrhunderts* (Tübingen, 2010).

[67] An edition of the prize question has recently been published in *Nützt es dem Volke, betrogen zu werden? Est-it utile au peuple d'être trompé? Die Preisfrage der Preußischen Akademie für 1780*, ed. H. Adler (Stuttgart-Bad Cannstatt, 2007).

[68] Cf. M. Kuehn, *Kant: A Biography* (Cambridge, 2001), 154ff.

[69] With regard to seventeenth century German school philosophy, this article is based on the most comprehensive account of it available, namely H. Holzhey, W. Schmidt-Biggemann (eds), in cooperation with V. Mudroch, *Die Philosophie des 17. Jahrhunderts*, vol. 4, *Das Heilige Römische Reich Deutscher Nation. Nord- und Ostmitteleuropa* (2 vols) (Basel, 2001), vol. 1, pp. 291–606, esp. the concise outline in Walter Sparn, 'Einleitung', in Holzhey, Schmidt-Biggemann (2001), pp. 293–295. With regard to university history, see N. Hammerstein, 'Die Universitäten. Geschichte und Struktur', in Holzhey, Schmidt-Biggemann (2001), pp. 295–302.

[70] See P. R. Blum et al., 'Die Schulphilosophie in den katholischen Territorien', in Holzhey, Schmidt-Biggemann (2001), pp. 302–391.

[71] See Blum, pp. 313–330.

[72] See the account in Blum, pp. 325–330.

[73] See Schmidt-Biggemann, 'Die Schulphilosophie in den reformierten Territorien', in Holzhey, Schmidt-Biggemann (2001), pp. 392–474, esp. p. 395.

[74] See W. Sparn, 'Die Schulphilosophie in den lutherischen Territorien', in Holzhey, Schmidt-Biggemann (2001), pp. 475–606, esp. pp. 487–493.

[75] See e.g. M. Sgarbi, *Logica e metafisica nel Kant precritico. L'ambiente intellettuale di Königsberg e la formazione della filosofia kantiana* (Frankfurt a/M, 2010), pp. 57–64.

[76] See, for the following as well, W. Röd, *Die Philosophie der Neuzeit 2. Von Newton bis Rousseau* (Munich, 1984), pp. 235–296.

[77] See C. Schwaiger, *Alexander Gottlieb Baumgarten – ein intellektuelles Porträt: Studien zur Metaphysik und Ethik von Kants Leitautor* (Stuttgart-Bad Cannstatt, 2011).

[78] With regard to this controversy, cf. also M. Wundt, *Die deutsche Schulphilosophie im Zeitalter der Aufklärung* (Tübingen, 1945), and L. W. Beck, *Early German Philosophy. Kant and His Predecessors* (Cambridge, MA, 1969), pp. 243–305.

[79] See G. Tonelli, *Kant's* Critique of Pure Reason *within the Tradition of Modern Logic* (Hildesheim, 1994), *passim*.

[80] See, also with regard to practical philosophy in general, W. Sparn, 'Die Schulphilosophie in den lutherischen Territorien', pp. 495–497.

[81] This has been emphasized recently by C. Schwaiger, *Kategorische und andere Imperative. Zur Entwicklung von Kants praktischer Philosophie bis 1785* (Stuttgart-Bad-Cannstatt, 1999), against the traditional view of Crusius's main role in leading Kant away from Wolff's eudaimonism.

[82] See **Refl** 6628, 1355, 6864, and 767 respectively. See further S. Fleischacker, 'Philosophy in moral practice: Kant and Adam Smith', *Kant-Studien* 82,3 (1991): 249–269, which is the first article-length treatment of the relationship between the two figures since A. Oncken, *Adam Smith und Immanuel Kant* (Leipzig, 1877). The *Reflexionen* had not been published when Oncken wrote, however, so the hard evidence for Smith's influence on Kant was limited to the Herz letter. This made it necessary for Oncken to treat the possibility that Smith influenced Kant as a mere speculation. Subsequent scholars – e.g. W. Eckstein, in his introduction to his 1926 German translation of TMS, and D. Raphael and A. Macfie, in their introduction to their 1976 edition of TMS – followed Oncken, and were therefore also hesitant to make any strong claims about Smith's importance to Kant. We can be considerably more confident about such claims today.

[83] Although WN was published in 1776, it did not become well-known in Germany (as in many other places) until the 1790s. See the discussion of reception of WN in Germany, as well as the passages in Kant that refer to WN, in S. Fleischacker, 'Values behind the market: Kant's response to the *Wealth of Nations*,' *History of Political Thought* 17,3 (1996): 379–407.

[84] For discussion of all these texts, see again S. Fleischacker, 'Values behind the market'.

[85] See S. Fleischacker, 'Philosophy in moral practice', but see also S. Darwall, 'Sympathetic liberalism: recent work on Adam Smith', *Philosophy and Public Affairs* 28,2 (1999): 139–164; S. Darwall, 'Equal dignity in Adam Smith', in *Adam Smith Review* I (2004): 129–134; L. Montes, *Adam Smith in Context* (Basingstoke/New York, 2004), ch. 4; M. A. Carrasco, 'Adam Smith's reconstruction of practical reason', *Review of Metaphysics* 58,1 (2004): 81–116; and C. Fricke, H.-P. Schütt (eds), *Adam Smith als Moralphilosoph* (Berlin/ New York, 2005).

[86] See A. Sen, *The Idea of Justice* (Cambridge, 2009) and S. Fleischacker, *A Third Concept of Liberty: Judgment and Freedom in Kant and Adam Smith* (Princeton, 1999).

3

SOURCES AND INFLUENCES

This chapter consists of a compilation of short essays on various philosophers and thinkers who can be seen to have directly influenced Kant's thinking. Leading figures such as Newton and Euler are included, from the world of science and mathematics, along with central philosophical figures such as Leibniz and Locke. The essays convey a sense of just how wide and varied the sources and influences which helped shape Kant's philosophy were – from his pre-Critical period, right up to and after the time of the publication of the *Critique of Pure Reason*. With some of the entries a list of further reading is provided that will enable the reader to undertake further research. – NH/DS

ARISTOTLE

Establishing the correspondence as well as the substantial differences between Kant and Aristotle rests to a large extent upon an evaluation of the historical context in which both their philosophical projects arose. For Kant, the rationalist conception of metaphysics, psychology and morality, was a historical given. Furthermore, → **Hume**, who famously woke Kant from his 'dogmatic slumber',

exercised an unquestionable influence on the development of the Critical philosophy. In Aristotle's case, on the other hand, it was his critique of → **Plato**'s doctrine of Ideas as well as scepticism that crucially informed his own philosophical views. The focus of Aristotle's metaphysics and theory of knowledge, chiefly articulated in the *Categories* and the *Metaphysics,* lies in his doctrine of substance, which is based on his view regarding the relation between language and reality. His psychology, presented in *On the Soul*, which is both a theory of knowledge and an anthropology, is directly linked up with his doctrine of substance.

To determine the difference with Kant, it is important to notice that Aristotle's notion of 'substance' is not a metaphysical concept that is part and parcel of the necessary stock of human faculties of the mind. Only in the course of the modern history of philosophy has the notion of 'substance' acquired the connotation of an adequate concept whose meaning is obvious. In → **Descartes**, → **Spinoza** and → **Leibniz** it is quite understandable how their interpretations of the concept of 'substance' led to the edifices of their respective foundationalist programmes.

Kant's thought is, in essence, a reaction to the debate between the empiricists and rationalists, in particular in regard to the use of such metaphysical concepts as 'substance' and 'cause'. He deems it necessary to subject the function and, accordingly, the use or applicability of the concept of 'substance' and other pure concepts to a Critical, transcendental-philosophical examination. What makes Kant's account different from Aristotle's is mostly due to the simple fact that, for Aristotle, 'substance' is not primarily a concept that requires either empirical or metaphysical application. Rather, in Aristotle, the term 'substance' or 'ousia' is used (1) to make explicit the relation between language or thought, on the one hand, and reality, on the other, in order subsequently to (2) clarify issues relating to the perceived abstractness and alleged independence of the ideas, which played such a fundamental role in Plato's thought.

Aristotle uses the term 'ousia' in two ways. First, in the sense of the real (subject) to which an enunciation relates in contrast to, second, the subject term in a proposition which is nothing but the form in which the 'real' is expressed. In this context, the term 'hypokeimenon' is also important in terms of its playing a supporting role; it is the substrate, the 'underlying', about which something is asserted.[1] Aristotle's analysis is notably concerned with differentiating what is in fact intrinsically connected: the subject term in a proposition and the reality that is enunciated by it. In a sense, Aristotle's method is descriptive rather than positing or seeking to determine a metaphysical foundation. It thus concerns a form of reflection which from the start remains in the immediacy of the relation between language and reality. This is different from the position of Kant's transcendental philosophy, which is in fact characterized by a certain distance from the immediacy of what is given (*in intentione obliqua* instead of *in intentione recta*).

In Aristotle's view, 'ousia', later called 'essence' or 'substance' because of what is implied by the supporting term 'hypokeimenon', points to 'relation' and the terms describing a relation. Aristotle's notion of substance is therefore entirely different in nature from the metaphysical conception of substance, which acquired the meaning of 'that which exists in and of itself', and constitutes the basic tenet of rationalist foundationalism. In connection herewith, Aristotle also crucially distinguishes between concepts, which are always abstract and universal, and the real essence of a thing. A concept never has real meaning just by virtue of itself, which is exactly why Aristotle is dissatisfied with Plato's realm of Ideas that are separate from the real world. In Aristotle's view, the difference between particulars and their essences need not result in an independent sphere or realm of Ideas.

Aristotle's method rests on a procedure of differentiation, much more than is the case in later traditions in philosophy. This particular method plays an important role also in the *Physics*, where he makes use of the multi-dimensional concept of 'causality', which is at the same time not restricted to 'efficient causality'.

It may be said that the problem of the *objectivity* of human knowledge first arose as a result of the disappearance of the technique that Aristotle introduced in order to make the relationship between language and reality explicit – this occurred most probably already with the arrival of Stoicism, but later Christian, metaphysical motifs have certainly played a pivotal role in this. There is a crucial difference between the sense and function of the categories with Aristotle, for whom they are concerned with 'ways of asserting', and later, more ontological interpretations of categories as 'ways of being' in terms of e.g. 'substance' and 'accidens' being forms in themselves. Aristotle sees the categories as from the outset connected with something as a concrete particular, a 'this here'. Accordingly, 'location' and 'time' play a concrete role in an assertion or judgment.

Kant, on the other hand, keeps a critical distance from the immediate, concrete in order to make explicit the necessary formal structure of finite human knowledge. Kant concentrates on both the formal aspects of sensible intuition and the forms of thought, to which he gives the Aristotelian label of 'categories' (CPR A79–80=B105), in contrast to – and in this sense Kant is more indebted to Plato – the ideas of reason, which are far removed from human experience.

There is a likeness of sorts between Kant and Aristotle in the way that both mark time in their painstaking analyses of the forms of knowledge, although the dynamics of analysis obviously differ. Importantly, however, Kant sees knowledge as resulting from the synthesis of given representations, which as so determined, as unified, first constitute, formally, an object. 'Object', then, corresponds with what is thought as 'determined' (cf. the definition of object at B137 in CPR). In Kant's account, the concept of 'synthesis', or 'synthetic unity of apperception', plays a crucial role and is closely linked to the function of the understanding. The most important reason why synthesis only first comes up with the account of the understanding and in fact defines 'thought' for Kant lies in the fact that, from the perspective of transcendental philosophy, one must start out from the object such as it is given in sensible intuition, viz. as a manifold of representations. Within the architectonic of Kant's system of thought, the principle of the unity of synthesis is contrasted with the manifold data in sensible intuition, which forms the empirical basis of knowledge.

By contrast, Aristotle sees no reason to connect synthesis to the understanding, for the sensed phenomenon is directly presented in sensibility as sensible awareness of unity. The thing we perceive is present before us by virtue of its distinguishable types of impressions (colour, sound and form), which are received simultaneously in our capacity for external perception. The impressions of a sensed thing are directly present and collectively constitute the thing we hold to be present before us. The *fact* of synthesis (unity) is incontrovertible and not explainable by the understanding alone, as it is for Kant. The perception of concrete things or particulars, in their spatiality, goes hand in hand with the structural features of the natural life-world, which is reflected by the human being as a spontaneously moving, living being. The involvement of the understanding is then but a reflection of the object's own form that is an integral part of its 'essence'.

In Aristotle, synthesis and structure thus rest on an a priori that is of an entirely different nature from Kant's conception of the synthetic a priori. Aristotle takes reality as primordially alterable and moving, which comports with taking the natural life-world and the human perspective within that context as the starting point for an analysis of nature, society and the moral life. Therefore, a sense of immediacy forms the basis of Aristotle's inquiry.

This can also be seen from Aristotle's account in the *Physics* and its typical explanations of kinds of movement, in the structure of the world as both earthly and heavenly spheres, and in the frequent reference to final causality or teleology in order to explain phenomena which in later philosophical traditions came to be seen as entirely explainable mechanically. From the perspective of these later accounts, 'finality' or 'purposiveness' can then no longer be regarded as *eo ipso* objective. The shift takes place when teleology begins to be regarded as a form of projection, whereby the human being projects the structure of his own perspective onto nature. In Kant, this results in critically departing from any type of explanation of reality or nature in terms of a necessary organic-systematic unity among natural phenomena. Purposiveness is then only relative to our own subjective perspective, as Kant points out in his account in **CJ**.

Similarly, Aristotle's ethics rests on a view of the natural recognizability of the good, of virtues that naturally belong to the human striving towards perfection. This changes with the loss of immediacy in modern philosophy. In Kant, the question of the *objectivity* of moral judgment arises, while at the same time the autonomy of the human being must be preserved. Kant's answer lies in the notion of rational self-legislation, which is not based on the value of 'natural' virtues as such. The natural pursuit of happiness no longer has an inner moral meaning for Kant, although the hope for happiness has not entirely been eradicated from the moral and religious perspective. – KJB/DS

FURTHER READING

S. Engstrom, J. Whiting (eds), *Aristotle, Kant and the Stoics: Rethinking Happiness and Duty* (Cambridge: Cambridge University Press, 1996).

O. Höffe, 'Ethik ohne und mit Metaphysik. Zum Beispiel Aristoteles und Kant', *Zeitschrift für philosophische Forschung* 61,4 (2007): 405–422.

H. Seidl, *Sein und Bewußtsein: Erörterungen zur Erkenntnislehre und Metaphysik in einer Gegenüberstellung von Aristoteles und Kant* (Hildesheim: Olms, 2001).

BACON, FRANCIS

The *Great Instauration* is the name Francis Bacon (1561–1626) gave to his monumental effort to reform natural philosophy into a practical science. According to its plan, the project was to consist of six parts. The first of these was intended by Bacon to provide an overview and classification of the extant sciences. The second part was intended to detail the proper method of scientific investigation. Complementing the second, the third part was intended to provide the material for practical knowledge in the form of histories, natural and experimental. Bacon also intended to supply, in the fourth part of the *Great Instauration*, examples for guidance in the application of the new method. The fifth part was intended to present an inventory of provisional truths discovered not through the new method, but with the ordinary method of inquiry and discovery. The sixth part of the project, what Bacon called 'Second Philosophy', or 'Practical Science', was intended to present and expound the truths discovered by the new method of science thus supplanting the fifth part and, indeed, all ill-begotten 'truth'.

Although Bacon had been working on it since at least 1592, the material he had produced at the time of his death in 1626 was not enough to complete the project, nor any single part thereof. The first three parts are most nearly complete, only fragments exist of parts four and five, and part six seems never to have even been begun by Bacon. Of the first three, the second part is the most important, not just philosophically, but also historically.

The material for the second part of the *Great Instauration* was provided by Bacon in 1620,[2] consisting of two books of aphorisms (although it is clear that he intended more): of the nine major topics introduced in the second half, only the first of seven that are relevant to this part of the project is treated in the remainder of the volume. Book I offers an unembellished examination of what he famously calls idols or false notions (*idola*), which 'not only block [people's] minds so that it is difficult for truth to gain access, but even when access has been granted and allowed [. . .] offer resistance and do mischief'.[3]

The 'Idols of the Tribe' are intellectual weaknesses generally inherent in human nature. These weaknesses include the tendency to suppose more order in nature than there actually is; the disposition of the mind to be misled by the errors and dullness of the senses; the mind's tendency to ignore exceptions to generally accepted principles; to be influenced by the emotions; and to continue in a direction of thought for which there is no evidence for doing so.

The 'Idols of the Cave or Den' are personal prejudices and biases. While some people are obsessed with the details, others are obsessed with the whole. While some look for differences, some look for similarities.

The 'Idols of the Marketplace' are tendencies to err due to the bewitchment of the mind by language. These are the most powerful idols: not only does reason affect words, but words also affect reason.

The 'Idols of the Theater' are tendencies to accept fictional systems of knowledge based on traditional but mistaken styles of learning. Bacon identifies and criticizes three systems of scientific knowledge in particular. The 'Sophistical system of philosophy', prevalent among what he calls the 'Rational School of philosophers', is based upon a weak empirical foundation: rational philosophers, such as → **Aristotle**, too hastily leave the realm of experience without duly ascertaining and diligently examining its data. 'The Empirical system of philosophy' is based on an empirical foundation that is too narrow: empirical philosophers duly ascertain and diligently examine empirical data, although the data examined are of insufficient quantity and quality. 'The Superstitious system of philosophy' is constructed through a mixture of philosophy with theology and traditions.

The *Great Instauration* requires that these idols be recognized and eradicated. In addition, it requires a new method through which it is possible to interpret, as opposed to anticipate, nature. In Book II of the *New Organon*, Bacon presents the method of what he calls 'true induction'.[4]

Figuring prominently in this method are 'illuminating experiments' (*experimenta lucifera*). Illuminating experiments are distinguished from 'fruit-bearing experiments'. The purpose of the latter is practical: to use nature for human ends. By contrast, the purpose of illuminating experiments is theoretical, namely to provide the critical instance or facts necessary to decisively decide between equally plausible hypotheses. Hence, they should be conducted at theoretical crossroads where the correct path is indeterminate.

As a lifelong student of natural philosophy, and one who owned a copy of the *New Organon*, Kant was no doubt familiar with the aim and method of Bacon's *Great Instauration*. To be sure, Kant's aim in **CPR** is unmistakably Baconian; its motto (Bii), which draws explicit attention to a new beginning in scientific inquiry, is taken from the Preface to the *New Organon*.

What is more, Kant's method in the same way 'imitates' Bacon's new scientific method. Kant undertakes an 'illuminating experiment', presented in the Antinomy of Pure Reason in **CPR**, in order to establish the facts necessary to decisively determine the correctness of the doctrine of transcendental idealism over against the doctrine of transcendental realism. This is the experiment of pure reason that Kant first introduces in his preface to the second edition of **CPR**. – BFS

FURTHER READING

S.-H. Kim, *Bacon und Kant* (Berlin/New York: de Gruyter, 2008).

BAUMGARTEN, ALEXANDER GOTTLIEB

Alexander Gottlieb Baumgarten was born in Berlin on 17 July 1714. He was educated in Berlin by Martin Georg Christgau, who taught him Hebrew and Latin poetry. In 1727 he moved to Halle an der Saale to study at the Waisenhaus under the direction of the Pietist pedagogue August Hermann Francke. In 1730, Baumgarten was enrolled in the University of Halle, where he studied theology and fine arts. During his university years, he became acquainted with Wolffian philosophy (→ **Wolff**), of which he was an original interpreter, but not a follower, for all of his life. He died on 26 May 1762.

With his *Meditationes philosophicae de nonnullis ad poema pertinentibus* (1735), Baumgarten founded a new philosophical discipline of aesthetics as the science of sensible knowledge. In 1739, he published his *Metaphysica*, which made him, at least according to Kant, the 'deepest' metaphysician of his time. He also published the *Aesthetica* in 1750, the *Initia philosophiae practicae primae* in 1760, and the *Acroasis logica* in 1761.

Baumgarten is probably the philosopher who had the single biggest influence on Kant, who for more than 40 years used his handbooks for his lectures on metaphysics, ethics and anthropology. Baumgarten's influence is particularly evident in Kant's metaphysical and aesthetic terminology.

A first impact of Baumgarten's terminology can be found in **ND**, from 1755, when Kant deals with the problem of existence and essence (**ND** 76). Kant criticizes Baumgarten's notion of 'existence' because it is not distinguishable from the concept of the 'possible', being the complement of essence according to all internal possibilities. Kant states that for existence not only all internal possibilities are necessary but also all the external ones, namely relations. In Baumgarten, the determination of all internal and external possibilities is the *omnimoda determinatio*, which corresponds to Kant's notion of individual existence.[5] Also **NM** shows Baumgarten's influence in the use of the concepts of '*something*' as equivalent to '*cogitabile*' and '*nihil negativum*' as '*irrepraesentabile*' (**NM** 171–172).

Kant recurs to this terminology in **CPR** when he defines the concepts of 'something' and 'nothing', which is based on §7 of Baumgarten's *Metaphysica*:

> The highest concept with which one is accustomed to begin a transcendental philosophy is usually the division between the possible and the impossible. But since every division presupposes a concept that is to be divided, a still higher one must be given, and this is the concept of an object in general (taken problematically, leaving undecided whether it is something or nothing). (A290=B346)

What probably had the greatest influence on Kant in the field of metaphysics is Baumgarten's doctrine of transcendentals. Baumgarten is the first prior to Kant to characterize the concept of 'transcendental' as 'logical' and 'essential' in opposition to the 'metaphysical' as 'real'.[6] In fact, in the Wolffian tradition, 'transcendental' was synonymous with 'metaphysical', and also Kant first used the term in this sense in the 1750s and in the early 1760s. But from the mid-1760s, Kant sharply distinguishes the 'logical' and 'transcendental' from the 'metaphysical' and the 'real', following Baumgarten's distinction, as is evidenced by, for example, **Refl 3765**. In the same note, Kant also associates 'the transcendental unity' with the thought that 'everything is not many [*ein iedes Ding ist nicht viel*]', which coincides with Baumgarten's definition of '*unicum transcendentale*'. Last but not least, in his *Acroasis logica*, Baumgarten used the concept of '*transcendentalis*' to denote the higher concepts which contained under them other concepts, similar to the way in which Kant defines the categories as the higher pure concepts of the understanding in **CPR**. Baumgarten was the first eighteenth-century philosopher before Kant to use the expression 'transcendental concept'.

Kant is also very close to Baumgarten in using the notion of spontaneity in the practical field in connection with the manifold meanings of freedom. According to Baumgarten, spontaneity is the capacity of self-determination according to an inner principle of the agent. Spontaneity differs from 'choice' (*arbitrium*), even if the latter is based on the former, for choice is the faculty to choose whether to follow the inner desire or not.

There are two kinds of *arbitrium*: (1) *arbitrium sensitivum* and (2) *liberum arbitrium*. The difference between the two conceptions of *arbitrium* consists in the different kinds of desire that determine actions. In cases where the inner desire is sensible, *arbitrium* is *sensitivum*, while in cases where it is rational, the *arbitrium* is *liberum*. Only in the latter sense, according to Baumgarten, is it possible to talk of *libertas* or *libertas moralis* proper.[7]

Kant is concerned with this problem in many places in **CPR**, **CPrR** and in several lecture notes. In **CPR** (A534=B562), Kant writes that a will, which is affected by sensible

representations, is *arbitrium sensitivum*, which is typical of higher animals. The human being's power of choice, insofar as they are rational beings, is *arbitrium liberum*, namely moral freedom or the faculty to act by means of mere reason, for freedom from sensibility does not necessarily imply an immediate reaction.

Also remarkable is the impact of Baumgarten's aesthetics on Kant. In **CPR** (A21=B35–36), Kant states that the Germans are the only people who use the word 'aesthetics' to designate what others call the critique of taste. Kant suggests to stop using this new name 'aesthetics' in the sense of a critique of taste, and to reserve the name 'aesthetics' for the doctrine of sensible cognition, following Baumgarten's suggestion. In this sense, aesthetics would have been a part of transcendental philosophy as well as of psychology.

Of course, Kant's transcendental aesthetics has nothing to do with Baumgarten, but the aesthetics of **CJ** seems to share some of his basic assumptions. First and foremost, for both Baumgarten and Kant aesthetics has the task to compensate for the limits of intellectual a priori knowledge, expanding knowledge to the cognition of the empirical and singular facts. Second, Kant takes from Baumgarten some key doctrines of his psychological aesthetics such as the distinction between an aesthetic judgment and an intellectual judgment, between the judgment of taste and the judgment of the agreeable and the disagreeable, between the universal *in concreto* and the universal *in abstracto*. – MS

FURTHER READING

K. Ameriks, 'The critique of metaphysics: Kant and traditional ontology', P. Guyer (ed.), *The Cambridge Companion to Kant* (Cambridge: Cambridge University Press, 1992), pp. 249–279.

A. Nuzzo, 'Kant and Herder on Baumgarten's *Aesthetica*', *Journal of the History of Philosophy* 44,4 (2006): 577–597.

E. Watkins (ed.), *Kant's Critique of Pure Reason. Background Source Materials* (Cambridge: Cambridge University Press, 2009), ch. 3.

CICERO, MARCUS TULLIUS

In view of the fact that the young Kant found himself strongly attracted to philology and Latin literature,[8] it is not surprising that his later moral philosophy is strongly influenced by Stoic ethics. In this respect, however, Seneca seems to have been a more important influence and source for Kant than Cicero, whom he considered a Stoic philosopher with regard to his moral philosophy, but more of a Platonist (→ **Plato**) with regard to his speculative philosophy (**JL** 31).

It is difficult to gauge Kant's assessment of Cicero exactly for a number of reasons. First, the capacity to distinguish accurately between Stoic doctrines original to Cicero, on the one hand, and doctrines which formed part of a common Stoic world view and could have been found by Cicero in Stoic handbooks and other sources, on the other, obviously presupposes highly developed philological skills. And Kant did not possess these skills. His training in ancient philosophy and literature had rather focused on the literary technique of the classical, i.e. Latin authors, and on their imitation, which in spite of his own vigorous critique of this attitude, Kant himself never left behind. For this reason, he actually never undertook a thorough systematic interpretation of any Stoic doctrine.

Secondly, it is not clear to what extent Kant was familiar with Cicero's writings. It is known that the study of Cicero's Letters, his Speeches and his dialogue *On Duties* formed part of Kant's education, but an edition of Cicero has not been found in his library. Moreover, *On Duties* does not deal with the themes of Stoic ethics which interested Kant in particular;[9] and again, it is doubtful whether the Stoic doctrines it presents are particular to Cicero or rather derive from the Stoic philosopher Panaetius.

On the basis of his mature writings, it becomes clear too that Kant was familiar with Cicero's *On the Ends of Good and Evil*.[10] Although this work is strongly influenced by the older Academy and the Peripatetic School, its fifth book, albeit inconclusive in its final position, most likely presents Cicero's own doctrine of virtue and of the highest good, but whether Kant was aware of this is doubtful.

Thirdly, Kant rarely quotes or refers to ancient authors, and when he does, he usually renders them imprecisely or erroneously.

It is certain though that Cicero exerted a decisive influence on Kant in a crucial stage of his philosophical development. In 1779, a reform of the Prussian (→ **Prussia**) educational system, in particular of the grammar schools, was proclaimed by the Minister of Education Karl Abraham von Zedlitz. Kant was of course familiar with the agenda of this reform, which intended to encourage the study of Plato and Latin writers and philosophers, and in addition to this to make the relevant writings available in German translation. One of the results of the latter objective was Christian Garve's translation of and commentary on Cicero's *De officiis*, published in 1783.[11]

Probably incited by Garve's derogatory review of his own **CPR** (→ **Garve-Feder review**), Kant wrote an extensive counter-review of Garve's book. This review was the basis for what eventually became Kant's **G** (1785).[12] Although **G** does not mention

Cicero by name, it aims to provide 'a decisive alternative' to Garve's ethics as well as to the ethics of Cicero as defended by Garve.[13] Kant's main objection to Cicero's concept of duty targets the position of Cicero and Garve that the duties of man follow from his nature, as nature provides man with reason, and that therefore man ought to follow nature in order to act morally. For both Cicero and Garve, this nature is affected by and has an effect on our social environment and social character. Kant rejects this view, for the duties of man, as citizens of the world (*Weltbürger*), must be universal and cannot be measured by the standard of our social nature. – EOO

FURTHER READING

U. Santoski, *Die Bedeutung antiker Theorien für die Genese und Systematik von Kants Philosophie* (Berlin/New York: de Gruyter, 2006).

CRUSIUS, CHRISTIAN AUGUST

In the middle of the eighteenth century Christian August Crusius (1715–1775) was the most important opponent of Christian → Wolff. Rather than opposing elements in Wolff's system, as many others did, Crusius established an entire system opposed to the Wolffian one. The main elements of this system were already present in Crusius' philosophical dissertations (published between 1739 and 1742).[14]

In general, Crusius was critical of the Wolffian rationalist pretensions and instead recognized and investigated the limitations of human understanding. He opposed the use of the mathematical method in philosophy, and rejected the ontological proof for the existence of God. In all these points, Kant was very much in the Crusian league from the

1760s onwards, although Kant never explicitly engaged with Crusius on these issues. He did so, however, with respect to his thoughts on the first principles of cognition.

Crusius presented a view of the supreme principles of human cognition that differed substantially from the standard Wolffian conception. He denied that the principle of contradiction forms the *single* supreme principle, and claimed that there are in fact three: the principle of contradiction, the principle of the inseparable ('what cannot be thought without each other cannot be without each other') and the principle of the uncombinable ('what cannot be thought with and next to each other cannot be with and next to each other').[15] The latter two principles, he argued, are characteristic of *human* understanding, and we need them to explain the truth of many cognitions. The principle of contradiction on its own, therefore, does not suffice for human cognition.

Regarding Wolff's principle of sufficient ground Crusius was equally critical. Crusius rejected its derivation from the principle of contradiction, and argued that it is merely a corollary of the principle of the inseparable.

Crusius' thought was very important for the development of Kant's views, especially in the pre-Critical period. In ND, Kant inclines to a Crusian position in his attacks on the Leibnizian-Wolffian interpretation of especially the principle of sufficient ground. Like Crusius, he does not consider the principle of contradiction to be the one supreme principle of cognition. Moreover, he repeats Crusius' criticism of the ambiguity of Wolff's term 'sufficient ground', preferring the term 'determining ground' instead – according to both a ground can be *sufficient* for many consequences, but it can be *determinate* for only one, as determinacy excludes the opposite of the consequence. Finally, like Crusius, he rejects both the derivation of the principle of determinate ground from the principle of contradiction and the unlimited application of the former – for Kant God's existence has no determining ground, as he exists absolutely necessarily.

However, Kant is critical of Crusius as well, as he rejects his arguments that free acts cannot have a determining ground; rather, he argues, they have their determining ground in the inclination of our conscious or unconscious desires and volitions. This does not deprive actions of their freedom, because the determining grounds are not external to the inclinations of the subject.

Later, in the Prize Essay (Inq), written in 1762, Kant still praises Crusius for noting that human cognition not only needs formal principles, but also material ones. These material principles are a number of propositions that Crusius derived from the nature of the understanding by means of the principles of the inseparable and the uncombinable, such as 'every substance is somewhere' and 'everything that comes to be, comes to be by a sufficient cause'.[16]

Although Kant is critical of the specific material principles that he brings forward, Crusius' idea that much of our cognition cannot be derived from the principle of contradiction alone but needs further principles was very important for the development of Kant's notion of synthetic a priori principles: shortly after writing the Prize Essay, Kant discovered the distinction between analytic and synthetic judgments. For this reason, some scholars, most notably L. W. Beck,[17] have suggested that Kant might have credited his awakening from his dogmatic slumber to Crusius just as well as to → Hume. Kant himself acknowledges a link to Crusius in Disc 245–246, but qualifies it by noting that Crusius only referred to the proof of certain metaphysical propositions without

offering a general treatment of the synthetic a priori.

In a 1789 letter to Reinhold (Corr-II 41), Kant expresses what can be considered his main criticism of Crusius, namely that he took a merely subjective necessity, arising from the incapability to think things differently, for an objective necessity. In the end, therefore, Kant could not agree with Crusius, but this cannot obliterate the important role Crusius played in his philosophical development. – JZ

FURTHER READING

H. Allison, 'Kant on freedom of the will', in P. Guyer (ed.), *The Cambridge Companion to Kant and Modern Philosophy* (Cambridge: Cambridge University Press, 2006), pp. 381–415.

E. Watkins, *Kant and the Metaphysics of Causality* (Cambridge: Cambridge University Press, 2005).

E. Watkins (ed.), *Kant's Critique of Pure Reason. Background Source Materials* (Cambridge: Cambridge University Press, 2009), ch. 4.

DESCARTES, RENÉ

Descartes' and Kant's philosophical projects are both very similar and very different. René Descartes (1596–1650) is often called the father of modern philosophy and undoubtedly one aspect of their connection is the idea that knowledge cannot be taken to simply arise from mere beliefs, assertions or sense impressions. Beliefs must be rationally justified for them to yield knowledge.

Descartes thought that only by pursuing a methodical inquiry into the foundations of truth could metaphysics be scientific in the same way that mathematics is. The classical formulation of his manner of investigating can be found in Descartes' *Discourse on Method* (1637), where he presents four rules always to abide by in one's investigations, the first of which – 'never to accept anything as true which I do not evidently know as being true' (AT VI, 18)[18] – was later, at the start of the Third Meditation of his *Meditations on First Philosophy* (1641), advanced as the succinct principle 'everything is true which I perceive very clearly and distinctly' (AT VII, 35). The work that Descartes undertook in the *Meditations* to apply the rigorous method he introduced in the *Discourse* amounted to providing a solid and universally valid foundation – in the words of the *Discourse*, 'the rock or loam' (AT VI, 29) – for the possibility of having certain knowledge of oneself as well as the world of objects around one.

The methodical character of Descartes' investigations in the *Meditations*, which progressively leads to the certainty of the cogito, the proof of God's existence and thence a justification of the propositions of our common knowledge, corresponds to the way that Kant considered **CPR** to be a 'treatise on the method' (Bxxii) of metaphysics, and that its 'synthetic method' (P 263) should provide metaphysics with a firm scientific footing. This concerns the crucial epistemological role of the subject in both their accounts. Kant writes, right after the above-quoted remark on method in the B-preface, that 'pure speculative reason [. . .] should measure its own capacity according to the different ways for choosing the objects of its thinking, [. . .] because [. . .] in *a priori* cognition nothing can be ascribed to the objects except what the thinking subject takes out of itself [. . .]', as a result of which metaphysics, like logic, 'has the rare good fortune' to be able to provide a systematic and complete foundation 'since

it has to do solely with principles' whose use is also determined by those same principles (Bxxii–xxiv).

The systematicity of metaphysics is thus intimately related to the self-reflective capacity of reason itself. The striking respect in which Descartes' procedure is similar to Kant's is that a particular mode of self-reflection or self-knowledge functions as the model for knowledge. For both, the reflecting cogito is central to the main argument concerning the possibility of foundational, or, rational knowledge.[19]

Of course, there are major differences between Descartes and Kant. One major difference concerns the way in which their very methods are de facto employed, which informs the manner in which the cogito functions in their respective arguments for the foundation of possible knowledge.[20] It is clear that Descartes' procedure is based on a radical form of scepticism, which however is more appropriately characterized as a method of unbending doubt.[21] Descartes exercises this doubt, not like 'the skeptics, who doubt purely for the sake of doubting' (AT VI, 29), but with a view to achieving certainty. By contrast, while some of Kant's arguments can plausibly be reconstructed as modes of argumentation by reductio,[22] Kant is rather unconcerned by sceptical challenges, insofar as he does not think that a knock-down argument against the sceptic would be the only viable and interesting philosophical demonstration of the possibility of knowledge. It is safe to say that the challenge of scepticism does not especially inform the main arguments of **CPR** and it is evident that the Transcendental Deduction of the categories, arguably the centrepiece of **CPR**, neither is anti-sceptical nor proceeds by means of methodical sceptical doubt as with Descartes.

This difference is reflected precisely in what their argumentations have in common, namely the central position of the cogito[23] in the deduction of knowledge. The Kantian 'I think' is only a formal representation that conveys the idea that what is called 'a higher unity' provides 'the ground of the unity of different concepts in judgments' (B131). In some sense, the Kantian 'I think' functions as the premise of the deductive argument, especially in its B-edition form, which by means of a step-by-step procedure leads to the conclusion of the synthetic a priori, that is, the applicability of the set of categories as the necessary conditions of any experience. The unity of apperception or 'I think' is the vehicle of reasoning, as it were, throughout the argumentation of the Deduction.

The order of reasoning in Kant's Deduction, then, appears different from that of Descartes' in the *Meditations*, as the cogito there does not feature as the premise with which Descartes' argument starts out, but rather only emerges as a preliminary conclusion at the end of a set of arguments.

Kant does not mention Descartes a lot in his published work.[24] The most important instance where Kant discusses Descartes is, apart from the Refutation of Idealism in the B-edition, in the context of rational psychology, that is, in the first-edition Paralogisms in **CPR** (A366ff.) and then again in a well-known note in the B-edition of the Paralogisms.

At A366ff., at the start of the Fourth Paralogism concerning the relation of the subject to outer objects, Kant criticizes Descartes' dualist position regarding the relation between consciousness and external appearances, the knowledge of which the problematic idealist, i.e. Descartes, only thinks possible through causal inference and hence vulnerable to doubt (this is argued by Descartes in the Third Meditation). Kant attacks the view that the consciousness of oneself would be more immediate than the perception of external objects.

Herewith, Kant appears to attack the very method of Descartes' radical doubt, or at least Descartes' procedure after having established the cogito and the *clare & distincte* principle at the start of the Third Meditation. For Descartes seems to presuppose the possibility of having ideas of things that I judge to be outside me, which might not in fact be ideas that have objective reference and hence derive in fact from things outside me. This does not necessarily mean that Descartes doubts the global existence of external objects (he doesn't), but he does seem to assume the epistemically privileged position of the mind as having self-knowledge as opposed to knowledge of bodies (including one's own body). He does so, in fact, in the very position of the meditator who, at the start of his meditation, puts everything to doubt and thus achieves self-certainty as a first piece of knowledge. But is the taking up itself of the position of the universal, radical doubter, prior to arriving at any conclusions ensuing from the doubt procedure, not dependent on the assumption of at least one's own *existence* as part of the world?

This is related to Kant's most detailed discussion of Descartes' cogito in a footnote in the B-Paralogism at B422–423n. There, Kant appears to endorse the claim made by Descartes that my existence is entailed by the proposition 'I think'. In fact, Kant says, my existence is already contained in the 'I think' and need not be inferred from it as a conclusion from an inference involving a major premise. That is, according to Kant the supposed inference would be: (1) Everything which thinks exists; (2) I think; (3) therefore, I exist. Kant holds, to the contrary, that my existence is in fact identical with, and not inferred from, my thinking.

But this charge against Descartes is historically not pertinent as Descartes himself does not think that an inference is at issue, as is clear from his replies to certain of the objections from his famous readers. Rather, the indubitability of my existence is necessarily involved in my thinking as something that I do; the proposition *cogito ergo sum* is in fact not an inference, based on the application of a prior universal rule, but a performance by a particular thinker or meditator.[25]

However, Kant's main point in this footnote (and in the main text to which the footnote is appended) is that Descartes, like the other rational psychologists, seems to ignore the fact that, as the very proposition *cogito ergo sum* makes clear, a conception of the self as an object without any empirical 'material for thinking' (B423n.) provided is in fact impossible. It is thus clear that Kant takes aim at Descartes' quintessential idea that in the very thought that I have of myself as thinker I have determinate knowledge of myself as a *thing*, a *res cogitans*, which is absolutely distinguishable from my body or any *res extensa*. It is therefore not so much the formal structure and epistemic role of the Cartesian cogito that Kant objects to, but the metaphysical conclusions that apparently Descartes draws from it.

The only other place where Descartes is explicitly mentioned in **CPR** is towards the end of Kant's account of the ontological proof of the existence of God (A602=B630). Kant's criticism of Descartes in this respect is chiefly related to Descartes' belief that based on a definition of God as the most perfect being, existence cannot be denied of God on pain of contradiction, since necessarily existence is possessed by a most perfect being as a being that possesses all properties, including existence. Kant famously refutes this as he denies that existence is a real predicate,

although Kant's criticism in **CPR** is actually directed at arguments attempting to prove a highest being, rather than a most perfect being (cf. by contrast **OPD** 156). At any rate, according to Kant, one can perfectly conceive of God without thereby analytically implying his existence.

However, Descartes makes an important distinction between various applications of the concepts of existence and essence (AT VII, 68) that Kant does not appear to have noticed (but cf. A596=B624); in the case of God, existence and essence are indeed mutually implicative but in all other cases existence and essence do not coincide; therefore, according to Descartes not all things of which I have an idea thereby necessarily exist. – DS

FURTHER READING

J.-M. Beyssade, 'Descartes' "I am a thing that thinks" versus Kant's "I think"', in D. Garber, B. Longuenesse (eds), *Kant and the Early Moderns* (Princeton: Princeton University Press, 2008), pp. 32–40.

M. Fichant, J.-L. Marion (eds), *Descartes en Kant* (Paris: PUF, 2006).

B. Longuenesse, 'Kant's "I think" versus Descartes' "I am a thing that thinks"', in D. Garber, B. Longuenesse (eds), *Kant and the Early Moderns* (Princeton: Princeton University Press, 2008), pp. 9–31.

EPICURUS AND EPICUREANISM

The picture which eighteenth-century Germany formed of Epicureanism was not based on a direct study of the ancient sources, including texts of Epicurus, but appears rather to be influenced by the presence of Epicureanism in contemporary French philosophy and English → **empiricism**. On this narrow basis, Kant valued Epicureanism above all because of its philosophy of nature, whose main tenets consist in the doctrine of atomism and the assumption of an empty space or vacuum. According to Kant, the Epicureans 'were the *best natural philosophers* among all the thinkers of Greece' (**JL** 30). This judgment can be explained by Kant's approval of the exclusively mechanistic constitution of nature that Epicurus defended. Kant praises Epicurus for his rigorous or 'pure empiricism' (**A466=B494**). In particular, Kant praises Epicurus for having proceeded 'more consistently in accord with his sensual system (for in his inferences he never exceeded the bounds of experience) than Aristotle and Locke' (**A854=B882**).

On the other hand, though, Kant feels compelled to criticize the doctrine of Epicurean philosophy of nature that introduces the idea of an 'accidental generation'. Throughout his works, he criticizes the induction of a theory of well-structured and well-organized nature obeying mechanical or teleological laws of nature from the accidental nature of things as 'absurd [*ungereimt*]' (**CJ** 391) or even, in particular in his earlier works, as 'impertinent [*unverschämt*]' (**NH** 227). In **CJ**, Kant argues extensively against any form of *generatio aequivoca*, i.e. 'the generation of an organized being through the mechanism of crude, unorganized matter' (**CJ** 419n.). According to Kant, this Epicurean model of explanation ignores 'the difference between a technique of nature and mere mechanism' resulting in 'blind chance [being] assumed to be the explanation' of the agreement of nature with 'our concepts of ends' (**CJ** 393).

As to his practical philosophy, Kant defends Epicurus against the charge of upholding a mere hedonism. On several occasions, Kant calls Epicurus a man with a high moral sense and draws attention to the fact that the principle of his moral theory is not intended to determine moral action, but rather to explain it (**CPrR** 116). Epicurus is a 'virtuous' man with an 'ever-cheerful heart', according to one qualification of Epicurus' moral attitude that Kant repeats more than once (here **CPrR** 116 and **MM** 485). Kant, however, has problems with the Epicurean connection of virtue with happiness, for the notion of virtue seems to be implied in the Epicureans' promotion of the individual's happiness. Epicurean happiness consists in the enjoyment of a highest pleasure regardless of any moral consideration; the maximum of happiness a fortiori consists in the satisfaction of a maximum of needs. The one who is happy has thus succeeded in achieving the highest good. The principle of happiness pivotal to Epicurean ethics is therefore in Kant's eyes completely mistaken (**CPrR** 126) as striving for happiness does not bring about 'a ground for a virtuous disposition (*Gesinnung*)' (**CPrR** 114).[26]

But even though the Epicurean moral principle is erroneous in view of grounding a moral theory, it is true in view of morality in general and in agreement with certain tenets of anthropology. Kant describes the principle of Epicurean morality repeatedly as 'self-love' (*Selbstliebe*), which he also finds in Helvétius and Mandeville.[27] Self-love, however, is not to be mistaken for 'selfish love' (*Eigenliebe*), which excludes others, as Epicurean self-love is the ground for the love of others and thus increases our pleasure.[28] According to the table of the 'Practical Material Determining Grounds *in the principle of morality*' in **CPrR**, the determining factor of the will in Epicurean ethics is what Kant calls a 'physical feeling', i.e. it is 'subjective' and thus empirical and not capable of providing a universal moral principle (**CPrR** 40). – EOO

EULER, LEONHARD

Leonhard Euler (1707–1783) was a Swiss mathematician of great repute who profoundly influenced his discipline's development.[29] Euler made contributions to standard areas of mathematics like number theory, algebra, analysis and geometry. But he also explored new areas such as graph theory[30] and differential geometry. And his work in mechanics, optics and acoustics established him also as a foremost applied mathematician. Altogether, this amounts to making Euler the most prolific mathematician of all time, with over 800 papers to his name.

However, it is worth noting that Euler's education was wide-ranging, and he obtained a master's degree in philosophy before focusing his energies on the full-time study of mathematics.[31] Euler also gets involved in important philosophical discussions in the eighteenth century, chiefly to defend science or the Holy Scriptures against philosophical attacks.[32] He thus criticizes the prevalent Wolffian (→ Wolff) system of monadology,[33] in particular because the notion that division of matter can be completed with some elementary monads is inconsistent with the infinite divisibility of matter, an issue which Kant discusses in the Second Antinomy.

This issue is one facet of what Speiser describes as the 'Euler-Kantian question',[34] namely that of the impact of physics on metaphysics. The rationalist tradition which dominated the philosophical scene in the mid-eighteenth century in Germany had it that philosophy must start from secure first principles. Its progress, for Wolff, is then governed by the principles of deduction, in the manner of a geometric proof. Once this logical chain reached concrete principles, these would be confronted with experience. Such confrontation could lead

to the need to revise the results of mechanics or geometry.

→ Newton's method was to start rather from the phenomena and ascend from these to first principles, using mathematics.[35] In 1748, in his essay *Reflections on Space and Time*,[36] Euler defends this conception, and this clearly influenced Kant, who endorses this view at **NM 167–168**.[37]

Another area in which Euler's dissatisfaction with the prevalent Wolffian metaphysics influenced Kant's thinking, is the issue of the nature of space. Up to 1768, Kant's writings essentially defend a relational view of the nature of space, namely the view that space is constituted out of relations between physical objects.[38] In 1768, however, in an essay on incongruent counterparts (**DS 37**), Kant appears to acknowledge Euler's 1748 essay on space and time,[39] in which he argues for absolute space on the basis of Newton's laws of motion. Euler contends that the relational theory of space cannot account for the motion in a straight line of a body under inertia because such a fixed direction cannot be explained in terms of all the other moving bodies of the universe.[40] Euler here mistakenly assumes the relational theory to refer to relations of *actual* bodies,[41] but his reflections were to feed into Kant's arguments for absolute space.

Kant, however, does not fully endorse the Newtonian conception of absolute space adopted by Euler (**NM 378**). Kant's position on this issue becomes clearer in **ID 398**, where he first introduces the idea that space has independent reality as a form of sensible intuition. This move represents the first step towards the full-blown transcendental idealist view of Kant's Critical philosophy.

This transformation of Kant's thought goes well beyond Euler, but the latter's epistemological views on the idea of space can be seen as pointing in a Kantian direction. Euler argues that one can only have ideas such as that of space through reflection. His disagreement with Wolff on this issue is echoed by Kant describing the Leibnizian (→ Leibniz) conception of space as resulting from a 'deception of transcendental reflection' (A275=B331). Moreover, Euler also understands the privileged role of space and time as conditions of experience, but, unlike Kant, he does not conclude to their transcendental ideality.[42]

Finally, an important influence of Euler upon Kant's late views should be noted. This is found in his theory of aether. In **OP**, Kant explains the role of heat in phase changes between the solid, liquid and gaseous states of matter in terms of the penetration of matter by a 'universally distributed, continuous, space-filling, perpetually vibrating'[43] fluid which he refers to as the caloric (*Wärmestoff*). This, Kant identifies with Euler's light-aether (*pulsus Aetheris*) (**OP-I** 523). Insofar as this caloric is viewed by Kant as providing 'a material principle of the unity of possible experience' (**OP-I** 585), it illustrates how, even at this late stage, Euler's influence stretches to the heart of Kant's philosophical enterprise. – CO

FURTHER READING

E. Watkins (ed.), *Kant's Critique of Pure Reason. Background Source Materials* (Cambridge: Cambridge University Press, 2009), ch. 5.

HERZ, MARCUS

Marcus Herz (1747–1803) was born in Berlin as the son of a Sofer or Jewish scribe. In 1762, he was sent to → **Königsberg** in order to train for a mercantile career. In 1766, however, he enrolled in the medical faculty of the University of Königsberg, the only faculty allowing Jewish students. Soon he realized that for him medicine was not meant to be more than a source of income, as his heart lay with philosophy. In Königsberg, he attended the lectures of Kant, with whom he soon developed a close friendship. This is borne out by the fact that Kant appointed Herz to respond to his inaugural dissertation (**ID**), thus opposing the will of the philosophy department.

Shortly afterwards, Herz had to abandon his studies in Königsberg due to financial reasons. Accompanied by a letter of recommendation by Kant for Moses → **Mendelssohn**, Herz returned to Berlin. Mendelssohn received him very warmly and soon afterwards they became close friends. The influence of Mendelssohn on Herz's philosophical development was probably as important as that of Kant and prompted him to harmonize both their philosophical systems.[44] In 1774, Herz received the degree of doctor in medicine from the University of Halle. In 1786 (or 1787), he was awarded the title 'Professor' by the Prussian (→ **Prussia**) king, an exceptional distinction in view of the fact that Herz was Jewish. Apart from widely acknowledged treatises on medical issues,[45] he authored several influential philosophical essays.

His early *Betrachtungen aus der spekulativen Weltweisheit* (Königsberg, 1771) discussed Kant's **ID** and had a huge impact on the reception of **ID** and of Kant's early philosophy in general.[46] This book has the form of a series of letters of a friend of the Kantian philosophy, and is obviously extremely well informed about the development of Kant's philosophy in the second half of the 1760s. It is of great historical value because here Herz elaborates on issues and debates which had remained implicit in **ID** itself. Herz shows that he is thoroughly familiar with Kant's lectures, to which many passages make reference more or less directly. *Betrachtungen* also gives an indication of the growing influence of Mendelssohn on Herz, to whom in particular the proof for the existence of the soul and Herz's critical remarks on Kant's elaborations on the principle of contradiction are indebted. In spite of his high expectations of Herz's book, Kant was in the end not entirely pleased with it and repudiated its portrayal of his own **ID** as being 'not very fortunate in expressing its meaning'.[47] Undoubtedly, this criticism was also informed by Kant's growing critical distance towards his own **ID**.

Herz's second philosophical essay *Versuch über den Geschmack und die Ursachen seiner Verschiedenheit* (Mitau-Leipzig, 1776) deals with aesthetics, more in particular with the German *Sturm und Drang* poetry that is evaluated from the perspective of a psychology of the faculty of aesthetic judgments. From this perspective, *Sturm und Drang* is to be valued as a creative accomplishment but not as art, for art 'requires a proportionate use of more powers, precise knowledge of the world and of the human soul'.[48] Kant received the second edition (1790) of this essay and regretted not having received it before completing the manuscript of **CJ**, for otherwise he would certainly have made use of some of Herz's insights.[49]

Apart from some interruptions, Kant and Herz maintained a correspondence which lasted into the 1790s. Most important from a philosophical point of view however are the letters from the 1770s, which offer essential insights into the conceptual genesis of **CPR**.[50]

Yet, although, starting in the late 1770s, Herz held private lectures in Berlin on Kant's logic, psychology and anthropology – before a notable audience among whom there were the Prussian Minister of Culture Von Zedlitz, the later Friedrich Wilhelm III, the Humboldt

brothers, Schiller, Goethe, Schleiermacher, Friedrich Schlegel and others – he gradually came to realize he did not fully comprehend the implications of Kant's Critical writings, which, in a letter to Kant (**Corr-II** 14ff.), he effectively acknowledged upon receiving his copy of Kant's **CPrR**.

Also historically relevant is the fact that Herz brought Kant into contact with Salomon Maimon,[51] whose manuscript of the *Versuch über die Transscendentalphilosophie* (1790) he sent to Kant. – EOO

HUME, DAVID

David Hume (1711–1776) was a Scottish philosopher who proceeded to investigate human nature by means of experience and observation rather than by means of a priori reasoning. According to Hume, the perceptions of the mind consist in impressions and ideas. Hume distinguished between these not in terms of their content, but in terms of their force and vivacity. Impressions are 'all our more lively perceptions, when we hear, or see, or feel, or love, or hate, or desire, or will'[52] while ideas are 'the faint images of [impressions] in thinking and reasoning'.[53] Hume went on to formulate the thesis that 'all our ideas or more feeble perceptions are copies of our impressions or more lively ones' (EHU 2.5).

Hume's copy thesis became a powerful tool in his investigation of the main concepts of metaphysics – concepts such as existence, substance, the self and causation.

In the case of the idea of the self, Hume used his copy thesis to argue against the Cartesian (→ **Descartes**) idea of the self as being a simple continuous substance. He argued that there is no impression that continues 'invariably the same, thro' the whole course of our lives' that could serve as the basis of the Cartesian idea of the self (T 1.4.6.2). Each of us is literally 'nothing but a bundle or collection of different perceptions, which succeed each other with an inconceivable rapidity and are in a perpetual flux and movement' (T 1.4.6.4). In turn, Hume argued, the identity we ascribe to this bundle of perceptions is a fiction produced by the imagination (T 1.4.6.15).

In tracing the idea of causation to its origin, Hume began by arguing that it must be derived from some relation among objects (rather than from some quality of objects). The three relations involved are contiguity, priority, and necessary connection. Necessary connection is the most important of these relations, and Hume traced the idea of necessary connection not to the objects or events themselves, but to a *feeling* that arises in the mind only through repeated experience. Hume argued that no impression of necessary connection can be found when we experience a single instance in which two objects are supposed to have a necessary connection (T 1.3.14, EHU 7.1). After repeatedly experiencing objects of the same sort being conjoined in the same way, however, 'the mind is carried by habit, upon the appearance of one event, to expect its usual attendant, and to believe that it will exist' (EHU 7.2.3). It is 'this customary transition of the imagination from one object to its usual attendant [that] is the sentiment or impression, from which we form the idea of power or necessary connexion' (EHU 7.2.3).

Hume further utilized his division of the perceptions of the mind into impressions and ideas to argue against the position that the foundation of our moral distinctions (good, evil, right, wrong, etc.) 'is nothing but a conformity to reason' (T 3.1.1.4). Hume argued that although through reason we discover truths about objects or ideas, reason by itself does not have an effect on either our passions

or our will (T 2.2.2 & 3.1.1). Moral distinctions, however, do have an effect on our passions and will – that is, '[m]orals excite passions, and produce or prevent actions' (T 3.1.1.6), so they must be grounded in something more than just reason. That something more is feeling or sentiment. In *An Enquiry Concerning the Principles of Morals* (1751), Hume wrote: 'This sentiment can be no other than a feeling for the happiness of mankind, and a resentment of their misery.'[54]

In Hume's epistemology, sentiment or feeling continued to play a central role. According to Hume, belief does not involve a difference in the content of an idea, but 'belief consists merely in a certain feeling or sentiment' (T App 2). 'An idea assented to *feels* different from a fictitious idea' (T 1.3.7.7). Ideas believed have 'an additional force and vivacity' (T 1.3.7.5) that has been transferred from impressions to ideas by means of custom. As a result, 'belief is more properly an act of the sensitive, than of the cogitative part of our natures' (T 1.4.1.8). Hume extended this conclusion beyond belief to probable reasonings. Hume claimed that 'all probable reasoning is nothing but a species of sensation. 'Tis not solely in poetry and music, we must follow our taste and sentiment, but likewise in philosophy' (T 1.3.8.12). In the *Treatise*, but not in the *Enquiry*, Hume even extended this to geometry, because, unlike arithmetic and algebra, geometry's 'first principles are still drawn from the general appearance of the objects' (T 1.3.1.4 see also T 1.2.417ff.). Hume did, however, distinguish knowledge from probability, but he also famously argued that 'all knowledge degenerates into probability' (T 1.4.1.1). Hume did not, however, repeat this argument in the *Enquiry*, where he drew the distinction between Relations of Ideas and Matters of Fact. There Hume wrote that relations of ideas, which include arithmetic, algebra *and* geometry, 'are discoverable by the mere operation of thought' (EHU 4.1.1).

Kant famously wrote that 'the remembrance of *David Hume* was the very thing that many years ago first interrupted my dogmatic slumber and gave a completely different direction to my researches in the field of speculative philosophy' (**P** 260). Although Kant's critique of Hume's position on causation gets the most attention, Kant also clearly responded to Hume's positions in other areas of metaphysics as well as epistemology, moral theory and aesthetics. German translations of Hume's two Enquiries became available in 1755. Although a translation of the conclusion to Book I of Hume's *Treatise* was published in the *Königsberger Zeitung* in 1771, a full translation of the *Treatise* wasn't published until 1790. Hume's views would also have been available to Kant at least through a 1772 translation of Beattie's *Essay on the Nature and Immutability of Truth* (1770) and Johann → **Tetens'** *Philosophische Versuche über die menschliche Natur und ihre Entwickelung* (1777). – SB

FURTHER READING

H. Allison, *Custom and Reason in Hume: A Kantian Reading of the First Book of the Treatise* (Oxford: Oxford University Press, 2008).

S. M. Bayne, *Kant on Causation: On the Fivefold Routes to the Principle of Causation* (Albany, NY: SUNY Press, 2004).

P. Guyer, *Knowledge, Reason and Taste: Kant's Response to Hume* (Princeton: Princeton University Press, 2008).

P. Kitcher, *Kant's Transcendental Psychology* (New York: Oxford University Press, 1990), esp. ch. 4.

M. Kuehn, 'Kant's conception of 'Hume's problem', *Journal of the History of Philosophy* 21 (1983): 175–193.

LEIBNIZ, GOTTLOB WILHELM

Leibniz (1646–1716) never published a treatise in which he systematically revealed all the details of his philosophical positions, and perhaps more importantly, many of his important writings were not published until after the eighteenth century. From the texts that would have been available to Kant, however, it is clear that Leibniz believed that reality is composed of simple substances that are unities.[55] This led to his rejection of the Cartesian (→ **Descartes**) notion of material substance, because Leibniz 'perceived that it is impossible to find *the principles of a true unity* in matter alone, or in what is only passive'.[56]

As a result, Leibniz held that we must think of these simple substances 'on the model of the notion we have of *souls*'.[57] These simple substances (or monads) therefore are capable of action and have perception and appetite.[58] It is only in terms of these internal characteristics that one monad is different from any other – Leibniz held that 'there are never two beings in nature that are perfectly alike, two beings in which it is not possible to discover an internal difference'.[59]

Whereas monads are simple unities, bodies are composites or aggregates – composed of, or grounded in, an infinity of monads.[60] As 'entities of aggregation' the unity bodies have 'is a mental one, and consequently their very being is also in a way mental, or phenomenal, like that of the rainbow'.[61]

Additionally, Leibniz held that given the Cartesian notion of a substance as 'a thing which exists in such a way as to depend on no other thing for its existence'[62] then there is no way to consistently explain 'how one substance can communicate with another created substance'.[63] Leibniz rejected the Spinozistic (→ **Spinoza**) single substance solution because it would ultimately entail that there is no human freedom,[64] and he rejected Malebranche's occasionalist solution because rather than providing an explanation, it simply amounts to an appeal to miracles.[65] Instead, Leibniz developed his view of pre-established harmony – holding that 'God originally created the soul (and any other real unity) in such a way that everything must arise for it from its own depths [*fonds*], through a perfect *spontaneity* relative to itself, and yet with a perfect *conformity* relative to external things'.[66] As a result, God 'brings it about that each simple substance has relations that express all the others, and consequently, that each simple substance is a perpetual, living mirror of the universe'.[67]

Although each simple substance 'represents the universe from its own point of view'[68], finite substances do so only confusedly.[69] All substances have an infinity of perceptions, but for finite substances, 'at every moment there is in us an infinity of perceptions, unaccompanied by awareness or reflection'.[70] Nevertheless, just as the noise of an individual wave contributes to the roar of the sea, each of these minute perceptions 'makes itself known only when combined confusedly with all the others'.[71]

According to Leibniz, however, some substances perceive things more or less distinctly than others. The perceptions of bare monads are not 'sufficiently distinct to be remembered'.[72] Souls (e.g. animals) have sensations – that is, they are substances 'where perception is more distinct and accompanied by memory'.[73] Finally, minds have reason, which enables them to have knowledge of necessary truths and to be capable of self-reflection.[74] Leibniz goes on to say that the reasonings of finite minds 'are based on *two great principles, that of contradiction* [. . .]

[*a*]*nd that of sufficient reason*'.[75] These in turn, Leibniz used to ground the distinction between necessary and contingent truths – that is, truths of reason and truths of fact.[76]

In his correspondence with Clarke, Leibniz also used the principle of sufficient reason to argue for his principle of the identity of indiscernibles,[77] and in turn used the principle of sufficient reason and the principle of the identity of indiscernibles to argue against the Newtonian theory of absolute space and in favour of a relational theory of space.[78]

Although Kant did famously write that 'the *Critique of Pure Reason* might well be the true apology for Leibniz' (**Disc** 250), in the Critical period Kant consistently criticized the main Leibnizian positions mentioned above. According to Kant, Leibniz's monadology, pre-established harmony, principle of sufficient reason, principle of the identity of indiscernibles, and his relational theory of space all revealed errors that could be attributed to a single root cause, namely, Leibniz's failure to recognize that understanding and sensibility are entirely distinct sources of cognitive content, both of which are essential for cognition.[79] As a result of this root error, 'Leibniz constructed an *intellectual system of the world*' (A270=B326) in which he 'compared all things with each other solely through concepts' (A270=B326), and intuition was 'intellectualized, i.e. transformed into mere confused concepts' (**PE** 282). – SB

FURTHER READING

A. Jauernig, 'Kant, the Leibnizians, and Leibniz', in B. Look (ed.), *The Continuum Companion to Leibniz* (London/New York: Continuum, 2011), pp. 289–309.

J. Mittelstraß, *Leibniz und Kant. Erkenntnistheoretische Studien* (Berlin/New York: de Gruyter, 2011).

LOCKE, JOHN

John Locke's influence on Kant is considerable, if not wholly direct. It is probable that most of Kant's knowledge of Locke was derived from → **Leibniz**'s *New Essays* or from → **Tetens**' work. Many of Kant's endeavours during the Critical period can be seen as being opposed to what he saw as a pervasive kind of 'transcendental realism' in philosophy, which, very briefly, is the metaphysical and epistemological position which claims that knowledge of objects in space can only be gained through some kind of direct contact of the mind with the things in themselves. In effect, transcendental realism is the position that tries to establish that knowledge of things in themselves *is* possible for finite human beings. Kant was keen to distance himself from all varieties of transcendental realism, and there is no doubt that he thought that Locke's *Essay Concerning Human Understanding* was a special case of the latter kind of philosophy.

Evidence of Kant's mistrust of Locke's philosophy can be gained by what he says in **CPR** concerning Locke's attempt to sensualize all concepts of the understanding (A271=B327), and when he refers to Locke as one who 'followed [Aristotle]' (A854=B882), thus linking Locke with the empiricist tradition. Kant has further reservations about Locke due to the fact that the latter seeks to derive pure concepts from experience alone. Not being content with this alone, Locke (according to Kant) goes even further, attempting to prove the existence of God and the immortality of the soul with an unerring mathematical precision (A854–855=B882–883).

Locke's denial of innate principles and innate ideas is interesting when contrasted with Kant's treatment of the same topic.

Kant's attitude towards innate ide plicated due to the fact that he rejects the claim of the rationalists, which is that certain kinds of clear and distinct ideas are bequeathed to us prior to experience. Kant seems to endorse a quasi-empiricist position at the start of **CPR** when he claims that 'all our cognition begins with experience' (B1). This Lockean sounding claim must be read in conjunction with what Kant goes on to say further on in the same passage, where he adds the proviso that not all knowledge actually arises through experience. What is clear from this, contrary to Locke's doctrine that all ideas can be traced back to a sensory source, is that Kant contends that the pure concepts of experience, as well as the pure forms of intuition, cannot be abstracted from any sensory source at all.

Locke's theory of space and time tends to receive little attention generally due to the immense importance of Kant's subsequent thinking on this subject. Locke thought that space was a simple idea given to us directly through experience of various kinds of distances, which are suggested to the mind. Such distances are perceived either between objects or within the internal space of the objects themselves. Our idea of time is more complicated, due to the fact that Locke defined time as a simple mode of our idea of duration. Various distances can be observed by reflecting on our internal sequence of ideas, which Locke calls succession. It is these various internal distances observed by the mind that Locke calls time. Kant keeps to Locke's basic distinction of viewing space as an external sense, whereas time is an inner sense.

Kant's major difficulty with Locke's theory of space and time really lies in the fact that, for the latter, these ideas are thought to be abstracted from experience. For Kant, space and time are the forms of our having an experience of objects at all. As forms of a priori intuition, they precede and make possible our knowledge of objects.

Another key area of interest for Kant, as far as Locke's philosophy is concerned, is the way in which we are led to an understanding of substance. Locke viewed our idea of substances of natural kinds of things as complex ideas compounded out of various simple ideas. Particular substances, for Locke, are products of the mind's acts of combining ideas into sorts of things; the 'species idea' is nothing but the abstracted idea of a combination of ideas which nominally agree with those qualities in things appearing in the world over time.

Kant's method diverges drastically from Locke's abstractive method, which becomes clear when we see that Kant instates the pure concept of 'inherence and subsistence' or 'substance' as well as the accompanying categorical form of judgment into the human understanding. Although the pure concept of substance is not an innate idea, according to Kant, it nevertheless can be classed as a kind of non-representational ground of our experience of things which appear in the world. So, whereas our idea of substance for Locke is and can only be a nominal kind, for Kant it acts as a pure concept that conditions our knowledge of appearances of the form of substance and accident, such that our appearances will conform to the conceptual structure of our understanding.

Kant cites Locke in **CPR** a number of times. Perhaps the most important section where Locke appears is the aforementioned note to the section Amphiboly of Concepts of Reflection (A260–A292=B316–B349). Kant refers to Locke's → **empiricism** as 'noogony', which, as a form of 'sensualism', is contrasted with Leibniz's intellectually motivated epistemology. Kant makes the pointed remark that both Locke and Leibniz failed to separate the understanding from sensibility, which led Locke to seek knowledge of things in the sensibility alone, while Leibniz was led to seek knowledge of things in the intellect alone. – NH

MEIER, GEORG FRIEDRICH

Georg Friedrich Meier was born in Ammendorf near Halle on 29 March 1718. During his youth, he was educated in a Pietist (→ **Pietism**) milieu and in 1730 he enrolled at the University of Halle, even though he only began his studies in 1735, finishing them in 1739. He started teaching at Halle in the Fall semester of 1739/40 as a *Privatdozent*, from 1746 to 1748 as an Extraordinary Professor and from 1748 to 1777 as Full Professor.

In 1754, he was ordered by Frederick William II (→ **Frederick the Great**) to teach John → **Locke**'s *Essay Concerning Human Understanding*, which Meier promptly did as is evidenced by his *Collegium über Locks Versuch vom menschlichen Verstande*. However, Meier spent all of his life commenting and writing companions on Christian → **Wolff** and Alexander Gottlieb → **Baumgarten**. Meier died on 21 June 1777.[80]

Kant was heavily influenced by Meier. He read his logic lectures for about forty years based on Meier's *Vernunftlehre* (1752) and his brief *Auszug aus der Vernunftlehre* (1752). Kant's own *Reflexionen* (**Refl**) and lectures on logic (**LL**) as well as **CPR** show a number of elements taken from Meier's handbooks. This is evident already from the terminology used by Kant: Kantian terms such as 'egoism', 'genius', 'horizon', 'system', 'party', 'popular', 'pure', 'doctrine of reason', and 'prejudice' all come from Meier.[81]

In particular, Meier was important for Kant because he mediated Locke's philosophy, helping to introduce Lockean issues such as the 'extent of human knowledge' and the 'degrees of assent' into Kant's philosophical framework.

Meier's influence on Kant can also be found in the conception of 'system' and 'architectonic' in **CPR**. Kant states that the 'architectonic' is the art of constructing a system. Kant specifies that only a systematic unity turns common knowledge into a science, that is, transforms a simple aggregate into a system. This systematic unity ensures that knowledge is not fragmentary, which is a crucial Kantian issue in conceiving of the possibility of a complete a priori knowledge. System is defined as the unity of various cognitions under one idea. The idea is the conception of the form of the whole, since because of it the extent of the manifold cognitions as well as the position of the parts among them can be determined (A832=B860). The idea is therefore fundamental in determining the end and the form of the whole. The form of the whole is 'therefore articulated (*articulatio*) and not heaped together (*coacervatio*)' (A833=B861).

Kant goes on to state that if we abstract from any content of knowledge, considered objectively, then all knowledge considered subjectively is either historical or rational (A836=B864). Historical knowledge is *cognitio ex datis*, while rational knowledge is *cognitio ex principiis*. It is historical when knowledge is not systematized according to principles. It is rational when it proceeds from principles and investigates a priori every possible knowledge. Kant takes these notions from the lectures on Meier's companion of logic. In §104 of *Auszug aus der*

Vernunftlehre, Meier writes that a doctrinal edifice (*Lehrgebäude, systema*) is a set of dogmatic truths, which are related to each other and which taken together form scientific knowledge as a whole. Meier adds that the truth of a doctrinal edifice requires that all its parts are related in such a way that each of them is a ground or a consequence of the others.[82]

In relation to the above-mentioned section of Meier's handbook, Kant is quoted as saying (**LL** 100) that a system is a multitude or manifold of various simple cognitions and truths combined together, such that taken together these constitute a whole, and that this system is either historical or rational. Kant comments on the same passage early in the 1770s in his lectures on logic (see **LL** 399–400). Unlike in the Logic Blomberg, in the Logic Philippi Kant raises the problem of an a priori ordering idea or principle and the necessity of a plan to set up the system,[83] and he does so by elaborating on his ideas about Meier's doctrines.

Meier is also Kant's source of the theory of logical prejudices, which are those prejudices that find their origin in the general configuration of human thought and speech. It was Meier who set the stage for Kant's idea of 'egoism' in the variants of 'logical', 'aesthetic', and 'moral' egoism. Kant was concerned about the consequences that 'private judgments' have with regard to the transcendental conditions of human cognition. Like Meier, Kant stresses the need to respect 'logical pluralism' and the necessity of a 'universal human reason' as a common ground of each individual human being.

As a result of his examination of the distortions produced by prejudices, Meier took great interest in the formative process of knowledge. In his *Beyträge zu der Lehre von den Vorurtheilen* (1766), he problematized

143

t relation by emphasizing
nsequences of prejudices
...wieage. Meier supports the idea that
the prejudice of experiential cognition is the
foundation of all other cognition according
to which all sensations represent to the mind
the configuration and quantity of an internal determination of the objects of the sensations. In this way, Meier distinguishes the
world of sense experience from the world of
the objects themselves, laying the foundation
for the Kantian distinction between the phenomenal and noumenal world.[84] – MS

NEWTON, ISAAC

Kant's reception of and engagement with
Newtonian physics spans across his entire
academic career, from the pre-Critical writings to **OP**, and can be clustered around
three main (albeit not exhaustive) themes:
(1) dynamical theory of matter; (2) absolute
space; (3) mechanics.

The first signs of Kant's reception of
Newtonian physics are in the short 1754 essay
EAR, where universal gravitation is presented
as the driving power of nature. A year later,
in **NH** Kant laid down a cosmogony 'according to the principles of Newton'. Although
no reference in **NH** is made to Newton's laws
of motion, Kant explained the formation of
celestial bodies out of primordial corpus-
cular matter, among which attraction and
repulsion would act. But, as Kant declared,
while attraction had been demonstrated by
Newton, repulsion was assumed only on the
basis of what he called unquestionable evidence coming from the dissolution of matter in vapours. Kant's early dynamical theory
of matter betrays, then, the double nature
of his debt to Newtonianism. By identifying

repulsion as a force at work primarily in fer-
mentations and vapours, Kant was implicitly
endorsing Newton's dynamical corpuscular-
ism as displayed in the *Opticks*.[85] Moreover,
the ether of the Queries of the *Opticks*, as the
matter of light, appears again in **F**, also from
1755, with the double connotation of being
the matter of light *and* of fire.

As far as space and mechanics are concerned, in the early essay **MR** (1758) Kant
endorsed a form of relationism, following
the tradition of → **Leibniz** and → **Wolff**
(whom he nonetheless criticized on the laws
of impact and collision).[86] Without mentioning Newton explicitly, Kant rejected the idea
of absolute space as an empty container of
bodies, and defined true motion as motion
always relative to other bodies. He also
introduced a principle of action and reaction
that was meant to correct the corresponding
Leibnizian-Wolffian principle, and was significantly different from Newton's one since
impressed forces were absent from Kant's
theory of motion.

In **DS**, from 1768, Kant articulated his
disagreement with relationalism by means
of the argument of incongruent counterparts: space cannot be defined in terms of
external relations among parts of matter,
because otherwise it would not be possible
to distinguish between left hand and right
hand, or any other incongruent counterparts.
Kant grounded that difference in an '*absolute
and original space*' (**DS** 383), which though
was not intended as a Newtonian substance,
but as a 'fundamental concept which first of
all makes possible all such outer sensation'
(**DS** 383), anticipating in this way somehow
the role that space plays in the Critical period
as a pure form of sensibility.

Kant's engagement with the three aforementioned Newtonian themes becomes the
object of mature reflection in the Critical

period, especially in **MFNS**. There is considerable and ongoing debate among scholars as to whether this text should be read as Kant's philosophical justification of Newton's mechanics as spelled out in the *Principia*.[87] There are in fact some important common elements but also differences between Newton and Kant such as the following:

(1) Kant's mature theory of matter clearly betrays its Newtonian origins by identifying attraction as an action at a distance through empty space (**MFNS** 512). Yet the balancing argument through which attraction and repulsion are introduced can be regarded as pre-Newtonian:[88] from a Newtonian point of view, spinning around its own axis would suffice to prevent matter from collapsing into one point due to attraction, without the need of introducing a counterbalancing repulsive force.

(2) In the chapter on Phenomenology, by rejecting absolute motion Kant differentiated himself from Newton's notion of absolute space, which could not be an object of experience 'for space without matter is no object of perception, and yet it is a necessary concept of reason, and thus nothing more than a mere *idea*' (**MFNS** 559). Kant argued that we can only have empirical representations of space, whereby matter as the moveable in space changes its relation with respect to space itself as a material moveable. The latter, in turn, can be regarded as contained into a bigger, yet still material space, and so on to infinity, with the result that 'all motion or rest can be relative only and never absolute' (**MFNS** 559). Absolute space then becomes the ideal limit of this open-ended sequence of nested material spaces.

(3) The chapter on Mechanics offers three laws of motion, whose relation to Newton's three laws remains a matter of debate among scholars. ▌ expresses the conservatioᵢ of matter, and as such does equivalent in Newton's laws,   ᵢ ᵣ second law bears important similarities with Newton's first law, although by 'inertia' Kant means 'lifelessness' of matter, and he mentions an 'external cause' for changes of inertial state but no impressed forces. Newton's second law, with the notion of impressed force, is strikingly absent from Kant's mechanics. And Kant's third law, i.e. action and reaction are always equal in all communication of motion, is once again not understood in terms of impressed forces, as in Newton.

Some scholars (most notably, Michael Friedman)[89] have explained away these differences between Newton and Kant by arguing that Newton's second law can indirectly be derived from Kant's third law, and that Kant's third law is in turn just a version of Newton's third law. Other scholars[90] have argued instead that the Leibnizian-Wolffian tradition, rather than Newton, provides the background against which we should read Kant's laws: in defending the view that reaction was not a passive force of resistance, Kant signalled that his main interlocutors were Leibniz and Wolff, who indeed identified reaction with a passive force of bodies called 'inertia'. Thus, the exact nature of Newton's influence on Kant's philosophy of natural science remains a matter of debate. – MM

PLATO

Kant's philosophy is not particularly known for its historical orientation. His critical project in philosophy entails an explicit breach with the preceding tradition of metaphysics. In his wish to make a new start in philosophy by means of a critical investigation of the human capacity for knowledge, Kant turns away from the older philosophy. He still acknowledges the 'great philosophers' of the past, but their authority is no longer taken for granted.

In Kant's Critical works, Plato is mentioned a few times in a significant way. In an interesting passage in the 'Introduction' of **CPR**, Kant refers critically to Plato as an example of the tendency of reason to free itself from the restriction of the senses in the mistaken assumption that knowledge would come easier in a 'free flight' without the resistance from the part of the senses. Kant writes:

The light dove, in free flight cutting through the air the resistance of which it feels, could get the idea that it could do even better in airless space. Likewise, Plato abandoned the world of the senses because it posed so many hindrances for the understanding, and dared to go beyond it on the wings of the ideas, in the empty space of pure understanding. He did not notice that he made no headway by his efforts, for he had no resistance, no support, as it were, by which he could stiffen himself, and to which he could apply his powers in order to get his understanding off the ground. (A5=B9)

Kant considers himself a critic of Platonism. For him, the fault of Platonism consists in the attempt of reason to elevate itself above the world of the senses in order to contemplate the Ideas in the supersensory realm of truth.

An interesting passage where Kant refers to the 'idea' of Plato is in the chapter on the Ideal of Pure Reason, in the second book of the Transcendental Dialectic (A568=B596). Kant introduces here the notion of an 'ideal'. An ideal is the single instantiation of an idea in its complete perfection. Kant compares such an 'ideal' with what in Plato is the transcendent idea (*Idee des göttlichen Verstandes*), that is, the true and perfect essence of each thing, which as such can only be an object of an intellectual intuition. It is clear that, for Kant, such Platonic ideas existing in a supersensory divine realm are not acceptable. Kant wants to bring back the divine ideas to the sphere of human reason, in which ideal notions function as regulative principles in a practical sense. So instead of transcendent ideas which are the object of an intellectual intuition, Kant speaks of ideas of pure reason which have but a regulative status.

In Kant's oeuvre, there is one work in which Plato is mentioned and discussed in a more than marginal sense. This is in the late polemical essay **PTS** from 1796, which Kant wrote on the occasion of the Platonist inspired critique by Schlosser of his philosophy. Schlosser published his critique of Kant together with a translation of the letters of Plato.[91] The famous Seventh Letter represents for Schlosser the paradigm of true divinely inspired philosophy. In this letter, Plato distinguishes between different degrees of knowledge. The highest and most perfect degree of knowledge concerns the 'thing itself in its truth', which is accessible by an immediate non-cognitive insight:

This knowledge is not something that can be put into words like other sciences; but after long companionship with it, as between teacher and pupil in joint pursuit of the subject, suddenly, like light flashing forth when a fire is kindled, it is born in the soul and straightway nourishes itself.

This is the mystical side of Plato which is popular with all kinds of theosophical and mystical conceptions of philosophy. This Plato is, according to Kant, 'the father of all enthusiasm [*Schwärmerei*] *by way of philosophy*' (**PTS** 398), that is, of the belief in the possibility of non-cognitive insight by way of inner feeling and intuition, a view which is entirely rejected by Kant.

Kant's objection to Plato concerns primarily the point of intellectual intuition. In Kant's view, Plato's philosophy is 'mystical', at least the Plato of the Letters: man closes his eyes in order to contemplate by means of the soul the higher truth of the ideas. Kant sees a link between Plato and the contemporary philosophers of sentiment (*Gefühlsphilosophen*) who in their appeal to an immediate feeling of the truth consider themselves to be exempt from the long and laborious way of conceptual thought. He disparages strongly the idea of a philosopher who does not have to work, but listens instead to his inner oracle.

The verdict on mysticism and enthusiasm, however, is not Kant's final word with regard to such a great and respected philosopher as Plato. Kant suggests that Plato is misused by the *Gefühlsphilosophen* such as Schlosser. Plato himself – that is, the serious Plato of the dialogues, not the 'mystagogue' of the dubious Seventh Letter – should have used the intellectual intuition only regressively in order to explain the possibility of synthetic knowledge a priori (see **PTS** 391n.). Here, Kant refers to the doctrine of ἀνάμνησις, by means of which Plato accounts for the non-empirical element in our knowledge. In this sense, Plato had already known the central question of all serious philosophy, viz. the question concerning the possibility of synthetic judgments a priori. In addition, Kant points out that Plato founded the Academy, which proves that he himself had recognized

the necessity of conceptual labour in philosophy. Kant's judgment of Plato is, thus, not merely negative. As source of inspiration of the *Gefühlsphilosophen*, especially on the basis of his Seventh Letter, he belongs to the camp of false and esoteric philosophy, of a philosophy of 'fire in the soul'. But there is another Plato, much more to be respected, one who has touched on, albeit hesitantly, the essential question of philosophy concerning the possibility of synthetic knowledge a priori. – RtV

FURTHER READING

R. Bubner, 'Platon der Vater aller Schwärmerei', in *Antike Themen und ihre moderne Verwandlung* (Frankfurt a/M: Suhrkamp, 1992), pp. 80–93.

R. Ferber, 'Platon und Kant', in A. Neschke-Hentschke (ed.), *Argumenta in dialogos Platonis, Teil 1. Platoninterpretation und ihre Hermeneutik von der Antike bis zum Beginn des 19. Jahrhunderts* (Basel: Schwabe, 2007), pp. 371–390.

H. Heimsoeth, 'Plato in Kants Werdegang', in H. Heimsoeth, D. Henrich, G. Tonelli (eds), *Studien zu Kants philosopher Entwicklung* (Hildesheim: Olms, 1967), pp. 124–143.

ROUSSEAU, JEAN-JACQUES

In 1756, → **Mendelssohn** translated Jean-Jacques Rousseau's *Discourse on Inequality* (1755) into German, and Johann Georg Hamann mentioned Rousseau in a December 1759 letter to Kant (**Corr-I** 30). The influence of Rousseau (1712–78) on Kant was profound, and it came most forcefully when Kant was about forty, as notes written in Kant's own copy of **Obs** around 1764–65 reveal. In those notes, he claimed that Rousseau stood to the moral world as → **Newton** did to the natural world (**Obs-R** 58–59). The Swiss thinker's influence on Kant was above all (but not exclusively) in anthropology and social philosophy, pedagogy, ethics and political philosophy.

In his writings in the 1750s, Kant mostly examined natural philosophy (physics and geography) and theoretical metaphysics. After reading the British empiricists (→ **Empiricism**) and especially Rousseau's *Émile* and *Of the Social Contract* (both published in 1762), Kant addressed the ends of *human* nature, intrigued by Rousseau's notion of the difference between natural and civilized human beings. Rousseau led Kant to reconsider the aims of the arts and sciences and especially philosophy, to think that philosophy should have practical and moral consequences, and to believe that knowledge for its own sake was not sufficient to justify intellectual pursuits.

On might think that the Swiss thinker did not influence **CPR**, which Kant was still composing when Rousseau died in 1778, but the very notion that reason was in need of a critique is in part traceable back to Rousseau's diagnoses that social ills were caused by a use of reason that overstepped its bounds, creating desires it could not satisfy. ('Diminish desires, and you will increase strength', Rousseau advised in *Émile*.) This arguably influenced Kant's claim that pure theoretical reason had a natural and inevitable tendency to fall into an illusory dialectic that could be properly understood, if not avoided (A298=B354). In the notes that reflect Rousseau's influence, Kant had defined metaphysics as 'the science of the limits of human reason' (**Obs-R** 181), and in the contemporaneous **DSS** (1766) Kant published this definition of metaphysics

(**DSS** 368). Rousseau's accounts of reason and alienation and the generally practical orientation of his philosophy also arguably influenced Kant's assertion that pure practical reason was primary vis-à-vis speculative reason (**CPrR** 119).

Anthropology and social philosophy. In late 1763 Kant saw the discovery of a boy roaming outside → **Königsberg** as confirmation of Rousseau's anthropology, as **EMH** (1764) showed. Kant's notes reveal that he was moved by Rousseau yet struggled not to be enchanted by his style and wit. Kant famously claimed that Rousseau 'set him straight' and inspired him to defend the rights of humanity, whereas before he had thought that one's worth was linked to intellectual achievements (**Obs-R** 44). He held that Rousseau was the first to discover 'the deeply hidden nature of humanity' and 'the secret law whose observation justifies Providence' (**Obs-R** 58–59), and that whereas 'belief in inequality also makes human beings unequal', only Rousseau's teaching could make it so that even the most learned philosopher did not see himself as better than the common man (**Obs-R** 176). Yet he had to keep reading Rousseau until the beauty of expression did not unsettle him and he could read again with reason (**Obs-R** 30). His reading proceeded in stages, from a first impression of finding an 'uncommon mental acuity, a noble flight of genius, and a sensitive soul', followed by the impression of 'alienation over strange and nonsensical opinions' that conflicted so strongly with general opinions that one was inclined to suppose that Rousseau only wanted to show off the magical power of his eloquence (**Obs-R** 43–44). This view of philosophical writing perhaps helps us better understand Kant's conscious adoption of a relatively dry and abstract style in the *Critiques*, as the → **Bacon** epigraph at the beginning of the B-edition of **CPR** demonstrates: *de nobis ipsis silemus* ('of our own person we will say nothing') (Bii).

Contrasting his method with Rousseau's 'synthetic' method, which began with the human being in the state of nature, Kant described his method as 'analytic' since it examined humans in the civilized condition (**Obs-R** 14). In the notes, Kant adopted a Rousseauian distinction between a primitive innocence, ignorant of artificial goods, and a wise innocence (**Obs-R** 77) that was familiar with, yet controlled, artificial impulses. Kant assessed the happiness of primitive humans not in order to 'return to the forests', but to see how far humanity had been artificially constructed and what had thereby been lost or gained (**Obs-R** 31; cf. **Anthr** 326). Likewise, in a published announcement of his lectures (1765), Kant distinguished between wise ('civilized') and primitive innocence, and urged us to understand human nature before attempting to state what should be done (**AL** 311–312; cf. **Anthr** 326–327). Kant agreed with Rousseau that the arts and sciences required a degree of corrupting luxury, but also believed they 'cultivated' us (**UH** 27). Although Kant agreed that social decorum could have a negative influence, he thought Rousseau failed to offer a compelling plan for bringing about the final, most important stage of humanity's development: moralization (**UH** 26; cf. **CBH** 116; **Anthr** 324). In addition, what Rousseau called *amour propre* emerged as Kant's key notions of self-conceit (**CPrR** 73), unsocial sociability (**UH** 20), and radical propensity to evil (**R** 28–32).

Kant held that Rousseau's writings seemed to conflict with each other and were often misinterpreted. Kant thought Rousseau's two *Discourses* correctly showed the unavoidable conflict of culture with our physical nature, but also that in *Émile* and *Of the Social Contract* and 'other writings', Rousseau sought to solve the harder problem of how to reconcile moral and natural predispositions (**CBH** 116). Yet Kant held that since the proper education of the youth and citizens had not yet been carried out, every ill and vice arose from this culture-nature conflict.

Pedagogy. Kant had worked as a private tutor for well-off families between 1747 and 1754, before returning to the Albertina University. Kant concluded **Obs** (1764), which even contained a footnote on Rousseau (**Obs** 246), with Rousseauian references to 'noble simplicity' and the 'as yet undiscovered secret of education' (**Obs** 255). Yet Kant's call to activate and raise the moral feeling in the breast of 'every young citizen of the world' revealed a cosmopolitanism that went beyond Rousseau.

The notes again showed a deeper, more critical reception of Rousseau. While Kant agreed with him that education should be 'free' and also 'make a free man' (**Obs-R** 167), Kant did not see how Rousseau's programme for the pupil Émile could be made practical for instruction in schools (**Obs-R** 29). Perhaps drawing from his experiences as a tutor, Kant considered Rousseau's ideas impractical since they were based on a tutor-governor model, for in order for schools to be possible, one must 'draw on' or extend *Émile* and show 'how schools could arise from it' (**Obs-R** 29). Yet Kant esteemed Rousseau's views on education, calling them the 'only means of bringing prosperity back to civil society' in an age of luxury, since political laws apparently did not suffice (**Obs-R** 175).

A Rousseauian, naturalist, and child-centred approach to teaching was ground for Kant's avid support of the Philanthropinum Institute established by Johann Bernard Basedow (1724–90) in Dessau in 1774,

149

as anthropology lecture notes reveal (**LA** 722–723). In **EPh,** Kant held that the proper educational method should be derived from nature and that schools should develop new methods that did not slavishly copy habit and tradition (**EPh** 449). In his pedagogy course, given four times between 1776 and 1787, Kant cited Rousseau often – for instance, to support his views that discipline should come before informative instruction and that the development of children's bodies through physical activity shapes them for society (**LP** 469; cf. 442).

Ethics and political philosophy. Kant's appeal to common moral knowledge in the first section of **G** shares the spirit of Rousseau's conviction that fundamental moral truth is just as accessible to common human reason as to philosophical reason. Moreover, there is a superficial resemblance between Kant's view of autonomy as the property of the will to be a law to itself (**G** 440) and to both Rousseau's *moral* liberty ('obedience to a law which we prescribe to ourselves') and *civil* liberty limited by the general will (*volonté générale*).[92] **G**'s Formula of Autonomy (**G** 431), and its variant, the Formula of the Realm of Ends (**G** 439), also sound somewhat like Rousseau's claim that citizens should be subject to laws that they themselves author. However, these notions are at most analogous. Rousseau's claim applies to legislators of a political law in a community of citizens, that is, to deliberation and the public process of voting in an ideal state, and he presents a political theory concerned with coercive laws of a state within a limited jurisdiction. A citizen can be 'forced to be free',[93] and a public authority exists to ensure that the laws are obeyed. Kant's ethical theory is based on autonomy as (non-coercive) inner legislation of the will. Here autonomy is ascribed to all rational beings,

not just to citizens of a particular political community (and it is not to be confused with autocracy, or self-mastery and control of inclinations). Kantian autonomy of the will is an internalization of what remains in Rousseau a political notion.

Like the author of *Of the Social Contract*, in **MM** Kant developed a social contract theory. Moreover, Kant's thoughts on global peace explicitly referred to Rousseau, who himself publicly endorsed a European alliance for peace (1761). However, Kant proposed a cosmopolitan (not just European) federation of states (**PP** 360, cf. **MM** 352), which he believed Rousseau ridiculed as fantastic – since Rousseau may have considered the league to be imminent (**UH** 24). In the notes, Kant had repudiated a general love of humanity since it could lead to chimerical, idle wishes (**Obs-R** 25), but his later theories of respect for humanity and human rights, so indebted to Rousseau, were arguably not subject to this criticism (**MM** 352). – RC

FURTHER READING

E. Cassirer, *Kant, Rousseau, and Goethe* (New York: Harper and Row, 1963).

K. Reich, 'Rousseau und Kant', in K. Reich, *Gesammelte Schriften*, ed. M. Baum (Hamburg: Meiner, 2001), pp. 147–165.

S. Shell, *Kant and the Limits of Autonomy* (Cambridge, MA: Harvard University Press, 2009).

S. Shell, R. Velkley (eds), *Kant's Observations and Remarks: A Critical Guide* (Cambridge: Cambridge University Press, 2012).

R. Velkley, 'Transcending nature, unifying reason: on Kant's debt to Rousseau', in O. Sensen (ed.), *Kant on Moral Autonomy* (Cambridge: Cambridge University Press, 2013), pp. 89–106.

SWEDENBORG, EMANUEL

Emanuel Swedenborg (1688–1772) was a widely published Swedish scientist, inventor, philosopher and Assessor of the College of Mines. In his fifties, Swedenborg experienced a spiritual crisis including a series of mystical visions, and he turned his attention to Biblical studies and theology. In April of 1745, these visions culminated in the experience of being chosen as a visionary. Swedenborg claimed that God had granted him access at will to the spiritual world and charged him with the task of revealing the inner meaning of the Bible. Swedenborg retired from public service in June 1745, and until the end of his life, he was principally engaged in writing and publishing exegetical, theological and visionary writings.

The first and most famous of Swedenborg's mature theosophical works is the *Arcana Coelestia*, published in 8 volumes between 1749 and 1756, in which Swedenborg explains the inner sense of every word of Genesis and Exodus. Between the exegetical chapters, Swedenborg offers accounts of his visionary journeys to heaven, hell and the spiritual world where he conversed with the spirits of human beings and the inhabitants of other planets.

Kant's surviving corpus contains explicit references to Swedenborg from 1763 to 1798.[94] Also, virtually every reference to enthusiasm (*Schwärmerei*) in Kant's corpus after 1764 can be interpreted as at least in part an allusion to Swedenborg. The first mention of Swedenborg is in a long letter dated 10 August 1763 (**Corr-I** 43–48), addressed to a young female friend, Charlotte von Knobloch, in which Kant reported on extensive research he had undertaken at her request on Swedenborg's reputation as a clairvoyant. The letter provides the most detailed descriptions extant of three famous clairvoyant feats, the so-called affairs of the Queen's Secret, the Lost Receipt and the Stockholm Fire, although all the events are attested to by other, independent sources.[95]

Kant makes it clear that he was not investigating Swedenborg just to please a lady. He was intensely interested in clairvoyance. He investigated the reports for about 18 months, corresponding with several individuals, including Swedenborg himself, and dispatching a friend, an English merchant based in → **Königsberg** with business in Sweden, to interview Swedenborg and several witnesses. He also parted with £7 (a considerable sum for him) for a set of the *Arcana Coelestia* (which had not yet arrived at the time he wrote the letter). Kant concludes, moreover, that after due investigation, he was quite convinced that Swedenborg had genuine clairvoyant powers.

According to Johann Gottfried → Herder's notes on Kant's **LM**, dating from 1763–64, Kant mentioned the *Arcana Coelestia* in his lectures.[96] In a letter to Moses → **Mendelssohn** dated 6 November 1764, Johann Georg Hamann reported that Kant was working on a review of the '*opera omnia*' of 'a certain Schwedenberg [sic]'.[97] This review grew into Kant's longest work on Swedenborg, the book **DSS**, published at the end of 1765 but dated 1766. **DSS** is one of the last of Kant's 'pre-Critical' writings, and it is the first in which he sketches out the agenda and basic tenets of his Critical philosophy.

Part I of **DSS**, 'which is dogmatic', consists of four chapters. Chapter 1, entitled 'A Tangled Metaphysical Knot that can be either Untied or Cut as One Pleases' (**DSS** 319), outlines Kant's early metaphysics and poses a problem brought home to him through his encounter with → **Rousseau**'s *Émile* and *On the Social Contract* in 1763: What is the place of the human soul – which possesses freedom, moral responsibility and intrinsic worth, not to mention aspirations to immortality – in Kant's materialistic metaphysics?

Chapter 2, entitled 'A Fragment of Occult Philosophy, the Purpose of which is to Reveal Our Community with the Spirit-World' (DSS 329), offers a dualistic resolution to this question, dividing the cosmos into material and spiritual worlds, the former governed by laws of necessity and the latter governed by laws of freedom. Man has dual citizenship and thus falls under both regimes. The moral problem is to live by the laws of freedom in the material world. Although Kant erects his account of the spirit world on metaphysical foundations, his blueprints clearly come directly from Swedenborg's *Arcana Coelestia*.

Chapter 3, entitled 'Anti-Cabbala – A Fragment of Ordinary Philosophy, the Purpose of which is to Cancel Community with the Spirit-World' (DSS 342), is a sceptical critique of the previous chapter from the point of view of the empiricist *Popularphilosophie* of the Berlin Enlightenment. This chapter must not be seen as representing Kant's own viewpoint. Indeed, the arguments he offers are rhetorically and logically self-refuting.[98] Kant does, however, accept one premise of this critique, namely that any notion of a spiritual world cannot be based upon a claim to mystical intuition, which is accessible only to the elect, but must instead rest on experiences and arguments that all men can understand.

In chapter 4, entitled 'Theoretical Conclusion Established on the Basis of All the Observations Contained in the First Part' (DSS 348–349), Kant proposes to begin again. His account of the spirit world may resolve the problems of his early metaphysics, but he accepts that it needs new, non-dogmatic, non-mystical foundations. Because theoretical reason has a tendency to overreach its grasp and launch itself into groundless speculation, Kant states that we must first

delimit its powers, tying reason to common experience before we philosophize. But since the idea of a spiritual world answers to some of the deepest needs of the human soul – the need to believe in our freedom, moral responsibility and survival after death – Kant argues that practical reason can provide grounds for belief that theoretical reason cannot.

Part II, 'which is historical', deals explicitly with Swedenborg, who is discussed in the most scathing terms. Chapter 1, entitled 'A Story, the Truth of which is Recommended to the Reader's Own Free Examination' (DSS 353), retells the stories of Swedenborg's three clairvoyant feats described in his letter to Charlotte von Knobloch. But in DSS, Kant treats them as mere unconfirmed rumours and does not mention his extensive research and attempts to corroborate them. Chapter 2, entitled 'Ecstatic Journey of an Enthusiast through the Spirit-World' (DSS 357), is a masterful condensation of the essence of Swedenborg's account of the spirit world in the *Arcana Coelestia*.

Chapter 3, entitled 'Practical Conclusion Drawn from the Treatise as a Whole' (DSS 368), returns to the idea that philosophy can guard itself from metaphysical absurdities like Swedenborg's only by first delimiting the powers of theoretical reason. Kant then concludes by recommending a turn to the practical. However, as we have seen from the conclusion of Part I of DSS, the turn toward practice can provide a new foundation for belief in a spiritual world.

DSS is the first work of Kant's in which the outlines of his mature Critical philosophy are set forth. But what role did Swedenborg play in the emergence of the Critical philosophy? Kant's dismissive treatment of Swedenborg in DSS naturally leads most scholars to conclude that he was merely chosen as a *reductio ad absurdum* of dogmatic metaphysics.[99] Some scholars, however, have noted a contradiction between **DSS** and Kant's respectful remarks about Swedenborg in his letter to Charlotte von Knobloch and student notes on his lectures on metaphysics. They have hypothesized that Kant may have dissembled his more positive views because Swedenborg was regarded as a heretic by the ecclesiastical establishment and as an enthusiast by the Enlightenment. Known sympathies with Swedenborg might have harmed Kant's academic career.[100] Mendelssohn clearly regarded Kant as being deceptive in **DSS**, and Kant's letter to Mendelssohn of 8 April 1766 (**Corr-I** 69–73) is an attempt at damage control.[101]

It can be argued, furthermore, that several crucial ideas of Kant's Critical system are influenced by Swedenborg. For instance, Swedenborg's account of the spiritual world contains a doctrine of the ideality of space and time, space and time being ways in which spiritual relations appear to finite, embodied knowers.[102] Also, Kant's doctrine of the 'kingdom of ends' derives from Swedenborg's spirit world. Indeed, Swedenborg even describes the spirit world as a kingdom of ends (*regnum finium*) in the *Arcana Coelestia*.[103]

DSS contains Kant's longest discussion of Swedenborg, but it was by no means his last. Numerous references to Swedenborg can be found in students' lectures notes (**LM** 113, 298–301, 447, 593, 689, 768, 897, and **LM-M/V** 919–920). These references appear in Kant's discussions of the state of the soul after death in the section on rational psychology. At **LM** 298–301, Kant's discussion of Swedenborg is detailed and highly respectful. Swedenborg's idea of the spirit world is here indeed described as 'quite sublime'.[104]

Furthermore, in **DRTBaum** 1325, Kant reportedly mentions Swedenborg's account of life on other planets and concludes: 'He appears, therefore, to have been a deliberate fraud'. In **LA** 284, Swedenborg is mentioned in connection with enthusiasm. In **LA** 1059, Swedenborg is offered as an example of the connection of genius and madness (*Wahnsinn*). Swedenborg is also mentioned in two *Reflexionen* from the 1770s: **Refl** 1486, where Swedenborg is cited as an example of enthusiasts and mystics who offer symbolic interpretations of the Bible, and **Refl** 5026, where Swedenborg is offered as an example of appeal to intellectual intuition.

In **CF** 46 and **Anthr** 191–192, Swedenborg is mentioned in connection with the symbolic interpretation of scripture, nature, and historical events.[105] Kant believes that Swedenborg's symbolic interpretation of scripture is a form of enthusiasm because it is based on a claim to special divine election and is thus not intersubjectively verifiable. Kant does, however, share Swedenborg's desire to interpret phenomena symbolically, but he argues that such interpretations must be based on his moral philosophy, which is intersubjectively verifiable.

Kant's interest in Swedenborg was intense, long-standing and philosophically fruitful. In particular, Swedenborg must be ranked alongside Rousseau as one of the prime influences on the emergence of Kant's Critical philosophy.[106] The Kant–Swedenborg relationship is, however, relatively unexplored and is thus fertile ground for future research. – GJ

FURTHER READING

M. David-Ménard, *La folie dans la raison pure: Kant lecteur de Swedenborg* (Paris: Vrin, 1990).

M. Grier, 'Swedenborg and Kant on spiritual intuition', in S. McNeilly (ed.), *On the True Philosopher and the True Philosophy – Essays on Swedenborg* (London: The Swedenborg Society, 2002), pp. 1–20.

G. Johnson, 'The tree of melancholy: Kant on philosophy and enthusiasm', in C. Firestone, S. Palmquist (eds), *Kant and the New Philosophy of Religion* (Bloomington: Indiana University Press, 2006), pp.43–61.

S. Meld Shell, *The Embodiment of Reason. Kant on Spirit, Generation, and Community* (Chicago: University of Chicago Press, 1996), ch. 5.

L. Thorpe, 'The realm of ends as a community of spirits: Kant and Swedenborg on the kingdom of heaven and the cleansing of the doors of perception', *The Heythrop Journal* 52,1 (2011): 52–75.

TETENS, JOHANN NICOLAUS

Johann Nicolaus (sometimes Nicolas) Tetens (1736–1807) was among the most influential German philosophers in the 1770s, mainly due to his voluminous *Philosophische Versuche über die menschliche Natur und ihre Entwickelung* (1777). He was a philosophy professor in Bützow and Kiel until 1789, when he left academia to embark on a second career as a public servant in the Danish finance ministry where he became, among other positions, vice director of the Danish national bank.

Tetens is a representative of a general empiricist tendency in German philosophy between the late 1750s and 1780s. Dissatisfied with rigid Wolffianism (→ **Wolff**), quite a few of his contemporaries – including figures such as Ernst Platner, Johann Georg Feder (→ **Garve-Feder review**), Christian Garve (→ **Garve-Feder review**) and, to a lesser extent, also Moses → **Mendelssohn** and Johann Georg

Sulzer – began discussing and appreciating British, Scottish and French → **empiricism** while, on the other hand, retaining much of the conceptual framework and the basic assumptions of the Wolffian tradition. It is in this context that Tetens is often called the 'German Locke' (→ **Locke**).[107] Tetens and his contemporaries, today largely unknown, are thus forerunners of Kant's endeavour to reconcile empiricism and rationalism. Tetens is also considered an important predecessor of developmental psychology.

Philosophische Versuche (like its shorter antecedent *Ueber die allgemeine speculativische Philosophie*, from 1775) is mainly intended as a work in empirical psychology (*Erfahrungs-Seelenlehre*). Structured rather loosely, it includes a broad range of issues such as the nature of representation (first essay), feelings, impressions and sensations (second essay), the origin of our cognition of the objective existence of things (fifth essay), the necessity of the universal truths of reason (seventh essay), spontaneity and freedom (twelfth essay) or man's perfectibility and development (fourteenth essay).

Tetens insists that all knowledge of reality is based on both observation and reasoning ('Raisonnement').[108] He aims at a synthesis of 'British observational' philosophy with 'French arguing' philosophy and the 'geometrical genius of Leibniz-Wolffian philosophy'.[109] Tetens argues: 'As much as I have taken care to avoid blending hypotheses into experiential propositions, I did not avoid drawing inferences and conclusions from the observations and thus conjoining them'.[110] According to Tetens, we have to 'pursue the course to which *Locke* has first guided us, with the torch of observation in his hand, to find the sensations from which the general notions are derived'.[111] He leaves no doubt that all concepts are derivative of sensations.[112]

With regard to psychology, Tetens renounces physiological anthropology which was flourishing at the time. Physiological anthropology is based on the attempt to explain mental features and events by modifications of the brain and the nervous system (without necessarily subscribing to a materialist ontology). Tetens instead prefers a Lockean 'observational method' that confines itself to what we observe in inner sense and abstains from further speculations.[113]

Tetens' peculiar attempt to synthesize rationalism and empiricism becomes obvious, for instance, when he criticizes → **Hume's** theory of causality. Tetens doubts that when we claim an event to be the cause of another one, we are merely associating ideas: 'Does not this connection of ideas include more, something that is the real reason to make the understanding judge: Here, we find cause and effect? Is the association of ideas not connected to a certain necessity, wherever it may have originated?'[114] Elsewhere, he argues in some detail that the idea of causal connection covers more than a connection, viz. an idea of dependence that is not included in Humean association.[115] Thus, the ideas of necessity and dependence are what reason irreducibly contributes to our concept of causality, according to Tetens.

Tetens discusses Kant's **ID** on various occasions, for instance with regard to the concept of space. Tetens argues that the concept of space as a whole is an individual idea, and he considers himself in agreement with Kant here: 'What else did *Herr Kant*, the profound philosopher who studies the understanding so acutely, intend to argue when he takes *space* to be an *intuitive idea*?'[116]

There is sufficient evidence that Kant has dealt with Tetens' views to a considerable degree. In letters to Marcus → **Herz** (**Corr-I** 270), Moses Mendelssohn (**Corr-I** 346) and Christian Garve (**Corr-I** 341) Kant suspects that only Tetens, besides Herz, Mendelssohn and Garve, could be in a position to fully grasp the importance of his Critical philosophy, requesting their assistance in explaining and disseminating his doctrine. Johann Georg Hamann notes in a letter to Johann Gottfried → **Herder** that Kant was making frequent use of Tetens' works while he was writing **CPR**;[117] in an earlier letter to Herder, he says that Kant is 'very full of' Tetens.[118]

However, Kant is also critical of Tetens. In another letter to Herz (**Corr-I** 232), he finds fault with the lack of structure and the redundancy especially of the second volume of *Philosophische Untersuchungen*. In **Refl** 4900, Kant distinguishes his own approach from that of both Tetens and Johann Heinrich → **Lambert**: 'I concern myself not with the evolution of concepts, like Tetens (all actions by means of which concepts are produced), nor with their analysis, like Lambert, but solely with their objective validity. I am not in competition with [*Mitbewerber*] these men.' – FW

FURTHER READING

H.-U. Baumgarten, *Kant und Tetens. Untersuchungen zum Problem von Vorstellung und Gegenstand* (Stuttgart: J. B. Metzler, 1992).

M. Kuehn, 'Tetens, Johann Nicolas', in H. Klemme, M. Kuehn (eds), *The Dictionary of Eighteenth Century German Philosophers* (London: Continuum, 2010), vol. 3, pp. 1163–1169.

S. Stapleford, 'A Refutation of Idealism from 1777', *Idealistic Studies* 40 (2010): 139–147.

E. Watkins, *Kant's Critique of Pure Reason. Background Source Materials* (Cambridge: Cambridge University Press, 2009), ch. 9.

WOLFF, CHRISTIAN

Christian Wolff (1679–1754) was the leading philosopher of the early German Enlightenment who contributed to forging the German philosophical vocabulary, the understanding of method and the architecture of a systematic philosophy adopted and criticized by Kant in almost equal measure. A teacher at the Pietist University of Halle until his expulsion in 1723 on the grounds of the threat his rationalist philosophy posed to religious orthodoxy, Wolff returned to his institution in 1740 upon the accession of → **Frederick the Great** to the throne of → **Prussia** as a symbol of the new 'enlightened' relationship between church and state. He produced two versions of his philosophical system, one written in the vernacular between 1713 and 1721 addressed to a broad German reading public and another more voluminous version in Latin written in exile between 1723 and 1740 for a European 'learned' audience. His system is the most plausible, historically specific candidate for the 'pure reason' criticized by Kant in **CPR**.

Wolff's reputation and influence among the general public and German universities was enormous for most of the eighteenth century, although they did not survive the constant and sustained level of criticism that culminated in Kant's Critical philosophy. While his thought was commonly paired with → **Leibniz** as the 'Leibnizian-Wolffian philosophy' it diverged considerably from that of his predecessor. While Wolff adopted the framework of degrees of perception ranging from obscure/confused to clear perception developed by Leibniz, it was without the latter's conviction that these degrees formed a continuum and were part of a dynamic unfolding of consciousness. He adopted the vocabulary of Leibniz, but put it to the service of a formal rationalism which came to characterize the early German Enlightenment and which Kant would describe as 'dogmatic'. The 'dogmatism' in question consisted in the centrality of the principle of contradiction from which Wolff derived subsequent concepts such as 'sufficient reason' and 'causality'. Accompanying the rational principle of contradiction was a view of enlightenment as the domination of the confusion of sense perception by the rational clarity of the understanding.

Wolff rested his entire philosophical system upon the principle of contradiction beginning accordingly with logic, then moving to metaphysics and thence to an ethics and politics. His commitment to rationalism is signalled by the titles of the parts of the system, all of which begin with the formula 'rational thoughts' (*vernünfftige Gedanken*). The Logic was published as *Rational Thoughts on the Powers of the Human Understanding and its Correct Use in the Knowledge of Truth* (1713), the Metaphysics as *Rational Thoughts on God, the World and the Human Soul as well as on Things Overall* (1719), the Ethics as *Rational Thoughts on Human Acts and Omissions for the Promotion of Happiness* (1720) and the Politics as *Rational Thoughts on Human Social Life and in particular the Commonwealth for the Promotion of the Happiness of the Human Species* (1721). A short overview of the system was published in 1728 as the *Preliminary Discourse on Philosophy in General*.[119] The most influential part of the system was the Metaphysics, which dominated the teaching of philosophy in Germany during the eighteenth century and provided the general overall structure for Kant's **CPR**, albeit with some significant and devastating specific changes such as the introduction of a 'Transcendental Aesthetic'.

Kant's assessment of Wolff's contribution was ambivalent: he could describe him, in **DSS**, as one 'who build[s] castles in the sky' (**DSS** 342) – a dogmatist out of contact with reality – as well as regarding him as a model for the methodical pursuit of systematic philosophy (cf. **CPR** Bxxxvi). Kant however, along with many other critics of his and the earlier generation of philosophers in Germany, could not accept the axiomatic quality of the principle of contradiction which for Wolff held that 'something cannot simultaneously be and not-be' (German Metaphysics, §6; translation mine). Kant's putting into question of the temporal assumptions contained in the word 'simultaneously' was prepared by a number of philosophers in the 1730s and 1740s, most notably → **Baumgarten** and → **Crusius**. He also accepted their critique of Wolff's view of sensible perception as but a confused variety of a rational perception of perfection.

His own critique of Wolff unfolded in four broad phases, the first in which he attempts to supplant Wolff's 'formal' with 'real' grounds of perception and reality, as in **LF** (1747), followed by a second in which he develops the distinction between sensible and intelligible sources of knowledge evident in **ID**. Kant's basing the Critical philosophy on the transcendental distinction between sensible and intelligible sources of knowledge and experience followed and was succeeded by a post-Critical defence of the achievements of the critiques against neo-Leibnizian and Wolffian critics such as → **Eberhard** in **Disc** and **PE**.

The most telling testimony to Kant's debt to Christian Wolff is **CPR** itself. The structure of **CPR** directly mirrors that of Wolff's German Metaphysics, making the former in many ways into a Critical gloss on the latter. Wolff's Metaphysics introduces the 'science of things in general' or ontology (general metaphysics) as the basis for the discussion of the objects of the sub-disciplines of metaphysics (special metaphysics), namely God (theology), the World (cosmology) and the Soul (rational and empirical psychology). Kant's 'Transcendental Analytic' was self-consciously cast as the Critical successor to 'ontology' (cf. B303=A247), and its achievement in setting the limits of knowledge and experience to appearances provided the basis for the critique of the sciences of theology, cosmology and psychology that make up the 'Transcendental Dialectic' of **CPR**.

Wolff's philosophy did not survive Kant's faithful demolition, in spite of the efforts of some of its defenders. By the time Hegel delivered his lectures on the history of philosophy, Wolff was a distant and unhappy memory. Yet his achievement in providing the vocabulary, structure and method of philosophy was vital for the invention of the Critical philosophy, and Wolff proved a worthy and resilient opponent for Kant. The significance of his work is not exhausted by its role as the pure reason or philosophical dogmatism opposed by Kant, as his contribution to the creation of philosophical German remains an enduring legacy and his controversial interest in Chinese philosophy is just one of the areas of his work that would reward fresh study. – HC

FURTHER READING

L. W. Beck, *Early German Philosophy: Kant and his Predecessors* (London: Thoemmes Continuum, 1996 [1969]).

H. Caygill, *Art of Judgement* (Oxford: Blackwell, 1989).

S. Grapotte, T. Prunea-Bretonnet (eds), *Kant et Wolff. Héritages et ruptures* (Paris: Vrin, 2011).

E. Watkins (ed.), *Kant's Critique of Pure Reason. Background Source Materials* (Cambridge: Cambridge University Press, 2009), ch. 1.

NOTES

[1] Cf. *Categories* v; *Metaphysics* vii, 1–4.

[2] Published as part of *Franciscus de Verulamio Summi Angliae Cancellaris Instauratio magna*, the *New Organon, or True Directions Concerning the Interpretation of Nature*. The edition used in this essay is Francis Bacon, *The New Organon*, ed. L. Jardine, M. Silverthorne (Cambridge, 2000).

[3] Bacon, *The New Organon*, Book I, XXXVIII.

[4] Bacon, *The New Organon*, Book II, XIV.

[5] See M. Sgarbi, *Logica e metafisica nel Kant pre-critico. L'ambiente intellettuale di Königsberg e la formazione della filosofia kantiana* (Frankfurt, 2010), pp. 95–102.

[6] See M. Sgarbi, 'The historical genesis of the Kantian concept of transcendental', *Archiv für Begriffsgeschichte* 53 (2011): 97–117.

[7] A. G. Baumgarten, *Metaphysica* (Halle, 1739), pp. 268–281.

[8] Cf. F. T. Rink, *Ansichten aus Immanuel Kant's Leben* (Königsberg, 1805), p. 19.

[9] Cf. K. Reich, *Kant und die Ethik der Griechen* (Tübingen, 1935); also in K. Reich, *Gesammelte Schriften*, ed. M. Baum et al. (Hamburg, 2001), pp. 113–146.

[10] The Latin title is *De finibus bonorum et malorum*.

[11] Cf. *Abhandlung über die menschlichen Pflichten in drey Büchern* (Breslau, 1783) and the commentary *Philosophische Anmerkungen und Abhandlungen zu Cicero's Büchern von den Pflichten* (Breslau, 1784).

[12] Cf. C. M. Gilbert, *Der Einfluß von Christian Garves Übersetzung Ciceros 'De Officiis' auf Kants 'Grundlegung der Metaphysik der Sitten'* (Regensburg, 1994).

[13] M. Kuehn, 'Kant and Cicero', in *Kant und die Berliner Aufklärung*, ed. V. Gerhardt, R.-P. Horstmann, R. Schumacher, vol. 3 (Berlin, 2001), p. 272.

[14] These were extended and integrated in his series of textbooks: on ethics (*Anweisung, vernünftig zu leben* [1744]), metaphysics (*Entwurf der notwendigen Vernunft-Wahrheiten, wiefern sie den zufälligen entgegen gesetzet werden* [1745]), logic (*Weg zur Gewißheit und Zuverlässigkeit der menschlichen Erkenntnis* [1747]), and physics (*Anleitung, über natürliche Begebenheiten ordentlich und vorsichtig nachzudenken* [1749]); quotations are from *Die philosophische Hauptwerke*, ed. G. Tonelli, S. Carboncini, R. Finster (Hildesheim, 1964–1987); translations are my own.

[15] Crusius, *Entwurf*, §15, pp. 26–27; cf. Crusius, *Weg zur Gewißheit*, §262, pp. 475–476.

[16] Crusius, *Weg zur Gewißheit*, §259, p. 469; cf. *Entwurf*, §31, p. 49, and §48, pp. 76–77.

[17] L. W. Beck, *Early German Philosophy. Kant and His Predecessors* (Cambridge, 1969), pp. 394–402.

[18] The edition of Descartes' work cited here is Descartes, *Oeuvres complètes*, ed. Adam & Tannery (AT) (Paris, 1996), followed by volume and page numbers; translations are mine.

[19] This view rests ultimately on their firm belief in what Descartes called the *lumen naturale* and what Kant regards as the a priori nature of reason, making both Kant and Descartes quintessential rationalists.

[20] The *locus classicus* for a comparative study of the Cartesian and Kantian cogito's is P. Lachièze-Rey, *L'idéalisme kantien* (Paris, 1931), ch. 1.

[21] Descartes speaks of 'obstinately' adhering to the doubting procedure: 'manebo obstinate in hac meditatione defixus' (AT VII, 23).

[22] Some also claim that, in particular in the Refutation of Idealism (which replaced the fourth Paralogism in the second edition of **CPR** and was in fact designed as a refutation of what Kant calls Cartesian 'problematic idealism'), Kant presents what has been called a transcendental argument that is anti-sceptical in nature.

[23] Notice that the famous *cogito ergo sum* does not appear as such in the *Meditations*. It occurs in this form in the *Discourse* ('Je pense, donc je suis') (AT VI, 33) and in the *Principles of Philosophy* ('Ego cogito, ergo sum') (AT VIII, 7). In the *Meditations* itself, the pivotal statement 'I am, I exist' occurs at AT VII, 25, 27.

[24] In Kant's so-called pre-Critical period, Descartes is specifically addressed in his first work **LF**, and only briefly mentioned by name in **NH**, **DSS**, **OPD**, and **Obs**. After **CPR**, in the Critical period Descartes is mentioned in **CJ** and **Anthr**.

25 See AT VII, 140–141. The *locus classicus* for a discussion of this topic is J. Hintikka, '*Cogito, ergo sum*: inference of performance?', *Philosophical Review* LXXI (1962): 3–32. See also the essential work on Descartes' philosophy of mind by H. Sarkar, *Descartes' Cogito. Saved from the Great Shipwreck* (Cambridge, 2003).

26 K. Düsing, 'Kant und Epikur. Untersuchungen zum Problem der Grundlegung einer Ethik', *Allgemeine Zeitschrift für Philosophie* 1,2 (1976): 39–58, argues that Kant does not do justice to the Epicurean principle of ἡδονή, for he does not make the crucial distinction between kinetic and katastematic lust.

27 Cf. **Refl 6894**, **LE 253** and **LE-M 621**.

28 Cf. **Refl 6894**.

29 The French mathematician and cosmologist Laplace referred to Euler as 'the master of us all', urging mathematicians to read him (W. Dunham, *Euler: The Master of Us All* [Washington, 1999], p. xiii).

30 Euler's pioneering work in setting up graph theory was triggered by the famous Königsberg bridge problem that exerted its citizens (and, one can speculate, Kant's family among them) in the first half of the eighteenth century. This is the problem of finding a path crossing each bridge once and only once and returning to its starting point (B. Hopkins, R. Wilson, 'The truth about Königsberg', in R. E. Bradley, C. E. Sandifer [eds], *Leonhard Euler: Life, Work and Legacy* [Amsterdam, 2007], p. 410).

31 This did not prevent Voltaire from referring to him as one who 'never learnt philosophy' (W. Dunham, *Euler: The Master of Us All*, p. xxvi). And the lack of esteem of his contemporaries for his philosophical acumen was well matched by Euler's disdain for philosophers (W. Breidert, 'Leonhard Euler and philosophy', in R. E. Bradley, C. E. Sandifer [eds], *Leonhard Euler: Life, Work and Legacy*, pp. 97–108).

32 W. Breidert, 'Leonhard Euler and philosophy', p. 100.

33 See A. Speiser, *Leonhard Euler und die Deutsche Philosophie* (Zürich, 1934), p. 8.

34 Speiser, *Leonhard Euler und die Deutsche Philosophie*, p. 9.

35 M. Friedman, *Kant and the Exact Sciences* (Cambridge, 1992), p. 15.

36 Euler, *Réflexions sur l'espace et le temps*, in *Opera Omnia*, ed. C. Carathéodory, Series Tertia, vol. 2 (Zürich, 1952), pp. 376–377.

37 Friedman, *Kant and the Exact Sciences*, p. 19. This view is discussed extensively in **Inq** 276–286.

38 From 1758 (see **MR 13–26**), Kant's views did however differ from Leibniz's in that his relational notion of space was now grounded on the analysis of motion, and the claim that there is a preferred reference frame (J. V. Buroker, *Space and Incongruence: The Origin of Kant's Idealism* [Dordrecht, 1981], pp. 43–47). Moreover, his understanding of the law of inertia and its incompatibility with Leibnizian monadology can be seen as influenced by Euler (H. Timerding, 'Kant und Euler', *Kant-Studien* 23 [1919]: 18–64).

39 See again Euler, *Réflexions sur l'espace et le temps*.

40 Euler, *Réflexions sur l'espace et le temps*, p. 381.

41 Buroker, *Space and Incongruence*, p. 51.

42 Breidert, 'Leonhard Euler and philosophy', p. 107.

43 Friedman, *Kant and the Exact Sciences*, p. 220.

44 For an account of Herz as Enlightenment philosopher, see M. L. Davies, *Identity or History? Markus Herz and the End of the Enlightenment* (Detroit, 1995).

45 Cf. *Briefe an Aerzte* (Berlin, 1777), p. 84; *Grundriß aller medicinischen Wissenschaften* (Berlin, 1782); *Versuch über den Schwindel* (Berlin, 1786, ²1791); and *Grundlage zu den Vorlesungen über die Experimental-Physik* (Berlin, 1787). On his remarkable career as physiologist, see C. M. Leder, *Die Grenzgänge des Marcus Herz. Beruf, Haltung und Identität eines jüdischen Arztes gegen Ende des 18. Jahrhunderts* (Münster/New York, 2007).

46 A modern edition has been published by E. Conrad et al. (Hamburg, 1990). The important *Wörterbuch zum leichteren Gebrauch der Kantischen Schriften*, compiled and written by Karl Christian Erhard Schmid (Jena, 1786 ff.) does not quote Kant's **ID**, but rather Herz's

essay when dealing with the Dissertation. See further on Herz and the Dissertation the essay 'Until 1781: Responses to Kant's 'Inaugural Dissertation' (1770)', this volume.

47 Kant in a letter to Nicolai dated 25 October 1773 (**Corr-I** 142; translation mine). Cf. Kant's letter to Herz of 7 June 1771 (**Corr-I** 123).

48 *Versuch über den Geschmack und die Ursachen seiner Verschiedenheit* (Mitau-Leipzig, 1776), p. 36; translation mine.

49 Cf. Kant's letter to Herz of 15 October 1790 (**Corr-II** 229).

50 Cf. the chapter on Herz in E. Watkins (ed.), *Kant's Critique of Pure Reason. Background Source Materials* (Cambridge, 2009), ch. 7, which contains translations of the letters as well as parts of *Betrachtungen* (translated as *Observations from Speculative Philosophy*).

51 See further on Maimon the essay 'First responses to the *Critique of Pure Reason*: the 1780s and later', this volume.

52 Hume, *An Enquiry Concerning Human Understanding*, ed. T. L. Beauchamp (Oxford, 1999), 2.3 (hereafter referred to as EHU).

53 Hume, *A Treatise of Human Nature*, ed. D. Fate Norton, M. J. Norton (Oxford, 2000), 1.1.1.1 (hereafter referred to as T).

54 Hume, *An Enquiry Concerning the Principles of Morals*, ed. T. Beauchamp (Oxford, 1998), Appendix 1.3.

55 See e.g. *Principles of Nature and Grace, Based on Reason* (henceforth PNG), §§1–2, original text in *Die philosophischen Schriften von Gottfried Wilhelm Leibniz*, ed. C. I. Gerhardt (Berlin, 1875–90), vol. 6, p. 598 (hereafter cited as G, followed by volume and page number[s]); translation from *G. W. Leibniz: Philosophical Essays*, trans. R. Ariew, D. Garber (Indianapolis, 1989), p. 207 (hereafter cited as AG followed by page number[s]).

56 *A New System of Nature* (henceforth NSN), G 4: 478, AG: 139.

57 NSN, G 4: 479, AG: 139.

58 PNG §1–2, G 6: 598, AG: 207; see also NSN, G 4: 479, AG: 139.

59 *Monadology* (henceforth M) §9, G 6: 608, AG: 214.

60 See e.g. M §1, §36, PNG §§1–3.

61 *New Essays on Human Understanding*, trans. & ed. P. Remnant, J. Bennett (Cambridge,

1981), p. 14; hereafter cited as NE followed by page number(s).

62 Descartes, *Principles of Philosophy*, I, 51, Adam & Tannery, vol. VIII, p. 24, translation from *The Philosophical Writings of Descartes*, vol. I, trans. Cottingham, Stoothoff, Murdoch (Cambridge, 1985), p. 210.

63 NSN, G 4: 483, AG:143.

64 See NSN, G 4: 485, AG: 144.

65 See NSN, G 4: 483, AG: 143.

66 NSN, G 4: 484, AG: 143.

67 M §56, G 6: 616, AG: 220.

68 PNG §3, G 6: 599, AG: 207.

69 M §60, G 6: 617, AG: 220.

70 NE 53.

71 NE 54.

72 PNG §4, G 6: 600, AG: 208.

73 M §19, G 6: 610, AG: 215.

74 PNG §§4–5, G 6: 600–601, AG: 208–209; M §§28–30, G 6: 611–612, AG: 216–217.

75 M §§31–32, G 6: 612, AG: 217.

76 M §§33–36, G 6: 612–613.

77 See Leibniz's fourth and fifth letters, G 7: 372, 393–394, AG: 327–328, 333.

78 See Leibniz's third and fourth letters, G 7: 363–364, 372, AG: 324–325, 328.

79 See especially the remark to the Amphiboly of the Concepts of Reflection (A268ff.=B324ff.) and **PE** 281ff., 372ff..

80 See R. Pozzo, *Georg Friedrich Meiers Vernunftlehre: eine historisch-systematische Untersuchung* (Stuttgart-Bad Cannstatt, 2000).

81 See N. Hinske, *Zwischen Aufklärung und Vernunftkritik: Studien zum Kantschen Logikcorpus* (Stuttgart-Bad Cannstatt, 1998).

82 Meier, *Auszug aus der Vernunftlehre* (Halle, 1752), 26.

83 **LL** 530–531; cf. **Refl** 2702; **JL** 72, 139.

84 See R. Pozzo, 'Prejudices and horizons: G. F. Meier's *Vernunftlehre* and its relation to Kant', *Journal of the History of Philosophy* 43 (2005): 185–202.

85 See M. Massimi, 'Kant's dynamical theory of matter in 1755, and its debt to speculative Newtonian experimentalism', *Studies in History and Philosophy of Science* 42,4 (2011): 525–543.

86 See M. Stan, 'Kant's early theory of motion: metaphysical dynamics and relativity', *The Leibniz Review* 19 (2009): 29–61.

[87] For an influential defence, see M. Friedman, *Kant and the Exact Sciences* (Cambridge, 1992).

[88] See D. Warren, 'Kant on attractive and repulsive force: the balancing argument', in M. Domski, M. Dickson (eds), *Discourse on a New Method. Reinvigorating the Marriage between History and Philosophy of Science* (Chicago, La Salle, IL, 2010), pp. 193–241.

[89] M. Friedman, *Kant and the Exact Sciences* (Cambridge, 1992).

[90] See E. Watkins, 'Kant's justification of the laws of mechanics', *Studies in History and Philosophy of Science* 29 (1998): 539–560.

[91] See J. G. Schlosser, *Platos Briefe* (Königsberg, 1795); trans. G. R. Morrow, *Plato's Epistles* (Indianapolis, IN, 1962).

[92] J. J. Rousseau, *Of the Social Contract*, Bk. I, ch. viii.

[93] J. J. Rousseau, *Of the Social Contract*, Bk. I, ch. vii.

[94] All of these references are translated by G. Johnson and G. Magee in G. Johnson (ed.), *Kant on Swedenborg: Dreams of a Spirit-Seer and Other Writings* (West Chester, PA, 2002); hereafter referred to as *Kant on Swedenborg*.

[95] See G. Johnson, *Kant on Swedenborg*, pp. 67–72. See also G. Johnson, 'A Commentary on Kant's *Dreams of a Spirit-Seer*', PhD dissertation (Washington, DC, 2001), ch. 2.

[96] G. Johnson, *Kant on Swedenborg*, pp. 73–75.

[97] G. Johnson, *Kant on Swedenborg*, pp. 113.

[98] See G. Johnson, '*Träume eines Geistersehers –* Polemik gegen die Metaphysik oder Parodie der Popularphilosophie?', in F. Stengel (ed.), *Kant und Swedenborg. Zugänge zu einem umstrittenen Verhältnis* (Tübingen, 2008), pp. 99–122 ; hereafter referred to as *Kant und Swedenborg*.

[99] I summarize the differing interpretations of DSS in G. Johnson, 'A Commentary on Kant's *Dreams of a Spirit-Seer*', ch. 1. For more recent interpretations, see F. Stengel (ed.), *Kant und Swedenborg*.

[100] I summarize such arguments in G. Johnson, 'Did Kant dissemble his interest in Swedenborg?', *The New Philosophy* 102 (1999): 529–560.

[101] G. Johnson, *Kant on Swedenborg*, pp. 83–86.

[102] G. Johnson, 'A Commentary on Kant's *Dreams of a Spirit-Seer*', ch. 7.

[103] G. Johnson, 'From Swedenborg's spirit world to Kant's kingdom of ends', *Aries: Journal for the Study of Western Esotericism* 9,1 (2009): 83–99. See also G. Johnson, 'Swedenborg's *positive* influence on the development of Kant's mature moral philosophy', in S. McNeilly (ed.), *On the True Philosopher and the True Philosophy: Essays on Swedenborg* (London, 2002), pp. 21–38.

[104] See G. Johnson, 'Kant on Swedenborg in the *Lectures on Metaphysics*: the 1760s and 1770s', *Studia Swedenborgiana* 10,1 (1996): 1–38; and 'Kant on Swedenborg in the *Lectures on Metaphysics*: the 1780s and 1790s', *Studia Swedenborgiana* 10,2 (1997): 1–26.

[105] G. Johnson, *Kant on Swedenborg*, pp. 108–109.

[106] G. Johnson, 'Kant, Swedenborg, and Rousseau: The synthesis of Enlightenment and esotericism in *Dreams of a Spirit-Seer*', in R. Geffarth, M. Meumann, M. Neugebauer-Wölk (eds), *Aufklärung und Esoterik: Wege in die Moderne*, forthcoming.

[107] First noted in K. Rosenkranz, *Geschichte der Kant'schen Philosophie* (Leipzig, 1840), p. 65.

[108] Tetens, *Ueber die allgemeine speculativische Philosophie* (Bützow/Wismar, 1775), in *Die philosophischen Werke*, ed. H.-J. Engfer, 4 vols. (Hildesheim, 1979–2005), here vol. IV, p. 18; translations from this work are my own.

[109] Tetens, *Ueber die allgemeine speculativische Philosophie*, p. 3.

[110] Tetens, *Philosophische Versuche über die menschliche Natur und ihre Entwickelung*, 2 vols. (Leipzig, 1777), in *Werke* I, p. xxix; translations from this work are my own. Some further passages are translated in E. Watkins (ed.), *Kant's Critique of Pure Reason. Background Source Materials* (Cambridge, 2009), ch. 9.

[111] Tetens, *Ueber die allgemeine speculativische Philosophie*, p. 72.

[112] Tetens, *Ueber die allgemeine speculativische Philosophie*, p. 49.

[113] Tetens, *Philosophische Versuche über die menschliche Natur und ihre Entwickelung*, *Werke* I, p. iv ff., *Werke* II, pp. 223–299.

114 Tetens, *Ueber die allgemeine speculativische Philosophie*, p. 74ff.

115 Tetens, *Philosophische Versuche über die menschliche Natur und ihre Entwickelung*, *Werke* I, pp. 312–327.

116 Tetens, *Ueber die allgemeine speculativische Philosophie*, p. 54n.

117 17 May 1779; J. G. Hamann, *Briefwechsel*, ed. A. Henkel (Wiesbaden, 1959), vol. 4, p. 81.

118 13 October 1777; J. G. Hamann, *Briefwechsel*, vol. 3, p. 377.

119 Trans. R. J. Blackwell (Indianapolis, 1963).

PART III:
KEY THEMES AND TOPICS

4

KEY THEMES AND TOPICS

This section consists of an A–Z entries list of key Kantian concepts, which are singled out for their particular technical usage in Kant's theoretical, practical and aesthetic philosophy and in his anthropology, philosophy of nature and philosophy of religion. Particularly those concepts and terms are addressed that are closely associated with Kant and thus have special significance in the context of his thought, or underwent semantic changes in Kant's philosophical language. Some of the key concepts are grouped together under more general topics. Also the familiar sections of core arguments in the *Critique of Pure Reason* are addressed under their known names, e.g. Analogies of Experience, Antinomies, Paralogisms, Proofs of the existence of God etc. Consistency overall has been sought while respecting the pluralist interpretive voices across the entries.

There are also provided here lists of further reading that will enable the reader to undertake further research on all major topics. Given the large number of secondary texts available on Kant, these are necessarily selective; emphasis has been placed on the most recent and accessible literature in English, German and occasionally French. A more extensive bibliography of the English

literature is provided elsewhere in this *Companion*.

The aim of this chapter is certainly not to be exhaustive but to provide the serious beginning student of Kant and the generally interested philosopher with the basic vocabulary that is required for an informed study of Kant's work. For more advanced scholarly research, one is advised to consult the three-volume *Kant-Lexikon*, edited by G. Mohr, J. Stolzenberg and M. Willaschek (Berlin/New York: de Gruyter, 2016). – DS

ABSTRACTION → LOGIC

AESTHETIC JUDGMENT

Kant's Critique of the Aesthetic Power of Judgment, the first part of **CJ**, has exerted an enormous influence on modern aesthetics. Yet some of its central claims remain a matter of controversy and its relation to the declared intentions of **CJ** as a whole, as they are presented in its 'Introduction', still seems to elude perspicuous understanding.

It is useful to distinguish aesthetic judgments into three kinds, according to their objects. The beauty of works of art is dealt with primarily in the discussion of art and genius (→ **art, genius**). The aesthetic sublime is dealt with in the Analytic of the Sublime of **CJ** (→ **sublime**). Despite the great importance of these discussions, Kant's primary focus seems to be – this, though, is a disputed matter – on the beauty of natural objects, examined in the Analytic of the Beautiful and the Deduction of Pure Aesthetic Judgments.

The Analytic presents a four-part definition of pure judgments of taste: (1) pure judgments of taste are not cognitive judgments that attribute the objective property of beauty to an object (→ **judgment**). They are subjective expressions of a distinct pleasure. Unlike expressions of sensual enjoyment or positive moral evaluation, judgments of beauty express a contemplative disinterested pleasure (→ **interest**).

(2) Although pure judgments of taste are singular and express a subjective pleasure, they lay claim to universal assent. This reveals that a subject making such judgments assumes that the mental capacities disinterestedly involved in them function in a similar manner in all other subjects. In this mental state, the understanding does not apply a concept to an intuition given in the → **imagination**. Rather, the understanding and the imagination are in a state which Kant characterizes as harmonious free play.

(3) The third moment examines this state further and describes it as 'the subjective purposiveness of representations in the mind of the beholder, which indicates a certain purposiveness of the representational state of the subject, and in this an ease in apprehending a given form in the imagination [. . .]' (**CJ** 227). The form of a representation of the imagination is felt somehow to fit or be made for the understanding and this state itself is described as purposive, yet it 'affords

absolutely no cognition [. . .] of the object' (**CJ** 228).

(4) Finally, Kant characterizes the universal assent that judgments of taste demand as necessary. But the 'necessity of the universal assent that is thought in a judgment of taste is a subjective necessity, which is represented as objective under the presupposition of a common sense' (**CJ** 239, heading) (→ **necessity**). Only on the assumption of a shared sensibility can a subject say of a judgment that 'everyone *should* agree with it' (**CJ** 239).

Two central and perhaps related controversies loom over the Analytic. Aesthetic pleasure is characterized as the mental state in which the understanding and the imagination interact in a state of harmonious free play. The precise characterization of this process is a matter of disagreement. On one interpretation, the understanding moves freely within a range of concepts that might be applied to a sensible manifold, without determining the manifold by means of them. According to a second interpretation, the understanding does determine the object of an aesthetic judgment conceptually, identifying it as the kind of thing it is, yet expresses the feeling that the object offers a greater unity or coherence than the application of these concepts demands. Both interpretations hold that aesthetic judgments somehow involve particular conceptual judgments. Thus, they might be seen as leading to the thought, often implicit and itself contested, that there is no essential difference between judgment of natural beauty and judgment concerning the beauty of art. For the appreciation of representational art clearly requires a conceptual ground.

These interpretations of the feeling of aesthetic pleasure, however, find only scant textual support. Kant says quite clearly and often that pure aesthetic judgments please 'without a concept' (**CJ** 219). Indeed, according to the prevalent reading, they express a sense of harmony or fit between a particular manifold given in the imagination and the understanding as a faculty. In this relation, the understanding employs no concepts. A central consequence of this interpretation is that judgments of beauty in nature and art are different in kind.

In the 'Introduction' to **CJ**, Kant claims that the assumption of the purposiveness of nature is a subjective condition of experience: 'The power of judgment thus also has in itself an *a priori* principle for the possibility of nature, though only in a subjective respect, by means of which it prescribes a law, not to nature (as autonomy), but to itself (as heautonomy) for reflection on nature.' (**CJ** 185–186)

Remarkably, a distinction is drawn between two types of reflective judgment that presuppose the teleological or conceptual purposiveness of nature and its aesthetic purposiveness respectively (**CJ** 188–194) (→ **teleology**). This raises the question of whether the aesthetic pleasure of feeling that certain sensible manifolds apprehended by the imagination are somehow purposive for the understanding is a subjective condition of experience. Is this why a critique of aesthetic judgment is an essential part of the Critical project?

Perhaps it is Kant's view that at the most fundamental, pre-conceptual level it is aesthetically pleasing spatial (or temporal) forms that we make into objects. It is pure judgments of taste that carve objects out of the manifold given in intuition. Furthermore, this aesthetic delineation of objects makes possible a first sorting of them into similarly shaped objects and so an account of our grasp of natural kinds. This suggestion finds confirmation in the discussion of the notion of a 'normal

idea', the spatial shape that would result if we were to superimpose a large number of members of a kind: 'This *normal idea* is not derived from the proportions taken from experience, as *determinate rules*; rather, it is in accordance with it that rules for judging first become possible. It is the image for the whole species [. . .].' (**CJ** 234)

The assumption of the aesthetic purposiveness of nature is then the assumption that the sensible manifolds that we find aesthetically pleasing will prove amenable to conceptual investigation. If this is right, then aesthetic judgment is a necessary condition of → **experience** and → **knowledge**, because it is the 'subjective condition of cognizing' (**CJ** 238) and the assumption of a common sense is a 'necessary condition of the universal communicability of our cognition' (**CJ** 239). Without the assumption that nature is aesthetically purposive the 'understanding could not find itself in it' (**CJ** 193).

In the Dialectic of the Aesthetic Power of Judgment, Kant appears to draw metaphysical conclusions from his analysis of judgments of natural beauty. The conflict between their demand for universal assent and their subjective and non-conceptual character is resolved by pointing to the idea of the aesthetic purposiveness of nature, which Kant here refers to as the 'supersensible substratum of humanity' (**CJ** 340). – IG

FURTHER READING

H. Allison, *Kant's Theory of Taste: A Reading of the Critique of Aesthetic Judgment* (Cambridge: Cambridge University Press, 2001).

H. Ginsborg, 'Lawfulness without a law: Kant on the free play of imagination and understanding', *Philosophical Studies* 25 (1997): 37–81.

P. Guyer, 'Kant's ambitions in the third *Critique*', in P. Guyer (ed.), *The Cambridge Companion to Kant and Modern Philosophy* (Cambridge: Cambridge University Press, 2006), pp. 538–587.

AMPHIBOLY

In → **Aristotle**, an amphiboly is a logical fallacy caused by the ambiguity of an expression. In the section 'On the Amphiboly of the Concepts of Reflection' in **CPR** (A260–A292=B316–349), Kant offers an account of how the main points in → **Leibniz**'s metaphysical system arise from a transcendental amphiboly. This is the fallacy of confusing appearances with objects of the pure understanding or noumena. The neglect to distinguish between them results from overlooking the distinction between two sources of cognition, sensibility and understanding. Leibniz thus treats all objects as noumena, which can be accounted for by purely conceptual means.

The cause of transcendental amphiboly is the neglect of transcendental reflection. In general → **logic**, reflection is the comparison of concepts. For logic, the source of a → **representation**, i.e. the question of which faculty it belongs to, is of no importance. By contrast, the task of transcendental reflection is to determine the cognitive source to which representations (and judgments based on them) belong, that is, whether they belong to the understanding or to sensibility. To thus determine the *topos* (place) of a putative cognition is a prerequisite for making philosophical claims. It is therefore a basic aspect of → **critique** (A263=B319).

For this purpose concepts of reflection are used. These consist of four pairs (corresponding to the four titles in the Table of Judgment): → **identity** and difference; agreement and opposition; the inner and the outer; and matter and → **form**. The concepts of reflection differ from categories in that categories determine objects (→ **deduction**), whereas reflection merely serves the initial task of finding the *topos* for a concept.

Kant examines the main points in Leibniz' metaphysics from the vantage point of the concepts of reflection. He attempts to show that Leibniz reached his results through a transcendental amphiboly. Leibniz, who 'intellectualized' the appearances (A271=B327), admits no role for sensibility, which he interprets as confused cognition.

Since he does not distinguish between the sources of cognition, Leibniz's reflection is merely logical. With respect to the first pair of reflective concepts (identity/difference), this leads to a metaphysical application of the principle of identity of indiscernibles. For concepts, the principle is valid, that is, if two concepts have the same internal determination, then they are identical. However, due to the amphiboly, Leibniz neglects differences that stem from sensibility. Space (→ **Transcendental Aesthetic**) enables two conceptually identical objects to exist at different places, so Leibniz's principle is invalid if taken as a law for appearances (A272=B328).

Reflecting on agreement and opposition, as applied to concepts, leads to the doctrine that reality is entirely positive and contains no opposition. But in the experienced world of appearances there exists real opposition, such as opposed forces. Kant also traces the rationalist belief that evil is mere privation to this confusion of appearances and objects of the understanding (noumena) (A273=B329).

As for the inner and the outer, objects of the understanding must have something inner which is independent of outer relations. This leads Leibniz to model his monads on our inner state, ascribing representations to them. Monads, as pure interiorities, must also lack real influence on each other, and be united only by means of predetermined harmony (A274–275=B330–331). Transcendental reflection, on the other hand, shows that a substance in space contains nothing absolutely internal, but consists in mere relations, due to the structure of space as a form of → **intuition** (B340=A284).

The relation between matter and form, finally, is reversed due to the amphiboly. For noumena, there must be matter for there to be form, and thus Leibniz assumes substances as ground for all possibility. As regards appearances, however, form precedes matter, since forms of intuition make possible the experience of objects (A267–268=B323–324). – MQ

FURTHER READING

M. Fichant, 'L'Amphibologie des concepts de la réflexion: la fin de l'ontologie', in V. Rohden et al. (eds), *Recht und Frieden in der Philosophie Kants. Akten des X. Internationalen Kant-Kongresses*, Band 1 (Berlin/New York: de Gruyter, 2008), pp. 71–93.

S. Heßbrüggen-Walter, 'Topik, Reflexion und Vorurteilskritik: Kants Amphibolie der Reflexionsbegriffe im Kontext', *Archiv für Geschichte der Philosophie* 86 (2004): 146–175.

M. Willaschek, 'Phaenomena/Noumena und die Amphibolie der Reflexionsbegriffe', in G. Mohr, M. Willaschek (eds), *Immanuel Kant. Kritik der reinen Vernunft*, in the series *Klassiker auslegen* (Berlin: Akademie Verlag, 1998), pp. 325–351.

ANALOGY

Kant talks of analogy in at least two ways. (1) There is the sense, common in the early modern logical tradition, in which analogy is characterized along with induction as an epistemically weaker form of inference, whereby one attempts to infer 'from the particular to the universal' (**LL** 287), and whose conclusions can never achieve a status of strict apodictic universality (→ **necessity**). Whereas an inductive inference postulates a single property of some observed objects to the entire set of those objects, analogical inferences postulate that insofar as two objects share some properties, those two objects share all their properties (**LL** 287).

Analogy is used in (2) a more developed sense in the Critical period, which follows the example of mathematical ratios in geometrical construction, i.e. $a:b :: c:x$. As regards mathematical ratios, Kant argues that 'if two members of the proportion are given the third is also thereby given, i.e., can be constructed' (A179=B222).

In philosophical analogies, in contrast, only 'the *relation* to this fourth member, but not *this* fourth *member* itself' (A179–180=B222) can be given or constructed. The allusion seems to be that analogy cannot be used to secure determinate → **knowledge**, such as the specific value of x, but can validate more indeterminate inferences, such as that given knowledge of a, b and the relation between them, we can infer from a given c that there must be a similar relation to an x, even though x is not (and perhaps could not) be an object of knowledge.

This model of analogy is used on different levels in the Critical system. While the principles of understanding are appropriately characterized as analogies, so too are the inferences that extend beyond the limits of possible → **experience**. Here, Kant suggests that characterization of the sphere beyond human experience can proceed through a process of 'symbolic anthropomorphism' (**P** 357). Such an inference takes the relation between known objects and posits it as existing between the sphere of possible experience and the sphere beyond possible experience.

The form of analogical inference finds a role throughout the Critical system, whether in regard to the characterization of the divine (**P** 357) (→ **proofs of the existence of God**), the understanding of the free will of human beings (**CPrR** 55–57) (→ **freedom**) or the purposiveness of nature which can only be characterized through the process of analogy, in comparison with the practice of the human artist (**FI** 240) (→ **teleology**). – JC

ANALOGIES OF EXPERIENCE

In **ID**, Kant asks for an explanation of 'how it is possible *that a plurality of substances should be in mutual interaction with each other*, and in this way belong to the same whole, which is called a world' (**ID** 407). This explanation is provided within the Critical system in the sections of **CPR** detailed as the Analogies of Experience.

The Analogies of Experience are the set of the principles of the understanding corresponding to the third class in the Table of the Categories, that of relation (A80=B106) (→ **deduction**). The categories under the heading of relation themselves correspond to the categorical, hypothetical and disjunctive forms of → **judgment**. Thus the principle of causality, for example, as discussed in the second analogy, is to be understood as the schematized application of the category of cause, which is an analogue of the hypothetical

form of judgment. Thus, the principles of the understanding 'are nothing other than rules of the objective use of the categories' (A161=B200).

As with all the principles however, the application of the schematized categories is discovered by way of argumentation to be a necessary and objective condition of the possibility of coherent → **experience**, and not merely a subjective employment of a concept. As Kant notes in **P** (**P** 258–259), the application of the concept of cause could be justified on the grounds of pragmatic expedience or perhaps even indispensability, but the genuine source of its objective validity is its role as a transcendental condition of experience.

Kant states that the general principle of the Analogies is that '[e]xperience is possible only through the representation of a necessary connection of perceptions' (A176=B218). As such, each of the Analogies concerns the manner in which the connection of representations within our experience is represented as manifesting a necessary connection. Since the schematized categories are nothing but the representation of temporal relations within the manifold of representations, the Analogies can be understood as detailing the sense in which temporal representation manifests different forms of necessary connection between our perceptions.

The result that Kant aims for is to demonstrate how a traditional metaphysical picture of the physical world as a community of causally interacting substances undergoing change within a spatiotemporal continuum can be articulated solely within the Critical vocabulary of necessary connection within the temporal order of representation.

A central claim that seems to play a role in the argument for each of the Analogies is that time itself cannot be perceived (e.g. B225, A192=B237, B257). Whereas time is, as argued in the → **Transcendental Aesthetic**, a fundamental representation within which all representation of objects takes place, it does not therefore present itself as a distinct object of perception. Thus, Kant will claim that the representation of the *modes* of time, i.e. the various temporal relations that manifest themselves in experience, can only take place via our representation of objects as they appear in time.

Kant states that the Analogies are to be understood as 'dynamical' principles of the understanding, which he states are concerned with the '*existence* of an appearance in general' (A160=B199). Dynamical principles are in one sense inferior to what Kant calls 'mathematical' principles (represented by the → **Axioms of Intuition** and → **Anticipations of Perception**) in that while the latter are 'unconditionally necessary', dynamical principles on the other hand are necessary 'only under the condition of empirical thinking in an experience' (A160=B199).

However, this restriction does not render the dynamical principles any less epistemically secure with regard to experience (A160=B200). While mathematical (or 'constitutive') principles serve to determine particular characteristics of related perceptions, dynamical principles – which Kant later characterizes as equivalent to a description of the dynamical principles as having a 'regulative' function – do not characterize the appearances themselves (e.g. in terms of extensive or intensive magnitude); rather, they concern relations between appearances which determine that, given a particular perception, there must be a relation to another existing perception that can be characterized in accordance with the modes of time (A179=B222).

The principle of the First Analogy (in the B-edition version) is as follows: 'In all change of appearances substance persists, and its

quantum is neither increased nor diminished in nature.' (B224) This section presents the case that time itself functions as the unchanging substratum within which all change, considered as a temporal relation manifested between objects, is represented.

The traditional metaphysical demand articulated by the concept of substance is, Kant claims, 'the substratum of everything real' (B225) and this demand can be satisfied by the role of time itself in the representation of an objective manifold for the possibility of coherent experience. The second clause of the principle, regarding the quantum of substance, is thought to follow from the preceding claim, whereby if time itself is unchanging, and time itself provides the role of substance, then since a diminution or increase in substance would entail a change in time itself, no such diminution or increase can occur.

The principle of the Second Analogy (again in the B-edition version) is that '[a]ll alterations occur in accordance with the law of the connection of cause and effect' (B232). Kant argues that the mere apprehension of two perceptions in a certain temporal order fails by itself to determine whether that temporal order is a result of it representing a genuine relation between the object(s) of those perceptions, or whether the order is a mere result of the order of the apprehensions of the perceiver – thus the order of the perceptions in mere consciousness is insufficient to determine whether that order represents an objective or subjective relation of the appearances.

Kant claims that the grasping of the conscious order as an objective relation must then result from the subject's contribution of the concept of cause, which demands that those perceptions be represented as manifesting a necessary and lawful relation, rather than a merely contingent association. Furthermore, without such a contribution, Kant holds that the manifold of appearance would fail to manifest the minimal order that allows for the coherence of experience itself (A188=B234).

The principle of the Third Analogy (in the B-version) states that '[a]ll substances, insofar as they can be perceived in space as simultaneous, are in thoroughgoing interaction' (B256). Simultaneity is defined by Kant as 'the existence of the manifold at the same time' (B257). The strategy of argumentation is broadly similar to that for the preceding analogies. From the mere subjective order of the manifestation of representations in our consciousness, we cannot infer the objective relation of those appearances as simultaneous, any more than we can infer their necessary succession, as in the Second Analogy.

Kant argues, then, that it must be the case that the concept of the reciprocal sequence of the perceptions (such that a reversal of the subjective time-order would not misrepresent the objective relation between them) must be applied so that the very notion of simultaneity, and thus the coherence of our experience, be possible (B258).

Together these principles secure the picture of empirical nature as a unified continuum of existing things ordered by necessary rules, i.e. undergoing law-like governance. The Analogies are taken by Kant to provide metaphysical foundations for the consolidation of Newtonian laws of mechanics (→ laws (of nature)/lawfulness, Newton). In MFNS, Kant takes the Analogies to provide a basis in general metaphysics for the first, second and third laws of mechanics (MFNS 541–553) (→ natural science). – JC

FURTHER READING

S. M. Bayne, *Kant on Causation. On the Fivefold Routes to the Principle of Causation* (Albany, NY: SUNY Press, 2004).

A. Melnick, 'Kant's proofs of substance and causation', in P. Guyer (ed.), *The Cambridge Companion to Kant and Modern Philosophy* (Cambridge: Cambridge University Press, 2006), pp. 203–237.

S. Rödl, *Kategorien des Zeitlichen* (Frankfurt a/M: Suhrkamp, 2005), esp. chs 4 and 5.

B. Thöle, 'Die Analogien der Erfahrung', in G. Mohr, M. Willaschek (eds), *Immanuel Kant. Kritik der reinen Vernunft*, in the series *Klassiker Auslegen* (Berlin: Akademie Verlag, 1998), pp. 267–296.

E. Watkins, 'The System of Principles', in P. Guyer (ed.), *The Cambridge Companion to Kant's 'Critique of Pure Reason'* (Cambridge: Cambridge University Press, 2010), pp. 151–167.

ANALYSIS (ANALYTIC)

Kant conceives of analysis in terms of the decomposition of a whole into its parts, although it also has the sense of a regress from consequence to ground (**ID** 388). The former sense can be seen in his accounts of conceptual analysis and of analytic → **judgment** in terms of concept-containment. In analyzing the predicate concept, its conceptual parts (or marks) are found to be parts also of the subject concept in an analytic judgment (A6–7=B10–11). Analysis in the latter sense is found in the characterization of the 'analytic method' as 'regressive', going from a given cognition to its conditions (**P** 276) (→ **method**).

Analysis consists in seeking out the marks of a concept (**LL** 757). Concepts are conceived of as conjunctions of conceptual marks, and by analyzing a concept one becomes conscious of the marks already thought in the concept (in that these marks become clear), which leads to the concept becoming distinct (cf. **JL** 34). If by analysis we were to discover all marks thought in a concept (including the marks of the marks), then we would have a complete definition of the concept. But 'the exhaustiveness of the analysis of my concept is always doubtful' (A728=B756), hence analyses will result in expositions rather than in strict definitions. In an exposition, a pragmatically sufficient number (though not all) of a concept's marks are given. Definitions and expositions are expressed in analytic judgments, since the marks in the predicate are found through analysis of the subject concept. Analytic judgments are thus called '*judgments of clarification*' (A7=B11).

In the 1760s, Kant came close to equating philosophy with conceptual analysis. At this point, he contrasts the synthetic method of mathematics with the analytic method of metaphysics: whereas mathematics arbitrarily defines its concepts, metaphysics starts from given concepts that have to be analyzed. This can be most difficult, as some concepts 'are scarcely capable of analysis at all' (**Inq** 280). In his Critical philosophy, Kant retains some of his earlier views on mathematics and conceptual analysis, but a major revision takes place in his conception of philosophical method. Analyzing 'the concepts that inhabit our reason *a priori*, is not the end [. . .] but only a preparation for metaphysics proper, namely extending its *a priori* cognition synthetically, and it is useless for this end, because it merely shows what is contained in these concepts' (B23). The primacy of → **synthesis** is also shown in Kant's claim that, even though they seem to be opposite actions, analysis always presupposes synthesis, 'for where the understanding has not previously combined anything, neither can it dissolve anything' (B130). Kant thus holds that the

synthetic unity of → **apperception** is 'the highest point' of the understanding, presupposed by the analytic unity of consciousness (B134).

In line with this, Kant thinks it much more important to analyze '*the faculty of understanding* itself, in order to research the possibility of *a priori* concepts' (A65=B90) than to analyze concepts in order to make them distinct. The former kind of analysis, called the Analytic of Concepts, is the task of → **transcendental** philosophy; its aim is to find the pure concepts of the understanding (A65–66=B90–91) (→ **deduction**). The Analytic of Concepts is followed by the Analytic of Principles, which gives the rules for applying the categories to appearances (A132=B171) (→ **Analogies of Experience, Anticipations of Perception, Axioms of Intuition**).

Kant's practical philosophy also contains an analytic. As practical reason does not concern the cognition of objects, but 'its own ability *to make them real*', its analytic proceeds in reversed order compared to that of theoretical reason (taken in a wide sense as including the Transcendental Aesthetic) (**CPrR** 89–90). Whereas the latter went from intuition via concepts to principles, the analytic of practical reason begins with the pure law.

In **CJ**, there is an Analytic of the Beautiful, an Analytic of the Sublime and an Analytic of the Teleological Power of Judgment, treating of these respective aspects of the reflecting power of judgment (→ **aesthetic judgment**). – MQ

ANALYTIC JUDGMENT → JUDGMENT

ANTHROPOLOGY

Anthropology, understood as the empirical study of human beings, forms part of several of Kant's works, e.g. his essays on history (**CBH, End, UH**), **MM**, especially the Doctrine of Virtue, and **R**. It is however systematically treated in **Anthr**, which is based on Kant's lectures on anthropology (**LA**), a very popular topic Kant taught for over 20 years. Yet, when **Anthr** first appeared, it was criticized for being unsystematic, for creating a profound problem for the coherence of Kant's moral philosophy and for the triviality of its observations. Assessing the soundness of these criticisms offers a useful way into this deceptively readable book.

In terms of Kant's overall philosophical project, the question 'What is the human being?' is a central one, so it is not surprising that Kant dedicates a volume to the subject. Alongside his lectures on anthropology, Kant offered lectures on physical geography (**PG**), a portion of which was devoted to the study of human beings as natural creatures in their natural environment.

But this is not the point of view of **Anthr**, which is 'pragmatic'. In **G**, the term 'pragmatic' is defined in contrast to 'technical', which refers to instrumental efficacy, and to 'moral'; 'pragmatic' refers to individual well-being and prudential planning for general welfare (**G** 416–417). Also in **G**, Kant announces the need for a practical anthropology, in the sense of casuistry, that is, of showing how his moral philosophy applies to particular cases (cf. **G** 412). Yet in his introduction to **Anthr**, he appears to revise these distinctions, linking the term 'pragmatic' with moral ends and discussing the empirical conditions of moral development, namely the 'investigation of what [the human being] as a free-acting being makes of himself, or can and should make of himself' (**Anthr** 119).

The book, then, helps to flesh out the moral commitments we have as rational and free creatures, addressing important issues concerning character, the moral role of human society, the formation of dispositions to act in certain ways, the empirical expression of moral personality and more generally the cultivation of psychological and social features that promote or facilitate the achievement of our moral vocation.

If the pragmatic perspective can be vindicated in terms of the overall architectonic of Kant's philosophy, a profound puzzle remains about the precise bearing of anthropological observations upon morality. These observations are drawn from a variety of sources, from personal experience of one's own past behaviour as well as that of others, travel books, memoirs and novels, and also, as regards national character and language. The behaviours, customs and habits Kant records and comments upon show how natural needs and traits are manifested and developed in different cultural contexts, mainly of course the contexts with which Kant was more immediately acquainted.

The overarching aim is to show how human beings can overcome their natural egoism, which can be aggravated in certain contexts, and cultivate human fellowship or '*pluralism*', a 'way of thinking in which one is not concerned with oneself as the whole world, but rather regards and conducts oneself as a mere citizen of the world' (**Anthr** 130).

The puzzle is to reconcile this empirical side with central tenets of Kant's moral philosophy (→ **morality**), namely that human beings may assert their transcendental → **freedom**, that is, the freedom from all empirical determination of their actions; that they ought to act autonomously, not as a result of received opinions, maxims, and such external influences, but only out of respect for the moral law (→ **categorical imperative**); and finally, that they can transform their moral personality by a 'change of heart', which differs from a change in practice that takes place 'little by little' (**R** 47).

Nevertheless, Kant also argues for the importance of the moral development of the empirical self both at the individual level and as regards society as a whole. So he clearly believes that a coherent account can be given that binds together pragmatic aims, broadly understood, and moral aims.

How **Anthr** is interpreted, then, depends on how the relation between the empirical and the noumenal self is treated in Kant's other works as well. The empirical Kant proved awkward for some of his contemporaries and was virtually ignored by subsequent scholars. Some recent work on the topic has opened up interesting interpretative and philosophical possibilities for integrating anthropological concerns into Kantian moral philosophy.

The charge of triviality resonates less with contemporary audiences, for whom the material, with its wide range of references (from Virgil to Voltaire), offers an interesting view of a historical period populated by characters some of whom are more enduring and recognizable than others. The charge levelled against Kant nowadays is that he promotes negative stereotypes of women and of non-white races. Some of the descriptive material on women is dated like all observations of this kind. Moral development regards women equally as all human beings without exception. What is different are the circumstances, roles and gender characteristics that facilitate, colour or impede this overarching aim.

When Kant turns to national character, his aim is to emphasize negative traits because he believes criticism helps us improve ourselves. So, for example, we find that the English are rude, and that the Spaniards resist reform and so forth. It is in his lectures on geography that Kant uses race in a biological sense, while making disparaging remarks about non-white races (**PG** 316). At the same time, he holds that all human beings have common descent and form 'one family' (**Refl** 1499) and that race diversity is down to environmental factors.

In **Anthr**, Kant's concern is the entire human race and its common vocation, which is to shape its own character and perfect itself, so that 'the human being, as an animal endowed with the *capacity of reason (animal rationabile)*, can make out of himself a *rational animal (animal rationale)*' (**Anthr** 321). – KD

FURTHER READING

P. Frierson, *Freedom and Anthropology in Kant's Moral Philosophy* (Cambridge: Cambridge University Press, 2003).

B. Jacobs, P. Kain (eds), *Essays on Kant's Anthropology* (Cambridge: Cambridge University Press, 2003).

R. Louden, 'Applying Kant's ethics: the role of anthropology', in G. Bird (ed.), *A Companion to Kant* (Malden, MA/ Oxford: Wiley-Blackwell, 2010), pp. 350–363.

H. Wilson, *Kant's Pragmatic Anthropology. Its Origin, Meaning, and Critical Significance* (Albany, NY: SUNY Press, 2006).

ANTICIPATIONS OF PERCEPTION

All of the categories are a priori concepts which serve as predicates in the synthetic a priori judgments or principles that determine the conditions for the possibility of experience of objects. So also the categories of quality, which are 'reality', 'negation' and 'limitation', and whose application *in concreto* are expounded in the Anticipations of Perception.

In conformity with the role of the categories of quality, which is to establish the reference to a possible → object, the Anticipations of Perception are concerned with the principle of a priori cognition of the 'matter of perception', viz. 'sensation' (B208=A167), and hence the application of the categories of quality to perceptions so as to establish their objective *reality*.

Of course, as Kant notes, it is impossible to anticipate a priori precisely that which can only be encountered in a posteriori → experience, viz. the matter of experience, but Kant argues that it is possible to determine that 'there is something which can be cognized *a priori* in every sensation, as sensation in general (without a particular one being given)' (A167=B209).

According to Kant's theory, 'perception is empirical consciousness, i.e., one in which there is at the same time sensation'. The objects of perception, appearances, do not only have an a priori side to them (pure spatiotemporal form) (→ **Transcendental Aesthetic**), but must also have a material component, namely 'the real' which affects the subject who is conscious of the object. This 'real' corresponds to the sensations in the subject (B209=A168), which in fact constitute the material aspect of a subject's empirical consciousness.

Therefore, the principle which anticipates empirical perception asserts that '[i]n all appearances the sensation, and the *real*, which corresponds to it in the object (*realitas phenomenon*), has an *intensive magnitude*, i.e., a degree' (A166). Since sensation is instantaneous, its apprehension does not rest on a successive synthesis, as with homogeneous quanta such as space and time, and is therefore not an extensive magnitude. But like the extensive magnitudes space and time, perception is also a 'continuous' or 'flowing' magnitude (B211=A170), for 'between reality in appearance and negation there is a continuous nexus of many possible intermediate sensations' (A168=B210; cf. A143=B182–183). The degree of consciousness in a multiplicity of perceptions can gradually increase or decrease until an approximation of zero (an actual zero degree of consciousness would mean the absence or negation of sensation, corresponding to the category of 'negation').

Sensation in perception is a merely subjective representation, but since sensation is connected to the real, any determination of the intensive magnitude of sensation is a determination of the empirical → **reality** of the object of perception, to which the sensation corresponds. Notice, however, that what is determined as real is that which is represented by a *concept* of reality, in fact 'a pure concept of the understanding' (B182=A143), and 'does not signify anything except the synthesis in an empirical consciousness in general' (A175=B217).

Importantly, Kant notes that if 'all reality in perception has a degree, between which and negation there is an infinite gradation of ever lesser degrees', then it is impossible to have an experience which proves 'an entire absence of everything real in appearance, i.e., a proof of empty space or of empty time' (A172=B214). The fact that 'the entire absence of the real in sensible intuition cannot itself be perceived' (ibid.) is important for showing that the standard assumption of natural philosophers 'that the *real* in space [. . .] is *everywhere one and the same*, and can be differentiated only according to its extensive magnitude' (A173=B215), which leads them to think that only assuming that volume 'is empty in all matter' can explain differences 'in the quantity of various kinds of matter in bodies that have the same volume' (trans. Kemp Smith), is 'merely metaphysical' and thus mistaken in Kant's view (ibid.). These differences can be accounted for because of the differences in intensive magnitude.

More generally, given the fact that Kant connects the anticipation of sensation in general to empirical consciousness in inner sense (A175–176=B217–218) doubts can be raised as to the possibility of being literally unconscious (in a first-order sense of consciousness), amounting to a negation=0 of the intensive magnitude of the quality of sensation, since no 'being' or 'real' would a fortiori correspond to zero degree of empirical consciousness in perception (cf. B414). In P, Kant observes that 'total unconsciousness' is in actual fact always 'psychological darkness', which should rather 'be regarded as a consciousness that is merely outweighed by another, stronger one' (P 307). This is important for assessing Kant's views regarding the existence of first-order consciousness in relation to transcendental self-consciousness (→ apperception). – DS

FURTHER READING

B. Longuenesse, *Kant and the Capacity to Judge* (Princeton: Princeton University Press, 1998), ch. 10.

ANTINOMIES

The faculty of → **reason** seeks the unconditioned for any conditioned knowledge (A409=B436). In the case of the appearances of outer sense (→ **inner/outer sense**), this leads it to posit the existence of the totality of conditions that defines the completeness of the world (A408=B434), which is the topic of rational cosmology. This, however, issues in apparently mutually contradictory statements: this is the Antinomy of Pure Reason (A407=B433). In the Antinomy, reason's search for the unconditioned is defined in terms of ascending series moving from conditioned to that which conditions it (A410–411=B437–438).

The Antinomy takes on different forms depending upon the nature of this regress. Kant identifies four antinomies corresponding to the groups of categories: there are thus two mathematical and two dynamical antinomies. For each antinomy, Kant presents a thesis and an antithesis, as well as proofs of these claims that should not rely upon the results of the → **Transcendental Aesthetic** or the Transcendental Analytic (→ **deduction, Analogies of Experience**).

These claims are so structured that the thesis locates the unconditioned ground in the world: it is *dogmatic* and broadly in line with the tradition of rationalist → **metaphysics**. The antithesis understands this ground in terms of the infinite totality of all the conditions: it is *empiricist* (A465–466=B493–494).

(1) In the First Antinomy (A426–433=B454–461), series of appearances are generated spatially by identifying larger regions conditioning a given region of space by containing it, or in time by identifying a previous time as conditioning the present one. The antinomy leads (A426–427=B454–456) to identifying a spatial boundary, or a first time (thesis), or on the contrary to the claim that the world is unlimited in space or time (antithesis).

(2) Instead of a regress in space or time, the parts of an object can be taken as conditions of the whole (Second Antinomy, A434–443=B462–471). This mereological series

leads (A434–435=B462–463) to identifying ultimate parts (thesis) or, on the contrary, claiming infinite divisibility (antithesis).

(3) One can identify a chain of causes for any given event (Third Antinomy, A444–451=B472–479). The thesis claims that there exists a non-natural causality that defines first causes of natural occurrences (A444–445=B472–473). The antithesis denies this, which means that the causal series is infinite (ibid.).

(4) Finally, one can seek that which is necessary for the existence of an appearance (Fourth Antinomy, A452–460=B480–488). The thesis argues for an absolutely necessary being that grounds all contingent appearances. The antithesis denies that there is anything else than an infinite series of contingent existential conditions which act as such a ground (A452–453=B480–481).

The apparent incompatibility of these pairs of thesis and antithesis shows that there is a problem with the speculations of rational cosmology. Kant provides an interpretation of the nature of the problem, a diagnosis of how it arises, and a solution to it. Kant interprets the Antinomy of Pure Reason in terms of a conflict of the faculties of reason and the understanding (A422=B450).

The antitheses are grounded in principles of the pure understanding, which are applied to the syntheses of the totality of the conditioned. This leads these antitheses to defining the unconditioned in terms of infinite regresses: a first cause (Third Antinomy), respectively a smallest part (Second Antinomy), for instance, cannot form part of the world of appearances. This follows from their incompatibility with the Second Analogy (→ **Analogies of Experience**), respectively the → **Anticipations of Perception**. The theses give precedence to the principle of reason according to which the totality of conditions

is given. This leads to defining the unconditioned in terms of an object in the world, which has to be finite to be cognizable.

Kant's diagnosis is that, in each case, both thesis and antithesis rely upon the totality of the series of appearances (finite in the thesis, and infinite in the antithesis) being given independently of our cognition. This is the nature of the transcendental illusion (→ **Dialectic**) that underpins both the theses and antitheses of the antinomies (A505–506=B533–534). This illusion is ultimately caused by reason's search for the unconditioned. It arises, however, because of the failure to distinguish between a condition's being given and its defining a task for our cognition.

Kant's Critical move is to ask about the possibility of such an unconditioned totality of conditions: he points out that it cannot be met with in space and time (A508=B536). The principle of reason according to which the totality of conditions is given does not, therefore, have a constitutive role for our experience: it is merely regulative (→ **regulative principles**).

The resolution of the antinomies then proceeds differently in the mathematical and the dynamical cases. In the first case, the totality of conditions defines an object, which is viewed as existing in itself (A504=B532). This is the world, identified by composition, in the First Antinomy, and the ultimate constituents of reality, identified by division, in the second. But this object is defined through a 'synthesis of homogeneous things' (A530=B558) in appearance, and does not define a thing in itself. As a result, the theses and antitheses of the first and second antinomies do not represent a contradiction, but a dialectical opposition (A504=B532), because both deal with an object which is mistakenly taken as given in itself. The theses and antitheses are thus both false.

In the case of the dynamical antinomies, the regresses in the theses lead to an unconditioned that is heterogeneous with the series, while the antitheses deny the existence of this heterogeneous term (A529–530=B557–558). As Kant indicates, 'the case can be *mediated* to the satisfaction of both parties' (A530=B558). Indeed, Kant can make use of the distinction between two perspectives, an empirical one (in the realm of appearances), and an intelligible one (in the realm of the in-itself), to allow a regress from the one perspective to lead to an unconditional condition (thesis), while from the other perspective the unconditional totality is the infinite series generated by the regress (antithesis).

The important Third Antinomy is thus resolved by a distinction between the intelligible point of view from which there is a non-natural causality defining first causes in the natural world, and the empirical one which admits of no other causality than that of nature (A530–537=B558–565): this defines Kant's solution to the free will/determinism problem (A538–557=B566–585) (→ **freedom**). The thesis and antithesis of the third and fourth antinomies are therefore both true, once their scope has been specified appropriately.

In the case of the mathematical antinomies, Kant makes an additional claim that leads to a conclusion that is of central importance to his whole enterprise in **CPR**. He claims that transcendental realism (TR) is not able to provide a resolution of the first and second antinomies. The problem for the transcendental realist is that he is faced with two possible options in each case, and that one of them must be true, because (1) they exhaust the list of possibilities for the determination in terms of the particular property at stake (boundedness or divisibility), (2) they are mutually exclusive, and (3) indeterminacy is not an available option.

The latter point is key here, and is a direct consequence of the fact that the world of objects is already given as fully determined for the transcendental realist. Insofar as the alternative to TR is the Critical perspective of → **transcendental idealism** (TI), for which objects first arise through conceptual determinations of the representations in intuition of the sensory manifold, the failure of TR to resolve the mathematical antinomies amounts to an indirect proof of the veracity of TI.

This important result may seem to depend crucially upon the validity of the proofs of the theses and antitheses. These are, however, generally regarded as problematic. The antithesis of the First Antinomy thus relies upon a → **principle of sufficient reason**. From the observation that there is no sufficient reason for the world to begin at any particular time or to be located in any determinate position in space, it follows that a bounded world has multiple situatability in space/time. Such indeterminacy is, of course, not thinkable in a realist framework. The endorsement of the principle of sufficient reason is problematic, although it is at least shared by Kant's immediate target, Leibnizian philosophy (→ **Leibniz**).

The verificationist principle underpinning the thesis of the First Antinomy is arguably more problematic. Here, the conclusion relies upon the impossibility of thinking the world as a *totum syntheticum*, i.e. a whole composed of parts given separately. Some argue however that this way of thinking the world is shared by the transcendental realist. Similar issues arise for the Second Antinomy, with defences of Kant by some commentators for the thesis, and some others for the antithesis.

If, however, the proofs are considered unsatisfactory, the antinomies can still function in support of TI. They could be seen as identifying states of affairs which conflict with aspects of our rationality. So, if either one of the thesis or antithesis of an antinomy were to be known to be true, the proofs show that we would not be able to grasp how this is possible: they would still 'remov[e] one inconceivability only to replace it with another' (A485=B513).

Insofar as these antinomies show that there is some way of making the thesis or antithesis appear inconceivable in the light of principles that it is natural and coherent for a rational being to adopt, they identify a problem for which TI has a solution while TR has none. It would, moreover, be irrational to adopt a framework (TR) which conflicts with rationality in this way.

This important result, together with the far-reaching consequences of the Third Antinomy for Kant's practical philosophy, ensures that the Antinomy of Pure Reason has a central role in Kant's Critical philosophy. – CO

FURTHER READING

N. Fischer (ed.), *Kants Grundlegung einer kritischen Metaphysik* (Hamburg: Meiner, 2010), pp. 243–311.

M. Grier, *Kant's Doctrine of Transcendental Illusion* (Cambridge: Cambridge University Press, 2001), ch. 6.

L. Kreimendahl, 'Die Antinomie der reinen Vernunft, 1. und 2. Abschnitt', in G. Mohr, M. Willaschek (eds), *Immanuel Kant. Kritik der reinen Vernunft*, in the series *Klassiker Auslegen* (Berlin: Akademie Verlag, 1998), pp. 413–446.

E. Watkins, *Kant and the Metaphysics of Causality* (Cambridge: Cambridge University Press, 2005), ch. 5.

A. Wood, 'The Antinomies of Pure Reason', in P. Guyer (ed.), *The Cambridge Companion to Kant's 'Critique of Pure Reason'* (Cambridge: Cambridge University Press, 2010), pp. 245–265.

APPEARANCE

At B34 in **CPR**, Kant defines an 'appearance' (*Erscheinung*) as 'an indeterminate object of an empirical → **intuition**'. An appearance is also called an object of perception (B207, 225), a 'possible object' (B459), or an object of possible → **experience** (B298). This contrasts, strictly speaking, with 'object' as the translation for *Gegenstand* (A109) or *Objekt* (B137) (→ **object**), which is a *determinate* object as a result of the application of the categories by means of an act of → **apperception** or the understanding, and is always a function of → **judgment**. Every 'object' is an 'appearance', but not every appearance is an object in the strict sense of the definition at B137. Sometimes, Kant may seem to use the terms 'object' and 'appearance' interchangeably, especially when used in the plural, but whenever Kant refers to appearances as the objects of our experience, he means to refer to the objects that we make judgments about, and that are ordered in accordance with the a priori laws of experience. Strictly speaking, appearances are that out of which experiences of objects are constructed by means of the categories, or as Kant famously says, appearances are spelled out 'according to a synthetic unity in order to be able to read them as experiences' (B370–371=A314; **P** 312–313).

This differentiation between 'appearance' and 'object' is connected with Kant's → **transcendental idealism**, and also points to the crucial distinction between intuition and concept (→ **logic**). As to the latter distinction in relation to appearance: for Kant, a *determinate* object of experience is never given in perception, on the basis of which we could conceptually form judgments about these objects that we perceive. The term 'appearance' indicates that an object is never merely given as such, but is always to some extent mind-dependent, i.e. 'appearing *to* some subject *s*'. A determinate object is basically the synthetic, conceptual unification of the appearance or manifold of appearances in intuition, so that the objects of our judgments are nothing but the appearances that are the undetermined objects of an empirical intuition *in abstraction from* the determination of them as objective by the pure concepts, i.e., categories. The term 'appearance' thus straddles the intuition-concept distinction.

This also explains why Kant can say that 'objects can indeed appear to us without necessarily having to be related to functions of the understanding' (A89=B122). Appearances 'nonetheless offer objects to our intuition', even if they were not found to 'accord with the conditions that the understanding requires for the synthetic unity' that establishes objective knowledge (A90=B122–3). This is a controversial passage, which has recently spawned a whole debate among conceptualist and nonconceptualist readers of the relation between appearance/intuition and conceptual activity. The central question is to what extent conceptual activity is involved in sensible intuition and whether appearances are in fact possible without the understanding. Sometimes, Kant argues as if appearances necessarily entail possible subsumption under the categories (A119). But it seems clear that, for Kant, appearances are not eo ipso objects *determined* by the understanding. Appearances can be *merely* subjective (B234–236=A189–191).

Kant sometimes also refers to determinate appearances as phenomena, to differentiate them from appearances generally: 'Appearances, to the extent that as objects they are thought in accordance with the unity of the categories, are called *phaenomena*' (A248–249). In **ID** (392–394), Kant

associated phenomena with the objects of sensible representations, 'of things as they appear', in contrast to intellectual representations, which represent 'things as they are'. He further specified that appearances precede the logical use of the understanding, while strictly speaking only objects of experience are phenomena, where experience is when 'several appearances are compared by the understanding'.

This introduces an idealist aspect. An object as phenomenon must be distinguished from a → **thing in itself** (B69). We only know things insofar as they *appear* to us, that is, *as* appearances (cf. Bxxv–xxvii, A34–35=B51, B59ff.=A42ff.; **P** 283, 286, 288–290). Appearances are not things in themselves (B66=A49; A101; A165=B206), therefore do not exist in themselves (B164; A505=B533), which seems to suggest their merely virtual existence in us (A127; A129) or that they are merely the appearing parts or aspects of things in themselves (B59=A42) (this constitutes the 'transcendental ideality of appearances'; A506=B534). Kant says that appearances are given only in an empirical synthesis (B527=A499), which means that their existence depends on the synthesis by the understanding. However, the precise relation between appearances and things in themselves is intensely disputed (see → **thing in itself**).

Notoriously, Kant also asserts that appearances are 'mere representations' (A490–491=B518–519; B522=A493–494; B535=A507; A563=B591; A537=B565; A104; A370, A372; A391), which might seem to imply that genuine objective → **reality** is denied of them. But objective reality is first conferred on the appearances by the understanding, whereas things in themselves precisely lack objective reality, namely a reality that is determinable *for* and *by* us. The fact that appearances are 'mere representations' thus does not make them any less real. Moreover, appearances are given in space, which 'with all its appearances, as representations', is also 'only in me', but in which 'the real, or the material of all objects of outer intuition is nevertheless *really* given' (A375). An appearance (*Erscheinung*) is therefore not 'mere illusion' (*Schein*) (B69, B349, B125, B157).

That in which the manifold of the appearance is 'ordered in certain relations', is the → **form** of the appearance. This form lies ready in the mind → **a priori** (B34=A20), and hence constitutes the necessary subjective aspect of an appearance. The mere form of appearance is → **pure** intuition (B36=A22), and it is twofold: i.e. the pure forms of intuition space and time (B50; A385–386), which are the pure forms of outer and inner appearances respectively (B38–39; B50; A385–386, A690=B718), and time is the 'a priori condition of all appearance in general' (B50) (→ **Transcendental Aesthetic**). An appearance can thus be an object of both inner and outer sense (→ **inner/outer sense**). The matter of appearance is what corresponds to sensation, which is the result of the affection of things, and is an a posteriori element of appearance that is independent of the a priori forms of the mind (B34=A20; **P** 284), so only for its form is an appearance dependent on the mind. – DS

Further Reading

L. Allais, 'Kant's idealism and the secondary quality analogy', *Journal of the History of Philosophy* 45,3 (2007): 459–484.

C. Marshall, 'Kant's appearances and things in themselves as qua-objects', *The Philosophical Quarterly* 63 (2013): 520–545.

G. Prauss, *Erscheinung bei Kant* (Berlin: de Gruyter, 1971).

APPERCEPTION (SELF-CONSCIOUSNESS)

In the B-Deduction, Kant defines pure apperception as 'that self-consciousness which, because it produces the representation *I think*, which must be able to accompany all others and which in all consciousness is one and the same, cannot be accompanied by any further representation' (B132). It is an 'unchanging consciousness' (A107) or the thought or awareness of the 'thoroughgoing identity of self-consciousness' (B135).

Pure apperception is distinguished from empirical apperception, which is derived from pure apperception 'under given conditions *in concreto*' (B140), is 'forever variable', and 'can provide no standing or abiding self in [the] stream of inner appearances' (A107). In contrast to pure apperception, empirical apperception is the accompaniment of individual (B133) rather than the totality of all my representations (B131) and thus has 'merely subjective validity' (B140). Therefore, empirical apperception is to be regarded as the subjective unity of consciousness, while pure apperception is an objective or transcendental unity of self-consciousness (B132, 139).

Pure apperception is self-consciousness *stricto sensu*, viz. an awareness of the thoroughgoing or numerical → **identity** of oneself as the person having that awareness (A107–108; B133). Hence, Kant speaks of pure apperception as the representation of the 'I think'. But it should be stressed that self-consciousness is for Kant in the first instance that type of consciousness which provides the ground for all other consciousness and is not to be equated with empirical self-consciousness, as it is itself unchanging and merely formal (cf. B422–423n.; **P** 333–334) (→ **Paralogisms**). Hence, it is also called original apperception (B132).

Quite appropriately, then, Kant uses the Leibnizian term *l'aperception* (cf. Leibniz, *Monadology* §14; *Principles of Nature and Grace*, §4) (→ **Leibniz**) to indicate that self-consciousness must be distinguished from the manifold states of first-order consciousness in internal perception, of which I can have a higher-order awareness. Kant frequently uses simply the term 'consciousness' when he speaks of apperception, but from the context it is clear that in such cases he means self-consciousness, not mere consciousness (cf. A103). Transcendental or pure apperception is a 'universal self-consciousness' (B133), which it is necessary to presuppose in order to have a self-conscious awareness of one's identical self.

Another aspect of pure apperception, which relates to synthesis, is its → **spontaneity** (B132) as opposed to the merely passive sense in which empirical apperception occurs, which Kant identifies with inner sense (A107) (→ **inner/outer sense**).

Pure apperception plays an important role in the → **deduction** of the categories. It is the function of unity that is required for the possibility of → **experience** as well as of the objects of experience. Pure apperception thus provides the basis for the objective unity that lies in the categories: 'The numerical unity of this apperception therefore grounds all concepts *a priori* [. . .].' (A107) Kant shows the interconnectedness between self-consciousness and possible experience of objects by demonstrating that an analytic unity of consciousness, that is, the thoroughgoing identity of apperception, rests on an implicit awareness of an *a priori* act of → **synthesis** among one's appearances (B133; A108).

This synthesis is not given, but is the result of an act by means of which a manifold of representations is combined into a unity, whose conception is the representation of 'the *identity of the consciousness in these representations*

itself' (B133). By the fact that 'the *analytic* unity of apperception is only possible under the presupposition of some *synthetic* one' (B133) Kant means that the act of apperceiving the manifold of representations by virtue of synthesizing them, viz. the synthetic unity of apperception, is cotemporaneous with the analytic unity or awareness of identity among one's representations. Synthesis is a *logically* prior condition of the analytic unity of self-consciousness. That is, a priori synthesis is both a necessary and sufficient condition for the representation of the analytical identity of self-consciousness. No analytic unity of the self obtains without a prior synthesis, but also no a priori synthesis fails to result in an analytic unity of apperception (cf. A108).

It is this implied, or 'antecedently conceived' (B133n.), synthesis or synthetic unity which provides the insight into the intertwinement between pure apperception and objective unity, as it is the a priori synthesis which constitutes the objective unity that makes both the self and the object of experience possible. It is thus the act of synthesis that yields an objective unity of representations (cf. B137; → **object, objectivity**). Objective unity is therefore analytically implied in pure apperception.

In the decade prior to the publication of **CPR** in 1781, specifically in the so-called *Duisburg Nachlass*, which are Kant's notes from 1775–76 (esp. **Refl 4674–4679**), Kant first experimented with the notion of apperception as the principle for a deduction of the categories but it is arguably only in the second version of the Deduction, published in 1787, that Kant actually manages to derive the categories from the principle of apperception by starting the argument with the so-called 'I think'-proposition, by means of which, as we saw above, Kant formally defines self-consciousness. It should be noted however that the ostensible analogy between self-consciousness and the way we must conceive of objects continues to be a highly controversial issue among Kant commentators. – DS

FURTHER READING

K. Ameriks, *Kant's Theory of Mind. An Analysis of the Paralogisms of Pure Reason*, new edition (Oxford: Clarendon Press, 2000).

K. Ameriks, 'Kantian apperception and the non-Cartesian subject', in *Kant and the Historical Turn. Philosophy as Critical Interpretation* (Oxford: Clarendon, 2006), pp. 51–66.

W. Carl, *Der schweigende Kant. Die Entwürfe zu einer Deduktion der Kategorien vor 1781* (Göttingen: Vandenhoeck & Ruprecht, 1989), esp. pt. III.

P. Guyer, *Kant and the Claims of Knowledge* (Cambridge: Cambridge University Press, 1987), esp. chs 3 and 5.

P. Kitcher, *Kant's Thinker* (New York: Oxford University Press, 2011).

H. Klemme, *Kants Philosophie des Subjekts* (Hamburg: Meiner, 1996).

D. Schulting, *Kant's Deduction and Apperception. Explaining the Categories* (Basingstoke/New York: Palgrave Macmillan, 2012).

knowledge is 'independent of all experience' (B2–3): it is → **pure**. A posteriori knowledge has its source in experience: it is empirical.

To identify the domain of a priori knowledge, Kant identifies its two characteristic features. In modal terms, it is necessary; in terms of its scope, it is strictly universal (B3–4). The latter is a covertly modal feature: it amounts to the claim that 'no exception at all is allowed to be possible' (B4). This modality is always understood in relation to experience, i.e. defined in terms of our type of cognition. The → **necessity** of a priori knowledge is therefore weaker than that of logical necessity; but its certainty is stronger than mere (empirical) psychological necessity (B5). It can be described as transcendental psychological necessity.

After briefly showing that there is a priori knowledge, e.g. → **mathematics** (B5), Kant outlines the central task of **CPR** as the examination of the possibility of a priori knowledge so as to circumscribe this cognitive domain (A2–6=B6–10). – CO

FURTHER READING

Ph. Kitcher, 'A priori', in P. Guyer (ed.), *The Cambridge Companion to Kant and Modern Philosophy* (Cambridge: Cambridge University Press, 2006), pp. 28–60.

APPREHENSION → SYNTHESIS

A PRIORI, A POSTERIORI

Kant introduces the distinction between a priori and a posteriori cognition in the first section of both introductions to **CPR** (A2=B2). This epistemological distinction characterizes → knowledge in relation to → experience. A priori

ART (GENIUS)

The first part of **CJ**, Critique of the Aesthetic Power of Judgment, draws a distinction between two sorts of judgment of beauty (**CJ** 229–231 [§16]; 311–313 [§48]): (1) pure judgments of taste are judgments of an object 'according to mere form' (**CJ** 229) (→ **form**); (2) adherent judgments of taste are 'ascribed to objects that stand under the concept of a particular end' (**CJ** 229). The first are the primary subject matter of the Analytic and their paradigmatic object is natural beauty (→ **aesthetic judgment**). Adherent judgments are the subject matter of the sections on beautiful art (esp. §§43–50 [**CJ** 303–320]) and their paradigmatic object is artistic beauty. Surprisingly, artworks cannot be the objects of pure judgments of taste. The notion of genius and the analysis of the creative process elucidates why this is so.

The creation of beautiful art harnesses two necessary and jointly sufficient abilities. One is the acquired skill to produce a work according to certain academic rules of representation. The other is genius, a rare innate talent to create the original content of the work, which is 'not yet known at all before the artist who made it' (**Anthr** 224). Thus, genius endows yet unborn artworks with original mental content or 'material', whereas the embodiment of this material in an object requires 'academically trained' skill (**CJ** 310).

A detailed characterization of this original content or, in Kant's terminology, new rule, is given in §49 (**CJ** 313–319). There are two elements to this rule: an aesthetic idea and an idea of reason. An aesthetic idea is a mental representation, the origin of which is the free creative power of the → **imagination**. The manner in which an aesthetic idea is created is, therefore, original (**Anthr** 224–225). Kant gives two alternative formulations as to why he names these representations ideas: the fact that they are sensible complements of ideas of reason and, consequently, their endlessly fertile indeterminacy.

Although the imagination initially draws the material for creating these representations from nature, they represent ideas of reason (→ **idea, ideas**). An idea of reason always designates a concept which far exceeds what can be given in intuition (A320=B377); as such,

its content is infinite. The mysterious mental ability to represent sensibly an idea of reason creates such abundance in the representation and its details that it is by definition never fully determinate, that is, the meaning of an artwork can never be fully articulated.

Genius is the distinct mental capacity that finds an original representation that is the sensible correlate of an idea of reason. The artist aspires to give concrete expression to this mental representation in an artwork. Thus, art is a product of intentional causality. The conception of its creator is the origin of its existence. An artwork is thus an end, the product of purposive activity (→ **teleology**). The end of a work of art is the concept of what it is meant to depict. The judgment of an artwork as beautiful always presupposes this end and concept. It is for this reason that the judgment is adherent or 'no longer purely aesthetic' (**CJ** 311). – AR

FURTHER READING

H. Allison, *Kant's Theory of Taste: A Reading of the Critique of Aesthetic Judgment* (Cambridge: Cambridge University Press, 2001), ch. 12.
P. Guyer, *Kant and the Claims of Taste*, second edition (Cambridge: Cambridge University Press, 1997).

AUTONOMY → FREEDOM

AXIOMS OF INTUITION

The discussion of the principle of the Axioms of Intuition is the first part of Kant's Analytic of Principles in **CPR** and thus marks the opening of the detailed schematization of the categories that was promised in the chapter on → **schematism**. The question of the applicability of the principles of → **mathematics** to experience has not been settled by Kant's argument for taking these principles to be synthetic a priori in the → **Transcendental Aesthetic** (B40–41). Kant turns to providing a justification for the applicability of the principles of mathematics to experience in the first two parts of the Analytic of Principles, which concern this section and the following one on the → **Anticipations of Perception**.

These two sets of principles are thus termed 'mathematical' not because they are principles within mathematics but rather because they are principles that make 'pure mathematics [. . .] applicable to objects of experience' (A165=B206). In the second edition of **CPR**, just prior to the Axioms, Kant adds a note indicating that the type of → **synthesis** involved in these 'mathematical' principles is a 'composition' in which the parts have no necessary connection to each other as when two triangles emerge from a division of a square (B201n). This synthesis is generally one of homogeneous elements but, in the case of the principle of the Axioms, it also concerns 'aggregates'.

As is the case with many of the other principles the statement of this one alters between the two editions of **CPR** with the A-version referring to 'appearances' in their intuition while the B-version merely discusses → **intuition**. Both versions, however, describe intuitions as being 'extensive magnitudes' by which is meant that they possess a representation whose whole only arises by means of combination of the parts (B203).

This conception of 'extensive magnitudes' is illustrated with the example of drawing a line in thought which is meant to show that to get the conception of what a line involves we have to bring it into being, something that cannot be done all at once. This point about the line is further suggested to apply to how we are able to describe a determinate sense of temporal objects since these also require that an aggregative synthesis take place.

This argument seems to refer back to the point in the A-Deduction concerning the unity of all temporal representation (A99). The point of insisting upon it is to suggest that empirical consciousness requires, in order to cognize anything at all, the same form of combination that is at work in generating mathematical objects and this is the reason for thinking that mathematical objects are cognizable within experience.

The principle of the Axioms of Intuition is explicitly presented as the basis of geometrical construction and Kant gives a series of statements that arise naturally as cardinal for Euclidean → **geometry** in this context (A162–163=B203). It is these latter that *are* the Axioms and the transcendental principle referring to 'extensive magnitudes' is the principle that makes possible their cognition.

Kant also distinguishes here between the principles of geometry and those of arithmetic pointing out that the latter, while synthetic like those of geometry, are not general as they do not describe objects that can be given in many different manners but only their particular possibility in one way. Kant's point here is that numerals are not capable of being represented in various ways, as for example triangles are. For something to be a part of an arithmetical addition it has to belong to a set that enables its classification with others of the same type.

Kant's philosophy of mathematics is intended to be given a ground by means of the defence of the principle of the Axioms but, while the philosophy of mathematics Kant presents has itself proved controversial, the transcendental principles underlying it have been more rarely treated to extended treatment. – GB

FURTHER READING

G. Banham, *Kant's Transcendental Imagination* (Basingstoke/New York: Palgrave Macmillan, 2006), ch. 6.
H. Klemme, 'Die Axiome der Anschauung und die Antizipationen der Wahrnehmung', in G. Mohr, M. Willaschek (eds), *Immanuel Kant. Kritik der reinen Vernunft*, in the series *Klassiker Auslegen* (Berlin: Akademie Verlag, 1998), pp. 247–266.
B. Longuenesse, *Kant and the Capacity to Judge* (Princeton: Princeton University Press, 1998), ch. 9.

CAPACITY TO JUDGE → JUDGMENT

CATEGORICAL IMPERATIVE (MORAL LAW)

In the first section of **G**, Kant proceeds by elimination to identify what is unconditionally good. Drawing on our moral intuitions, his investigation homes in on the good → **will** as the only thing that is good in itself, and independently of anything else (**G** 393). The latter condition implies that the good will's action cannot be motivated by any inclination, but only by reason (**G** 396). The concept of duty (→ **duty, duties**) is then introduced to explain the moral worth of the good will: the good will's action must be in accordance with and from duty (**G** 397). Finally, Kant unpacks the notion of duty by noting that to do one's duty involves acting in conformity to a law (the moral law), and out of respect for it (**G** 400).

In the second section of **G**, Kant translates this common understanding of morality in terms of rules or principles that will constitute the synthetic a priori judgments of practical rationality (**G** 412, 420). Considering how rules operate as imperatives in practical rationality (**G** 413), Kant notes that we have no difficulty making sense of hypothetical imperatives. Either in the form of rules of skill spelling out how to contribute to advancing a specific purpose ('Use a serrated knife to cut bread'), or counsels of prudence where the end of happiness is assumed ('Avoid excess'), they are essentially unproblematic because analytic (**G** 416–419).

But unconditional goodness is not goodness with respect to the pursuit of a certain end (**G** 416). The command which enjoins us to do what is morally good cannot therefore be hypothetical, but must be categorical. For a categorical imperative, however, the question of its possibility arises (**G** 419).

Kant proceeds to settle it by exhibiting the content of such an imperative. In line with section I, Kant claims that morality requires our maxim of action to conform to a practical law (**G** 420). Since all that characterizes this law is that it is universally valid, he claims that a maxim which conforms to it must be universalizable. And since action on the law must be motivated by respect for the law, it is the universalizability of the maxim that must provide the motive for morally worthy action. Kant expresses this motivational constraint in terms of the requirement that it be possible simultaneously to will that this maxim be universal law (**G** 420–421).

In the examples (**G** 421–423), Kant chooses to illustrate the application of the Formula of Universal Law (FUL), by referring to a modified version. Here, the requirement is the more usable one that one act as though one's maxim were to become a universal law of nature (**G** 421).

Kant shows how the FUL can be used to identify what is forbidden by the moral law. There are essentially two ways in which a maxim can fail to pass the test of the FUL (**G** 424). These are generally known as the contradiction in conception (CC) and the contradiction in the will (CW). Both tests essentially rely upon there being basic rules of practical rationality. According to this 'logic of the will', there is a contradiction in willing an end and not having the means to achieve it.

In the CC case, willing the universalization of the maxim amounts to willing a situation in which some means required by the end of one's action are no longer available. In the CW case, the agent thereby wills that certain means which foster the pursuit of her ends not be available. Thus, willing that all agents break their promises when convenient amounts to willing a situation in which promises will no longer be accepted. This contradicts (CC) the purpose of profiting from breaking one's promise (**G** 422).

In the second case (CW), the contradiction is located, not in the universalization itself, but rather between this universalization and the agent's pursuits of her ends. Thus, willing that no-one provide help to those in need amounts to willing that one never be helped, even when this would serve one's ends (**G** 423).

As a result, the duties defined by these contradictions are of different strength and scope. The first define perfect and strict duties, such as that of self-preservation. There is no room for interpretation here, and the obligation can be discharged. The second define imperfect and broad duties, as the duty to cultivate one's talents. There is scope for inclinations to guide our choices and the obligation cannot be discharged.

Kant's FUL is only the first form of the categorical imperative. Noting that all human action is directed to an end, that of dutiful action has to be objective and hold for all rational beings (**G** 428). Only persons have absolute worth, so humanity is the only possible objective end. Kant characterizes humanity as the ability to formulate ends for one's actions.

This gives rise to the Formula of Humanity (FH), which enjoins us never to treat others as means only, but always also as ends (**G** 429). This formula is useful in dealing with certain cases of immoral actions that the FUL is not able to exhibit as forbidden. Its ability to deal with such maxims stems from the fact that it is the end of humanity which bestows value upon the agent's ends.

As a result, natural actions such as suicide can be dealt with using the FH. Kant shows that a maxim of committing suicide when life becomes unbearable does not pass the FH test (**G** 429). Indeed, an agent's end of making one's life bearable to the end acquires its value from that of the humanity of the agent. To destroy his agency is to destroy the source of this value, which exhibits a contradiction in terms of practical rationality.

Kant provides two more formulations of the categorical imperative, each designed to add a different dimension to its content. The Formula of Autonomy adds a reflexive dimension, i.e. defining how a moral agent should view herself, namely as an autonomous legislator (**G** 432) (→ **spontaneity**). The formula of the → **kingdom of ends** adds an inter-subjective dimension through the conception of the legislator as a member of a realm of autonomous legislators (**G** 433–436). Both formulas, which Kant presents without derivation, bring the categorical imperative closer to our intuitions.

There have been a number of objections to Kant's conception of the categorical imperative. Most prominently, Hegel claimed that some prior knowledge of the good is required, else the good will could be wrong about what is good. Hegel also seems to think an appeal to the value of certain institutions (e.g. promising) is required if the categorical imperative is to successfully reject maxims such as that of breaking one's promises. But this gets the order wrong: the categorical imperative defines what is right, and doing what is right, because one sincerely holds it to be right, is morally worthy.

Focusing on the FUL, Hegel claimed that it is empty as it cannot, for instance, rule out universal egoism. This however overlooks the fact that it is not rational to pursue an end and simultaneously not to want to be helped to achieve it – or the end has been wrongly formulated in the first place.

Many objections, such as Mill's claim that a notion of universal utility must be presupposed when carrying out the FUL test, fail largely because of problematic interpretations of the notion of contradiction in conception. These problems have been tackled in different ways in the literature, although issues remain however, in particular that of how specific a maxim of action should be for the FUL testing procedure. – CO

FURTHER READING

S. Kerstein, 'Deriving the formula of universal law', in G. Bird (ed.), *A Companion to Kant* (Malden, MA/ Oxford: Wiley-Blackwell, 2010), pp. 308–321.

C. Korsgaard, *Creating the Kingdom of Ends* (Cambridge: Cambridge University Press, 1996), pt. I.

C. Onof, 'A framework for the derivation and reconstruction of the categorical imperative, *Kant-Studien* 89 (1998): 410–427.

J. Timmermann, *Kant's Groundwork of the Metaphysics of Morals: A Commentary* (Cambridge: Cambridge University Press, 2007).

A. Wood, 'The supreme principle of morality', in P. Guyer (ed.), *The Cambridge Companion to Kant and Modern Philosophy* (Cambridge: Cambridge University Press, 2006), pp. 342–380.

A. Wood, 'Kant's formulations of the moral law', in G. Bird (ed.), *A Companion to Kant* (Malden, MA/ Oxford: Wiley-Blackwell, 2010), pp. 291–307.

CATEGORIES → DEDUCTION

CAUSALITY → ANALOGIES OF EXPERIENCE, LAWS (OF NATURE)/ LAWFULNESS

CHOICE → WILL

CLEAR/OBSCURE → REPRESENTATION

COGNITION → KNOWLEDGE

COMBINATION → SYNTHESIS

COMPARISON → LOGIC

CONCEPT → LOGIC

CONSCIOUSNESS → REPRESENTATION, APPERCEPTION, ANTICIPATIONS OF PERCEPTION

COSMOLOGICAL PROOF → PROOFS OF THE EXISTENCE OF GOD

COSMOPOLITAN, COSMOPOLITANISM

The notion of cosmopolitanism already appears in **UH** (1784), where Kant shows that there are grounds to look at history as an irregular yet inexorable unfolding of a plan leading to a universal condition of peace between individuals and states. He argues that after the repeated experience of the desolation caused by war, humans will be compelled to create institutions – the state at the domestic level and the federation of states at the international level – capable of regulating their antagonism and to create a condition of stable peace, or, as he puts it, a 'cosmopolitan condition of public state security' (**UH** 26).

Similarly, Kant talks in **TP** (1793) of a 'cosmopolitan constitution [*Weltbürgerliche Verfassung*]' (**TP** 310) or 'cosmopolitan commonwealth [*Weltbürgerliches gemeines Wesen*]' (**TP** 311), which is again the peaceful, orderly, juridical condition that mankind will achieve when international right has been fully implemented.

In **PP** (1795) and in **MM** (1797), however, Kant introduces the notion of 'cosmopolitan right [*Weltbürgerrecht*]' indicating something different and more specific. → **Right** (*Recht*) is now a tripartite notion denoting state right, international right and cosmopolitan right. Cosmopolitan right concerns the rules that all nations should adopt in the treatment of individuals who enter foreign countries. These rules of hospitality accord visitors the 'right to visit' (**PP** 358) and prescribe that strangers be treated without hostility when they arrive on someone else's territory. However, cosmopolitan right does not grant strangers a right to become members of the hosting country. In fact, they can be 'turn[ed] away' (**PP** 358), if this can be done without endangering their life. It does grant them a right 'to *visit* all regions of the earth' while

they attempt 'to establish a community with all' (**MM** 353).

In **PP**, Kant claims that cosmopolitan right is both (a) a condition of the accomplishment of the cosmopolitan constitution and (b) 'a supplement to the unwritten code of the right of a state and the right of nations necessary for the sake of any public rights of human beings' (**PP** 360). This is so because a right to visit enables peaceful interactions between foreigners. It also enables international commerce, which makes wars between economically interdependent countries particularly costly and thus unlikely. Through cosmopolitan right 'distant parts of the world can enter peaceably into relations with one another, which can eventually become publicly lawful and so finally bring the human race ever closer to a cosmopolitan constitution' (**PP** 358).

Cosmopolitan right is one of Kant's most important innovations in legal theory. While the natural law tradition introduced the normative elements of what would then become (and still is) international positive right, Kant refuses to limit himself to the dichotomy state/interstate right and proposes a tripartite division, thus adding the novel concept of cosmopolitan right. Kant thinks that individuals hold rights against states and other individuals independently of their citizenship. Universal hospitality – a matter of right, not of philanthropy – pertains to humans *qua* humans. This means that although there is as yet no global state that can enforce the rights of individuals as citizens of the world, individuals nonetheless possess rights ultimately resting on the intrinsic dignity of human beings.

In the absence of a global institution that could enforce these rights, either in the form of a universal republic – which Kant at times seems to consider the best global institutional form – or in the form of a Federation of States – which at times he seems to consider a more prudent surrogate, cosmopolitan right establishes standards of respect that are not only just but also conducive to the cosmopolitan condition. Cosmopolitan right, in this sense, anticipates the 1948 Universal Declaration of Human Rights and the normative principles on which contemporary global institutions such as the UN are based. – LC

FURTHER READING

D. Archibugi, 'Immanuel Kant, cosmopolitan law and peace', *European Journal of International Relations* 1,4 (1995): 429–456.

J. Bohman, M. Lutz-Bachmann (eds) *Perpetual Peace: Essays on Kant's Cosmopolitan Ideal* (Cambridge: Cambridge University Press, 1997).

O. Höffe, *Kant's Cosmopolitan Theory of Law and Peace*, trans. A. Newton (Cambridge: Cambridge University Press, 2006).

P. Kleingeld, *Kant and Cosmopolitanism* (Cambridge: Cambridge University Press, 2011).

CRITIQUE

Kant begins **CPR** with a diagnosis of the state of → **metaphysics** in his days. Metaphysics is the science of → **reason** as such, which is a kind of → **knowledge** that must, according to Kant, be scientific in a strict sense. The very first pages of the 'Preface' in the second edition **CPR** make clear that Kant thinks that the prevailing schools of philosophy, rationalism and → **empiricism**, give conflicting accounts of the nature of metaphysics.

This situation reflects the fact that metaphysics is clearly not yet founded on a secure scientific footing. Other domains of science such as → **logic** and → **mathematics** developed with a better understanding of what we can discover in an object in conformity with its conception. Accordingly, Kant thinks that a 'Copernican revolution' is necessary in metaphysics, which means that reason enacts an experiment with itself by virtue of systematically criticizing unfounded philosophical presumptions (→ **method**). This means that reason must subject itself to a critique of its own capacity (A738=B766; cf. Bxxxv-xxxvi; A65–66=B90–91).

The elementary presumption of metaphysics seems to be that knowledge 'must conform to the → **object**' (Bxvi). Kant posits the opposite hypothesis: the object of knowledge must → **a priori** conform to our cognition. The experiment that reason enacts with itself consists in critically analyzing the character and scope of its own concepts and seeking its own 'objective reality' in relation to the object of cognition. This results in what one may call a relativism 'with a positive accent'. Our concepts must not be taken as determinations of things in themselves for we can only know for certain that they are the forms in which we as finite beings must de facto intuit and think them.

In a letter to Marcus Herz of 21 February 1772 (**Corr-I** 130), Kant formulated the fundamental Critical problem for the first time as the problem of how our representations, that is, pure concepts of the understanding as well as forms of → **intuition**, may be said to relate to the objects of our experience, the solution to which is expounded in detail in **CPR**. His analysis starts in the 'Introduction' to **CPR** with the observation that there is no doubt 'that all our cognition begins with experience' (B1), but that importantly not all cognition arises from → **experience**.

In this respect, Kant makes a crucial distinction between the → **form** and the matter of experience. When considering the architectonic structure of **CPR** it becomes evident what kind of criteria are at stake in the → **transcendental** analysis of theoretical knowledge. It is the critical investigation of reason in *its* relation to an empirical reality that remains bound to the object as directly given in intuition, as → **appearance**. The object as appearance must be characterized in respect of its *form*, more specifically, the forms of space and time (→ **Transcendental Aesthetic**).

Crucial for this analysis is the distinction Kant makes between these forms as putative forms of things and as they appear to us. These forms belong to things as we perceive them but they should not in fact be thought as belonging to things in themselves (→ **thing in itself**). Why, after all, should something that is elementary for things as we know them be interpreted as something we take as necessary in an absolute, say 'transcendental', sense?

The distinction that is made here is vital for the steps that Kant takes to restrict the unmotivated and unfounded claims of traditional metaphysics, which takes the forms of sensibly perceiving things to apply to them absolutely. In the same way the necessary forms of thought, the categories of the understanding, are examined with regard to their specific function and application.

As becomes clearer in the chapter on the Principles of the Pure Understanding, the entire Critical perspective is built on the correlation between a priori principles of the understanding and their real correlate: the structure of the object as object of experience. The ground of our knowledge of objects lies in the way we can a priori show the correlation between reason and object. It is in this respect that the separation between phenomena and noumena (→ **transcendental idealism**) is necessary, implying that the absolute or 'unconditioned necessity' is 'for human reason [. . .] the true abyss' (A613=B641; cf. **LPöl**

1032–1033), wherein no cognizable structure can be discerned. This is the basis of Kant's critique of a metaphysical self-knowledge of the soul (→ **Paralogisms**), the → **proofs of the existence of God** and rational knowledge of our moral and psychological → **freedom**.

The general goal of Kant's critique is to break with all kinds of dogmatism and scepticism. However, the concept of things as we have to think of them (as 'noumena') remains not only admissible, but is even unavoidable; the notion of 'noumenon' is a concept that sets critical limits to sensibility (B311–312). The methodological distinction between phenomena and noumena is thus the key to **CPR** as a treatise on the method of a Critical metaphysics. – KJB

FURTHER READING

S. Gardner, *Kant and the Critique of Pure Reason* (London/New York: Routledge, 1999), chs 1 and 2.

D. Hogan, 'Kant's Copernican turn and the rationalist tradition', in P. Guyer (ed.), *The Cambridge Companion to Kant's 'Critique of Pure Reason'* (Cambridge: Cambridge University Press, 2010), pp. 21–40.

D. Schulting, 'Kant's Copernican analogy: beyond the non-specific reading', *Studi Kantiani* xxii (2009): 39–65.

DEDUCTION (CATEGORIES)

In arguably the centrepiece of **CPR**, the Transcendental Deduction of the Categories (henceforth TD), Kant aims to demonstrate the justified use of the necessary a priori concepts of objective → **experience**. These a priori concepts are called categories. The most important categories, which are listed in the Table of the Categories (A80=B106) in four classes of each three 'moments', are those of relation, i.e. substance, causality and community, which play a crucial role in the → **Analogies of Experience.**

In TD, Kant wants to show not only that the categories are justifiably used – this concerns the so-called *quid juris* question of TD (see **CPR** §13 [A84–92=B116–124]) – but also that they are the necessary a priori conditions for the possibility of objective experience. These two goals are interconnected.

TD appears in two versions in **CPR**, commonly referred to as the A- and B-Deductions corresponding to the first (1781) and second (1787) editions of **CPR**. Although Kant himself stated (Bxxxviii) that the changes he made in the B-version were only presentational, it is clear that there are more dissimilarities than Kant would have us believe, so much so that some commentators focus entirely on the A-version (such as Heidegger) and some on the B-version of **CPR**. Nevertheless, the objective of both versions of TD appears to be the same: to show that experience is only possible on condition of the applicability of the categories.

Before Kant proceeds to show that the categories do indeed apply to any possible experience in the actual TD (which starts at A95 and B129 respectively), Kant addresses several preliminary issues in the preceding sections (§§9–14). §§9–12 are usually referred to as the Metaphysical Deduction (MD). Although there is no heading thus named, Kant retrospectively refers to these sections with that designation at B159.

In MD, Kant provides definitions for the terms he will use in TD and first lists, in a Table of Categories, the various categories that will be shown, in TD, to apply necessarily to experience. This table is derived from a table of → **judgment** in accord with a guiding thread (A79=B104–105), which shows that

the categories rest on the same function of the understanding on which the logical functions for judgment rest (→ **synthesis**), and in fact completely coincide with the latter (B159; cf. **P** 305). The Table of the Categories is modelled on the Table of Judgment in the sense that the categories are 'grounded on logical functions in judgments' (B131) and express these same functions for judgment insofar as they refer to an object outside thought. More precisely, categories 'are concepts of an object in general, by means of which its intuition is regarded as *determined* with regard to one of the *logical functions* for judgments' (B128).

There are some controversial issues concerning the precise function of MD in relation to the main goal of TD. This concerns, among other things, the fact that only 12 functions of judgment are listed and that these presumably exhaust the series of possible functions for judgments. Kant thinks that if we proceed in accordance with a principle then we can derive fully a priori all the necessary elementary functions of judgment, and based on them, the necessary concepts of experience. This has been roundly criticized as it would appear that at any rate the use of the forms of judgment, and hence the categories, is always already assumed in any putative a priori demonstration of their derivability. However, this objection rests on the assumption that a deduction in the proper sense must be something like a derivation from an indisputable basic logical principle so as to constitute a genuine proof and that the demonstration conflates with experience itself.

Without delving further into the intricacies of MD and aforementioned issues, it is important to note that Kant wants to show that there is a link between the way that we think and form judgments on the basis of concepts, which are functions of thought (cf. A68=B93), and the way in which we refer to objects outside our thoughts. Put succinctly, Kant aims to show the intimate connection between the subjective conditions of thought and the objective conditions of knowledge or experience (A89–90=B122). The genuine challenge that Kant's TD presents, which makes it an argument belonging to a → transcendental → logic, is the counterintuitive claim that by analyzing the structure of discursive thought and, also fully a priori, the way that human beings are answerable to sensory input we can come to know all that which makes experience of an object possible, independently of that experience or reference to the object itself.

TD is furthermore a *transcendental* deduction (a *quaestio juris*), and not an empirical one (a *quaestio facti*), as the demonstration concerns not the material origin of the categories or the fact that they are used but the rightfulness of their use, that is to say, their justified applicability to objective experience. If Kant can show that indeed the categories are applicable to experience, by showing that they make experience possible, then he will have shown their legitimate use.

If we look at the actual argument of the more streamlined B-Deduction, it is apparent that Kant divides the proof into what has been called 'two steps'. It is controversial how exactly these two 'steps' are connected, but it is at any rate clear what the respective arguments are in each of these two steps. The first step runs through §15–20 and presents the argument concerning the necessary conditions for the representation of an object in general. The argument proceeds roughly as follows:

1. Combination, which is the representation of a synthetic unity of the manifold of representations in an intuition and is required for possible reference to an object, can never occur by means of

the senses or be derived from the objects (B134), but requires an act of spontaneous → synthesis (§15).

2. The synthetic unity achieved by this act of synthesis involves a 'higher' unity.

3. The higher unity is 'the *I think* [which] must be able to accompany all my representations' (§16), which shows an analytic truth with regard to the → identity of my self-consciousness (S) (→ apperception).

4. S requires an a priori synthesis, i.e. a 'transcendental unity of self-consciousness' (TUS), since S by itself is a purely formal unity and contains no manifold.

5. TUS is the consciousness of an a priori synthesis (B135; cf. A108).

6. TUS is an objective unity of consciousness (OUC) (§17; cf. §18).

7. OUC constitutes the concept of an → object as 'that in the concept of which the manifold of a given intuition is united' (B137).

8. OUC determines the objective validity of representations and defines a judgment (B141).

9. All unitary intuitions are determined in regard to the logical functions of judgment.

10. The categories are these logical functions insofar as the manifold is determined in regard to them.

11. Therefore, the categories apply to a united manifold in an intuition (§20).

In the second step, which runs from §21 to §26, Kant argues for the necessary application of the categories to objects of human sensible, i.e. spatiotemporal, experience. The second step thus provides an argument for the possibility of, not the mere conception, but rather the perception of an actual empirical object (cf. §22). In the important §24, Kant differentiates between figurative and intellectual synthesis so as to indicate the difference between the synthesis of representations in general, which yields the pure concept of an object, and the synthesis of empirical representations in human sensibility that enables the experience of a sensible object. Kant then argues in §26 that it is the act of synthesis itself in sensibility – that is, a synthesis of space and time as a priori forms of intuition (→ **Transcendental Aesthetic**) – which establishes the synthetic unity of a spatiotemporal object of sensible intuition. Any empirical apprehension of a *sensible object* is therefore subject to the a priori synthesis of the understanding, and a fortiori stands under the categories. By virtue of the same act of synthesis that determines any manifold in general, the understanding determines sensible intuition and hence the unity of space and time itself, being the necessary forms of sensible intuition, as themselves objects of perception. This concludes the argument towards the legitimation of the use of the categories in regard to objective experience.

Towards the end of §26, Kant elaborates on the results of the deduction of the categories by arguing that 'all appearances of nature' stand under the categories. Nature itself depends on the categories, which form the 'original ground of its necessary lawfulness' (→ **laws (of nature)/lawfulness**). But only *'nature in general*, as lawfulness of appearances in space and time' is concerned here, as *'natura formaliter spectata'* (B165), not nature in terms of its 'particular laws' (B165), which is *'natura materialiter spectata'* (B163).

In conclusion, in TD Kant's general argument is that (1) objects can only be thought by means of the categories; (2) objects can only be known in combination with intuition; (3) intuition is for us always sensible, so that (4) knowledge is always empirical and that (5) therefore, knowledge is only possible of objects of experience. This in turn concludes the argument for the justified use of the categories, as it is hereby shown that categories make knowledge possible by being limited to the domain of objects of experience.

It is not only in **CPR** that one encounters a deduction; also in the other *Critiques* are provided deductions. In **CPrR** (42ff.) the deduction concerns the principles of pure practical reason (→ **morality**) and in **CJ** (279ff.) the deduction involves the question concerning the legitimacy of pure aesthetic judgments of taste (→ **aesthetic judgment**). – DS

FURTHER READING

W. Carl, 'Kant's first drafts of the Deduction', in E. Förster (ed.), *Kant's Transcendental Deductions* (Stanford: Stanford University Press, 1989), pp. 3–20.

P. Guyer, 'The Deduction of the Categories. The metaphysical and transcendental deductions', in P. Guyer (ed.), *The Cambridge Companion to Kant's 'Critique of Pure Reason'* (Cambridge: Cambridge University Press, 2010), pp. 118–150.

B. Longuenesse, 'Kant on a priori concepts. The metaphysical deduction of the categories', in P. Guyer (ed.), *The Cambridge Companion to Kant and Modern Philosophy* (Cambridge: Cambridge University Press, 2006), pp. 129–168.

D. Schulting, *Kant's Deduction and Apperception. Explaining the Categories* (Basingstoke/New York: Palgrave Macmillan, 2012).

DESIRE → INTEREST

DIALECTIC

The Transcendental Dialectic is the second and largest part of the Logic in **CPR**. Yet its importance is sometimes underestimated in comparison to the Analytic, the first part of the Logic. The Dialectic covers a range of important topics, such as the transcendental ideas (→ idea, ideas), the → Paralogisms, the → Antinomies and the Ideal of Pure Reason (→ transcendental ideal), discussed in two introductions (on reason's transcendental illusion), two books (on the concepts or ideas and the dialectical inferences of pure → reason) and an appendix (on the regulative use of the ideas of pure reason and the final aim of the natural dialectic of human reason) (→ regulative principles).

These topics are analyzed in the context of what Kant calls a critique of transcendental (or dialectical) illusion, that is, a transcendental investigation into pure reason's natural tendency to transgress the boundaries of → knowledge or sensible cognition enforced in the Analytic:

The second part of the transcendental logic must [...] be a critique of this dialectical illusion, and is called transcendental dialectic, not as an art of dogmatically arousing such illusion [. . .], but rather as a critique of the understanding and reason in regard to their hyperphysical use, in order to uncover the false illusion of their groundless pretensions and to reduce their claims to invention and amplification, putatively to be attained through transcendental principles, to the mere assessment and evaluation of the pure understanding, guarding it against sophistical tricks. (A63–64)

Kant's conception of dialectic can therefore best be understood from his theory of transcendental illusion or, more adequately, his theory of pure reason as the seat of a transcendental illusion, since one of the central (at least interpretive) complications of this theory seems to consist precisely in the fact that although it would ground and explain the necessary dialectical (hence illegitimate) reasoning of rationalist metaphysics, transcendental illusion is inherent to pure reason itself and must consequently be critically accounted for on the level of a *critique* of pure reason (→ critique).

In fact, two basic elements in Kant's theory of pure reason seem to be essential to his conception of dialectic. On the one hand, there is the 'supreme principle of pure reason' (B365), at one point formulated as follows: 'If the conditioned is given, then through it a regress in the series of all conditions for it is *given* to us *as a problem.*' (B526) This principle marks the demand or need for systematic unity and completeness of knowledge (→ system), and ultimately for the unconditioned, that belongs to the very nature and calling of pure reason and thus somehow has to be fulfilled, if only in the sense of an infinite task.

On the other hand, Kant insists that (the same) pure reason is the seat of transcendental illusion: '[I]n our reason [. . .] there lie fundamental rules and maxims for its use, which look entirely like objective principles, and through them it comes about that the subjective necessity of a certain connection of our concepts on behalf of the understanding is taken for an objective necessity, the determination of things in themselves.' (B353)

The factor that seems to complicate the project of the Dialectic most profoundly, however, stems from Kant's repeated assertion that transcendental illusion, contrary to empirical and logical illusions, is not an artificial or avoidable one, but a natural and unavoidable one that 'irremediably [*unhintertreiblich*]' (B354) attaches to human reason. Kant holds therefore that the Dialectic is limited to uncovering the transcendent judgments by which rationalist metaphysics is characterized: it can never bring about that transcendental illusion, unlike empirical or logical illusions, should disappear and cease to be an illusion – even if the Critical philosopher is no longer deceived by it. – JV

FURTHER READING

K. Ameriks, 'The critique of metaphysics: the structure and fate of Kant's Dialectic', in P. Guyer (ed.), *The Cambridge Companion to Kant and Modern Philosophy* (Cambridge: Cambridge University Press, 2006), pp. 269–302.

M. Grier, *Kant's Doctrine of Transcendental Illusion* (Cambridge: Cambridge University Press, 2001).

R.-P. Horstmann, 'Der Anhang zur transzendentalen Dialektik', in G. Mohr, M. Willaschek (eds), *Immanuel Kant. Kritik der reinen Vernunft*, in the series *Klassiker Auslegen* (Berlin: Akademie Verlag, 1998), pp. 525–545.

M. Willaschek, 'Kant on the necessity of metaphysics', in V. Rohden et al. (eds), *Recht und Frieden in der Philosophie Kants. Akten des X. Internationalen Kant-Kongresses*, Band 1 (Berlin/New York: de Gruyter, 2008), pp. 285–307.

DIFFERENCE → IDENTITY, AMPHIBOLY

DISPLEASURE, PLEASURE → SUBLIME, AESTHETIC JUDGMENT

DUTY, DUTIES

Kant treats morally good actions as 'duties' in the sense that, ultimately, they are good not because particular individuals happen to need, want or enjoy them or because particular authorities happen to demand them, but for further reasons that are universal and unconditional – that is, for the distinctively moral reasons that he describes with his formulas (→ **categorical imperative**). He also thinks that moral goodness consists not simply in doing one's duties, but in doing them precisely because they are morally good, rather than for other reasons. He calls this doing one's duty 'from duty', rather than acting 'in conformity with duty' but 'from inclination'.

In **G** he also claims that it is clearer that one acts from duty when one lacks other reasons for doing one's duty – as, for instance, when one's own troubles or lack of emotional involvement tell against helping others or when more immediate enjoyments tempt one to neglect the duty to stay healthy (**G** 397–398). However, he also denies that one can ever establish with certainty whether oneself or others acted from duty – indeed, he suspects that we are often over-charitable in attributing morally good reasons to ourselves (**G** 406–408; **TP** 284–285; **MM** 392–393, 441, 446–447).

Besides distinguishing between duties to oneself and duties to others and between duties to do actions and duties to refrain from actions, Kant makes two different distinctions between kinds of duties. In **G** he distinguishes between 'perfect', or 'narrow', duties and 'imperfect', or 'wide', ones on the grounds that only the latter kind allow for exceptions for the sake of other, non-moral reasons.

With reference to four examples, he also claims that the formula of universal law (→ **categorical imperative**) treats the two kinds of duties differently: our duties to promise honestly and not to commit suicide are perfect, he claims, because one cannot coherently conceive of everyone doing the opposite, whereas our duties to cultivate our own talents and to help others are imperfect because one can conceive of everyone doing the opposite, but nonetheless not want them to (G 421–424, 421n.).

He uses the same examples to make a corresponding claim about the formula of the end in itself – namely, that a duty is perfect when its opposite considers affected agents merely as 'things' or 'means' to satisfy inclinations, while a duty is imperfect when its opposite considers affected agents as 'ends in themselves' (→ kingdom of ends), but without actively promoting these ends (G 429–430).

In MM, on the other hand, Kant distinguishes political from ethical duties, or duties of justice from duties of → virtue, on the grounds that the former are duties merely to do or refrain from certain actions, since one can be coerced to fulfil them, whereas the latter are duties to recognize certain reasons for action, which cannot be coerced. Ethical duties are therefore 'imperfect' or 'wide', he claims, not because they allow for exceptions for the sake of non-moral reasons, but only because they leave some 'playroom' in terms of precisely which actions fulfil or neglect them and thus allow for exceptions for the sake of fulfilling other duties (MM 214, 218–221, 231, 239, 375, 382, 390–391, 410–411).

Kant also presents our manner of judging what our duties are in two different ways. In his treatments of the four examples in G, he simply tests specific reasons in specific circumstances against the formulas. But his account in MM is more systematic. There he claims that in reasoning over specific cases, we must balance the requirements of different duties against each other, particularly by prioritizing political duties over ethical ones and more general duties over more specific ones.

The generality of duties is a matter of their applicability – he derives our most general duties by considering whether the most general reasons, those applicable to human beings generally, might be consistent with the formulas in the most general human circumstances, and he claims that more specific duties are to be derived by considering more specific reasons in more specific circumstances (MM 216–217, 224, 390–391, 403–404, 468–469; LE 536–538). – TB

FURTHER READING

M. Baron, *Kantian Ethics Almost Without Apology* (Ithaca, NY: Cornell University Press, 1995), pt. 2.

O. O'Neill, 'Instituting principles: between duty and action', in M. Timmons (ed.), *Kant's Metaphysics of Morals: Interpretive Essays* (Oxford: Oxford University Press, 2002), pp. 331–343.

J. Timmermann, 'Acting from duty: inclination, reason and moral worth', in J. Timmermann (ed.), *Kant's Groundwork of the Metaphysics of Morals. A Critical Guide* (Cambridge: Cambridge University Press, 2009), pp. 45–62.

EMPIRICAL REALISM → REALITY

END(S) → CATEGORICAL IMPERATIVE, DUTY, FREEDOM, INTEREST, TELEOLOGY

ENLIGHTENMENT

Kant's essay E is widely regarded as giving expression to the highest ideal of the age of Enlightenment, namely the progressive liberation of reason from superstition and censorship. The essay appeared in the December 1784 issue of the *Berlinische Monatsschrift*, the journal of the Berlin Wednesday Society, one of the many learned societies active in Berlin at the time. The society met regularly to discuss scientific and political events but also topics of broad intellectual interest, such as the benefits and dangers of freethinking or the role of religion in contemporary society.

Kant's essay, as its title indicates, was prompted by a question posed by Johann Friedrich Zöllner, in a piece published a year earlier in the then newly established journal. Zöllner, one of the leading lights of the Berlin Enlightenment, argued that the question 'what is enlightenment?' is 'almost as important as the question what is truth' and 'yet I have nowhere found it answered!'

Kant rises to this challenge with a concise and resonant reply: 'Enlightenment is human being's emergence from his self-incurred minority' (E 35). He also provides a motto for enlightenment: '*Sapere aude*! Have courage to make use of your *own* understanding!' (E 35) Because of its powerful message and accessible tone, Kant's essay on enlightenment is one of few among his works, together perhaps with **G**, to have found a wide non-specialist audience. However, to properly understand Kant's answer to the question of enlightenment an appreciation of his broader philosophical commitments is necessary.

Kant's essay makes a diagnosis and then proposes a treatment. The diagnosis is 'self-incurred minority [*selbst verschuldeten Unmündigkeit*]'. The sometime translation of the German terms *mündig* and *unmündig* as 'mature' and 'immature' respectively, gives the misleading impression that Kant refers to an organic process. The adjective *mündig*,

however, does not have connotations of ripeness. It is connected to the word for mouth, *Mund*, and is specifically used to designate the coming of age, that is, having reached an age at which a person is legally recognized as independent, as having rights and responsibilities, in short, as having a 'voice'.

Kant's conception of immaturity or minority has a precise sense; it is the 'inability to make use of one's own understanding without direction from another' (E 35). The inability Kant identifies has nothing to do with lack of capacity. Rather it has to do with a settled disposition to defer to the opinions of those who 'set themselves up as [. . .] guardians' and who have 'kindly taken it upon themselves to supervise' the rest of us (ibid.). The notion of 'guardian' has an obvious Platonic reference. → **Plato** entrusts the 'guardians' with the protection and government of the ideal city, because they know the Good and are able to discriminate between right and wrong (*Republic* 375a–376c).

What Kant is saying here is that our own claim to think for ourselves can be rightfully asserted. He uses the legal term '*naturaliter maiorennes*', which means those who have come of age by virtue of nature and indicates that, having reached a certain age, a person is recognized by law as an adult and as no longer in need of supervision by a guardian.

The treatment proposed in the essay is nothing short of revolutionary. To take the first steps to maturity all that is needed is enlightenment, which consists in the 'freedom to make *public use* of one's reason' (E 36) (→ **reason**). This use of reason is one anyone can make, Kant insists. So we are all invited to suspend our habitual reliance on external authority and assert the rights of our own reason. This is not mere self-assertion, however. Rather, we are asked to submit our reasoning to a putatively universal public.

Historically, the idea was revolutionary because it asks for freedom from censure and from censorship for all communications. Kant's examples of such communications include criticisms of military discipline, of the tax system, and the church. In addition, publicity liberates reason from being put to the service of specific interest groups, and this means not just those who set to abuse reason to suit their ends, but also those who profess to serve it, such as members of enlightened societies who selectively publicize their communications or of scientific academies who set themselves up as modern day oracles.

The idea of a public use of reason is also conceptually revolutionary. Kant holds that reason's 'authority [*Ansehen*]' (A738=B766) rests on → **freedom**. Freedom is to be understood not only negatively as absence of constraints, but also positively as consisting precisely of those constraints that test our reasoning and so justify reason's 'claim [*Ausspruch*]' (ibid.) on us.

Relevant here is the notion of → **critique** employed in Kant's major philosophical works: enlightenment understood as public use of reason amounts to a popular critique of reason, a way, that is, to achieve self-critical thinking in all matters. The theoretical underpinning for the notion of 'publicity' employed here is provided by Kant's conviction that only the equivalent of a universalizability test for reasoning can challenge self-serving maxims of thinking.

The goal is to achieve 'liberal' (**Anthr** 200) or 'broad-minded' thinking, which Kant characterizes as the ability to 'think in the position of everyone else' (**CJ** 294). Such thinking has an ineradicable practical dimension. It requires being 'in communication with human beings' (**Anthr** 200) and so addressing a real public and being challenged by it.

Much of the contemporary criticism of the enlightenment project fails to take into account the distinctive nature of Kant's own interpretation of enlightenment as a practice of thinking with others. Kantian enlightenment is not a rationalist utopia. It is a practice of communication through which everyone takes responsibility for promoting the fragile and difficult freedom of the public use of reason.

It is these broader concerns that account for the continuing interest and relevance of Kant's interpretation of enlightenment. Kant seeks to show that the interest his contemporaries should take in their own enlightenment and the commitments this involves, to reason inclusively and publicly, are a matter of 'treat[ing] the human being, *who is now more than a machine*, in keeping with his dignity' (**E** 42). – KD

FURTHER READING

K. Deligiorgi, *Kant and the Culture of Enlightenment* (Albany, NY: SUNY Press, 2006).

P. Niesen, *Kants Theorie der Redefreiheit* (Baden-Baden: Nomos 2008).

O. O'Neill, *Constructions of Reason: Explorations of Kant's Practical Philosophy* (Cambridge: Cambridge University Press, 1989).

ENTHUSIASM

In the Kantian philosophical lexicon, the English term 'enthusiasm' can express both the German terms *Enthusiasmus* and *Schwärmerei*. However, from the beginning of the 1760s, Kant differentiates between the two concepts as → **Herder**'s annotations to Kant's lectures testify (**LE** 175–177). In a footnote in **Obs** Kant writes:

> Fanaticism [*Schwärmerei*] must always be distinguished from *enthusiasm* [*Enthusiasmus*]. The former believes itself to feel an immediate and extraordinary communion with a higher nature, the latter signifies the state of the mind which is inflamed beyond the appropriate degree by some principle, whether it be by the maxim of patriotic virtue, or of friendship, or of religion, without involving the illusion of a supernatural community. (**Obs** 251n.; cf. **DSS** 348, 365)

What distinguishes fanaticism from enthusiasm is the belief in the implication of a supernatural and divine cause in the determination of the activity of the mind. In particular, Kant has in mind the British moral philosophers such as Shaftesbury and also → **Pietism**.

In the contemporary essay **EMH**, Kant gives concrete examples from morality by distinguishing enthusiasm from fanaticism and considering the latter as a negative aspect of the life of the mind, which is deceived by false appearances (or chimeras):

> This two-sided appearance of fantasy in moral sensations that are in themselves good is *enthusiasm* [*Enthusiasmus*], and nothing great has ever been accomplished in the world without it. Things stand quite differently with the *fanatic* (*visionary*, *enthusiast* [*Schwärmer*]). The latter is properly a deranged person with presumed immediate inspiration and a great familiarity with the powers of the heavens. Human nature knows no more dangerous illusion. (**EMH** 267)

In **CJ**, Kant asserts that enthusiasm arises when the idea of the good is connected with affect. 'This state of mind', Kant says, 'seems to be sublime, so much so that it is commonly maintained that without it nothing great can be accomplished'. In particular, enthusiasm is 'aesthetically sublime, because it is a stretching of the powers through ideas, which give the mind a momentum that acts far more powerfully and persistently than the impetus given by sensory representations' (**CJ** 272).

Fanaticism, instead, is 'a delusion of being able to see something beyond all bounds of sensibility, i.e., to dream in accordance with principles (to rave with reason) [. . .]' (**CJ** 275). In **CF**, Kant explains the anthropological importance of the concept of 'enthusiasm':

> [T]he passionate participation in the good with affect, i.e., enthusiasm (although not to be wholly esteemed, since all affect as such deserves censure), provide[s] through this history the occasion for the following remark which is important for anthropology: genuine enthusiasm always moves only toward what is ideal and, indeed, to what is purely moral, such as the concept of right, and it cannot be grafted onto self-interest. (**CF** 86; trans. amended)

In this last moral sense enthusiasm is referred to also in **CPrR** (cf. **CPrR** 157) and it is extremely important for Kant's ethics and philosophy of history. – MS

FURTHER READING

R. Clewis, *The Kantian Sublime and the Revelation of Freedom* (Cambridge: Cambridge University Press, 2009), pp. 169–214.

P. Fenves (ed.), *Raising the Tone of Philosophy. Late Essays by Immanuel*

Kant, Transformative Critique by Jacques *Derrida* (Baltimore: Johns Hopkins University Press, 1999).

G. Johnson, 'The tree of melancholy: Kant on philosophy and enthusiasm', in C. Firestone, S. Palmquist (eds), *Kant and the New Philosophy of Religion* (Bloomington, IN: Indiana University Press, 2006), pp.43–61.

S. Meld Shell, *The Embodiment of Reason. Kant on Spirit, Generation, and Community* (Chicago: University of Chicago Press, 1996), pt. 5.

ETHER → NATURAL SCIENCE, EULER

ETHICAL COMMONWEALTH (ETHICAL COMMUNITY) → RELIGION

EVIL → RADICAL EVIL

EXALTATION → ENTHUSIASM, PIETISM

EXPERIENCE (SENSIBILITY)

Kant uses the notion 'experience' in two ways. It means either (1) perception and what is given through it, and that which is abstracted from perceptions by means of induction, which is the indispensable basis and necessary ground of all empirical → knowledge (B1) or, far more frequently, (2) the 'correspondence of perceptions' (**Refl** 2741) or 'connected perceptions' (B161) constituting such knowledge; experience in the latter sense is a necessary connection or synthesis of perceptions (A176=B218; P 275 [§5]). For Kant, experience and knowledge are inextricably bound up.

Although he admits that it may not be immediately obvious, or recognized by some of his modern predecessors, Kant holds that 'experience [. . .] contains two very heterogeneous elements, namely a *matter* for cognition from the senses and a certain *form* for ordering it from the inner source of pure intuiting and thinking' (A86=B118) (→ **form**).

On Kant's view, without both these material and formal conditions, an objective unity of representations and thus experience, in the second above-mentioned sense, itself is not possible. Kant often talks about 'possible experience' (e.g. B73, B127) or 'the possibility of experience', which indicates that Kant's main concern are the *conditions of possibility* of both the experience of objects and the objects of experience (B197=A158) rather than *mere* experience.

Kant believes that failure to recognize this led philosophers such as → **Locke** and → **Hume** to mistaken positions regarding the source of our concepts and our cognition. Locke and Hume fail to recognize that there are formal conditions necessary for the possibility of experience, as they think that material conditions alone are sufficient to produce experience. Kant believes that for them 'the senses do not merely afford us impressions but also put them together, and produce images of objects [. . .]' (A120n.).

On this view, experience is something we have independently of any subsequent actions of either the understanding (→ **judgment, deduction**) or → **imagination**. As a result of failing to recognize that experience 'is a composite of that which we receive through impressions and that which our own cognitive faculty [. . .] provides out of itself' (B1), Kant believes that the empiricists are led to the conclusion that ultimately all of our concepts and cognition have their source in our senses.

With a correct understanding of experience, however, Kant believes there is room to hold that some of our concepts, such as the pure concepts of understanding, are not derived from the senses, but instead have their source in the understanding itself. He also believes that a proper understanding of experience will enable him to explain the possibility of synthetic a priori cognition – it is rooted in the formal conditions of experience and so our synthetic a priori theoretical cognition is grounded in what is required for the possibility of experience.

Kant opposes the empiricist view (→ empiricism) that the senses not only provide us with impressions, but also with the way they are connected. One of Kant's most fundamental assertions is that 'the *combination* (*conjunctio*) of a manifold in general can never come to us through the senses' (B129). Instead, 'all combination [. . .] is an action of the understanding' (B130).

As a result, according to Kant, 'experience itself is a kind of cognition requiring the understanding, whose rule I have to presuppose in myself before any object is given to me, hence *a priori*' (Bxvii). Experience is not something simply given as a fact to which we must then apply our understanding. Instead, experience is only first made possible through the synthetic activity (→ synthesis) of the imagination and understanding.

Once the necessary contribution of the understanding in the production of experience is recognized, however, it would nonetheless be a mistake to conclude on that basis that experience can arise through the intellect alone – this is a mistake Kant believes → Leibniz was led into as a result of his intellectualizing space and time. For sensibility is also an essential component of experience.

In order to have experience at all, there must be *something* to experience. As Kant puts it, right at the beginning of the introduction to CPR (B1), '[t]here is no doubt whatever that all our cognition begins with experience', by means of which 'the cognitive faculty [is] awakened into exercise'.

The sense of experience meant here is the above-mentioned first sense and concerns the sensations of outer and inner sense (→ inner/outer sense) that are the *matter* of experience.

It is also important to note, however, that according to Kant, sensibility does not just contribute to the material conditions of experience. For it is essential to realize that, along with the pure concepts of understanding, the pure forms of sensibility, i.e. space and time (→ Transcendental Aesthetic), are a component of the formal conditions of experience. In order for sensations to be either outer or inner, this already presupposes the representations of respectively space and time (although being sensations outer sensations are also always in time). According to Kant, then, outer and inner experience is only possible through the representations of space and time.

The formal and material conditions of experience play a crucial role in the → Analogies of Experience and in the → Postulates of Empirical Thinking in General (A218=B265ff.). According to the first postulate, if something fits within the framework of the formal conditions of experience, then it is possible. According to the second postulate, if something can be connected with the material conditions of experience (i.e. with perception), then it is actual. Finally, according to the third postulate, if something 'is determined through the connection of perceptions in accordance with concepts, then the object is called necessary' (A234=B286–287). – SB

FURTHER READING

S. M. Bayne, *Kant on Causation. On the Fivefold Routes to the Principle of Causation* (Albany, NY: SUNY Press, 2004), ch. 1.

A. Collins, *Possible Experience. Understanding Kant's Critique of Pure Reason* (Berkeley/Los Angeles: University of California Press, 1999).

H. Ginsborg, 'Kant and the problem of experience', *Philosophical Topics* 34 (2006): 59–106.

FAITH (HISTORICAL, REVEALED, RATIONAL) → RELIGION

FANATICISM → ENTHUSIASM

FIGURATIVE SYNTHESIS → SYNTHESIS

FORM, FORMAL

Kant takes up the Aristotelian distinction between form and matter and gives it a central place in his philosophy. Matter is the determinable, form its determination (A266=B322); matter counts as the given, form as 'a manner of thinking of that which is given' (A279=B335). The relation between form and matter is one of the four pairs of concepts of reflection (→ Amphiboly). Kant claims that transcendental reflection is 'a duty' for those who want to 'judge anything about things *a priori*' (A263=B319), and he further holds that the concepts of form and matter are inseparably 'bound up with every use of the understanding', and 'ground all other reflection' (A266=B322), so the form/matter distinction can be taken to be the fundamental operative tool of the Critical philosophy.

In → logic, the matter (or content) of a → judgment is its constituent concepts, whereas the relation between the concepts (as expressed by the copula) constitutes the form of the judgment (A266=B322). From the point of view of the understanding, matter must precede form. In transcendental reflection, this order is reversed. Appearances are not things in themselves, putatively cognized by the pure understanding (→ transcendental idealism). Sensible → intuition is shown to have forms of its own, and therefore 'a formal intuition (of space and time)' (A268=B324) precedes the matter of intuition (i.e. sensations). Forms of intuition are thus a priori, and in general the concept of form is closely linked to the → a priori.

With regard to the understanding, the Table of Judgment maps its 'mere form' (A70=B95), and the corresponding categories are the forms for 'thinking of an object in general' (A51=B75), or 'the pure form of the use of the understanding in regard to objects in general' (A248=B305). As for reason, its demand for 'absolute *unity*' (A334=B391) leads to dialectical illusion (→ Dialectic); its pure ideas can be taken as forms without content. When critically used, however, they serve as regulative ideas, forming cognition into a → system, under 'the form of a whole' (A832=B860) (→ regulative principles).

Form and matter are also key concepts in Kant's practical philosophy. Practical universal laws determine the → will 'not by their matter but only by their form' (CPrR 27). Only the lawgiving form of the maxim is moral, whereas a will determined by the matter of its maxim (e.g. one's own happiness) is in opposition to the principle of → morality (CPrR 25).

In aesthetics, the judgment of taste is formal. Beauty concerns the form of the object (CJ 279). A judgment that asserts the agreeableness of an object is a judgment of sense (a 'material aesthetic judgment'), not a judgment of taste (CJ 223) (→ **aesthetic judgment**). – MQ

FURTHER READING

R. Pippin, *Kant's Theory of Form* (New Haven: Yale University Press, 1982).

FORMS OF INTUITION (PURE INTUITION) → INTUITION

FREEDOM

Kant conceives of freedom primarily in terms of the autonomy, or self-legislation, of the will. By → **will** he means one's ability to act for reasons and he considers autonomy to consist in taking this ability itself – whether one's own or others' – as a reason for action. He also thinks that this autonomy coincides with moral goodness, such that an autonomous will is also a 'good will'.

He emphasizes these claims in presenting his basic understanding of → **morality** in **G** and particularly with his formulas of the end in itself and autonomy. The formula of the end in itself describes a morally good action as one done considering each affected agent as an 'end in itself' (→ **kingdom of ends**) – that is, as something of such value that he or she may not be used merely as a 'thing' or a 'means' for satisfying one's own or others' inclinations.

The examples that he gives in presenting this formula show that, for Kant, to consider each affected agent as an end in itself is to consider each affected agent's will as itself providing reasons to do or refrain from action – as when one refrains from making false promises because others could not consent to this, helps others to get what they want because they consider these things to

make them happy or cultivates one's own skills because this improves one's own ability to act for reasons (**G** 428–430).

The formula of autonomy emphasizes that one's will is thus autonomous, or self-legislating, in the sense that the reasons for which one acts fundamentally concern only the will, something which one appreciates simply as and because one is a will, rather than for other, contingent reasons (**G** 431–433; **CPrR** 33–41).

Kant considers the will's autonomy also to presuppose the will's freedom in the sense of its being undetermined by antecedent causes. He appeals to his → **transcendental idealism** to claim that we need not consider ourselves merely as objects of possible experience, subject to determination by antecedent causes, and that we may consider, if not experience, ourselves otherwise. He also argues that in acting according to moral reasons, and so achieving autonomy, the will causes actions in a way that differs from that of antecedent causes of changes in the objects of possible experience and is thus underdetermined by such causes (**CPrR** 28–29; **G** 450).

In some passages, he also argues that this freedom is manifested in a variety of other ways – in acting for reasons, whether moral or not (A532–534=B560–562, A800–803=B828–831; **P** 344–347; **G** 455–457), in producing 'ideas' (→ **idea, ideas**) that go beyond the objects of possible experience (**G** 447–463), or in being responsible for actions in the sense of their being within one's 'control' (**CPrR** 94–100) – and in **G** he argues that this freedom implies the will's autonomy, since the only alternative to determination by antecedent causes is such moral self-determination (**G** 446–447) (→ **spontaneity**). But in **CPrR** he insists that this freedom must be considered simply as a presupposition of autonomy and cannot be demonstrated independently (**CPrR** 3–7, 28–33, 42–56, 93–99, 103–106).

Kant also provides an account of political freedom, particularly in **MM**. He distinguishes this freedom from the autonomy of the will on the grounds that politics, or justice, concerns only what can be coerced by others and is therefore a matter only of actions and not of the reasons for which we do them. He claims that we each have a basic right not to be coerced, but only insofar as this is consistent with everyone else's equal freedom of action – thus, he claims, coercion can be justified to protect such freedom (**MM** 214, 218–221, 230–233, 237–239).

In **MM** he proceeds to argue for a range of freedoms in this sense, from the property and family rights of individuals to the legislative and international rights of states (→ **right**). Elsewhere, he also limits his speculations about human progress to such freedoms, on the grounds that while natural and social circumstances may make our actions more just, autonomy can be achieved only by the will itself (**UH** 21–29; **CBH** 118–126; **CJ** 359–445; **TP** 310–312; **PP** 360–361, 365, 366). – TB

FURTHER READING

H. Allison, *Kant's Theory of Freedom* (Cambridge: Cambridge University Press, 1990).

H. Allison, 'Kant on freedom of the will', in P. Guyer (ed.), *The Cambridge Companion to Kant and Modern Philosophy* (Cambridge: Cambridge University Press, 2006), pp. 381–415

K. Flikschuh, *Kant and Modern Political Philosophy* (Cambridge: Cambridge University Press, 2000).

A. Reath, 'Kant's Critical account of freedom', in G. Bird (ed.), *A Companion to Kant* (Malden, MA/Oxford: Wiley-Blackwell, 2010), pp. 275–290.

GEOMETRY

Geometry is the body of synthetic a priori knowledge whose validity is guaranteed by the status of → **a priori** → **intuition** conferred upon the representation of space by Kant (B40–42) (→ **Transcendental Aesthetic**). As Kant explains, geometry's a priori status is not analytic (B16), but involves the exhibition of concepts through a priori intuitions (A714=B743). That the shortest line between two points is the straight line does not follow from an → **analysis** of the concept 'straight'. It requires an ostensive construction in pure intuition whereby the → **synthesis** of the generated manifold is brought under geometric concepts according to the categories of quantity.

If carried out empirically (e.g. on paper), this construction generates a particular object which must however serve 'to express the concept without damage to its universality' (A714=B742). Since '[n]o image of a triangle would ever be adequate to the concept of it' (A141=B180), what is therefore at stake is the construction of a concept in pure intuition (A714=B742), i.e. the schema (A141=B180) (→ **schematism**). This notion of schema allows Kant to avoid the temptation of mathematical realism: there is no intuition of a universal, but the universal is exhibited through the construction of an instance of the formal intuition of a particular (A714=B742).

Kant's geometry is Euclidean (cf. **Refl** 9). Historically, this view is not surprising. In the nineteenth century, hyperbolic (Lobachevsky) and elliptic (Riemann) geometries were developed, which deny Euclid's fifth postulate. Whereas in Euclidean geometry there is one and only one line parallel to a given straight line and passing through a point external to it, in hyperbolic geometry there are infinitely many such parallel lines, and in elliptic geometry there are none.

Some commentators view Kant's pronouncement on the logical possibility of denying fundamental mathematical propositions (B14) as creating the conceptual space for non-Euclidean geometry. Others see his geometry as necessarily Euclidean insofar as geometric results are obtained by construction in space, and such constructions are Euclidean. While the former view generally mistakenly sees Kant as a forerunner of axiomatic geometry, the latter overlooks the distinction between space as form of intuition and as geometrical space.

Two observations are useful with regard to the issue of Kant and non-Euclidean geometry. First, Kantian examples of Euclidean plane geometry (A717ff.=B745ff.) easily let us overlook the distinction between geometrical image and a priori spatial intuition. The latter is a transcendental condition of spatial images which instantiate it. But the actual generation of images involves empirical conditions connected with the specificity of our perceptual apparatus, and this may explain the Euclidean framework's privileged status.

The suggestion is therefore that the fact that our images are Euclidean is ultimately a feature of our perception that is related to our embodiment in space, and to the convention of how to formalize it. It is therefore not a priori, thus distinguishing a posteriori applied geometry from a priori pure geometry. This does not involve the mistaken claim that our perceptual geometry is Euclidean, but rather the observation that Euclidean

geometry is a particularly suitable conventional choice, e.g. according to a criterion of simplicity.

Second, this would leave us with the possibility of other ways of intuiting non-Euclidean figures, e.g. by making use of models of elliptic and hyperbolic geometry in Euclidean space. This would amount to different ways of schematizing geometrical concepts than suggested at A141=B180. The resulting formal intuitions would represent non-Euclidean geometrical concepts; the generated images are both Euclidean and ostensive constructions (under the selected model). Such constructions share properties with both Kant's ostensive and symbolic constructions (A717=B745) (→ mathematics).

Our formal intuition of perceptual space is three-dimensional, and this feature is important for Kant's interest in incongruent counterparts. Kant first discusses them in the pre-Critical essay DS (1768), which argues against → Leibniz's relational view of space. According to Kant, counterparts such as the right and the left hand are spatial objects for which all internal relations are identical, but which are not superposable. That is to say, it is not possible to turn the one into the other using a rigid continuous transformation.

Kant's argument successfully shows that this property of incongruence depends upon the nature of space as a whole. Kant concludes that this invalidates the Leibnizian relational theory of space. In ID (1770), Kant examines the epistemological implications of this conclusion. Knowledge of space cannot be intellectual: sensibility does not therefore provide a confused type of knowledge, but is rather a distinct source of cognition.

The Critical Kant concludes (A283=B339) that, since the relational properties of things in themselves must only be dependent upon their intrinsic properties, spatial objects are not things in themselves. This provides grounds for his much discussed claim that '[s]pace does not represent any property of things in themselves, nor does it represent them in their relation to one another' (A26=B42), and thus addresses the famous 'neglected alternative' of the proof of → **transcendental idealism** in the Transcendental Aesthetic. – CO

FURTHER READING

M. Friedman, 'Geometry, construction and intuition in Kant and his successors', in G. Sher, R. Tieszen (eds), *Between Logic and Intuition. Essays in Honor of Charles Parsons* (Cambridge: Cambridge University Press, 2000), pp. 186–218.

F. Kjosavik, 'Kant on geometrical intuition and the foundations of mathematics, *Kant-Studien* 100,1 (2009): 1–27.

A. Moretto, 'Philosophie transcendantale et géométrie non-euclidienne', in *Kant et les Mathématiques*, in the series *Les Cahiers philosophiques de Strasbourg* 26 (2009): 117–140.

H. Poincaré, 'On the foundations of geometry', in W. Ewald (ed.), *From Kant to Hilbert: A Source Book in the Foundations of Mathematics*, vol. II (Oxford: Oxford University Press, 1996), pp. 982–1011.

L. Shabel, 'Kant's argument from geometry', *Journal of the History of Philosophy* 42,2 (2004): 195–215.

GOD → PROOFS OF THE EXISTENCE OF GOD

GOOD → MORALITY

GOOD WILL → WILL

GUIDING THREAD → DEDUCTION

HAPPINESS → MORALITY, RELIGION, VIRTUE/VIRTUES

HIGHEST GOOD → RELIGION, MORALITY

I THINK → APPERCEPTION

IDEA, IDEAS

In CPR, Kant's concept of an idea (*Idee* or *Vernunftbegriff*) is exclusively linked to pure → **reason** and its concepts, just like the concept of a category (*Kategorie* or *Verstandesbegriff*) is linked to the understanding and the concept of an intuition (*Anschauuung*) to sensibility, and chiefly discussed in the first book of the → **Dialectic** ('On the concepts of pure reason').

The overall objective of this theoretical discussion of pure reason's ideas is clearly to ground and secure the system of practical philosophy, namely

that of making the terrain for these majestic moral edifices level and firm enough to be built upon; for under this ground there are all sorts of passageways [. . .] left over from reason's vain but confident treasure hunting, that make every building insecure. It is the transcendental use of pure reason, of its principles and ideas, whose closer acquaintance we are [. . .] obligated to make, in order properly to determine and evaluate the influence and the worth of pure reason. (B375–376)

For these reasons, it is already on the theoretical level that Kant gives a positive account or regulative defence of the transcendental – not the (illegitimate) transcendent – use of pure reason, that is, its transcendental ideas and its system of transcendental ideas. One interesting formulation of this account or defence goes as follows:

> [T]he pure rational concepts [*Vernunftbegriffe*] of the totality in a synthesis of conditions are necessary at least as problems of extending the unity of the understanding, if possible, to the unconditioned, and they are grounded in the nature of human reason, even if these transcendental concepts lack a suitable use *in concreto* and have no other utility than to point the understanding in the right direction so that it may be thoroughly consistent with itself when it extends itself to its uttermost extremes. (B380)

Generally speaking, transcendental ideas have to do with 'the unconditioned synthetic unity of all conditions in general' for reasons of heuristics and consistency, but Kant specifies that they can be brought 'under *three classes*, of which the *first* contains the absolute (unconditioned) *unity* of the *thinking subject*, the *second* the absolute *unity* of the *series* of *conditions of appearance*, the *third* the absolute *unity* of the *condition of all objects of thought in general*', so that 'pure reason provides the ideas for a transcendental doctrine of the soul (*psychologia rationalis*), a transcendental science of the world (*cosmologia rationalis*), and [. . .] a transcendental cognition of God (*theologia transcendentalis*)' (B391–392). And it is by means of this tripartite classification of progressively unifying ideas – soul, world and God – that pure reason brings all its cognitions into a → **system**.

However, two important characteristics of Kant's theory of ideas should be stressed. First, there is no objective deduction of these transcendental ideas possible, such as in the case of the categories (→ **deduction**), since ideas are not related to any object that

could be given corresponding to them; the only applicable method of demonstrating the legitimate function of transcendental ideas seems to be 'a subjective introduction [*Anleitung*] to them from the nature of our reason' since the transcendental ideas serve only for 'ascending [*Aufsteigen*] in the series of conditions to the unconditioned, i.e., to the principles' (B393–394).

Secondly, Kant's conception of a system of ideas is developed from his theory of judgment, similar to the way he proceeds in the Deduction, namely through a differentiation of the different types of relation between subject and predicate in a judgment of reason:

> There will be as many concepts of reason [*Vernunftbegriffe*] as there are species of relation represented by the understanding by means of the categories; and so we must seek an *unconditioned*, *first*, for the *categorical* synthesis in a *subject*, *second* for the *hypothetical* synthesis of the members of a *series*, and *third* for the *disjunctive* synthesis of the parts in a *system*. There are [. . .] just as many species of syllogism [*Arten von Vernunftschlüssen*], and in each of them prosyllogisms proceed to the unconditioned: one, to a subject that is no longer a predicate, another to a presupposition that presupposes nothing further, and the third to an aggregate of members of a division such that nothing further is required for it to complete the division of a concept. (B379–380)

This judgment-oriented way of Kant's argumentation can hardly be underestimated since it is in terms of the dialectical inferences of pure reason that the → **Paralogisms**, → the **Antinomies**, the Ideal of Pure Reason (→ **transcendental ideal**) and most of the other issues of the Dialectic are discussed. – JV

FURTHER READING

N. Klimmek, *Kants System der transzendentalen Ideen* (Berlin/New York: de Gruyter, 2005).

M. Rohlf, 'The Ideas of Pure Reason', in P. Guyer (ed.), *The Cambridge Companion to Kant's 'Critique of Pure Reason'* (Cambridge: Cambridge University Press, 2010), pp. 190–209.

IDEALISM → TRANSCENDENTAL IDEALISM

IDENTITY

Kant sometimes characterizes the distinction between analytic and synthetic judgments in terms of identity: in affirmative analytic judgments 'the connection of the predicate with the subject is thought through identity', whereas judgments 'in which this connection is thought without identity are to be called synthetic' (A7=B10–11; trans. amended) (→ judgment). This means that the marks contained in the predicate concept of an analytic judgment are identical to (some of) those in the subject concept (→ analysis). Such comparison of the contents of concepts rests on reflection: 'identity and difference' is one of the four pairs of concepts of reflection (A261=B317) (→ Amphiboly).

Kant employs transcendental reflection, which locates the cognitive source of a representation, for criticizing the Leibnizian principle of the identity of indiscernibles. According to → Leibniz, two concepts with the same internal determinations are identical, and since he 'believed himself able to cognize the inner constitution of things by comparing all objects only with the understanding and

the abstract formal concepts of its thinking' (A270=B326), he concluded that things with identical conceptual determinations must be numerically identical. Through transcendental reflection, Kant by contrast distinguishes between concepts and intuitions. Sensible objects have spatiotemporal locations, which cannot be derived from their conceptual determinations. Therefore, two things can be 'fully similar and equal' to each other and yet occupy different places, as the parts of space are 'entirely indifferent with regard to the inner determinations of the things' (A272=B328). The principle of the identity of indiscernibles, though valid for concepts, is thus 'no law of nature' (A272=B328).

Kant also discusses identity in connection with → apperception. The possibility to think a concept, i.e. an identical feature in different representations (analytical unity), depends on the synthetic unity of consciousness (→ synthesis). Identity among representations thus requires that the manifold is united, i.e. 'the *analytical* unity of apperception is only possible under the presupposition of some *synthetic* one' (B133). Without this original synthetic apperception 'I would have as multicolored, diverse a self as I have representations' (B134); it therefore grounds the 'thoroughgoing identity of self-consciousness' (B135).

In the section on the → Paralogisms in CPR, Kant criticizes the rationalist doctrine of the thinking subject as a simple substance. The apperceptive identity of consciousness cannot prove the 'identity of person' (A365) pertaining to a noumenal substance. – MQ

FURTHER READING

K. Ameriks, *Kant's Theory of Mind. An Analysis of the Paralogisms of Pure Reason*, new edition (Oxford: Clarendon Press, 2000), ch. 4.

IMAGINATION

In the mid-1770s, Kant includes the faculty of imagination (*das Vermögen der Einbildung*) among the six faculties (illustration, imitation, anticipation, correlation, imagination and cultivation) of the formative faculty (*Bildungsvermögen*), 'which is a faculty for making out of ourselves cognitions which in themselves nevertheless have the form according to which objects would affect our senses' (**LM** 235). The faculty of imagination in particular 'is the faculty for producing images from oneself, independent of the actuality of objects, where the images are not borrowed from experience' (**LM** 237). This formative faculty as a whole Kant locates within sensibility (*Sinnlichkeit*), the lower faculty of cognition, which he in turn distinguishes from 'the higher faculty of cognition, [which] is threefold: *understanding* [*Verstand*], *power of judgment* [*Urtheilskraft*], and *reason* [*Vernunft*]' (**LM** 241).

By the time of **CPR**, the imagination's location within the faculties of cognition has changed. Instead of placing imagination within sensibility, Kant now holds that 'sense, imagination, and apperception' are the 'three original sources (capacities or faculties of the soul), which contain the conditions of the possibility of all experience, and cannot themselves be derived from any other faculty of the mind' (A94).

Imagination is contrasted with sensibility in that whereas sensibility is 'the *receptivity* of our mind to receive representations insofar as it is affected in some way' (A51=B75), imagination (i.e. productive imagination) involves → **spontaneity** and it is an active 'faculty for determining the sensibility *a priori*' (B151–152). Imagination is also contrasted with understanding in that while both are active faculties involving spontaneity, understanding enacts an intellectual →

synthesis whereas imagination enacts a figurative synthesis.

Heidegger has famously argued in his *Kant und das Problem der Metaphysik* that imagination is not simply one faculty among equals (see the essay on Heidegger in the section 'Reception and Influence', this volume). Instead, according to Heidegger, the transcendental power of imagination is the common root Kant writes about when he tells us that 'there are two stems of human cognition, which may perhaps arise from a common but to us unknown root, namely sensibility and understanding [. . .]' (A15=B29).

In **CPR**, the function of the imagination has also been transformed. Image formation is still part of the role of imagination and it is still true that '[i]magination is the faculty for representing an object even without its presence in intuition' (B151), but a crucial addition to the role of imagination is the function of synthesis. Kant writes that '[s]ynthesis in general is [. . .] the mere effect of the imagination, of a blind though indispensable function of the soul, without which we would have no cognition at all, but of which we are seldom even conscious' (A78=B103).

The synthesis of the imagination is a figurative synthesis that can either be a priori or empirical. When discussing the a priori synthesis of imagination, Kant typically calls it the productive imagination. When this productive imagination is aimed at determining the form of sensibility a priori in accordance with the unity of apperception, this is called the transcendental synthesis of imagination and is as such necessary for the possibility of experience (e.g. A123; B151–152). The synthesis of the reproductive imagination, however, 'is subject solely to empirical laws, namely those of association, and that therefore contributes nothing to the explanation of the possibility of cognition *a priori* [. . .]' (B152).

In the Critical period, Kant also calls the imagination the faculty of presentation (*das Vermögen der Darstellung*) (see e.g. **CJ** 232, and **CJ** 244–245). In **CPR** this function of the imagination takes prominence in the chapter 'On the Schematism' (→ **schematism**), where Kant explains, for the case of determinative → **judgment**, the general procedure by which imagination exhibits a determinate concept in intuition. In the case of → **aesthetic judgment**, which is a merely reflective rather than determinative judgment, however, Kant holds that imagination is not constrained by the understanding to exhibit a determinate concept, but instead the imagination is free and 'it schematizes without a concept' (**CJ** 287). The satisfaction of these judgments is not grounded on intuitions being subsumed under a concept, but instead it is grounded on a feeling that arises when the free play of the imagination 'is in harmony with the [understanding] *in its lawfulness*' (**CJ** 287). – SB

FURTHER READING

G. Banham, *Kant's Transcendental Imagination* (Basingstoke/New York: Palgrave Macmillan, 2006).

J. Kneller, *Kant and the Power of Imagination* (Cambridge: Cambridge University Press, 2007).

R. Makkreel, *Imagination and Interpretation in Kant. The Hermeneutical Import of the Critique of Judgment* (Chicago: University of Chicago Press, 1990).

J. M. Young, 'Kant's view of the imagination', *Kant-Studien* 79 (1988): 140–164.

**IMMATURITY (*UNMÜNDIGKEIT*) →
ENLIGHTENMENT**

**IMPERATIVE → CATEGORICAL
IMPERATIVE**

**INCLINATION → DUTY/DUTIES,
MORALITY, WILL**

**INCONGRUENT COUNTERPARTS →
GEOMETRY**

INNER/OUTER SENSE

Kant's notion of sensibility is divided into inner sense and outer sense. Outer sense is that by means of which 'we represent to ourselves objects as outside us, and all as in space' (B37). Inner sense is that 'by means of which the mind intuits itself, or its inner state' (ibid.). However, while intuiting itself the mind does not thereby have an intuition of the soul as a determinate object (→ **Paralogisms**); this marks out a major difference between Kant and his predecessors regarding self-consciousness. A distinction must be made between the self that intuits itself in terms of being self-consciously aware of one's representing and the self that putatively determines the substance underlying one's representing.

Outer sense is a formal designation that makes it possible to regard 'certain sensations to be related to something outside me' (B38), that is, to represent those sensations being related such as to constitute reference to an external spatial object. The pure form of outer sense is space, which 'comprehends all things that may appear to us externally' (B43) (→ **Transcendental Aesthetic**).

Inner sense is in some sense more fundamental than outer sense. The → **form** of inner sense is time, which is therefore the form of *all* appearances (B51), whereas space is only the form of *outer* appearances. In other words, all representations, whether of inner or outer 'objects', belong to the mind and thus to inner sense. Time, Kant says, is the 'immediate condition of the inner intuition (of our souls), and thereby also the mediate condition of outer appearances' (B50=A34). However, the representations of outer sense 'make up the proper material with which we occupy our mind' (B67). They are the actual matter of all our representations.

The → form of → intuition is, Kant tells us, nothing other than 'the way in which the mind is affected by its own activity', that is, 'affected through itself' (B67–68) and this makes it an inner sense (B68). The subject as → appearance is the object of this inner sense (B68), not the subject as its own self-activity. But the question is 'how a subject can internally intuit itself' (ibid.). Kant notes that → apperception or self-consciousness is only a simple representation through which nothing manifold is given; if a manifold were given in it, then the inner intuition would be intellectual and would be identical to apperception. But as apperception is merely simple, 'an inner perception of the manifold that is antecedently given in the subject' (B68), independently of the spontaneity of the mind, is required. This justifies the distinction between self-consciousness as spontaneous self-activity (→ spontaneity) and the way the mind is affected by it in inner sense, and is thus passive.

At B153ff. Kant reiterates the argument from B68 and notices that it might strike one as paradoxical that we only intuit ourselves 'as we are internally affected' by ourselves. How can the same 'I' be both passive and active?

To explain this, Kant again sharply discriminates between inner sense and apperception. The function of apperception, the activity of the understanding, is not a faculty of intuition

but merely a function of unity among one's representations in an intuition that is *given* to it. Apperception, 'under the designation of a transcendental synthesis of the imagination', 'exercises that action on the *passive* subject' (B153). The inner sense, which is mere form of intuition, containing no synthetic unity, is in this way affected by the act of apperception, which combines and hence determines the manifold in inner sense.

Inner sense is also central to the argument of the → **Refutation of Idealism**, where Kant attempts to undermine the ostensible threat of idealism, and which continues to occupy Kant's mind afterwards, judging by the numerous *Reflexionen* that Kant wrote in the years after the publication of the second edition of **CPR**, which reflect on the problem of idealism (see esp. **Refl 5655** and **LenFr** in relation to inner sense). – DS

FURTHER READING

H. Allison, *Kant's Transcendental Idealism. An Interpretation and Defense*, revised & enlarged edition (New Haven: Yale University Press, 2004), ch. 10, pt. I.

G. Mohr, *Das sinnliche Ich. Innerer Sinn und Bewußtsein bei Kant* (Würzburg: Königshausen & Neumann, 1991).

INTELLECT → JUDGMENT (UNDERSTANDING)

INTELLECTUAL SYNTHESIS → SYNTHESIS

INTEREST

For Kant, the notion of 'interest' is of importance in a variety of contexts. Most generally, interest drives a finite rational agent towards an end: it is the 'dependence of a contingently determinable will on principles of reason' (**G** 413n; see also **G** 460n, **MM** 212, **CJ** 204, 207).

By way of a deep-seated analogy, Kant speaks of the interests of our faculties: 'Reason, as the faculty of principles, determines the interest of all the powers of the mind but itself determines its own' (**CPrR** 119–120). → **Reason** is by nature architectonic; its most fundamental end is to discover an absolute foundation for → **knowledge** (A474ff.=B502ff.) (→ **system**). This speculative interest leads it uncritically to claim knowledge of what lies beyond the bounds of → **experience**, in particular, to the → **Paralogisms**, → **Antinomies** and → **proofs of the existence of God** (A340ff.=B398ff.). However, the psychological, cosmological and theological ideas do have a necessary regulative role in leading reason towards systematic unity (A671=B699) (→ **regulative principles, system**).

The discussion of the conditions and limits of knowledge answers the first of the three questions that unite all interests of reason: '1. What can I know? 2. What should I do? 3. What may I hope?' (A805=B833). The second question is answered by moral theory (→ **morality**); it does not lead reason beyond its bounds. The third reveals that its practical interest reaches farther than the theoretical. The moral imperative cannot be separated from the hope for happiness and thus from the belief that a wise creator rewards morality and that the striving for it is endless (**CPrR** 122–132). Theoretical reason cannot prove moral → **freedom**, God's existence or the soul's immortality. Reason's interest is 'complete in practical use alone' (**CPrR** 121).

Central to Kant's practical philosophy is the distinction between pathological interests in natural ends that satisfy desires and a pure moral interest that is simply the feeling of '*respect* for the law' (**G** 401n). However, it is far from easy to comprehend the interest that explains the legislation of an autonomous will and the role that the feeling of respect plays in moral agency (**CPrR** 71–89, esp. 79–81; see also **MM** 399–403) (→ **categorical imperative**). Were a sceptic to ask us why morality has 'a worth so great that there can be no higher interest anywhere [. . .] we could give him no satisfactory answer' (**G** 449ff.; cf. **G** 459–463). Kant's ultimate answer seems simply to be that the law interests us because it arises 'from our proper self' (**G** 461).

Kant lays great emphasis on the claim that judgments of taste are disinterested (**CJ** 203–205) (→ **aesthetic judgment**). Although they are expressions of pleasure, it is neither merely sensual nor moral (**CJ** 205–211). Finding a thing beautiful (or → **sublime**) is 'merely *contemplative*, i.e., a judgment [. . .] indifferent with regard to the existence of an object [. . .]' (**CJ** 209). Nevertheless, it is 'also not directed to concepts; for the judgment of taste is not a cognitive judgment [. . .]' (**CJ** 209). Aesthetic judgment expresses pleasure in the interaction of our mental faculties.

From the disinterestedness of aesthetic judgments follows their claim to universality (**CJ** 211–212) and the difficulty of judging objects purely aesthetically. Though aesthetic judgments are essentially disinterested, the beauty of → **art** promotes our natural interest in sociability and finding nature beautiful is a mark of interest in the good (**CJ** 296–303). – IG

INTUITION

The term 'intuition' (*Anschauung*), whose Latin cognates are already introduced by Kant in **ID** (387, 396, 402–403) to differentiate a sensible form of → **knowledge** that is irreducible to intellectual (conceptual)

knowledge, denotes a direct reference to a particular or → **object**, which cannot be captured by a concept. In Kant's theory of concepts (→ **logic**), a concept is always a general or universal → **representation**, never a representation of a singular thing. An intuition is 'immediately related to the object and is singular', whereas a concept is always 'mediate, by means of a mark, which can be common to several things' (A320=B377; cf. A19=B33; **ID** 396). 'That representation [...] which can only be given through a single object, is an intuition' (B47=A32). Hence, unlike concepts an intuition is not a discursive representation, which can be represented of a plurality of objects. Only by means of sensibility can intuitions, through which alone objects can be presented to us, be given.

Three criteria for intuitions can be identified: (1) the *immediacy* criterion; (2) the *singularity* criterion; and (3) the *dependency* criterion.

The first criterion concerns the above-noted aspect of the direct relation of an intuition to its object, unlike a concept, which is only indirectly related to an object by means of other concepts or by means of an intuition (A68=B93). The second aspect, as noted, indicates that an intuition picks out a particular. The third concerns an often ignored element, namely the fact that intuitions only exist on the basis of a given object. An intuition 'takes place only insofar as the object is given to us' (A19=B33). That is, the existence of an intuition is dependent on the existence of an object (i.e. an as yet undetermined object or appearance) (B72; **P** 281). By contrast, a concept need not depend on an actually existing object (the concept of a unicorn, say).

While Kant sharply distinguishes between intuitions and concepts, whose roles must not be mixed up (A52=B76), he also importantly argues for their necessary connection to the extent that knowledge should arise from it; Kant famously says that intuitions without concepts are blind, and that concepts without intuitions are empty (A51=B75). This dictum in fact conveys the idea that only intuitions are the means by which empirical content is provided – that is, that an immediate relation to the perceived object by way of sensations is established – whereas concepts are the forms necessary to objectively determine this content.

Nevertheless, intuitions are not just empirical *content*, but also have a necessary → **form**. Hence, Kant distinguishes between → **pure** and empirical intuition, where the former is the necessary form of the latter. An intuition is empirical if it contains a manifold of sensations, which is the matter of an intuition. Furthermore, the object of an empirical intuition is an → **appearance**. On the other hand, 'pure intuition contains merely the form under which something is intuited' (A50=B74), and is → **a priori**. Pure intuition is the 'pure form of sensibility' (A20–21=B34–35), and contains nothing but relations (B66–67).

The two pure intuitions at the centre of Kant's argument in the → **Transcendental Aesthetic** are space and time (B38–40, 46–47). Already in **ID**, published eleven years prior to **CPR**, it is argued that space (as well as time) is a pure intuition and is the 'very form of all sensory intuition' (**ID** 402–403). Space and time are the 'formal principle[s] of our intuition', i.e. 'the condition under which something can be the object of our senses', hence the 'condition of sensitive cognition' (**ID** 396). Space and time as mere *forms of intuition* become *formal intuitions* – and so objects in their own right, which in the case of space can be studied in → **geometry** – under the influence of the → **synthesis** of the → **imagination** (B160–1n.).

It should be noted that an intuition is not a single representation or a sensation, but an objective perception (B376–377=A320; **LM** 484). One can have an intuition of an object, without needing a concept or the capacity to judge (A89–91=B122–123; **JL** 33). However, for an intuition to refer objectively in the strict sense, a synthesis of the imagination is required, which is not given in the manifold itself (B129–131; B134; B151–152); and without thinking, 'mere intuition' does not yet constitute a real relation to an object (B309; cf. A111). An intuition gives us the object, with the understanding it is thought, that is, subsumed under concepts in judgements. An intuition is a necessary condition, though not a sufficient condition for objective knowledge. It is then the argument of the Transcendental Deduction of the categories (→ **deduction**) to argue that intuition and concept must be combined to establish the possibility of objective → **experience**.

For Kant, intuition is always sensible and hence passive (**ID** 396); unlike for the German idealists, who were intrigued by Kant's suggestion of the possibility of an 'intuitive understanding' which is active and original (**CJ** 406), for Kant intellectual intuition is not a possible way of intuiting for human beings. Intellectual intuition is a mode of original intuition, 'through which the existence of the object of intuition is itself given' (B72), whereas by contrast sensible intuition is dependent on an already given object through the manifold of representations that are affected by it. At various places in the Transcendental Deduction and elsewhere (B135; B138–139; B145; B159; A230=B283; cf. **CJ** 402–403, 405–406), Kant explicitly contrasts sensible and intellectual intuition to point out the incontrovertibly *discursive*, *non-intuitive* nature of our, human mode of conceptual cognition, which requires the receptivity of sensible representations

in order to relate to objects (A19=B33; B298=A239). – DS

FURTHER READING

L. Allais, 'Kant, non-conceptual content and the representation of space', *Journal of the History of Philosophy* 47,3 (2009): 383–413.

L. Falkenstein, *Kant's Intuitionism: A Commentary on the Transcendental Aesthetic* (Toronto: Toronto University Press, 1995), Part I.

S. Grüne, *Blinde Anschauung. Die Rolle von Begriffen in Kants Theorie sinnlicher Synthesis* (Frankfurt a/M: Klostermann, 2009).

JUDGMENT (UNDERSTANDING)

The notion of judgment forms the backbone of Kant's philosophy. It is a central concept of both **CPR** and **CJ**. At A132=B171, Kant distinguishes between, on the one hand, the understanding 'as the faculty of rules' and, on the other hand, 'the power of judgment [*Urteilskraft*]' as 'the faculty of *subsuming* under rules'. However, Kant also appears to define the understanding as a 'faculty for judging' (A69=B94). This is so because he takes the understanding to be a faculty for thinking, which means that it is a way of cognizing through concepts. And given that concepts rest on functions, by which Kant means 'the unity of the action of ordering different representations under a common one' (A68=B93), and given that 'the understanding can make no other use of these concepts than that of judging by means of them' (ibid.) – i.e. concepts are 'predicates of possible judgments' (A69=B94) – an act of the understanding, or act of thought, comes down to an act of judgment, defined as the capacity to subsume under rules. 'Therefore, thinking is the same as judging' (**P** 304).

This analysis forms the basis of Kant's claim in the guiding thread (A79=B104–105) that '[t]he same function [i.e. 'the same understanding', D.S.] that gives unity to the different representations *in a judgment* also gives unity to the mere synthesis of different representations *in an intuition*', which yields the pure concepts of the understanding, the categories (→ **deduction, synthesis**). That is to say, the elementary functions for judgment, which are listed in the Table of Judgment, correspond in a strong sense to the pure concepts by means of which the connection between the understanding and a determinate → **object** is made possible.

The elementary functions for judgments are what, apart from the modal forms, makes up the content of a paradigmatic subject–predicate judgment. The quantitative moments concern the predicate of a judgment being attributed to either all, some or a particular thing(s) that are/is subsumed under the subject. The qualitative moments relate to whether the copula in a judgment is affirmative, negative or infinite. Furthermore, a judgment is characterized by three possible relations among its predicates: either it is categorical, hypothetical or disjunctive.

These elementary unitary forms correspond to the categories being those very same forms in respect of their relation to the intuition of an object. This is why Kant identifies, at a crucial stage in the argument in the Transcendental Deduction (§19) (→ **deduction, object**), a judgment as 'nothing other than the way to bring given cognitions to the *objective* unity of apperception' (B141; cf. **MFNS** 476n. and **Refl** 5933), i.e. the way that by means of the concepts of the

understanding (the categories) predicates are related such that they refer to a determinate object of intuition that is subsumed under the subject predicate. As Kant is reported to have said in **LL** 928: 'A judgment is the representation of the way that concepts belong to one consciousness universally[,] objectively.'

In **FI** and **CJ**, Kant makes a distinction between a 'determinative' judgment and a 'merely reflecting' judgment, corresponding to the determining and reflecting powers of judgment respectively (**FI** 211; cf. **CJ** 179). For Kant, this distinction is important for arguing for the possibility of finding among the multiplicity of the empirical objects of nature a common ground for their unity and arriving at empirical concepts and their thorough interconnection into empirical laws. Other than with determinative judgment in the context of establishing the possibility of determinate knowledge, where 'its transcendental schematism serves it [. . .] as a rule under which given empirical intuitions are subsumed' (**FI** 212) so as to provide an object for the judgment, the reflecting power of judgment 'proceeds with given appearances, in order to bring them under empirical concepts of determinate natural things [. . .] in accordance with the general but at the same time indeterminate principle of a purposive arrangement in a system' (**FI** 213–214).

The power of judgment in its 'merely reflective' mode proceeds empirically and ascends from the particular to the general and unlike judgment in its determining mode, which subsumes the particular under a universal, it does not yield a determinate concept of an object. Therefore, a reflective judgment is not objectively but merely subjectively necessary. Examples of such judgments are → **aesthetic judgment** and teleological judgment (→ **teleology**).

In potential conflict with the account of judgment in **CPR** is the distinction Kant makes in **P**, published three years before Kant first defined judgment as an objective unity of representations in **MFNS** (476n.), between judgments of experience and judgments of perception. The former are '*empirical judgments, insofar as they have objective validity*', whereas the latter 'are *only subjectively valid*' and 'do not require a pure concept of the understanding, but only the logical connection of perceptions in a thinking subject' (**P** 298). Judgments of perception do not appear to be consistent with the definition of judgment provided in §19 of **CPR**.

Most importantly, although the grounding of both reduces to the same original synthetic unity of apperception (cf. B133–134n.), Kant differentiates sharply between analytic and synthetic judgment (A6ff.=B10ff.). Analytic judgments are merely clarificatory in that they are propositions whereby the predicate is already implicitly contained in the subject term of the judgment and can be made explicit by means of conceptual → **analysis** alone. The sole principle on which analytic judgments rest is the → **principle of (non-)contradiction.** The reference to any underlying intuition of an object is otiose as it does not contribute to the understanding of the relation between subject and predicate, which is merely conceptual.

A synthetic judgment, by contrast, is a judgment where the predicate is not already contained in the subject; synthetic judgments do not rest on strict conceptual identity among their predicates. The predicate really amplifies knowledge that is not already contained in the subject term of a judgment (cf. **JL** 111; **P** 266–268). That which increases the knowledge beyond the information contained in the predicates must be something 'in addition to the concept of the subject [. . .] on which the understanding depends in cognizing a predicate that does not lie in that concept as nevertheless belonging to it' (A8).

This something is → **experience**, from which analytic judgments are, by contrast, entirely independent for their comprehension.

All judgments of experience are synthetic. However, not all synthetic judgments are empirical judgments of experience, i.e. a posteriori. Crucially, Kant also talks about synthetic a priori judgments (→ **synthesis**). These judgments are amplificatory but nonetheless → **a priori**, and do therefore not depend on experience. Typical synthetic a priori judgments are 'Everything that happens has its cause' (A9=B13) or such mathematical judgments as '7+5=12' (B15) or 'The straight line between two points is the shortest' (B16) (→ **mathematics, geometry**). The principle that makes these judgments possible is what is expressed by the synthetic a priori.

In natural science, synthetic a priori judgments are precisely the principles which enable objective empirical experiences and form the subject content of the chapter in **CPR** that deals with the 'synthetic principles of pure understanding' (B197ff.=A158ff.) (→ **Axioms of Intuitions, Anticipations of Perception, Analogies of Experience**). – DS

FURTHER READING

B. Longuenesse, *Kant and the Capacity to Judge* (Princeton: Princeton University Press, 1998).

JUDGMENT OF TASTE → AESTHETIC JUDGMENT

KINGDOM OF ENDS

By 'kingdom', or better 'realm [*Reich*]', Kant understands 'a systematic union of various rational beings through common laws' (**G** 433). Rational beings, for Kant, are characterized by two features: (1) they determine freely their own ends and (2) they can follow the moral law. This last capacity grounds their intrinsic dignity. As Kant puts it: 'Morality, and humanity insofar as it is capable of morality, is that which alone has dignity.' (**G** 435)

If we think of this 'systematic union' by abstracting from the particular ends rational beings may have in virtue of their inclinations, rational beings are thought of merely as subject to the moral law (the sole 'common law' that remains if such abstraction is made). We thus arrive at the notion of kingdom of ends:

> [A]ll rational beings stand under the *law* that each of them is to treat himself and all others *never merely as means* but always *at the same time as ends in themselves.* But from this there arises a systematic union of rational beings through common objective laws, that is, a kingdom, which can be called a kingdom of ends (admittedly only an ideal) [. . .]. (**G** 433)

In this kingdom, not only do rational beings treat each other as ends in themselves, but they are also the authors of the laws to which they are subject. If a member is 'not subject to the will of any other' (**G** 433) and if 'he is a completely independent being, without needs and with unlimited resources adequate to his will' (**G** 434), then this member belongs to the kingdom as a sovereign (*Oberhaupt*). Therefore, rational yet finite beings such as ourselves belong to the kingdom as members and as legislators. An infinite rational being such as God belongs to it as sovereign.

Although 'only an ideal' (**G** 433), the notion of kingdom of ends plays a crucial role in Kant's ethical system. In fact, it is intrinsically connected to the very idea of → **morality**.

'Morality', Kant says, 'consists [. . .] in the reference of all action to the lawgiving by which alone a kingdom of ends is possible' (**G** 434). Acting morally, in other words, means acting as if we were members (legislators and at the same time subjects) of a kingdom of ends. A rational, autonomous being cannot but see himself as member of a kingdom of ends.

To deny such membership would be tantamount to denying one's transcendental → **freedom**, that is, one's ability to legislate from the universal point of view required by the moral law, which in turn would be tantamount to denying one's own personality.

The close relationship between the idea of the kingdom of ends and that of morality is also made evident by the fact that one of the formulas of the → **categorical imperative** turns on this notion, namely that 'every rational being must act as if he were by his maxims at all times a lawgiving member of the universal kingdom of ends' (**G** 438). Stated as an imperative this becomes: '[A]ct in accordance with the maxims of a member giving universal laws for a merely possible kingdom of ends.' (**G** 439)

This formula brings to light one of the crucial dimensions of moral agency, namely the necessity in our moral reasoning to rise to the level of an ideal legislator of an equally ideal kingdom to enact laws which could earn acceptance by a community of fully rational agents.

Interestingly, in **CPrR**, Kant clarifies that we should not think of ourselves as sovereigns in the kingdom of ends, at least if this implies failing to recognize our inferior position as creatures in this kingdom, that is, as beings that necessarily stand under the authority of the law. As Kant puts it:

> We are indeed lawgiving members of a kingdom of morals possible through freedom [. . .] but we are at the same time

subjects in it, not its sovereign, and to fail to recognize our inferior position as creatures and to deny from self-conceit the authority of the holy law is already to defect from it in spirit, even though the letter of the law is fulfilled. (**CPrR** 82–83)

We are authorized to think of ourselves as legislators of the kingdom, because the moral law springs from our own reason, but not as sovereigns. The law in fact presents itself with absolute authority and exacts subordination. It is an absolute command (albeit self-imposed), quite different from the discretionary power usually associated with the idea of sovereignty. – LC

FURTHER READING

K. Flikschuh, 'Kant's kingdom of ends: metaphysical, not political', in J. Timmermann (ed.), *Kant's Groundwork of the Metaphysics of Morals: A Critical Guide* (Cambridge: Cambridge University Press, 2009), pp. 119–139.

C. Korsgaard, *Creating the Kingdom of Ends* (Cambridge: Cambridge University Press, 1996), pt. I.

J. Timmermann, *Kant's Groundwork of the Metaphysics of Morals. A Commentary* (Cambridge: Cambridge University Press, 2007).

KNOWLEDGE (COGNITION)

In the so-called *Stufenleiter*, an 'objective perception', that is, a perception that refers to an → **object**, is defined as knowledge (*Erkenntnis*) or cognition, which 'is either an intuition or a concept (*intuitus vel conceptus*)' (B376=A320), corresponding to sensibility and the understanding respectively, or what Kant intriguingly refers to as the 'two stems of human cognition, which may perhaps arise from a common but to us unknown root' (B29).

However, Kant states that knowledge in the strict sense can only arise from the combination of → **intuition** and concept, as '[t]houghts without content are empty, [and] intuitions without concepts [. . .] blind' (A51=B75). More in particular, knowledge or cognition, according to Kant in a late essay, 'is a judgment from which proceeds a concept that has objective reality, i.e., to which a corresponding object can be given in experience' (**PE** 266). Furthermore, knowledge is → **transcendental** when it concerns not objects but the faculty of knowledge itself in respect of its a priori application to things (A11–12, cf. **P** 293).

The various forms of knowledge that Kant recognizes depend on the various forms of → **judgment**. One can distinguish four basic types of knowledge. Knowledge, like judgment, can be analytic, synthetic, a posteriori or → **a priori**. Analytic knowledge is purely formal (cf. **JL** 111), 'from mere concepts' (A47=B64; cf. A7–8). 'With analytic cognition I make a given concept distinct' (**LL** 845). It rests essentially on the → **principle of (non-)contradiction**. Knowledge is synthetic when the predicate of the judgment is not a part of the subject. A posteriori knowledge consists in empirical judgments drawn from → **experience**, whereas a priori knowledge is independent of all perception and all experience. These four types of knowledge were already identified by Kant in a reflection dating from around 1770: 'All knowledge is based in either empirical or rational principles; the latter are either logical or real.' (**Refl** 4162)

Kant's question concerning the possibility of knowledge in general reduces to the central question of his theoretical philosophy: 'How are synthetic judgments *a priori* possible?' (B19) The question can be rephrased as follows: Can one speak of a priori synthetic (non-analytic) judgments which are both necessary and universally valid? How is it possible for there to be any sort of necessity of or within experience?

'To know is to judge something and hold it to be true with certainty' (**LL** 148). All knowledge consists in the recognition of a → **necessity**. Such necessity is at once formal and material. Apodictic judgments express a lawfulness that does not in any way abstract from the given material of the actual (→ **laws (of nature)/lawfulness**). Necessity in this sense consists in the framing of the real in accordance with a rule; it is the relation of an object to thinking insofar as thinking determines the being of the object itself. An apodictic judgment is one that, like the conclusion of a syllogism, can never be contingent, but rather contains necessity in itself: '[T]he conclusion is always accompanied with the consciousness of necessity and consequently has the dignity of an apodeictic proposition.' (**JL** 122)

The formal unity of consciousness, or the transcendental unity of apperception (→ **apperception**), is the highest presupposition of all necessary synthetic connections of the sensibly given manifold and, as a result, the necessary ground of the objectivity of knowledge (cf. B137) (→ **object, objectivity**). Things in themselves, on the other hand, which abstract from all connection with experience, cannot be known (→ **transcendental idealism; thing in itself**).

The two most basic forms of rational knowledge are expounded at the beginning of the Transcendental Doctrine of Method in the section of the **CPR** called the Discipline of Pure Reason. Specifically, the two forms of rational knowledge are philosophical knowledge 'from concepts', which considers the particular only in the universal, and mathematical knowledge 'from the construction of concepts', which, by contrast, considers 'the universal in the particular, indeed even in the individual, yet nonetheless *a priori* and by means of reason' (A714=B742). Philosophical knowledge is divided into pure and empirical cognition (A840=B868). It is sub-divided further into propaedeutic and → **metaphysics**, the latter comprising the metaphysics of nature and the metaphysics of morals (cf. A841=B869).

In contrast to the rationalists, who derive all knowledge from a single principle (the principle of non-contradiction), and the empiricists (→ **empiricism**), who gladly renounce the programme of systematizing knowledge, Kant wrestled with the question of architectonic and the systematic unity of knowledge intensively for his entire life (→ **system**). Questions concerning the taxonomy of knowledge are prominent in Kant's thinking from **DSS** onwards. – GM/SS

LAWS (OF NATURE), LAWFULNESS

In Kant's theoretical philosophy, the faculty of understanding is identified as the 'source of the laws of nature' (A127). Through the understanding and its categories the manifold of appearances, coming from the pure forms of sensible → **intuition**, is conceptually determined. Appearances (→ **appearance**) become objects of → **experience**, ultimately, by virtue of the unity of apperception as the transcendental ground for the lawfulness of nature (→ **deduction, apperception**). Hence, all empirical laws can be regarded as 'particular determinations of the pure laws of the understanding' (A128). Although empirical laws do not completely derive from the understanding, the 'necessary lawfulness of all appearances in an experience' (A127) derives nonetheless from the understanding.

The question then arises as to how nature with its empirical laws can possibly conform to the understanding, without deriving completely from it. The solution lies in Kant's system of the principles of pure understanding. They provide rules for the objective use of the categories, namely rules that explicate how a given category applies to particular appearances and transform them into objects of experience.

Patterned upon the table of categories, Kant's table of principles of the understanding includes: (1) → **Axioms of Intuition** (corresponding to the category of quantity); (2) → **Anticipations of Perception** (corresponding to the category of quality); (3) → **Analogies of Experience** (corresponding to the category of relation); and (4) → **Postulates of Empirical Thinking in General** (corresponding to the category of modality) (→ **experience**).

The Analogies of Experience are of particular relevance to the issue of the laws of nature. They are principles that allow the representation of the manifold of appearances 'as it is objectively in time' (B219). That is to say, they concern the existence and the relation of appearances to one another according to the three temporal modes of persistence, succession, and simultaneity. Accordingly, the first Analogy is the principle of the persistence of substance (A182). The second is the principle of temporal sequence according to the law of causality (B233). The third is the principle of simultaneity according to the law of interaction or community (B257).

Patterned upon the three Analogies of Experience, Kant offered three laws of

mechanics as metaphysical principles of pure → **natural science**, in the third chapter of **MFNS**. Kant's first mechanical law follows the first Analogy of Experience (persistence of substance) in claiming that the 'the total quantity of matter remains the same, neither increased nor diminished' (**MFNS** 541). Based on the Second Analogy (causality), Kant's second mechanical law reads: 'Every change in matter has an external cause. (Every body persists in its state of rest or motion, in the same direction, and with the same speed, if it is not compelled by an external cause to leave this state).' (**MFNS** 543) And based on the third Analogy (interaction, or community) the third mechanical law is formulated thus: 'In all communication of motion, action and reaction are always equal to one another.' (**MFNS** 544)

Kant scholars have long debated the extent to which Kant's three mechanical laws are equivalent to → **Newton's** three laws of motion, given the notable absence of Newton's second law in Kant's mechanics. A related, and more general debate concerns the extent to which the Second Analogy is meant to capture the temporal succession of events as causally determined either in a loose sense or in accordance with universal and necessary causal laws; and whether the law-governedness of nature is ultimately due to the faculty of understanding with its constitutive principles, or to the faculty of reflective judgment with its → **regulative principles**.

Indeed, in **FI** Kant reassigned the lawfulness of nature to the faculty of reflective judgment as the faculty that searches for empirically determined concepts under which given particulars can be subsumed. The faculty of understanding can only provide objects of experience and particular empirical laws. But given the '*infinite multiplicity* of empirical laws and such a *great heterogeneity of forms* of nature', a principle of the faculty of reflective judgment is required to warrant the 'thoroughly lawlike interconnection, i.e., empirical unity of these experiences' (**FI** 203).

Kant called it the principle of the purposiveness of nature, as a regulative principle without which 'the systematic unity in the thoroughgoing classification of particular forms in accordance with empirical laws would not be possible' (**FI** 219) (→ teleology). It is not a constitutive principle, since it does not provide the necessary condition of possibility of any experience. But it complements the faculty of understanding in making possible our knowledge of nature as a lawful system. – MM

FURTHER READING

H. Allison, 'Causality and causal laws in Kant: a critique of Michael Friedman', in *Idealism and Freedom. Essays on Kant's Theoretical and Practical Philosophy* (Cambridge: Cambridge University Press, 1996), pp. 80–91.

G. Buchdahl, 'The conception of lawlikeness in Kant's philosophy of science', in L. W. Beck (ed.) *Kant's Theory of Knowledge* (Dordrecht: Kluwer, 1974), pp. 128–150.

M. Friedman, 'Causal laws and the foundations of natural science', in P. Guyer (ed.) *The Cambridge Companion to Kant* (Cambridge: Cambridge University Press, 1992), pp. 161–199.

LOGIC (CONCEPT, THOUGHT, SYLLOGISM)

Logic is for Kant the science of 'the formal rules of all thinking' (Bix), and is grounded in the faculties of understanding and →

reason. The understanding is characterized as the faculty of concepts (A160=B199), of thought (A50–51=B74–75), and of rules (A132=B171), whereas reason, the capacity for principles (A299ff.=B356ff.), is in its logical use the faculty of making inferences from rules. Kant's conception of logic is broadly Aristotelian (including some propositional logic). Kant famously claims that logic has been 'unable to take a single step forward' since the time of → **Aristotle** (Bviii), though it can 'gain in regard to *exactness, determinateness* and *distinctness*' (**JL** 20). Kant follows the traditional tripartite division of logic as concerned with concept, → **judgment**, and inference. These are linked to the three aspects of the higher cognitive faculty: the understanding, the power of judgment, and reason, respectively (A130=B169).

Kant divides logic into general logic and particular logic. The former abstracts from all objects, whereas the latter consists of rules for 'a certain kind of objects' (of a special science) (A52=B76). General and formal logic, which disregards the content of cognition, is pure (i.e. strictly → a priori). Pure logic has therefore nothing to do with psychology, which is considered in 'applied' logic (A53=B77).

A further distinction is that between general (but merely formal) and → **transcendental** logic. The latter takes account of the conditions for cognizing objects a priori. As general logic gives the clue for finding the categories, it plays a most important role in Kant's philosophy (→ **deduction**), even if general logic as purely formal is of limited cognitive importance. As concerned solely with → **form**, it is not sufficient for cognizing the → **truth** of a synthetic judgment, which depends on its → **object**. Mistaking general logic for an organon, which is a sufficient condition for the acquisition of contentful cognition, constitutes dialectic, the logic of illusion (A61=B85) (→ **Dialectic**).

Kant's theory of concepts starts from the critical division of the cognitive faculties. A concept is a general → **representation** mediately linked to objects, whereas an → **intuition** is a singular representation immediately connected to its object (A19=B33; **JL** 91). This goes against the rationalist doctrine of singular concepts; for Kant, a concept is essentially general. It contains marks that are common to several objects (**LL** 752).

Concepts are generated by certain acts of the understanding: comparison, reflection and abstraction. In comparing for instance a spruce, a willow and a linden, their differences are attended to. Reflection involves noticing what they have in common, and abstraction, finally, is the isolating of these common marks (e.g. the possession of a trunk, branches and leaves), leaving out the differences, so that the concept 'tree' is acquired (**JL** 94–95). This account, which is close to that of the Wolffians (→ **Wolff**), may appear artificial: noticing differences (comparison) seems to involve noticing what the objects have in common (reflection). But rather than meaning three successive stages, Kant perhaps points to conditions for acquiring and having a concept: this requires the ability to notice both similarities and differences, and to abstract from the differences.

Kant's theory of concepts develops the Cartesian and Leibnizian-Wolffian distinctions concerning clarity and distinctness. A concept is clear if a person is conscious of it (**JL** 33; **LL** 702). Clear concepts can be distinct or indistinct. A concept is distinct if the person is clear about its content, i.e. the marks of which it is composed (cf. **JL** 34). To make a concept distinct is to analyze it into its constituents. Distinctness comes in degrees. A complete → **analysis** would result

in a definition; but for given concepts we cannot be certain of having achieved that (A728=B756). An incomplete analysis of a concept is called an exposition (A729=B757). Kant also countenances obscure, as opposed to clear, concepts (i.e. unconscious ones) (**LL** 702).

Relative to their intension (Kant uses the term 'content'), concepts can be hierarchically ordered. The higher concepts are poorer and the lower ones richer in intension. So for instance, 'metal' is above 'gold'. Since the latter concept is a specification of the former, and 'gold' contains all the marks of 'metal' plus additional ones, its intension is richer. The extension of 'gold' – the concepts below it in the hierarchy, or as Kant often says, 'contained under' it – is on the other hand less than the extension of the higher concept 'metal'. Intension and extension are thus inversely proportional (**JL** 95; **LL** 925).

Kant is sometimes unclear as to whether the extension is the concepts located under a concept in the hierarchy, or rather the objects falling under it (the modern sense of 'extension'). The hierarchical ordering of concepts can also be expressed in the terminology of genus and species (**JL** 96–97). A higher concept is a genus for that which is under it (its species), but is itself a species under a higher concept, *its* genus (**LL** 911).

Similar views are frequently met in Kant's contemporaries (→ **Meier**); they go back to Aristotle's doctrine of genus and species and the conceptual trees of Porphyry. Kant deviates from one strand of this tradition by stressing that there can be no individual concepts at the bottom of the hierarchy. Concepts can always be further specified (**LL** 927). The hierarchical model of concepts is the background to the distinction of analytic and synthetic judgments. In an analytic → **judgment**, the predicate's marks are contained in the subject, and conceptual containment is modelled in such hierarchies.

Concepts are combined into judgments (in accordance with the elementary forms systematized in the Table of Judgment). To make logical inferences from judgments is the task of reason. In its logical use, it is the capacity to infer (or draw a conclusion) from a premise, insofar as the inference is mediate, that is, requires another premise. Inferences of reason (syllogisms) consist of a major and a minor premise from which the conclusion is drawn (A304=B361; A330=B386). In contrast, a direct or immediate inference (for instance of 'Some B are A' from 'All A are B') is an inference of the understanding (*Verstandesschluss*) (A303=B360). Here, conclusion and ground share the same matter but differ in form (**LL** 769), whereas in a syllogism the conclusion differs from the ground as to matter, i.e. the pair of concepts in the conclusion is not found together in any of the premises.

There are three forms of syllogism: the categorical, the hypothetical and the disjunctive (A304=B361). Each of these has as major premise a judgment of one of the three relational forms in Kant's Table of Judgment. Examples of the types of syllogism are 'All A are B, All C are A, therefore all C are B' (categorical); 'If A then B, A, therefore B' (hypothetical); and 'A is either B or C, A is not B, therefore A is C' (disjunctive). The hypothetical and the disjunctive inferences do not belong to Aristotelian syllogistic, but conform to Kant's wider characterization of the syllogism as a mediate inference from a premise serving as a rule (A304=B360–361).

Kant calls the major premise in a categorical syllogism (e.g. 'All philosophers are learned') the rule, whereas the minor premise (e.g. 'Locke is a philosopher') puts the cognition it expresses 'under the condition of the rule' (A304=B360). This means that its subject term, 'Locke', is subsumed under the predicate 'philosopher', which is the 'condition' (i.e. subject term) of the major premise (the rule). Reason is thus able to determine 'Locke' through the predicate of the rule, and infer that Locke is learned (cf. A304=B360–361).

The major premise of a syllogism is itself conditioned, and presupposes further conditions from which it follows. Obviously, this would be the case also for such further conditions. Only if the totality of conditions could be given would reason's demand for the unconditioned be satisfied (A307=B364). This ascending series from condition to further conditions consists of prosyllogisms, in which the major premise of a given syllogism is inferred as conclusion from higher premises (A331=B387–388). The descending series from the conditioned to further inferences, through episyllogisms, where the conclusion of a syllogism is used as premise for a new syllogism, can also be continued indefinitely, but it is not important for reason. For reason seeks grounds; and a given judgment is grounded on its premises and not on its potential consequences (A331ff.=B388ff.). – MQ

FURTHER READING

B. Longuenesse, *Kant and the Capacity to Judge* (Princeton: Princeton University Press, 1998), pt. II.

R. Stuhlmann-Laeisz, *Kants Logik* (Berlin/ New York: de Gruyter, 1976).

**MAJORITY, MATURITY →
ENLIGHTENMENT**

MANIFOLD → SYNTHESIS

MARK, CHARACTERISTIC (*MERKMAL*)
→ LOGIC

MATHEMATICS

Mathematical knowledge interests Kant for two reasons. First, it forms a paradigmatic case of synthetic a priori knowledge (B14–17) (→ **synthesis**), and as such is a problematic type of → **knowledge** (A10), whose validity **CPR** sets out to ground (B20). Second, mathematical knowledge stands both as a model for, and in contrast to, philosophical knowledge (→ **method**).

On the one hand, the success of mathematics (and → **natural science**) is presented by Kant (Bx–Bxv) as standing in contrast to the disarray characterizing metaphysical speculation (Bxiv), and thus functions as a model for future metaphysics (Bxvi). On the other hand, mathematical knowledge is differentiated from philosophical knowledge insofar as the latter is '*rational cognition* from *concepts*', whereas 'mathematical cognition [is] that from the *construction* of concepts' (A713=B741).

Kant starts addressing the *quid juris* question regarding mathematical knowledge in the → **Transcendental Aesthetic** (B41). → **Geometry**, the science of space, represents Kant's favourite example of mathematical knowledge, largely because geometric constructions are ostensive.

But arithmetic occupies a very central place in Kant's account of cognition insofar as 'number is nothing other than the unity of the synthesis of the manifold of a homogeneous intuition in general' (A143=B182). Thus number, as the schema of magnitude, provides a rule for the generation of time, and is thus involved in the → **synthesis** of apprehension of any object.

Kant gives us an account of why arithmetical truths are synthetic a priori. Famously, Kant explains how, when adding 7 and 5, one makes use of an intuitive representation (e.g. fingers or points) of 7 to which one consecutively adds 5 times one unit to obtain 12 (B15–16). This construction in → **intuition** is meant to show that the concept of '12' cannot be found by mere → **analysis** of the concepts of '7' and '5', hence that the judgment '7+5=12' is synthetic (B16).

To understand the meaning of the synthetic nature of arithmetic, it is instructive to see the failure of attempts such as → **Leibniz's** to show that such propositions of arithmetic are analytic: Leibniz's proof relies upon the covert use of non-analytic principles (associativity and commutativity of addition). The view that Kant has an axiomatic conception of arithmetic would be incompatible with some of Kant's statements (A163–164=B204), and in any case, insufficient to account for the role of intuition.

A key problem though is the question how the timeless truths of arithmetic can depend upon a construction *in* time. The answer lies in recalling that number is defined by Kant as '[t]he pure schema of magnitude' (A142=B182). That is, number 'n' is a rule for the construction of intuitions of collections of n objects. When summing 7 and 5, the combined use of the rules for 7 points and 5 points leads to the construction in intuition of a number of points that, according to the rule for construction of 12, can be identified as that number.

The spelling out of the word 'synthetic' to find out how many letters it contains is an analogous synthetic construction. It is only by applying the rules for spelling that word and counting up to 9 that one comes by the synthetic truth that the number of letters in that word is 9. This is how mathematical cognition arrives at the universal (conceptual) through the particular (intuition).

Unlike the ostensive constructions of geometry, algebraic symbols no longer refer to objects, so algebraic construction in intuition is symbolic (A717=B745). This may seem like a weaker sense of construction in intuition, particularly in view of the centrality of the geometric paradigm in Kant's writings. But there is a sense in which algebraic constructions are paradigmatic for mathematical construction in intuition, as it is quantity itself (*quantitas*), rather than the magnitude of some object (as *quantum*), that is at stake. If algebra and geometry represent two poles of the notion of mathematical construction, arithmetic lies in between. Arithmetical constructions are ostensive, but I construct numbers of objects, not numbers themselves, which are schemata, i.e. representations of construction rules. Insofar as the construction operates on numerals that refer to rules, it is also symbolic. Whether ostensive, symbolic, or both, all mathematical constructions are in spatial intuition for Kant. – CO

FURTHER READING

G. Brittan, 'Kant's philosophy of mathematics', in G. Bird (ed.), *A Companion to Kant* (Malden, MA/ Oxford: Wiley-Blackwell, 2010), pp. 222–235.

R. Butts, 'Rules, examples and constructions. Kant's theory of mathematics', *Synthese* 47,2 (1981): 257–288.

C. Parsons, 'Kant's philosophy of arithmetic', in C. Posy (ed.), *Kant's Philosophy of Mathematics – Modern Essays* (Dordrecht: Kluwer, 1992), pp. 43–79.

L. Shabel, 'Kant's philosophy of mathematics', in P. Guyer (ed.), *The Cambridge Companion to Kant and Modern Philosophy* (Cambridge: Cambridge University Press, 2006), pp. 94–128.

J. M. Young, 'Kant on the construction of arithmetical concepts', *Kant-Studien* 73 (1982): 17–46.

MAXIM → CATEGORICAL IMPERATIVE

METAPHYSICAL DEDUCTION → DEDUCTION

METAPHYSICS

'This much is certain: whosoever has once tasted of critique forever loathes all the dogmatic chatter with which he previously had to put up with out of necessity, since his reason was in need of something and could not find anything better for its sustenance.' (P 366)

Kant here identifies his entire work as the turning point in the resolution and rebirth of metaphysics. It is through transcendental philosophy that the progress of metaphysics from a natural disposition of → reason (P 279; cf. B21, Bxxxi) – which falsely assumes a second world of substances behind the visible appearances – to metaphysics as science first becomes possible. The fundamental question of CPR is this: How are synthetic a priori judgments (→ judgment, synthesis) possible? The success or failure of metaphysics depends on the solution of this central problem (B19).

In CPR – which, according to a letter to Marcus → Herz from 11 May 1781, contains the '*metaphysics of metaphysics*' (Corr-I 269) – Kant shows that traditional metaphysics as the science of the first, general principles of things (ontology), as well as the speculative investigation of the soul (→ **psychology**) (→ **Paralogisms**), the world (cosmology) (→ **Antinomies**) and God (theology) (→ **proofs of the existence of God**), is no longer possible. Ontology can no longer be a science of things in themselves (→ **transcendental idealism**), but rather – as Critical ontology – it is the science of the a priori conditions under which alone the objects of experience can be known (→ **object/objectivity, experience, deduction**).

The metaphysical pretensions of speculative reason to have knowledge of the soul, the world and God are finally put to rest in the Transcendental → **Dialectic** of **CPR**. The old metaphysical dispute concerning the soul, the world and God – the three branches of *metaphysica specialis*, in contrast to ontology as *metaphysica generalis*, according to the Wolffian division (→ **Wolff**) – is nevertheless carried further by Kant through consideration of the theoretical presuppositions of morals within the so called Postulates of Pure Practical Reason in **CPrR** (→ **morality**).

Kant held lectures on metaphysics for 40 years (from the Winter semester of 1755/56 to the Winter semester of 1795/96) at the Albertus University in → **Königsberg**. In August 1770 he was named Professor Ordinarius of Logic and Metaphysics. Kant's chosen text was → **Baumgarten**'s *Metaphysica*. This gave him the opportunity to present his criticisms and his new conception of metaphysics before the students, though his views were presented most clearly in his own writings.

In **ND**, Kant denies the existence of a highest principle (*pace* Wolff and Baumgarten), and rejects as mistaken the assumed equivalence of *ratio actualitatis* and *ratio veritatis*. The philosophical foundations of the subjectivism and empiricism of Christian August → **Crusius**, who had proposed an anti-Wolffian

metaphysics, are criticized here as well. Problems of natural philosophy (the theory of fire, of heaven, of monads, of wind, etc.) (→ **natural science**) are dealt with by the young Kant always with a view to the radical reform of metaphysics.

In the first lectures that have been handed down to us (the *Metaphysik Herder* of 1762–1764 [**LM**]), Kant directs a number of criticisms against metaphysics as it was then practiced. It is 'hard', he complains. It is poorly presented – a 'plague of souls'. It is also 'dry' because very abstract. But most significantly, it is uncertain: The irresolvable dispute between → **Leibniz** and Clarke is for Kant the clearest demonstration of the undecidability of metaphysical questions (**LM** 157). The following comment from the *Prize Essay* of 1764 (→ **Academy prize essay**) is apposite: 'Metaphysics is without doubt the most difficult of all the things into which man has insight. But so far no metaphysics has ever been written.' (**Inq** 283)

Metaphysicians have always tried to import the method of → **mathematics** into philosophy – an impossible move, according to Kant, for at least two reasons: (1) While in mathematics a small number of definitions serve as the primary indemonstrable concepts, in metaphysics various indemonstrable propositions must furnish the primary data. (2) Mathematics is easier than metaphysics and partakes of a greater degree of intuition (cf. **Inq** 296). Its immediate relation to intuition is in fact the feature of mathematics that distinguishes it most clearly from philosophy.

In the Second Reflection of **Inq** (283ff.), Kant tries to validate the method of metaphysics by modelling it on the method of Newtonian physics (→ **Newton**) rather than mathematics – though this tendency is arguably present in all of his writings from 1755 onwards.

In the lectures on metaphysics of the winter semester 1765/66, Kant placed his commentary on the empirical psychology of Baumgarten before the commentary on ontology and the other parts of metaphysics. This is a clear indication of the tendency to psychologize and anthropologize philosophy, which occurred both in his thoughts as well as explicitly in his writings of the period.

This subjectifying tendency is, however, always accompanied by deep reflection on the possibility of transforming the foundations of metaphysics. One can even say that the decisive thoughts which led Kant to re-conceive the whole of metaphysics are implicit in his original conception of mathematics. His criticisms of dogmatism and → empiricism in fact pertain in the first instance to the 'logicistic' understanding of → geometry and arithmetic. The task of revising metaphysics requires bringing mathematics within the sphere of experience, something that Kant accomplished both in **DS** (1768) as well as **ID** (1770).

Kant's most pointed criticism of traditional metaphysics occurs not in **CPR** but in **DSS**, a work which contains an ironic and sometimes amusing comparison between metaphysics and the art of spirit-seeing (→ **enthusiasm, Swedenborg**). At the beginning of the third chapter (in the so-called 'Anti-Cabbala'), an account of the immaterial world is dismissed outright as a vision of reason. But metaphysics is also defined here positively as the science of the boundaries of the faculty of knowledge (cf. **DSS** 351, 368). In **DSS**, Kant – inspired by Newton and → **Rousseau** – sketches the basic idea for his later division of metaphysics into the metaphysics of nature and the metaphysics of morals, a classification which brings ethics for the first time into the system of metaphysics.

There are two possible causes of anything that happens in the world. An event can be the result of physical determination or of free action (→ **freedom**). Kant develops the entire system of a new metaphysics on the basis of the fundamental antinomy between nature and freedom (→ **Antinomies**): 'Metaphysics is divided into the metaphysics of the *speculative* and the *practical* use of pure reason, and is therefore either *metaphysics of nature* or *metaphysics of morals*. The former contains all rational principles from mere concepts (hence with the exclusion of mathematics) for the *theoretical* cognition of all things; the latter, the principles which determine *action and omission a priori* and make them necessary.' (A841=B869)

Preserving the Hellenistic division of philosophy into three sciences – logic, physics and ethics – Kant distinguishes at the beginning of **G** between formal philosophy, or logic, which is 'occupied only with the form of the understanding and of reason itself and with the universal rules of thinking in general', and material philosophy, or metaphysics, 'which has to do with determinate objects and the laws to which they are subject' (**G** 387). Since these are either → **laws of nature** or laws of freedom, metaphysics is further subdivided into a theoretical part – the metaphysics of nature, or physics – and a practical part – the metaphysics of morals, or ethics.

In the notes for the Academy prize question of 1795 on the progress of metaphysics in Germany since the time of Leibniz and Wolff (which were printed posthumously in 1804), Kant identifies dogmatism, scepticism and empiricism as the 'three stages which philosophy had to traverse in its approach to metaphysics' (**PE** 264). There are, according to Kant, two hinges on which the new metaphysics turns: '*First*, the doctrine of the ideality of space and time, which in regard to theoretical principles merely points toward the super-sensible, but for us unknowable

[...]; *second*, the doctrine of the reality of the concept of freedom, as that of a knowable super-sensible, in which metaphysics is still only practico-dogmatic.' (**PE** 311) – GM/SS

FURTHER READING

K. Ameriks, 'The critique of metaphysics: Kant and traditional ontology', in P. Guyer (ed.), *The Cambridge Companion to Kant* (Cambridge: Cambridge University Press, 1992), pp. 249–279.

N. Fischer (ed.), *Kants Grundlegung einer kritischen Metaphysik* (Hamburg: Meiner, 2010).

J. Van Cleve, *Problems from Kant* (New York: Oxford University Press, 1999), chs 10–13.

METHOD

In **P**, Kant makes a distinction between the 'critical method' and 'the dogmatic method' (**P** 308), where the Critical method provides a means to investigate the a priori principles of experience 'completely and according to a principle' *'from the nature of the understanding itself'*, rather than dogmatically *'from the things themselves'* (**P** 308). At the same time, the Critical method assures that 'only *as objects of experience* are all things necessarily subject *a priori*' to the principles of experience, not as things in themselves, which is the central purport of Kant's → **transcendental idealism**. This intimate connection between the possibility of → **a priori** cognition and the limitation of → **knowledge** to the objects of possible → **experience** is the differentiating characteristic of Kant's Critical method (→ **Critique**).

In the preface to the second edition, Kant expounds on the significance of the properly methodical nature of **CPR**, which he calls a 'treatise on the method' (Bxxii) of → **metaphysics** as science. He repeats here again the nature of the Critical method as having to do with a reversal in the way a priori cognition, the business of metaphysics, can be made possible as opposed to the many attempts in traditional, dogmatic metaphysics to extend knowledge synthetically. Kant does this by enacting a thought experiment, which he presents as analogous to the way Copernicus made advances in astronomy possible (Bxvi; cf. Bxviii n.). The thought experiment relates to the way, similar to the account in **P**, in which it is suggested that only an antecedent analysis of the subjective conditions of thought will provide apodictic insight into the a priori relation between subject and → **object**. The acceptance of this hypothesis results in what Kant calls 'the altered method of our way of thinking' (Bxviii).

Despite the ostensibly hypothetical nature of the thought experiment in the B-Preface, Kant however insists that '[c]riticism is not opposed to the *dogmatic procedure* of reason in its pure cognition as science'. For Kant, science, and thus metaphysics, 'must always be dogmatic, i.e., it must prove its conclusions strictly *a priori* from secure principles' (Bxxxv). The sense in which it is opposed to dogmatic metaphysics is that rather than presuming to be able to obtain (synthetic) knowledge purely on the basis of conceptual → **analysis**, reason must first critically inquire 'in what way and by what right it has obtained' the principles by means of which it acquires pure cognition (Bxxxv).

This procedure also explains the crucial distinction that Kant makes in **P** (**P** 263, 274ff., 278ff.) between the analytic and synthetic methods, or regressive and progressive methods respectively. Analysis 'proceeds from that which is sought as if it were given, and ascends to the conditions under which alone it is possible' (P 276n.), i.e. from consequent to ground, whereas conversely → **synthesis** proceeds from ground to consequent. Kant makes clear that while **P** is sketched out after the analytical method, **CPR** itself must be synthetic, that is, start from a principle rather than from a given in experience, which in the case of **P** is the fact of → **natural science** and → **mathematics**, the grounds of whose possibility is inquired into by regressive analysis. Only the synthetic, progressive method, however, constitutes a genuine philosophical → **proof**, which accepts no data 'except reason itself' and thus 'develop[s] cognition out of its original seeds without relying on any fact whatever' (P 274).

This is somewhat similar to the remark Kant makes in the B-Preface, namely that what in the Preface had been proposed 'as a hypothesis' (i.e. the Copernican thought experiment), must 'in the treatise itself [. . .] be proved not hypothetically but rather apodictically from the constitution of our representations of space and time and from the elementary concepts of the understanding' (Bxxii n.). Proofs in philosophy must always be 'ostensive' (A789=B817), albeit not in the mathematical sense, as Kant makes sufficiently clear in the Transcendental Doctrine of Method, the second main part of **CPR**, which however only takes up one-sixth of the whole of **CPR**.

In the first chapter of this part, on the Discipline of Pure Reason, Kant explicates the distinctive method of the transcendental philosophy. He defines discipline as having the task of limiting and eventually eradicating the 'compulsion through which the constant propensity to stray from certain rules is limited' (A709=B737). Although it makes a negative contribution,

the faculty of reason 'badly needs a discipline to constrain its propensity to expansion beyond the narrow boundaries of possible experience' (A711=B739). Unlike the Transcendental Dialectic which focused upon the content of the claims made by reason in its use beyond these boundaries, the discipline looks at the method that reason employs.

In a first section on the dogmatic use of reason, Kant compares the warranted employment of reason in mathematics with 'that by means of which one seeks the same certainty in philosophy' (A713=B741). He rejects the notion that the difference between philosophy and mathematics could lie in the first dealing with quality while the latter has quantity as its object (A714=B742). While it is true that mathematics constructs magnitudes (or even magnitude in algebra), it does not deal with quality simply because the latter requires empirical intuition (A715=B743), which is also lacking for pure concepts of reason.

Rather, mathematics exhibits its concepts in pure intuition, by construction, i.e. through a homogeneous synthesis which considers its objects merely as quanta (A723=B751) (→ **Transcendental Aesthetic**). The success of the mathematical method leads to the expectations that it could be successful in pure philosophy (A724ff.=B752ff.). Philosophy cannot exhibit its concepts in pure intuition (A722=B750), and appeal to empirical intuition cannot yield a priori knowledge. But this leaves a task for philosophy, namely to explore the principles 'of the synthesis of possible empirical intuitions' (A722=B750): this defines '*rational cognition* from concepts, which is called *philosophical*' (A724=B752). Such conceptual cognition pertaining to the possibility of being given objects in empirical intuition amounts to philosophy 'knowing its bounds' (A727=B755). It can usefully be interpreted as definitive of what has generally become known as 'transcendental arguments', i.e. the identification of necessary conditions for having experience of a certain kind.

Kant examines definitions, axioms and demonstrations in turn, to show that 'none of these elements, in the sense in which the mathematician takes them, can be achieved or imitated by philosophy' (A726=B754). A priori concepts such as those the philosopher deals with, cannot be defined because one cannot be certain that one has originally exhibited 'the exhaustive concept of a thing within its boundaries' (A727=B755). Moreover, in philosophy, there are no synthetic a priori principles which are immediately certain, hence no axioms (A732=B760). Finally, since philosophy can only 'consider the universal *in abstracto* (through concepts)' while mathematics does this '*in concreto* (in the individual intuition)', demonstrations, which are apodictic proofs in intuition, are impossible in philosophy (A734=B762). This concludes Kant's case for claiming that the dogmatic use of pure reason, based as it is upon direct synthetic propositions from concepts alone, 'is inappropriate per se' (A737=B765). – DS/CO

FURTHER READING

N. Hinske, 'Die Rolle des Methodenproblems im Denken Kants', in N. Fischer (ed.), *Kants Grundlegung einer kritischen Metaphysik. Einführung in die 'Kritik der reinen Vernunft'* (Hamburg: Meiner, 2010), pp. 343–354.

A. Moore, 'The Transcendental Doctrine of Method', in P. Guyer (ed.), *The Cambridge Companion to Kant's*

'Critique of Pure Reason' (Cambridge: Cambridge University Press, 2010), pp. 310–326.

D. Schulting, 'Kant's Copernican analogy: beyond the non-specific reading', *Studi Kantiani* xxii (2009): 39–65.

B.-S. Wolff-Metternich, *Die Überwindung des mathematischen Erkenntnisideals. Kants Grenzbestimmung von Mathematik und Philosophie* (Berlin/New York: de Gruyter, 1995).

MINORITY → ENLIGHTENMENT

MORAL LAW → CATEGORICAL IMPERATIVE

MORAL WORTH → MORALITY

MORALITY

Kant considers morality to be fundamentally a matter of one's reasons for choosing to act as one does – what he calls one's → will – rather than one's actions themselves or their consequences. To be morally good, then, one must not only do what is morally good, but do so for morally good reasons, rather than other ones.

He also holds that morally good reasons do not ultimately concern what oneself or others happen to need, want or enjoy as individuals or moral authorities that one may happen to believe in, such as God, conscience or convention. Indeed, he holds that morally good reasons override any such reasons for doing things. For instance, he thinks that one should be honest or help the needy not just because it happens to benefit oneself or others or to be considered honourable or caring – rather, one should do these things because they are good in a further, universal and unconditional way.

In Kant's terms, to have a good will one must act not only 'in conformity with duty' (→ **duty, duties**) but also 'from duty' rather than 'from inclination' (**G** 397–399), and one's duties are 'categorical imperatives' (→ **categorical imperative**), rather than 'hypothetical' ones based on contingent needs, wants, pleasures, or authorities (**G** 414–420).

In **G**, Kant describes the reasons that make an action morally good in terms of four formulas. The first, the formula of universal law, describes the reason for which one does a morally good action as a reason for which one could want all others to do the same action in similar circumstances – in other words, it is a reason for which one could want it to be a 'universal law' (→ **categorical imperative**) to do this action in these circumstances.

For example, Kant argues that it is morally wrong to make a false promise or ignore the needy for self-interest because if everyone were to do the same no one would trust one's promise or help oneself in turn, and this would conflict with one's self-interest. One could not, then, want it to be a 'universal law' to do these things for self-interested reasons (**G** 402–403, 421–424; **CPrR** 27–28).

The second formula, the formula of the end in itself, describes a morally good action as one done considering each affected agent an 'end in itself' (→ **kingdom of ends**) – that is, as something of such value that he or she may not be used merely as a 'thing' or a 'means' to satisfy one's own or others' inclinations. Kant argues that this formula too explains why making a false promise or not helping the needy is morally wrong, since a promisee could not consent to being deceived nor a needy person accept that his or her needs be ignored (**G** 427–431).

The other two formulas, those of autonomy (→ **freedom**) and the → **kingdom of ends**, emphasize a corollary of this – namely, that, since the reason for which one does a morally good action fundamentally concerns only affected agency, it is a reason that one appreciates simply as and because one is an agent, rather than a reason concerning something else that one may or may not appreciate. In this sense, Kant thinks that in doing what is morally good for morally good reasons one is 'autonomous' or 'self-legislating' and constructs a systematic 'kingdom' of agents, reasons and actions with other agents (**G** 431–436, 440–445; **CPrR** 33).

In **MM** Kant proceeds to derive two kinds of general moral requirements, political and ethical. Since political requirements are those that one can be coerced to fulfil by others, he treats them as requirements merely to do, refrain from, or allow certain actions, rather than to do so for certain reasons (**MM** 214, 218–221, 231, 239). He identifies these actions as those which ensure that any one agent's freedom of action does not impinge on others' equal freedom – in his terms, '[a]ny action is *right* if it can coexist with everyone's freedom in accordance with a universal law' (**MM** 230–233, 237–238).

He argues in particular that property rights (→ **right**) to things are limited by the finite nature of the earth, such that one person's coming to own an un-owned thing, while necessary for his or her freedom of action, also diminishes others' similar freedom – it follows, he claims, that we must consider things as if they were originally owned 'in common' by all affected agents. To secure these property rights, he further argues, we must obey a state that also ensures our equality and consent (**MM** 245–270, 311–318).

Ethical requirements or virtues (→ **virtue**), on the other hand, are requirements to recognize certain reasons for action, and Kant claims that they consequently leave us some playroom in terms of precisely which actions might be considered to fulfil or neglect them (**MM** 379–380, 383–384, 389–390, 394–395). He argues that each of us is ethically required to pursue his or her own perfection as an agent – by, among other things, cultivating mental and physical capacities and the performance of duties simply 'from duty' – and also to consider others' needs, wants and pleasures – particularly, given the needy nature of human beings, by promoting what others consider necessary for their own overall happiness (**MM** 385–388, 391–394, 417–468).

Regarding happiness, in **CPrR** Kant also argues that, since happiness is deserved only to the extent that one is morally good, we must postulate God as the cause of this deserved happiness and the soul's immortality as allowing us to progress towards deserving it. He calls this combination of moral goodness and happiness 'the highest good' (**CPrR** 107–148) (→ **religion**).

Along with his derivations of general moral requirements, in **MM** Kant also presents our moral reasoning in a more systematic way than in **G**. Rather than simply testing specific reasons in specific circumstances against the formulas, as he does in discussing his examples in **G**, in **MM** he presents moral reasoning as a balancing of different morally good reasons against each other.

In particular, he claims that political requirements are to be prioritized over ethical ones and more general requirements prioritized over more specific ones. He derives general requirements by considering whether general reasons – those applicable to human beings generally – might be consistent with the formulas in general human circumstances – such as the finite nature of the earth or the needy nature of human beings – while claiming that more specific requirements are to be derived by considering more specific reasons in more specific circumstances (**MM** 216–217, 224, 390–391, 403–404, 468–469; **LE** 536–538).

Given his emphasis on reasons for action, however, it is notable that Kant denies that we can ever establish with certainty whether or not an agent acted for morally good reasons, even in our own cases (**G** 406–408; **TP** 284–285; **MM** 392–393, 441, 446–447). Indeed, he suspects that we are often overcharitable in attributing morally good reasons to ourselves (**G** 407), limits his hopes for moral progress to the skills and inclinations that might lead us to do morally good actions for non-moral reasons (**CJ** 429–445; **TP** 308, 310; **PP** 360–361, 365, 366; **Anthr** 324, 327–330), and even argues that we are all evil (→ **radical evil**) in the sense that, although we recognize morally good reasons, we always prioritize other reasons over them (**R** 19–44). But he insists that we can and ought always to pursue moral goodness and to reason morally nonetheless (**G** 407–408; **TP** 284–288; **R** 41, 44–45).

Kant also attempts to justify his basic understanding of morality in two different ways. In **G** he argues that we should consider our reasoning as free (→ **freedom**) in the sense of undetermined by antecedent causes, since we need not consider ourselves merely as objects of possible experience, subject to determination by antecedent causes, and our reasoning displays its freedom in producing ideas (→ **idea, ideas**) that go beyond such objects. If we consider our reasoning to be free, he further claims, then we must also consider it to recognize moral reasons in his sense, since the only alternative to determination by antecedent causes is such moral 'self-determination' (**G** 446–463).

In **CPrR**, however, he denies that the freedom of our reasoning can be demonstrated and claims simply that morality is a 'fact of reason', that it implies the freedom of our reasoning, and that this freedom can be admitted as something beyond possible experience (**CPrR** 3–7, 28–33, 42–56, 93–99, 103–106). He thus leaves the ultimate justification for his understanding of morality to common sense, just as in **G**, before arguing from reasoning's freedom, he derives this understanding from the common sense notion of the goodness of a 'good will' (**G** 392–394, 403–405, 437, 444–445; **CPrR** 8). – TB

FURTHER READING

H. Allison, *Kant's Theory of Freedom* (Cambridge: Cambridge University Press, 1990), esp. pts 2 and 3.

J. Timmermann, A. Reath (eds), *Kant's Critique of Practical Reason. A Critical Guide* (Cambridge: Cambridge University Press, 2010).

M. Timmons (ed.), *Kant's Metaphysics of Morals: Interpretative Essays* (Oxford: Oxford University Press, 2002).

A. Wood, *Kant's Ethical Thought* (Cambridge: Cambridge University Press, 1999).

A. Wood, 'The supreme principle of morality', in P. Guyer (ed.), *The Cambridge Companion to Kant and Modern Philosophy* (Cambridge: Cambridge University Press, 2006), pp. 342–380.

MOTIVE, INCENTIVE (*TRIEBFEDER*) → CATEGORICAL IMPERATIVE

NATURE → LAWS (OF NATURE)/ LAWFULNESS, NATURAL SCIENCE

NATURAL SCIENCE

Kant's reflections on natural science occupy a prominent role within his transcendental project and span over Kant's entire academic career. In his first work **LF**, Kant latched onto the then ongoing debate between Cartesians and Leibnizians on *vis viva* (what we now call kinetic energy). The engagement with → **Newton**'s physics began in 1755 with **NH**, where Kant put forward a cosmogony 'according to Newtonian principles' and explained the formation of celestial bodies out of a primordial *nebula* (anticipating Laplace's nebular hypothesis).

From Newton's *Opticks* Kant borrowed the idea of the ether as the matter of light, to which he added the property of being also the matter of fire in his 1755 essay **F**. Scholars have read Kant's endorsement of Newtonian physics as signalling his departure from both the Leibnizian-Wolffian metaphysical dynamics and the Crusius-Knutzen theory of → **physical influx** (→ **Crusius**).

Against the former Kant argued in **PhM**, where he defended the view that bodies consist of physical monads as 'spheres of activity', i.e. centres of attractive and repulsive forces. In **ND**, from 1755, Kant argued against the theory of physical influx, i.e. the Pietist school of thought that claimed that the ground of physical change was to be found in the bare existence of physical substances.

Kant's engagement with natural science continued throughout the pre-Critical period (see **MR; DS**), and culminated in the Critical period with **MFNS**, published in 1786, as an attempt to implement the transcendental apparatus developed five years earlier in **CPR**. The extent to which **MFNS** ties in with the Transcendental Analytic of **CPR** remains a matter of debate (→ **laws (of nature)/ lawfulness**).

In the preface to **MFNS**, Kant distinguishes between proper and improper natural science. The former 'treats its object wholly according to *a priori* principles, the second according to laws of experience' (**MFNS** 468). Kant took chemistry to be an example of the latter category, which lacked apodictic certainty. Kant's concern was instead with proper natural science, whose apodictic certainty presupposes a metaphysics of nature, i.e. pure a priori principles underlying the empirical part. Metaphysics of nature focuses on the empirical concept of matter and brings all the determinations of the concept of matter under the a priori concepts of the understanding (→ **deduction**).

The basic determination of the empirical concept of matter is motion as the object of outer sense (→ **inner/outer sense**). Hence natural science is ultimately a doctrine of motion and its metaphysical foundations are brought under four chapters (Phoronomy, Dynamics, Mechanics and Phenomenology), corresponding respectively to the four titles of categories: quantity, quality, relation and modality.

Phoronomy takes motion as a 'pure *quantum* in accordance with its composition' (**MFNS** 477). Motion is here considered only kinematically, i.e. with respect to speed (defined as a scalar quantity), direction and composition of motions. Matter is considered as a material point and all motions are rectilinear motions, whose composition with regard to their respective speeds and directions falls under three possible cases (**MFNS** 490). Two motions (with equal or unequal speeds) either (1) constitute a new motion along the same line and the same direction in one body; or (2) constitute a new motion along the same line, when combining motions of opposite directions; or (3) form an angle, when motions along different rectilinear lines are combined.

Dynamics considers motion 'as belonging to the *quality* of matter, under the name of an original moving force' (**MFNS** 477). Matter is here defined as 'the *moveable* insofar as it *fills* a *space*' through a particular moving force (**MFNS** 496). By reasoning a priori about properties of matter, Kant introduced two moving forces, attraction and repulsion. Attraction causes matter to approach other matter. Repulsion causes matter to repel other matter.

The repulsive force is characterized as an original expansive force 'also called *elasticity*' (**MFNS** 500) through which matter's impenetrability is explained. In other words, matter resists penetration dynamically, i.e. via a force of repulsion, not via its solidity. Kant argued that if there were only repulsive force as an original expansive force, matter would disperse itself to infinity. Hence, there must be a counteracting attractive force, through which matter impels another to approach it. On the other hand, no attraction is possible without repulsion because, if only attraction existed, all matter would coalesce into a point and space would be empty. While repulsion manifests itself as a contact force or a surface force (via impenetrability), attraction acts at a distance through empty space as a penetrating force.

Mechanics takes matter 'in *relation* to another through its own inherent motion' (**MFNS** 477). Matter is here defined as 'the moveable insofar as it, as such a thing, has moving force' (**MFNS** 536). The moving forces in this chapter are those that set matter in motion and communicate motion between bodies, although mechanics presupposes dynamics – e.g. the original attractive force is said to be 'the cause of universal gravitation' as a mechanical force (**MFNS** 541).

Kant calls mass the quantity of matter (intended as the moveable present in a certain space), and calls quantity of motion what is now called momentum (i.e. the product of mass and speed). Three laws of mechanics follow (for their statements → **laws (of nature)/ lawfulness**). The first law is about quantity of matter being conserved. The second law is a version of Newton's law of inertia, with the important difference that Kant defined matter's inertia as 'nothing else than its *lifelessness*, as matter in itself' (**MFNS** 544), and does not consider inertia as the cause of a body's resistance (**MFNS** 551). The third law is a variant of the law of action and reaction (→ **Newton**).

Phenomenology 'determines matter's motion or rest merely in relation to the mode of representation or *modality*' (**MFNS** 477). Matter is defined as 'the moveable insofar as it, as such a thing, can be an object of experience' (**MFNS** 554). For matter to be an object of experience the faculty of understanding has to determine it with respect to the predicate of motion. Kant identified three possible predicates, corresponding to the three categories of modality (possibility, actuality and necessity). The 'rectilinear motion of a matter with respect to an empirical space' (**MFNS** 555) is said to be a possible predicate. Thus, absolute motion, as motion of matter not with respect to an empirical space or other matter external to it, is said to be impossible.

Circular motion (as a continuous change of rectilinear motion) is an actual predicate. Finally, an opposite and equal motion for every motion of a body is said to be a necessary predicate (given the third law of mechanics). To prove the physical impossibility of empty space, Kant speculated that the cohesion of matter could be due to the ether distributed everywhere in the universe (**MFNS** 564).

Kant's speculations on the ether find their ultimate expression in **OP**. In continuity with **F**, the ether is identified as both the matter of heat (also called caloric) and the matter of light (**OP-II** 214). The existence of the ether is transcendentally deduced so as to allow the transition from the metaphysical foundations of natural science to physics (**OP-I** 218). In **OP**, Kant's aim was indeed to go beyond attraction and repulsion as established a priori in **MFNS** towards physics as 'the systematic investigation of nature as to [*durch*] empirically given forces of matter' (**OP-II** 298). The search for a system of empirically given forces of matter remains a regulative idea of reason (→ **regulative principles**) in line with Kant's later view of nature as a lawful system. – MM

FURTHER READING

E. Förster, *Kant's Final Synthesis* (Cambridge, MA: Harvard University Press, 2000).

M. Friedman, *Kant and the Exact Sciences* (Cambridge, MA: Harvard University Press, 1992).

M. Friedman, *Kant's Construction of Nature. A Reading of the* Metaphysical Foundations of Natural Science (Cambridge: Cambridge University Press, 2013).

M. Massimi (ed.), *Kant and Philosophy of Science Today* (Cambridge: Cambridge University Press, 2008).

E. Watkins (ed.), *Kant and the Sciences* (New York: Oxford University Press, 2001).

E. Watkins, *Kant and the Metaphysics of Causality* (Cambridge: Cambridge University Press, 2005).

NECESSITY

Necessity belongs – along with its opposite, contingency – to the categories of modality. Although only the twelfth and final category within the table of pure concepts of the understanding (A80=B106), necessity plays an enormously significant role within **CPR** insofar as it provides at the same time the definition of the → **a priori** (B4; A633=B661). The category necessity is derived from apodictic judgments, which alone – in contrast to problematic judgments (of possibility) and assertoric judgments (of actuality) – express objective and universally valid knowledge.

In contrast to belief and opinion, → **knowledge** consists in the awareness of necessity: '[W]hat I *know* [. . .], I hold to be *apodeictically certain*, i.e., to be universally and objectively necessary (holding for all).' (**JL** 66) The capacity to recognize necessities is → **reason**. Specifically, reason is the faculty of drawing inferences, and conclusions inferred always express some sort of necessity. Strict necessity is, according to Kant, the mark of a priori judgments.

In the Critical system, possibility corresponds to → **form**, actuality to matter; necessity expresses the connection between form and matter. In the case of arithmetic (→ **mathematics**) and → **geometry**, pure form can do without matter. Leaving matter out of account, consideration of form alone yields a complete description of the contents of these two sciences and their necessary truths.

By contrast, judgments in the philosophy of nature cannot be made without reference to matter. In this case, objects are considered 'necessary' when reason recognizes that they are given in accordance with the universal laws of experience (→ **laws (of nature)/lawfulness**). Accordingly, the third Postulate of Empirical Thought reads: 'That whose connection with the actual is determined in accordance with general conditions of experience is (exists) *necessarily*.' (A218=B266)

The transcendental examination of the concept of necessity in the third Postulate reduces to the analysis of the connections of appearances 'in accordance with the dynamical law of causality' (B280=A228). Four principles (*in mundo non datur hiatus, saltus, casus* and *fatum*), which clarify again the fourfold grouping of the categories, are structurally constrained by the law of causality. All necessity in nature is conditioned – rather than blind – and so all necessity is comprehensible. The possibility of any determination of the existence of the absolute is clearly ruled out through the presentation of the principles of continuity in the third Postulate. That nothing can be either conceived or intuited as necessary in itself by the human understanding is demonstrated by Kant in the → **Antinomies**.

Necessity and objectivity are one and the same not only in a theoretical , but also in a practical, sense: 'bonitas actionis est necessitas obiectiva. bonitas actionis contingentis est necessitatio obiectiva.' (**Refl** 6926) In the second note to the third section of **CPrR**, the distinction between two forms of necessity (physical and practical) – and the attendant distinction between two different concepts of law – is described as the single 'most important distinction' to be considered in practical investigations (**CPrR** 26).

This distinction in fact reflects the fundamental cleavage between the metaphysics of nature and the metaphysics of morals, which, in the mid-1760s, already characterized the sketch for a new metaphysics in **DSS** as well as the definition – crucial for the Critical project – of the Third Antinomy. → **freedom** and necessity exclude each other by turns, according to Kant.

In the note to the sixth section of **CPrR** (directly before the introduction of the categorical imperative in §7), Kant asks how consciousness of the moral law in general is possible (→ morality, categorical imperative). His answer – decisive for the whole of practical philosophy – is as follows: 'We can become aware of pure practical laws just as we are aware of pure theoretical principles, by attending to the necessity with which reason prescribes them to us and to the setting aside of all empirical conditions to which reason directs us.' (CPrR 30)

Of beauty, as Kant says in §18 of CJ, one thinks that it has a necessary connection to satisfaction (→ aesthetic judgment). '[T]his necessity is of a special kind: not a theoretical objective necessity [. . .] nor a practical necessity [. . .]. Rather, as a necessity that is thought in an aesthetic judgment, it can only be called *exemplary*, i.e., a necessity of the assent of *all* to a judgment that is regarded as an example of a universal rule that one cannot produce.' (CJ 236–237) In this case it has to do with a subjective necessity, conditioned by the idea of a common sense. According to the title of §22: 'The necessity of the universal assent that is thought in a judgment of taste is a subjective necessity, which is represented as objective under the presupposition of a common sense.' (CJ 239) – GM/SS

FURTHER READING

J. Van Cleve, *Problems from Kant* (New York: Oxford University Press, 1999), ch. 2.

NOUMENON, NOUMENA → THING IN ITSELF, TRANSCENDENTAL IDEALISM

OBJECT, OBJECTIVITY

The concept of 'object' (*Gegenstand, Objekt*) is the centre around which Kant has organized **CPR**. At a crucial stage in the argument of the → **Deduction** Kant defines an object as 'that in the concept of which the manifold of a given intuition is united' (B137). In the A-Deduction, Kant speaks of the 'transcendental object', as 'that which in all our empirical concepts in general can provide relation to an object, i.e., objective reality' (A109). But this definition is not the premise of Kant's argument. The objectivity of knowledge, and so what is an object at all, is the key point that must rather be explained.

Although Kant formulated the Critical problem formally in terms of the general question how synthetic judgments a priori could be possible (B19) – which represent the kind of knowledge that especially metaphysics presupposes – his explanation of human knowledge is in fact both broader and deeper than an analysis of synthetic a priori judgment.

It is in the Transcendental Deduction of the categories (TD) that Kant demonstrates that the whole project turns on the explanation of the aspect of the → **synthesis** of representations as an essential element in human knowledge. Without synthesis our representations would be a chaotic stream of impressions. → **Knowledge** of an object in the strong sense is reflected in the type of 'synthesis' of representations that is found in a → **judgment** as such. The essential step lies in determining the implications of the objective unity of a synthesis of representations as distinguished from a merely subjective connection of representations (cf. B136–142) (→ **apperception**), which is based solely on the laws of association of the human mind as they had been explained by David → **Hume**.

Hume distinguished two kinds of proposition that relate to two areas of knowledge:

relations between matters of fact and relations of ideas. He concluded that the nature of the certainty of the knowledge of matters of fact is of a completely different kind from that of pure relations of ideas as such. Hume showed at any rate that there is no strictly logical or a priori explanation possible of relations of matters of fact but only a psychological reference to a tendency of the mind to assume a → **necessity** of sorts in the sequence of factual events. The character of the 'necessary connection' of some cause and some effect is, however, logically always contingent.

By contrast, Kant thinks he must bring the problem to another level and interpret the problem in terms of a → **transcendental** foundation of the objectivity of human knowledge that is to be distinguished from an explanation in terms of the laws of association of the mind. For Kant, the central question is: What is the formal character, the meaning, and implication of an objective unity of representations in a synthetic judgment?

In §19 of the B-version of TD (B140–142), Kant focuses on the fact that through the copula 'is' a judgment shows its intrinsic intentional character that is entirely missed when one explains the objectivity expressed in a judgment in terms of a contingent association of ideas, as Hume does. A judgment, which is in essence 'synthetic' – all judgments ultimately rest on a synthesis of concepts – and is 'nothing other than the way to bring given cognitions to the *objective* unity of apperception' (B141), means something different from a merely subjectively linked succession of representations.

The concepts in a judgment function as subject and predicate in relation to each other and as such in relation to an object that is 'thought' or determined as to its own character. Judgment, in itself, means thinking something *as* an 'object'. The concept of object has its own import as Kant stresses constantly against Hume: it implies 'thinking' something, thinking something formally as 'determined', that is, as something that is such and such for me. For Kant, judgment and object thus are intimately connected.

In this context, Kant focuses on the role of the self, more in particular, the way I myself am 'implicated' in the formal analysis of the objectivity of knowledge (→ **apperception**). He is not interested in what I accomplish actively in the construction of propositions but rather in the way that something is thought as an 'objective unity' or as an object 'for me' (B138). This 'me' or this form of self-consciousness does not refer to a kind of self-perception whereby I am involved in or literally know my own different acts. The 'me' that is crucial in this case is the 'me' that is just 'implicated', so to speak, in the 'objective character' of something that is thought as something (for me). Put differently, it is a 'me' that is derivative of the determination of the object. This 'me' is always essentially 'implicit' in the conception of an object.

Thus, Kant's argument in §§17 and 19 of TD stresses the 'immanent' strong connection between the concept of 'object' and a kind of self-consciousness that does not imply an empirical soul-substance but functions only as a 'relational' concept of sorts in the formal analysis of objectivity.

Importantly, Kant associates objects with appearances (→ **appearance**) as the only things that can be known, in contrast to things in themselves (→ **thing in itself; transcendental idealism**). This is of course connected with his view of objects as functions of judgment, and hence as dependent on the subjective conditions of thought. – KJB

FURTHER READING

H. Allison, *Kant's Transcendental Idealism.*
An Interpretation and Defense, revised and
enlarged edition (New Haven: Yale University
Press, 2004), ch. 7, esp. pts I and II.

OBJECTIVE UNITY → OBJECT/
OBJECTIVITY, APPERCEPTION,
SYNTHESIS

ONTOLOGY → METAPHYSICS

ONTOLOGICAL PROOF → PROOFS OF
THE EXISTENCE OF GOD

OUTER SENSE → INNER/OUTER SENSE

PARALOGISMS

In the section 'Paralogisms of Pure Reason',
Kant attacks the extravagant claims of
rational psychology. Rational → psychology, as a discipline that purports to offer a
priori cognition of the human soul in particular, was first introduced among the topics of → metaphysics by → Wolff, though
Kant directs his criticism in the chapter
rather widely, targeting claims by a number
of thinkers, including → Descartes and →
Mendelssohn, on topics of long-standing
philosophical interest, such as the soul's substantiality and simplicity.

Kant can be seen to adopt a twofold
strategy against the rational psychologist.
First, he disputes the particular metaphysical claims made about the soul, arguing
that they cannot be taken to be informative
about the soul's nature insofar as the idea
of the soul has no other grounding than the
'I think'.

Second, Kant conjectures diagnostically
that the basis for the rational psychologist's
error in thinking that a merely logical subject (the 'I' of the 'I think') (→ apperception)
could constitute the foundation for synthetic
cognition lies in transcendental illusion in
accordance with which that subject naturally
seems to be a real subject of thinking.

Through each of the four paralogisms presented in the chapter, Kant attempts to show
that a central metaphysical claim on the part
of the rational psychologist is in fact the
conclusion of a formally invalid argument.
In particular, Kant thinks the reasoning
offered by the rational psychologist suffers
from a fallacy of equivocation inasmuch as
a concept is made use of in different senses
throughout the argument.

For example, in the First Paralogism, the
rational psychologist supplies the following
argument for the substantiality of the soul:

[1] That the representation of which is the
absolute subject of our judgments, and
hence cannot be used as the determination of another thing, is *substance*.
[2] I, as thinking being, am the *absolute subject* of all my possible judgments, and this
representation of Myself cannot be used
as the predicate of any other thing.
[3] Thus I, as thinking being (soul), am *substance*. (A348)

According to Kant, in the major premise
(1) the concept of substance is made use of
in its transcendental signification, that is, in
the sense in which it would apply to things
in general, whereas in the minor premise (2)
and conclusion (3) the same concept is made
use of in its empirical signification, that is, as
it would apply to things as they appear.

This latter use is unwarranted, however,
since we have no sensible intuition of the
soul that might ground it. This makes the

syllogism a paralogism, or an inference that is false according to its → **form** (cf. **JL** 135; §90) (→ **logic**); thus, the rational psychologist cannot pretend to offer synthetic cognition of the soul's substantiality in this way.

Kant adheres to this general line of criticism throughout the Paralogisms, but he also spares room for attacking the inferences that the rational psychologist sought to draw from these initial claims.

In the Second Paralogism, Kant tackles the traditional argument for the soul's simplicity, namely, that a unified thought requires a single unifying thinker, pointing out that this argument rests on an unfounded claim that a multitude of representations must be contained in a single thinking subject to constitute a thought. In addition, Kant disputes the cogency of the rational psychologist's further inference from the soul's simplicity to its immateriality, arguing that while the soul's simplicity might distinguish it from matter considered as an appearance, it cannot serve to distinguish it from the ground of matter considered as it is in itself.

In the Third Paralogism, Kant takes issue with the rational psychologist's demonstration of the soul's personality, where this is understood as its capacity to be 'conscious of the numerical identity of its Self in different times' (A361). Although Kant allows that we are, through transcendental → **apperception**, conscious of our own numerical → **identity** through all time, he rejects the rational psychologist's claim that this amounts to an empirical consciousness of our persistence through time and, as such, a synthetic cognition of the soul's personality. Together, these criticisms undermine the rational psychologist's attempts to demonstrate the soul's immortality, where this consists in the soul's incorruptibility and continued personality after death.

Finally, in the Fourth Paralogism Kant considers the rational psychologist's argument for the ideality of external things insofar as the existence of these things, unlike that of the soul, is known only mediately. Against this, Kant argues that his own doctrine of → **transcendental idealism**, in accordance with which things in space and time 'are all together to be regarded as mere representations and not as things in themselves' (A369) allows for the immediate perception of external things (inasmuch as they are mere representations). However, in the → **Refutation of Idealism** added to the second edition of **CPR**, Kant offers a different line of argument.

Kant recognized that, in order to be persuasive, he must also explain *how* it is that the rational psychologist could have been misled into thinking that a merely formal representation could be the object of synthetic cognition. This is precisely the role of Kant's doctrine of transcendental illusion (→ **Dialectic**), as he claims that the soul naturally and unavoidably seems to be given empirically, giving rise to the temptation to take 'the unity in the synthesis of thoughts for a *perceived* unity in the subject of these thoughts' (A402; emphasis added).

It is precisely insofar as the soul holds out the illusory appearance of being given in inner → **intuition** that Kant thinks it serves as the 'transcendental ground for inferring falsely' (A341=B399) on the part of the rational psychologist. Having fallen prey to this illusion, the rational psychologist subsequently takes the subsumption of the soul under a category in its empirical signification to be warranted, and Kant will allow nonetheless that there is a sense in which the soul can be understood to be a simple, identical substance, though only insofar as these concepts are taken in their transcendental significations. Even then, however, these claims are not inferred of the soul but lie 'already in every thought itself' (A354). – CD

FURTHER READING

K. Ameriks, *Kant's Theory of Mind: An Analysis of the Paralogisms of Pure Reason*, new edition (Oxford: Clarendon Press, 2000).
C. Dyck, *Kant and Rational Psychology* (Oxford: Oxford University Press, 2014).
U. Thiel, 'The critique of rational psychology', in G. Bird (ed.), *A Companion to Kant* (Malden, MA/ Oxford: Wiley-Blackwell, 2010), pp. 207–221.
J. Wuerth, 'The Paralogisms of Pure Reason', in P. Guyer (ed.), *The Cambridge Companion to Kant's 'Critique of Pure Reason'* (Cambridge: Cambridge University Press, 2010), pp. 210–244.

PEACE → COSMOPOLITAN, COSMOPOLITANISM

PERCEPTION → EXPERIENCE, ANTICIPATIONS OF PERCEPTION, ANALOGIES OF EXPERIENCE, REPRESENTATION

PHENOMEN(A)(ON) → TRANSCENDENTAL IDEALISM

PHYSICO-THEOLOGICAL PROOF → PROOFS OF THE EXISTENCE OF GOD

PLEASURE → AESTHETIC JUDGMENT

POSTULATES OF EMPIRICAL THOUGHT IN GENERAL

The Postulates of Empirical Thought in General (A218–235=B265–287) are the fourth group of synthetic a priori principles of experience, next to the → **Axioms of Intuition** and the → **Anticipations of Perception**, which are also called the mathematical principles, and the → **Analogies of Experience**, which are called the dynamic principles (B199=A160). The Postulates deal with the schematized (→ **schematism**) categories of modality 'possibility', 'actuality' and 'necessity', that is, with the restriction of them to their merely empirical use (A219=B266). Kant refers to the postulates as mere regulative principles, like the Analogies of Experience, but the way in which the postulates are applied as principles is very different from both the Analogies and the Axioms.

Whereas the previous set of principles dealt with the manner in which the schematized categories are related to appearances (→ **appearance**), or objects (→ **object**), directly, the aim of the postulates is to explicate the manner in which the modal concepts of the understanding 'express the relation of the concept *to the faculty of knowledge*' (A219=B266; emphasis added). That is to say, the postulates concern the ways in which objects are assumed to exist *in relation to* the subject of knowledge. Unlike the other principles, the postulates thus do not make any claims as to how objects of → **experience** are constituted themselves or how objects relate to each other. Rather, they express whether, in relation to our subjective cognitive capacity, an object of our cognition is to be regarded as 'possible', as 'actual' or as 'necessary'. The principles of modality thus do not 'augment' the concept of a thing; hence, they can be called postulates (A234–235=B287).

The first postulate concerns the application of the category of *possibility* in an empirical judgment: that is possible 'which agrees with the formal conditions of experience' (A218=B265). Kant is concerned to show how for something to be a possible object of knowledge at all, it must at least fall under the general formal conditions of knowledge, that is, the forms of → **intuition**, space and time (→ **Transcendental Aesthetic**), and the categories (→ **deduction**).

The postulate of the *actuality* of things is bound up with 'the material conditions of experience (of sensation)' (A218=B266); an object must be given a posteriori in a sensible intuition and must thus be sensibly perceived, for any concept of an object, in accordance with the categories, to be about a really existing object (B268–269=A221–222). 'Perception [...] is the sole characteristic of actuality' (A225=B273). The postulate of actuality thus concerns the requirement of 'the connection of the object with some actual experience, in accordance with the analogies of experience' (B272=A225).

The third postulate concerns the way the category of *necessity* is to be schematized in connection 'with the actual as determined in accordance with universal conditions of experience' (A218=B266). That is to say, the third postulate unites the two postulates of possibility and actuality, and thus indicates that, necessarily, we can only have knowledge of actual objects that conform to the conditions of possible experience.

The schematization of the concept of possibility relates to the formal subjective conditions of experience that enable objective experience. Hence, it is different from a merely *logical* understanding of possibility, which would only involve the absence of contradiction, i.e. that the thought of an object does not contradict the formal rules of thinking. This alone, however, does nothing to help us understand whether something is *objectively* or *really* possible. Whether something is objectively or really possible involves 'the conditions of space and of its determination' (A221=B268), which is as much as to say that to grasp the real possibility of something requires seeing it as standing under the formal conditions of intuition, as well as the concepts of the understanding that concern quantity, quality and relation and determine what is given in intuition.

The important point with the postulate of the actuality of things is that any cognition of a thing must be mediated by our perceptions, also when it is something objective that cannot immediately be perceived by means of the senses, such as a magnetic field, whose existence must be inferred from its connection with actual perceptions within possible experience (cf. B521=A493), i.e. that 'magnetic matter' really exists can be inferred from the existence of perceivable 'attracted iron filings' (B273=A226), for which only a magnetic field could be responsible.

It is at this point in his discussion of the postulates that Kant refers to previous systems of idealist thought (in particular → **Descartes**), which have cast serious doubts over the existence of external objects and over the fact that we immediately perceive objects in experience, as Kant has pointed out in his discussion of the postulate of actuality. Such external world scepticism would threaten to undermine the Critical principles of experience, which is the main reason why Kant inserts a section on the → **Refutation of Idealism** in the B-version of **CPR**, in which he attempts to allay the sceptical worry, before turning to the postulate of → **necessity**.

By the postulate of necessity, Kant means that 'it pertains to material necessity in existence', and 'not [to] the merely formal and logical necessity in the connection of concepts' (B279=A226). That is, any really existing object can only be known through the perception of it in conformity with 'general laws of experience' (B279=A227), more particularly 'in accordance with laws of causality' (B279=A227). This means that the existence of the object cannot be known 'fully a priori' (B279=A226). Kant maintains that the necessity of which we have knowledge only concerns the relation between actual appearances, so that we only know the necessity of '*effects in nature*' (A227=B280). Therefore, the postulate of necessity is only about the hypothetical necessity of the relation between objects of possible experience, not about the absolute necessity of the existence of things. – NH/DS

FURTHER READING

P. Guyer, 'The Postulates of Empirical Thinking in Genreal and the Refutation of Idealism', in G. Mohr, M. Willaschek (eds), *Immanuel Kant. Kritik der reinen Vernunft*, in the series *Klassiker Auslegen* (Berlin: Akademie Verlag, 1998), pp. 297–324.

G. Motta, *Die Postulate des empirischen Denkens überhaupt* (Berlin/New York: de Gruyter, 2012).

PRINCIPLE OF IDENTITY OF INDISCERNIBLES → IDENTITY

PRINCIPLE OF (NON-) CONTRADICTION

In the 'Introduction' to **CPR**, in the section 'On the division of general logic into analytic and dialectic', Kant clarifies his understanding of → **truth** and agrees with the traditional notion of truth as correspondence or 'agreement of cognition with its object' (B82=A58). This is what in scholastic philosophy is known as the dictum *veritas est adaequatio rei et intellectus*. This nominal definition of truth is granted by Kant, although it does not provide 'the general and certain criterion of the truth of *any cognition*' (ibid.; emphasis added). Kant asks what it is that makes the intellect correspond to the → **object** of → **knowledge**.

The difficulty with determining a criterion of truth is that it must at the same time be general to be valid for all objects and be particular so as to hold for any particular object, the content with which truth is precisely concerned. To ask 'a sufficient and yet at the same time general sign of truth' (A58=B83) seems a tall order.

Kant therefore distinguishes between the content or matter and → **form** of cognition, and accordingly makes a distinction between 'material (objective) truth' (A60=B85) and 'the form of truth' (A59=B84), with which not two kinds of truth are meant but two formally separable aspects of truth. This is to avoid 'a material use of the merely formal principles of pure understanding through empty sophistries' (A63=B88).

The 'merely logical criterion of truth, namely the agreement of a cognition with the general and formal laws of understanding and reason' (A59=B84) is the principle of non-contradiction, or the principle of contradiction as Kant labels it. The principle amounts to the thought that 'no predicate pertains to a thing that contradicts it' (B190=A151). In modern parlance: of some *a* of which is asserted F cannot also be asserted ¬F. It is the '*conditio sine qua non*' or 'negative condition of all truth' (A59–60=B84; cf. B190=A151). But 'for all that a judgment may be free of any internal contradiction, it can still be either false or groundless' (A151=B190).

The first use of the principle is thus a negative one, i.e. in order 'to ban falsehood and error', which makes it a necessary condition of all thought. But it also serves a positive role, as it is the sufficient condition for analytic → judgment (A151=B190–191; cf. P 267), '[f]or the contrary of that which as a concept already lies and is thought in the cognition of the object is always correctly denied, while the concept itself must necessarily be affirmed of it, since its opposite would contradict the object' (ibid.).

But the principle cannot be used materially; it is not sufficient for objective cognition. Some other principle must be presupposed which will provide the sufficient ground of knowledge (→ **principle of sufficient reason**).

In one of his earliest works, **ND**, Kant elaborated on the supreme principle of metaphysics and made the case for two reciprocal principles, the principle of affirmative truths ('whatever is, is') and one for negative truths ('whatever is not, is not'), which basically come down to one supreme principle, namely the principle of → **identity** (ND 389), on which the principle of contradiction, viz. the principle of negative truths, is based. Incidentally, in **ND** Kant still formulates the principle of contradiction in quasi-temporal terms that he refutes in **CPR**: '[I]t is impossible that the same thing should simultaneously be and not be.' (**ND** 391; cf. B191–193=A152–153)˙ – DS

PRINCIPLE OF SUFFICIENT REASON

There is a reason for everything that is. In Proposition IV of **ND** (**ND** 392), Kant takes aim at the main support of Wolffian rationalism (→ **Wolff**) insofar as he breaks the principle of sufficient reason (*principium rationis determinantis, vulgo sufficientis*) down into (1) the principle of antecedently determining grounds – the 'reason *why*' (*ratio cur*), or the 'ground of being or coming to be' (*ratio fiendi vel existendi*) – and (2) the principle of consequentially determining grounds – the 'ground that' (*ratio quod*), or 'ground of knowing' (*ratio cognoscendi*).

Kant asserts the necessary validity of the principle of the determination of a thing through its cause: 'Nothing which exists contingently can be without a ground which determines its existence antecedently.' (**ND** 396; heading) At the end of the work, Kant derives two further principles from the principle of sufficient reason: the principle of succession (Proposition XII) and the principle of co-existence (Proposition XIII).

In the Critical period, the principle of sufficient reason loses its ontological character and is construed as the fundamental a priori principle of the determination of the possibility of → **experience** itself. This idea is clearly anticipated in several reflections from the so-called *Duisburg Nachlass* (1774–1775): 'Everything that happens [. . .] cannot be specifically determined in the time in which it occurs except by means of a rule. [. . .] Thus the principle of sufficient reason is a *principium* of the rule of experience, namely for ordering it.' (**Refl 4680**; cf. **Refl 4682**)

Ontology as the science of things in themselves is impossible, according to Kant, and 'must give way to the modest [. . .] analytic of the pure understanding' (B303=A247). The Transcendental Analytic is meant to show that true, discursive knowledge of things is nevertheless possible. The principle of sufficient reason cannot, strictly speaking, be proven (see A783=B811). But Kant singles out the proof of the principle of causality in the Second Analogy of Experience (→ **Analogies of Experience**) as a surrogate for a proof of the principle of sufficient reason: 'All alterations occur in accordance with the law of the connection of cause and effect.' (B232) Kant regards this as the most important condition for the possibility of the objects of experience: 'Thus the principle of sufficient reason is the ground of possible experience, namely the objective cognition of appearances with regard to their relation in the successive series of time.' (A200–201=B246) – GM/SS

FURTHER READING

B. Longuenesse, 'Kant's deconstruction of the principle of sufficient reason', in *Kant on the Human Standpoint* (Cambridge: Cambridge University Press, 2005), pp. 117–142.

PRODUCTIVE IMAGINATION →
IMAGINATION, SYNTHESIS

PROOF

Within the 'Systematic Representation of all Synthetic Principles of Pure Understanding' (A158=B197) Kant presents the proof of the → **Axioms of Intuition**, the proof of the → **Anticipations of Perception** and the three proofs of the → **Analogies of Experience**. The possibility of attaining, synthetically and a priori, to certain → **knowledge** of things must be established here. Only by this means can thorough and orderly knowledge of things arise. Kant explains later in the Discipline of Pure Reason: 'Without attention to this proofs, like water breaking its banks, run wildly across

the country, wherever the tendency of hidden association may happen to lead them.' (A783=B811)

Such → **transcendental** proofs are subject to completely different constraints than are the synthetic a priori principles of → **mathematics**, which can be drawn immediately from → **pure** → **intuition** (cf. A782=B810). Transcendental proofs amount to nothing more than a demonstration that without certain connecting concepts of the understanding → **experience** itself, and consequently the objects of experience, would not be possible. But this does not imply that transcendental proofs are directed towards objects. Rather, they are meant to establish 'the objective validity of the concepts and the possibility of their synthesis a priori' (A782=B810) (→ **deduction**).

As a precaution against the dogmatic use of → **reason**, Kant lays down three rules to be observed in the carrying out of philosophical proofs:

(1) No transcendental proofs may be attempted 'without having first considered whence one can justifiably derive the principles on which one intends to build' (A786=B814).
(2) There can be only one proof for any transcendental proposition (see A787=B815ff.).
(3) Such proofs must not be 'apagogic' (disproving the opposite), but rather 'ostensive' (making evident the truth of the transcendental proposition directly). This yields not only certainty, but also insight into the sources (the objective ground) of the certainty (see A789=B817ff.).

The three main divisions of the → **Dialectic**, viz. the → **Paralogisms**, the → **Antinomies** and the Ideal of Pure Reason (→ **transcendental ideal, proofs of the existence of God**) are

247

devoted to exposing the counterfeit proofs of pure reason which violate these three rules each in their own way. – GM/SS

PROOFS OF THE EXISTENCE OF GOD

Kant's justly famous critique of the physico-theological, cosmological and especially ontological proofs of God's existence is best known in its Critical version published in **CPR** (A583–A642=B611–670). But it is preceded by an at least as equally important version of his critique of the proofs in **OPD**, published some 18 years earlier, which in turn is preceded, by some eight years, by a short argument similar in nature in Proposition VII in **ND** 395–396. Other than in **CPR**, in **ND** and **OPD** Kant still thinks it possible to provide what he considers the only possible ground for a positive proof of God's existence, which as such does not reappear in **CPR**.

OPD is important for various reasons. Historically, Kant's famous belief that existence is not a predicate finds its first expression here (**OPD** 72). Secondly, for a systematic understanding of Kant's pivotal claims regarding material possibility in the section on the → **transcendental ideal** (A571–583=B579–611), which precedes the discussion of the actual proofs, one must have recourse to the core argument of **OPD**, to which it is heavily indebted. The argument from possibility, which Kant presents in **OPD**, is refashioned in such a way that an inference from the necessity that something absolutely necessary exists to God as the unique exemplification of this is no longer deemed valid in its Critical version.

In **OPD**, the ground for a proof of God's existence is thus offered on the basis of an argument from possibility. Kant argues that although absolutely necessary existence or being cannot be explained purely by means of the → **principle of (non-)contradiction**, which concerns what he calls the 'internal possibility' of concepts (**OPD** 77), absolutely necessary existence can be inferred from the necessary 'material element' of the possibility of conceivability. The former rests on the logical → **necessity** in the predicates entailing that what is self-contradictory is absolutely impossible, and the latter concerns the sufficient condition of the conceivability of concepts, or their 'absolute real necessity' (**OPD** 82). By this latter, Kant means that there must be something given for what is conceivable for if material possibility is annulled, then all possibility is annulled. That is to say, if nothing exists, then nothing is possible. Of course, one can deny the existence of a single contingent thing, but one cannot consistently deny *all* existence. Although, as Kant says, 'there is no *internal* [logical, D.S.] contradiction in the negation of all existence' (**OPD** 78; emphasis added), '[o]n the other hand, to say that there is a possibility and yet nothing real at all is self-contradictory'. Therefore, necessarily something exists for there to be something to be possibly thought for if 'all existence is denied, then all possibility is cancelled as well' (**OPD** 79).

Kant then proceeds to argue, not entirely convincingly, for the existence of an *absolutely* necessary being; in one of its versions, the argument runs as follows:

[1] All possibility presupposes something actual in and through which all that can be thought [*alles Denkliche*] is given.
[2] Therefore, there is a certain actuality, the cancellation of which would itself cancel all internal possibility whatever.

[3] But that, the cancellation of which eradicates all possibility, is absolutely necessary [*schlechterdings nothwendig*].

[4] Therefore, something exists absolutely necessarily [*absolut nothwendiger Weise*]. (**OPD** 83; trans. amended)

From thereon, Kant argues that only one being can fit the bill of absolutely necessary existence and that it has all the necessary characteristics that in fact define the idea of God, among which there is supreme reality, which is the 'real ground' upon which 'all possible reality' is dependent (**OPD** 85).

The pre-Critical Kant thus thinks it still justified to infer from the necessity of an absolutely necessary being, which is an *ens realissimum*, to the absolutely necessary existence of God as its personification. But the Critical Kant of **CPR** no longer deems the inference valid or indeed that there must be *some being* (cf. A586–587=B614–615; cf. A675=B703) that absolutely necessarily exists, rather than is 'a mere creature of [reason's] own thinking' (A584=B612), an '*ens rationis*' (A681=B709). Nonetheless, Kant continues to believe that reason quite naturally seeks an 'immovable rock of the absolutely necessary', which serves as that which 'alone can complete series of conditions carried out to their grounds' (A584=B612), and to which 'the concept of a being having the highest reality would be best suited' (A586=B614) (→ **Dialectic**).

In **OPD**, before going on to offer his positive argument, detailed above, Kant first introduces his central, and most famous, argument that existence is not a predicate – an argument also central to the account concerning the impossibility of the ontological proof in **CPR** – and that any proof of God's existence cannot be based on the premise that a denial of God's existence would be conceptually or logically contradictory (**OPD** 81). Kant makes an important distinction between the relation between the predicates of a thing and the relation of the existing thing to the subject that judges about the thing. This latter relation is what Kant calls the absolute positing of the thing with all its predicates (**OPD** 82).

If I assert the proposition 'God is omnipotent', then it is only the logical relation between concepts that is thought, since it is an explanation of the concept 'God'. No existence of God is thereby posited (**OPD** 74). It is a true judgment, even if one were not to acknowledge God's existence. By contrast, the judgment 'God exists', or 'God is an existent thing' (**OPD** 74), is not the expression of a relation between a predicate and the subject term of a judgment. More properly – and herein Kant's analysis of existence shows to be a clear precursor of the modern notion of existential quantification – one should analyze this judgment as stating 'Something existent is God', or more precisely, '[T]o an existing thing belong those predicates, which taken together we designate by means of the expression "God"' (**OPD** 74; trans. amended). This analysis is repeated in **CPR**.

Importantly, against what he takes to be the traditional ontological argument Kant points out that, once something is posited as existent, existence is not a predicate added to the totality of predicates that a *possible* thing possesses; 'nothing more is posited in an existent thing than is posited in a merely possible one' (**OPD** 75), although of course 'more is posited through an existent thing', that is, an *actual* thing is more than a possible thing, because this 'involves the absolute positing of the thing itself as well' (**OPD** 75; cf. Kant's Critical account of the hundred actual thalers compared to hundred possible thalers at A599=B627).

A very similar, albeit much condensed and less clear, argument is offered in **CPR** when Kant addresses the transcendental or ontological proof (A594ff.=B622ff.; see also **LPöl**, which are from the period after the publication of the first edition of **CPR**). In Kant's view, the classical a priori proof that existence cannot be denied of the highest reality, namely God, on pain of contradiction can be dismissed on the grounds that a distinction must be heeded between absolute positing and the relative (logical) positing of concepts, the latter of which entails that positing the subject while at the same time cancelling the predicate that belongs essentially to it is contradictory but the former of which can perfectly well be negated without a contradiction ensuing. So existence as belonging to a highest reality, which is an absolutely necessary being, cannot be proved purely on the basis of the principle of non-contradiction. Also, the ontological argument, if it is presumed to be analytic, crucially rests on a conflation of the categories of 'reality' and 'existence' (A597=B625). At any rate, the attempt 'to think existence through the pure category alone', without having recourse to a posteriori experience, makes it impossible to 'assign any mark distinguishing it from mere possibility' (A601=B629).

Next to the one transcendental, i.e. a priori, argument Kant considers the two classical a posteriori arguments, i.e. the cosmological and physico-theological proofs (which Kant had also addressed in **OPD**).

The cosmological proof is a proof that argues from contingency to an absolutely necessary being, referred to by Kant as → **Leibniz's** 'proof *a contingentia mundi*' (A604=B632). In his presentation of the argument, Kant however does not mention contingency, although he does refer to it in a footnote to the proof, which he circumscribes

in succinct form as follows: '[1] If something exists, then an absolutely necessary being also has to exist. [2] Now I myself, at least, exist; [3] therefore, an absolutely necessary being exists.' (ibid.) Kant says that 'the minor premise contains an experience', whereas the inference is from experience to 'the existence of something necessary'. In the footnote to this passage, Kant indicates that in its classical formulation the proof is indeed concerned to show that 'everything *contingent* must have a cause, which, if it in turn is contingent, must likewise have its cause, until the series of causes [. . .] has to end with an absolutely necessary cause, without which it would have no completeness' (A605=B633n.).

According to Kant, the force of the cosmological proof rests on the ontological proof, which makes the reference to experience in its premise in fact superfluous. And since the ontological proof has been dismissed, Kant does not think that the cosmological proof succeeds either.

The ostensible difference with the ontological argument is that the cosmological argument is not an a priori proof but neither is it empirical in the same way that the physico-theological is, which 'uses observations about the particular constitution of this sensible world of ours for its ground of proof' (A605=B633).

The physico-theological proof (A620ff.=B648ff.) draws Kant's praise but as with the foregoing proofs he argues that it must be rejected as a philosophical proof. The proof, today often referred to as the argument from design, is premised on the observation that the world shows clear signs of 'immeasurable [. . .] manifoldness, order, purposiveness, and beauty' that can only be explained by an order that pertains contingently to the world and which therefore points to a 'sublime and wise' (A625=B653) unitary self-subsisting cause external to the world as well as proportionate to it.

But despite its popular reputation, which Kant is loath to ridicule, there is a fatal flaw in the physico-theological proof since it moves from anthropomorphic reasoning based on empirical experience to the postulation of a highest being, God, whose determinate concept it cannot establish and for which it must have recourse to the a priori, ontological proof. Also, the physico-theological proof could only establish that there must be an architect, not that he is also the creator of the world.

Kant thus dismisses all of the above proofs, which he thinks exhaust the possible kinds of theoretical proof of God's existence. The concept of a highest being can only function as a 'regulative principle of reason' (A619=B647) (→ regulative principles). He does however proffer a positive argument for the necessary postulation of God in **CPrR** and **CJ** based on moral and, in the latter case, also natural teleology.

In **CJ** (441–442), Kant argues that the concept of a supreme intelligence, by analogy with human intelligence, is required to be able to conceive of the 'purposive arrangements' of nature, given the way our discursive faculties are constituted, although this concept cannot be theoretically determined to pertain to an actual intelligent designer (→ teleology).

In **CPrR**, in chapter 5 of section 2 of the Dialectic (**CPrR** 124–132), Kant aims to undergird the moral teleology that assures that the moral world and the realm of nature can be seen to coincide by postulating God's existence. Only the actuality of 'a highest original good, namely of the existence of God' (**CPrR** 125) is the guarantee 'for a necessary connection between the morality and the proportionate happiness of a being [. . .]

who [. . .] cannot by his own powers make it harmonize thoroughly with his practical principles' (**CPrR** 124–125; cf. **CJ** 442ff.) (→ morality, religion).

Lastly, in **OP** Kant makes the prima facie new claim that the God of moral theology only exists as a moral postulate (**OP-II** 116) and that the notion of God designates no 'substance different from man' (**OP-I** 21). – DS

FURTHER READING

P. Byrne, *Kant on God* (Aldershot: Ashgate, 2007), chs 2, 3 and 5.

A. Chignell, 'Kant, modality, and the most real being', *Archiv für Geschichte der Philosophie* 91,2 (2009): 157–192.

W. Forgie, 'Kant and existence. *Critique of Pure Reason* A600/B628', *Kant–Studien* 99 (2008): 1–12.

L. Kreimendahl, 'Einleitung' to I. Kant, *Der einzig mögliche Beweisgrund zu einer Demonstration des Daseins Gottes*, ed. L. Kreimendahl & M. Oberhausen (Hamburg: Meiner, 2011), pp. XIII–CXXIX.

J. Van Cleve, *Problems from Kant* (New York: Oxford University Press, 1999), ch. 12.

A. Wood, *Kant's Rational Theology* (Ithaca, NY: Cornell University Press, 2009 [1978]).

PSYCHOLOGY

For Kant, the object of its investigation defines the discipline of psychology, which is the thinking subject (A334=B391). While Kant negotiates the diverse views of → **Wolff**, → **Baumgarten**, → **Meier**, → **Locke**, → **Hume** and → **Tetens** in developing his concept of psychology, his own inquiries into the cognitive capacities of human beings occurs at an extremely abstract level. Instead of examining the particular mechanisms of memory or imaginative visualization, Kant is interested in the capacities of the human mind insofar as they are considered as basic powers of → representation (e.g. A86=B118).

For Kant, human beings are both receptive agents, i.e. passive recipients of stimuli manifested through intuitive representations (→ **inner/outer sense**), on the one hand, and spontaneous discursive agents (→ **spontaneity**), i.e. active agents employing conceptual representations, on the other. Kant does conduct an investigation into the powers of the thinking subject, and to that extent he is interested in psychology as he has defined it, although his inquiries are of a nature such that they are crucially distinct from the other forms of psychological inquiry that he recognizes, i.e. rational psychology and empirical psychology.

For Kant, transcendental inquiry into the nature of the thinking subject requires careful delineation of the difference between such an inquiry and the inquiries pursued by empirical and rational psychologists. Kant describes empirical psychology as the attempt to cognize the human soul from our experience, and rational psychology as the attempt to characterize the human soul from concepts alone (cf. **LM** 263).

The latter inquiry, which Kant comes to reject as part of his rejection of the Leibnizian-Wolffian paradigm of rationalist → **metaphysics**, seeks to establish key features of the human soul – its immateriality, simplicity, identity and immortality – through syllogistic inference from the initial premise of the very concept of a thinking self (A345=B403) (→ **Paralogisms**).

Spontaneous concept-use can be understood as the capacity to employ concepts in manners not simply determined as patterned reactions to received stimuli. In this sense, the subject matter of transcendental psychology is distinct from that of empirical psychology, which concerns the psychological mechanisms of association and habit insofar as they govern the practice of → **judgment**.

Lockean psychology, for example, affords the human mind the process of association as a central cognitive capacity in the formation of judgments about empirical objects. The capacity for association is expressed by Kant as the capacity for reproduction in the → **imagination**. The capacity for associating different representations under a particular rule presupposes the capacity to first render those representations as associable, as manifesting a basic affinity such that their connection via association can take place (A100–102). Kant's transcendental psychology thus concerns the conditions under which the observable processes of empirical psychology can take place.

In investigating the nature of the thinking subject, Kant focuses upon the 'I' that can act as the subject of all empirical judgments. As such, the 'I' is not determined by the particular content of any individual empirical judgment but is rather that which accompanies all such judgments and which, Kant argues, makes such judgments first possible. In this way, the psychological investigation of the thinking 'I' is also a transcendental investigation (A343=B401).

Another difference between empirical and transcendental psychology concerns the fact that the subject matter of empirical psychology is the observable empirical self (**P** 337). The empirical self is one conditioned in time, and the act of self-observation is similarly a temporally conditioned act. The process of self-examination itself, Kant claims, has the tendency to alter the object of one's examination, such that one cannot grasp unalterable truths regarding one's own self through temporal acts of introspective observation (**MFNS** 471). Transcendental psychology, on the other hand, proceeds via argumentation to uncover the features of the transcendental self that must be operative in order for self-consciousness (→ **apperception**) per se to be possible.

Finally, Kant claims that the type of cognition with which he is concerned, namely → a **priori** cognition, cannot be examined through the methodology of empirical psychology. A priori cognition involves apodictic certainty, i.e. → **necessity** (B4), whereas empirical psychology can only concern itself with facts regarding what is or has been the case, and not what must be the case (A86–87=B119). To uncover the sources of a priori cognition, a different kind of inquiry into our cognitive powers must be pursued. Kant holds this to be true of all a priori judgments, including aesthetic ones (**CJ** 266).

Despite Kant's own achievements with regard to the transcendental conditions of the thinking subject, he ultimately rejects the possibility that empirical psychology could ever achieve the status of a science, properly so called (**MFNS** 471). Apart from the fact that its methodology precludes it from achieving a priori cognition, Kant also holds that since empirical psychology is ultimately concerned with the self as inner appearance, it is not amenable to mathematical quantification of its solely temporal dimension, which is for Kant a necessary feature of genuine science. – JC

FURTHER READING

G. Hatfield, 'Empirical, rational and transcendental psychology: psychology as science and as philosophy', in P. Guyer (ed.), *The Cambridge Companion to Kant* (Cambridge: Cambridge University Press, 1992), pp. 200–227.

T. Sturm, 'How not to investigate the human mind: Kant on the impossibility of empirical psychology', in E. Watkins (ed.), *Kant and the Sciences* (New York: Oxford University Press, 2001), pp. 163–184.

PURE

A cognition (or representation) is pure if it is 'not mixed with anything foreign to it' (A11); more specifically, if no sensation is intermixed with it (A11; A20=B34). 'Pure' is thus very close to → a **priori** in meaning, and these two terms are often used interchangeably. Purity is also closely related to → **form** (in contrast to matter). But occasionally Kant takes care to demarcate purity as a further specification under the concept 'a priori'. This makes it possible for there to be non-pure a priori judgments. Such a judgment contains a concept linked to → **experience**. For instance, the a priori judgment 'Every alteration has its cause' is not pure in this more restrictive sense, since the concept of alteration 'can be drawn only from experience' (B3; cf. **UTP** 183–184).

An important task of Kant's Critical project is to isolate pure uses of faculties, as well as pure types of → **judgment** and → **representation** in the different areas of philosophy. As regards sensibility, its pure forms are found by abstraction of all matter (i.e. sensation) from → **intuition**. In this way, pure intuition is uncovered, and with it the pure forms of sensibility (space and time) (cf. A20–21=B34–35) (→ **Transcendental Aesthetic**). A corresponding investigation of the understanding as to its form leads to the discovery of its pure concepts (the categories) (→ **deduction, judgment**). The pure concepts presuppose pure → **apperception**, whose synthetic unity is 'the highest point' of the understanding (B132–134). → **Reason** too has its pure concepts, namely the transcendental → **ideas** (A321=B378).

In Kant's moral philosophy, a main task is to show that pure reason can be practical, i.e. capable of determining the → **will** against all empirical inclinations (**CPrR** 15) (→ **morality**). Pure practical reason is governed by the pure moral law (→ **categorical imperative**), which is binding for all rational beings.

Also in Kant's aesthetics purity plays a crucial role. Beauty is expressed in a pure → **aesthetic judgment** (pure judgment of taste). As independent of any conceptual determination of the object, and not influenced by feelings of agreeableness, this is grounded only on the 'purposiveness of the form' (**CJ** 223).

Apart from establishing pure principles and cognitions, Kant's Critical philosophy also examines unwarranted claims of purity, as is manifest from the title of **CPR**. The critique of pure theoretical reason surveys reason's attempts to surpass the limits of cognition and diagnoses the transcendental illusion causing these attempts (→ **Dialectic**). 'Pure reason', as the target of → **critique**, denotes the transcendent metaphysics exemplified by rationalism (→ **Wolff**). – MQ

PURE INTUITION → INTUITION

PURPOSIVENESS → TELEOLOGY

QUID JURIS → DEDUCTION

RADICAL EVIL

The term 'radical evil' first appears in Kant's article 'On the Radical Evil in Human Nature' (*Berlinische Monatsschrift*, April 1792, pp. 323–385), which one year later is published as the first part of **R** (1793/1794). It has been the subject of debate ever since whether or not Kant's notion of radical evil implies a rupture with respect to, especially, his practical philosophy or Critical ethics developed during the 1780s.

Some critics also suggest that Kant's notion of radical evil is not radical enough to account for 'absolute evil' (in particular in view of the excessive atrocities of the twentieth century), especially since Kant seems to rule out the possibility of what he calls diabolic evil (cf. esp. **R** 35, 37). However, before endorsing or challenging such criticisms, the specific radicality of Kant's notion of radical evil should be acknowledged, in particular against the background of his moral philosophy (→ **morality**).

The first thing to emphasize, then, is that radical evil concerns a natural propensity in human nature, as conceptually opposed to human nature's original predisposition to the good. Kant defines a propensity as 'the subjective ground of the possibility of an inclination [. . .], insofar as this possibility is contingent for humanity in general'. He writes further: 'It is distinguished from a predisposition in that a propensity can indeed be innate yet may be represented as not being such: it can rather be thought of [. . .] (if evil) as brought by the human being upon himself.' (**R** 29)

This concept of propensity is explicated by using a legal and deontological terminology, because Kant is interested in a propensity to genuine evil, i.e., moral evil, which, since it is only possible as the determination of a free power of choice and this power for its part can be judged good or evil only on the basis of its maxims, must reside in the subjective ground for the possibility of the deviation of the maxims from the moral law. And, if it is legitimate to assume that this propensity belongs to the human being universally [. . .], the propensity will be called a *natural* propensity of the human being to evil. (**R** 29)

The radicality of the Kantian conception lies in the fact that it not only concerns a general weakness or a shortcoming of human nature, nor merely an impurity of the human heart, refusing to adopt the moral law (→ **categorical imperative**) alone as its sufficient incentive, but 'the *perversity* (*perversitas*) of the human heart, for it reverses the ethical order as regards the incentives of a free power of choice' – a perversity or reversal by which 'the mode of thinking [*Denkungsart*] is [. . .] corrupted at its root (so far as the moral disposition [*Gesinnung*] is concerned) [. . .]' (**R** 30; translation amended).

It is this morally evil propensity that deserves the predicate radical insofar as 'it corrupts the ground of all maxims; as natural propensity, it is also not to be *extirpated* through human forces, for this could only happen through good maxims [. . .]' (**R** 37). Simultaneously, Kant maintains that 'it must equally be possible to *overcome* [*überwiegen*] this evil, for it is found in the human being as acting freely' (**R** 37). This is why he forcefully argues that the ground of evil should not be situated in the sensible nature (*Sinnlichkeit*) of the human being, but neither in a corruption (*Verderbnis*) of morally legislative reason itself.

But, if a human being is corrupt in the very ground of his maxims, how is a restoration (*Wiederherstellung*) of the original predisposition to the good at all possible? The only way to reconcile propensity and predisposition is 'by saying that a revolution is necessary in the mode of thinking [*Denkungsart*] but a gradual reform in the mode of sense [*Sinnesart*] [. . .] and [that both] must therefore be possible [. . .] to the human being' (**R** 47–48).

Insofar as we are able to reverse the supreme ground of our maxims by which we were evil human beings, we are in principle receptive to the good, but are not yet good human beings: I can only hope, through hard labour, to find myself upon the path of constant progress from bad to better – without acquiring any insight into 'the depths of [my] own heart (the subjective first ground of [my] maxims)' since it is 'inscrutable [*unerforschlich*]' to me (**R** 51).

According to Kant, the thesis of an innate, radical evil means essentially this: 'We cannot start out in the ethical training of our connatural moral disposition to the good with an innocence which is natural to us but must rather begin from the presupposition of a depravity of our power of choice in adopting maxims contrary to the original ethical predisposition; and, since the propensity to this [depravity] is inextirpable, with unremitting counteraction against it.' (**R** 51)

In all this, it is important to keep in mind that, for Kant, the battle against evil is not so much a problem of (or within) the individual, but from the outset an issue with social and political dimensions and implications. – JV

FURTHER READING

S. Anderson-Gold, P. Muchnik (eds), *Kant's Anatomy of Evil* (Cambridge: Cambridge University Press, 2009).

M. Forschner, 'Über die verschiedenen Bedeutungen des "Hangs zum Bösen"', in O. Höffe (ed.), *Immanuel Kant. Die Religion innerhalb der Grenzen der bloßen Vernunft*, in the series *Klassiker Auslegen* (Berlin: Akademie Verlag, 2011), pp. 71–90.

P. Rossi, *The Social Authority of Reason. Kant's Critique, Radical Evil, and the Destiny of Humankind* (Albany, NY: SUNY Press, 2005), ch. 4.

RATIONAL FAITH → RELIGION

REALITY (OBJECTIVE REALITY)

Reality is the equivalent of the German *Realität*, whereas Kant's term *Wirklichkeit* is usually translated as 'actuality'. Actuality means '[t]hat which is connected with the material conditions of experience' (B266). Everything is actual which 'stands in one context with a perception in accordance with the laws of the empirical progression' (A493=B521). Actuality does not refer to things in themselves but to the objects of perception, which exist 'only in experience, and [. . .] do not exist at all outside it' (A492–493=B521).

Actuality is to be identified with the modal category of 'existence' (*Dasein*) (A80=B106), whereas 'reality' is one of the categories of quality (→ **Anticipations of Perception**). So when Kant speaks of the reality of things he does not, or not in the first instance, mean the reality, or more precisely, the actuality of the objects of → **experience**. Reality, as category, is attributed to the things judged about in terms of the objective determination of the manifold of sensations that are involved in any particular empirical → **judgment**. On the other hand, however, reality must be seen as more than determinate objects of experience, that is, the appearances in experience.

That is to say, Kant makes a distinction between the reality of phenomena, i.e. the objects of experience, and the *realitates noumena*, which are putative 'example[s] of [. . .] pure and non-sensible reality' (B338n.). Kant refers to reality as *realitas phenomenon* and as *realitas noumenon* in the → **Amphiboly** section, where the former relates to 'realities in → **appearance**' and the latter to reality as 'represented only through the pure understanding' (B320). In a *Reflexion*, Kant links this to another distinction, namely between 'absolute' and 'comparative' reality (**Refl 5826**), whereby absolute reality concerns what 'in respect of a thing in general belongs to Being'. In **Refl 4182**, Kant makes clear that reality is either comparative or absolute and that *realitas phenomenon* is not absolute. The latter does not immediately refer to the thing in itself but is only that to which the category of reality is attributed, which is in fact 'the synthesis in an empirical consciousness in general' (A175=B217). The reality meant here corresponds to sensation (B207).

However, in the Schematism chapter Kant asserts that that which corresponds to sensation is 'the transcendental matter of all objects, as things in themselves (thinghood, reality)' (B182=A143). The term 'thinghood' is the English translation of the German *Sachheit*, which Kant equates with 'reality' (B602) in the transcendental sense, i.e. reality regarded as 'transcendental matter' or the noumenal thing in itself rather than as the sensible matter of perception. Only the former is reality in the absolute sense.

By 'objective reality', Kant understands the relation of cognition to an → **object** (A155–156=B194–195), which amounts to an object being 'given in some way', which 'is nothing other than to relate its representation to experience (whether this be actual or still possible)' (ibid.). In other words, '[t]he *possibility of experience* is therefore that which gives all of our cognitions *a priori* objective reality' (ibid.). It is in fact the synthetic unity of concepts in synthetic a priori propositions that establishes objective reality by providing them a 'third thing, namely a pure object' (B196=A157). Similarly, at A109 Kant argues that '[t]he pure concept of this transcendental object [...] is that which in all of our empirical concepts in general can provide relation to an object, i.e., objective reality'.

These distinctions are related to Kant's discrimination between empirical realism and transcendental realism, the former of which he associates with his own → **transcendental idealism**. Empirically real is that which is conditioned by the → **pure** forms of human cognition, which leads Kant to claim that space and time are not transcendentally real (B52–53), but only objectively or empirically real, which comports with their transcendental ideality. – DS

REASON

In → **Baumgarten**'s *Metaphysica*, which Kant used as a course textbook, 'ratio', which is translated as 'ground' (Pars I, *ontologia* §14), is the principle of connectedness of all things. Knowledge of these grounds is ontology or, as Baumgarten indicates, 'architectonic' (ibid., §4), which consists of principles of cognition as well as of objects of knowledge. Kant adopts from his predecessors the idea of an architectonic order of rational knowledge but radically revises it, giving up on the ambition to build 'a tower that would reach the heavens', and offering his readers instead

a modest dwelling 'just roomy enough for our business on the plane of experience' (A707=B735).

The task of surveying reason's cognitive claims takes shape both in his major philosophical works and in his contributions to contemporary debates through his 'popular' essays. A common thread throughout is the notion of → **critique**, that is, the self-examination of reason in order to ascertain which of its claims are 'rightful', viz. valid and rightfully presented for our assent, and which are 'groundless pretensions' (Axi) and must be rejected.

In **CPR**, Kant calls upon reason to undertake 'the most difficult of all its tasks, namely that of self-knowledge' (Axi). That reason is capable of self-knowledge is central to Kant's conception of both philosophical and popular uses of reason. In the domain of → **metaphysics**, or of 'pure reason', Kant's stance is shaped by his analysis of the failure of classical rationalism to establish that a priori reflection yields substantive truths and that it is a reliable procedure of philosophical justification.

Self-knowledge results in the repudiation of certain claims to metaphysical knowledge, a topic analyzed in the Transcendental → **Dialectic** of **CPR**. The negative conclusion of the Transcendental Dialectic is that reason affords us no insights of its own. At the same time, Kant is keen to establish that reason is not 'inactive', as → **Hume** claimed, but capable of self-reflection, self-criticism and, crucially, of offering us guidance in the practical sphere.

Accordingly, the positive conclusion that can be drawn from the Transcendental Dialectic is that reason is capable of setting its own boundaries. The limits of rational reflection are not something we discover, as a brute fact of our human constitution, but rather something which can be accounted for rationally. Reason, as Kant puts it, is 'not like a pupil' who indiscriminately copies his teacher's words, but rather like 'an appointed judge who compels witnesses to answer the questions he puts to them' (Bxiii).

Reason's role in the practical sphere is similarly one of critical scrutiny. In sharp contrast to moral sceptics and naturalists, Kant affirms reason's right to guide our actions. Reason is end-setting in the sense that it enables agents to subject to rational scrutiny the ends they set out to pursue, not just the means they may use to pursue them. Consistently with the conclusions of **CPR**, Kant does not present reason as equipping us with a vision of the good, but rather, with a way of testing our maxims. The law of pure practical reason stipulates that 'the maxim of your will could always hold at the same time as a principle in a giving of universal law' (**CPrR** 30).

Although Kant acknowledges that his theoretical and, in large part, also his moral writings are technical, and that 'the public need take no interest' in such 'subtle investigations' (**CPrR** 163), his aim in setting human reason on a critical path is to secure it from dogmatism and from scepticism. Kant identifies dogmatism with classical rationalism and scepticism with Hume (cf. A856). There are parallels in the general employment of reason.

The dogmatist resembles the popular genius, who 'pleased with its bold flights' mesmerizes his audience into 'enthusiasm' (**OT** 145) (→ **enthusiasm**). The sceptical equivalent is loss of all regard for the bonds of reason and degeneration 'into a misuse and a presumptuous trust in the independence of its faculties from all limitations' (**OT** 146). To avoid such pitfalls, lawful yet critical thinking is of the essence.

In works such as **OT** or **E**, Kant formulates in non-technical terms what it is for our ordinary reasoning to be subject to critical scrutiny. As in **CPR**, at issue is the preservation of reason's authority. When we say of a course of action or a belief that it is rational in everyday life we mean something like 'it makes sense', that we endorse it in some way and think it worthwhile. In Kant's words, reason and rational argument are held in high esteem among 'the common people' (A749; trans. Kemp Smith).

The question then is: to what does reason owe its prestige? In the domain of pure reason, Kant shows that dogmatic faith in reason can lead to irrationality, to contradictions and → **paralogisms**. It is only through the process of critique that reason is able to uphold its authority.

Critical scrutiny is not just the preserve of the philosophical architect, however, it is vital also for the everyday use of reason. Kant's conception of a public use of reason, the freedom to engage in critical discussion in public, is the practical upshot of this basic commitment. As Kant argues, '[r]eason must subject itself to critique in all its undertakings, and cannot restrict the freedom of critique through any prohibition without damaging itself [. . .]' (A738). Freedom is however not anarchy. The enemy of reason is not just 'civil compulsion' and fear of '*one's own investigation*', but also 'lawlessness in thinking' (**OT** 144–145).

While Kant does not lay down any laws for the general employment of reason, he formulates a basic test for critical reasoning: whenever we are urged to accept something, we must ask ourselves whether it is possible to transform either the reason for accepting it or the rule that follows from what is accepted into 'a universal principle for the use of [one's own] reason' (**OT** 146n.). It is through such effort, Kant believes, that we may, as a species, shape our character, bring to fruition our rational abilities and become a 'rational animal' (**Anthr** 321). – KD

FURTHER READING

S. Engstrom, *The Form of Practical Knowledge: A Study of the Categorical Imperative* (Cambridge, MA: Harvard University Press, 2009).
S. Gardner, 'The primacy of practical reason', in G. Bird (ed.), *A Companion to Kant* (Malden, MA/Oxford: Wiley-Blackwell, 2010), pp. 259–274.
O. O'Neill, 'Vindicating reason', in P. Guyer (ed.), *The Cambridge Companion to Kant* (Cambridge: Cambridge University Press, 1992), pp. 280–308.
S. Neiman, *The Unity of Reason: Rereading Kant* (New York: Oxford University Press, 1994).

RECEPTIVITY → SPONTANEITY

REFLECTION → LOGIC

REFLECTION, CONCEPTS OF → AMPHIBOLY

REFLECTIVE JUDGMENT → AESTHETIC JUDGMENT, JUDGMENT

REFUTATION OF IDEALISM

Kant's Refutation of Idealism, which is found in the B-version of **CPR** (B274–279), is explicitly concerned with distancing the → transcendental idealism of CPR from what he calls the '*problematic* idealism' (B274) of → **Descartes**, and the '*dogmatic* idealism' of Berkeley (B274). It is clearly the case that Kant also intends the Refutation to oppose all forms of transcendental realism, which is the view that the mind can know objects as they are in themselves – that is, either by directly intuiting their essence in some sense, or by claiming knowledge of real objects existing independently of the mind (see A369) (→ **thing in itself**).

Not only is Kant concerned, in the Refutation, with defeating a brand of external world scepticism associated with the rationalism of Descartes, but it is clear that he is also challenging a brand of empirical scepticism that one finds in the philosophy of → **Hume** (see Hume, *Treatise of Human Nature*, Bk 1, pt. IV, §II, 'Of scepticism with regard to the senses'). In the B-Preface, in a note (Bxxxix n.) that is intended to supplement the argument of the Refutation, Kant claims that it is a 'scandal of philosophy' that a proof for the existence of external objects has as yet not been forthcoming. So in essence, the Refutation is important for Kant as a positive argument in itself, but, importantly, it is also designed to distance the theory of knowledge put forward in **CPR** from those systems of thought mentioned above.

It is important to mention that Kant inserts the Refutation in the → **Postulates of Empirical Thought** section of the B-edition of **CPR**. This placement is significant due to the fact that the Postulates are inextricably bound up with the modal categories of experience in general. The modal categories of possibility, actuality and → **necessity** are employed in order to 'express only the relation [of the concept] to the faculty of cognition' (A219=B266). Given that the Refutation appears at the end of the Second Postulate, which deals with 'cognizing the *actuality* of things' (B272=A225), we can clearly see that one of its main concerns is to emphasize the centrality of the a priori conditions required for our knowledge of things.

The main content of the Refutation argument can be found in one condensed paragraph at B275–276, along with an important accompanying passage contained in the B-Preface (Bxli). The Theorem basically tells the reader exactly what the argument hopes to achieve overall, which is that if I am conscious of my own existence, as empirically determined, then this proves that I am also aware of objects existing outside of my mind in space.

The Proof starts with the basic claim that what I am most immediately aware of is my own conscious existence: 'I am conscious of my existence as determined in time.' (B275) What Kant is aiming to do at this point is to seemingly offer a tacit agreement with the sceptic's claim that it is almost beyond reproach that I am conscious of my ideas, which appear in successive moments in time. It follows from this that the sceptic maintains that I can never actually be certain of the existence of objects external to the mind. Kant then argues, in the second premise of the Proof, that if I accept the first premise (which appeases the sceptic), then one can only accept it if a condition can be found for the changing states of mind which I undergo.

It is at this point that a remarkable turnaround in the argument ensues, because Kant at once demands that the immediacy of our inner consciousness is only possible if 'something *persistent* in perception' (B275) can be found. In many ways, this is the point in the argument where Kant's claim that 'the game that idealism plays has [. . .] been turned against it' (B276) is most significant. In other words, in order for the empirical idealist to claim that what is immediately known are our own inner representations, something must be perceived outside of us, i.e. in an 'outer sense' (→ **inner/outer sense**).

Building on the above, Kant continues his argument by insisting that the permanent something is made possible through a 'thing' outside me (B275) and then by 'actual things' (ibid.) perceived outside me. The perception of these 'actual things' leads to a key point in the argument, in the penultimate sentence of the paragraph, when Kant claims that my 'consciousness [of my existence] in time' (B276) is inextricably bound up with 'the existence of the things outside me' (ibid.), which condition such time-consciousness. These 'things' stand in as perceptual surrogates for the unchanging permanent structure, which are perceived in space – the realm of outer sense. Kant can now say that my own consciousness in time is 'at the same time an immediate consciousness of the existence of other things outside me' (ibid.).

An intriguing aspect of the Refutation is how Kant separates the role of the → **imagination** from our intuition of space. Claiming that the faculty of → **intuition** would be 'annihilate[d]' (B277n.) should there be no outer sense, Kant argues that without an a priori grasp of something given through pure receptivity there would be no imagination.

It is clear, however, that in order even only to imagine something as outer, that is, to present it to sensibility in intuition, we must already have an outer sense, and must thereby immediately distinguish the mere receptivity of an outer intuition from the → **spontaneity** which characterizes every act of imagination (B277). – NH

FURTHER READING

D. Emundts, 'The Refutation of Idealism and the distinction between phenomena and noumena', in P. Guyer (ed.), *The Cambridge Companion to Kant's 'Critique of Pure Reason'* (Cambridge: Cambridge University Press, 2010), pp. 168–189, pt. I.

P. Guyer, *Kant and the Claims of Knowledge* (Cambridge: Cambridge University Press, 1987), pt. IV.

S. Stapleford, *Kant's Transcendental Arguments: Disciplining Pure Reason* (London/New York: Continuum, 2008), ch. 3.

REGULATIVE PRINCIPLES

The importance of Kant's distinction between constitutive and regulative principles, which respectively relate to the constitution of experiential cognition (→ **knowledge**) and to the mere regulation thereof, can hardly be underestimated since it touches upon the basic structure of his Critical philosophy. In fact, no extensive comment seems to be needed to show that whereas constitutive principles apply legitimately only to the understanding, regulative principles apply to pure → **reason** itself and, therefore, are exemplarily discussed in the → **Dialectic**, the second part of the Logic in **CPR**.

According to Kant's definition, a regulative principle of reason is a rule (Latin: *regula*) prescribing a regress in the series of conditions of possibility for (spatiotemporally) given appearances. That is to say, it concerns not the possibility of (experiential) cognition of objects, as with the constitutive principles of the understanding, but at the same time it does not go fully beyond all possible experience either, as would be the case with a (theoretically unjustifiable) *constitutive* principle of reason. It is then merely a principle that regulates or postulates 'the greatest possible continuation and extension of possible experience', as Kant writes (B537), in terms of a legitimate and consistent account of the subjectively necessary elements of thinking, such

as heuristic ones, that are transcendentally presupposed (see B544).

For one thing, Kant argues that philosophical concepts like → **necessity** and contingency are not objectively valid since they do not pertain to or concern things (i.e. appearances) themselves. They can however be justified as subjective principles of reason, because these concepts or principles encourage and impel us to keep on searching for further (necessary) grounds of what is contingently given, and thus remind us never to assume anything empirical as an unconditioned endpoint of our analysis (cf. B644).

Interestingly, Kant also appeals to his notorious 'as if'-argument to explicate the regulative character of the *summum ens* by stating that '[t]he ideal of the highest being is [. . .] nothing other than a *regulative principle* of reason', and that one should 'regard all combination in the world *as if* it arose from an all-sufficient necessary cause, so as to ground on that cause the rule of a unity that is systematic and necessary according to universal laws' (B647). Clearly, for Kant such a statement implies no assertion of anything existing that is objectively necessary, but precisely denotes a mere formal regulative principle, although he warns that it is unavoidable, by means of what is called a 'transcendental subreption', 'to represent this formal principle to oneself as constitutive, and to think of this [systematic] unity hypostatically' (B647). Thus, it is absolutely crucial to keep in mind that regulative principles involve the constant danger of transcendental illusion (→ **Dialectic**), that is, of mistaking them for constitutive ones by forgetting their objective indeterminacy.

Another example mentioned by Kant could be illuminating from a historical viewpoint, namely that of what he calls 'the widely respected law of the *ladder of continuity* among creatures, made current by Leibniz and excellently supported by Bonnet' (B696). Even though the observation and study of the order of nature could never present this law or principle, i.e. 'the principle of affinity', as something that can be asserted to be objectively true, he argues that the method for the investigation of the order of nature in conformity with such a principle is 'a legitimate and excellent regulative principle of reason', which 'without determining anything, [. . .] only points the way toward systematic unity' (B696) (→ **system**).

Finally, one must point to a distinction that Kant makes – and, in his view, has great importance for transcendental philosophy – between two ways of thinking regarding one and the same presupposition, namely that there can be a 'satisfactory reason for assuming something relatively (*suppositio relativa*), without being warranted in assuming it absolutely (*suppositio absoluta*)'. This distinction seems particularly relevant since the first type of presupposition applies in the case of a regulative principle, 'for which we assume a supreme ground merely with the intention of thinking the universality of the principle all the more determinately [*um desto bestimmter die Allgemeinheit des Princips zu denken*]' (B704). Regulative principles do therefore not imply any absolute assumption regarding the real, or objective, existence of such a supreme or underlying ground, which has only the status of a transcendental → **idea** or → **transcendental ideal**.

The fact that numerous text passages may be cited to illustrate Kant's concept of regulation already shows the general consistency of his views on the need for and status of regulative principles. – JV

FURTHER READING

M. Grier, *Kant's Doctrine of Transcendental Illusion* (Cambridge: Cambridge University Press, 2001), ch. 8.

R.-P. Horstmann, 'Der Anhang zur transzendentalen Dialektik (A642/B670–A704/B732). Die Idee der systematischen Einheit', in G. Mohr, M. Willaschek (eds), *Immanuel Kant. Kritik der reinen Vernunft*, in the series *Klassiker Auslegen* (Berlin: Akademie Verlag, 1998), pp. 525–545.

F. Rauscher, 'The appendix to the Dialectic and the Canon of Reason: The positive role of reason', in P. Guyer (ed.), *The Cambridge Companion to Kant's Critique of Pure Reason* (Cambridge: Cambridge University Press, 2010), pp. 290–309.

RELIGION (HIGHEST GOOD)

In **R**, Kant's philosophical conception, and analysis of, the phenomenon of religion depends heavily on a fundamental distinction, as well as a rather strict hierarchy, between two concepts of religion and religious community.

On the one hand, there is the essentially moral and universal concept of pure 'rational religion' or 'religion of reason' (*Vernunftreligion*), also called pure 'rational faith' (*Vernunftglaube*) or pure 'religious faith' (*Religionsglaube*), or 'natural religion' (*natürliche Religion*), or even simply the 'one (true) religion' (**R** 107). This concept corresponds to the idea of an ethical commonwealth or community according to the laws of → **virtue** (*nach Tugendgesetzen*), which in human history can never be fully attained – due to the → **radical evil** in human nature – but only gradually approximated, as well as to a universal, purely invisible church, or a kingdom of God, beyond civil society or legal institutions, which would ultimately satisfy the unity and universality claims of religion.

On the other hand, there is the essentially historical and statutory concept of 'ecclesiastical faith' (*Kirchenglaube*), also called 'historical faith' or 'statutory religion', 'statutory faith' or 'revealed faith' (*Offenbarungsglauben*), or indeed 'revealed religion' (*geoffenbarte Religion*). This concept corresponds to the different organized churches or various religious denominations, including all their particular beliefs and rites, that exist or have existed (or, for that matter, might exist) positively and visibly in the course of human history.

Famously, in the preface to the second edition (1794) of **R**, Kant uses the image of concentric circles to indicate the relation between his two concepts of religion or faith:

> Since [. . .] *revelation* can at least comprise also the pure *religion of reason*, whereas, conversely, the latter cannot do the same for what is historical in revelation, I shall be able to consider the first as a *wider* sphere of faith that includes the other, a *narrower* one, within itself (not as two circles external to one another but as concentric circles); the philosopher, as purely a teacher of reason (from mere principles *a priori*), must keep within the inner circle and, thereby, also abstract from all experience. (**R** 12)

This picture of two concentric circles, the inner circle of pure rational religion and the wider circle of historical revelation, already reveals the philosophical primacy and priority of pure rational religion. Since, in Kant's view, pure rational religion represents the true inner kernel or final destination of any (possible) historical religion, all historical elements, particular beliefs or religious rites

and cults in the wider sphere should be critically evaluated by the moral and universal standards of the inner one. Moreover, they should ultimately be used for instrumental or provisional reasons only, as a means (or 'vehicle') to an end, namely in order to gradually approximate these a priori standards.

It is important to note that Kant starts his discussion of religion against the background of his Critical practical philosophy (→ **morality**), in particular his doctrine of the moral law (→ **categorical imperative**). Recall, for instance, two famous statements in the preface to the first edition (1793) of **R** regarding, on the one hand, the foundational role of morality and, on the other, the supplementary or functional role of religion, namely for the sake of (the possibility of) morality's efficacy in the world.

First, Kant states that 'morality really has no need of an end for right conduct' since the moral law 'that contains the formal condition of the use of freedom in general suffices to it'. Nevertheless, 'it cannot possibly be a matter of indifference to reason how to answer the question, *What is then the result of this right conduct of ours?*' (**R** 4–5).

Secondly, Kant adds that reason's own interest in the efficacy of the moral law in the world entails 'the idea of an object that unites within itself the formal condition of all such ends as we ought to have (→ **duty**) with everything which is conditional upon ends we have and which conforms to duty (happiness proportioned to its observance)'. What Kant means here is the notion 'of a highest good in the world', the possibility of which presupposes 'a higher, moral, most holy, and omnipotent being' (**R** 5), who alone is able to unite duty and happiness.

What appears to be crucial to Kant's approach, however, is to acknowledge the appropriate order between duty and happiness, between moral foundation and moral end, namely that the idea of a highest good 'rises out of morality and is not its foundation; that it is an end which to make one's own already presupposes ethical principles' (**R** 5). One could of course argue whether, or to what extent, Kant remains completely faithful to these programmatic statements on the relation between morality and religion, between duty and happiness, and on the idea of a highest good in the world and the need of assuming 'a higher, moral, most holy omnipotent being'.

However, there are no profound reasons to doubt the global consistency and coherence of Kant's philosophy of religion, as well as the validity of its major concerns. In essence, it is a theory of morally and rationally warranted hope. Kant writes:

Reason says that whoever does, in a disposition of true devotion to duty, as much lies within his power to satisfy his obligation (at least in a steady approximation toward complete conformity to the law), can legitimately hope that what lies outside his power will be supplemented by the supreme wisdom *in some way or other* (which can render permanent the disposition to this steady approximation). (**R** 171)

The implications of Kant's theory become particularly evident when looking at his views on specific religious issues. Priestcraft (*Pfaffentum*), for instance, is unmasked by Kant as 'a regime in the counterfeit service [*Afterdienst*] of the good principle' (**R** 175) since it is supposed to involve 'the constitution of a church to the extent that a fetish-service [*Fetischdienst*] is the rule; and this always obtains wherever statutory commands, rules of faith and observances, rather than principles of morality, make up the groundwork and the essence of the church' (**R** 179).

And similar arguments are presented against religious worship and religious cult, as being forms of obtaining favour (*Gunstbewerbung*) that obstruct and pervert the moral principle that '[a]part from a good life-conduct, anything which the human being supposes that he can do to become well-pleasing to God is mere religious delusion and counterfeit service of God' (**R** 170–171). – JV

FURTHER READING

J. DiCenso, *Kant, Religion, and Politics* (Cambridge: Cambridge University Press, 2011).

J. DiCenso, *Religion within the Boundaries of Mere Reason. A Commentary* (Cambridge: Cambridge University Press, 2012).

J. E. Hare, *The Moral Gap. Kantian Ethics, Human Limits and God's Assistance* (Oxford: Clarendon Press, 1997), pt. I.

O. Höffe (ed.), *Immanuel Kant. Die Religion innerhalb der Grenzen der bloßen Vernunft*, in the series *Klassiker Auslegen* (Berlin: Akademie Verlag, 2011).

M. Kuehn, 'Moral faith and the highest good', in P. Guyer (ed.), *The Cambridge Companion to Kant and Modern Philosophy* (Cambridge: Cambridge University Press, 2006), pp. 588–629.

L. Pasternack, *Kant on Religion within the Boundaries of Mere Reason* (London, New York: Routledge, 2013).

A. Wood, 'Religion, ethical community, and the struggle against evil', in C. Payne, L. Thorpe (eds), *Kant and the Concept of Community* (Rochester, NY: University of Rochester Press, 2011), pp. 121–137.

REPRESENTATION

'Representation' is the English translation of the Latin *repraesentatio*, which in Kant's German is rendered *Vorstellung*. In **OPD** Kant writes that 'the word "representation" is understood with sufficient precision and employed with confidence, even though its meaning can never be analyzed by means of definition' (**OPD** 70) and in **JL** he states that representation 'cannot be explained at all' (**JL** 34).

Despite this, the concept of 'representation' is crucial for understanding Kant's thought. In fact, in general 'representation' for Kant is a genus that characterizes the faculty of cognition, as it is used in the Wolffian School, especially in → **Baumgarten** and → **Meier**, since cognition always presupposes representation. In a famous letter of 21 February 1772 to → **Herz**, Kant announces that a central concern of his philosophy will be the investigation into answering the question 'What is the ground of the relation of that in us which we call "representation" to the object?' (**Corr-I** 130) (→ **object**).

In **CPR**, representations in general are said to be 'inner determinations of our mind in this or that temporal relation' (B242=A197). In the section 'On the ideas in general' of the Transcendental Dialectic, Kant seems to suggest, in the so-called *Stufenleiter* (B376–377=A320), that 'representation' is indeed the central concept of his transcendental philosophy, which puts us on the way to answering the above-mentioned question.

From the progression of the *Stufenleiter* it can be inferred that not every representation is eo ipso a conscious representation, i.e. a perception, and that there are thus also unconscious representations (cf. **Corr-II** 52). But most importantly, it is clear from the progression passage that only if the representation refers not just to an inner determination of the mind but also to a mind–external object, then it yields a cognition, i.e. a representation that has an object.

A representation is furthermore an → **intuition** when it is singular and immediately refers to the object (*repraesentatio singularis*), while it is a concept or a universal representation (*repraesentatio per notas communes*) or reflected representation (*repraesentatio discursiva*) (**JL** 91), when it refers to the object by means of the mediation of a mark.

In **CPR**, Kant further argues that representations are either → **pure** or empirical. Pure representations are representations in which 'nothing is to be encountered that belongs to sensation' (A20=B34). Empirical representations contain sensation, which presupposes the actual presence of the object (cf. A50=B74). A representation can also be either clear or obscure. A representation 'is clear if the consciousness in it is sufficient for *a consciousness of the difference* between it and others', while it is obscure 'if this consciousness suffices for a distinction, but not for a consciousness of the difference' (B415n.). → **Logic** deals only with clear but not with obscure representations, and it does not show how representations arise, but merely how they agree with logical → **form** (cf. **JL** 33).

All clear representations can be distinguished in regard to distinctness and indistinctness. If there is consciousness 'of the whole representation, but not of the manifold that is contained in it, then the representation is indistinct' (**JL** 34). A distinct representation can be either sensible, when it 'consists in the consciousness of the manifold in intuition', or intellectual, when it 'rests on the analysis of the concept in regard to the manifold that lies contained within it' (**JL** 35). – MS

**RESPECT → MORALITY,
CATEGORICAL IMPERATIVE**

RIGHT

In Kant's writings, the German noun *Recht*
and adjective *recht* translate into English as
'right' or 'justice' and 'just' respectively. *Recht*
means either a system of laws that govern the
external relationships between individuals –
and in this sense it comes close to what we
now call justice – or *a* right, i.e. one of the
rights established by those laws. The adjective *recht* qualifies actions that conform to
those laws. The crucial meaning is therefore
the first one while the others depend on it.

Kant spells out the content of right (in
the first sense) in the part of **MM** entitled
Metaphysical First Principles of the Doctrine
of Right. There, he asserts that by right he
does not mean to refer to 'what the laws in
some country at some time prescribe' (**MM**
229). This is a question that the jurist must
answer. Kant is rather interested in the philosophical question of 'whether what these
laws prescribed is also right, and what the
universal criterion is by which one could
recognize right as well as wrong (*iustum et
iniustum*)'. The universal principle of right
says that 'any action is *right* if it can coexist
with everyone's freedom in accordance with
a universal law, or if on its maxim the freedom of choice of each can coexist with everyone's freedom in accordance with a universal
law' (**MM** 229–230).

To understand why this alone constitutes
the universal principle of right one needs to
recall the conclusions Kant reached in other
areas of his philosophical system, and especially in his moral philosophy (→ **morality**).
There Kant argued that humans are autonomous beings, i.e. capable of authentic moral
agency. In autonomy lies the source of their

dignity, the basis of the respect due to them,
and the ground of the innate or natural right
they have, i.e. the right to → **freedom**, understood as 'independence from being constrained by another's choice' (**MM** 237).

A just system of laws has to take into
account this innate right and treat humans
accordingly. From these premises the universal principle of right follows analytically.
Each citizen is entitled to the largest sphere
of free agency possible with the sole limiting
condition that the same amount of freedom
be secured to all other citizens. Any limitation of the freedom of each that does not
arise from the necessity of securing the same
amount of freedom to all others is wrong.
Any coercion exercized by the state, then, is
legitimate if and only if it is aimed at securing for all citizens the same amount of freedom and impeding arbitrary enlargements
of one person's freedom at the expense of
others'.

In Kant's opinion, the universal principle
of right is valid for any culture, tradition, or
group because it rests on → **reason** (a faculty
common to all humans). It is not inferred
from a sociological survey of actual juridical
systems existing around the world. Since it is
universally valid, it can be used as a test of
the justice of any existing system of laws.

In **MM** Kant distinguishes between private right and public right. Private right
encompasses the rights we have in the state
of nature, while public right is 'the sum of the
laws which need to be promulgated generally
in order to bring about a rightful condition'
(**MM** 311). That there are rights against others in the state of nature – a claim in contrast
with the Hobbesian tradition – is a direct
consequence of that moral quality (autonomy) that Kant, as we saw, attributes to all
humans. It is ultimately because humans are
autonomous and therefore worthy of respect

that they can legitimately claim to be entitled (to have a right) to certain treatment by other individuals or groups.

Kant's account of private right begins with an analysis of the conditions on which things could be 'mine or yours'. Kant thinks that anyone can acquire and own property (a piece of land or any other object of choice) – a tenet in direct contrast with feudalism and slavery. This possibility follows directly from the pre-political, innate right to external freedom. In the section 'Postulate of practical reason with regard to rights', he argues that if one were denied *in principle* the possibility of acquiring and owning an object, then one would be deprived of the means with which to exercize one's external freedom. As he puts it: '[F]reedom would be depriving itself of the use of its choice with regard to an object of choice, by putting *usable* objects beyond any possibility of being *used*.' (**MM** 250)

In a state of nature something external can thus be mine or yours, but, says Kant, 'only provisionally' (**MM** 256). A provisionally rightful possession becomes 'conclusive' only if the state of nature is overcome and a civil condition is created. The moral status of the state as well as the → duty for anyone who lives side by side with others to enter the civil condition rest on the fact that the state protects rights already present in the state of nature. They do not depend on some empirical fact about human nature, such as its propensity to violence.

Public right has three main subdivisions: state right, the right of nations (or international right) and cosmopolitan right (→ cosmopolitan, cosmopolitanism). State right spells out how a state should look in order to guarantee humans' pre-political entitlements. The state must (1) recognize the freedom, equality and independence of all members, (2) be a republic, i.e. a state characterized by

a division of powers (legislative, executive, judiciary) and by the fact that all its citizens *could consent* to the enacted laws.

The second subdivision of public right – the right of nations – defines the rules that should govern international relations. Since nations stand to one another very much like individuals in the state of nature, Kant argues that they should enter a 'universal *association of states*', where 'rights come to hold *conclusively* and a true *condition of peace* [will] come about' (**MM** 350).

The third and final subdivision of public right – cosmopolitan right – concerns the rules all nations should adopt in the treatment of foreign individuals, especially those who visit for the sake of commerce or cultural exchange. Individuals hold, Kant thinks, a right 'to *visit* all regions of the earth' (though not to stay), while they try 'to establish a community with all' (**MM** 353). Cosmopolitan right is one of Kant's most important innovations in legal theory and is recognized as laying the foundations for contemporary declarations and treatises of human rights. – LC

FURTHER READING

B. S. Byrd, J. Hruschka, *Kant's Doctrine of Right. A Commentary* (Cambridge: Cambridge University Press, 2010).

O. Höffe (ed.), *Immanuel Kant: Metaphysische Anfangsgründe der Rechtslehre*, in the series *Klassiker Auslegen* (Berlin: Akademie Verlag, 1999).

W. Kersting, *Wohlgeordnete Freiheit. Immanuel Kants Rechts- und Staatsphilosophie*, third edition (Paderborn: mentis, 2007).

R. Pippin, 'Mine and thine? The Kantian state', in P. Guyer (ed.), *The Cambridge Companion to Kant and Modern*

Philosophy (Cambridge: Cambridge University Press, 2006), pp. 416–446.

SCHEMATISM

'On the schematism of the pure concepts of the understanding' is a notoriously difficult, but important section of **CPR**. The schematism deals with the way in which concepts and intuitions are related. It concerns the subsumption of objects under concepts. The need for special explanation arises because of Kant's theory of concepts (→ **logic**) combined with his position that '[i]n all subsumptions of an object under a concept the representations of the former must be homogeneous with the latter [. . .]' (A137=B176).

According to Kant, all our cognition 'contains two very heterogeneous elements, namely a *matter* for cognition from the senses and a certain *form* for ordering it [. . .]' (A86=B118) (→ **form**). Intuitions and concepts are the two distinct necessary elements of all our cognition. A concept is a discursive → **representation** that 'is always something general, and something that serves as a rule' for unifying representations (A106). Conversely, intuitions are imagistic representations that provide the specific particular content of our cognition (→ **intuition**).

On the one hand, then, subsumption under a concept requires that the representation of an object be homogeneous with the concept, but, on the other hand, Kant's theory of concepts requires that intuitions and concepts are two distinct types of mental representation – that is, they are heterogeneous. Kant's task in the schematism chapter is to explain, in the light of this heterogeneity, how subsumption under a concept is possible.

According to Kant, subsumption under a concept requires the use of a schema.

If concepts and intuitions were ultimately a single type of mental representation, as they were for his predecessors, e.g. → **Leibniz** and → **Hume**, then there would be no apparent problem explaining how subsumption works. If, for example, they were both like images (à la Hume), they would be genuinely homogeneous, so the intuition and concept could be directly compared. However, when concepts and intuitions are different types of mental representation (heterogeneous), there must be some third thing that can mediate between them (A138=B177) – something that transforms the discursive content in a concept into determinate intuitive content. This third thing is a schema and Kant holds that a concept 'is always related immediately to the schema of the imagination, as a rule for the determination of our intuition in accordance with a certain general concept' (A141=B180).

According to Kant, the schema of a concept is the 'representation of a general procedure of the imagination for providing a concept with its image' (A140=B179–180) (→ **imagination**). With empirical concepts, 'the *image* is a product of the empirical faculty [*Vermögen*] of productive imagination' (A141=B181). For example, with the concept of a dog 'my imagination can specify the shape of a four-footed animal in general, without being restricted to any single particular shape that experience offers me or any possible image that I can exhibit *in concreto*' (A141=B180).

With mathematical concepts, for example the concept of a triangle, the schema 'signifies a rule of the synthesis of the imagination with regard to pure shapes in space', and 'is a product and as it were a monogram of pure *a priori* imagination' (A141–142=B180–181).

Schemata for pure concepts, however, are not rules for producing spatial images.

According to Kant, '[t]he schema of a pure concept of the understanding, on the contrary, is something that can never be brought to an image at all, but is rather only the pure synthesis, in accord with a rule of unity according to concepts in general, which the category expresses, and is a transcendental product of the imagination, which concerns the determination of the inner sense in general, in accordance with conditions of its form (time) in regard to all representations [. . .]' (A142=B181).

That is, in the case of a pure concept, the schema produces, or is, a transcendental time determination (A138–139=B177–178). For example, the schema for the pure concept of substance is 'the persistence of the real in time', '[t]he schema of actuality is existence at a determinate time', and '[t]he schema of necessity is the existence of an object at all times' (A144–145=B183–184).

The schematism chapter is important because in the Transcendental Deduction (→ **deduction**) Kant has proven that experience is only possible through the categories, but in the Analytic of Principles (→ **Analogies of Experience, Axioms of Intuition, Anticipations of Perception**) the goal is to prove that those categories have objective use (A161=B200), that is, application to spatiotemporal objects. To do this, the conditions for subsumption under a concept must be specified and this is what schemata do. 'Thus the schemata of the concepts of pure understanding are the true and sole conditions for providing them with a relation to objects, thus with significance [*Bedeutung*] [. . .]' (A145–146=B185).

For all of its importance for Kant's theory of concepts and the Analytic of the Principles, the biggest concern with Kant's exposition of the schematism is his lack of explanation of the precise details of the procedure. Kant in fact tells us that 'their mere form is a hidden art in the depths of the human soul, whose true operations we can divine from nature and lay unveiled before our eyes only with difficulty' (A141=B180–181).

This lack of detail becomes particularly acute with the schemata for the categories. With the schemata for pure concepts, Kant forgoes the 'dry and boring analysis of what is required for transcendental schemata of pure concepts of the understanding in general' (A142=B181), and he simply lists their schemata without any argument for their correctness. – SB

FURTHER READING

H. Allison, *Kant's Transcendental Idealism. An Interpretation and Defense*, revised and enlarged edition (New Haven: Yale University Press, 2004), ch. 8.

S. Bayne, *Kant on Causation. On the Fivefold Route to the Principle of Causation* (Albany, NY: SUNY Press, 2004), ch. 1.

M. Pendlebury, 'Making sense of Kant's schematism', *Philosophy and Phenomenological Research* 55,4 (1995): 777–797.

SCIENCE → NATURAL SCIENCE, METAPHYSICS, CRITIQUE

SELF-ACTIVITY → SPONTANEITY

SELF-LEGISLATION → FREEDOM

SENSATION → ANTICIPATIONS OF PERCEPTION

SENSIBILITY → EXPERIENCE

SPACE → TRANSCENDENTAL AESTHETIC, GEOMETRY, ANTINOMIES

SPONTANEITY

Kant contrasts spontaneity with receptivity, where spontaneity is the way in which an empirical object is cognized by means of the representations that are first received by the mind (A50=B74). Cognition arises from these two 'fundamental sources of the mind', that is, from the combination of the spontaneity and receptivity of the power of representation (B130–131). More precisely, it is 'concepts [which] are [. . .] grounded on the spontaneity of thinking, as sensible intuitions are grounded on the receptivity of impressions' (B93), whose combination yields → knowledge.

The spontaneity of cognition is the understanding determining the manifold, rather than being the determinable, which is the manifold given to it (B150–152; see also B156–157n.). The spontaneity of the determinative understanding is uncaused, that is, itself not further determinable as to its cause, but is also only a spontaneously determining cause relative to the receptivity in empirical intuition and therefore cannot be determined absolutely (cf. B430).

Spontaneity is linked to Kant's notion of a priori → synthesis. The spontaneity of thought rests on the idea that because a concept rests on a function, viz. the unity of an action of ordering different representations under a common one (A68=B93), our thought or understanding must first run through the manifold of impressions, given by means of receptivity, in order to have a unified representation. This action is synthesis, which is required for the combination of a manifold of representations to form an objective unity that refers to an object of possible experience. In abstraction from a concrete empirical manifold and its unification in an act of synthesis, the act of thought is 'merely the logical function and hence the sheer spontaneity of combining the manifold of a merely possible intuition' (B428).

However, the 'sheer spontaneity' of thought, 'taken in itself' (ibid.) does not imply a theoretical grasp of the *absolute* spontaneity of the thinking agent, the 'I', that is, as itself an uncaused cause in the absolute, metaphysical sense (→ **Paralogisms**). Nevertheless, in contrast to the relative spontaneity of thought in theoretical cognition, reason always seeks 'an *absolute* causal *spontaneity* beginning *from itself*' (A446=B474), a cause that is uncaused by the causal chain of natural mechanisms (cf. A533=B561; A445ff.=B473ff.) (→ **Antinomies**). Such a cause has particular relevance in relation to the possibility of transcendental → **freedom**.

This notion of transcendental freedom as a self-determining cause outside the 'continuous natural chain' (**CPrR** 95) plays a crucial role in the way we must conceive of ourselves as rational agents, who rather than possessing the relative spontaneity of a 'turnspit' (**CPrR** 97) – where freedom would for instance consist merely in the subjective representation of the '*mechanism* of nature', a kind of '*automaton* [. . .] *spirituale*' (ibid.) – must be seen as having 'absolute spontaneity' to freely will an action (**CPrR** 48; cf. **LM** 269).

In the latter case, the agent possesses the capacity of 'pure self-activity [*Selbstthätigkeit*]' of reason, by means of which he 'distinguishes himself from all other things, even from himself insofar as he is affected by objects' (**G** 452). This must be seen in contrast to the self-activity of the understanding, which 'though [. . .] does not, like sense, contain merely representations that arise when we are *affected* by things (and are thus passive), yet [. . .] can produce from its activity no other concepts than those which serve merely *to bring sensible representations under rules*' (G 452). Here, self-activity rests on the function of combination that the understanding must operate in order for a given manifold of representations to have a synthetic structure, which is 'not given through objects' (B130). Self-activity in this sense is thus merely relative to the need for combination of the sensible manifold in receptivity that the manifold itself does not contain. → **Reason**, on the other hand, shows to be 'a spontaneity so pure that it thereby goes *far beyond* anything that sensibility ever can afford it' (G 452; emphasis added).

Kant thus appears to discriminate between the spontaneity involved in the act of understanding, which is linked to receptivity, and the absolute spontaneity of reason, which is far removed from it. Herein, Kant's concept of spontaneity must be distinguished from that of his successors such as Fichte and Hegel, who clearly conflated the two capacities. – DS

FURTHER READING

H. Allison, 'Kant on freedom: A reply to my critics', in *Idealism and Freedom. Essays on Kant's Theoretical and Practical Philosophy* (Cambridge: Cambridge University Press, 1996), pp. 109–128, esp. pt. IV.
H. Allison, 'Autonomy and spontaneity in Kant's conception of the self', in H. Allison, *Idealism and Freedom*, pp. 129–142.
R. Pippin, 'Kant on the spontaneity of mind', in *Idealism as Modernism. Hegelian Variations* (Cambridge: Cambridge University Press, 1997), pp. 29–55.

SUBLIME

In the early work **Obs**, Kant presents an anthropological examination that distinguishes the feeling of the beautiful from the sublime. The first section of this work examines the different manners in which various objects arouse these pleasurable feelings. The second and third sections extend these observations and draw from them distinct features of human beings in general and of the two sexes (**Obs** 211–227, 228–243).

Roughly, sublimity has to do with moral and noble qualities and is diametrically opposed to the ridiculous, while beauty is closely associated with refinement and tenderness and is opposed to disgust. The last section offers a differentiation between national characteristics, based on the particular proportions of beauty and sublimity in them.

In the Critical period, the Analytic of the Sublime in **CJ** draws a comparison between the beautiful and the sublime as the two types of pure → **aesthetic judgment**. They are both characterized as unique feelings that are the affective aspect of a particular relation between two cognitive faculties. Therefore, although they are triggered by natural objects or events, their 'satisfaction does not depend on a sensation [. . .] nor on a determinate concept' (**CJ** 244). Both judgments are characterized as singular, disinterested, universally valid, subjectively purposive and necessary.

The sublime is awakened by an amorphous object, which appears to be extensively unlimited, and is therefore related to the quantity of the representation. It is a feeling 'that arises only indirectly' (**CJ** 245). Specifically, judgments of the sublime involve a negative interaction between the → **imagination** and → **reason**. The imagination apprehends the object, but its lack of → **form** is contrapurposive and our finite imagination is inadequate to encompass it. The imagination comes face to face with its own boundaries. Therefore, sublimity is felt as displeasure. Indirectly however, the mind 'is incited to abandon sensibility and to occupy itself with ideas that contain a higher purposiveness' (**CJ** 246).

The sublime is divided into two forms: (1) the mathematical sublime is related to the faculty of cognition, whereas (2) the dynamical sublime is related to the faculty of desire (**CJ** 247). Each of these judgments expresses a different disposition of the mind to its failure of representation and provokes a distinctive idea of reason. Both are 'similar to the moral disposition' (**CJ** 268).

The mathematical sublime is aroused by a representation of 'raw nature' (**CJ** 253) that is absolutely or incomparably great. The imagination fails in its attempt to estimate aesthetically such a totality. But '*even to be able to think* the given infinite without contradiction requires a faculty in the human mind that is itself supersensible' (**CJ** 254). Reason is the capacity that redirects the mind to attempt to grasp this totality by means of the 'idea of the absolute whole' (**CJ** 260). Sublimity, then, is the feeling of respect for the 'superiority of the rational vocation of our cognitive faculty over the greatest faculty of sensibility' (**CJ** 257).

The dynamical sublime, conversely, is provoked by a fearful representation of natural power (**CJ** 260). Its immeasurability exposes our vulnerability and 'physical powerlessness' (**CJ** 261). But indirectly, it makes us recognize that as moral subjects we are not threatened by and, therefore, are independent of and indeed superior to nature (**CJ** 261–262). – AR

FURTHER READING

H. Allison, *Kant's Theory of Taste: a Reading of the Critique of Aesthetic Judgment* (Cambridge: Cambridge University Press, 2001), ch. 13.

R. Clewis, *The Kantian Sublime and the Revelation of Freedom* (Cambridge: Cambridge University Press, 2009).

P. Crowther, *The Kantian Sublime. From Morality to Art* (Oxford: Oxford University Press, 1989).

J.-F. Lyotard, *Lessons on the Analytic of the Sublime*, trans. E. Rottenberg (Stanford: Stanford University Press, 1994).

SUBSTANCE → ANALOGIES OF EXPERIENCE, PARALOGISMS

SYNTHESIS (SYNTHETIC A PRIORI)

The concept of synthesis is central to Kant's Critical philosophy, in particular to the arguments of the → **Deduction** and the → **Analogies** in CPR. It forms the core of his analysis of the possibility of → **knowledge**. Synthesis accounts for the possibility of establishing a unity in a manifold of representations, which in the series of states of consciousness 'would never constitute a whole' (A103), from which alone cognition can arise, without it. Kant follows → **Hume** in believing that the unity of representations is not ipso facto given with the successive generation of a manifold of representations. Neither is the analytic unity among subordinated series of conceptual representations sufficient for our thoughts to yield knowledge of objects.

This is so because of the nature of our discursive thought. If we did not recognize in consciousness *that* a unity obtains among the multitude representations, any representation, 'as contained in one moment', would just be an 'absolute unity' (A99), rather than a synthetic whole. '[E]very individual representation' would be 'isolated and separated' (A97) from every other. Therefore, 'in order for *unity* of intuition to come from this manifold [. . .], it is necessary first to run through and then take together this manifoldness [*Mannigfaltigkeit*], which action I call the synthesis of apprehension' (A99).

In fact, the way in which the manifold 'as such, and indeed as contained *in one representation*' (ibid.) can be represented is by means of a discursive synthesis, namely 'through [. . .] successive addition of one to the other' (A103). In other words, the very manifold can only be *conceived as manifold* through synthesis, which gives it unity.

In the run-up to the Deduction, in §10, where Kant provides the clue to the discovery of the categories, Kant defines synthesis as 'the action of putting different representations together with each other and comprehending their manifoldness in one cognition' (A77=B103). Although at first Kant describes synthesis in general as 'the mere effect of the imagination, of a blind though indispensable function of the soul' (B103=A78) (significantly, in his own copy of **CPR** Kant substitutes 'understanding' for 'soul'), later he makes clear that synthesis is always either an act of the understanding (B130), or an effect of the understanding (B151–152). At any rate, 'pure synthesis [. . .] yields the pure concept of the understanding' (A78=B104), i.e. the category, which is an *a priori* synthesis, or a 'synthesis in accordance with concepts (ibid.). The set of the categories are the set of the functions of a priori synthesis.

Whereas in the A-Deduction Kant appears to differentiate more obviously between the various aspects of a priori synthesis – 'synthesis of apprehension in the intuition', 'synthesis of reproduction in the imagination' and 'synthesis of recognition in concepts' (A98–100) – so that it thus seems as if separable acts of synthesizing are involved of which only the last is an act of the understanding, in the B-Deduction it is made sufficiently clear that all a priori syntheses come down to 'an action of the understanding' (B130).

This is only logical, as Kant means a priori synthesis as an original unitary ground of cognition, more fundamental than which no ground can be given. It is this original unity, also called 'the original-synthetic unity of apperception' (B131, heading) (→ **apperception**) that 'makes the concept of combination', and hence any synthesis, 'first possible' since nothing is combined if not by an act of combination (B131). This possibility rests on the → **spontaneity** of the act of synthesizing of the manifold of representations so as to yield a unity among one's representations that constitutes conceptual knowledge.

Later in the B-Deduction, Kant differentiates between intellectual synthesis and figurative synthesis, also called transcendental synthesis of the → **imagination** (B151–152), which accounts for the difference between respectively the a priori combination of conceptual representations in a judgment and the equally a priori combination of representations in a concrete empirical intuition, which together give a judgment objective validity. The figurative synthesis in productive imagination is then not a distinct act of combination, but 'an effect of the understanding on sensibility' (B152) or the way the understanding affects → **inner sense** (B155).

The a priori synthesis of the productive imagination, which is the spontaneity of the understanding that affects inner sense, must be distinguished from the reproductive imagination, 'whose synthesis is subject solely to empirical laws, namely those of association', which belongs not to transcendental philosophy but to → **psychology** (B152; cf. B139–140).

The synthetic a priori plays a pivotal role in all of Kant's arguments in **CPR** after the Deduction, in particular of course in the chapter that deals with the synthetic a priori principles that govern possible experience, viz. the → **Axioms of Intuitions** →, the → **Anticipations of Perception,** the → **Analogies of Experience** and the → **Postulates of Empirical Thinking in General.**

But the concept of synthesis also plays a significant role in the Dialectic, in particular in the First and Second → **Antinomies** and in the → **transcendental ideal,** where Kant argues for an even more fundamental synthesis than the synthesis of the understanding, namely a 'synthesis of all predicates which are to make up the complete concept of a thing'; this synthesis constitutes the 'transcendental presupposition [. . .] of the material *of all possibility*, which is supposed to contain *a priori* the data for the *particular* possibility of every thing' (A572–573=B600–601).

Here, synthesis is not meant as the formal necessary condition of conceiving of a unified manifold of representations so as to determine an → **object** as → **appearance,** but as the metaphysical condition, viz. the principle of thoroughgoing determination, that first enables the individual thing in its very being, as a → **thing in itself.** This synthesis involves a concept, or → **idea,** which can never be exhibited *in concreto,* in contrast to the synthesis of the pure concept of the understanding that by means of an empirical intuition can thus be exhibited. – DS

FURTHER READING

H. Hoppe, *Synthesis bei Kant* (Berlin/New York: de Gruyter, 1983).

P. Kitcher, *Kant's Thinker* (New York: Oxford University Press, 2011), ch. 8.

B. Longuenesse, *Kant and the Capacity to Judge* (Princeton: Princeton University Press, 1998), chs 1, 2, 8 and 9.

D. Schulting, *Kant's Deduction and Apperception. Explaining the Categories* (Basingstoke/New York: Palgrave Macmillan, 2012).

SYNTHETIC A PRIORI (JUDGMENT) → **SYNTHESIS, JUDGMENT, ANALOGIES OF EXPERIENCE**

SYNTHETIC JUDGMENT → **JUDGMENT**

SYSTEM

The notion of 'system' is, for Kant, intrinsically linked with scientific knowledge: a systematic unity makes a system out of an aggregate of → **knowledge,** which then serves as the basis for scientific knowledge (B860ff.). 'System' here means the unity of various cognitions (as parts) under an → **idea** (B860; cf. B673). This idea, which is a concept of → **reason,** determines a priori the limits of its parts as well as their place within the whole. The intrinsic relationship between whole and parts, as well as between the parts themselves, ensures that the system will only expand through internal differentiation, like an organism, and not through an external addition of parts (B860ff.).

Furthermore, the → **form** of a system is not an external feature of reason, but reason itself, for reason is by nature architectonic (e.g. B502, 673, 676, 835) and systematic (B765ff.). In this subjective respect, reason aims at totality: with reason we form a unity out of our cognitions. Hence reason, in the broad sense, deals with itself (cf. e.g. B708).

Systematicity is a general characteristic of both philosophy and scientific knowledge. Undoubtedly, Kant thought of Euclidean → **geometry**, Aristotelian → **logic**, or the mechanics of → **Newton** and Kepler, as paradigmatic systems. However, for methodological reasons such systems cannot adequately deal with the question of their *foundation*. Especially the mathematical → **method** with its axiomatic-deductive proofs (→ **proof**) shows crucial shortcomings in the way it can scientifically justify its own axioms, or, presuppositions.

Kant, therefore, introduces a new method for philosophy, namely → **transcendental** philosophy. Contrary to many of his predecessors, for Kant the ground of the validity of a system cannot be a system external to reason itself. The system of knowledge and the system of what is known, respectively the subject and object of knowledge, must be intrinsically related.

However, for Kant the systematic unity of reason itself does not have a constitutive function. On the contrary, the unity of reason has merely a regulative function that unites the knowledge of the understanding. Consequently, Kant denies that the unity of reason has objective reality. The system as architectonic unity thus is merely a regulative → **idea** of reason (→ **regulative principles**). The unity of reason remains a postulate; it is not the concept of an object of possible experience, but the idea of the thoroughgoing unity of knowledge gained by understanding (B670ff.).

In **CJ** Kant broadens his concept of a system, as nature too is now taken, by virtue of the power of reflective judgment, to be a system (→ **teleology**). But he holds on to the regulative status of this unity. In **OP**, Kant then tries to transform the subjective unity into an objective one.

As far as the internal structure of the system of transcendental philosophy is concerned, according to Kant it consists of, roughly speaking, a level of → **critique** and a level of → **metaphysics**, also called 'doctrine'. In conformity with this general structure, Kant's final system of philosophy has three critical parts and two doctrinal parts: the critical parts provide a radical foundation for the determination of the objects to be determined in the doctrinal parts.

In particular, it was Kant's view that the unity of reason merely has a regulative, subjective character which inspired the development of post-Kantian idealism towards a conception of a system of philosophy that should overcome Kant's dualistic model of constitutive and regulative principles. The post-Kantians strived for a higher form of unity of reason: one that incorporates a constitutive function. Reason then turns out not to be a system in a merely subjective way aiming at systematization, but reason is also a system in an objective sense: it is the constitutive foundation for possible objectivity, and hence not only regulative for the knowing subject. – CK

FURTHER READING

P. Abela, 'The demands of systematicity: rational judgment and the structure of nature', in G. Bird (ed.), *A Companion to Kant* (Malden, MA/Oxford: Wiley-Blackwell, 2010), pp.408–422.

H. Fulda, J. Stolzenberg (eds), *System der Vernunft. Kant und der deutsche Idealismus. Bd. 1, Architektonik und System in der Philosophie Kants* (Hamburg: Meiner, 2001).

P. Guyer, *Kant's System of Nature and Freedom: Selected Essays* (Cambridge: Cambridge University Press, 2005).

N. Rescher, *Kant and the Reach of Reason* (Cambridge: Cambridge University Press, 2000), ch. 4.

TABLE OF CATEGORIES → DEDUCTION

TABLE OF JUDGMENT → DEDUCTION, JUDGMENT

TASTE → AESTHETIC JUDGMENT

TELEOLOGICAL JUDGMENT → TELEOLOGY, JUDGMENT

TELEOLOGY (PURPOSIVENESS, END)

Teleology or purposiveness is essential to descriptions of rational agency and seems to be unproblematic. This is not at all the case in descriptions of natural laws and processes (→ **laws (of nature)/lawfulness**), which according to the canons of modern science are blind rather than purposive.

Teleological notions and ideas are prevalent in Kant's works. They appear already in the pre-Critical period (most notably perhaps in **OPD** 87–89; see also **ND** 412–416).

In the Critical period, teleology is important in two related contexts. First, the assumption that organisms are to be viewed teleologically or purposively is fundamental in the biological papers on race (**DR, HR, UTP**) and it underwrites Kant's conception of universal history and the development of humankind: '*All natural predispositions of a creature are determined sometime to develop themselves completely and purposively* [. . .] An organ that is not to be used, an arrangement that does not attain to its end, is a

contradiction in the teleological doctrine of nature.' (**UH** 18)

It is, however, only in the Analytic of the Teleological Power of Judgment of **CJ** that Kant systematically elaborates the claim that organisms (including human beings), their organs, systems and capacities are viewed as if they were designed to serve ends.

Second, in the 'Appendix' to the Transcendental Dialectic of **CPR** and in the 'Introduction' to **CJ**, Kant appears to claim that the assumption of the purposiveness of nature is a necessary transcendental condition of experience and knowledge generally. We necessarily regard nature *as though* it were made to be known by our distinctive cognitive faculties. Although his language can sometimes be misleading, Kant consistently regards teleology as an assumption only, however, and never asserts that there *are* teleological forces or purposive beings in nature; nowhere does he contradict the modern scientific commitment to blind mechanistic causality.

It is of great importance to see that the point of departure of the Analytic in **CJ** is the fact that we commonly speak of organisms as if they were self-organizing beings. For this fundamental fact implies in itself that we view them as goal-directed. Kant writes: '*An organized product of nature is that in which everything is an end and reciprocally a means as well*. Nothing in it is in vain, purposeless, or to be ascribed to a blind mechanism of nature.' (**CJ** 376)

Again, despite such misleading language, Kant is not asserting that certain natural objects *are* purposive. Teleology is simply the conceptual framework through which we judge these objects. Kant writes:

[I]n teleology we certainly talk about nature as if the purposiveness in it were intentional, but at the same time ascribe this intention to nature, i.e., to matter, by which we would indicate (since there can be no misunderstanding here, because no intention in the strict sense of the term can be attributed to any lifeless matter) that this term signifies here only a principle of the reflecting, not of the determining power of judgment, and is thus not meant to introduce any special ground of causality [. . .]. (CJ 383)

Although we describe organisms teleologically, all natural laws and so all scientific explanations are mechanistic, as Kant asserts:

It is of infinite importance to reason that it not allow the mechanism of nature in its productions to drop out of sight and be bypassed in its explanations; for without this no insight into the nature of things can be attained. (CJ 410)

Apparently, Kant never argues for the claim that we must judge certain objects as purposive. He simply assumes we do. Moreover, organic life is not a necessary phenomenon (CJ 193–194, 359–360). What then grounds his claim that teleological judgment is necessary? On the prevalent interpretation, Kant claims that the assumption that nature is purposive for our cognitive capacities directs us to search for more general and more specific empirical regularities and so erect a more unified and comprehensive → system of knowledge. This methodology is indeed a presupposition of the empirical investigation of nature. But it is not a necessary condition of any empirical → experience and cannot properly be said to be → transcendental.

On the stronger and controversial reading, the very employment of any empirical universal concept presupposes that nature is constituted by such universal regularities and is, in this manner, purposive for our

discursive minds. Our very employment of universal empirical concepts attributes to nature a greater unity than a finite mind can ever encounter. The assumption that nature is purposive for our conceptual minds is thus a necessary condition of our employment of any empirical concept. This may explain why Kant claims that the 'principle of the purposiveness of nature (in the multiplicity of its empirical laws) is a transcendental principle' (CJ 181).

Finally, in the Methodology of the Teleological Power of Judgment, Kant argues that the purposiveness we attribute to any organism necessarily leads to the question why it exists and this, in turn, to the idea of the ultimate end of creation. The human being as moral is 'alone capable of being a final end, to which the whole of nature is teleologically subordinated' (CJ 436). Thus, there is 'a *physical teleology* which gives our theoretically reflecting power of judgment a sufficient basis for assuming the existence of an intelligent world-cause' (CJ 447). This theoretical argument is the counterpart of the argument of Kant's practical philosophy for the highest good as the final end of creation, which is a '*moral teleology*' (CJ 447). – IG

FURTHER READING

I. Geiger, 'Is the assumption of a systematic whole of empirical concepts a necessary condition of knowledge?', *Kant-Studien* 94 (2003): 273–298.

I. Geiger, 'Is teleological judgment (still) necessary? Kant's arguments in the Analytic and in the Dialectic of Teleological Judgment', *British Journal for the History of Philosophy* 17 (2009): 533–566.

P. McLaughlin, *Kant's Critique of Teleology in Biological Explanation* (Lewiston, NY: Edwin Mellen, 1990).

M. Quarfood, 'The antinomy of teleological judgment', in M. Quarfood, *Transcendental Idealism and the Organism* (Stockholm: Almqvist & Wiksell, 2004), pp. 160–208.

THING IN ITSELF

In the Preface to the B-edition of **CPR**, Kant first contrasts appearances (→ **appearance**) with 'things as they are in themselves' (Bxx), and then explains that his Critical approach (→ **critique**) to the problem of pure speculative reason has the consequence that 'we can have cognition of no object as a thing in itself' (Bxxvi). Kant's justification for the latter claim follows from his proofs, in the → **Transcendental Aesthetic**, that space (A26=B42) and time (A32=B49) do not represent properties of things in themselves; as a result, we do not gain cognitive access to things in themselves when we acquire → **knowledge** of spatiotemporal objects. The notion of 'thing in itself' is thus introduced to refer to things as they are independently of our cognition.

This can be interpreted in a number of ways: (a) as a purely methodological claim, namely that the objects of our spatiotemporal knowledge can be considered independently of this spatiotemporal mode of access, i.e. as they are in themselves; (b) as a metaphysical claim about the different modes of access to what we know as spatiotemporal objects, which defines a perspective upon them that transcends cognition, and from which they are viewed as they are in themselves; (c) as a metaphysical claim about the nature of things

which belong to a world that is distinct from our spatiotemporal world of appearances; (d) as a metaphysical claim about the nature of things which do not thereby define a world that is distinct from that of our spatiotemporal objects. These are the methodological and metaphysical two-aspect theories, the two-world, and the two-perspective theories respectively, which have become standard in the Anglophone Kant literature (→ **transcendental idealism**).

While no knowledge of reality in itself is possible, Kant does allow for us to have thoughts about things as they are in themselves (Bxxvi); he adds that in so doing, we would be thinking of them as that which appears as the objects of our spatiotemporal → **experience** (ibid.). In thinking of things in themselves, a useful tool is the concept of the 'transcendental object' (B63; A109), by which Kant refers to the general conceptual structure of an → **object**. Kant sometimes uses this to refer to things in themselves (A380; B506; B522; A613–614=B641–642), but, importantly, no knowledge claim is made through this use, not even that the thing in itself is an object of any particular sort.

To think of things in themselves is to think of an intelligible world, and in the → **Dialectic** of **CPR**, Kant will both dismantle the claims made by traditional → **metaphysics** of cognitive access to truths about the soul, the world, and God, while showing in what way reason necessarily forms ideas about the intelligible world which regulate the progress of our knowledge (→ **Paralogisms**; → **Antinomies**; → **proofs of the existence of God**; → **regulative principles**). Barring cognitive access to the intelligible world has a further systematic function in Kant's Critical system: as Kant puts it, 'I had to deny knowledge in order to make room for faith' (Bxxx): Kant shows that belief in God and the immortality of the soul are required by → **morality** (A809–811=B837–839; **CPrR** 121–133).

Our epistemic situation with respect to things in themselves is, however, not only characterized by the prohibition of knowledge (A42=B59). Indeed, first, while it is not possible to know anything about things in themselves, there is evidence that Kant endorsed the minimal claim that things in themselves exist (**P** 315), although this is a contentious issue among commentators. It is however initially not clear how it is possible to make such a claim, as it seems to go beyond the bounds of knowledge established in the Analytic of **CPR**.

Second, if we are to think of things in themselves as appearing as spatiotemporal objects, for such appearances to come about it is necessary that our sensibility be first affected (A19=B33): this is a transcendental condition of appearing. This relation of affection is typically interpreted as involving things in themselves having a causal impact upon us, although there are interpreters who rather understand spatiotemporal objects as the prime candidates for what affects us, and others who view the need for a combination of both, i.e. hold a theory of double affection.

These two controversial issues of the existence of, and affection by, things in themselves, come together in a way that Kant's contemporary Friedrich Jacobi (1743–1819) famously deemed to amount to an inconsistency in Kant's Critical system. Jacobi complained that, while it is not possible to enter this system without presupposing the existence of the thing in itself, neither is it possible to affirm its existence within the system. There are, additionally, arguably grounds for viewing such existence claims as denied by Kant himself. Kant considers the possibility of objects of knowledge that are not phenomenal, i.e. not objects of our sensible intuition. These he calls noumena, and while noumena are characterized only negatively (B306), one can also consider a positive characterization of noumena as objects of a non-human non-sensible type of cognition, i.e. of an intellectual intuition or intuitive understanding (B307). Kant clearly says that we cannot claim that positive noumena exist (A286–287=B343). Such a denial of the possibility of existence claims about noumena in the positive sense does not, however, translate into a denial that things in themselves exist unless these things are thereby claimed to be objects of some sort (noumena). Rather, Jacobi's claim that it is not possible to claim that things in themselves exist can be refuted by pointing to the difference between determinate knowledge of things in themselves (which is denied by Kant) and indeterminate knowledge of something that affects us, something, of which we cannot even say that it is an object but is nonetheless presupposed as a ground for knowledge.

Jacobi's complaint set the scene for the post-Kantian dismissive attitude to things in themselves. The German Idealists Schelling and Hegel dispensed with the notion of thing in itself altogether by seeking a ground to their systems of thought that does not appeal to anything beyond thought. Schopenhauer, on the contrary, did away with the denial that knowledge of things in themselves is a possibility, by claiming that in fact reality in itself is 'the Will', as opposed to the representations to which we have access in our normal cognition. – CO

FURTHER READING

Adickes, E., *Kant und das Ding an sich* (Berlin: Pan, 1924).

Allison, H., *Kant's Transcendental Idealism: An Interpretation and Defense*, revised and enlarged edition (New Haven: Yale University Press, 2004), ch. 3.

Prauss, G., *Kant und das Problem der Dinge an sich* (Bonn: Bouvier, 1974).

Schulting, D., J. Verburgt (eds), *Kant's Idealism. New Interpretations of a Controversial Doctrine* (Dordrecht: Springer, 2011).

THOROUGHGOING DETERMINATION → TRANSCENDENTAL IDEAL

TIME → TRANSCENDENTAL AESTHETIC, ANTINOMIES, SCHEMATISM

TRANSCENDENT → TRANSCENDENTAL

TRANSCENDENTAL

Kant generally uses the notion 'transcendental' to restrict the scope of a subject in terms of the a priori requirements for → **experience**, which have their origin in our cognitive faculties rather than in objects. So, for example, Kant writes that 'I call all cognition transcendental that is occupied not so much with objects but rather with our mode of cognition of objects insofar as this is to be possible *a priori*' (B25) (→ **a priori, a posteriori**). Thus, transcendental logic, as opposed to general → **logic**, which applies to all 'representations wherever they may have originated', is restricted to representations that 'are originally given *a priori* in ourselves' (A56=B80).

Transcendental, however, can also modify the use or employment of a transcendental principle. It is given transcendental employment when we attempt to apply it to something that is not an object of possible experience – when we give it 'a use that reaches out beyond the boundaries of experience' (A296=B352–353).

Both senses of transcendental are to be contrasted with the term transcendent. A transcendent principle is one that inherently denies that our theoretical cognition is limited to the boundaries of experience. On the contrary, it is 'a principle that takes away these limits, which indeed bids us to overstep them, [and therefore] is called transcendent' (A296=B353). – SB

TRANSCENDENTAL AESTHETIC (INTUITION, SPACE, TIME)

Kant's epistemology is constructed upon a model of cognition that assumes a distinction between the faculties of sensibility and understanding – with the addition of the faculty of → **reason** to account for the role of theory in → **knowledge**. The separation between sensibility and the understanding reflects a distinction between two types of → **representation**, intuitions and concepts. Intuitions are characterized as immediate representations of an object (A19=B33), but also as the representation of a particular (A32=B47–48) (→ **intuition**). Both characteristics distinguish intuitions from concepts: concepts are universal representations, which represent objects only through the mediation of intuitions (A19=B33).

In making this distinction, Kant apportions a passive role to sensibility, in contrast to the active role of the understanding discussed in the Transcendental Analytic (B129–130) (→ **spontaneity**). Sensibility thus has the function of receiving a manifold of sensations, which are located spatially and temporally in an intuitive representation (A20=B34).

In the Transcendental Aesthetic, Kant's task is to examine intuitive representations, with the aim of identifying any eventual a priori contribution made by intuitions to the cognition of objects. Unlike the Transcendental Analytic, which first has to identify concepts that have a transcendental function (this occurs in the so-called Metaphysical Deduction; → **deduction**), the intuitions of space and time are already known to be the subject matter of the Transcendental Aesthetic.

On the other hand, unlike the categories, the nature of space and time as intuitive representations is problematic. Aside from dealing with this issue (A24–25=B39–40; A31–32=B47–48), the 'Metaphysical Exposition' establishes the → **a priori** nature of the representations of space and time. This identifies them as having a → **transcendental** function in cognition, and as accounting for the possibility of certain synthetic a priori judgments (e.g. those of → **geometry** in the case of space, B40–41).

Kant presents two arguments for the intuitive nature of the representations of space (and similar arguments in the case of time). The part-whole relations of space are characterized by containment of parts in a unique all-encompassing space which is logically prior to them. In the case of a concept, the relation is different: the concept's intension is defined by a set of marks (A320=B377) that are its parts; but these marks are prior to the concept. Correlatively, the whole of space prior to all these parts is unique; this is not the case for a concept since the concept as a whole always refers to a potential multiplicity of instances, its extension (→ **logic**).

Aside from the part–whole relation, space differs from a conceptual representation in that it is infinite (in the sense of limitless: its quantum is infinite). Our understanding

could not grasp a concept defined by an infinite number of marks. A concept's extension could be infinite, but this would amount to an infinity of instances *under* the concept. By contrast, an infinity of parts is thought *within* space (B39–40): only an intuition could thus be infinite.

As we shall see, Kant's claim that the representations of space and time are a priori is at the core of his → **transcendental idealism**. His arguments are aimed at philosophers holding sensationist or constructivist theories of spatiotemporal cognition, chiefly → **Leibniz** and → **Locke**. The latter view spatial relations as deriving from non-spatial relations respectively of monads and sensible data (and the same goes for time).

Focusing on space (the case of time is analogous) in his first argument, Kant draws attention to the impossibility of constructing spatial relations out of non-spatial ones: space is not derived from empirical data. What space allows is the representation of the data in intuition as relating to things that are taken 'not merely as different but as in different places' (A23=B38). In particular, space has the transcendental function of enabling the representation of purely numerical differences in outer sense (→ **identity**).

The priority of space with respect to empirical data and its necessity in experience are confirmed in the second argument. Kant's claim that 'one can never represent that there is no space' (A24=B38) establishes its → **necessity**, while the claim that 'one can very well think that there are no objects to be encountered in it' (ibid.) confirms its priority.

The 'Transcendental Exposition' shows why the representation of space must be an a priori intuition if the science of geometry is to be possible. Insofar as geometric judgments are amplificatory, and not merely clarificatory

(A7=B10–11; B14–17), they must be synthetic (→ **judgment**). This is only possible if spatial representations enable us to go 'beyond the concept' (B41): they must be intuitions. And insofar as geometric knowledge is apodictic, these intuitions must be a priori.

Important metaphysical conclusions are derived from these epistemological considerations (A26=B42; A32–33=B49–50). Insofar as the intuition of space is a priori, space 'represents no property at all of any things in themselves nor any relation of them to each other' (A26=B42). If space is to have the transcendental functions described above, its representation cannot be derived from things in themselves (→ **thing in itself**).

Therefore, no Leibnizian (relational) or Newtonian (absolutist) (→ **Newton**) theory of space could account for the role of the representation of space described above. This, however, seems to leave a big gap in the argument to the conclusion that things in themselves are not spatial. If it has been shown that space is one of the 'subjective condition[s] of sensibility' (A26=B42), there remains the neglected alternative (raised by Reinhold and, most famously, Trendelenburg) that space should also be a property of things in themselves.

If space (and time), and the 'extended beings' in it, are transcendentally ideal, Kant claims that space also possesses 'empirical reality' (A26–28=B42–44) (→ **reality**). That is, judgments about objects located in space are valid as long as they are understood to refer to the human standpoint, i.e. as long as it is understood that these things 'be taken as objects of our sensible intuition' (ibid.).

As indicated above, the Transcendental Aesthetic must consider intuitions in abstraction from concepts. In the → **Axioms of Intuition**, Kant shows how the manifold in intuition is first synthesized under the categories of quantity. This occurs 'through the synthesis of the manifold through which the representations of a determinate space or time are generated' (B202), i.e. the synthesis of composition of homogeneous parts of the single space. Such a → **synthesis** is thought in the concept of magnitude, so that the appearances we perceive are all 'extensive magnitudes' (B203).

It is this synthesis that Kant refers to in a famous footnote in the Transcendental Deduction (B160–161n.), where he explains that it is presupposed by the unity of space. This defines space as a 'formal intuition', aside from its general role as 'form of intuition' for the manifold of sensations. Although this synthesis makes concepts of space (as in geometry) possible, its unity 'precedes all concepts' (B161n.). The meaning of this claim is much discussed in the literature. What it suggests is the possibility of considering syntheses under a given category (here, categories of quantity) which do not issue in a conceptual determination; this has important implications for the question of non-conceptual content in Kant. – CO

FURTHER READING

H. Allison, *Kant's Transcendental Idealism: An Interpretation and Defense*, revised and enlarged edition (New Haven: Yale University Press, 2004), ch. 5.

J. V. Buroker, *Kant's Critique of Pure Reason. An Introduction* (Cambridge: Cambridge University Press, 2006), ch. 3.

L. Falkenstein, *Kant's Intuitionism* (Toronto: Toronto University Press, 1995).

C. Onof, D. Schulting, 'Space as form of intuition and as formal intuition. On the note to B160 in Kant's *Critique of Pure Reason*', *The Philosophical Review* 124,1 (2015).

L. Shabel, 'The Transcendental Aesthetic', in P. Guyer (ed.), *The Cambridge*

Companion to Kant's 'Critique of Pure Reason' (Cambridge: Cambridge University Press, 2010), pp. 93–117.

TRANSCENDENTAL APPERCEPTION → APPERCEPTION

TRANSCENDENTAL DEDUCTION → DEDUCTION

TRANSCENDENTAL DIALECTIC → DIALECTIC

TRANSCENDENTAL IDEA → IDEA, IDEAS

TRANSCENDENTAL IDEAL

The doctrine of the transcendental ideal is not among the most frequently debated ones in Kant scholarship. Yet it plays quite an important role in understanding the general status of the → Dialectic and even the nature of Kant's → transcendental idealism. Not least, the doctrine of the transcendental ideal of reason is intrinsically connected to the principle of thoroughgoing determination since it is this principle for which the ideal of reason is supposed to serve as transcendental prototype.

In order to grasp the function of the transcendental ideal, it is crucial to recall Kant's definition of an ideal:

[S]omething that seems to be even further removed from objective reality than the idea is what I call the *ideal*, by which I understand the idea not merely *in concreto* but *in individuo*, i.e., as an individual thing which is determinable, or

even determined, through the idea alone. (B596)

This definition shows that the concept of an ideal is linked exclusively to the → **ideas** and principles of reason (→ **regulative principles**), and only indirectly or analogously to the understanding's categories and principles (→ **deduction, Analogies of Experience**). Therefore, the object of reason's ideal is to be found 'only in reason', whereby the ideal does not signify 'the objective relation of an actual object to other things, but only that of an *idea* to *concepts*' (B606–607). In fact, the ideal of reason concerns only what Kant calls an 'object in the idea' (B698–699; B724–725), or a 'scheme' (B702, 707, 710–712, 725, 727) for the sake of an idea or principle of reason, such as the principle of thoroughgoing determination.

At the same time, the fact that the object of reason's ideal is explicated in theological terms (e.g. as *ens realissimum*, *ens originarium*, *ens summum* and *ens entium*), and especially Kant's statement that 'the ideal of pure reason is the object of a transcendental *theology*' (B608), seems to worry some scholars. This statement is best understood in terms of the apparently transcendental question that is formulated by Kant towards the end of the section: 'How does reason come to regard all the possibility of things as derived from a single possibility, namely that of the highest reality, and even to presuppose these possibilities as contained in a particular original being [*Urwesen*]?' (B609)

On the one hand, Kant asserts that the answer to this question suggests itself on the basis of the Analytic by stating, first, that the possibility of empirical objects, i.e. appearances, is a relation of these objects to our thought, in which the → **form** can be thought a priori while what materially makes up the → **reality** in them has to be given through sensation. Secondly, however, there seems to be more at stake in Kant's analysis of the ideal when he writes that 'the material for the possibility [*Materie zur Möglichkeit*] of all objects of sense has to be presupposed as given in one sum total [*Inbegriffe*]' and that 'all possibility of empirical objects, their difference from one another and their thoroughgoing determination, can rest only on the limitation [*Einschränkung*] of this sum total' (B610).

Thus, Kant claims that the principle of thoroughgoing determination presupposes, as its grounding condition, a transcendental substrate, a non-empirical notion of materiality, which in turn is identified with the idea of an *omnitudo realitatis*. He writes:

[I]f the thoroughgoing determination in our reason is grounded on a transcendental substratum, which contains as it were the entire storehouse of material from which all possible predicates of things can be taken, then this substratum is nothing other than the idea of an All of reality [*All der Realität*] (*omnitudo realitatis*). (B603)

In a sense, Kant's doctrine of the transcendental ideal centres on the insight that it is only in the case of *omnitudo realitatis* that reason produces the thoroughgoing determination of what is thought in the idea and hence is capable of a genuine ideal. Kant even describes this in terms of the notorious notion of the → thing in itself, by asserting that '[t]hrough this possession of all reality [*Allbesitz der Realität*]' is a representation possible of 'the concept of a *thing in itself* which is thoroughly determined' (B604).

At the same time, from the concept of an *ens realissimum* which is the concept of 'an individual being' that is determined by means of each of all possible predicates that absolutely belong to it, it follows that the idea of *omnitudo realitatis* not just concerns a transcendental ideal, but also 'the one single genuine ideal of which human reason is capable', as it is 'only in this one single case an – in itself universal – concept of one thing thoroughly determined through itself, and cognized as the representation of an individual' (ibid.).

On the other hand, due to what Kant calls a transcendental illusion, irremediably attached to human reason (→ **Dialectic**), we have a natural propensity to hypostatize and personify the idea of the sum total of all reality. Kant writes that such a hypostatization and personification come about because, time and again, we dialectically, that is, illegitimately though unavoidably, transform 'the *distributive* unity of the use of the understanding in experience, into the *collective* unity of a whole of experience' and subsequently 'from this whole of appearance [. . .] think up an individual thing containing in itself all empirical reality', which we then confuse 'with the concept of a thing that stands at the summit of the possibility of all things, providing the real conditions for their thoroughgoing determination' (B610–611).

That is also the reason why Kant stresses that the objective of the Dialectic is not just 'to describe the procedure of our reason and its dialectic', but also 'to discover its sources, so as to be able to explain this illusion itself [. . .]; for the ideal we are talking about is grounded on a natural and not a merely arbitrary idea' (B609). Thus the doctrine of the transcendental ideal affirms the need, at the level of the Dialectic, to give a fundamental explanation for reason's dialectical proceedings. – JV

FURTHER READING

J. Ferrari, 'Das Ideal der reinen Vernunft', in G. Mohr, M. Willaschek (eds), *Immanuel Kant. Kritik der reinen Vernunft*, in the series *Klassiker Auslegen* (Berlin: Akademie Verlag, 1998), pp. 491–521.

M. Grier, 'The Ideal of Pure Reason', in P. Guyer (ed.), *The Cambridge Companion to Kant's 'Critique of Pure Reason'* (Cambridge: Cambridge University Press, 2010), pp. 266–289.

J. Verburgt, 'How to account for reason's interest in an ultimate prototype? A note on Kant's doctrine of the transcendental Ideal', in D. Schulting, J. Verburgt (eds), *Kant's Idealism. New Interpretations of a Controversial Doctrine* (Dordrecht: Springer, 2010), pp. 237–254.

TRANSCENDENTAL IDEALISM (APPEARANCE, THING IN ITSELF, PHENOMENA, NOUMENA)

Transcendental idealism centres on a distinction between things as they appear to us, or appearances, and things as they are in themselves. Kant argues that we cannot have cognition of things as they are in themselves, and that things as they appear to us are 'mere representations' (A30=B45), which are in some way limited to human cognition, or a human standpoint. The things that appear to us, to which our knowledge is limited, are objects in space and time which causally interact with our senses (→ **thing in itself; appearance**).

Thus, Kant argues that we cannot have knowledge of non-spatiotemporal things, such as God, or Cartesian souls, and that objects in space and time are in some sense representations which exist in relation to human cognition. Transcendental idealism is first fully presented and argued for in **CPR**, and features to some extent in almost all Kant's subsequent works.

Kant presents transcendental idealism as a completely revolutionary position, which he compares to the Copernican revolution in astronomy. He says that Copernicus had the revolutionary thought that what appear to be movements of heavenly bodies around the earth might in fact be attributed to the movement of the earth, the position from which we observe the heavenly bodies (Bxvi–Bxvii).

Similarly, Kant proposes that we attribute some of what appear to be features of the objects of experience to the experiencing subject, or to the point of view from which we cognize the world. Kant argues that this revolution in thinking about the relation between subjects and the objects of cognition will enable us to resolve the question of whether and how → **metaphysics** is possible, to explain the a priori conditions of empirical → **knowledge,** to avoid Cartesian scepticism, to show that metaphysical and scientific knowledge of God (→ **proofs of the existence of God**), free → **will** (→ **freedom**) and immortality (→ **Paralogisms**) is not possible, while showing that free will is metaphysically possible, and making room for the ideas of God, free will and immortality playing a role in our thinking and morality.

The main places where Kant presents and argues for the position are the → **Transcendental Aesthetic,** which concerns space and time, and the → **Antinomies,** which is part of his critique of traditional metaphysics. In these sections, he defines transcendental idealism, respectively, as making the following claims:

[A]bsolutely nothing that is intuited in space is a thing in itself, and that space is not a form that is proper to anything in itself, but rather that objects in themselves are not known to us at all, and that what we call outer objects are nothing other than mere representations of our sensibility, whose form is space, but whose true correlate, i.e., the thing in itself, is not and cannot be cognized through them, but is also never asked after in experience. (A30=B45)

[E]verything intuited in space or in time, hence all objects of an experience possible for us, are nothing but appearances, i.e., mere representations, which, as they are represented, as extended beings or series of alterations, have outside our thoughts no existence grounded in itself. (A490–491=B518–519)

Thus, central to understanding the position is making sense of what it means to say that objects in space are mere representations, giving an account of Kant's reasons for thinking that we cannot know things in themselves, as well as an account of what his commitment to things in themselves amounts to – that is, whether it is a commitment to an actually existing aspect of → reality.

In the → Transcendental Aesthetic, Kant argues that our representation of space (and then, in parallel arguments, time) is → a priori (not derived from experience) and is an → intuition. The role of intuition, according to Kant, is to give us the objects about which we think, something, Kant believes, concepts could never do. Kant argues that space and time are the a priori forms of our intuition, and concludes from this that space 'represents no property at all of any things in themselves' (A26=B42) and that '[s]pace is nothing other than merely the form of all appearances of outer sense, i.e., the subjective condition of sensibility, under which alone outer intuition is possible for us' (ibid.). A priori intuition is supposed to explain the possibility of synthetic a priori knowledge (→ synthesis, Analogies of Experience), and to lead to idealism.

In the Antinomies, Kant argues that the way we think about the world in the pursuit of empirical knowledge drives us unavoidably to contradictory conclusions, when we try to think about the extent of the world in space and time, the divisibility of matter, freedom of the will, and the first cause of the world. He argues that contradictions arise because we only ever have knowledge of things which are conditioned (dependent), but seek total explanations which require something unconditioned (something which would not need further explanation), and we assume that if we are given something conditioned, the unconditioned will also be given (→ Dialectic).

Our empirical thinking seems both to involve and not to involve the idea of the unconditioned, leading us to contradictory claims about the empirical world thought as a totality. Kant argues that positing his proposed distinction between things in themselves and appearances enables us to resolve this contradiction: we have knowledge of appearances only, which contain nothing which is unconditioned. The idea that where there are conditioned things there must be something unconditioned appears to us only as a principle of reason (→ regulative principles), but it is not in fact true of the spatio-temporal world of which we have experience. While we need to give the principle a role in our thinking, we need not think that it is true of the world we experience.

In addition to talking about things as they appear to us and things as they are in themselves, Kant talks about phenomena and noumena. Phenomena are objects which are given to our senses and which have been thought through the categories (→ deduction). Noumena are objects which are known by a pure intellect, without sense experience. Kant explains his notion of things in themselves by distinguishing between a positive and a negative sense of the term 'noumenon'. The positive notion of noumenon is the notion of a distinct kind of object: one which is not spatio-temporal, and which does not affect our senses, but rather would be known by the intellect alone. Putative examples of such an object would be God, Cartesian souls, Leibnizian monads, and, perhaps, platonistically understood numbers.

Kant argues that we cannot have knowledge of such objects, including knowledge that there are any, and do not even really understand what such objects would be. In the negative sense, however, the notion of noumena refers to the things of which we have knowledge (through sense experience), thought of in abstraction from what we know about them through the senses. Kant says that the notion of things as they are in themselves should be understood in terms of the notion of noumena in the negative sense.

Kant explicitly distances his position from Berkeleian idealism, which he sees as an example of the position he calls empirical idealism, which doubts the existence of objects in space, or denies that we cognize them immediately (A369; A491=B519). Kant says that space and objects in space are ideal in a *transcendental* sense, saying that space 'is nothing as soon as we leave aside the condition of the possibility of all experience, and take it as something that grounds the things in themselves' (A28=B44). At the same time, he insists that objects in space are real, and that we have immediate experience of them, as opposed to inferring their existence as the causes of certain merely mental states. – LA

FURTHER READING

L. Allais, 'Kant's argument for transcendental idealism in the Transcendental Aesthetic', *Proceedings of the Aristotelian Society* 110,1 (2010): 47–75.

L. Allais, 'Kant's idealism and the secondary quality analogy', *Journal of the History of Philosophy* 45,3 (2007): 459–484.
H. Allison, 'Transcendental realism, empirical realism and transcendental idealism', *Kantian Review* 11 (2006): 1–27.
D. Schulting, J. Verburgt (eds), *Kant's Idealism. New Interpretations of a Controversial Doctrine* (Dordrecht: Springer, 2010).

**TRANSCENDENTAL LOGIC →
DEDUCTION, JUDGMENT**

**TRANSCENDENTAL REFLECTION →
AMPHIBOLY**

**TRANSCENDENTAL UNITY OF SELF-
CONSCIOUSNESS → APPERCEPTION**

TRUTH

According to the nominal definition of truth, truth is 'the agreement of cognition with its object' (A58=B82). The → object is the common ground of intersubjective agreement, 'through which the truth of the judgment is proved' (A821=B849).

Despite the wealth of passages where Kant equals truth to agreement with the object (e.g. A237=B296; LL 219, 718, 823), there is some controversy as to whether Kant really adheres to a correspondence theory of truth, or if he only refers to it in a preliminary fashion. It might seem more plausible to construe Kant's view as a coherence theory of truth, since idealism can be taken to hold that the objects of cognition are subordinated to the subject and therefore cannot serve as independent truthmakers (→ transcendental idealism). But this interpretation is based on too subjective a construal of Kant's idealism. Its empirical realism countenances objects with which judgments can agree. The a priori determinations of objects prescribed by the categories and forms of → **intuition** are taken by Kant to be conditions for the possibility of true and false judgments about objects. In that sense, the Transcendental Analytic is a '*logic of truth*' (A131=B170), making cognition of objects possible. Coherence is a feature of the systematicity of cognition (→ **system**) required by → **reason**, rather than of truth as such.

A couple of qualifications are needed here, however. First, agreement with the object does not explain the truth of *analytic* judgments (→ **judgment**). Such a judgment lacks a corresponding object, since its predicate merely repeats marks contained in its subject concept, and therefore amounts to a conceptual analysis of the subject concept. Its truth can be cognized through the law of contradiction alone (A151=B190) (→ **principle of (non-) contradiction**). The explanation of the truth of an analytic judgment lies in its formality (→ **form**). In addition to a synthetic judgment's material agreement with its object, truth has a 'formal aspect' that 'consists in agreement with the laws of the understanding' (A294=B350). Although this can refer to the principles of transcendental logic which determine the form of an empirical object, it also applies to general → **logic**, so that a statement true merely in virtue of logic can be said to agree with the formal conditions of thought rather than to an object (cf. A59=B84).

Second, there are passages where Kant may seem to cast doubt on the adequacy of the received definition of truth (A57–60=B82–84; JL 50–51). However, what is here in critical focus is not correspondence, but the notion of a general criterion of truth. Such a criterion would be 'valid of all cognitions without any distinction among their objects' (A58=B83). But that would amount to abstracting from all content or relation to an object, and yet such content is

what truth consists in (according to the received definition). It is in this sense, as a demand for a general and sufficient criterion, that the question '*What is truth?*' is absurd and leads to absurd answers, a situation Kant compares to the sight of 'one person milking a billy-goat while the other holds a sieve underneath' (A58=B82–83).

From an ethical point of view, truthfulness is 'the greatest virtue in the world' (LL 62). Though one can be mistaken as to the truth of what one says, 'one can and must stand by the *truthfulness* of one's declaration or confession, because one has immediate consciousness of this'; for as regards what we hold as true, we do not need to compare it with an object, but only 'with the subject (before conscience)' (MT 267). Kant holds that truthfulness is a → **duty**, however great the disadvantage it may lead to (SRL 426); notoriously, this is a duty towards everyone, even to a murderer at our door. – MQ

FURTHER READING

G. Prauss, 'Zum Wahrheitsproblem bei Kant', in G. Prauss (ed.), *Kant. Zur Deutung seiner Theorie von Erkennen und Handeln* (Cologne: Kiepenheuer & Witsch, 1973), pp. 73–89 [also in *Kant-Studien* 60,2 (1969): 166–182].

A. Vanzo, 'Kant on the nominal definition of truth', *Kant-Studien* 101,2 (2010): 147–166.

UNCONDITIONED, THE → **ANTINOMIES, IDEA/IDEAS, REGULATIVE PRINCIPLES**

UNDERSTANDING → **JUDGMENT, KNOWLEDGE**

UNITY OF CONSCIOUSNESS → **APPERCEPTION**

VIRTUE, VIRTUES

The Doctrine of Virtue is the second part of Kant's **MM**, that in which he treats the general ethical, rather than political, requirements of → morality. There he defines virtue as the strength with which one prioritizes morally good reasons over other reasons, and vice as the prioritizing of the latter reasons when they conflict with the former.

Kant thus considers virtue and vice to be matters of one's reasoning, rather than of one's dispositions or habits of feeling or understanding, and allows that one can be neither virtuous nor vicious, if one prioritizes moral reasons without the strength associated with virtue.

He also claims that, since they concern reasons and not only actions, virtues and vices both leave some playroom in terms of precisely which actions reflect them (cf. **MM** 379–380, 383–384, 389–390, 394–395, 399–410).

Kant proceeds to identify specific virtues as specific morally good reasons and specific vices as the reasons which oppose them, and to divide virtues and vices into two kinds according to the basic reasons, or 'ends', that they concern. He argues in particular for a range of virtues and vices concerning human beings generally, irrespective of their more specific circumstances.

Those concerned with 'perfecting' one's own agency prohibit suicide and self-harm, erotic fantasizing, drunkenness and gluttony, lying, avarice, and servility, and promote the cultivation of one's mental and physical capacities and one's performance of morally good actions for morally good reasons. Kant considers it a vice to be servile, for instance, because moral reasons consider all affected agents equally – in his terms, they consider all affected agents as 'ends in themselves' (→

kingdom of ends), rather than as valuable only relative to inclinations that they might be used as a 'thing' or 'means' to satisfy (**MM** 434–437).

The general virtues and vices concerned with others' happiness, on the other hand, prohibit arrogance, defamation, and ridicule and promote beneficence, gratitude and sympathy. For example, Kant regards beneficence as a virtue because moral reasons are those for which one could want everyone to act in similar circumstances, and considering others only self-interestedly would conflict with one's own self-interest when one finds oneself in need (**MM** 453).

He denies that virtues and vices can concern other ends than one's own perfection and others' happiness, since one inevitably pursues one's own happiness and others' agency can be perfected only by themselves. But he claims that more specific virtues and vices can be derived by considering more specific circumstances (**MM** 384–389, 468–469). – TB

FURTHER READING

L. Denis, 'Kant's conception of virtues', in P. Guyer (ed.), *The Cambridge Companion to Kant and Modern Philosophy* (Cambridge: Cambridge University Press, 2006), pp. 505–537.

L. Denis (ed.), *Kant's 'Metaphysics of Morals': A Critical Guide* (Cambridge: Cambridge University Press, 2010).

O. O'Neill, 'Kant's virtues', in R. Crisp (ed.), *How Should One Live? Essays on the Virtues* (Oxford: Oxford University Press, 1996), pp. 77–97.

M. Timmons (ed.), *Kant's Metaphysics of Morals: Interpretative Essays* (Oxford: Oxford University Press, 2002), chs 1 and 12–17.

WILL (CHOICE)

For Kant, the 'will' (*Wille*) is the ability to act for reasons. He defines 'life', or 'desire', as the ability to act intentionally, and 'choice' (*Willkür*) as this ability insofar as it is motivated and aware of circumstances. The 'will', then, is the particular kind of 'choice' that is motivated by reasons.

Kant thus allows that choice need not always be rational – indeed, he considers animals to choose without reasoning and he admits that human reasoning can be suspended, obstructed or distorted by feelings. He also considers our reasoning, or will, itself to be concerned in part with our non-rational motivations, or inclinations.

Consequently, while he considers us able to act for reasons and thus 'free' from determination by the non-rational, Kant describes reasons as 'imperatives' or 'constraints' for us in the sense that we do not necessarily obey them. He claims that only a 'holy' will, one not subject to feelings and non-rational motivations, would not regard reasons in this way (cf. **G** 412–414; **CPrR** 19–20, 32–33; **MM** 211–214, 222; and on the limits of human reasoning cf. **R** 29n.; **MM** 407–408; **Anthr** 251–275).

A 'good will' for Kant is one that acts for reasons of a specifically moral kind. Rather than 'hypothetical' reasons concerning how best to pursue our non-rational motivations, these reasons are 'categorical' (→ **categorical imperative**) ones concerned with will itself, something that Kant thinks motivates us simply as and because we are wills. He therefore presents a good will as one that acts for reasons which concern what is good for willing as such – such as consent, skills, or what is included in a rational sense of 'happiness' – and thus express the will's own 'autonomy', or 'self-legislation' (**G** 393–399, 414–445) (→ **freedom**).

In **R** he also argues that the 'good' or 'evil' (→ **radical evil**) character of a will must be considered as a basic choice, underlying all others, about whether to prioritize morally good reasons over others (**R** 19–44). – TB

FURTHER READING

H. Allison, *Kant's Theory of Freedom* (Cambridge: Cambridge University Press, 1990), chs 5–8.

J. Timmermann, *Kant's Groundwork of the Metaphysics of Morals: A Commentary* (Cambridge: Cambridge University Press, 2007).

A. Wood, *Kant's Ethical Thought* (Cambridge: Cambridge University Press, 1999), chs 2 and 4.

PART IV:
RECEPTION AND INFLUENCE

5

RECEPTION AND INFLUENCE

This chapter presents a series of short essays on the reception of Kant's work, in particular his Inaugural Dissertation from 1770 and the first publication of the *Critique of Pure Reason* in 1781, in the period 1770–1802. The main figures treated here that were important for the development and early reception of Kant's philosophy and that can be loosely grouped under the often used historical label of post-Kantianism – although most of them were certainly not card-carrying Kantians – are Lambert, Schultz, Mendelssohn, Herz, Garve and Feder, Hamann, Maimon, Jacobi, Reinhold, Schulze, the early Schelling, Diez, Flatt, Rapp, Fichte and the early Hegel. The emphasis here is on these thinkers' reception of Kant's work, not their own philosophies.

A second set of essays addresses the influence Kant's thought exerted on later developments in philosophy in the second half of the nineteenth and early twentieth centuries, in particular Schopenhauer, neo-Kantianism and Heidegger's influential phenomenological reading. A final set of articles gives an overview of mainstream contemporary Kantianism, both in theoretical philosophy and ethics.

With each essay a list of further reading is provided that will enable the reader to undertake further research in a specific area

of scholarship on the reception and influence of Kant's thought. – DS

UNTIL 1781: RESPONSES TO KANT'S INAUGURAL DISSERTATION (1770)

In his treatise *On the Form and Principles of the Sensible and Intelligible World*, known as the Inaugural Dissertation of 1770 (**ID**), Kant claims that time and space are subjective forms, rooted in the nature of the human mind rather than pertaining to things in themselves, and that as a result our cognition of the sensible world is distinct in kind from the cognition of the intelligible world. Kant argues for the subjectivity of time and space by showing that conceiving either as an object or as a determination of an object, whether an accident or relation, cannot account for the character of the representation that we have of each.

With respect to time, for instance, Kant argues that the idea we have of it could not have been acquired through use of the senses but is in fact presupposed in any such use. So, against those, like Leibniz, who have claimed that our ideas of succession arise from our (confused) representation of the series of actual things existing one after the other, Kant claims that 'I only understand the meaning of the little word *after* by means of the antecedent concept of time [. . .] [for] those things come *after* one another which exist at *different times*' (**ID** 399).

In addition, Kant points out that our representation of time is singular rather than general, and that it cannot be analyzed into characteristic marks, both of which imply that the idea of time could not be a discursive representation. Altogether, these features, which also pertain to the representation of space, imply that the ideas of time and space could only be pure intuitions and from this it is inferred that neither is something 'objective and real' but only 'the subjective condition which is necessary, in virtue of the nature of the human mind, for the co-ordinating of all sensible things in accordance with a fixed law' (**ID** 400).

Given this, things in time and space are to be regarded as phenomena, and their cognition, even when it involves the use of the understanding, is to be distinguished from the cognition of noumena, or things considered apart from these sensible forms. According to Kant, it has been the failure to recognize and enforce this distinction that has led to persistent errors in metaphysics.

Kant rightly considered his account of the status of time and space, his take on the distinction between phenomena and noumena, and his diagnosis of the errors in metaphysics to be original and important philosophical contributions. For this reason, he sent his Dissertation to a number of prominent intellectuals, including Johann Heinrich Lambert (1728–1777), a scientist, mathematician, and philosopher; Johann Georg Sulzer (1720–1779), known primarily for his work in aesthetics; and Moses Mendelssohn (1729–1786), the famous philosopher,

theologian, and literary critic. In addition, a review of **ID** was published late in 1771 in the *Königsbergische gelehrte und politische Zeitungen* by Johann Schultz (1739–1805), a court chaplain and professor of mathematics in Königsberg.

As was to be expected, Kant's arguments for the status of time and space as pure intuitions, and his conclusion that they are not objective and real but merely subjective forms, proved the most controversial. Kant's respondents raised a number of problems with these claims, ranging from minor quibbles to serious challenges. Sulzer, for instance, objected that time and space are 'constructed concepts' in that they include the notion of order and that it was duration and extension that should be considered 'absolutely simple concepts' (**Corr-I** 112), a point echoed by Lambert (at least with regard to duration; cf. **Corr-I** 108).

More substantively, Schultz objected to Kant's claim that space and time are only forms of the sensible world, arguing that from the fact that these are intuitions it does not follow that they do not extend to intellectual things. Indeed, Schultz contends that there is good reason to think that space and time are also forms of the intelligible world. With respect to space, Schultz claims that the intellectual concept of 'subject' as a mere relation (to its accidents) or general notion falls short of the complete concept of substance, which also includes the thought of an absolutely singular existing thing, and for which Schultz argues the intuition of the subject in space is required.[1]

As it relates to time, Schultz contends that the subject's persistence (a temporal predicate) is required to conceive of the unchangeable as well as the changeable: 'every alteration requires the persistence of the subject and a succession of opposed states, and even for the existence of the unalterable the persistence of the subject is required, although without the succession of opposed states.'[2]

Significantly, Schultz was not the only critic to challenge Kant's claim that time, as a subjective form, does not apply to intelligible objects as both Lambert and Mendelssohn raise a similar objection in their comments on **ID**. Both reject Kant's case for the subjectivity of time, arguing that while we might deny the reality and objectivity of space, we cannot possibly deny the reality and objectivity of time since, at the very least, we cannot deny that changes occur in the thinking subject's own representations. Lambert, who was the first to respond with this criticism in his letter of 13 October 1770, puts the objection in the following way:

The trouble seems to lie only in the fact that one must simply think time and duration and not define them. All changes are bound to time and are inconceivable without time. *If changes are real, then time is real*, whatever it may be. *If time is unreal, then no change can be real*. I think, though, that even an idealist must grant at least that changes really exist and occur in his representations, for example, their beginning and ending. Thus time cannot be regarded as something unreal. (**Corr-I** 107)

Mendelssohn, in his response to Kant in a letter of 25 December 1770, offers much the same criticism but draws the key contrast more sharply:

For several reasons I cannot convince myself that time is something merely subjective. Succession is to be sure at least a necessary condition of the representations of finite minds. But finite minds are not only subjects; they are also objects of representations, both those of God and those of their fellow minds. Consequently succession is to be regarded as something objective. (**Corr-I** 115; trans. amended)

As Mendelssohn counters, we might convince ourselves that time is subjective if we limited our consideration to the perspective of the representing subject since, from that perspective, there is no basis for determining whether the temporal order of our representations is grounded in their objects or in ourselves.

Nonetheless, the claim that time is subjective cannot be sustained when we consider the representing subject as itself an object of representation on the part of other minds. This is because, considered from the perspective of such minds, including God's, the representing subject does not merely represent objects successively but is also itself the subject of successive representations. Accordingly, the representing subject must be recognized as itself really changing with respect to these representations and, therefore, time (as applying in this way to the subject) must be objective and real.

Given their illustrious sources, these objections could not but be taken seriously by Kant, and his first replies to his critics are found in the well-known letter to Markus Herz of 21 February 1772. Against Schultz's contention that space might equally be a condition of the intelligible world, and as such be objective, Kant explains that the complete analysis of space yields no substances, nor connections among those substances, that might serve as a real ground for this representation, and, therefore, that space could not possibly be objective (**Corr-I** 133–134).

Concerning the objection raised by Lambert, Mendelssohn and Schultz, Kant confesses that it 'has made me reflect considerably' (**Corr-I** 134) but argues that its implausibility becomes evident once we consider how it might be applied to objects in space:

> Why does one not accept the following parallel argument? Bodies are real (according to the testimony of outer sense). Now, bodies are possible only under the condition of space; therefore space is something objective and real that inheres in the things themselves. The reason lies in the fact that it is obvious, in regard to outer things, that one cannot infer the reality of the object from the reality of the representation, but in the case of inner sense the thinking or the existence of the thought and the existence of my own self are one and the same. (**Corr-I** 134)

Just as no one would accept that bodies are real based solely on the testimony of outer sense (and so that space, as the condition of bodies, is also real), so we should not accept that changes in the thinking subject are real based solely on the testimony of inner sense (and so that time, as the condition of such changes, is also real). Accordingly, there is no reason to think that because the thinking subject is represented as in time through inner sense that it really is in time.

Whatever the merits of this particular line of response, Kant evidently continued to reflect on the objection as he would return to it in **CPR** in the 'Elucidation' that follows the discussion of time in the Transcendental Aesthetic (A37=B53–54).

It bears noting that not all of the reaction to Kant's Dissertation was of a critical tenor. Herz himself, a former student of Kant and the original respondent to **ID**, published his *Betrachtungen aus der speculativen Weltweisheit* in 1771, a text that amounts to a commentary on Kant's work, though one that extends Kant's analysis in significant ways.

In particular, Herz contends that while Kant denies space and time objective reality, they are nonetheless not thereby reduced to wholly ideal entities but must be accorded at least a reality in the subject. Herz argues that the objective reality of a relation, as involving a comparison of two things, has to have its ground either in one of the things that are being compared or in both taken together. But Herz rules each of these options out, concluding instead that 'with all relations some subject must be presupposed which compares these objects with one another and, from the differences it perceives in the effects of both, brings forth a simple result [i.e. the relation]'.[3]

Interestingly, Herz proceeds to use this as a basis for demonstrating the simplicity of the thinking subject that is thereby presupposed. As he argues, the thinking subject could not consist in a number of parts, because if it did then the representations that are compared in the relation would be distributed among the parts and we would have to posit a further subject in order to institute the comparison that results in the relation. While the posit of this subject might be postponed for as long as one wishes, in the end one will require 'a simple being [. . .] which is in the position of representing to itself various objects at the same time and bringing forth from their comparison a single result'.[4]

Kant praised Herz's text as a 'discerning and deeply thoughtful little book' (**Corr-I** 132), and it is certainly possible that its claims about the nature and centrality of the thinking subject exercised an important influence on the direction of Kant's thought in the 1770s, the so-called silent decade at the end of which Kant published **CPR**. – CD

FURTHER READING

L. Falkenstein, 'Kant, Mendelssohn, Lambert and the subjectivity of time', *Journal of the History of Philosophy* 21 (1991): 227–251.

H. Klemme, 'Kants Wende zum Ich', *Zeitschrift für philosophische Forschung* 53 (1999): 509–529.

A. Laywine, 'Kant on sensibility and the understanding in the 1770s', *Canadian Journal of Philosophy* 33,4 (2003): 443–482.

A. Laywine, 'Kant's laboratory of ideas in the 1770s', in G. Bird (ed.), *A Companion to Kant* (Malden, MA/Oxford: Wiley-Blackwell, 2010), pp. 63–78.

FIRST RESPONSES TO THE *CRITIQUE OF PURE REASON*: THE 1780S AND LATER

THE GARVE-FEDER REVIEW

Kant often expressed dissatisfaction about the reception of the Critical philosophy. Certainly, things did not begin well. The first published review of **CPR**, which appeared anonymously in the *Zugabe zu den Göttingschen Anzeigen von gelehrten Sachen* in 1782, inspired bitter polemics in **P**, which Kant published in 1783, exposing the reviewer's failure to understand **CPR** and challenging him '*to emerge from being incognito*' (**P** 379).

Kant's challenge initiated correspondence with Christian Garve (1742–1798). Garve confessed to reviewing **CPR** for the Göttingen journal, yet disowns the review published therein (**Corr-I** 328). For Garve's submission was substantially rewritten by Johann Georg

Heinrich Feder (1740–1821) – who bears responsibility for 'the breath of pure animosity' and 'incoherence' of the Göttingen review (respectively **Corr-I** 329–330 and 337). Nevertheless, when Garve's original manuscript later appeared in the *Allgemeine deutsche Bibliothek*, evidence suggests that Kant was no more impressed with it.[5]

Garve misreads Kant's 'appearances' as synonymous with Hume's 'impressions', and thus misinterprets Kant as claiming that space and time are 'forms of sensation',[6] and that the delimitation of reason's cognition-geared application excludes, not only cognition of supersensible entities, but also cognition of any self-subsistent object over and above our impressions.[7] Garve therefore misinterprets **CPR** as attempting to solve 'the mystery' concerning how 'in the face of the total dissimilarity of representations and objects (if the later exist), the former still lead to the latter and seem to afford knowledge of them'.[8] Garve's original manuscript thus suffers from four of the faults for which Kant castigates the Göttingen review in **P**, namely:

(1) Failing to recognize that **CPR** aimed at answering the question concerning the possibility of metaphysics (**P** 372–373); (2) failing to appreciate the question concerning the possibility of synthetic cognition a priori (**P** 377); (3) failing to appreciate the role of transcendental idealism (**P** 375–377); and (4) unjustifiably accusing **CPR** of providing no 'sure criterion for distinguishing truth from illusion in experience' (**P** 375).[9]

However, while Garve misread Kant as a Humean, Feder misread him as a Berkeleyan. Feder's interpolations thus draw analogies between transcendental idealism and Berkeleyan phenomenalism, and yet, in nonetheless recognizing that the former 'encompasses spirit and matter in the same manner', describes it as a '*higher* idealism' that 'transforms the world and ourselves into representations'.[10]

We can therefore understand why Garve was embarrassed by the 'incoherence' of the Göttingen review. For it ended up as, not only a *misguided*, but also an *inconsistent* polemic, sometimes misreading Kant as a Humean for whom objects outside our impressions are rationally indemonstrable, while also accusing Kant of the Berkeleyan claim that objects outside our impressions are impossible.

Kant explicitly responds to Feder's charges of Berkeleyanism in **P**,[11] but does not similarly respond to Garve's Humean misreadings. Yet, perhaps Kant's many claims throughout **P** concerning how 'criticism' is intended as a 'solution' to Humean scepticism (which are almost entirely absent from the first edition of **CPR**[12]) constitute such a response.

These claims set the agenda for **CPR**'s reception within the decade to come. In those years, Kant's defenders as much as his opponents questioned the extent to which he succeeded in silencing the sceptic, often arguing that radical reconfigurations of Kantian doctrine are required for the Critical philosophy to achieve this – reconfigurations which led to the emergence of German Idealism in the 1790s.

INVESTIGATIONS INTO THE 'COMMON ROOT': HAMANN, REINHOLD AND MAIMON

While the Göttingen review was the first published review of **CPR**, it was not the first review ever composed. The first review was completed on 1 July 1781 (just six weeks after publication of **CPR**) by Johann Georg Hamann (1730–1788). Hamann developed his criticisms of Kant in order to complete, in 1784, a text entitled *Metakritik über den Purismum der reinen Venunft*, which, in being circulated among leading

thinkers, exerted a 'considerable subterranean influence'.[13]

Hamann's focus upon later sections of **CPR**, in particular 'The Discipline of Pure Reason', means that, even in 1781, he recognizes that Kant attempts some kind of 'answer' to Hume by forging a 'middle path' between dogmatism and scepticism.[14] As a self-confessed Humean, however, Hamann remains unimpressed, and claims that Kant unduly sides with dogmatism by insisting upon the autonomy of reason. Hamann thus refers to Kant's suggestion that 'sensibility and understanding [. . .] spring from a common, but to us unknown, root' (A15=B29) to make the Humean claim that an investigation into this 'common root' would reveal that *impressions* constitute the 'transcendental root' from which *all* concepts are abstracted.[15]

Likewise, in the *Metakritik*, he appeals to Hume's Berkeleyan argument that, contra Locke, 'all general ideas are nothing but particular ones, annexed to a certain term, which gives them a more extensive signification'[16] to dismiss Kant's claim to a faculty of a priori concepts. Kant's claim is the product of a 'purification' which erroneously interprets reason as independent of (1) 'all tradition and custom and belief in them', (2) 'experience and its everyday induction' and (3) 'language'.[17]

In regard to the latter, Hamann suggests that, had Kant attended to how 'the entire faculty of thought [is] founded on language'[18] and thus how all thought depends upon the 'visible and audible',[19] he would have realized that our intellectual faculties are rooted in the sensible. Hamann thus dismisses Kant's enquiry into 'the possibility of the human cognition of objects of experience *without* and *before* any experience and [. . .] the possibility of a sensible intuition *before* any sensation of an object' as an enquiry into a 'double *im*-possibility'.[20]

Hamann's review was published twenty years later in the *Beyträge zur leichtern Uebersicht des Zustandes der Philosophie* by Karl Leonhard Reinhold (1757–1823),[21] who, in the late 1780s, attained fame by also investigating the 'common root' of our cognitive faculties. Far from intending to support Hume's position, however, Reinhold hoped to inoculate the results of Kant's Critical philosophy from the Humean sceptic – or, indeed, the objections of anyone of opposed philosophical persuasions.

Reinhold believed that this could be achieved by means of a foundationalist reconfiguration of the Critical philosophy, and he believed that this was required insofar as the results of CPR were founded upon controversial presuppositions which it lacked the resources to make universally accepted.

Reinhold called this investigation the *Elementarphilosophie*, which he defined as 'the science of the *entire faculty of representation as such*'.[22] It provides an investigation into the 'common root' of our faculties insofar as it concerns 'the representations of sensibility, understanding and reason [. . .] *simply qua representations*',[23] i.e. that which is 'common' to every conscious state and conscious datum.[24] The first, that is, foundational, principle of this science – the 'principle of consciousness' – is thus drawn from the '*fact*' of 'consciousness as such' or 'mere representation' and asserts that '*in consciousness representation is distinguished through the subject from object and subject and is referred to both*'.[25]

As the ultimate explanatory ground of all knowledge, this principle is 'self-determined' and 'self-explanatory'[26] and, insofar as it expresses nothing but the 'fact of consciousness' of which everyone is immediately certain,

it is universally binding (*allgemeingeltend*),[27] since anyone who understands it must recognize its indubitable truth. Reinhold thus endeavours to derive Kant's many presuppositions from this principle in the hope of raising the results of the Critical philosophy beyond all possible doubt.[28]

As Reinhold promulgated the *Elementarphilosophie*, another investigation into the 'common root' was conducted by Salomon Maimon (1753–1800) in his *Versuch über die Transzendentalphilosophie* (1790). There, Maimon characterizes himself as an 'empirical sceptic' and a 'rational dogmatist'.[29] He is an 'empirical sceptic' insofar as, like Hume, he doubts whether natural science contains any a priori principles, while he is a 'rationalist dogmatist' insofar as he believes that, to explain the possibility of mathematical cognition, transcendental philosophy must appeal to the resources of Kant's rationalist predecessors.

The question concerning mathematical cognition demands a better explanation of how the (apparently) heterogeneous faculties of sensibility and understanding interact than that provided by Kant. Maimon thus advocates re-appropriating the Leibnizian conception of space and time, which, qua forms of intuition, he declares to be confused representations produced by the imagination of beings endowed with merely 'finite understanding'.

However, for an 'infinite understanding' – of which our understanding is a limitation[30] – space and time are originally concepts of the objective *difference* of things, which it simultaneously thinks and produces. *Understanding* thus constitutes the 'common root' of our cognitive faculties; sensibility merely providing confused representations of concepts of *objects of thought* and *thought relations*.

Are There any A Priori Synthetic Truths? Maimon's Humean Doubts

In **P**, Kant reproached the Göttingen review for not appreciating the question concerning synthetic cognition a priori; one had to appreciate that question, Kant implied, to understand why he embraced transcendental idealism. Nonetheless, it was soon recognized that, in this regard, Kant simply begged the question against the Humean sceptic. For Kant simply *presupposed* that we possess synthetic cognition a priori, and thus had little to say to a Humean, who, in holding all a priori truths to be analytic and all synthetic truths to be a posteriori, was under no obligation to accept any of the results of Kant's investigation into the possibility of synthetic cognition a priori.

A case in point is mathematical cognition: Kant presupposed that this is a priori synthetic and failed to justify the validity of this presupposition to the bulk of his initial readership who, under the influence of Hume or Leibniz, were convinced it was analytic. Likewise, he had little to say to those who denied the apriority of mathematical truths, such as the 'many mathematicians' who, at the time, considered them as 'hypothetical'.[31]

This worried Reinhold, who maintains that **CPR** lacks resources to convince the Humean or Leibnizian that mathematical judgments are not analytic, since Kant derived the distinction between intuition and concept, requisite for any such argument, from the very assumption that mathematical judgments are a priori synthetic.[32]

Just such a problem, for Reinhold, justifies his *Elementarphilosophie*. For the *Elementarphilosophie* endeavours to prove that mathematical judgments are a priori synthetic *from* the distinction between intuition and concept, and proves the distinction

between intuition and concept *from* the principle of consciousness. As Reinhold believes that Humeans and Leibnizians must accept the principle of consciousness, he hopes that, by its means, he can convince them of the synthetic apriority of mathematical truths.

Reinhold's foundationalism failed to convince Maimon, however, who allied himself with Hume and Leibniz in maintaining that all a priori cognition is derived from the principle of non-contradiction. Maimon admits that for a 'finite understanding' such judgments may appear synthetic, but insists that for the 'infinite understanding' they are analytic.

He claims that we only believe mathematical judgments to be synthetic insofar as their subject is either 'badly defined' or 'not defined at all' and says that demonstrating that they are analytic would be a not impossible, albeit laborious, task.[33] He also denies that natural science contains any synthetic cognition a priori to follow Hume in claiming that all its truths are a posteriori.

Indeed, in his *Versuch einer neuen Logik oder Theorie des Denkens* he castigates Kant for lumping together two very *dissimilar* questions, i.e. the questions concerning the possibility of (1) pure mathematics and (2) a (supposed) *physica pura*, under the rubric of the question concerning a priori synthetic judgments, as *if* they possessed an essential similarity.[34]

For Maimon these questions are very different since (1) in referring to determinate objects mathematical judgments can be illustrated 'through construction' (e.g. every straight line is the shortest because, in being constructed, every straight line must acquire the predicate of being the shortest), whereas (2) the judgments of a (supposed) *physica pura* never refer to determinate objects and cannot be illustrated through construction.[35]

Maimon thus argues that even if the causal law is an a priori principle applicable to objects of experience in general, it does not legitimate cognition of necessary connections between determinate objects, and the most coherent explanation of 'synthetic judgments that refer to *determinate objects of actual experience*'[36] is that provided by Hume.

However, that Hume's position can also explain judgments concerning objects of experience in general leads Maimon to conclude his *Versuch einer neuen Logik* with the claim that 'in my opinion [. . .] the categories are designed not for empirical employment, but only for the employment in the determination a priori of the objects of mathematics'.[37]

MAIMON ON THE QUID FACTI AND THE QUID JURIS

Maimon expressed doubts about whether we employ a priori concepts to cognize objects of experience when he writes to Kant concerning 'the question quid facti?' that '[y]ou seem to have touched on this, but it is, I think, important to answer it fully, on account of the Humean skepticism' (**Corr-II** 17). Kant described the question *quid facti* – with reference to Locke's *Essay* – as demanding physiological explanation of our '*possession* of pure knowledge' (A87=B119) to distinguish it from the Transcendental Deduction's *quid juris* question, which demands explanation of how a priori concepts are applicable within experience.

Maimon grants the former question more significance, since he recognizes that, in focusing upon *how* pure knowledge of experience is possible, Kant does not answer Hume's doubts concerning such pure knowledge. Kant may have attempted to answer Hume in the Second Analogy with his argument

that our ability to distinguish an objective succession of appearances from a subjective succession of apprehended perceptions is the product of a cognition of necessary connection enabled by the category of causality, but Maimon questions this account for the following reasons:

(1) He denies that we possess any sure criterion for distinguishing an objective succession of appearances from a subjective succession of perceptions. For if we compare a supposedly objective succession of *b* following *a* with a subjective succession of *c* following *a* we find that *in themselves* these successions are indistinguishable. We might believe that the succession of *a* to *b* is objective because of its irreversibility, but this does not provide an adequate criterion for distinguishing it from *a* to *c*, since, when I apprehend *c* following *a*, it is just as impossible that I could at the same time apprehend *a* following *c* as it is that I could apprehend *a* following *b*.[38]

(2) He maintains that our commonsensical pretension to distinguish necessarily connected events from contingent sequences of perceptions can be based, as Hume maintained, only on experience. E.g. 'the stove in the room has been lit and then we notice that outside snow has fallen'[39]. Common sense maintains that the warming of the air and the snowfall are objectively real events, so why do we believe that the former illustrates necessary connection while the latter does not? For Maimon this can only be based upon past experience, as Hume claimed.

(3) If we have no criterion to distinguish an objective succession of appearances from a subjective succession of perceptions other than fallible inductive inferences from past experience, the possibility that we possess nothing but subjective successions of perceptions cannot be ruled out.[40] Garve's objection

that **CPR** does not provide a sure criterion for distinguishing truth from illusion (see above), cannot therefore, albeit for different reasons, be ruled out decisively.

The *Versuch über die Transzendentalphilosophie*, despite doubting the fact of experience (in the Kantian sense), still maintains that Kant's categories possess objective validity as 'conditions of perception'.[41] There, for example, Maimon argues that the category of causality has objective validity as a condition of possibility of alteration, and is therefore a condition of possibility of even subjective sequences of perceptions.[42] Transcendental philosophy must explain this objective validity by demonstrating how categories are valid of empirical intuition, i.e. by answering the *quid juris* question.

Nevertheless, Maimon's transcendental philosophy rules out transcendental arguments concerning the possibility of experience (since he doubts that we possess 'experiential propositions'), to focus upon transcendental arguments concerning the possibility of 'mathematical propositions'.[43] Maimon thus refers to himself within a letter to Kant as enlarging the scope of the *quid juris* question. For Kant, the *quid juris* concerned the application of a priori categories to a posteriori intuitions; and the connection between the categories and a priori intuitions established within mathematical propositions was seen by Kant as a resource for the solution to the former problem rather than as generating another problem.

Maimon however objects that 'even if they are a priori, intuitions are still heterogeneous with concepts of understanding'[44] to conclude that the *quid juris* must be extended to the categories' application to a priori intuition. The solution to this problem provides resources for the further problem concerning the categories' application to a posteriori intuitions.

For Maimon, the forms of intuition and categories are not fundamentally heterogeneous, since the former are originally concepts. He thus claims that in thinking forms of intuition we do not apply the categories directly to them, but rather think the relations of things in general which would be thought by an infinite understanding. What, however, are those 'things', the concepts of their relations of which constitute the objective ground of intuitions of space and time? Maimon here refers to '*ideas of the understanding*' which, in a letter to Kant (**Corr-II** 16), he claimed to have introduced to answer the *quid juris*.

He insists that the diversity of empirical intuition compels us to assume a corresponding diversity among its objective grounds and declares that the objective grounds of both the matter and form of intuitions are imminently contained within them as elements from which they are composed. These elements are '*ideas* of understanding' since we can never be conscious of them insofar as consciousness presupposes their synthesis.[45]

As elements of synthesis they complement the '*idea* of reason', i.e. the idea of a 'complete synthesis', which, for Maimon, is the idea of an infinite understanding. They are 'useful for resolving the question *quid juris*?'[46] because they enable Maimon to explain the application of the categories to empirical intuitions by appeal to our participation within the infinite understanding's conceptual grasp of the things which it produces.[47] Only in this way, Maimon believes, does the *quid juris* attain a satisfactory answer.[48]

THE PROBLEMATIC STATUS OF THINGS IN THEMSELVES: JACOBI'S AND SCHULZE'S CRITIQUE OF KANT'S IDEALISM

Maimon's description of the 'ideas of understanding' as noumena and the perceptible objects compounded from them as phenomena shows how he avoids the claim that the material content of intuitions is 'given' by things in themselves.[49] He thus obviates the (supposed) contradictions in Kant's account of the ground of the material content of intuition, which were highlighted by Friedrich Heinrich Jacobi (1743–1819) in his *David Hume über den Glauben, oder Idealismus und Realismus*, published in 1787.

Jacobi takes up Kant's claim that the material content of intuition is received by our passive faculty of sensibility to ask about the 'objects' producing these sensations. These cannot be empirical objects, Jacobi concludes, since, for Kant, they are merely the product of a synthesis of the manifold.[50] They must therefore be things in themselves; and since 'the word sensibility [. . .] would be meaningless [. . .] if the concepts [. . .] of causality and dependence were not already contained in the concept of it *as real and objective determinations*'[51] it follows, according to Jacobi, that Kant presupposes that the material content of intuition is 'given' through the causal affection of things in themselves.

As Jacobi observes, however, such a presupposition contradicts the Critical philosophy's conclusion that we possess no knowledge of things in themselves, neither regarding whether they conform to the principle of sufficient reason, nor whether they even exist.[52] He thus concludes that '*without* that presupposition I could not enter into the system, but *with* it I could not stay within it',[53] for it is impossible 'to reconcile the presupposition of objects that produce impressions on our senses [. . .] with a hypothesis intent on abolishing all grounds by which the presupposition could be supported'.[54]

Five years later, similar claims were made by the Humean Gottlob Ernst Schulze

(1761–1833) in his anonymously published sceptical attack on the Critical philosophy, *Aenesidemus oder über die Fundamente der von dem Herrn Professor Reinhold in Jena gelieferten Elementar-Philosophie: Nebst einer Verteidigung des Skeptizismus gegen die Anmaßungen der Vernunftkritik.*

Schulze accuses Kant's claims that we are affected by things in themselves of begging the question against Hume's claim that such affection is rationally indemonstrable.[55] In this regard, Schulze contends, Kant proceeds just like a rationalist metaphysician in tacitly accepting an isomorphism between *thought* and *being* to infer from our propensity to *think* of many representations as the product of things in themselves *the conclusion that* they do indeed have such an origin.

Yet, for Schulze, Kant is more objectionable than a rationalist metaphysician because of the prima facie contradiction between (1) his presupposition that the affection of things in themselves occasions empirical intuitions, and (2) his argument that the categories of *actuality* and *causality* are only applicable to those very intuitions.[56]

THE INCOHERENCE OF FORMALISM

Kant's failure to establish the existence of things in themselves provokes Schulze to restate Garve's objection that **CPR** does not provide a sure criterion for distinguishing truth from illusion in experience.[57] This objection demonstrates how Schulze, like Garve, misreads Kant's 'appearances' as referring to congeries of sensations structured by the mind, so that the reality of cognition of experience is only secured insofar as they correspond with things in themselves. Schulze thus misinterprets Kant as a representationalist still committed to a correspondence theory of truth.

As such, one of his final criticisms of the doctrine of things in themselves concerns how any correspondence between them and their appearances is even conceivable. Schulze writes:

to be [. . .] convinced of the fact that, according to the principles of the critical philosophy, cognition of empirical sensation [. . .] may not possess an actual relation to things outside us [. . .] one need only, after having dissolved the representation of a sensible object into the marks from which it is constituted, abstract those which, according to the critical philosophy, belong merely to the form of cognition [. . .]. How much remains after abstraction of all these forms [. . .] as matter for cognition? It might be nothing. Therefore according to the most recent dogmatic system [i.e. the critical philosophy] [. . .] the representation of an empirical object is [. . .] compounded from forms of cognition; it could thus appropriately be called *formalism* [. . .] to indicate its differences from other dogmatic systems.[58]

Towards German Idealism: Schelling's Reaction in the 1790s

The influence of the Humean sceptics' reception of Kant is well illustrated by the *Allgemeine Uebersicht der neuesten philosophischen Litteratur* that Friedrich Wilhelm Joseph Schelling (1775–1854) wrote for the *Philosophisches Journal einer Gesellschaft Teutscher Gelehrten*. There, Schelling (1) highlights misinterpretations of Kant that should be avoided and (2) draws upon some of Kant's early critics to offer an interpretation of 'what [Kant] *had* to have intended if his philosophy was to prove internally cohesive'.[59] In so doing, Schelling points

towards directions pursued by himself and other German Idealists.

Schelling borrows Schulze's term 'formalism'[60] to disparage the position of those who – according to Schelling – misread Kant as claiming that 'the *form* of our cognitions originate within *ourselves* whereas their *matter* is given to us *from the outside*'.[61] Such misreadings, Schelling observes, are responsible for the assumption that Kant accounts for the material content of empirical intuition as the product of the affection of things in themselves, which, as Jacobi and Schulze pointed out, contradicts his critical restriction of the categories of actuality and causality to appearances.

Like Maimon, Schelling attempts to free Kant from this contradiction by denying that he ever appealed to things in themselves to explain the origins of experience.[62] According to Schelling, Kant could have in no way intended that things in themselves possess such a role, first, because **CPR** maintains that 'everything that is for us an object or thing has become object etc. only within an original synthesis of intuition'[63]; and secondly because that would reduce Kant to being an inconsistent Humean. In regard to the latter, Schelling remarks how for the 'Formalists'

the world bears no affinity to our spirit [*Geiste*] other than that of a contingent affect. Nevertheless *such* a world [. . .] they claim to govern with laws that [. . .] have been implanted in the understanding. As the supreme legislators of nature [and] with the full consciousness that the world is comprised of things in themselves, they impose these concepts and laws of the understanding onto these things in themselves [. . .] and this world of eternal and determinate nature obeys their speculative decree. [. . .] Hume, the sceptic, first had claimed what is now being attributed to Kant.

Yet Hume readily admitted that all our natural sciences amount to deception, [and] that all laws of nature constitute but a routine of our imagination. This was consistent philosophy. And Kant is supposed to have done no more than repeat Hume so as to now render him, who had been consistent, inconsistent.[64]

Schelling's 'non-formalist' interpretation of Kant draws upon many of Maimon's suggestions for how transcendental philosophy should be reconfigured. Just as Maimon accused Kant of promulgating an 'indolent philosophy' with respect to time and space, insofar as he simply presupposed that they are 'original forms' without investigating whether they might originate within some prior ground,[65] so Schelling denies that we 'simply bring along [the forms of space and time] as something finished and ready-made for the purpose of intuition'.[66]

For Schelling, investigation into the prior ground of these forms of intuition provides – just as it did for Maimon – 'a hint [regarding] the most complete account of the essence of intuition (of its material)',[67] which can explain the material content of empirical intuition without recourse to 'that fantasy of the brain [Hirngespinnst] that has tormented our philosophers for so long – viz. the things in themselves'.[68]

Furthermore, to obviate the objection that critical idealism is an inconsistent Humeanism, Schelling follows Maimon's rationalist dogmatism in denying the absolute heterogeneity of the form and matter of empirical intuitions to argue that both arise inseparably united as a result of the 'self-intuition of a spirit [Geistes]' or 'absolute subject',[69] which – akin to the relationship between Maimon's infinite understanding and our own understanding – 'contains

the essence of an individual nature (of selfhood [Ichheit])'.[70] – RF

FURTHER READING

F. Beiser, *The Fate of Reason: German Philosophy from Kant to Fichte* (Cambridge, MA: Harvard University Press, 1987).

E. Förster, *The Twenty-Five Years of Philosophy* (Cambridge, MA: Harvard University Press, 2012).

M. Frank, '*Unendliche Annäherung': Die Anfänge der philosophischen Frühromantik* (Frankfurt a/M: Suhrkamp, 1997).

P. Franks, *All or Nothing. Systematicity, Transcendental Arguments, and Skepticism in German Idealism* (Cambridge, MA: Harvard University Press, 2005).

R.-P. Horstmann, *Die Grenzen der Vernunft. Eine Untersuchung zu Zielen und Motiven des Deutschen Idealismus*, third edition (Frankfurt a/M: Klostermann, 2004), esp. pt. II: 'Vom Buchstaben zum Geist. Die Rezeption der Kantischen Philosophie durch F. H. Jacobi und die Deutsche Idealisten'.

M. Kuehn, 'Kant's Critical philosophy and its reception – the first five years (1781–1786)', in P. Guyer (ed.), *The Cambridge Companion to Kant and Modern Philosophy* (Cambridge: Cambridge University Press, 2006), pp. 630–663.

KANTIANISM IN THE 1790S: FROM REINHOLD TO HEGEL

REINHOLD'S MAJOR IMPETUS

It would appear beyond doubt that the Critical philosophy of Immanuel Kant is, in general, of great importance to the philosophical development of German Idealism. Historically, however, its importance to post-Kantian philosophy is often overstated. One must keep in mind, for example, that until 1790 only a handful of books on the Critical philosophy had appeared, most of them also critical of it.

In institutional terms, though, among the first attempts to establish Kantian philosophy academically, in the mid-1780s the University of Jena made the Critical philosophy compulsory for students in the faculty of philosophy.[71] Due to this curricular reform and the subsequent appointments of Karl Leonhard Reinhold and Johann Gottlob Fichte, the Salana soon became one of the leading German universities.

The main figure behind this reform was Christian Gottfried Schütz, who was the founder of the most successful journal of this period, the *Allgemeine Literatur-Zeitung*, which was also committed to the general propagation of Kantian philosophy. However, after the publication of **CPR**, it took more than four years until in July/August 1785 a first positive assessment of Kantian philosophy appeared. The lengthy review in the *Allgemeine Literatur-Zeitung* was based largely on the at that time only obtainable exposition of **CPR**, the *Erläuterungen über des Herrn Professor Kant Critik der reinen Vernunft* (1784), written by the court chaplain of Königsberg, Johann Schul[t]z.

For the earliest reception of the Critical philosophy this book proved far more important than **CPR** itself. Virtually all classical German writers and philosophers from the beginning got acquainted with the key issues of **CPR** through reading this book, with the noticeable exception of Fichte.

Fichte was one of the very few who, in 1790, studied the *Critiques* firsthand and also understood their content and intention more or less in its literal sense. In 1792, he got acquainted with Reinhold's foundational philosophical programme, which was the initial motivation behind his own foundational philosophy of the *Grundlage der gesamten Wissenschaftslehre* (1794). Fichte's adaptation of Kantian philosophy is virtually the inverse of its adaptation by the students in the *Tübinger Stift* (most famously, Hölderlin, Hegel, and Schelling). Initially, they in fact do not deal with Kant's Critical philosophy directly, but as mediated by the aforementioned interpretive work of Schulz and the writings of Reinhold.

Reinhold was one of the very first who, in the second half of the 1780s, adopted the philosophy of Kant. His interest was aroused by the aforementioned review in the *Allgemeine Literatur-Zeitung*. One year after this review had been published, Reinhold's first two of in all eight 'Letters on the Kantian philosophy' appeared between August 1786 and September 1787 in the *Teutsche Merkur*. Journalistically, these 'Letters' proved a huge success. It is no exaggeration to say that it is thanks to them that the Kantian philosophy was put on the philosophical agenda.

Reinhold's 'Letters', however, are anything but a concise exploration of the more technical tenets of the Critical philosophy. Rather, they deal very broadly with the more general question of its usefulness (*Nutzen*). It is by virtue of this question that Reinhold made the extremely difficult insights of the Critical philosophy accessible for the learned audience of his time. Due to its specific orientation, but also due to the fact that **CPR** itself plays a relatively minor role in the 'Letters', from the very beginning the debate around the Critical philosophy followed a pattern that was more in line with the interests of Reinhold himself rather than those of the Critical philosophy strictly speaking.

In an engaging way, Reinhold summarized the results of the Critical philosophy and fitted them in with the programme that he himself had pursued since his time in Vienna.[72] It has often been claimed that Reinhold only popularized Kant's thought, which consequently led to the general disregard of his own philosophy. Such views, however, fail to do justice to Reinhold's historical importance.

According to Reinhold, the chief merit of the Critical philosophy is that it frees us from blind faith and false religious beliefs, and that it thus paves the way towards an enlightened society. The Kantian philosophy purifies the Christian religion that had been corrupted by self-opinionated dogmatism and the self-serving clergy. Reinhold's main point in this regard is that philosophy, by means of a critical approach to reason, is able to achieve what Christianity originally had brought into the world by means of the heart.

This was, of course, not the intention behind Kant's own philosophical programme. Nevertheless, just a cursory look at Hegel's early philosophy shows that Reinhold propounded philosophical ideas that could not but wake the young students of the *Stift* 'from their dogmatic slumber'. In Reinhold's view, Critical philosophy was to be seen as paving the way for a new religion, which was propagated some years later in the so-called *Älteste Systemprogramm des deutschen Idealismus.*

PIVOTAL MINOR FIGURES: DIEZ, FLATT, RAPP

The importance of Reinhold's philosophy for understanding the development of Kantian philosophy cannot be underestimated. One of the early leading Kantians in the *Stift*, Immanuel Carl Diez (1766–1796), writes in regard to Reinhold's second main work, his *Versuch einer neuen Theorie des menschlichen Vorstellungsvermögens* (1789),[73] that it was through this book that

he became familiar with **CPR**.[74] From Diez' correspondence we may conclude that he also discussed Reinhold's 'Letters' with his fellow students.

Another important source for the reception of Kantian philosophy in the *Stift* are the lectures of the philosophy professor Johann Friedrich Flatt (1759–1821). In a lecture most probably attended by Hegel and Hölderlin he offers a concise guideline for studying Kant. Flatt repeatedly recommends Schulz' *Erläuterungen* and Reinhold's 'Letters', while Reinhold's *Versuch* he only recommends with reservations.

Flatt's main criticism is directed against Reinhold's attempt in the *Versuch* to provide a foundation for the results of **CPR**. Virtually all students, however, rejected Reinhold's foundationalism (*Grundsatzphilosophie*) as well as Fichte's more substantial attempt at providing such a foundation. In this respect it is significant that Hegel approached the early discussions on this subject matter with indifference.[75]

It is noticeable that, towards the end of 1790, two factions of Kantians came to the fore in the *Stift*. The one faction leans heavily on Reinhold's *Versuch* for its understanding of Kant, while the other is inspired primarily by Reinhold's 'Letters'. The first group includes the radical Kantians, especially the aforementioned Diez.

On the basis of his reading of Kant, Diez reaches the conclusion that divine revelation is impossible and consequently he refuses to acknowledge the authority of the Lutheran confessions of faith. In 1792, he moves to Jena to study medicine. For his friends and fellow students in the *Stift*, but also for the younger generation of students, Diez's action proved too extreme.

In response, the other faction adhered to Reinhold's aim in the 'Letters' to try and bring about a reconciliation of Kantian philosophy and the insights of the theology of G. C. Storr, who emphatically asserted the necessity of divine revelation. The most important representative of Storrian theology is Gottlob Christian Rapp (1763–1794), whose writings have been studied intensively by Hegel during his time in Bern and profoundly influenced his early thought.[76]

For this second group, the discussion of the moral argument, brought up by Flatt already in the late 1780s, was of crucial importance. Flatt rejects the Kantian moral argument, but only because it is considered by Kant as the only possible proof for the existence of God and immortality. In contrast to what he sees as its one-sidedness, Flatt states that Kant's argument is a merely subjective proof which cannot lay claim to any 'objective validity and necessity'. This culminates in Flatt's charge of blind faith encapsulated in the Kantian dictum 'I want there to be a God [*ich will, daß ein Gott sey*]'.[77]

In fact, Flatt denounces Kantian philosophy generally as 'subjective idealism' – notice that this will become the central criticism levelled by Hegel and Schelling against both Kant and Fichte. Flatt, however, not only criticizes the Kantian approach, on the basis of its shortcomings he himself also attempts to argue for the proof of revelation as presented by the Storr school. His main argument is that Kant's one-sided moral argument must be bolstered by a physico-theological proof in conjunction with a cosmological proof.

RAPP, HEGEL AND KANTIAN MORALITY

In early 1795, Schelling complains in a letter to Hegel about the excitement of the self-proclaimed Kantians in the *Stift* dwelling on the moral argument.[78] Hegel replies that he is occupied with extending the moral-theological proof with a physico-theological proof, a project that Schelling positively welcomes.[79] Although at that point the details of Hegel's project have yet to be worked out, it is striking that Hegel proclaims a plan of action against the one-sidedness of Kant's moral proof that is remarkably similar to that of his teacher Flatt.

At the time of this correspondence, Hegel is also occupied with a lengthy essay by Rapp on Kant's notion of the moral incentive (*Triebfeder*).[80] Rapp is a relatively unknown, but nonetheless pivotal figure in the Kant debate in the *Stift*. Just before he became *Repetent* in the *Stift* he studied with Reinhold in Jena during 1790. His philosophical concern was to reconcile Kantian philosophy with the theology of the Storr school. For this reconciliation he leans heavily on Reinhold's 'Letters', but not without criticism.

According to Reinhold, the merit of the Critical philosophy was that it redeemed the 'religion of the pure heart' by establishing a new 'religion of pure reason'.[81] Rapp argues that the way of the heart cannot be elevated by reason, i.e. by virtue of the Kantian moral argument. The heart, though, remains indispensible for moral motivation, for it occupies an intermediate position between sensibility and the moral law by means of which it is able to inform the 'sensuous inclinations of the subject' with an incentive that is both sensuous and moral.[82]

The heart, that is, the love of the heart, is thus to be considered the mediator between sensibility and the moral law. This mediating faculty is required, because sensuous inclinations can only be opposed by a morally informed incentive acting in the sensible realm itself. The heart becomes a loving heart first by upbringing. The unconditional love for us felt by our fathers implants requited love in our hearts enabling us to follow their laws by virtue of a loving heart. The laws of our fathers, however, do not necessarily correspond to the moral law. Therefore, Christianity provides the example of a loving father and the fulfilment (πλήρωμα) of the moral law in the real life of God's beloved Son. Since this example has originally been provided for mankind, it is no longer necessary for each of us to perform the hard task of a compulsory love for the divine lawgiver; it is enough to be 'infatuated' with the testimony of the real life of Jesus Christ revealing in man's hearts that to follow the law is no longer a cold demand of moral reason, but an easy demand of the heart.

It is Rapp's intent to replace the 'frigidity' of the moral law and likewise the cold feeling of respect (*Achtung*) of Kantian moral philosophy by the mediating reality of a loving heart that is informed by the moral law. Only such a heart can affect us genuinely and can oppose our manifold sensuous inclinations. Kantian morality, by contrast, stays within the realm of the intellect and does not affect the sensible realm where genuine actions are performed. Thus, Kantian transcendental philosophy cannot go beyond its own intellectual bounds and is thus unable to have any impact on the real world that is in great need of being transformed, at least according to many of the students of the *Stift*.

The programmatic claims of Rapp converge in Hegel's fragment *Der Geist des Christentums*. Hegel writes: 'To complete subjection [*Knechtschaft*] under the law of an alien Lord, Jesus opposed not a partial subjection under a law of one's own, the self-coercion of Kantian virtue [*Tugend*], but virtues without lordship and without submission, i.e., virtues as modifications of love [. . .] as modifications of one living spirit [*Geist*].'[83] According to Hegel too, we are in

need of a principle that mediates between sensibility and morality in order to bring about a virtuous sentiment.

The origin of the post-Kantian idealist tradition is thus not the result of a direct discussion and confrontation with Kant, but rather is the effect of debates initiated by Reinhold's reception of the Kantian philosophy and its problems highlighted against the backdrop of Storrian theology.

THE LIMITED ROLE OF FICHTE

The commonly assumed influence of Fichtean philosophy must be put into perspective. It is certainly true that Fichte's *Versuch einer Kritik aller Offenbarung* (1792) immediately became the object of intense study in the *Stift*. Its central argument, however, that revelation is not only possible but also necessary for the sustainability of the moral order, was not shared by the students of the *Stift*.

The Storrian Friedrich Gottlieb Süßkind (1767–1829) argues in a lengthy essay that Fichte's proof of the possibility of revelation is a recipe for reinstalling orthodox theology,[84] which was an imminent peril that had to be averted. Hegel expresses a very similar criticism in relation to his plan of expanding the moral argument with physico-theology, as Fichte 'restores the old-fashioned way of proving in [Christian] dogmatics'.[85] The general charge of dogmatism against Fichte's *Wissenschaftslehre* is also brought by Hölderlin, for Fichte in his theory aims to go beyond the fact of consciousness. In his fragment 'Seyn, Urtheil und Modalität' this critique is specified insofar as, in Hölderlin's view, being cannot be subordinated to self-consciousness.

Post-Kantian idealism is not a linear development from Kant to Hegel. Things are far more complicated than this influential historical interpretive model suggests. Although without Kant's Critical philosophy it is indeed impossible to understand the later developments in German philosophy, its direct historical influence, however, is easily overrated if one does not address the impact of the interpretation of Kantian thought by Reinhold and the Storrians.

The philosophy of Fichte is a special case within this development. Contrary to his contemporaries, he approached Kant's philosophy more directly, even to an extent that his anonymously published *Versuch einer Kritik aller Offenbarung* was initially widely – even by Reinhold – considered to be a publication from Kant himself.

When Fichte came into contact with Reinhold's writings, he was fascinated by his attempt to establish the whole system of knowledge on the basis of one primary principle. He was ignorant about the fact that by 1792 Reinhold's foundational philosophy had already come under heavy attack, for which Diez was to a large extent responsible.

However, when Fichte presented his far more advanced foundational philosophy in the form of his *Wissenschaftslehre* (1794) the *Stift*-ians had sharpened their critical assets. The younger Hegel, Hölderlin and Schelling never embraced Fichte's *Wissenschaftslehre*; they already believed they had to hand the philosophical means that would supersede subjective idealism in either its Kantian or Fichtean mode.

In conclusion, with regard to post-Kantian idealism, at least two different lines of development must be distinguished. One line leads via Reinhold's *Grundsatzphilosophie* to Fichte and the other via Reinhold's 'Letters' to Hegel's absolute idealism. For the latter development Fichte was of minor importance. – EOO

FURTHER READING

K. Ameriks, *The Fate of Autonomy. Problems in the Appropriation of the Critical Philosophy* (Cambridge: Cambridge University Press, 2000).

F. Beiser, *German Idealism: The Struggle against Subjectivism 1781–1801* (Cambridge, MA: Harvard University Press, 2008).

D. Henrich, *Grundlegung aus dem Ich. Untersuchungen zur Vorgeschichte des Idealismus. Tübingen – Jena 1790–1794*, 2 volumes (Frankfurt a/M: Suhrkamp, 2004).

R.-P. Horstmann, 'The reception of the *Critique of Pure Reason* in German Idealism', in P. Guyer (ed.), *The Cambridge Companion to Kant's Critique of Pure Reason* (Cambridge: Cambridge University Press, 2010), pp. 329–345.

K. Marx, *The Usefulness of the Kantian Philosophy. How Karl Leonhard Reinhold's Commitment to Enlightenment Influenced His Reception of Kant*, in the series *Reinholdiana*, vol. 1 (Berlin/New York: de Gruyter, 2011).

K. L. Reinhold, *Letters on the Kantian Philosophy*, ed. K. Ameriks (Cambridge: Cambridge University Press, 2006).

HEGEL'S APPROPRIATION OF KANT'S THEORETICAL PHILOSOPHY IN THE JENA PERIOD

KANT'S 'AUTHENTIC IDEALISM'

Throughout his oeuvre, Hegel consistently stressed the necessity to distinguish between, on the one hand, the 'spirit' or 'principle' of Kant's thought, and, on the other hand, the 'letter' of Kant's philosophy, or its actual execution. In spirit or principle, Hegel believes that Kant's philosophy contains a core of potentially 'authentic' or 'true idealism'.[86] In its specific execution however, Hegel deems it fundamentally insufficient. Kant's idealism remains a 'subjectivism' insofar as it affirms the opposition between concept (*Begriff*) and being (*Sein*). In this way, Hegel alternates between praise for the potential of the principle of Kantian thought, and criticism of its actual execution.

The meritorious principle which Hegel takes to guide Kant's thought is that philosophy should consist in a self-justification of reason. For Hegel, this means that self-consciousness must show itself to be the implicit unity of all explicit conceptual oppositions. However, Kant succeeded in developing such an 'authentic idealism' only from a 'limited standpoint [*eingeschränkten Standpunkt*]'.[87]

Hegel identifies several aspects of Kantian thought which contain this 'authentic Idea of Reason'.[88] First, it is expressed in the question guiding **CPR**: 'How are synthetic judgments a priori possible?' The turn with which Kant set out to put metaphysics on the 'secure course of a science' (Bxviii), consisted in the hypothesis that objects conform to our knowledge, rather than the other way around. That is to say, Critical philosophy must involve an investigation into the ways in which the object of experience must be thought in accordance with the rules of the understanding.

The ways in which the object must be thought are expressed by the categories, on which rests any synthetic judgment a priori. Hegel writes: 'The determinations of thought or *concepts of the understanding* make up the *objectivity* of experience [*Erfahrungserkenntnisse*]. They contain *relations* only [*überhaupt*], and therefore through them *synthetic* judgments a priori

are formed.'[89] By shifting in this way the focus of the inquiry from the *content* of an experience to its *form* (the 'relations' under which any object of experience must necessarily be thought), Kant manages, in his intentions at least, to break through the opposition between the subjective and the objective, since, in Hegel's words, for Kant '[t]he objectivity here means the element of *universality* and *necessity*, i.e. of the determinations of thought themselves – the so-called *a priori*'.[90] From this point of view, Kant's philosophy is true idealism because objectivity is taken *in terms of* the determinations of thought, rather than as simply opposed, or external, to them.

Secondly, for this same reason, Hegel finds in Kant's philosophy a core of true idealism 'insofar as it shows, that neither the concept in isolation nor intuition in isolation is anything at all; that intuition by itself is blind and the concept by itself is empty'.[91] Since for Hegel any self-justification of reason must entail that subjectivity recognize itself as absolute (i.e. the implicit unity of what is explicitly opposed), Hegel takes Kant's stipulation that neither intuitions nor concepts can by themselves yield knowledge to be fully justified.

Lastly, it is above all in the Transcendental Deduction that Hegel recognizes in Kant's philosophy an authentic idealism: 'It is one of the profoundest and truest insights to be found in the Critique of Reason that the *unity* which constitutes the *essence of the concept* is recognized as the *original synthetic* unity *of apperception*, the unity of the "*I think*", or of self-consciousness.'[92]

THE IMPLICIT PRINCIPLE OF SPECULATION

The greatest merit of Kant's turn in metaphysics is that it asserts that the 'highest point'

(**CPR** B134n) of the justification of knowledge is to be found in self-consciousness, as Hegel approvingly observes: 'The principle of speculation is the identity of subject and object, and this principle is most definitely articulated in the deduction of the forms of the intellect (*Verstand*).'[93]

This principle is a principle of speculation, since as the *implicit*, speculative, identity of subject and object, or of concept and being, consciousness cannot be thought in terms of either side of that opposition. According to Hegel, however, Kant's standpoint is 'limited', precisely because it restricts the validity of the principle of the understanding itself to appearances only, excluding from its domain things in themselves, based on his infamous doctrine of the unknowability of things in themselves. This means that, for Hegel, the discovery of the speculative identity of subject and object reverts back to one side of that opposition: although Kant distinguishes the 'objective' from the 'subjective' unity of consciousness (cf. **CPR** B139–140), Kant's Critical philosophy will never be able to go beyond subjectivism because of this restriction of the validity of that unity.

The Ontological Proof of God's Existence

The specific form of Hegel's critique of Kant's execution of the self-justification of reason is well brought out in his treatment of Kant's critique of the ontological proof of the existence of God. It is here that what Hegel takes to be the essential trait of Kant's Critical subjectivism comes to light most prominently, viz. an affirmation of the *opposition* between thought and being.

Kant's criticism of the ontological proof rests precisely on the assumption that the categories are restricted to possible experience, that is, that their application only holds for a given empirical manifold of representations. Since with the concept of God an object is thought which by definition cannot be given in experience, its existence can ex hypothesi never justifiably be known on this ground.

The only thing that *can* be shown, according to Kant, is (1) the necessary regulative function of the *idea* of God, and (2) the necessity to postulate God's existence as a demand of practical reason. For Kant, the ontological proof rests entirely on the deduction of existence from concepts. But since for Kant existence (*Dasein* or *Wirklichkeit*) is a category with a restricted use, judging that something exists can never be justified on the basis of thought alone but always requires empirical intuition.

Beyond Kant's Subjectivism

For Hegel, herein lies the very core of Kantian subjectivism: it is an explicit affirmation of the opposition between thought and being. This, however, is not a 'false' or 'wrong' opposition, and Hegel indeed sees its explication by Kant as highly valuable. Its merit, at this point, consists in the expression of that difference 'in its highest abstraction and in its truest form',[94] since at bottom all knowledge consists precisely in the implicit or speculative identity of thought and being.

That this identity cannot be 'known' as per the rules of the understanding Hegel takes to be one of Kant's 'excellent discoveries [*vortreffliche Entdeckung*]'.[95] Yet to state that, because of this, this speculative principle is nothing for knowledge, that it stands over against knowledge and cannot itself be brought before consciousness, is where Hegel refuses to follow Kant.

In Hegel's view, knowledge precisely consists in this very absolute identity, and a true self-justification of reason will have to bring every opposition (most especially the difference in its 'highest abstraction' – as between thought and being) back to consciousness itself. The Kantian 'I think' as the highest point of the Deduction potentially expresses this insight into the truly synthetic *absolute* identity of the subjective and the objective, but remains abstract or formal once the restriction of its validity reverts the 'I' back to the merely subjective. A truly synthetic concept of self-consciousness must, according to Hegel, recognize its dependence on the content of its specific determinations, which leads to a much more differentiated concept of self-consciousness (ultimately, in his later philosophy, as 'spirit'), rather than it being merely a formal rule of the understanding with restricted validity.

The same problem holds for Kant's categories: they must remain formal and will never be more than 'static, dead pigeonholes of the intellect [*ruhenden toten Fächern der Intelligenz*]',[96] whereas a true self-justification of reason must be able to show how each category flows dynamically from consciousness itself, which can be explained by focusing on the way in which each category implies, and brings with it, its own opposite.

In this way, although much of Hegel's thought on objectivity clearly bears the hallmarks of Kant's major discoveries, the project of transcendental philosophy changes significantly from the Kantian project of the self-justification of reason in terms of a restriction and limitation of the understanding to possible experience into the path or development of consciousness towards fully self-conscious 'spirit', by tracing the dynamic logic of reason's own determinations and categories and therewith progressively recognizing itself as *absolute* subjectivity.

Hegel's early intuitions regarding such a project receive their first systematic exposition, in all their theoretical and also practical-philosophical facets, in his major work *Phenomenology of Spirit* of 1807, and are carried through in the *Science of Logic* and afterwards. – JdJ

FURTHER READING

K. Ameriks, *Kant and the Fate of Autonomy. Problems in the Appropriation of the Critical Philosophy* (Cambridge: Cambridge University Press, 2000), pt. IV.

W. Bristow, *Hegel and the Transformation of Philosophical Critique* (Oxford: Oxford University Press, 2007).

R.-P. Horstmann, 'Hegels Konzeption von Rationalität – die Verbannung des Verstandes aus dem Reich der Wahrheit', in *Die Grenzen der Vernunft. Eine Untersuchung zu Zielen und Motiven des Deutschen Idealismus,* third edition (Frankfurt a/M: Klostermann, 2004), pp. 123–142.

R. B. Pippin, *Hegel's Idealism. The Satisfactions of Self-Consciousness* (Cambridge: Cambridge University Press, 1989), pt. I.

D. Schulting, 'Hegel on Kant's synthetic a priori in *Glauben und Wissen*', in *Hegel-Jahrbuch 2005: Glauben und Wissen. Dritter Teil,* ed. A. Arndt, K. Bal & H. Ottman (Berlin: Akademie Verlag, 2005), pp. 176–182.

S. Sedgwick, *Hegel's Critique of Kant* (Oxford: Oxford University Press, 2012).

SCHOPENHAUER'S RECEPTION OF KANT

SCHOPENHAUER ENCOUNTERS KANT

With his father's apparent suicide in 1805, Arthur Schopenhauer (1788–1860) was released from what he saw as his depressing destiny in the family merchant business. Turning to the study of medicine and physiology, Schopenhauer soon became enthralled by philosophy, especially Kant and Plato. Under G. E. Schulze's tutelage in Göttingen, Schopenhauer read Kant first-hand and became acquainted with the criticisms that had been levelled for two decades at the Critical philosophy. In 1811, Schopenhauer moved to Berlin to study with Fichte, but he soon became disappointed in Fichte's lectures finding them obscure to the point of obscurantism.[97] Worse still, Schopenhauer thought Fichte (as well as Schelling and Hegel) had steered philosophy back to the kind of rationalist project thoroughly discredited by the First *Critique*. For these and other reasons, Schopenhauer harboured a career-long hostility to Schelling, Fichte and Hegel (in order of increasing disdain) of which he made no secret.

Schopenhauer was the first 'back to Kant' philosopher. His aim was to 'take up directly from Kant' in order to modify and offer a self-consistent transcendental idealist system.[98] This has not generally been recognized by commentators since Schopenhauer makes greater knowledge claims concerning the thing in itself than Kant ever thought possible, namely, in addition to the world as representation, there is another side of the coin, as it were, the *world as will*. In order to see how Schopenhauer thought he could stay true to Kant's transcendental idealism while identifying the Kantian thing in itself with will – conceived as a non-teleological and thus 'blind' striving – one must turn to Schopenhauer's reception of Kant's epistemology.

MODIFICATIONS TO KANT'S EPISTEMOLOGY

In his doctoral dissertation, *The Fourfold Root of the Principle of Sufficient Reason* (1813–14;

revised 1847), Schopenhauer argues for several modifications and simplifications of Kant's picture of the cognitive faculties. The understanding should not be construed as the faculty for thinking intuitions through pure and empirical concepts. Rather, it non-conceptually transforms sensory intuitions into a world of experience ordered in space, time and causality. On Schopenhauer's view, basic human sensory experience is not-yet-conceptualized and is similar – with variations for different sensory organs – to that of non-human animals. The fact that non-human animals do not use language and thus seem to lack concepts but nonetheless perceive and act intelligently constitutes evidence, in Schopenhauer's view, for construing the understanding as operating non-conceptually. Distinctive to human cognition is the faculty of reason, but in contrast to Kant, according to Schopenhauer reason is *nothing but* the faculty that abstracts concepts from experience and imposes four modes of explanation, that is, the four roots of the principle of sufficient reason, onto experience as well as onto our judgments.[99]

This changed picture of the cognitive faculties means that while Schopenhauer agrees with Kant in the view that 'concepts without intuitions are empty' he disagrees with the view that 'intuitions without concepts are blind' (**CPR** A50–51=B74–75). On the contrary, intuitions without concepts form a class of knowledge he calls 'feeling' (*Gefühl*) or 'intuitive knowledge' (*intuitive Erkenntniß*) as opposed to conceptual knowledge (*Wissen*).[100]

IDENTIFICATION OF THE THING IN ITSELF AS 'WILL'

The best summary of Schopenhauer's reception of Kant's metaphysics is to be found in the Appendix to the first volume of his magnum opus *The World as Will and Representation* (1818, revised with a second volume in 1844;

third edition 1859) titled 'Critique of the Kantian Philosophy'. Here we gain a sense of the Kantian views from which Schopenhauer never wavered: He asserts that 'Kant's greatest merit is to distinguish between appearance and thing in itself – by proving that the *intellect* always stands between us and things, which is why we cannot have cognition of things as they may be in themselves'.[101] Another doctrine from which he never departs is Kant's distinction between the empirical and intelligible character, which Schopenhauer considers 'one of the most excellent things anyone has ever said'.[102] We also get a sense of how Schopenhauer interpreted Kant's version of transcendental idealism from the fact that he praises the exposition of it in **P** and asserts the superiority of the first edition of the First *Critique* over the second, claiming that the latter spoiled its insights.

To put things in contemporary scholarly terms, Schopenhauer thought that the best way to understand Kant's transcendental idealism is as a 'two-worlds' or 'causality' view rather than as a 'two-aspects' or 'identity' view.[103] Interestingly, Schopenhauer's own version of transcendental idealism is well characterized as a *metaphysical* version of a two-aspects or identity view: The world has two sides, the world as we represent it, and the way it is in itself, as will. But these two sides are not related causally, rather, the world of representation is the 'objectification' of the world as will.

To arrive at this view, Schopenhauer reconfigured transcendental idealism in a way that would avoid the criticism levelled famously by Jacobi and Schulze that Kant had unjustifiably applied the category of causality to things in themselves. Further, Schopenhauer adhered very strictly to the notion that space, time and causality are *exclusively* forms that the subject imposes to structure the world of representation. Accordingly, there are at

least two things, for Schopenhauer, we can know about the thing in itself: It is *not* spatiotemporal and it may *not* be understood as causally related to phenomena. It is the strict adherence to the *exclusive* subjectivity of space and time as well as to the claim that space and time constitute the principle of individuation that leads Schopenhauer to argue that Kant should have talked only about unindividuated 'thing in itself' in the singular, although strictly speaking the thing in itself is not 'one' in the way an object is one, nor in the way a concept is one, rather, the will is 'one in the sense that it lies outside of [...] the possibility of multiplicity'.[104]

Notwithstanding his agreement with Kant that we can never have direct cognition of the thing in itself, there is a very special instance of knowledge – one's first-personal insight into acts of volition – that is immediate in the sense that it is not mediated by the forms of space or causality, but which is still known in 'the form of time, as well as that of being known and of knowing in general'.[105] Schopenhauer believes the distinctive immediacy of an individual's epistemic access to her own body in acts of willing licenses an identification of the thing in itself with will. In a revealing passage Schopenhauer writes:

> It is nonetheless fair to say that we are only using a denomination from the superior term [a *denominatio a potiori*] that gives the concept of will a broader scope than it has had before. [...] no word [could] designate the concept of this genus. Accordingly, I will name the genus after its most important species; the more intimate and immediate cognition we have of this species leads to the mediated cognition we have of all the others.[106]

The rhetorical device that Schopenhauer explicitly employs to call the thing in itself 'will' is the *denominatio a potiori*, literally, 'receiving its name from what is better, superior or greater'. What Schopenhauer offers us is metonymical insight into the thing in itself. He is trying to get us to widen the extension of the concept of 'will' which we know from our nearly immediate experience of willing beyond the bounds of possible sensation to the thing in itself, and invites his readers to do this on the strength of their special insight into their own wills.

This is the same kind of sensible confirmation by way of a felt connection that Kant affirms in §59 of the Critique of Aesthetic Judgment (**CJ** 351ff.), namely the notion that beauty is a symbol of morality, except that the Schopenhauerian connection is not to be brought about by the felt recognition of structural analogies, but rather, by felt *contiguity*; that is, we gain insight into the nature of the thing in itself *by being* part of the in-itself, and by experiencing *ourselves* in the least mediated way available.[107] Another place to look in Kant for the origin of Schopenhauer's metonymical mode of making the thing in itself sensible is **CJ** 338–346 (§§56–57), where Kant resolves the antinomy of taste by invoking the 'supersensible substratum of appearance'. Here as well, Kant sees a role for feeling (aesthetic feeling) in making the rational idea of the thing in itself sensible without being able to provide a *direct* intuition thereof.

AESTHETICS

Schopenhauer faults Kant's aesthetic theory for its focus on *judgments* rather than on aesthetic *experience,* but applauds it for giving the correct 'general method of investigation' for aesthetics. The correct method is the largely subjective method of investigating the elements in human nature which, when stimulated in a certain way, prompt us to judge an object as beautiful or sublime, as opposed to the largely objective investigations of Aristotle, Burke, Winckelmann, Lessing and Herder.[108] Kant's theory of the sublime comes in for high praise, however, and in his *Studienhefte* entry on the Third *Critique* (1808–11), one sees that Schopenhauer was clearly moved by it: 'How true and fine is what he says about the sublime!' He qualifies this appraisal only as follows: '[O]nly a few things in his language and the fatal faculty of reason [*die fatale Vernunft*] are to be overlooked.'[109]

Affinities between their views include the conception of aesthetic experience as disinterested and a focus on both nature and art. This follows in the tradition of eighteenth century aesthetics, although Schopenhauer understands aesthetic experience more particularly as 'will-less' (*willenlos*). In addition, Schopenhauer's theory of the sublime is really a transformation of Kant's theory that retains the distinction between the mathematical and dynamical sublime, the mixed painful/pleasurable nature of the experience that is theorized as a kind of oscillation between, on the one hand, fear (dynamical) or frustration (mathematical) and, on the other, exaltation in the felt recognition of a supersensible quality in ourselves. The main difference between their respective accounts derives from Schopenhauer's excision of the role of reason – '*die fatale Vernunft*' – in the experience.[110]

Yet, Schopenhauer departs from Kant's aesthetic theory in several ways. Schopenhauer sees a greater *cognitive* import of the experience of the beautiful and sublime than did Kant. In place of Kant's cognitive free-play in an experience of beauty, Schopenhauer sees a 'perception of Ideas', the ideas being the essential features of the phenomenal world. Since the perception of Ideas is a somewhat rare form of intuitive knowledge, this renders art highly significant from a cognitive perspective. The most significant art form on his view is music. Absolute music, that is, non-programmatic music without a text, for Schopenhauer bypasses the Ideas and affords a 'copy of the will' by expressing universal human emotions and strivings shorn of any particular context in the phenomenal world. Like first-personal volitional insight – the basis on which Schopenhauer identifies the world in itself with 'will' – absolute music is experienced only in time, without the mediation of other forms of cognitive conditioning such as space and causality. It thus affords, for Schopenhauer, the *closest* – though still not entirely immediate – access we can have to the nature of the in-itself of the world.

ETHICAL THOUGHT

Schopenhauer's most pronounced departure from Kant concerns his ethical thought. In his essay 'On the Basis of Morality' (1840, published with his essay 'On the Freedom of the Will' in 1841) Schopenhauer spends the entire first half of the essay offering a highly critical assessment of Kant's ethics before giving his positive account of the basis of morality. Schopenhauer argues that Kant begs the question by assuming that morality has an imperatival form, and anticipating G. E. M. Anscombe's criticism, continues that a 'moral law' makes little sense without the notion of a divine or worldly *lawgiver*. Further, Schopenhauer does not think reason can play the moral lawgiver role due to its being merely a faculty for abstracting concepts from and imposing on experience the four forms of *explanatory* reasoning (the four roots of the PSR). Relatedly, Schopenhauer does not think reason can legitimately be seen as the ground for any 'causality through freedom' insofar as this idea involves illegitimately predicating causality beyond the bounds of sense. Finally, Schopenhauer is outraged by the fact that Kant's ethics does not include non-rational animals directly as objects of proper respect, and believes it seriously ethically defective accordingly.

The basis of morality for Schopenhauer is instead the feeling of compassion. Compassion involves feeling the suffering (or prospective suffering) of another as if it were one's own, and thus motivates one to try to relieve (or to prevent) that suffering. Unlike sentimentalist views, however, Schopenhauer believes there is a metaphysical basis that grounds the normativity of this feeling. Whereas persons of predominantly egoistic and malicious character see a 'thick partition' between themselves and others, the compassionate person recognizes the fundamental connection among all living beings.

This connection may be interpreted in a robustly metaphysical fashion as a felt recognition of the unindividuated nature of the in-itself of the world as will, or it may be interpreted axiologically as the felt recognition of inherent value in all living beings. If one favours the latter interpretation (as this author does) one might see a greater affinity after all between Kant and Schopenhauer's ethical views: Schopenhauer's view that all living beings have inherent value may be seen as a transformation of Kant's view of rational nature as having inherent value. On both interpretations, the compassionate person, for Schopenhauer, 'sees the world aright' (to borrow Wittgenstein's phrase), that is, insofar as she responds compassionately to the suffering of others, she tracks the way things really are. – SSh

FURTHER READING

P. Guyer, 'Schopenhauer, Kant, and the methods of philosophy', in C. Janaway (ed.) *The Cambridge Companion to Schopenhauer* (Cambridge: Cambridge University Press, 1999), pp. 93–137.

P. Guyer, 'Schopenhauer, Kant and compassion', *Kantian Review* 17,3 (2012): 403–429.

C. Janaway, 'Necessity, responsibility and character: Schopenhauer on freedom of the will', *Kantian Review* 17,3 (2012): 431–457.

M. Kossler, 'The "perfected system of criticism": Schopenhauer's initial disagreements with Kant', *Kantian Review* 17,3 (2012): 459–478.

S. Shapshay, 'Schopenhauer's transformation of the Kantian sublime', *Kantian Review* 17,3 (2012): 479–511.

S. Shapshay, 'Schopenhauer's aesthetics and philosophy of art', *Philosophy Compass* 7,1 (2012): 11–22.

'BACK TO KANT': NEO-KANTIANISM

To come to grips with neo-Kantianism as a philosophical movement, it is important to see that neo-Kantianism primarily understands philosophy as a science of foundations. As such, neo-Kantianism underscores the basic intention of metaphysics to address fundamental questions concerning our understanding of the world and ourselves.

From a historical point of view, Plato is an important sparring partner for the neo-Kantians. For Plato showed that we can only understand the foundations of both things and our knowledge of them, if we assume that ideas transcend sensible experience. The neo-Kantians thus agreed with Plato that philosophy should be idealism. However, although he tried to understand ideas as principles, Plato's classical metaphysical position insufficiently differentiates between being and knowledge, ontology and logic. He understands ideas as themselves a type of being, i.e. general, transcendent, non-sensible, and proper being.

Kant's project of transcendental philosophy makes an end to such a reification of ideas. The domain of philosophical foundations, 'the transcendental' so to speak, is discovered to be a domain of principles that are the ground for the validity of thought and action as such. These principles should not be understood as representing a type of entity or *being*, but rather as the basis of the comprehension of what it is to describe something as possessed of the quality of *validity*. That is, they must be seen as conditions that first enable and direct our thought and action. Thus, principles are to be seen as preceding experience without losing their intimate relation to experience. Put in more general terms, any putative ontology presupposes a transcendental logic.

For Kant, knowledge has its ground in the cognitive relation which is defined in terms of the a priori conditions that make knowledge and the objects of knowledge first possible. The objective validity of these conditions lies in their function to enable possible experience.

THE SPIRITUAL BACKGROUND

This systematic link to the history of philosophy is only one aspect of neo-Kantianism. Another aspect concerns the fact that a philosopher never operates in a cultural vacuum, but is also always imbued with the spirit of his own age. Neo-Kantianism is also a reaction to its own cultural context and seeing it from this perspective is important to interpreting it. The cultural or spiritual context of neo-Kantianism is a complex one. I will highlight one important line of influence.

This line starts with Hegel's death as a historical date that has symbolic meaning for the history of philosophy: German Idealism had lost its leading spiritual position in Germany. Henceforth, natural science, a more historical orientation, realism, and the general 'loss of illusions' gradually came to dominate intellectual culture and this provoked a kind of post-idealistic identity crisis. With Hegel's death his philosophy and the Hegelian conception of the unity of facticity and meaning, of reason and reality, gradually lost purchase. As a result, not only the influential theme of 'worldview' (*Weltanschauung*) suggesting a situated perspective on totality could spring up and grow popular, but also all kinds of naturalism and scientific reductionism, evoking loss of meaning, of the richness and depth of life, sprouted. The ghost of nihilism, of a metaphysical void, dawned.

This spiritual background points already to neo-Kantianism as it tried to overcome the above-sketched post-idealistic gap between 'is' and 'ought'. The situation becomes even more complex as the empirical sciences appeared to be emancipated from philosophy and became wholly independent. The question arose: why then still philosophy?

NEO-KANTIANISM AS EPISTEMOLOGY

By the mid-nineteenth century, marking out and making sense of the field of properly philosophical investigations had become problematic. This problem leads us directly to the beginning of neo-Kantianism. In reaction to the identity crisis of philosophy, neo-Kantianism, both in its early and its mature forms, makes a case for the rehabilitation of philosophy.

This rehabilitation starts with a clear commitment to epistemology (*Erkenntnistheorie*) as the ultimate foundational discipline of both philosophy and the other sciences. To be sure, this does not imply a reduction of philosophy to epistemology: neo-Kantian philosophy is about culture in the broad sense, not just about knowledge and science in the narrow sense. With respect to the rehabilitation of philosophy, the neo-Kantians, as the epithet suggests, return to Kant.

Of course, many regard neo-Kantianism as primarily an epistemological Kantian movement. There are many reasons for doing so. Widespread topical and methodological uncertainty in the universities led philosophers such as Eduard Zeller and scientists like Hermann von Helmholtz to attempt to provide philosophy with its own topic and its own method, while at the same time discussing the methods and principles of the non-philosophical sciences, which were developing ever so rapidly in their time. Such attempts led to what at the end of the 1870s became known as the Marburg and Southwest Schools of neo-Kantianism. Fairly soon these schools came to dominate the epistemological debates of the nineteenth century. It is therefore not entirely untrue to see neo-Kantianism as primarily an epistemological movement.

However, more recent research on neo-Kantianism suggests that this view is responsible for much confusion about neo-Kantianism. Especially the cultural-philosophical nature of neo-Kantianism as a reaction to a crisis has, as a result, been insufficiently acknowledged. Recent research has emphasized that questions regarding world view were in fact the driving force behind the 'logical' preoccupations of the neo-Kantians. Despite the major differences in approach, it is a modern philosophy of culture that unites the Marburg and Southwest neo-Kantians.

The interpretation of Kant's philosophy is equally part of this goal.

PHILOSOPHY AS WELTANSCHAUUNG

The concept of 'worldview' (*Weltanschauung*) serves as an abbreviation for the problem of the validity of values and hence points to the dispute about how culture is to be shaped. Nihilism, the loss of faith in the rationality of the world and the values assumed to be valid, is not only a major challenge for neo-Kantianism, but also a concern of many other scientists and thinkers towards the end of the nineteenth century.[111]

To understand neo-Kantianism properly, however, it is important that the emphasis on the cultural-philosophical aspect does not lead one to disregard the specific way in which the neo-Kantians put culture on the philosophical agenda. Not just *that* neo-Kantianism can be understood as a philosophy of culture and that it understands itself as such, but also *how* it is to be seen as a philosophy of culture is what explains the peculiar nature and unity of neo-Kantianism as well as its relation to Kant and ultimately its argumentative potential.

'BACK TO KANT'

The labels 'neo-Kantianism' or 'Critical philosophy' (*Kritizismus*) are best restricted to the Marburg School – whose main representatives are Hermann Cohen, Paul Natorp, and Ernst Cassirer – and the Southwest German School, also called the Baden School or Heidelberg School – whose protagonists were in particular Wilhelm Windelband, Heinrich Rickert, Emil Lask, and Bruno Bauch. Both schools are formed towards the end of the 1870s. The Marburg and Southwest Schools represent the mature

theories of neo-Kantian philosophy. (Of course there also exist broader conceptions of neo-Kantianism; some identify as many as seven sub-schools.)

The famous dictum 'back to Kant', originating with Otto Liebmann,[112] one of the pathfinders for neo-Kantianism, encapsulates in a concise and programmatic way the determined recourse to Kant of the leading neo-Kantians. However, Kantian motifs can be found not only in neo-Kantianism, but in almost every philosophical school of thought in the nineteenth and twentieth centuries (at least in the continental tradition).[113] Therefore, an additional feature marking out neo-Kantianism is needed. Windelband formulated a dictum not less famous than that of Liebmann: 'To understand Kant rightly means to go beyond him'. For the leading figures of neo-Kantianism this dictum means that the return to Kant is not a mere reproduction of his historical position; to understand Kant means to further the development of philosophy with the help of Kant.

However, the tendency to advance philosophy by Kantian means is not specific to neo-Kantianism. One must think here of German idealists such as Fichte and Hegel. Another additional feature is therefore needed to determine the specific nature of neo-Kantianism.

THE PROBLEM OF VALIDITY

At the centre of the efforts of the neo-Kantians, as indicated earlier, is the problem of validity (*Gültigkeit, Geltung*). Taking the validity of our theoretical and non-theoretical – practical, aesthetic, religious – endeavours as its theme constitutes the core of neo-Kantian philosophy. For neo-Kantianism, philosophy *is* the theory of validity. In developing a theory of validity, the neo-

Kantians emphasize a fundamental aspect of Kant's Critical philosophy, namely that the determinacy of human endeavours, being products of reason, is to be established by means of a determination of the *principles* of their validity.

Neo-Kantians thus especially appreciate Kant's insight into the problem of validity (cf. the *quid juris* issue in the Transcendental Deduction of the categories). At the same time, they find it important to develop further Kant's concept of philosophy, rather than resort to metaphysical speculation as did the German idealists or regard the method of philosophy in terms of a positivistic approach to the nature of validity. Neo-Kantians therefore do not only recover Kant's contribution to philosophy but their aim is to renew it in the light of a different constellation of philosophical problems from Kant's.

Against post-Kantian German Idealism, neo-Kantians stress that philosophy should not study things qua their being, but focus on the validity of thinking things qua their being. In some respects, one could see Hegel's logic as a development of Kant's transcendental logic. On this reading, Hegel's analysis of the determinations of thought leads to a fundamental set of a priori conditions. For the neo-Kantians, however, Hegel's logical system is not just a whole of logical conditions for the validity of thoughts; they reproach him for having conceptualized thought as itself a metaphysical reality of spirit. In their view, Hegel contaminates the radical foundations of modernity with classical metaphysics, hence departing from the framework of Kantian transcendental philosophy.

Instead of taking the conditions of validity of the thought of reality again as itself a reality, the neo-Kantians discriminate sharply between validity and being. Hence, they try to correct the assumed metaphysical position of Hegel by harking back to Kant's critical arguments. According to the neo-Kantians, validity and being are related to each other in such a way that, following Kant, being has its foundation in validity, and ontology in epistemology. According to their understanding of Kant's transcendental philosophical method, philosophy takes as point of departure the given, i.e. a concrete experience, or the fact (*Faktum*) of culture in order to establish its principles, or as Kant would put it, the conditions of its possibility.

PURE VERSUS EMPIRICAL SUBJECT

For the neo-Kantians, as presumed successors of Kant, philosophy does not take as its theme the world in terms of a direct relation to objects, as do the non-philosophical sciences. They do not assume the 'I' or 'consciousness' to be an empirical phenomenon, nor do they take the relation between such empirical phenomena and the world to be a philosophical topic. Rather, philosophy aims at determining the validity structure of experience. Time and again, neo-Kantians criticize all kinds of metaphysical, psychological, physiological and what nowadays is called (neo)-structuralist and evolutionary-biological conceptualizations of epistemology, or, more comprehensively, of the philosophy of culture. Such attempts understand knowledge as an ontic relationship. According to the neo-Kantians, these deficient conceptualizations, including their agnostic and relativistic implications, deprive epistemology of its fundamental thematic: the validity of knowledge.

Neo-Kantians exclude the empirical subject and its anthropological and metaphysical connotations from study insofar as they primarily focus on a 'pure subject'. This subject, in the sense of the whole of the principles of validity (a priori structures, values, etc.), is understood as the foundation of all that can be valid and hence as the ground for the possibility of objectivity. By means of this strategy, which discriminates sharply between, on the one hand, a 'pure' subject as foundation of objectivity and an 'empirical' subject which is grounded in that normative foundation, on the other, the neo-Kantians try to overcome what they consider to be certain exaggerated positions or naïve, objectivist worldviews be they called naturalism, materialism, psychologism, empiricism, positivism, logicism, fideism, historicism, *Lebensphilosophie*, or nihilism.

Philosophy of Culture

As in theoretical philosophy, the relation between the unconditional norm of the pure subject and its conditional fulfilment by the empirical subject equally plays a central role in the philosophy of culture. This proportional relation of validity makes clear that the duality of facticity and meaning, of reason and reality, of 'is' and 'ought', is grounded on premises that turn out to be false.

We may illustrate this through Heinrich Rickert's concept of 'meaning'. Meaning is conceptualized as the recognition by the finite rational being called 'man' of unconditionally valid theoretic and non-theoretic values. The reciprocal relation of implication, and the one-sided relation of foundation between the norm and that for which the norm is, absolute demand and finite fulfilment, principle and the concrete, implies of course that the human production of meaning is characterized by finitude.

Therefore, the neo-Kantians deny that the duality of subject and object as between an empirical subject and an inner or outer world is fundamental to epistemology. They

develop another kind of relationship that not only turns out to be more fundamental, but also proves to be of great importance to the development of a philosophy of culture.

Starting the philosophical analysis with given cultural phenomena or spheres of culture, which implicitly contain objective validity claims, does not imply that the premise of the analysis is a *Faktum* that is stipulated dogmatically as valid. Rather, the analysis takes such 'facta' as problematic, as a validity claim that is in need of philosophical evaluation. According to the neo-Kantians' understanding of the method of transcendental philosophy, the original determinacy of the different spheres of culture is to be known via an oblique, validity-reflexive disclosure of the constituents of meaning of those spheres of culture, i.e. of the principles of validity of those claims.

The Primacy of 'Ought'

Like Kant, the neo-Kantians understand culture as a system of meaning in order to provide a conceptual account of 'the world of man'. With this they aim to show reason itself to be the governing principle of our world, of culture.

Take the case of the Southwest School of neo-Kantianism. Unlike the Marburg School, the Southwest School did not fall victim to the 'narrow intellectualist' focus of Cohen, who restricted philosophical analysis mainly to the cultural fact of scientific knowledge, although the later development of the Marburg School broadened the scope of analysis as can be seen in the work of Natorp and Cassirer. From the start, however, the Southwest School takes culture in its widest sense.

The Southwest School conceives of culture as determined by values. From a philosophical point of view, what is called theoretical culture ('knowledge') has a logical and a systemic primacy. Already in theoretical philosophy it turns out that *theoretical* culture rests on a range of theoretical values (a priori structures, principles), which determines the validity of theoretical endeavours. The values that comprise the value 'truth' ought to be normative for the thoughts of empirical subjects in order to assure that their thought yields knowledge of objects, i.e. that thought is objective. This logical relation within the realm of theoretical culture is then transported to other spheres of culture: these too consist of subjects who acknowledge values.

In this sense, the Southwest School neo-Kantians propagate the primacy of 'ought' (*Sollen*), a primacy of practical reason in its most radical, and not just in its practical sense, namely in the sense that it encompasses *all* dimensions of reason. They propagate a philosophy of values as a philosophy of culture.

Numerous historical and systematic studies of the first decades of the twentieth century make clear that the Southwest School is to be seen as a comprehensive philosophy of values. But they also make clear that the concept of value is a fundamental concept: philosophy itself is essentially about values. The idea of living through a metaphysical crisis fits in well with this systematic perception. After all, the exploration of values should contribute to the overcoming of the post-German-Idealist divide between values and reality that threatened to make human orientation both practically impossible and theoretically incomprehensible. The philosophy of values acts against the culture of nihilism by showing that there are values that are objectively valid.

Hence, the concept of 'value' – and closely related concepts like 'meaning', 'ought', 'validity' – has a meaning that goes

far beyond its *methodological* function in the constitution of the subject matters of the arts and humanities. It points to the aforementioned *metaphysical* dimension that contains the grounds of our thoughts and actions.

The debate is thus not so much about the validity and status of some traditional values. Rather, against the background of the post-Idealist conception of reality as value-free and without meaning, the debate focuses primarily on the foundations of our understanding of the world and ourselves. Values traditionally treated by metaphysics, such as truth and morality, unity and plurality, value and reality, function as a framework to enable our understanding of, and dealings with, the world. Hence, the philosophy of values operates against the background of nihilism and aims at elucidating the principles of human existence and the world that humans live in.

In conclusion, the main schools of neo-Kantianism take the basic problem of philosophy to be that of the validity of our theoretical and non-theoretical endeavours. This problem is to be solved through a determination of the principles of validity. These principles are what make up the sphere of the 'transcendental'. The transcendental domain, therefore, is not to be confused with the psychology of an empirical subject or with the metaphysics of an absolute reality.

Far from declaring the world we live in to be meaningless, the neo-Kantians aim to bring to light the philosophical foundations of the world. Hence, they try to understand the rationality of our world and its meaning. The concept of culture functions as a universal and fundamental framework, a framework that was once occupied by metaphysics. This framework is now freed from ontological premises yet is still able to counteract nihilism. – CK

FURTHER READING

A. Chignell (ed.), 'On going back to Kant', special issue on neo-Kantianism in *The Philosophical Forum* 39,2 (2008): 109–298.
M. Heinz, C. Krijnen (eds), *Kant im Neukantianismus: Fortschritt oder Rückschritt?* (Würzburg: Königshausen & Neumann, 2007).
S. Luft, R. Makkreel (eds), *Neo-Kantianism in Contemporary Philosophy* (Bloomington, IN: Indiana University Press, 2010).
D. Pätzold, C. Krijnen (eds), *Der Neukantianismus und das Erbe des deutschen Idealismus* (Würzburg: Königshausen & Neumann, 2002).
K. Pollok, 'The "Transcendental Method". On the reception of the *Critique of Pure Reason* in neo-Kantianism', in P. Guyer (ed.), *The Cambridge Companion to Kant's Critique of Pure Reason* (Cambridge: Cambridge University Press, 2010), pp. 346–379.

HEIDEGGER'S ONTOLOGICAL READING OF KANT

In the spring of 1929, Martin Heidegger and Ernst Cassirer famously discussed their views of Kant's **CPR** before an audience of philosophers and students who had come to Davos from all over Europe. Heidegger, aged 39, had acquired great fame through his Marburg lecture courses and the publication of *Being and Time* two years earlier.

Although he had lectured on Kant's **CPR** during the winter of 1927/1928, Heidegger had not yet engaged with this text in writing. Davos offered him a pre-eminent opportunity to challenge the neo-Kantian approaches to Kant which had dominated German academic philosophy from the 1870s onwards. It should be recalled, however, that neo-Kantianism was already waning, not in the least because Kant's account of pure intuition and a priori principles was considered to have been refuted by Einstein's relativity theory.

Trying to reconcile Kant and Einstein, Cassirer had contributed to this debate by means of various publications. However, at Davos the stakes of the debate were quite different. In order to defend Hermann Cohen's legacy against Heidegger's ontological reading of **CPR**, Cassirer focused on its humanistic and idealistic elements rather than on Kant's alleged foundation of physics. Yet, as most of the participants would have realized, his revision of neo-Kantianism was no match for Heidegger's radical new philosophical voice. From now on, Heidegger was to lead the way – not just away from neo-Kantianism, but also from the phenomenology of Edmund Husserl, who until recently had regarded Heidegger as one of his most promising pupils.

Heidegger's ontological reading of **CPR** also helped him to clarify his own approach to philosophy, not least by marking the difference between it and both Cohen's chiefly epistemological interpretation of Kant and Husserl's focus on transcendental consciousness. Drawing from his earlier lecture series and the lectures he gave in Davos, he published *Kant and the Problem of Metaphysics* in 1929. His other, less famous, texts on Kant consist of various published lecture courses partly or primarily devoted to Kant, including *Basic Problems of Phenomenology* (1927), *Phenomenological Interpretations of*

Kant's Critique of Pure Reason (1927/1928), and *What is a Thing?* (1935/1936). The latter text was first published as a book in 1962, shortly after Heidegger wrote the essay – included in *Pathmarks* – entitled 'Kant's Thesis about Being' (1961).

What these texts have in common is their emphasis on Kant's engagement with ontology and metaphysics at large in **CPR**. However, this aspect of Heidegger's approach to Kant was less revolutionary than it may seem today, for in the early 1920s commentators such as Heinz Heimsoeth and Max Wundt had elaborated on this issue as well. The true novelty of Heidegger's work rather lay in his effort to track down the very source of the mode of thought that traditionally was called ontology. In *Being and Time*, Heidegger had conceived of this source as temporality. In *Kant and the Problem of Metaphysics*, to which the rest of this essay is confined, Heidegger radicalizes what he regards as Kant's insight into this source in such a way that it yields the same result as the analytic of human finitude elaborated in *Being and Time*.[114]

This procedure – called 'destruction' in *Being and Time* – is characteristic of Heidegger's engagement with the philosophical tradition in general. In a first movement, Heidegger opposes mainstream interpretations of classical texts in order to lay bare the insights he believed to have been achieved by the philosopher under discussion. Articulating, secondly, the unsaid in that which is being said[115], he attempts to retrieve an insight that informs the history of philosophy, yet which it had never been able to appropriate. What philosophy should face rather than repress, according to Heidegger, is the radical finitude of human life.[116]

Since Kant's account of knowledge affirms this finitude at least to a certain extent, Heidegger could regard his reading of Kant

as a 'productive appropriation' of the basic thrust of Kant's thought.[117] Yet, as we will see, he also considered Kant to have recoiled from the insight he had reached in the first edition of **CPR**. In what follows I discuss the main stages of Heidegger's attempt to retrieve and radicalize this insight. Given the limits of this essay, I will not dwell on those elements of his reading that obviously violate the meaning of Kant's own formulations.

THE 'CRITIQUE' AS A FOUNDATION OF ONTOLOGY

Attacking neo-Kantianism head on, Heidegger asserts that **CPR** has nothing to do with a theory of experience or an epistemology.[118] In his view, Kant rather seeks to uncover the inner possibility of any ontological knowledge, that is, of the horizon that allows us to relate to something as an object of experience in the first place.[119] This horizon is constituted, according to Kant, by the basic synthetic a priori principles that derive from the categories. As Heidegger points out, Kant aimed to demonstrate why these categories cannot be used to acquire a priori knowledge of the soul, the world as such, and God, as special metaphysics had always purported to do.

He argues, however, that Kant's criticism of special metaphysics (*metaphysica specialis*) did not entail a rejection of former metaphysics per se. Quite the contrary: metaphysics *qua* general metaphysics, or ontology, had always investigated the concepts constitutive of our knowledge of beings as such. Since the Transcendental Analytic investigates the possibility of using such concepts to acquire knowledge of objects, this part of **CPR** might well be considered to reflect on the very possibility of ontology.[120] Seen in this way, **CPR** contains not just a critique of special metaphysics, but also provides the discipline formerly called ontology with its proper foundation. **CPR**, Heidegger notes, is 'the foundation of metaphysics in that it reveals the essence of ontology'.[121]

INTUITION

Given his opposition to neo-Kantianism, Heidegger understandably puts great emphasis on the role of intuition in **CPR**. Cohen and his followers had downplayed the role of the Transcendental Aesthetic by reinterpreting space and time as categories in the logical sense of the term.[122]

Heidegger, by contrast, takes Kant to mean that human beings relate to the world primarily and necessarily by means of intuition, which means that their relation to objects is essentially receptive.[123] On this view, discursive thought only has the task of clarifying and ordering the contents perceived by the senses.

Heidegger even goes so far as to state that thought stands essentially in the service of intuition.[124] It is intuition, as it were, that uses the understanding to achieve its own goal, namely, to reveal beings as objects. Its dependence on the understanding – *qua* means – to achieve this goal is indicative of the finitude of human thought as such.[125]

This does not entail, however, that human thought is not creative at all. What it creates, *qua* pure understanding, are the synthetic a priori principles that reveal the ontological structure of beings qua possible objects of experience.[126] It creates, in other words, the 'horizon of objectivity' that allows something to appear as an object in the first place.[127]

THE IMAGINATION

But is it really the understanding, or the understanding alone, to which Kant assigns the creation of this very horizon? According to Heidegger, Kant's texts by no means warrant this view. Evidently, it was crucial for Kant to present intuition and thought as the two complementary 'sources' or 'stems' of our capacity to acquire knowledge of something,[128] for the rationalist metaphysics he opposed purported to possess a priori knowledge of things based on thought alone. Yet in the Transcendental Deduction, Kant also conceived of pure imagination as a basic faculty of the soul that underlies all a priori knowledge (A124).[129] Moreover, he repeatedly notes that pure intuition, pure imagination and pure apperception together produce the synthetic a priori cognition of objects that precedes empirical knowledge.[130]

For Heidegger, however, imagination is not just one of these three elements. Insofar as human thought produces synthetic a priori principles, it does not relate to things 'out there', but presents to itself the possible ways in which representations can be unified or turned into objects of knowledge. Kant, Heidegger argues, attributes this synthetic activity primarily to pure imagination.[131] Accordingly, it is primarily by dint of pure imagination that we can conceive of beings as possible objects of experience. Heidegger takes this to imply that both pure intuition and pure understanding (or transcendental apperception) are merely derivative forms of imaginative synthetic activity.[132] Their mysterious 'common root', in other words, turns out to be none other than pure imagination.[133]

As Heidegger points out, Fichte and Schelling had interpreted Kant's conception of pure imagination in a similar vein.[134] Yet whereas the German Idealists went on to identify this imagination with reason,[135] Heidegger moves into the opposite direction. For, on his view, Kant's remarks on pure imagination precisely contest the hegemony of thought celebrated by neo-Kantians and German idealists alike.

He holds, moreover, that Kant opposed this hegemony in an even deeper sense than he himself was ready to admit. Confronted with the 'abyss' opened up by his insight into the nature of pure imagination, Kant in the second edition of **CPR** conceived of its activity as a mere function of the understanding, thus removing the incongruity between the content of **CPR** and its architectonic division into Transcendental Aesthetic and Transcendental Logic.[136]

THE SCHEMATISM

Heidegger puts pure imagination central stage in order to highlight the role of the transcendental schemas it produces. In his view, **CPR** as a whole hinges on Kant's account of the schematization of the categories.[137] According to Kant, each category articulates a particular way of connecting representations. Categories only have meaning, however, insofar as their content can be translated into rules that tell us how to unify representations that affect our inner sense one after the other, that is, occur in time.

Thus, the schema of the category 'substance' tells us that we must a priori determine something in our successive representations as persisting, or unchangeable, in order to constitute something as an object at all.[138] This means for Kant that the schemas constitute particular determinations of time *qua* pure intuition.[139]

Accordingly, Heidegger regards the transcendental schemas as rules that bring about the horizon within which something can present itself as an object in the first place.[140] In this sense, the schemas can be said to constitute the true ground of any metaphysics. As such, they also explain why categories cannot be used to turn putative 'things' such as the soul, the world as such, and God into objects

of knowledge. Indeed, as was noted above, Kant reflected on the horizon of objectivity produced by the transcendental schemas primarily to oppose former special metaphysics.

Heidegger suggests, however, that this very horizon constrains philosophical questioning in a more radical way than Kant could admit. Human life, for example, cannot be turned into an object of knowledge by means of schematized categories. If the ontological horizon revealed by Kant entails that beings can only appear as objects of experience, then philosophy – concerned with the being of beings – should not only affirm the necessity of this horizon insofar as scientific knowledge is concerned, but also oppose its predominance within the realm of philosophy. That is why Heidegger in *Being and Time* as well as in the last part of *Kant and the Problem of Metaphysics* proposes that philosophy first of all reflect on the horizon of any understanding of being.[141]

TEMPORALITY

In *Being and Time*, Heidegger aimed to expose the limits of this horizon by arguing that it tends to constrain our understanding of being to that which is constantly present. Constant presence, in its turn, refers to a particular mode of what Heidegger calls temporality. Since Kant's account of the schematism highlights the constitutive function of time qua form of all representations, Heidegger starts from this account to argue that the horizon within which being can merely present itself as constant presence relies on a certain form of temporality.

He realized, however, that this step involved a 'more primordial repetition'[142] of Kant's own foundation of metaphysics, since, in his eyes, Kant's conception of time remained dependent on the traditional definition of time in terms of successive now-moments.[143] Yet, on the other hand, Kant also conceived of time as 'pure self-affection'.[144] Drawing on the latter element of Kant's conception of time, Heidegger suggests that any synthesis enacted by the understanding presupposes such a primordial self-affection. On his reading, even transcendental apperception, the intellectual principle of any synthetic activity, relies on a determination of the inner sense in terms of time.[145]

For Heidegger, accordingly, Kant conceived of time not just as the form in which representations necessarily present themselves to us, but also as the non-intellectual form of self-determination that opens up the space within which beings can be understood as possible objects of experience in the first place. If this is the case, then the threefold distinction between transcendental apperception, time *qua* self-affection and pure imagination – a distinction that prevails in Kant's own account – dissolves into a form of pure imagination that is temporal through and through.[146]

In conclusion, Heidegger admitted the violent nature of his reading of Kant already in *Kant and the Problem of Metaphysics* itself.[147] But even though this work is driven by questions foreign to **CPR**, it can be argued that it offers valuable insights not just into Heidegger's own thought, but also into aspects of Kant's transcendental philosophy which mainstream commentaries too often ignore, reject or misconstrue.

All details aside, moreover, Heidegger's engagement with Kant is very similar to Kant's own engagement with the philosophical tradition. Kant, as we have seen, criticized the effort of metaphysics to achieve knowledge of the soul, the world as such, and God by means of concepts that are merely suitable to turn phenomena into objects of knowledge.

On the other hand, he aimed to preserve those elements of the metaphysical tradition that he regarded as pertinent to the modern, scientific worldview of his time. In a similar way, Heidegger retrieved elements of Kant's philosophy that allowed him to criticize the objectifying tendency of the scientific, technological and philosophical forms of thought characteristic of late modernity. Seen in this way, Heidegger may well have been more faithful to the 'spirit' of Kant's philosophy than his texts suggest. – KdB

FURTHER READING

W. Blattner, 'Laying the ground for metaphysics', in C. B. Guignon (ed.), *The Cambridge Companion to Heidegger*, 2nd enlarged edition (Cambridge: Cambridge University Press, 2006), pp. 149–176.

D. Dahlstrom, 'The *Critique of Pure Reason* and continental philosophy: Heidegger's interpretation of transcendental imagination', in P. Guyer (ed.), *The Cambridge Companion to Kant's Critique of Pure Reason* (Cambridge: Cambridge University Press, 2010), pp. 380–400.

P. Gorner, 'Phenomenological interpretations of Kant in Husserl and Heidegger', in G. Bird (ed.), *A Companion to Kant* (Malden, MA/Oxford: Wiley-Blackwell, 2010), pp. 500–512.

F. Schalow, *The Renewal of the Heidegger-Kant Dialogue: Action, Thought, and Responsibility* (Albany, NY: SUNY Press, 1992).

C. M. Sherover, *Heidegger, Kant, and Time* (Bloomington, IN/London: Indiana University Press, 1971).

M. Weatherston, *Heidegger's Interpretation of Kant: Categories, Imagination and*

Temporality (Basingstoke: Palgrave Macmillan, 2002).

ANALYTICAL KANTIANISM

Analytic Kantianism here refers to the influence of Kantian ideas on philosophy in the analytic tradition, as opposed to interpretations of Kant by analytically oriented philosophers. To the extent that analytic philosophy, in its early stages, was a specific programme oriented around logical analysis, it was not engaged with the history of philosophy, and was officially opposed to almost all central doctrines and concerns of Kantianism.

However, in the broader sense in which it refers to a style of philosophy which dominated English-speaking philosophy departments in the twentieth century, analytic philosophy became increasingly interested in the history of philosophy in general and Kant in particular, and parts of Kant's philosophy had a large influence on central figures such as Peter Strawson, Wilfred Sellars and Hilary Putnam.

As a specific programme, analytic philosophy was centrally and originally associated with the logicism of Bertrand Russell and Gottlob Frege, the empiricism and positivism of A. J. Ayer, Rudolf Carnap and the Vienna Circle, and subsequently with the naturalism of W. V. Quine. Logicism was the project of attempting to reduce mathematics to logic; positivism the rejection as meaningless of claims that lack empirical content, and Quinean naturalism questioned of all a priori knowledge. This programme was therefore explicitly and firmly opposed to central Kantian claims, discussed below.

Most philosophers who consider themselves to be working in an analytic tradition no longer accept the main goals and claims of the original programme, and the term 'analytic philosophy' now has a broader, partly institutional sense, in which it refers more to an approach to philosophy than to a particular set of doctrines, or to a particular use of the method of analysis. In analytic philosophy in the broader sense, the strict focus on logical analysis becomes an emphasis on conceptual clarity, the programme of logicism gives way to an emphasis on the importance of logic as a central part of philosophy, and the positivism of the early project shifts to a broad naturalism and respect for the natural sciences.

Kantianism is an important strand in analytic philosophy in the broader sense. Kant is also a central figure in analytic ethics; analytic Kantian ethics is a topic in its own right, and will be mentioned only briefly here.

KEY TENETS OF KANT'S PHILOSOPHY

Logicism, Carnapian empiricism and Quinean naturalism centrally rejected key tenets of Kant's Critical philosophy. Kant presents **CPR** as addressed to the question: how is synthetic a priori knowledge possible? He thinks that if metaphysics is to be possible, there must be synthetic a priori knowledge, since metaphysical claims must be substantive, and not merely logical, but are not claims within empirical science.

His solution to this question has three parts, which Kant sees as inseparably interconnected: the idea of a priori intuition, transcendental idealism and so-called 'transcendental arguments'. Kant thinks all substantive (synthetic) knowledge claims concern objects which it is possible for us to have presented to us in immediate, singular representations, which he calls intuitions. Without intuitions, we may have coherent conceptual thought, but these thoughts will not succeed in being about any actual object.

Like all synthetic claims, synthetic a priori claims require objects which can be given to us in intuition, but since the claims are a priori, these objects cannot be presented to us merely empirically, through objects affecting our senses. Kant's solution is to propose that we have a priori intuition: representations which are singular and immediately present to us, yet which do not depend on sense experience. Kant argues that space and time are the a priori intuitions, or the a priori forms of our intuition. A priori intuition makes synthetic a priori knowledge possible: such knowledge is either a priori knowledge of the structure of space and time – in which case its 'objects' are the pure forms given to us in a priori intuition; or knowledge of a priori conditions of cognizing spatiotemporal objects – in which case its objects are empirical, spatiotemporal objects.

Kant thinks that the idea that space and time are the a priori forms of our intuition leads to the complicated position he calls transcendental idealism, according to which the only objects of which we can have knowledge are spatiotemporal objects which affect our senses, and these objects are in some sense dependent on the standpoint of human cognition, or essentially connected to the possibility of our being presented with them (representing them).

Kant then thinks we can establish certain synthetic a priori metaphysical claims by demonstrating them to be necessary conditions of the possibility of experience. What can be known a priori to be a necessary condition of the possibility of experience is true of all objects of experience; since spatiotemporal objects are essentially connected to our experience of them, this enables us to establish certain necessary truths about spatiotemporal objects.

While Kant does not use the term, the argumentative strategy of defending synthetic a priori claims by showing them to be conditions of the possibility of experience has come to be referred to as a transcendental argument. A transcendental argument defends a controversial claim by showing it to be a condition of the possibility of a less controversial claim.

In sum, Kant's project is characterized by the inclusion of a kind of idealism, a belief in a sharp and exhaustive analytic-synthetic distinction, and a belief in more than one kind of necessity, since both analytic a priori and synthetic a priori claims have some kind of necessity, so logical necessity is not the only necessity.

While Kant's project is in a certain sense a critique and rejection of metaphysics (substantive a priori knowledge of non-spatiotemporal objects such as God and Cartesian souls), it can also be seen as doing metaphysics in another sense, in that it aims to come up with necessary truths, known a priori, about the spatiotemporal world.

From the Early Analytic Programme's Rejection of Kant to Strawson's Defence

The early analytic programme rejected all of these aspects of Kant's position. The aim of logicism was to reduce mathematics to logic, thereby doing away with Kant's need to invoke intuition, and rejecting the idea of synthetic a priori knowledge (although Frege continued to accept Kant's view of geometry). In addition to its positivism, the empiricism of the Vienna circle was also centred around the idea that the only a priori knowledge is knowledge of analytic truths, and the only kind of necessity is logical necessity. Both movements explicitly rejected metaphysics.

Quine's naturalism attacked the last central Kantian claims about synthetic a priori knowledge, in rejecting the idea of a sharp analytic-synthetic distinction, and questioning the idea of any kind of a priori knowledge. Thus, in its central, original programme, twentieth century analytic philosophy was in almost no sense Kantian.

If any one figure changed this picture, it was the Oxford philosopher P. F. Strawson. Strawson was an analytic philosopher both institutionally and in terms of his commitment to analysis, his concern with logic, his rejection of idealism and of synthetic a priori knowledge. However, Strawson was seriously and centrally engaged with Kant, most notably in his controversial, brilliant and enormously influential book about Kant, *The Bounds of Sense*,[148] and his no less remarkable earlier book *Individuals*,[149] arguably a work of Kantian metaphysics.

While Strawson defended the analytic-synthetic distinction against Quine, he mostly discarded Kant's central notion of synthesis, thought that Kant had no clear and general conception of the synthetic a priori and that transcendental idealism was incoherent and the chief obstacle to a sympathetic reading of **CPR**. However, Strawson took a number of central ideas from Kant, which he impressively developed in his own work, and which influenced subsequent analytic philosophy. In addition to reviving interest in these ideas, Strawson's work, arguably, reignited the interest of analytic philosophers in the history of philosophy in general and Kant in particular.

A central aspect of Strawson's Kantianism is the idea of metaphysics as an investigation of the limiting framework of ideas and principles required by empirical knowledge, and implicit in any coherent conception of experience, together with belief in a universal human conceptual scheme, and the philosophical interest of exploring it. He revived Kant's attack on the coherence of minimal empiricism, rejecting the attempt to provide a foundation for ordinary experience and/or science from sense data, and foregrounding the unavoidability of experience-level concepts such as the concept of a physical object. He defended the central Kantian idea of an essential connection between the experience of a self-conscious agent and perception of spatio-temporal objects. He brought back into philosophical view Kant's so-called transcendental arguments.

STRAWSON'S INFLUENCE

Strawson's work influenced a generation of philosophers who did not work directly on Kant, but whose work was Kantian in a distinctive sense. This included the rejection of a minimal empiricism and a sense-data conception of experience, the idea of consciousness and self-consciousness as playing a central role in philosophy (as opposed to a primary focus on brain-processes) and a rejection of scientific reductivism.

There was, for a while, significant interest in the potential of transcendental arguments. Like Strawson, and in contrast to the development of Kant's thought by the German idealists, analytic Kantianism mostly tried to develop key Kantian ideas without Kant's idealism. There was a lot of interest in exploring the idea of space and time as central to experience of an objective world, for example in the work of Gareth Evans, Quassim Cassam and John Campbell.[150] Analytic Kantians often rejected a Cartesian account of perceptual experience, according to which the mental states that perception involves do not require the actual existence and presence of the objects of perception to consciousness. In an interesting circle, this trend in philosophy of perception has come to influence a number of contemporary interpreters of Kant.

AMERICAN KANTIANISM

Two of the towering figures of analytic philosophy in the United States, Wilfrid Sellars and Hilary Putnam, self-consciously worked with at least some Kantian ideas. In an exception to the lack of interest analytic Kantians had in Kant's transcendental idealism, Putnam has produced a variety of positions which aim to preserve parts of Kant's transcendental idealism, while rejecting Kant's account of the thing in itself. Sellars relates his work explicitly to Kant in his 1968 book, *Science and Metaphysics: Variations on Kantian Themes*.[151] Although firmly a naturalist, Sellars rejected reductive naturalism and minimal empiricism. While developing a different response to the problem than Kant's, Sellars was concerned with what is arguably the central problem of Kant's Critical philosophy: reconciling the perspectiveless, impersonal view of the world presented to us by science, and, in particular, physics, and the value-laden view of free, rational human agents central to morality.

Resolving this apparent conflict has also been a concern of John McDowell, who is influenced by Strawson and Sellars, and explicitly engages with some parts of Kant's project, in his *Mind and World*.[152] Like Sellars, McDowell develops Kantian ideas in arguing that inner sensory experience can have no cognitive force in the absence of conceptualization, rejects a minimal empiricism, and a Cartesian conception of perceptual experience. McDowell has developed the Kantian idea of the opposition between intuitions (singular mental representations given to us through the world affecting our senses) and concepts (general, structured mental representations which are essentially constituents of judgments), and Kant's famous claim that 'intuitions without concepts are blind',

to argue that perceptual experience cannot present us with objects, and thus have representational content, in the absence of the application of concepts.

Conceptualism has been a popular position in analytic philosophy of perception for some time. More recently, however, the conceptualist reading of Kant has been questioned, with some commentators arguing that Kant's account of intuition needs to be understood as a kind of non-conceptual content, and that intuitions present us with particulars independently of the contribution of concepts.[153]

ANALYTIC ETHICS

While the early analytic programme rejected metaphysics, metaphysics is a thriving and central part of contemporary analytic philosophy, with Kantianism featuring as one strand among many. In contrast, in analytic ethics, Kantianism is one of the three positions most focused on, the other two being utilitarianism and virtue ethics. In the early analytic movement, which was dominated by positivism, there was not much interest in ethics, since there was widespread suspicion of the status of ethical claims.

Most focus was on semi-sceptical metaethical theories, such as emotivism, and subsequently, in response, on attempts to respond to moral sceptics and to the egoist. Since then, however, Kantian ethics has become a centre of focus in analytic ethics. An important influence in this was the work of John Rawls.[154] Rawls, and some of his followers, reads Kant from the point of view of liberalism and constructivism, but contemporary analytic Kantian ethics includes many points of view and topics, including substantial work on Kant's moral psychology.[155] – LA

FURTHER READING

H.-J. Glock (ed.), *Strawson and Kant* (Oxford: Oxford University Press, 2003).

R. Hanna, *Kant and the Foundations of Analytic Philosophy* (Oxford: Oxford University Press, 2001).

J. O'Shea, 'Conceptual connections: Kant and the twentieth-century analytic tradition', in G. Bird (ed.), *A Companion to Kant* (Malden, MA/Oxford: Wiley-Blackwell, 2006), pp. 513–526.

R. Stern (ed.), *Transcendental Arguments: Problems and Prospects* (Oxford: Oxford University Press, 1999).

K. Westphal, 'Kant's *Critique of Pure Reason* and analytic philosophy', in P. Guyer (ed.), *The Cambridge Companion to Kant's Critique of Pure Reason* (Cambridge: Cambridge University Press, 2010), pp. 401–430.

ANALYTIC APPROACHES TO KANT'S ETHICS

Interpretations of Kant's ethics in the Anglo-American philosophical tradition have been very varied in terms of their assessment of the meaning, value and import of Kant's central contributions to the subject. A number of issues have been explored but focus on the nature of Kant's universalization tests, the relationship between the different formulas of the categorical imperative, deontology and the primacy of the right over the good have, until relatively recently, been the dominant topics in the reception of Kant's ethics by Anglo-American writers. In relation to these topics, there have been a consistent set of questions and problems, some of which have produced stable received interpretations and others which have not.

KANT'S UNIVERSALIZATION TESTS

The understanding of Kant's appeal to universalization tests for the construction of morally acceptable maxims of action has been one of the most controversial areas although Marcus Singer[156] arguably succeeded in making this topic central to the understanding of Kant's ethics at the cost of introducing confusions. Finding a way of characterizing the test of universalization in such a way that it both describes something substantively and yet also does so in such a way as to make a purely formal process of judgment possible has proved remarkably difficult. The usual tendency has been to focus on the examples Kant gives of moral judgment in the second part of **G**, where Kant treats the same four examples (suicide, promising, cultivation of talents and beneficence) twice in relation to two apparently different formulations of the categorical imperative.

While the application of the test of universalization is thought in all cases to turn on the lack of consistency involved in maxims that are not truly universalizable there is nonetheless thought to be a difference between the first two examples and the second two given that while suicide and false promising are taken to require direct types of contradiction, the second two examples of failure to cultivate one's talents or to act beneficently are, on the contrary, taken not to involve such types of contradiction.

The result of the attention to these examples has been to produce a distinction between 'contradiction in conception' and 'contradiction in the will'.[157] The distinction between these types of contradiction is one that requires itself, however, a ground for why agents should view these contradictions as serious. This question in turn leads to viewing the two types of contradiction as examples of lack of consistency in relation to something fundamental but disagreement has persisted concerning what this fundamental reference is concerned with. One of the earliest ways of understanding it, and one which has proved resilient, is in relation to purposes by means of a teleological law of consistency of purposes. A version of this was first promoted by Herbert Paton[158] and appeal to such a notion also featured in Bruce Aune's work[159] but, in relation at least to the contradiction in conception test, has been challenged, not least by Richard Galvin.[160]

The contradiction in conception test has been more generally understood as involving notions of either practical contradiction or logical contradiction. The practical contradiction view, like the teleological contradiction view, does involve reference to purposes but, unlike the teleological contradiction view, abstracts these from nature and relates them solely to the agent's intentions. However, as Christine Korsgaard admits, a lot then depends on how the statement of maxims is given and this makes the practical contradiction view controversial.[161] This problem of the determination of the maxim afflicts even the logical contradiction test and the latter has the further problem of not obviously offering substantive material for moral judgments.[162]

If the contradiction in conception test is controversial, the contradiction in the will test has appeared more appealing due to its more substantive appearance.[163] One of the reasons for this is clearly because the contradiction in the will test is connected to Kant's formula of humanity with the reference to persons as ends in themselves, a reference often taken to be one of the most generally important parts of Kant's ethics.[164] However, this does also resurrect questions about the kind of teleological appeal that might be involved in Kant's ethics, albeit without the reference to 'nature' that Paton appeared to import being required.[165]

Further, some have objected that such a reference to 'purposes' in Kant requires him to affirm a conception of value that is inherently at odds with the Kantian approach.[166] The problem of asserting the contradiction in the will test over the contradiction in conception test thus concerns the way it appears to affect the understanding of the general structure of Kant's moral theory and this shows that the discussion over the understanding of the universalization tests cannot be viewed in isolation from the assessment of the meaning and import of the distinct formulas of the categorical imperative.

THE FORMULAS OF THE CATEGORICAL IMPERATIVE

Since Paton there has been a sustained dispute concerning how many formulations of the categorical imperative Kant presents in **G**, with Paton suggesting that there were five separate formulas although Kant himself appears to indicate there are only three. If much of the controversy concerning universalization has been based on the appeal to examples that Kant makes in the second part of **G**, the same work presents, allegedly, some other formulas that Kant does not connect to examples or therefore use in practical assessment of actions. Some commentators have, in fact, rejected the general contention that it is the point of the categorical imperative to be used in practical assessment of actions[167] but this kind of view tends to be based mainly on an intuitionist view of ethics (such as was classically given by W.D. Ross[168]).

While this type of reading of Kant's ethics has been revived in recent years[169] it remains a minority response to Kant, not least because it is a clear revisionary reaction to his work that undermines any justificatory appeal of the categorical imperative in ethics.[170] If such a view is not to be adopted, however, there remains the need to account for Kant's appeal to notions such as the 'kingdom of ends' and 'autonomy' in his discussion of the categorical imperative. In accounting for this, it is possible to take the former notion as part of the overall work of ethics[171] while the latter idea, as central to Kant's general view of freedom, can, by contrast, be argued to unite a number of disparate themes in Kant's philosophy.[172] The general problem of how to think the relationship between the formulas overall has, however, certainly not been solved.[173]

DEONTOLOGY AND THE PRIORITY OF THE RIGHT

The general view of Kant's ethics which until recently was the received interpretation is that it is a form of deontology that asserts the priority of the right over the good. In order to explain both this interpretation and the challenges that have recently been presented to it, however, it is necessary to indicate the distinction that exists between deontology as a general claim and the assertion of the priority of the right over the good as a specification of it.

Samuel Freeman has articulated this distinction in terms of the parts of moral theory stating that there is a distinction between the *content* of its principles, the means of *justifying* them and the ways in which the principles are *applied*. According to Freeman, deontology is a thesis concerning the *content* of moral principles, while the conception of the priority of the right over the good with

which it is often confused concerns instead the *justification* of principles and the account of their *application* is meant to describe how the principles justified will be connected to given matters.[174]

The point of this distinction is to suggest that deontologists are committed to a pluralist conception of the good while the assertion of the priority of the right is meant to show a procedure for constraining the way in which heterogeneous goods can be related to thus providing us with an understanding of which goods are *permissible*.[175] Viewed in this way the key point for normative ethics is not so much deontology itself (which emerges as a meta-ethical thesis on this view) as the priority of the right over the good.

Recent writers have subjected the attribution to Kant of deontology to some critical scrutiny with Barbara Herman[176] using Kant's claims about the good will in the first part of **G** to argue for a view of rational agency as containing an ultimate internal condition that we have to value. On Herman's view, there is a need for a 'grounding' conception of value in order to account for the right-making characteristics of action and to give motivational force to moral conduct.

Paul Guyer, in contrast to Herman, tends to conflate deontology with the priority of the right over the good as Guyer takes deontological theories to require a constraint of the good by the right.[177] This runs into the problem that, when discussing the 'fact of reason' in **CPrR**, Kant clearly asserts the need for the good to be determined after the moral law and through it (**CPrR** 63). In response, Guyer stresses the notion that freedom is the locus of value for Kant and that the notion of autonomy incorporates both the notions of value and duty. However, Guyer's interpretation is clearly revisionist in requiring rejection of Kant's argument in **CPrR** in favour of the appeal to the good will in **G** though the value of this good will is still found in freedom.

The most radical challenge to the conception of Kantian deontology comes, however, not from Herman or Guyer but rather from David Cummiskey, who articulates a case for 'Kantian consequentialism'.[178] Cummiskey's view, like Guyer's, is explicitly revisionist since it is not here the claim that Kant himself was a consequentialist but rather that a consistently worked-out normative theory of the Kantian type will be consequentialist even though Kant's 'foundational' theory is not consequentialist. The point of Cummiskey's interpretation is to present the 'foundational' theory of Kant as involving formalism and the derivation of the categorical imperative (or the content of his principles on Freeman's view), the normative theory, by contrast, as the place where the *justification* is provided and this justification is taken by Cummiskey to be amenable to consequentialist interpretation. Although Cummiskey's interpretation is certainly controversial,[179] it is far from alone in articulating a view of Kant that makes his ethics amenable to consequentialist readings.[180]

These successive challenges to the received interpretation of Kant's ethics have not gone without challenge and there is a series of gradations that have led to the consequentialist reading since Guyer earlier suggested a kind of maximization involved in Kant's ethics, at least with regard to freedom. The denial of a place in ethical theory for this thesis of maximization is part of the understanding of deontology, at least on John Rawls' influential (and arguably Kantian) view.[181]

However, Rawls' commitment to the notion of 'primary goods' does seem to contravene deontology as understood on Herman's construal since it allows for a notion of value independently of the simple appeal to willing. Similarly, Andrews Reath, in his defence of the priority of the right over the good, does allow for value commitments to be brought into pure practical reason which appears to contravene deontology positively understood.[182] Reath, however, rejects the appeal to the good will as a source of value[183] on the grounds that what makes the good will good is only its conformity to law.

MORAL AGENCY

The dispute concerning deontology and the priority of the right shows further strains over how to combine Kant's formalism with a moral content that has substantive force and the formalist readings of Kant have tended to appeal consistently to the sense that the only 'good' available on Kantian premises concerns conformity to law. In some sense, this conformity to law is clearly central to Kant's general normative theory though the basis of it as a picture of rational agency requires a response to questions about the structure of reasons for action.[184]

Such responses have been forthcoming, notably in Korsgaard[185] but these defences have tended to be open to objection both by those committed to a stronger form of externalist view[186] and by those who want to articulate a more clearly psychologistic view of Kant generally.[187] There are also defences of Kant's view that are more strongly metaphysical than Korsgaard suggests.[188] The relationship of Kant's moral psychology to these general problems is surely at present under-developed, not least because, as Gary Banham[189] pointed out in some detail, the general topic of Kantian moral psychology has been, until recently, neglected despite its significance in the Doctrine of Virtue.

A 'WIDER' VIEW OF KANT'S ETHICS

As my stress thus far has shown, the general nature of the focus on Kantian ethics has tended to be based on the interpretation of G with only passing attention to **CPrR**.[190] The reasons for this restrictive focus have included the lack of provision, until recently, of English editions of a number of Kant's works though Mary Gregor[191] was pioneering in her attention to **MM**. Focus upon **MM** brings with it attention to both Kant's philosophy of right and a concern with his relation to contemporary virtue ethics.

The former belongs to Kant's political philosophy, which has recently been treated to evaluations that make evident its difference from contemporary political philosophy[192] and which provide both reconstructive attention to his view of public right[193] and to his relation to the traditions of jurisprudence.[194] However, it is arguable that the task of relating the political philosophy more closely to the general picture of Kant's practical philosophy is, as yet, in its infancy with systematic relations between the supreme principle of right and the categorical imperative still unresolved.

The view of Kant's virtue ethics is, likewise, still in process of formation with attention to duties to oneself,[195] humility[196] and virtue in general[197] only recently available. There is, further, as yet, no systematic study of the entirety of **MM** from the analytic tradition. Due to these lacunae, it is evident that analytic treatment of Kantian ethics has much work left to do but the debates within it are notable both for their seriousness and for the degree of attention to detail they commonly involve. – GB

FURTHER READING

R. Dean, *The Value of Humanity in Kant's Moral Theory* (Oxford: Oxford University Press, 2006).

P. Guyer, *Kant's System of Nature and Freedom* (Cambridge: Cambridge University Press, 2005).

T. Hill (ed.), *The Blackwell Guide to Kant's Ethics* (Malden, MA/Oxford: Wiley-Blackwell, 2009).

C. Korsgaard, *Creating the Kingdom of Ends* (Cambridge: Cambridge University Press, 1996).

A. Wood, *Kantian Ethics* (Cambridge: Cambridge University Press, 2007).

KANTIAN NORMATIVITY IN RAWLS, KORSGAARD AND CONTINENTAL PRACTICAL PHILOSOPHY

Aside from the scholarly discussions concerning the interpretation of Kant's ethical writings, Kant's ethics has exerted a major influence upon twentieth century philosophy in the broadly analytic tradition. These range from innovations in the way the history of ethics and meta-ethics informs contemporary ethical debates to the development of substantial theories of practical normativity. Here, we focus upon the figures of John Rawls, Jürgen Habermas, Karl-Otto Apel and Christine Korsgaard.

KORSGAARD (I)

One of Korsgaard's contributions to contemporary analytic ethics has been to provide an interpretation of Kant's ethics which views its analysis of obligation as the culmination of a historical progression involving several traditions (which continue into the twentieth century). In analyzing the question of why there are moral obligations,[198] she first distinguishes the 'voluntarist' tradition (Hobbes, Pufendorf) for which obligations result from a legislator's will and the contract binding agents to it. The realist tradition (Clarke, Price, Moore, Prichard, Nagel) she presents as responding originally to the regress arising from the further question of what makes such a contract with the legislator binding. More generally, it would seem that whatever answer is given to the normative question, it leads to such a regress insofar as whatever grounds are provided, their normative force can be questioned. To avoid scepticism about moral obligation, the realist draws such questioning to a close by appealing to moral properties as real features of the world whose normativity is intrinsic.

Additionally, according to Korsgaard, there is a third tradition which can be traced back to Hume, and includes Bernard Williams (and to an extent Bentham and Mill) for which the proper way to address scepticism is to show how moral values are endorsed under different points of view (e.g. self-interest, human flourishing). If such 'reflective endorsement'[199] can be used to give an account of why there is moral obligation in general, it is not sufficient to explain why one is morally obligated in any particular case of decision-making. This is where Kant's notion of autonomy is required. Korsgaard interprets Kant's concept of normativity as defined in terms of endorsement by the reflecting self-conscious agent. This identifies normative reasons as laws of the agent's freedom. And, going somewhat beyond Kant, she argues that the kind of laws that are normative for an agent as those which define the agent's practical conception of herself.

If this places Kant's ethics in a tradition of reflective endorsement ethics, it also shows him to be a voluntarist, with the source of obligation lying in the agent's own will; and it identifies moral commands as intrinsically normative as the realist has it.

Aside from this original work on Kant's place among different traditions in ethics, Korsgaard's reconstruction of Kant's foundational claims arguably enables us to understand how Kant's ethics informed the development of new ethical theories in the twentieth century.[200] In her attempt to reconstruct the Kantian grounding of ethics, Korsgaard finds that Kant's appeal to the fact of reason proof (**CPrR** 47) can only work if the 'highest good' is given as a goal of rationality, together with the conception of moral law, as a fact of reason.[201] This notion of the highest good is too thick a teleological notion to meet with universal assent. Apparently no other notion is available to Kant to play an analogous grounding role, since he draws exclusively upon the content of rationality. This suggests that with some transformation of the content of Kant's ethical principles, minimal grounding assumptions ('thicker' than mere rationality) that meet with universal assent could be sought.

This provides one way of interpreting important developments in twentieth-century practical philosophy in the Kantian tradition. Rawls, on the one hand, and Apel and Habermas, on the other, have sought to construct frameworks for universal normative practical principles which are directly inspired by Kant. These authors appeal to some constructive process to generate the principles that all agents will take as binding. In so doing, they replace the grounding role of Kantian teleological assumptions either with universal desires (Rawls) or non-moral normative constraints (Apel and Habermas) that underpin the constructive process.

JOHN RAWLS

Rawls distances himself from Kant insofar as he views the test of the Formula of Universal Law (the CI test) as rejecting the maxim of charity in the same way as it rejects the maxim of universal egoism, i.e. because of a contradiction in the will.[202] That is, insofar as Rawls takes 'willing' to mean 'wanting', he argues that one could not will to be committed to a maxim of charity that would conflict with the pursuit of our other ends. This leads to a concern with moral scepticism, i.e. a threat to the normative force of moral laws.[203]

To generate morally binding principles, Rawls injects the notion of willing with 'true human needs', which are taken to define wants that are universally valid for human beings.[204] This follows from Rawls's claim that mere rational willing will not suffice to generate principles: the agents' desires and priorities must be taken into account. This thickening of the agent to include true human needs has the advantage of transforming the test procedures using the Formula of Universal Law into the making of rational choices committed to securing these basic needs.[205] This involves a move away from Kant's formal tests, which reflects Rawls's uneasiness with the formal and a priori aspects of Kant's ethics.[206]

Rawls's solution for an impartial form of rational choice is to consider an a-historical ideal situation, the original situation, from which we can decide which kind of social contract would produce a fair and just society. This situation is characterized by an ignorance of the particular features of the agents involved in the decision-making, as well as of their place in the future social arrangements.

For Rawls, the question about what is fair must be agreed upon in this ideal state.[207] And this notion of fairness will then define normative constraints. This approach defines an important strand in twentieth-century practical philosophy, contractualism.[208]

The Rawlsian notion of 'ideal state' is however not unproblematic. Much as Rawls seeks to thicken the rational agent to take into account wants and priorities, the way these essential needs are identified could be questioned. That is, insofar as Rawls abandons Kant's notion of rational agent, what is taken as legitimately defining agents' true human needs will have an impact upon decision-making in the ideal state.

A corresponding problem arguably arises for the very notion of person which replaces Kant's rational agent. For instance, Nozick argues that if we are to distribute benefits and burdens among agents, this assumes boundaries between persons and assets are clearly defined.[209] These are however not given, and potentially difficult to draw insofar as real individuals are always already found with assets. As soon as persons as properly situated, i.e. with certain assets, are considered, there is no reason why this existing distribution of assets should meet with general assent. The apparently neutral idea of a fair decision in an ideal situation as definitive of a normative conception of justice can therefore be questioned because it does not properly represent the situatedness of the agents and how this might affect what they take to be their true human needs. It is therefore not clear how Rawls's proposal can in fact lead to a consensus.

APEL AND HABERMAS

The notion of an ideal process generating principles that would be binding for those involved in this process also underpins Apel's and Habermas's work.[210] They require that an ideal discussion between all members of a society provide the grounds upon which decisions will be made as to what rules the participants will then be bound by. The question again is whether the starting points of these approaches are uncontroversial and therefore are appropriate for the task of grounding ethical obligations. That is why Apel and Habermas try to minimize the assumptions their discourse ethics rely upon to a set of basic claims about communication.

In particular, Apel thus discusses a transcendental grounding for his ethics: the conditions of the ideal discussion are presupposed by everyday argumentative discourse.[211] Apel takes over from Habermas four validity claims defining the ideal conditions of human discourse. These are that meaning, truth, truthfulness and normative correctness are features of our everyday discourse, which human beings accept insofar as they are members of a linguistic community. Whenever someone speaks, he aims to utter something meaningful. Some truth claim(s) is (are) also involved, either directly, or through the assumptions made by the speaker. At some point in the communicative exchange, there must be something that one assumes represents what the speaker believes to be true, i.e. where the speaker exhibits truthfulness. In communicating with others, the speaker appeals to a shared sense of validity, which defines a normative correctness.

For Apel, these claims are necessarily universal.[212] Apel is thus in effect replacing Kant's transcendental subject with the consideration of an ideal communication community. Against Rorty, he argues that if one were to contravene any of the features of discourse that he and Habermas identify in their validity claims, one would be involved

in a performative self-contradiction. For Apel, these validity claims thus identify transcendental-pragmatic conditions of argumentation.

Apel takes these claims further than Habermas, as he argues that insofar as a speaker takes it as a normative constraint that he is able to justify the claims he makes to his interlocutors, normative correctness thereby grounds ethical normativity.[213] And Apel adds that this normativity binds the speaker insofar as he seeks the consensus not only of his language community, but also of the whole community of mankind.[214] For Apel, such transcendental reflection takes us further than the problem of grounding ethical normativity. It can also enable us to formulate moral norms. In particular, Apel formulates his own substitute for Kant's formula of universal law.[215]

Such a proposal for an overhaul of Kantian ethics can be criticized on Kantian grounds,[216] but also on systematic grounds. Habermas thinks that rules which are inherent to discourse and argumentation cannot be claimed to be valid for action beyond discourse.[217] He therefore does not adhere to Apel's programme for a strong grounding of ethics that characterizes Apel's transcendental-pragmatic approach.

For Habermas, a weaker grounding can be achieved by noting that there are universal pragmatic presuppositions of speech acts resulting from the agent's know-how. Such presuppositions can be identified through empirical enquiry. It is not clear however why, given the different ways in which these presuppositions can be characterized, an investigation into these presuppositions should give rise to universally valid ethical norms.

If Apel's proposal for grounding ethical normativity in one's belonging to a language community is thus taken to task by Habermas for an unwarranted exportation of normativity of human discourse into the realm of the practical, it may be worth exploring whether this normativity cannot be understood in a deeper sense as a feature of rational agency, and thus inherent both to discourse and to practical decision-making.

KORSGAARD (II)

Korsgaard makes a move along these lines, by drawing upon the notion of reflective endorsement which places rational discourse at the heart of practical decision making. As we saw above, her account of the historical position of Kantian ethics leads to viewing it as the culmination of a tradition of reflective endorsement. Normativity for Korsgaard lies in the endorsement by the self-reflecting agent. To get from here to obligation, Korsgaard makes three moves.

The first is closely connected to Kant's argument for the Formula of Humanity. Korsgaard argues that, insofar as one values anything at all, one must thereby value the source of such values, namely oneself as a human being. Recognizing that this gives us no obligations towards others, she does not attempt to move from self-interested reasons to concern for others. Rather, she draws upon Wittgenstein's private language argument to argue for the publicity of reasons: there are, for Korsgaard, no private reasons that could not be translated into a communicable form. And the third step consists in following Nagel's lead in arguing that another's reasons will therefore feature in my practical thinking and define obligations insofar as the other is thereby recognized as a person like me.[218]

Even if we accept the Wittgensteinian move at the heart of Korsgaard's argument,

it is not clear how much can be achieved by such a line of reasoning. Her first move is a transcendental argument which establishes that the value of humanity must feature in my decision-making. Her argument is that, if I value X, and X can be described as a partial 'consequence' of Y, then I am obligated to value Y also.

Although this argument has been challenged,[219] another worry is that it is not clear how Korsgaard can account for the normative force of ethical commands. Cohen points to what he calls, after Hobbes, the problem of the sovereign.[220] Although the sovereign is bound by the laws he makes, he can alter these laws. It would therefore seem that if the source of normativity for Korsgaard is human, then she has no answer to this problem. And indeed, when she identifies the sense of one's practical identity as defining normative constraints for an agent, what is apparently lacking is something like Kant's appeal to a faculty of reason at the transcendental level as the only way of binding the agent. For Kant, in the moral realm, we are subjects rather than sovereigns (**CPrR** 82). To these criticisms, Korsgaard responds that a legislating agent cannot alter the law at will, since universality constraints apply.[221]

This claim relies upon accepting that she can derive universality constraints from her minimal premises. Her interesting detailed account of this claim draws upon an understanding of the agent as wanting to see himself as having a causally effective will.[222] This is at the heart of the agent's sense of identity. This view however amounts to endorsing a teleological premise in which a proto-existentialist pursuit of an agent's identity is substituted for the role played by the pursuit of the highest good in her earlier reconstruction of Kant's fact of reason proof.

Korsgaard's introduction of the agent's practical identity is a key development of Kantian ethics that takes account of standard criticisms of its alienating features (Hegel, Williams) by absorbing some of the tradition of reflective endorsement ethics. What it shares with Rawls, Habermas and Apel's approaches is a rejection of Kant's alleged formalism and the metaphysical commitments of his notion of the a priori. This tradition of Kantian ethics is thus largely divorced from the investigation of transcendental idealism as an alternative to naturalism. This may make it more attractive to many, but one might wonder with Cohen whether, 'if morality is merely human, then it is optional as far as rationality is concerned'.[223] – CO

Further Reading

K.-O. Apel, 'Discourse ethics, democracy, and international law: Toward a globalization of practical reason', *American Journal of Economics and Sociology* 66,1 (2007): 49–70.

K. Baynes, *The Normative Grounds of Social Criticism: Kant, Rawls and Habermas* (Albany, NY: SUNY Press, 1992).

P. Gilabert, 'Considerations on the notion of moral validity in the moral theories of Kant and Habermas', *Kant-Studien* 97,2 (2006): 210–227.

O. O'Neill, 'Constructivism in Rawls and Kant', in S. Freeman, *The Cambridge Companion to Rawls* (Cambridge: Cambridge University Press, 2002), pp. 347–367.

A. Wellmer, 'Ethics and dialogue: Elements of moral judgment in Kant and discourse ethics', in A. Wellmer, *The Persistence of Modernity*, trans. D. Midgley

(Cambridge, MA: MIT Press, 1991), pp. 113–231.

NOTES

1. J. Schultz, *Exposition of Kant's Critique of Pure Reason* [incl. Schultz's review of **ID**], trans. and ed. J. C. Morrison (Ottawa, 1995), p. 169 [hereafter referred to as *Exposition*].
2. J. Schultz, *Exposition*, pp. 168–169.
3. M. Herz, *Betrachtungen aus der speculativen Weltweisheit* (Königsberg, 1771), p. 66 [hereafter referred to as *Betrachtungen*]; all translations from this text are my own.
4. M. Herz, *Betrachtungen*, p. 74.
5. See Hamann's letter of 8 December 1783 to Herder, in J. G. Hamann, *Briefwechsel*, ed. W. Ziesemer, A. Henkel (Wiesbaden, 1955–1957), pp. v, 107.
6. B. Sassen (ed.), *Kant's Early Critics: The Empiricist Critique of the Theoretical Philosophy* (Cambridge, 2000), p. 61.
7. B. Sassen, *Kant's Early Critics*, p. 59.
8. B. Sassen, *Kant's Early Critics*, p. 60.
9. Kant thus refers to Garve's claim that 'neither the concepts of space and time, nor the categories combined with them, are particular to the conditions of alertness and sensation in which alone we assume existing objects; we can find them also in novels, fantasies, and dreams, even in the fantasies of the insane. Whenever we dream, we see what is represented [. . .] in accord with the laws of our spirit, and yet we do not in the end recognise it as actual' (B. Sassen, *Kant's Early Critics*, p. 76).
10. B. Sassen, *Kant's Early Critics*, pp. 53–54.
11. Kant interprets Berkeley as a 'Platonist' or 'enthusiast' who claims that 'all cognition through the senses and experience is nothing but sheer illusion, and there is truth only in the ideas of pure understanding and reason', and shows that such a claim is diametrically opposed to **CPR**'s conclusion that '[a]ll cognition of things out of mere pure understanding or pure reason is nothing but sheer illusion, and there is truth only in experience' (**P** 374).
12. In the 1781 edition, Hume is not mentioned at all until 'The Discipline of Pure Reason'.

13 F. Beiser, *The Fate of Reason: German Philosophy from Kant to Fichte* (Cambridge, 1987), p. 38.

14 See J. G. Hamann, *Sämtliche Werke: Historisch-kritische Ausgabe*, ed. J. Nadler (Vienna, 1949–1957), vol. III, p. 279 [hereafter referred to as HKA]. All translations are my own.

15 See Hamann, HKA, p. 278.

16 Hamann, HKA, p. 283.

17 Hamann, HKA, p. 284.

18 Hamann, HKA, p. 286.

19 Hamann, HKA, p. 288.

20 Hamann, HKA, p. 285.

21 See Karl Leonhard Reinhold, *Beyträge zur leichtern Uebersicht des Zustandes der Philosophie beym Anfange des 19. Jahrhunderts* (Hamburg, 1801), vol. I, pp. 206–212.

22 Reinhold, *Über das Fundament des philosophischen Wissens*, ed. W. Schrader (Hamburg, 1978), p. 71 [hereafter referred to as *Über das Fundament*]. All translations are my own.

23 Reinhold, *Über das Fundament*, p. 72.

24 Reinhold, *Über das Fundament*, pp. 74–75.

25 Reinhold, *Beiträge zur Berichtigung bisheriger Mißverständnisse der Philosophen. Erster Band, das Fundament der Elementarphilosophie betreffend*, ed. F. Fabbianelli (Hamburg, 2003), pp. 98–99, and 113 respectively. See also Reinhold, *Über das Fundament*, pp. 77–78.

26 Reinhold, *Über das Fundament*, pp. 82–83.

27 See Reinhold, *Beiträge zur Berichtigung*, p. 233.

28 See further the essay 'Kantianism in the 1790s: from Reinhold to Hegel', this volume.

29 Maimon, *Gesammelte Werke* (Hildesheim, 1965–1976), vol. II, p. 432 [hereafter referred to as GW followed by volume and page numbers]. All translations are my own.

30 See Maimon, GW, pp. 64–65.

31 See Reinhold, *Beiträge zur Berichtigung*, p. 199.

32 Ibid.

33 Maimon, GW, vol. II, pp. 178–179.

34 Maimon, GW, vol. V, pp. 473–475.

35 Maimon, GW, vol. V, pp. 470 and 490–491.

36 Maimon, GW, vol. V, p. 490.

37 Maimon, GW, vol. V, 495–496.

38 See Maimon, GW, vol. II, pp. 187–188.

39 Maimon, GW, vol. II, p. 371.

40 Maimon, GW, vol. II, p. 372.

41 Maimon, GW, vol. II, p. 215. This claim sits uncomfortably alongside Maimon's conclusion to his later *Versuch einer neuen Logik* (see Maimon, GW, vol. V, pp. 495–496).

42 See Maimon, GW, vol. II, pp. 215–217 and 372.

43 See Maimon, GW, vol. II, pp. 363–364.

44 Maimon, GW, vol. II, p. 64.

45 Maimon, GW, vol. II, pp. 415–416.

46 Maimon, GW, vol. II, p. 355.

47 See Maimon, GW, vol. II, pp. 355–356.

48 Maimon, GW, vol. II, p. 82.

49 Maimon, GW, vol. II, p. 32.

50 See F. H. Jacobi, *Werke* (Darmstadt, 1968–1980), vol. II, pp. 301–302. All translations are my own.

51 Jacobi, *Werke*, vol. II, pp. 303–304.

52 Jacobi, *Werke*, vol. II, pp. 307–310.

53 Jacobi, *Werke*, vol. II, p. 304.

54 Jacobi, *Werke*, vol. II, p. 307.

55 See G. E. Schulze, *Aenesidemus oder über der von Herrn Professor Reinhold in Jena gelieferten Elementarphilosophie: Nebst einer Verteidigung des Skeptizismus gegen die Anmaßungen der Vernunftkritik*, ed. M. Frank (Hamburg, 1996), p. 183 [hereafter referred to as *Aenesidemus*]. All translations are my own.

56 See Schulze, *Aenesidemus*, p. 184.

57 Schulze thus writes that 'as long as the existence of [things in themselves] is uncertain, we are unable to decide anything about whether that which we experience in our present life constitutes more than a mere illusion' (Schulze, *Aenesidemus*, p. 259).

58 Schulze, *Aenesidemus*, p. 263–264.

59 F. W. J. Schelling, *Historisch-Kritische Ausgabe* (Stuttgart, 1976–), vol. IV, p. 102 [hereafter referred to as HKA]. All translations are my own.

60 Schelling, HKA, vol. IV, p. 90–92.

61 Schelling, HKA, vol. IV, p. 82. From his accompanying remarks – see e.g. Schelling, HKA, vol. IV, p. 91 – it is clear that Schelling has Reinhold's version of the Critical philosophy very much within his sights.

62 Schelling, HKA, vol. IV, p. 73. For Maimon's related claims see Maimon, GW, vol. V, p. 435.

63 Schelling, HKA, vol. IV, p. 73.

64 Schelling, HKA, vol. IV, pp. 78–79.

[65] Maimon, GW, vol. V, p. 479.

[66] Schelling, HKA, vol. IV, p. 73.

[67] Schelling, HKA, vol. IV, p. 74.

[68] Schelling, HKA, vol. IV, p. 75.

[69] Schelling, HKA, vol. IV, p. 85.

[70] Schelling, HKA, vol. IV, p. 87.

[71] Cf. H. Schröpfer, *Kants Weg in die Öffentlichkeit. Christian Gottfried Schütz als Wegbereiter der kritischen Philosophie* (Stuttgart-Bad Cannstatt, 2003).

[72] Cf. my 'Einleitung', chs 3 and 4 in K. L. Reinhold, *Versuch einer neuen Theorie des menschlichen Vorstellungsvermögens*, vol. 1 (Hamburg, 2010).

[73] An English translation has recently appeared under the title *New Theory of the Human Capacity for Representation*, trans. and ed. T. Mehigan, B. Empson (Berlin/New York, 2010).

[74] D. Henrich (ed.), *Immanuel Carl Diez, Briefwechsel und Kantische Schriften. Wissensbegründung in der Glaubenskrise Tübingen – Jena (1790–1792)* (Stuttgart, 1997), p. 176.

[75] Cf. the report by Leutwein in D. Henrich, 'Leutwein über Hegel. Ein Dokument zu Hegels Biographie', in *Hegel-Studien* 3 (1965): 39–77.

[76] Cf. M. Brecht, 'Die Anfänge der idealistischen Philosophie und die Rezeption Kants in Tübingen (1788–1795)', in H. Decker-Hauff (ed.), *500 Jahre Eberhard-Karls-Universität Tübingen. Beiträge zur Geschichte der Universität Tübingen 1477–1977* (Tübingen, 1977), pp. 381–428.

[77] J. F. Flatt, *Briefe über den moralischen Erkenntnisgrund der Religion überhaupt, und besonders in Beziehung auf die Kantische Philosophie* (Tübingen, 1789), pp. 16 and 72 respectively.

[78] Schelling, HKA, vol. III/1, p. 16. That this does not refer to the teachers in the *Stift* is shown by M. Franz, 'Johann Friedrich Flatts philosophisch-theologische Auseinandersetzung mit Kant', in ». . . *an der Galeere der Theologie«? Hölderlins, Hegels und Schellings Philosophiestudium an der Universität Tübingen*, ed. M. Franz, in the series *Schriften der Hölderlin-Gesellschaft*, Bd. 23/3 (Tübingen, 2007), pp. 189–222.

[79] Schelling, HKA, vol. II, pp. 19, 21.

[80] G. C. Rapp, 'Ueber die moralischen Triebfedern, besonders die der christlichen Religion', in *Allgemeines Repertorium für empirische Psychologie und verwandte Wissenschaften*, ed. I. D. Mauchart, vol. 1, continued in vol. 2 (1792), pp. 130–156 and 133–220 [hereafter referred to as 'Ueber die moralischen Triebfedern']. Hegel's occupation with this essay is attested to by his letter on Christmas Eve, 1794 to Schelling; see Schelling, HKA, vol. III/1, p. 14.

[81] K. L. Reinhold, *Letters on the Kantian Philosophy*, ed. K. Ameriks (Cambridge, 2005), p. 33.

[82] Rapp, 'Ueber die moralischen Triebfedern', p. 151.

[83] G. W. F. Hegel, *Werke*, vol. 1: *Frühe Schriften* (Frankfurt a/M, 1971, 1986), pp. 359–360; trans. in T. M. Knox (ed.), *Early Theological Writings* (Philadelphia 1971, 1996), p. 244.

[84] Cf. my 'Hegel zwischen Fichte und der Tübinger Fichte-Kritik', in C. Krijnen, D. H. Heidemann (eds), *Hegel und die Geschichte der Philosophie* (Darmstadt, 2007), pp. 171–190. Storrian theology is not a branch of such orthodoxy, as has been made clear in M. Franz, ''Tübinger Orthodoxie'. Ein Feindbild der jungen Schelling und Hegel', in S. Dietzsch, G. F. Frigo (eds), *Vernunft und Glauben. Ein philosophischer Dialog der Moderne mit dem Christentum* (Berlin, 2006), pp. 141–160.

[85] Schelling, HKA, vol. III/1, p. 19.

[86] See Hegel, *Differenz des Fichteschen und Schellingschen Systems der Philosophie*, in *Hauptwerke*, vol. 1 (Hamburg, 1999), p. 5 [hereafter referred to as *Differenzschrift*]; trans. W. Cerf, H. Harris, *The Difference between Fichte's and Schelling's System of Philosophy* (Albany, 1977), p. 79 [hereafter referred to as *Difference*].

[87] Hegel, *Verhältnis des Skeptizismus zur Philosophie*, in *Hauptwerke*, vol. 1, p. 223 [hereafter referred to as *Skeptizismus*]; all translations of this essay are my own.

[88] Hegel, *Glauben und Wissen*, in *Hauptwerke*, vol. 1, p. 326; trans. W. Cerf, H. S. Harris, *Faith and Knowledge* (Albany, 1977), p. 69.

[89] *Encyclopaedia of the Philosophical Sciences in Basic Outline*, §40 [hereafter referred to as *Encyclopaedia*]; all translations of this work are my own.

90 Hegel, *Encyclopaedia*, §41.
91 Hegel, *Glauben und Wissen*, p. 326; *Faith and Knowledge*, p. 68; translation amended.
92 Hegel, *Science of Logic*, trans. G. di Giovanni (Cambridge, 2010), p. 515.
93 Hegel, *Differenzschrift*, p. 6; *Difference*, p. 80.
94 Hegel, *Skeptizismus*, p. 223.
95 Hegel, *Skeptizismus*, p. 224.
96 Hegel, *Differenzschrift*, p. 5; *Difference*, p. 80.
97 For a detailed account of Schopenhauer's disillusionment with Fichte's philosophy, see R. Safranski, *Schopenhauer and the Wild Years of Philosophy*, trans. E. Osers (London, 1989), ch. 8.
98 A. Schopenhauer, *The World as Will and Representation*, volume I, trans. and ed. J. Norman et al. (Cambridge, 2010), p. 443, henceforth WWR I.
99 See *The Fourfold Root of the Principle of Sufficient Reason*, Chapter 5; WWR I: Section 3.
100 WWR I: Sections 10–11.
101 WWR I: 444.
102 WWR I: 535.
103 For a clear account of these two interpretations of transcendental idealism see A. Wood, *Kant* (Malden, MA, 2005), ch. 4.
104 WWR I: 138.
105 *The World as Will and Representation*, volume II, trans. E. F. J. Payne (New York, 1966), p. 197.
106 WWR I: 135–6.
107 For a full argument for this interpretation see my 'Poetic intuition and the bounds of sense: metaphor and metonymy in Schopenhauer's philosophy', *European Journal of Philosophy* 16,2 (2008): 211–229.
108 WWR I: 560–1.
109 WWR I: 562, and *Manuscript Remains in Four Volumes*, ed. A. Hübscher, trans. E. F. J. Payne (Oxford, 1988), vol. II: 320.
110 For the full argument see my 'Schopenhauer's transformation of the Kantian sublime', *Kantian Review* 17,3 (2012): 479–511.
111 E.g. H. Bergson, G. Sorel, E. Durkheim, W. Dilthey, M. Weber, G. Simmel, R. Michels, G. Mosca and V. Pareto.
112 In his book *Kant und die Epigonen* (Stuttgart, 1865), in which he compared the German idealists, Herbart, Fries and Schopenhauer with the Critical philosophy of whose 'absoluteness' and 'certainty' (p. 13) he was convinced, Liebmann wrote at the end of each chapter: 'Hence, we must return to Kant [*Also muß auf Kant zurückgegangen werden*].'
113 The influence of Kantian thought can be found in post-Kantian German Idealism, in the work of J. F. Fries, J. F. Herbart, R. H. Lotze, E. Laas, R. Avenarius and E. Mach, in W. Dilthey, K. Jaspers and M. Heidegger, the Frankfurt School, the transcendental pragmatics of K.-O. Apel, and even in post-modern philosophers like J.-F. Lyotard and M. Foucault.
114 See K. de Boer, *Thinking in the Light of Time. Heidegger's Encounter with Hegel* (Albany, NY, 2000) for an interpretation of *Being and Time* and related texts that focuses on the issue of temporality.
115 Heidegger, *Kant and the Problem of Metaphysics*, trans. R. Taft (Bloomington, 1990, 1997), p. 201/140 [hereafter referred to as KPM]; the page references are to the English translation and the original German edition respectively, separated by a slash.
116 cf. KPM 21/15, 32/22.
117 KPM 20/14.
118 KPM 16–17/11.
119 KPM 16/10.
120 KPM 11/7.
121 KPM 15/10; cf. 125/88.
122 KPM 145/102; cf. 51/36.
123 KPM 25/18.
124 KPM 22/15.
125 KPM 24/17.
126 KPM 30/21, 38–39/26–27.
127 KPM 84/59; cf. 119/84.
128 KPM 135/95.
129 Cf. KPM 134/95.
130 KPM 135/95.
131 KPM 84/59.
132 KPM 142/99–100, 151/106.
133 KPM 137–138/96; cf. A15=B29.
134 KPM 137/96–97.
135 cf. KPM 197/138.
136 KPM 164–169/115–118.
137 KPM 89/63.
138 See A144=B183; cf. KPM 107–108/76.
139 Cf. KPM 197/138.
140 KPM 103/73, 108/76.
141 Cf. KPM 224–226/157–158.
142 KPM 220/154.

143 KPM 200/140.

144 KPM 200/140; cf. B156.

145 KPM 189–191/132–134.

146 KPM 196/137.

147 KPM 202/141.

148 P. F. Strawson, *The Bounds of Sense. An Essay on Kant's Critique of Pure Reason* (London, 1966).

149 P. F. Strawson, *Individuals. An Essay in Descriptive Metaphysics* (London, 1959).

150 See J. Campbell, *Reference and Consciousness* (Oxford, 2002), Q. Cassam, *Self and World* (Oxford, 1997), Q. Cassam, *The Possibility of Knowledge* (Oxford, 2007), and G. Evans, *The Varieties of Reference* (Oxford, 1982).

151 W. Sellars, *Science and Metaphysics: Variations on Kantian Themes* (Atascadero, 1992 [1968]).

152 J. McDowell, *Mind and World* (Cambridge, MA, 1994, ²1996); see also McDowell, *Having the World in View: Essays on Kant, Hegel, and Sellars* (Cambridge, MA, 2009)

153 R. Hanna, 'Kant and non-conceptual content', *European Journal of Philosophy* 13 (2005): 247–290; R. Hanna, 'Kantian non-conceptualism', *Philosophical Studies* 137 (2008): 41–64; L. Allais, 'Kant, non-conceptual content and the representation of space,' *Journal of the History of Philosophy* 47,3 (2009): 383–413.

154 J. Rawls, *A Theory of Justice* (Cambridge, MA, 1971).

155 See further the essays 'Analytic Approaches to Kant's Ethics' and 'Kantian Normativity in Rawls, Korsgaard and continental practical philosophy', this volume.

156 M. Singer, *Generalization in Ethics* (New York, 1961).

157 See e.g. O. O'Neill, *Acting on Principle* (New York, 1975).

158 H. Paton, *The Categorical Imperative* (Chicago, 1948).

159 B. Aune, *Kant's Theory of Morals* (Princeton, 1979).

160 R. Galvin, 'Ethical formalism: the contradiction in conception test', *History of Philosophy Quarterly* 8,4 (1991): 387–408.

161 C. Korsgaard, 'Kant's formula of universal law', *Pacific Philosophical Quarterly* 66 (1985): 24–47.

162 See however S. Engstrom, *The Form of Practical Knowledge: A Study of the Categorical Imperative* (Cambridge, MA, 2009) for one of the most recent attempts to suggest otherwise.

163 See A. Wood, *Kant's Ethical Thought* (Cambridge, 1999) and A. Wood, *Kantian Ethics* (Cambridge, 2007).

164 R. Dean, *The Value of Humanity in Kant's Moral Theory* (Oxford, 2006).

165 H. Paton, *The Categorical Imperative* (Chicago, 1948); P. Guyer, 'Ends of reason and ends of nature: the place of teleology in Kant's ethics', *Journal of Value Inquiry* 36 (2002): 161–186.

166 A. Reath, 'Value and law in Kant's moral theory', *Ethics* 114 (2003): 127–155.

167 T. C. Williams, *The Concept of the Categorical Imperative: A Study of the Place of the Categorical Imperative in Kant's Ethical Theory* (Oxford, 1968); P. Stratton-Lake, *Kant, Duty and Moral Worth* (London/New York, 2000).

168 W. D. Ross, *Kant's Ethical Theory* (Oxford, 1954).

169 R. Audi, *The Good in the Right: A Theory of Intuition and Intrinsic Value* (Princeton, 2004).

170 See C. Onof, 'Moral worth and inclinations in Kantian ethics', *Kant Studies Online*, posted 7 April 2011.

171 C. Korsgaard, *Creating the Kingdom of Ends* (Cambridge, 1996).

172 S. Holtmann, 'Autonomy and the kingdom of ends', in T. Hill (ed.), *The Blackwell Guide to Kant's Ethics* (Oxford/New York, 2009), pp. 102–118, which should be compared with P. Guyer, 'Kant on the theory and practice of autonomy', in P. Guyer, *Kant's System of Nature and Freedom: Selected Essays* (Cambridge, 2005), pp. 115–145.

173 See the essays in P. Guyer (ed.), *Kant's Groundwork of the Metaphysics of Morals: Critical Essays* (Lanham, 1998) for various accounts of the formulas.

174 See S. Freeman, 'Utilitarianism, deontology, and the priority of the right', *Philosophy and Public Affairs* 23,4 (1994): 313–349, which however says little about application.

175 This also connects to Silber's conception of the *summum bonum* as composed for Kant of heterogeneous goods. See J. Silber, 'Kant's conception

176 of the highest good as immanent and transcendent', *Philosophical Review* 68 (1959): 469–492.

176 B. Herman, 'Leaving deontology behind', in B. Herman, *The Practice of Moral Judgment* (Cambridge, MA, 1993), pp. 208–240.

177 P. Guyer, 'Morality of law and morality of freedom', in P. Guyer, *Kant on Freedom, Law and Happiness* (Cambridge, 2000), pp. 129–171.

178 D. Cummiskey, *Kantian Consequentialism* (Oxford, 1996).

179 See J. Timmermann, *Kant's Groundwork of the Metaphysics of Morals: A Commentary* (Cambridge, 2007).

180 See very recently D. Parfit, *On What Matters*, 2 vols. (Oxford, 2011).

181 J. Rawls, *A Theory of Justice* (Oxford, 1971).

182 A. Reath, 'Value and law in Kant's moral theory', *Ethics* 114 (2003): 127–155.

183 This is also present in R. Dean, *The Value of Humanity in Kant's Moral Theory* (Oxford, 2006)

184 B. Williams, 'Internal and external reasons', in B. Williams, *Moral Luck* (Cambridge, 1982), pp. 101–113.

185 C. Korsgaard, *The Sources of Normativity* (Cambridge, 1996).

186 R. Jay Wallace, *Normativity and the Will: Selected Essays on Moral Psychology and Practical Reason* (Oxford, 2006).

187 W. Waxman, *Kant's Model of the Mind: A New Interpretation of Transcendental Idealism* (Oxford, 1991).

188 R. McCarty, *Kant's Theory of Action* (Oxford, 2009).

189 G. Banham, *Kant's Practical Philosophy: From Critique to Doctrine* (Basingstoke/New York, 2003).

190 H. Allison, *Kant's Theory of Freedom* (Cambridge, 1990) concentrates on freedom in general, including in the theoretical philosophy.

191 M. Gregor, *Laws of Freedom: A Study of Kant's Method of Applying the Categorical Imperative in the Metaphysik der Sitten* (Cambridge, 1963).

192 K. Flikschuh, *Kant and Modern Political Philosophy* (Cambridge, 2000).

193 A. Ripstein, *Force and Freedom: Kant's Legal and Political Philosophy* (Cambridge, MA, 2009).

194 B. S. Byrd, J. Hruschka, *Kant's Doctrine of Right: A Commentary* (Cambridge, 2010).

195 L. Denis, *Moral Self-Regard: Duties to Oneself in Kant's Moral Theory* (New York, 2001).

196 J. Grenberg, *Kant and the Ethics of Humility: A Story of Dependence, Corruption and Virtue* (Cambridge, 2005).

197 A. M. Baxley, *Kant's Theory of Virtue: The Value of Autocracy* (Cambridge, 2011).

198 C. Korsgaard, *The Sources of Normativity*, ed. O. O'Neill (Cambridge, 1996).

199 C. Korsgaard, *The Sources of Normativity*, p. 89.

200 C. Onof, 'Reconstructing the grounding of Kant's ethics: a critical assessment', *Kant-Studien* 100,4 (2009): 496–517.

201 C. Korsgaard, *Creating the Kingdom of Ends* (Cambridge, 1996), p. 169.

202 See J. Rawls, *Lectures on the History of Moral Philosophy*, ed. B. Herman (Cambridge, MA, 2000), pp. 172–173 [hereafter referred to as *Lectures*].

203 See J. Rawls, *Lectures*, p. 149.

204 J. Rawls, *Lectures*, pp. 174–175.

205 See K. Budde, 'Rawls on Kant: Is Rawls a Kantian or Kant a Rawlsian?', *European Journal of Political Theory* 6 (2007): 348.

206 See K. Budde, 'Rawls on Kant', p. 352.

207 See J. Rawls, *A Theory of Justice* (Oxford, 1971).

208 Scanlon is a key figure of contractualism; see T. Scanlon, *What We Owe to Each Other* (Cambridge, MA, 1988). Scanlon's contractualism is less Kantian than Rawls's, and so is not examined here: Scanlon seeks principles that no-one can reasonably reject, rather than principles that all would agree to, as Rawls does. He also provides a substantive account of the ground of morality, rather than attempt to ground practical constraints outside morality.

209 R. Nozick, *Anarchy, State and Utopia* (New York, 1974). For an important response to Nozick, see J. Wolff, *Robert Nozick. Property, Justice and the Minimal State* (Cambridge, 1991).

210 See K.-O. Apel, 'Diskursethik als Verantwortungsethik – eine postmetaphysische Transformation der Ethik Kants', in J. Schönrich, Y. Kato (eds), *Kant in der*

Diskussion der Moderne (Frankfurt a/M, 1996), pp. 326–359 [hereafter referred to as 'Diskursethik']; K.-O. Apel, *Karl-Otto Apel: Selected Essays. Volume II: Ethics and the Theory of Rationality*, ed. E. Mendieta (New Jersey, 1996) [hereafter referred to as *Selected Essays*]; and J. Habermas, 'Diskursethik – Notizen zu einem Begründungsprogramm', in *Moralbewußtsein und kommunikatives Handeln* (Frankfurt a/M, 1983), pp. 53–126.

[211] See K.-O. Apel, 'Diskursethik', p. 332.

[212] See K.-O. Apel, *Selected Essays*, pp. 196–197.

[213] See K.-O. Apel, *Selected Essays*, pp. 198–199.

[214] See K.-O. Apel, *Selected Essays*, p. 195.

[215] See K.-O. Apel, *Selected Essays*, p. 206.

[216] See O. Höffe, 'Kantian skepticism toward transcendental ethics of communication', in S. Benhabib, F. Dallmayr (eds), *The Communicative Ethics Controversy* (Cambridge, MA, 1990), pp. 193–219.

[217] See J. Habermas, 'Discourse ethics: notes on a program of philosophical justification', S. Benhabib, F. Dallmayr (eds), *The Communicative Ethics Controversy* (Cambridge, MA, 1990), pp. 60–110.

[218] See T. Nagel, *The Possibility of Altruism* (Princeton, 1970).

[219] See G. A. Cohen, 'Reason, humanity, and the moral law', in C. Korsgaard, *The Sources of Normativity*, ed. O. O'Neill (Cambridge, 1996), 186.

[220] G. A. Cohen, 'Reason, humanity, and the moral law', pp. 170–174.

[221] See C. Korsgaard, *The Sources of Normativity*, p. 235.

[222] See C. Korsgaard, *The Sources of Normativity*, pp. 228–229.

[223] See C. Korsgaard, *The Sources of Normativity*, p. 188.

PART V:
BIBLIOGRAPHY

6

KANT BIBLIOGRAPHY

The literature on Kant is very large and constantly growing so it is necessarily the case that this bibliography is selective but the selection is aimed at providing for the reader reference to the major recent works on each aspect of Kant's philosophy, at least with regard to English-language contributions. Only very selective attention has been paid to work in other languages with the result that the overwhelming focus is on works in English. However, this bibliography is rare in presenting works on each of the major elements of the Critical division of Kant's works in addition to incorporating wide material on the background, context and influence of the Critical philosophy. – GB/DS

1. KANT'S WORKS IN GERMAN

The standard critical edition of Kant's works, which provides the pagination for all volumes cited in this Companion other than the *Critique of Pure Reason* is Kant's gesammelte Schriften, edited by the *Königlich Preußische Akademie der Wissenschaften*, subsequently *Deutsche* and then *Berlin-Brandenburg Akademie der Wissenschaften* and which is generally simply referred to as the *Akademie*

edition (see further the List of Abbreviations in this volume).

2. ENGLISH TRANSLATIONS

The Cambridge Edition of Kant's work, which has been appearing since 1992, edited by Paul Guyer and Allen Wood, has gained authority as the source for many of Kant's works and includes translations of lectures and notes that were, until very recently, not available at all in English. The edition of the *Critique of Pure Reason*, published in 1998, has not, however, decisively replaced the long-classic translation by Norman Kemp Smith (1929) (published by Palgrave Macmillan). The 2007 edition of Kemp Smith also includes an extensive bibliography of English-language work on the *Critique* but does not entirely overlap with this one as it is more focused than this. Alongside these two translations of the *Critique* an important third one, by Werner Pluhar, has also appeared (1996). Hackett, the publishers of Pluhar's edition of the *Critique of Pure Reason*, have further published translations by him of the *Critique of Judgment* and the *Critique of Practical Reason*. Hackett and Cambridge University

Press thus offer competing translations of the central Critical works. For a list of translations of Kant's works into English, see P. Guyer (ed.)(2010), pp. 668–673.

3. BIOGRAPHIES OF KANT

Cassirer, E., *Kant's Life and Thought* (New Haven: Yale University Press, 1981 [1918]).

Gulyga, A., *Immanuel Kant: His Life and Thought* (Boston: Birkhauser, 1987).

Kuehn, M., *Kant: A Biography* (Cambridge: Cambridge University Press, 2001).

Stuckenberg, J. W. H., *The Life of Immanuel Kant* (Lanham, MD/London: University Press of America, 1986 [1882]).

4. INTRODUCTIONS TO KANT

Altman, M., *A Companion to Kant's Critique of Pure Reason* (Boulder: Westview, 2008).

Broad, C. D., *Kant: An Introduction* (Cambridge: Cambridge University Press, 1978).

Buroker, J. V., *Kant's Critique of Pure Reason: An Introduction* (Cambridge: Cambridge University Press, 2006).

Callanan, J., *Kant's Groundwork of the Metaphysics of Morals: An Edinburgh Philosophical Guide* (Edinburgh: Edinburgh University Press, 2013).

Dicker, G., *Kant's Theory of Knowledge: An Analytical Introduction* (Oxford: Oxford University Press, 2005).

Dudley, W. & K. Engelhard (eds), *Immanuel Kant: Key Concepts* (Durham: Acumen, 2011).

Ewing, A. C., *A Short Commentary on Kant's Critique of Pure Reason* (Chicago: University of Chicago Press, 1938).

Gardner, S., *Kant and the Critique of Pure Reason* (London/New York: Routledge, 1999).

Guyer, P., *Kant* (London/New York: Routledge, 2006).

Hall, B., *The Arguments of Kant's 'Critique of Pure Reason'* (Lanham, MD: Lexington, 2011).

Hartnack, J., *Kant's Theory of Knowledge* (London/Toronto: Macmillan, 1968).

Hughes, F., *Kant's 'Critique of Aesthetic Judgment': A Reader's Guide* (London/New York: Continuum, 2009).

Körner, S., *Kant* (Harmondsworth: Penguin, 1955).

Luchte, J., *Kant's 'Critique of Pure Reason': A Reader's Guide* (London: Continuum, 2007).

O'Shea, J., *Kant's Critique of Pure Reason: An Introduction and Interpretation* (Durham: Acumen, 2012).

Robinson, D., *How is Nature Possible? Kants Project in the First Critique* (London/New York: Continuum, 2011).

Rosenberg, J., *Accessing Kant: A Relaxed Introduction to the 'Critique of Pure Reason'* (Oxford: Oxford University Press, 2005).

Savile, A., *Kant's Critique of Pure Reason: An Orientation to the Central Themes* (Oxford: Blackwell, 2005).

Scruton, R., *Kant: A Very Short Introduction* (Oxford: Oxford University Press, 2001).

Segdwick, S., *Kant's Groundwork of the Metaphysics of Morals: An Introduction* (Cambridge: Cambridge University Press, 2008).

Uleman, J. K., *An Introduction to Kant's Moral Philosophy* (Cambridge: Cambridge University Press, 2010).

Walker, R. C. S., *Kant* (London: Routledge & Kegan Paul, 1978).

Ward, A., *Kant: The Three Critiques* (Cambridge: Polity, 2006).

——, *Starting with Kant* (London/New York: Continuum, 2012).

Wenzel, C. H., *An Introduction to Kant's Aesthetics* (Oxford/New York: Wiley-Blackwell, 2005).

Wilkerson, T. E., *Kant's Critique of Pure Reason* (Oxford: Clarendon Press, 1976).

Wood, A. W., *Kant* (Oxford/New York: Wiley-Blackwell, 2005).

5. MULTI-AUTHOR EDITED COLLECTIONS ON KANT

Anderson-Gold, S. & P. Muchnik (eds), *Kant's Anatomy of Evil* (Cambridge: Cambridge University Press, 2009).

Baiasu, S., S. Pihlstrom & H. Williams (eds), *Politics and Metaphysics in Kant* (Cardiff: University of Wales Press, 2011).

Beck, L. W. (ed.), *Kant Studies Today* (Chicago/La Salle, IL: Open Court, 1967).

—— (ed.), *Kant's Theory of Knowledge* (Dordrecht: D. Reidel, 1974).

Beiner, R. & J. Booth (eds), *Kant & Political Philosophy* (New Haven: Yale University Press, 1993).

Bird, G. (ed.), *A Companion to Kant* (Oxford: Blackwell, 2006).

Bohman, J. & M. Lutz-Bachmann (eds), *Perpetual Peace: Essays on Kant's Cosmopolitan Ideal* (Cambridge: MIT Press, 1997).

Bruxvoort Lipscomb, B. & J. Krueger (eds), *Kant's Moral Metaphysics* (Berlin/New York: Gruyter, 2010).

Butts, R. E. (ed.), *Kant's Philosophy of Physical Science* (Dordrecht: D. Reidel, 1986).

Chadwick, R. & C. Cazeaux (eds), *Immanuel Kant: Critical Assessments*, 4 vols. (London/New York: Routledge, 1992).

Cicovacki, P. (ed.), *Kant's Legacy* (Rochester: University of Rochester Press, 2001).

Clewis, R. (ed.), *Reading Kant's Lectures* (Berlin/New York: de Gruyter, 2015).

Cohen, A. (ed.), *Kant's Lectures on Anthropology: A Critical Guide* (Cambridge: Cambridge University Press, 2014).

—— (ed.), *Kant on Emotion and Value* (London/New York: Palgrave Macmillan, 2014).

Cohen, T. & Guyer, P. (eds), *Essays in Kant's Aesthetics* (Chicago: University of Chicago Press, 1982).

Dancy, R. M. (ed.), *Kant and Critique* (Dordrecht: Kluwer, 1993).

Denis, L. (ed.), *Kant's 'Metaphysics of Morals': A Critical Guide* (Cambridge: Cambridge University Press, 2010).

Elden, S. & E. Mendieta (eds), *Reading Kant's Geography* (Albany, NY: SUNY Press, 2011).

Emundts, D. (ed.) *Self, World, and Art. Metaphysical Topics in Kant and Hegel* (Berlin/New York: de Gruyter, 2013).

Engstrom, S. & J. Whiting (eds), *Aristotle, Kant and the Stoics: Rethinking Happiness and Duty* (Cambridge: Cambridge University Press, 1996).

Firestone, C. & S. Palmquist (eds), *Kant and the New Philosophy of Religion* (Bloomington, IN: Indiana University Press, 2006).

Firestone, C. & N. Jacobs (eds), *In Defense of Kant's Religion* (Bloomington, IN: Indiana University Press, 2008).

Fischer, N. (ed.), *Kants Grundlegung einer kritischen Metaphysik* (Hamburg: Meiner, 2010).

Förster, E. (ed.), *Kant's Transcendental Deductions* (Stanford: Stanford University Press, 1989).

Giordanetti, P., R. Pozzo & M. Sgarbi (eds), *Kant's Philosophy of the Unconscious* (Berlin/New York: de Gruyter, 2012).

Goy, I. & E. Watkins (eds), *Kant's Theory of Biology* (Berlin/New York: de Gruyter, 2014).

Gram, M. S. (ed.), *Kant: Disputed Questions* (Chicago: Quadrangle Books, 1967; second expanded edition, Atascadero: Ridgeview Publishing, 1984).

—— (ed.), *Interpreting Kant* (Iowa City: University of Iowa Press, 1982).

Guyer, P. (ed.), *The Cambridge Companion to Kant* (Cambridge: Cambridge University Press, 1992).

—— (ed.), *Kant's Groundwork of the Metaphysics of Morals: Critical Essays* (Lanham, MD: Rowman & Littlefield, 1998).

—— (ed.), *Kant's Critique of the Power of Judgment: Critical Essays* (Lanham, MD: Rowman & Littlefield, 2003).

—— (ed.), *The Cambridge Companion to Kant and Modern Philosophy* (Cambridge: Cambridge University Press, 2006).

—— (ed.), *The Cambridge Companion to Kant's 'Critique of Pure Reason'* (Cambridge: Cambridge University Press, 2010).

Harper, W. A. & R. Meerbote (eds), *Kant on Causality, Freedom, and Objectivity* (Minneapolis: University of Minnesota Press, 1984).

Heidemann, D. (ed.), *Kant and Non-Conceptual Content* (Abingdon/New York: Routledge, 2012).

Hill, T. E. (ed.), *The Blackwell Guide to Kant's Ethics* (Oxford: Blackwell, 2009).

Höffe, O. (ed.), *Grundlegung der Metaphysik der Sitten: Ein kooperativer Kommentar* (Frankfurt a/M: Vittorio Klostermann, 1989).

Höwing, T. (ed.), *The Highest Good in Kant's Philosophy* (Berlin/New York: de Gruyter, 2015).

Horn, C. & D. Schönecker (eds), *Groundwork for the Metaphysics of Morals* (Berlin/New York: de Gruyter, 2006).

Jacobs, B. & P. Kain (eds), *Essays on Kant's Anthropology* (Cambridge: Cambridge University Press, 2003).

Jost, L. & J. Wuerth (eds), *Perfecting Virtue: New Essays on Kantian Ethics and Virtue Ethics* (Cambridge: Cambridge University Press, 2011).

Kennington, R. (ed.), *The Philosophy of Immanuel Kant* (Washington, DC: Catholic University Press, 1985).

Kitcher, P. (ed.), *Kant's Critique of Pure Reason* (Lanham, MD: Rowman & Littefield, 1998).

Kneller, J. & S. Axinn (eds), *Autonomy and Community: Readings in Contemporary Kantian Social Philosophy* (Albany, NY: SUNY Press, 1998).

Kukla, R. (ed.), *Aesthetics and Cognition in Kant's Critical Philosophy* (Cambridge: Cambridge University Press, 2006).

Lyre, H. & O. Schliemann (eds), *Kants 'Prolegomena': Ein kooperativer Kommentar* (Frankfurt a/M: Klostermann, 2012).

Massimi, M. (ed.), *Kant and Philosophy of Science Today* (Cambridge: Cambridge University Press, 2008).

Michalson, G. (ed.), *Kant's 'Religion within the Boundaries of Mere Reason': A Critical Guide* (Cambridge: Cambridge University Press, 2014).

Mohanty, J. N. & R. W. Shahan (eds), *Essays on Kant's Critique of Pure Reason* (Norman: University of Oaklahoma Press, 1982).

Ouden, B. den & M. Moen (eds), *New Essays on Kant* (New York: Peter Lang, 1987).

Palmquist, S. (ed.), *Cultivating Personhood: Kant and Asian Philosophy* (Berlin/New York: de Gruyter 2010).

Parret, H. (ed.), *Kants Ästhetik/Kant's Aesthetics/L'esthétique de Kant* (Berlin/New York: Walter de Gruyter, 1998).

Parrini, P. (ed.), *Kant and Contemporary Epistemology* (Dordrecht: Kluwer, 1994).

Payne, C. & L. Thorpe (eds), *Kant and the Concept of Community* (Rochester, NY: University of Rochester Press, 2011).

Penelhum, T. & J. MacIntosh (eds), *The First Critique: Reflections on Kant's Critique of Pure Reason* (Belmont: Wadsworth, 1969).

Posy, C. (ed.), *Kant's Philosophy of Mathematics* (Dordrecht: Kluwer, 1992).

Reath, A. & J. Timmermann (eds), *Kant's Critique of Practical Reason: A Critical Guide* (Cambridge: Cambridge University Press, 2010).

Rockmore, T. (ed.), *New Essays on the Precritical Kant* (Amherst, NY: Humanity, 2001).

Rorty, A. & J. Schmidt (eds), *Kant's 'Idea for a Universal History with a Cosmopolitan Aim': A Critical Guide* (Cambridge: Cambridge University Press, 2012).

Roth, K. & C. Surprenant (eds), *Kant and Education: Interpretations and Commentary* (London/New York: Routledge, 2011).

Rothfield, P. (ed.), *Kant after Derrida* (Manchester: Clinamen Press, 2003).

Schaper, E. & W. Vossenkuhl (eds), *Reading Kant: New Perspectives on Transcendental Arguments and Critical Philosophy* (Oxford: Blackwell, 1989).

Schott, R. M. (ed.), *Feminist Interpretations of Immanuel Kant* (University Park: Penn State University Press, 1997).

Schulting, D. & J. Verburgt (eds), *Kant's Idealism: New Interpretations of a Controversial Doctrine* (Dordrecht: Springer Science, 2011).

Sensen, O. (ed.), *Kant on Moral Autonomy* (Cambridge: Cambridge University Press, 2012).

Shell, S. Meld & R. Velkley (eds), *Kant's Observations and Remarks: A Critical Guide* (Cambridge: Cambridge University Press, 2012).

Thompson, M. (ed.), *Imagination in Kant's Critical Philosophy* (Berlin/New York: de Gruyter, 2013).

Timmermann, J. (ed.), *Kant's Groundwork of the Metaphysics of Morals: A Critical Guide* (Cambridge: Cambridge University Press, 2009).

Timmons, M. (ed.), *Kant's Metaphysics of Morals: Interpretative Essays* (Oxford: Clarendon Press, 2002).

Timmons, M. & S. Baiasu (eds), *Kant on Practical Justification: Interpretative Essays* (Oxford: Oxford University Press, 2013).

Trampota, A., O. Sensen & J. Timmermann (eds), *Kant's 'Tugendlehre': A Comprehensive Commentary* (Berlin/New York: de Gruyter, 2013).

Walker, R. C. S. (ed.), *Kant on Pure Reason* (Oxford: Oxford University Press, 1982).

Watkins, E. (ed.), *Kant and the Sciences* (Oxford: Oxford University Press, 2001).

Williams, H. (ed.), *Essays on Kant's Political Philosophy* (Chicago: University of Chicago Press, 1992).

Wolff, R. P. (ed.), *Kant: A Collection of Critical Essays* (Garden City: Doubleday Anchor, 1967).

Wood, A. W. (ed.), *Self and Nature in Kant's Philosophy* (Ithaca, NY: Cornell University Press, 1984).

Yovel, Y. (ed.), *Kant's Practical Philosophy Reconsidered* (Dordrecht: Kluwer, 1989).

6. CONTEXT AND RECEPTION OF KANT'S WORK

Allison, H. E., *Lessing and the Enlightenment* (Ann Arbor, MI: University of Michigan Press, 1966).

——, *The Kant-Eberhard Controversy* (Baltimore: Johns Hopkins University Press, 1973).

——, 'Kant's critique of Spinoza', in R. Kennington (ed.), *The Philosophy of Spinoza* (Washington, DC: Catholic University of America Press, 1980), pp. 199–227.

Altmann, A., *Moses Mendelssohn: A Biographical Study* (London: Routledge & Kegan Paul, 1973).

Al-Azm, S., *The Origins of Kant's Arguments in the Antinomies* (Oxford: Oxford University Press, 1972).

Ameriks, K., *Kant and the Fate of Autonomy: Problems in the Appropriation of the Critical Philosophy* (Cambridge: Cambridge University Press, 2000).

——, *Kant and the Historical Turn: Philosophy as Critical Interpretation* (Oxford: Clarendon Press, 2006).

——, *Kant's Elliptical Path* (Oxford: Clarendon Press, 2012).

Anderson, R. L., 'The Wolffian paradigm and its discontent: Kant's containment definition of analyticity in historical context', *Archiv für Geschichte der Philosophie* 87 (2005): 22–74.

Bailey, T., 'Nietzsche the Kantian?', in K. Gemes & J. Richardson (eds), *The Oxford Handbook of Nietzsche* (Oxford: Oxford University Press, 2013), pp. 134–159.

Banham, G. 'The continental tradition: Kant, Hegel, Nietzsche', in J. Mullarkey & B. Lord (eds), *The Continuum Companion to Continental Philosophy* (London/New York: Continuum, 2009), pp. 33–52.

Baumgarten, H.-U., *Kant und Tetens* (Stuttgart: Metzler, 1992).

Beck, L. W., *Early German Philosophy: Kant and His Predecessors* (Cambridge, MA: Harvard University Press, 1969).

Beiser, F., *The Fate of Reason: German Philosophy From Kant to Fichte* (Cambridge, MA: Harvard University Press, 1987).

——, *German Idealism: The Struggle Against Subjectivism, 1781–1801* (Cambridge, MA: Harvard University Press, 2002).

Berg, H. v.d., 'Wolff and Kant on scientific demonstration and mechanical explanation', *Archiv für Geschichte der Philosophie* 95,2 (2013): 178–205.

Boehm, O., *Kant's Critique of Spinoza* (New York: Oxford University Press, 2014).

Boer, K. de, 'Transformations of transcendental philosophy: Wolff, Kant, and Hegel', *Bulletin of the Hegel Society of Great Britain* 63/64 (2011): 50–79.

Bristow, W., *Hegel and the Transformation of Philosophical Critique* (Oxford: Oxford University Press, 2007).

Bubner, R., 'Platon der Vater aller *Schwärmerei*', in *Antike Themen und ihre moderne Verwandlung* (Frankfurt a/M, Suhrkamp, 1992), pp. 80–93.

Buroker, J. V., *Space and Incongruence: The Origin of Kant's Idealism* (Dordrecht: D. Reidel, 1981).

Butts, R. E., 'The grammar of reason: Hamann's challenge to Kant', *Synthese* 75 (1988): 251–283.

Carrasco, M. A., 'Adam Smith's reconstruction of practical reason', *Review of Metaphysics* 58 (2004): 81–116.

Cavallar, G., 'Kant's judgment on Frederick's enlightened absolutism', *History of Political Thought* 14 (1993): 103–132.

Caygill, H., *Art of Judgement* (Oxford: Blackwell, 1989).

Chignell, A. (ed.), 'On going back to Kant', special issue on neo-Kantianism, *The Philosophical Forum* 39, 2 (2008): 109–298.

Dahlstrom, D., 'The *Critique of Pure Reason* and continental philosophy: Heidegger's interpretation of transcendental imagination', in P. Guyer (ed.) (2010), pp. 380–400.

Darwall, S., 'Sympathetic liberalism: recent work on Adam Smith', *Philosophy and Public Affairs* 28,2 (1999): 139–164.

Davies, M. L., *Marcus Herz and the End of the Enlightenment* (Detroit: Wayne State University Press, 1995).

Di Giovanni, G., 'Kant's metaphysics of nature and Schelling's *Ideas for a Philosophy of Nature*', *Journal of the History of Philosophy* 17 (1979): 197–215.

——, 'The first twenty years of critique: the Spinoza connection', in P. Guyer (ed.) (1992), pp. 417–448.

——, 'Hume, Jacobi, and common sense: an episode in the reception of Hume at the time of Kant', *Kant-Studien* 89 (1998): 44–58.

——, 'Faith without religion, and religion without faith: Kant and Hegel on religion', *Journal of the History of Philosophy* 41,3 (2003): 365–383.

——, *Freedom and Religion in Kant and His Immediate Successors: The Vocation of Humankind, 1774–1800* (Cambridge: Cambridge University Press, 2005).

Dixon, R. A., 'Johann Nicolas Tetens: a forgotten father of developmental psychology?', *International Journal of Behavioral Development* 13 (1990): 215–230.

Domsky, M. 'Kant and Newton on the a priori necessity of geometry', *Studies in the History and Philosophy of Science* 44,3 (2013): 438–447.

Ducheyne, S., 'Kant and Whewell on bridging principles between metaphysics and science', *Kant-Studien* 102,1 (2011): 22–45.

Dunham, W., *Euler: The Master of Us All* (Washington: The Mathematical Association of America, 1999).

Düsing, K., 'Kant und Epikur. Untersuchungen zum Problem der Grundlegung einer Ethik', *Allgemeine*

Zeitschrift für Philosophie 1/2 (1976): 39–58.

——, 'Constitution and structure of self-identity: Kant's theory of apperception and Hegel's criticism', *Midwest Studies in Philosophy* 8 (1983): 409–431.

——, 'The reception of Kant's doctrine of postulates in Schelling's and Hegel's early philosophical projects', in M. Baur & D. Dahlstrom (eds), *The Emergence of German Idealism* (Washington, DC: Catholic University of America Press, 1999), pp. 201–237.

Ertl, W. '"Ludewig" Molina and Kant's libertarian compatibilism', in M. Kaufmann & A. Aichele (eds), *A Companion to Luis de Molina* (Leiden: Brill, 2014), pp. 405–445.

——, '"Nothing but representations" — A Suárezian way out of the mind?', in S. Bacin et al. (eds), *Kant und die Philosophie in weltbürgerlicher Absicht. Akten des XI. Internationalen Kant-Kongresses*, vol. 5 (Berlin/New York: de Gruyter 2013), pp. 429–440.

——, 'Kant and the early modern scholastic legacy: New perspectives on transcendental idealism', in H. Busche (ed.), *Departure for Modern Europe. A Handbook of Early Modern Philosophy (1400–1700)* (Hamburg: Meiner 2011), pp. 1178–1193.

Garber, D. & B. Longuenesse (eds), *Kant and the Early Moderns* (Princeton: Princeton University Press, 2008).

Falkenstein, L., 'Kant, Mendelssohn, Lambert and the subjectivity of time', *Journal of the History of Philosophy* 29 (1991): 227–251.

——, 'The great light of 1769 – a Humean awakening? Comments on Lothar Kreimendahl's account of Hume's influence on Kant', *Archiv für Geshichte der Philosophie* 77 (1995): 63–79.

Fleischacker, S. 'Philosophy in moral practice: Kant and Adam Smith', *Kant-Studien* 82,3 (1991): 249–269.

——, 'Values behind the market: Kant's response to the *Wealth of Nations*', *History of Political Thought* 17 (1996): 379–407.

——, *A Third Concept of Liberty: Judgment and Freedom in Kant and Adam Smith* (Princeton: Princeton University Press, 1999).

Förster, E., *The 25 Years of Philosophy* (Cambridge, MA: Harvard University Press, 2012).

Forster, M., *After Herder* (Oxford: Oxford University Press, 2012).

Frank, M., *'Unendliche Annäherung': Die Anfänge der philosophischen Frühromantik* (Frankfurt a/M: Suhrkamp, 1997).

Franks, P. W., *All or Nothing: Systematicity, Transcendental Arguments and Skepticism in German Idealism* (Cambridge, MA: Harvard University Press, 2005).

Friedman, M. & A. Nordmann (eds), *The Kantian Legacy in Nineteenth-Century Science* (Cambridge, MA: MIT Press, 2006).

Fulda, H. F. & J. Stolzenberg (eds), *System der Vernunft. Kant und der deutsche Idealismus*, Bd. 1, *Architektonik und System in der Philosophie Kants* (Hamburg: Meiner, 2001).

Gardner, S., 'Schopenhauer's contraction of reason: Clarifying Kant and undoing German Idealism', *Kantian Review* 17,3 (2012): 375–401.

Geiger, I., *The Founding Act of Modern Ethical Life. Hegel's Critique of Kant's Moral and Political Philosophy* (Stanford: Stanford University Press, 2007).

Glock, H.-J. (ed.), *Strawson and Kant* (Oxford: Clarendon Press, 2003).

Gorner, P., 'Phenomenological interpretations of Kant in Husserl and Heidegger', in G. Bird (ed.) (2006), pp. 500–512.

Gregor, M., 'Baumgarten's *Aesthetica*', *Review of Metaphysics* 37,2 (1983): 357–385.

Guyer, P., *Knowledge, Reason, and Taste: Kant's Response to Hume* (Princeton: Princeton University Press, 2008).

——, 'Schopenhauer, Kant and compassion', *Kantian Review* 17,3 (2012): 403–429.

Haag, J. & M. Wild (eds), *Übergänge – diskursiv oder intuitiv? Essays zu Eckart Försters "Die 25 Jahre der Philosophie"* (Frankfurt a/M: Klostermann, 2013).

Hanna, R., *Kant and the Foundations of Analytic Philosophy* (Oxford: Clarendon Press, 2001).

Heinz, M. & C. Krijnen (eds), *Kant im Neukantianismus: Fortschritt oder Rückschritt?* (Würzburg: Königshausen & Neumann, 2007).

Henrich, D., *Grundlegung aus dem Ich. Untersuchungen zur Vorgeschichte des Idealismus. Tübingen – Jena 1790–1794*, 2 vols. (Frankfurt a/M: Suhrkamp, 2004).

Holden, T., *The Architecture of Matter: From Galileo to Kant* (Oxford: Clarendon Press, 2004).

Horstmann, R. P., *Die Grenzen der Vernunft. Eine Untersuchung zu Zielen und Motiven des Deutschen Idealismus*, third edition (Frankfurt a/M: Klostermann, 2004).

Höffe, O., 'Ethik ohne und mit Metaphysik. Zum Beispiel Aristoteles und Kant', *Zeitschrift für philosophische Forschung* 61,4 (2007): 405–422.

——, 'The reception of the *Critique of Pure Reason* in German Idealism', in P. Guyer (ed.) (2010), pp. 329–345.

Jenkins, S., 'Hegel on space: A critique of Kant's transcendental philosophy', *Inquiry* 53 (2010): 326–355.

Jong, W. R. de, 'Kant's analytic judgments and the traditional theory of concepts', *Journal of the History of Philosophy* 33,4 (1995): 613–641.

Klemme, H., 'Kants Wende zum Ich', *Zeitschrift für philosophische Forschung* 53 (1999): 509–529.

Kossler, M., 'The "perfected system of criticism": Schopenhauer's initial disagreements with Kant', *Kantian Review* 17,3 (2012): 459–478.

Kreimendahl, L., *Kant – Der Durchbruch von 1769* (Cologne: Dinter, 1990).

Kuehn, M., 'Kant's conception of Hume's problem', *Journal of the History of Philosophy* 21 (1983): 175–193.

——, *Scottish Common Sense in Germany, 1786–1800: A Contribution to the History of Critical Philosophy* (Kingston/Montreal: McGill-Queens University Press, 1987).

——, 'The Wolffian background of Kant's Transcendental Deduction', in P. A. Easton (ed.), *Logic and the Workings of the Mind* (Atascadero: Ridgeview, 1997), pp. 229–250.

——, 'Christian Thomasius and Christian Wolff', in R. H. Popkin (ed.), *The Columbia History of Western Philosophy* (New York: Columbia University Press, 1999), pp. 472–475.

——, 'Kant's Critical philosophy and its reception – the first five years (1781–1786)', in P. Guyer (ed.) (2006), pp. 630–664.

——, 'Tetens, Johann Nicolas', in H. Klemme & M. Kuehn (eds), *The Dictionary of Eigtheenth Century*

German Philosophers, vol. 3 (London: Continuum, 2010), pp. 1163–1169.

Laywine, A., *Kant's Early Metaphysics and the Origins of the Critical Philosophy* (Atascadero: Ridgeview, 1993).

——, 'Kant in reply to Lambert on the ancestry of metaphysical concepts', *Kantian Review* 5 (2001): 1–48.

——, 'Kant on sensibility and the understanding in the 1770s', *Canadian Journal of Philosophy* 33,4 (2003): 443–482.

——, 'Kant's laboratory of ideas in the 1770s', in G. Bird (ed.) (2006), pp. 63–78.

——, 'Kant's metaphysical reflections in the *Duisburg Nachlass*', *Kant-Studien* 97 (2006): 79–113.

Lenoir, T., 'Kant, Blumenbach, and vital materialism in German biology', *Isis* 71 (1980): 77–108.

Look, B., (ed.), *The Continuum Companion to Leibniz* (London: Continuum, 2011).

Lord, B., *Kant and Spinozism* (Basingstoke/New York: Palgrave Macmillan, 2011).

Manchester, P. 'Kant's conception of architectonic in its historical context', *Journal of the History of Philosophy* 41,2 (2003): 187–207.

Massimi, M., 'Kant's dynamical theory of matter in 1755, and its debt to speculative Newtonian experimentalism', in *Studies in History and Philosophy of Science* 42,4 (2011): 525–543.

McCumber, J., *Understanding Hegel's Mature Critique of Kant* (Stanford: Stanford University Press, 2014).

Mittelstrass, J., *Leibniz und Kant* (Berlin/New York: de Gruyter, 2011).

Montes, L., *Adam Smith in Context* (Basingstoke/New York: Palgrave Macmillan, 2004).

Nuzzo, A. 'Kant and Herder on Baumgarten's *Aesthetica*', *Journal of the History of Philosophy* 44 (2006): 577–597.

——, 'Transformations of freedom in the Jena Kant-reception, 1785–1794', *The Owl of Minerva* 32,2 (2001): 135–167.

O'Shea, J., 'Conceptual connections: Kant and the twentieth-century analytic tradition', in G. Bird (ed.) (2006), pp. 513–526.

Pinkard, T., *German Philosophy 1760–1860: The Legacy of Idealism* (Cambridge: Cambridge University Press, 2002).

Piper, W. B., 'Kant's contact with British empiricism', *Eighteenth-Century Studies* 12 (1978–1979): 174–189.

Pippin, R. B., *Hegel's Idealism. The Satisfactions of Self-Consciousness* (Cambridge: Cambridge University Press, 1989).

Pollok, K., 'The "transcendental method". On the reception of the *Critique of Pure Reason* in neo-Kantianism', in P. Guyer (ed.) (2010), pp. 346–379.

Polonoff, I., *Force, Cosmos, Monads and Other Themes of Kant's Early Thought* (Bonn: Bouvier, 1973).

Pozzo, R. 'Prejudices and horizons: G. F. Meier's Vernunftlehre and its relation to Kant', *Journal of the History of Philosophy* 43 (2005): 185–202.

Radner, M., 'Unlocking the second antinomy: Kant and Wolff', *Journal of the History of Philosophy* 36 (1998): 413–441.

Reiss, H., 'Kant's politics and the enlightenment: reflections on some recent studies', *Political Theory* 27 (1999): 236–273.

Rockmore, T. (ed.), *Heidegger, German Idealism, and Neo-Kantianism* (New York: Humanity Books, 2000).

Ross, G. M. & T. McWalter (eds), *Kant and His Influence* (Bristol: Thoemmes, 1990).

Sarmiento, G., 'On Kant's definition of the monad in the *Monadologia physica* of 1756', *Kant-Studien* 96 (2005): 1–19.

Sassen, B., 'Critical idealism in the eyes of Kant's contemporaries', *Journal of the History of Philosophy* 35 (1997): 421–455.

—— (ed.), *Kant's Early Critics: The Empiricist Critique of the Theoretical Philosophy* (Cambridge: Cambridge University Press, 2000).

Schalow, F., *The Renewal of the Heidegger-Kant Dialogue: Action, Thought, and Responsibility* (Albany, NY: State University of New York Press, 1992).

Schaller, W. E., 'From the *Groundwork* to the *Metaphysics of Morals*: what happened to morality in Kant's theory of justice?', *History of Philosophy Quarterly* 12 (1995): 333–345.

Schlipp, P. A., *Kant's Pre-Critical Ethics*, second edition (Evanston: Northwestern University Press, 1960).

Schmidt, J., 'What Enlightenment was: how Moses Mendelssohn and Immanuel Kant answered the *Berlinische Monatsschrift*', *Journal of the History of Philosophy* 30 (1992): 77–101.

—— (ed.), *What is Enlightenment? Eighteenth Century Answers and Twentieth Century Questions* (Berkeley/ Los Angeles: University of California Press, 1996).

——, 'Civility, Enlightenment, and society', *American Political Science Review* 92 (1998): 419–427.

Schneewind, J., *The Invention of Autonomy: A History of Modern Moral Philosophy* (Cambridge: Cambridge University Press, 1998).

Schönfeld, M., *The Philosophy of the Young Kant. The Pre-Critical Project* (New York: Oxford University Press, 2000).

Schulting, D., 'Hegel on Kant's synthetic a priori in *Glauben und Wissen*', in A. Arndt, K. Bal & H. Ottman (eds), *Hegel-Jahrbuch 2005: Glauben und Wissen. Dritter Teil* (Berlin: Akademie Verlag, 2005), pp. 176–182.

Sedgwick, S. (ed.), *The Reception of Kant's Critical Philosophy: Fichte, Schelling and Hegel* (Cambridge: Cambridge University Press, 2000).

Sedgwick, S., 'Hegel's critique of Kant: an overview', in G. Bird (ed.) (2006), pp. 473–485.

——, *Hegel's Critique of Kant* (Oxford: Oxford University Press, 2012).

Seidl, H., *Sein und Bewußtsein: Erörterungen zur Erkenntnislehre und Metaphysik in einer Gegenüberstellung von Aristoteles und Kant* (Hildesheim: Olms, 2001).

Shapshay, S., 'Schopenhauer's transformation of the Kantian sublime', *Kantian Review* 17,3 (2012): 479–511.

Stan, M., 'Kant's early theory of motion: metaphysical dynamics and relativity', *The Leibniz Review* 19 (2009): 29–61.

Stapleford, S., 'A refutation of idealism from 1777', *Idealistic Studies* 40 (2010): 139–146.

Stern, R. *Understanding Moral Obligation. Kant, Hegel, Kierkegaard* (Cambridge: Cambridge University Press, 2012).

Thiel, U., 'Between Wolff and Kant: Merian's theory of apperception', *Journal of the History of Philosophy* 34 (1996): 213–232.

Thorpe, L., 'Is Kant's realm of ends a *unum per se*? Aquinas, Suárez, Leibniz and Kant on composition', *British Journal for the History of Philosophy* 18 (2010): 461–485.

Tonelli, G., 'Conditions in Königsberg and the making of Kant's philosophy', in A. J.

Bucher et al. (eds), *Bewusst-sein* (Bonn: Bouvier, 1975).

———, *Kant's 'Critique of Pure Reason' Within the Tradition of Modern Logic* (Hildesheim: Olms, 1994).

Townsend, D., 'From Shaftesbury to Kant: the development of the concept of aesthetic experience', *Journal of the History of Ideas* 48 (1987): 287–305.

Van der Zande, J., 'In the image of Cicero: German philosophy between Wolff and Kant', *Journal of the History of Ideas* 56 (1995): 419–442.

———, 'The microscope of experience: Christian Garve's translation of Cicero's *De Officiis* (1783)', *Journal of the History of Ideas* 59 (1998): 75–94.

Walford, D., 'The aims and method of Kant's 1768 *Gegenden im Raume* essay in the light of Euler's 1748 *Réflexions sur l'Espace et le Temps*', *British Journal for the History of Philosophy* 7,2 (1999): 305–322.

———, 'Towards an interpretation of Kant's 1768 *Gegenden im Raume* essay', *Kant-Studien* 92 (2001): 407–439.

Ward, K., *The Development of Kant's View of Ethics* (Oxford: Blackwell, 1972).

Watkins, E. (ed.), *Kant's 'Critique of Pure Reason': Background Source Materials* (Cambridge: Cambridge University Press, 2009).

Waxman, W., *Kant and the Empiricists: Understanding Understanding* (Oxford: Oxford University Press, 2005)

Weatherston, M., *Heidegger's Interpretation of Kant: Categories, Imagination and Temporality* (London/New York: Palgrave Macmillan, 2002).

Westphal, K., 'Kant's *Critique of Pure Reason* and analytic Philosophy', in P. Guyer (ed.) (2010), pp. 401–430.

Wolff, R. P., 'Kant's debt to Hume via Beattie', *Journal of the History of Ideas* 21 (1960): 117–123.

Zammito, J. H. *The Genesis of Kant's Critique of Judgment* (Chicago: University of Chicago Press, 1992).

———, *Kant, Herder and the Birth of Anthropology* (Chicago: University of Chicago Press, 2002).

Zoeller, G., 'From innate to a priori: Kant's radical transformation of a Cartesian-Leibnizian legacy', *The Monist* 72 (1989): 222–235.

———, 'Lichtenberg and Kant on the subject of thinking', *Journal of the History of Philosophy* 30 (1992): 417–441.

7. KANT'S THEORETICAL PHILOSOPHY

Abaci, U, 'Kant's *Only Possible Argument* and Chignell's real harmony', *Kantian Review* 19,1 (2014): 1–25.

Abela, P., 'Putnam's internal realism and Kant's empirical realism: the case for a divorce', *Idealistic Studies* 26 (1996): 45–56.

———, *Kant's Empirical Realism* (Oxford: Clarendon Press, 2002).

———, 'Kantian walls and bridges: challenging the integrationist model of the relation between theoretical and practical reason', *British Journal for the History of Philosophy* 10,4 (2002): 591–616.

Achourioti, T. & M. van Lambalgen, 'A formalization of Kant's transcendental logic', *The Review of Symbolic Logic* 4,2 (2011): 254–289.

Adams, R., 'Things in themselves', *Philosophy and Phenomenological Research* 57 (1997): 801–825.

Adkins, B., 'The satisfaction of reason: the mathematical/dynamical distinction in the *Critique of Pure Reason*', *Kantian Review* 3 (1999): 64–80.

Adorno, T. W., *Kant's Critique of Pure Reason* (Cambridge: Polity Press, 2001 [1995]).

Al-Azm, S. J., *Kant's Theory of Time* (New York: Philosophical Library, 1967).

——, 'Absolute space and Kant's First Antinomy of pure reason', *Kant-Studien* 59 (1968): 151–164.

——, *The Origins of Kant's Arguments in the Antinomies* (Oxford: Clarendon Press, 1972).

Alexander, P., 'Incongruent counterparts and absolute space', *Proceedings of the Aristotelian Society* 85 (1984/5): 1–21.

Allais, L., 'Kant's transcendental idealism and contemporary anti-realism', *International Journal of Philosophical Studies* 11 (2003): 369–392.

——, 'Kant's one world', *The British Journal for the History of Philosophy* 12,4 (2004): 655–684.

——, 'Intrinsic Natures: a critique of Langton on Kant', *Philosophy and Phenomenological Research* LXXIII (2006): 143–169.

——, 'Kant's idealism and the secondary quality analogy', *Journal of the History of Philosophy* 45,3 (2007): 459–484.

——, 'Kant, non-conceptual content, and the representation of space', *Journal of the History of Philosophy* 47,3 (2009): 383–413.

——, 'Kant's argument for transcendental idealism in the Transcendental Aesthetic', *Proceedings of the Aristotelian Society* 110,1 (2010): 47–75.

——, 'Transcendental idealism and metaphysics: Kant's commitment to things as they are in themselves', *Kant Yearbook* 2 (2010): 1–32.

——, 'Transcendental idealism and the Transcendental Deduction', in D. Schulting & J. Verburgt (eds) (2011), pp. 91–108.

——, 'Idealism enough: Response to Roche', *Kantian Review* 16,3 (2011): 375–398.

——, 'Kitcher on the Deduction', *Philosophy and Phenomenological Research* 87,1 (2013): 229–236.

Allison, H. E., 'Kant's concept of the transcendental object', *Kant-Studien* 59 (1968): 165–186.

——, 'Transcendental idealism and descriptive metaphysics', *Kant-Studien* 60 (1969): 216–233.

——, 'Kant's non-sequitur', *Kant-Studien* 62 (1971): 367–377.

——, 'Kant's transcendental humanism', *The Monist* 55 (1971): 182–207.

——, 'Kant's critique of Berkeley', *Journal of the History of Philosophy* 11 (1973): 43–63.

——, 'Transcendental affinity – Kant's answer to Hume', in L. W. Beck (ed.) (1974), pp. 119–127.

——, 'The *Critique of Pure Reason* as transcendental phenomenology', in D. Ihde & R. Zaner (eds), *Dialogues in Phenomenology* (The Hague: Martinus Nijhoff, 1975), pp. 136–155.

——, 'Kant's refutation of realism', *Dialectica* 30 (1976): 223–253.

——, 'The non-spatiality of things in themselves for Kant', *Journal of the History of Philosophy* 14 (1976): 313–321.

——, 'Things in themselves, noumena, and the transcendental object', *Dialectica* 32 (1978): 41–76.

——, 'Transcendental schematism and the problem of the synthetic a priori', *Dialectica* 35 (1981): 57–83.

——, 'Practical and transcendental freedom in the *Critique of Pure Reason*', *Kant-Studien* 73,3 (1982): 271–290.

——, *Kant's Transcendental Idealism: An Interpretation and Defense* (New Haven: Yale University Press, 1983).

——, 'Incongruence and ideality', *Topoi* 3 (1984): 169–175.

——, 'Causality and causal laws in Kant: a critique of Michael Friedman', in Allison (1996), pp. 80–91.

——, *Idealism and Freedom: Essays on Kant's Theoretical and Practical Philosophy* (Cambridge: Cambridge University Press, 1996).

——, 'Where have all the categories gone? Reflections on Longuenesse's reading of Kant's Transcendental Deduction', *Inquiry* 43,1 (2000): 67–80.

——, *Kant's Transcendental Idealism: An Interpretation and Defense*, Revised and Expanded Edition (New Haven: Yale University Press, 2004).

——, 'Transcendental realism, empirical realism, and transcendental idealism', *Kantian Review* 11 (2006): 1–28.

——, *Custom and Reason in Hume: A Kantian Reading of the First Book of the Treatise* (Oxford: Oxford University Press, 2008).

——, *Essays on Kant* (Oxford: Oxford University Press, 2012).

Ameriks, K., 'Kant's Transcendental Deduction as a regressive argument', *Kant-Studien* 69 (1978): 273–287.

——, 'Kant and Guyer on apperception', *Archiv für Geschichte der Philosophie* 65 (1983): 174–186.

——, 'From Kant to Frank: the ineliminable subject', in K. Ameriks & D. Sturma (eds), *The Modern Subject* (Albany, NY: SUNY Press, 1995), pp. 217–230.

——, *Kant's Theory of Mind: An Analysis of the Paralogisms of Pure Reason*, new edition (Oxford: Oxford University Press, 2000 [1982]).

——, 'Problems from Van Cleve's Kant: Experience and Objects', *Philosophy and Phenomenological Research* 66 (2003): 196–202.

——, *Interpreting Kant's Critiques* (Oxford: Oxford University Press, 2003).

——, 'The critique of metaphysics: the structure and fate of Kant's Dialectic', in P. Guyer (ed.) (2006), pp. 269–302.

——, *Kant and the Historical Turn* (Oxford: Clarendon Press, 2006).

——, *Kant's Elliptical Path* (Oxford: Clarendon Press, 2012).

Anderson, A., 'On the practical foundation of Kant's response to epistemic skepticism', *Kant-Studien* 89 (1998): 145–166.

Anderson, D., 'The neglected analogy', *The Southern Journal of Philosophy* 21 (1983): 481–488.

Anderson, E., 'Kant, natural kind terms, and scientific essentialism', *History of Philosophy Quarterly* 11 (1994): 355–373.

Anderson, J. C., 'Kant's paralogism of personhood', *Grazer Philosophische Studien* 10 (1980): 73–86.

Anderson, R. L., 'Synthesis, cognitive normativity and the meaning of Kant's question, "How are synthetic cognitions a priori possible?"', *European Journal of Philosophy* 9,3 (2001): 275–305.

——, 'It adds up after all: Kant's philosophy of arithmetic in the light of the traditional logic', *Philosophy and Phenomenological Research* LXIX,3 (2004): 501–540.

Aquila, R., 'Kant's theory of concepts', *Kant-Studien* 65 (1974): 1–19.

——, 'Kant's phenomenalism', *Idealistic Studies* 5 (1975): 108–126.

——, 'Two kinds of transcendental arguments in Kant', *Kant-Studien* 67 (1976): 1–19.

——, 'The relationship between pure and empirical intuition in Kant', *Kant-Studien* 68 (1977): 275–289.

——, 'Things in themselves and appearances: intentionality and reality in Kant', *Archiv für Geschichte der Philosophie* 61 (1979): 293–308.

——, 'Personal identity and Kant's Refutation of Idealism', *Kant-Studien* 70 (1979): 259–278.

——, 'Intentional objects and Kantian appearances', *Philosophical Topics* 12 (1981): 9–38.

——, *Representational Mind: A Study in Kant's Theory of Knowledge* (Bloomington: Indiana University Press, 1983).

——, *Matter in Mind: A Study of Kant's Transcendental Deduction* (Bloomington: Indiana University Press, 1989).

——, 'Imagination as a "medium" in the *Critique of Pure Reason*', *Monist* 72 (1989): 209–221.

——, 'Unity of apperception and the division of labour in the Transcendental Analytic', *Kantian Review* 1 (1997): 17–52.

——, 'Hans Vaihinger and some recent intentionalist readings of Kant', *Journal of the History of Philosophy* 41 (2003): 231–250.

——, 'The singularity and the unity of transcendental consciousness in Kant', *History of European Ideas* 30 (2004): 349–376.

Arens, P., 'Kant and the understanding's role in imaginative synthesis', *Kant Yearbook* 2 (2010): 33–52.

Aschenbrenner, K. A., *Companion to Kant's 'Critique of Pure Reason'*:

Transcendental Aesthetic and Analytic (London/Lanham: University of America Press, 1983).

Bader, R., 'The role of Kant's Refutation of Idealism', *Archiv für Geschichte der Philosophie* 94,1 (2012): 53–73.

Baiasu, S., 'Space, time, and mind-dependence', *Kantian Review* 16,2 (2011): 175–190.

Baiasu, S. & M. Grier, 'Revolutionary versus traditionalist approaches to Kant: some aspects of the debate', *Kantian Review* 16,2 (2011): 161–173.

Baldner, K., 'Is transcendental idealism coherent?', *Synthese* 85,1 (1990): 1–23.

——, 'Causality and things in themselves', *Synthese* 77 (1988): 353–373.

Baldwin, T. 'Kantian modality', *Proceedings of the Aristotelian Society* 76 (supplement) (2002): 1–24.

Banham, G., *Kant's Transcendental Imagination* (Basingstoke/New York: Palgrave Macmillan, 2006).

Bardon, A., 'Temporal passage and Kant's Second Analogy', *Ratio* 15 (2002): 134–153.

——, 'Kant's empiricism in his Refutation of Idealism', *Kantian Review* 8 (2004): 62–88.

——, 'Kant and the conventionality of simultaneity', *British Journal for the History of Philosophy* 18,5 (2010): 845–856.

——, 'Time-awareness and projection in Mellor and Kant', *Kant-Studien* 101 (2010): 59–74.

Barker, M., 'The proof-structure of Kant's A-deduction', *Kant-Studien* 92,3 (2001): 259–282.

Barker, S., 'Appearing and appearances in Kant', *Monist* 51 (1967): 426–441.

Bauer, N., 'Kant's subjective deduction', *British Journal for the History of Philosophy* 18,3 (2010): 433–460.

——, 'A peculiar intuition: Kant's conceptualist account of perception', *Inquiry* 55,3 (2012): 215–237.

Baum, M., 'The B-deduction and the Refutation of Idealism', *Southern Journal of Philosophy* 25 (supplement) (1986): 89–107.

Bayne, S. M., 'Objects of representation and Kant's Second Analogy', *Journal of the History of Philosophy* XXXII, 3 (1994): 381–410.

——, 'Kant's answer to Hume', *British Journal for the History of Philosophy* 8,2 (2000): 207–224.

——, *Kant on Causation: On the Fivefold Routes to the Principle of Causation* (Albany, NY: State University of New York Press, 2004).

Beck, L. W., 'Kant's theory of definition', *The Philosophical Review* 65,2 (1956): 179–191.

——, 'The Second Analogy and the principle of indeterminacy', *Kant-Studien* 57 (1966): 199–205.

——, *Essays on Kant and Hume* (New Haven: Yale University Press, 1978).

——, 'Kant on the uniformity of nature', *Synthese* 47 (1981): 449–464.

Bell, D., 'Some Kantian thoughts on propositional unity', *Aristotelian Society Supplementary Volume* LXXV (2001): 1–16.

Bencivenga, E. 'Identity, appearances, and things in themselves', *Dialogue* 23,3 (1984): 421–437.

——, 'Knowledge as a relation and knowledge as an experience in the *Critique of Pure Reason*', *Canadian Journal of Philosophy* 15,4 (1985): 593–615.

——, 'Understanding and reason in the First *Critique*', *History of Philosophy Quarterly* 3 (1986): 195–205.

——, *Kant's Copernican Revolution* (New York: Oxford University Press, 1987).

——, 'Kant is on my side: a reply to Walker', *Philosophical Inquiry* 13,3–4 (1991): 62–69.

Bennett, J., *Kant's Analytic* (Cambridge: Cambridge University Press, 1966).

——, 'Strawson on Kant', *The Philosophical Review* 77,3 (1968): 340–349.

——, *Kant's Dialectic* (Cambridge: Cambridge University Press, 1974).

Berg, H. v.d., 'Kant's conception of proper science', *Synthese* 183,1 (2011): 7–26.

——, *Kant on Proper Science: Biology in the Critical Philosophy and the Opus postumum* (Dordrecht: Springer, 2013).

Bermudez, J. L., 'The unity of apperception in the *Critique of Pure Reason*', *European Journal of Philosophy* 2 (1994): 213–240.

——, 'Scepticism and the justification of transcendental idealism', *Ratio* 8,1 (1995): 1–20.

Bernecker, S., 'Kant on spatial orientation', *European Journal of Philosophy* 20,4 (2012): 519–533.

Bernstein, J., 'Imagination and lunacy in Kant's First *Critique* and *Anthropology*', *Idealistic Studies* 27 (1997): 143–154.

Bird, G., *Kant's Theory of Knowledge* (London: Routledge & Kegan Paul, 1962).

——, 'Kant's transcendental idealism', in G. Vesey (ed.), *Idealism: Past and Present* (Cambridge: Cambridge University Press, 1982), pp.71–92.

——, 'Kant's transcendental arguments', in E. Schaper & W. Vossenkuhl (eds) (1989), pp.21–39.

——, 'McDowell's Kant', *Philosophy* 71 (1996): 219–243.

——, 'Kantian myths', *Proceedings of the Aristotelian Society* 71 (1996): 245–251.

——, 'Editorial review: Kant and contemporary epistemology', *Kantian Review* 1 (1997): 1–16.

——, 'Kantian themes in contemporary philosophy II', *Proceedings of the Aristotelian Society* 72 (supplement) (1998): 131–151.

——, 'The trouble with Kant', *Philosophy* 74 (1999): 587–594.

——, 'The Paralogisms and Kant's account of psychology', *Kant-Studien* 91 (2000): 129–145.

——, *The Revolutionary Kant: A Commentary on the Critique of Pure Reason* (Chicago/La Salle, IL: Open Court, 2006).

——, 'Another puzzle about Kant's idealism', *Studi kantiani* XXIII (2010): 11–22.

——, 'Replies to my critics', *Kantian Review* 16,2 (2011): 257–282.

——, 'Repy to Edward Kanterian', *Kantian Review* 18,2 (2013): 289–300.

Biro, J. I., 'Kant and Strawson on transcendental synthesis', *New Scholasticism* 53 (1979): 486–501.

Blatnik, E., 'Kant's refutation of anti-realism', *Journal of Philosophical Research* 19 (1994): 127–146.

Blecher, I., 'Kant on formal modality', *Kant-Studien* 104,1 (2013): 44–62.

Blomme, H., 'The completeness of Kant's Metaphysical Exposition of Space', *Kant-Studien* 103,2 (2012): 139–162.

Boehm, O., 'Kant's regulative Spinozism', *Kant-Studien* 103,3 (2012): 292–317.

Boer, K. de, 'Pure reason's enlightenment: Transcendental reflection in Kant's first *Critique*', *Kant Yearbook* 2 (2010): 53–74.

——, 'Kant's multi-layered conception of things-in-themselves, transcendental objects, and monads', *Kant-Studien* 105,2 (2014): 221–260.

Booth, E., 'Kant's critique of Newton', *Kant-Studien* 87 (1996): 149–165.

Bossart, W. H., 'Kant and some metaphysicians', *Kant-Studien* 55,1 (1964): 20–36.

——, 'Kant's doctrine of the reciprocity of freedom and reason', *International Philosophical Quarterly* 8 (1968): 334–355.

——, 'Kant's Transcendental Deduction', *Kant-Studien* 68 (1977): 383–403.

——, 'Kant's "Analytic" and the two-fold nature of time', *Kant-Studien* 69,3 (1978): 288–298.

Bowman, B., 'A conceptualist reply to Hanna's Kantian non-conceptualism', *International Journal of Philosophical Studies* 19,3 (2011): 417–446.

Bristow, W. F., 'Are Kant's categories subjective?', *Review of Metaphysics* 55,3 (2002): 551–580.

Brittan, G., *Kant's Theory of Science* (Princeton: Princeton University Press, 1978).

——, 'Kant's philosophy of mathematics', in G. Bird (ed.) (2006), pp. 222–235.

——, 'Graham Bird *The Revolutionary Kant*: introduction', *Kantian Review* 16,2 (2011): 211–219.

Broad, C. D., 'Kant's First and Second Analogies of experience', *Proceedings of the Aristotelian Society* 26 (1926): 189–210.

——, 'Kant's theory of mathematical and philosophical reasoning', *Proceedings of the Aristotelian Society* 42 (1941–2): 1–24.

——, 'Kant's mathematical antinomies', *Proceedings of the Aristotelian Society* 55 (1954–5): 1–22.

Brook, A., 'Imagination, possibility, and personal identity', *American Philosophical Quarterly* 12 (1975): 185–198.

——, 'Kant's a priori methods for recognizing necessary truths', *Canadian Journal of Philosophy* 22 (supplement) (1992): 215–252.

——, *Kant and the Mind* (Cambridge: Cambridge University Press, 1994).

——, 'Critical notice of *Kant's Intuitionism*', *Canadian Journal of Philosophy* 28 (1998): 247–268.

——, 'Kant, cognitive science and contemporary neo-Kantianism', *Journal of Consciousness Studies* 10–11 (2004): 1–25.

Brueckner, A., 'The anti-sceptical epistemology of the Refutation of Idealism', *Philosophical Topics* 19 (1991): 31–45.

Bubner, R., 'Kant, transcendental arguments, and the problem of deduction', *Review of Metaphysics* 28 (1975): 453–467.

Buchdahl, G., 'Causality, causal laws and scientific theory in the philosophy of Kant', *British Journal for the Philosophy of Science* 16,63 (1965): 187–208.

——, 'The relation between "understanding" and "reason" in the architectonic of Kant's philosophy', *Proceedings of the Aristotelian Society* 67 (1967): 209–226.

——, *Metaphysics and the Philosophy of Science* (Oxford: Blackwell, 1969).

——, 'Gravity and intelligibility: Newton to Kant', in R. Butts & J. W. Davis (eds), *The Methodological Heritage of Newton* (Toronto: University of Toronto Press, 1970), pp. 74–102.

——, 'Transcendental reduction', *Akten des 4. internationalen Kant-Kongresses (1974)*, part 1, ed. G. Funke & J. Kopper (Berlin: de Gruyter, 1974): 28–44.

——, 'The conception of lawlikeness in Kant's philosophy of science', in L. W. Beck (ed.) (1974), pp. 128–150.

——, 'Science and God: the topology of the Kantian world', *The Southern Journal of Philosophy* XXX (supplement) (1992): 1–24.

——, *Kant and the Dynamics of Reason* (Oxford: Blackwell, 1992).

Bunch, A., '"Objective validity" and "objective reality" in Kant's B-deduction of the categories', *Kantian Review* 14,2 (2010): 67–92.

Butts, R. E., 'Rules, examples and constructions. Kant's theory of mathematics', *Synthese* 47,2 (1981): 257–288.

——, *Kant and the Double Government Methodology* (Dordrecht: D. Reidel, 1984).

Byrne, P., *Kant on God* (Aldershot: Ashgate, 2007).

Caimi, M., 'The logical structure of time according to the chapter on the Schematism', *Kant-Studien* 103,4 (2012): 415–428.

Callanan, J., 'Kant's transcendental strategy', *The Philosophical Quarterly* 56 (2006): 360–381.

——, 'Normativity and the acquisition of the categories', *Bulletin of the Hegel Society of Great Britain* 63,1 (2011): 1–26.

——, 'Kant on nativism, scepticism and necessity', *Kantian Review* 18,1 (2013): 1–27.

Caranti, L., 'Kant's criticism of Descartes in the "Reflexionen zum Idealismus" (1788–1793)', *Kant-Studien* 97 (2006): 318–342.

——, *Kant and the Scandal of Philosophy* (Toronto: University of Toronto Press, 2007).

Carl, W., *Der schweigende Kant. Die Entwürfe zu einer Deduktion der Kategorien vor 1781* (Göttingen: Vandenhoeck & Ruprecht, 1989).

———, 'Kant's first drafts of the deduction of the categories', in Förster (ed.)(1989), pp. 3–20.

———, 'Apperception and spontaneity', *International Journal of Philosophical Studies* 5 (1997): 147–163.

Carrier, M., 'Kant's relational theory of absolute space', *Kant-Studien* 83 (1992): 399–416.

———, 'How to tell causes from effects: Kant's causal theory of time and modern approaches', *Studies in History and Philosophy of Science* 34 (2003): 59–71.

Carson, E. 'Kant on intuition in geometry', *Canadian Journal of Philosophy* 27,4 (1997): 489–512.

———, 'Kant on the method of mathematics', *Journal of the History of Philosophy* 37,4 (1999): 629–652.

Cassam, Q., 'Transcendental arguments, transcendental synthesis and transcendental idealism', *The Philosophical Quarterly* 37 (1987): 355–378.

———, 'Inner sense, body sense, and Kant's "Refutation of Idealism"', *European Journal of Philosophy* 1,2 (1993): 111–127.

———, *Self and World* (Oxford: Clarendon Press, 1997).

———, *The Possibility of Knowledge* (Oxford: Clarendon Press, 2007).

Cassirer, H. W., *Kant's First Critique* (London: Allen & Unwin, 1954 [reprinted 1968 and 1978]).

Castaneda, H. N., 'The role of apperception in Kant's Transcendental Deduction of the categories', *Noûs* 24 (1990): 147–157.

Chance, B., 'Sensibilism, psychologism, and Kant's debt to Hume', *Kantian Review* 16,3 (2011): 325–349.

———, 'Scepticism and the development of the Transcendental Dialectic', *British Journal for the History of Philosophy* 20,2 (2012): 311–331.

Chepurin, K., 'Kant on the soul's intensity', *Kant Yearbook* 2 (2010): 75–94.

Chiba, K., *Kants Ontologie der raumzeitlichen Wirklichkeit* (Berlin/New York: de Gruyter, 2012).

Chignell, A., 'Kant, modality, and the most real being', *Archiv für Geschichte der Philosophie* 91,2 (2009): 157–192.

———, 'Causal refutations of idealism', *The Philosophical Quarterly* 60,240 (2010): 487–507.

———, 'Real repugnance and belief about things-in-themselves: A problem and Kant's three solutions', in Krueger & Lipscomb (2010), pp. 177–210.

———, 'Causal refutations of idealism revisited', *The Philosophical Quarterly* 61,242 (2011): 184–186.

———, 'Real repugnance and our ignorance of things-in-themselves: a Lockean problem in Kant and Hegel', *International Yearbook of German Idealism* 7 (2011): 135–159.

———, 'Kant, real possibility, and the threat of Spinoza', *Mind* 121,483 (2012): 635–675.

———, 'Kant and the 'monstrous' ground of possibility: A reply to Abaci and Yong', *Kantian Review* 19,1 (2014): 53–69.

Cicovacki, P., 'An aporia of a priori knowledge', *Kant-Studien* 82,3 (1991): 349–360.

———, 'On the normative aspect of concepts as rules', *Idealistic Studies* 25 (1995): 25–49.

Collins, A., *Possible Experience: Understanding Kant's Critique of Pure Reason* (Berkeley: University of California Press, 1999).

Crawford, P. D., 'Kant's theory of philosophical proof', *Kant-Studien* 53,3 (1961–62): 257–268.

Cuffaro, M., 'The Kantian framework of complementarity', *Studies in History and Philosophy of Modern Physics* 41 (2010): 309–317.

——, 'Kant and Frege on existence and the ontological argument', *History of Philosophy Quarterly* 29,4 (2012): 337–354.

Cummins, P., 'Kant on outer and inner intuition', *Noûs* 2 (1968): 271–292.

De Pierris, G., 'Kant and innatism', *Pacific Philosophical Quarterly* 68 (1987): 285–305.

Dicker, G., *Kant's Theory of Knowledge* (New York: Oxford University Press, 2004).

——, 'Kant's Refutation of Idealism', *Noûs* 42,1 (2008): 80–108.

——, 'Kant's Refutation of Idealism: a reply to Chignell', *The Philosophical Quarterly* 61,242 (2011): 175–183.

——, 'Kant's Refutation of Idealism: Once more unto the breach', *Kantian Review* 17,2 (2012): 191–195.

Dickerson, A. B., *Kant on Representation and Objectivity* (Cambridge: Cambridge University Press, 2004).

Doyle, J. P., 'Between transcendental and transcendent: the missing link?', *Review of Metaphysics* 50,4 (1997): 783–815.

Dryer, D. P., *Kant's Solution for Verification in Metaphysics* (London: George Allen & Unwin, 1966).

Dummett, M., 'Frege and Kant on geometry', *Inquiry* 25 (1982): 233–254.

Duncan, H., 'Inertia, the communication of motion, and Kant's third law of mechanics', *Philosophy of Science* 51 (1984): 93–119.

Dunlop, K., '"The unity of time's measure": Kant's reply to Locke', *Philosophers' Imprint* 9,4 (2009): 1–31.

——, 'Kant and Strawson on the content of geometrical concepts', *Noûs* 46,1 (2012): 86–126.

Dyck, C., 'Empirical consciousness explained: Self-affection, (self-)consciousness and perception in the B Deduction', *Kantian Review* 11 (2006): 29–54.

——, 'The divorce of reason and experience: Kant's Paralogisms of Pure Reason in context', *Journal of the History of Philosophy* 47 (2009): 249–275.

——, 'The Aeneas argument: personality and immortality in Kant's Third Paralogism', *Kant Yearbook* 2 (2010): 95–122.

——, 'Kant's Transcendental Deduction and the ghosts of Descartes and Hume', *British Journal for the History of Philosophy* 19,3 (2011): 473–496.

——, *Kant and Rational Psychology* (Oxford: Oxford University Press, 2014).

Earman, J., 'Kant, incongruous counterparts, and the nature of space and space–time', *Ratio* 13 (1971): 1–18.

Edgar, S., 'The explanatory structure of the Transcendental Deduction and a cognitive interpretation of the first *Critique*', *Canadian Journal of Philosophy* 40 (2010): 285–314.

Edwards, J., *Substance, Force and the Possibility of Knowledge* (Berkeley/Los Angeles: University of California Press, 2000).

Engel, M. S., 'Kant's Copernican analogy: a re-examination', *Kant-Studien* 54,3 (1963): 243–251.

Engelland, C., 'The phenomenological Kant: Heidegger's interest in transcendental philosophy', *Journal of the British Society for Phenomenology* 41,2 (2011): 150–169.

England, F. E., *Kant's Conception of God* (New York: Humanities Press, 1968 [1929]).

Engstrom, S., 'The Transcendental Deduction and scepticism', *Journal of the History of Philosophy* 32 (1994): 359–380.

——, 'Unity of Apperception', *Studi kantiani* XXVI (2013): 37–54.

Ertl, W., 'Hume's antinomy and Kant's critical turn', *British Journal for the History of Philosophy* 10,4 (2002): 617–640.

Evans, J. C., 'Two-steps-in-one-proof: the structure of the Transcendental Deduction', *Journal of the History of Philosophy* 28 (1990): 553–570.

Evans, J. D. G., 'Kant's analysis of the paralogism of rational psychology in *Critique of Pure Reason* Edition B', *Kantian Review* 3 (1999): 99–105.

Everitt, N., 'Kant's discussion of the ontological argument', *Kant-Studien* 86 (1995): 385–405.

Falkenstein, L. 'Spaces and times: a Kantian response', *Idealist Studies* 16 (1986): 1–11.

——, 'Kant's argument for the non-spatiotemporality of things in themselves', *Kant-Studien* 80 (1989): 265–283.

——, 'Kant's account of sensation', *Canadian Journal of Philosophy* 20 (1990): 63–88.

——, 'Was Kant a nativist?', *Journal of the History of Ideas* 51 (1990): 573–597.

——, 'Kant's account of intuition', *Canadian Journal of Philosophy* 21,2 (1991): 165–193.

——, *Kant's Intuitionism: A Commentary on the Transcendental Aesthetic* (Toronto: University of Toronto Press, 1995).

——, 'Kant's empiricism', *Review of Metaphysics* 50 (1997): 547–589.

——, 'A double-edged sword? Kant's refutation of Mendelssohn's proof of the immortality of the soul and its implications for his theory of matter', *Studies in History and Philosophy of Science* 29 (1998): 561–588.

——, 'Hume's answer to Kant', *Noûs* 32,3 (1998): 331–360.

——, 'Localizing sensations: a reply to Anthony Quinton's trouble with Kant', *Philosophy* 73,3 (1998): 479–489.

——, 'Langton on things in themselves', *Kantian Review* 5 (2000): 49–64.

Ferrari, J., 'Das Ideal der reinen Vernunft', in G. Mohr & M. Willaschek (eds), *Immanuel Kant. Kritik der reinen Vernunft*, in the series *Klassiker Auslegen* (Berlin: Akademie Verlag, 1998), pp. 491–521.

Ferrarin, A. 'Construction and mathematical schematism. Kant on the exhibition of a concept in intuition', *Kant-Studien* 86 (1995): 131–174.

——, 'Kant's productive imagination and its alleged antecedents', *Graduate Faculty Philosophy Journal* 18 (1995): 65–92.

——, 'Lived space, geometric space in Kant', *Studi Kantiani* XIX (2006): 11–30.

Fincham, R., 'Transcendental idealism and the problem of the external world', *Journal of the History of Philosophy* 49,1 (2011): 221–241.

Findlay, J. N., *Kant and the Transcendental Object: A Hermeneutic Study* (Oxford: Clarendon Press, 1981).

——, 'The central role of the thing-in-itself for Kant', *The Philosophical Forum* 13 (1981): 51–65.

Forgie, J. W., 'Kant on the relation between the cosmological and the ontological arguments', *International Journal for Philosophy of Religion* 34,1 (1993): 1–12.

——, 'Kant and existence. *Critique of Pure Reason* A600/B628', *Kant–Studien* 99 (2008): 1–12.

Förster, E., 'Kant's Refutation of Idealism', in A. Holland (ed.), *Philosophy, Its History and Historiography* (Dordrecht: D. Reidel, 1985), pp. 287–303.

——, 'Is there a "gap" in Kant's critical system?', *Journal of the History of Philosophy* 25,4 (1987): 533–555.

——, 'Kant's notion of philosophy', *Monist* 72 (1989): 285–304.

——, *Kant's Final Synthesis* (Cambridge, MA: Harvard University Press, 2000).

——, 'Reply to Friedman and Guyer', *Inquiry* 46,2 (2003): 228–238.

——, *The Twenty-Five Years of Philosophy* (Cambridge, MA: Harvard University Press, 2012).

Forster, M., *Kant and Skepticism* (Princeton: Princeton University Press, 2008).

——, 'Kant's philosophy of language?', *Tijdschrift voor Filosofie* 74,3 (2012): 485–511.

Freyenhagen, F., 'Reasoning takes time: on Allison and the timelessness of the intelligible self', *Kantian Review* 13,2 (2008): 67–84.

Friedman, M., 'Kant on concepts and intuitions in the mathematical sciences', *Synthese* 84,2 (1990): 213–257.

——, *Kant and the Exact Sciences* (Cambridge, MA: Harvard University Press, 1992).

——, 'Causal laws and the foundations of natural science', in P. Guyer (ed.) (1992), pp. 161–199.

——, 'Exorcising the philosophical tradition', *The Philosophical Review* 105,4 (1996): 427–467.

——, 'Kantian themes in contemporary philosophy (I)', *Proceedings of the Aristotelian Society*, supplementary volume 72 (1998): 111–130.

——, 'Logical form and the order of nature', *Archiv für Geschichte der Philosophie* 82 (2000): 202–215.

——, 'Geometry, construction and intuition in Kant and his successors', in G. Sher & R. Tieszen (eds), *Between Logic and Intuition: Essays in Honor of Charles Parsons* (Cambridge: Cambridge University Press, 2000), pp. 186–218.

——, *Dynamics of Reason* (Chicago: University of Chicago Press, 2001).

——, 'Kant, Kuhn, and the rationality of science', *Philosophy of Science* 69 (2002): 171–190.

——, 'Eckhart Förster and Kant's *Opus Postumum*', *Inquiry* 46 (2003): 215–227.

——, 'Transcendental philosophy and mathematical physics', *Studies in History and Philosophy of Science* 34 (2003): 29–43.

——, 'Kant, scepticism and idealism', *Inquiry* 49,1 (2006): 26–43.

——, 'Kant on geometry and spatial intuition', *Synthese* 186,1 (2012): 231–255.

——, 'Newton and Kant: Quantity of matter in the *Metaphysical Foundations of Natural Science*', *Southern Journal of Philosophy* 50,3 (2012): 482–503.

——, *Kant's Construction of Nature: A Reading of the 'Metaphysical*

Foundations of Nature' (Cambridge: Cambridge University Press, 2013).

Fugate, C., *The Teleology of Reason: A Study of the Structure of Kant's Critical Philosophy* (Berlin/New York: de Gruyter, 2014).

Fulkerson-Smith, B. A., 'On the apodictic proof and validation of Kant's revolutionary hypothesis', *Kantian Review* 15,1 (2010): 37–56.

Geiger, I., 'Is the assumption of a systematic whole of empirical concepts a necessary condition of knowledge?', *Kant-Studien* 94 (2003): 273–298.

Genova, A. C., 'Kant's three critiques: a suggested analytical framework', *Kant-Studien* 60,2 (1969): 135–146.

———, 'Kant's epigenesis of pure reason', *Kant-Studien* 65,3 (1974): 259–273.

———, 'The purposive unity of Kant's critical idealism', *Idealistic Studies* 5 (1975): 177–189.

———, 'Kant's notion of transcendental presupposition in the first *Critique*', *Philosophical Topics* 12 (1981): 99–126.

———, 'Good transcendental arguments', *Kant-Studien* 75,4 (1984): 469–495.

George, R., 'Kant's sensationism', *Synthese* 47 (1981): 229–255.

———, 'Van Cleve and Kant's Analogies', *Philosophy and Phenomenological Research* 66 (2003): 203–210.

Gibson, M., 'A revolution in method, Kant's "Copernican hypothesis" and the necessity of natural laws', *Kant-Studien* 102,1 (2011): 1–21.

Ginsborg, H., 'Kant and the problem of experience', *Philosophical Topics* 34 (2006): 59–106.

———, 'Empirical concepts and the content of experience', *European Journal of Philosophy* 14,3 (2006): 349–372.

———, 'Was Kant a nonconceptualist?', *Philosophical Studies* 137,1 (2008): 65–77.

Glouberman, M., 'Kant on receptivity: form and content', *Kant-Studien* 66,3 (1975): 313–330.

———, 'Conceptuality: an essay in retrieval', *Kant-Studien* 70,4 (1979): 383–408.

———, 'Reason and substance: the Kantian metaphysics of conceptual positivism', *Kant-Studien* 70,4 (1982): 1–16.

———, *The Origins and Implications of Kant's Critical Philosophy* (Lewiston: Edwin Mellen, 1990).

———, 'Rewriting Kant's Antinomies: a meta-interpretive discussion', *The Philosophical Forum* 25 (1993): 1–18.

Gochnauer, M., 'Kant's Refutation of Idealism', *Journal of the History of Philosophy* 12 (1974): 195–206.

Goldberg, N. J., 'Do principles of reason have "objective but indeterminate validity"?', *Kant-Studien* 95,4 (2004): 404–425.

Goldman, A., *Kant and the Subject of Critique: On the Regulative Role of the Psychological Idea* (Bloomington, IN: Indiana University Press, 2012).

Golob, S., 'Heidegger on Kant, time and the "form" of intentionality', *British Journal for the History of Philosophy* 21,2 (2013): 345–367.

Gomes, A., 'Is Kant's Transcendental Deduction of the categories fit for purpose?', *Kantian Review* 15,2 (2010): 118–137.

———, 'Kant and the explanatory role of experience', *Kant-Studien* 104,3 (2013): 277–300.

———, 'Kant on perception: Naïve realism, non-conceptualism and the B-Deduction', *The Philosophical Quarterly* 64 (254) (2014): 1–19.

Gram, M. S., 'Kant's First Antinomy', *The Monist* 51 (1967): 511–518.

——, *Kant, Ontology and the A Priori* (Evanston: Northwestern University Press, 1968).

——, 'How to dispense with things in themselves (I) and (II)', *Ratio* 18 (1976): 1–15 & 107–123.

——, 'The crisis of syntheticity', *Kant-Studien* 7 (1980): 155–180.

——, 'Intellectual intuition: the continuity thesis', *Journal of the History of Ideas* 42 (1981): 287–304.

——, 'The skeptical attack on substance: Kantian answers', *Midwest Studies in Philosophy* 8 (1983): 359–371.

——, *The Transcendental Turn* (Gainesville: University Press of Florida, 1984).

Grayeff, F., *Kant's Theoretical Philosophy* (Manchester: Manchester University Press, 1970 [1951]).

Greenberg, R., *Kant's Theory of A Priori Knowledge* (University Park, PA: Penn State University Press, 2001).

——, 'Necessity, existence and transcendental idealism', *Kantian Review* 11 (2006): 55–77.

——, *Real Existence, Ideal Necessity* (Berlin/New York: de Gruyter, 2008).

Greenwood, J. D., 'Kant's Third Antinomy', *International Philosophical Quarterly* 30 (1990): 43–57.

Greenwood, T., 'A non sequitur of numbing grossness', *Kant-Studien* 72,1 (1981): 11–30.

Grier, M., 'Illusion and fallacy in Kant's First Paralogism', *Kant-Studien* 84 (1993): 257–282.

——, 'Kant on the illusion of a systematic unity of knowledge', *History of Philosophy Quarterly* 14,1 (1997): 1–28.

——, 'Transcendental illusion and transcendental realism in Kant's Second Antinomy', *British Journal for the History of Philosophy* 6,1 (1998): 47–70.

——, *Kant's Doctrine of Transcendental Illusion* (Cambridge: Cambridge University Press, 2001).

——, 'The revolutionary interpretation of the Analytic of Concepts', *Kantian Review* 16,2 (2011): 191–200.

——, 'The ideal of pure reason', in P. Guyer (ed.) (2010), pp. 266–289.

Griffith, A., 'Perception and the categories: A conceptualist reading of Kant's *Critique of Pure Reason*', *European Journal of Philosophy* 20,2 (2012): 193–222.

Grüne, S., *Blinde Anschauung. Die Rolle von Begriffen in Kants Theorie sinnlicher Synthesis* (Frankfurt a/M: Klostermann, 2009).

——, 'Is there a gap in Kant's B Deduction?', *International Journal of Philosophical Studies* 19,3 (2011): 465–490.

Guyer, P., 'Kant on apperception and a priori synthesis', *American Philosophical Quarterly* 17 (1980): 205–212.

——, 'Kant's intentions in the Refutation of Idealism', *Philosophical Review* 92 (1983): 329–383.

——, 'The failure of the B-deduction', *Southern Journal of Philosophy* XXV (supplement) (1986): 67–84.

——, *Kant and the Claims of Knowledge* (Cambridge: Cambridge University Press, 1987).

——, 'The Postulates of Empirical Thinking in General and the Refutation of Idealism', in G. Mohr & M. Willaschek (eds), *Immanuel Kant. Kritik der reinen Vernunft* (Berlin: Akademie Verlag, 1998), pp. 297–324.

——, 'Space, time and the categories: The project of the Transcendental Deduction', in R. Schumacher (ed.), *Idealismus als Theorie der Repräsentation?* (Paderborn: Mentis, 2001), pp. 313–338.

——, 'Kant on common sense and scepticism', *Kantian Review* 7 (2003): 1–37.

——, 'Kant's answer to Hume?', *Philosophical Topics* 31 (2003): 127–164.

——, *Kant's System of Nature and Freedom: Selected Essays* (Cambridge: Cambridge University Press, 2005).

——, *Knowledge, Reason, and Taste: Kant's Response to Hume* (Princeton: Princeton University Press, 2008).

——, 'The deduction of the categories. The metaphysical and transcendental deductions', in P. Guyer (ed.) (2010), pp. 118–150.

Hacyan, S., 'On the transcendental ideality of space and time in modern physics', *Kant-Studien* 97 (2006): 382–395.

Hahn, R., *Kant's Newtonian Revolution in Philosophy* (Carbondale: Southern Illinois University Press, 1988).

Hall, B., 'Appearances and the problem of affection in Kant', *Kantian Review* 14,2 (2010): 38–66.

——, 'A dilemma for Kant's theory of substance', *British Journal for the History of Philosophy* 19,1 (2011): 79–109.

——, *The Post-Critical Kant: Understanding the Critical Philosophy Through the Opus Postumum* (Oxford/ New York: Routledge, 2014).

Hanna, R., 'Kant's theory of empirical judgment and modern semantics', *History of Philosophy Quarterly* 7 (1990): 335–351.

——, 'The trouble with truth in Kant's theory of meaning', *History of Philosophy Quarterly* 10 (1993): 1–20.

——, 'A Kantian critique of scientific essentialism', *Philosophy and Phenomenological Research* 58,3 (1998): 497–528.

——, 'How do we know necessary truths? Kant's answer', *European Journal of Philosophy* 6 (1998): 115–145.

——, 'The inner and the outer: Kant's "Refutation" reconsidered', *Ratio* 13 (2000): 146–174.

——, 'Why gold is necessarily a yellow metal', *Kantian Review* 4 (2000): 1–47.

——, 'Kant, truth and human nature', *British Journal for the History of Philosophy* 8,2 (2000): 225–250.

——, 'Mathematics for humans: Kant's philosophy of arithmetic revisited', *European Journal of Philosophy* 10 (2002): 328–353.

——, 'Kant and nonconceptual content', *European Journal of Philosophy* 13,2 (2005): 247–290.

——, 'Kant, causation, and freedom', *Canadian Journal of Philosophy* 36 (2006): 281–306.

——, *Kant, Science, and Human Nature* (Oxford: Clarendon Press, 2006).

——, 'Kant's non-conceptualism, rogue objects, and the gap in the B deduction', *International Journal of Philosophical Studies* 19,3 (2011): 399–415.

——, 'The Kantian's revenge: On Forster's *Kant and Skepticism*', *Kantian Review* 17,1 (2012): 33–45.

——, 'Kant, Hegel, and the fate of non-conceptual content', *Hegel Bulletin* 34,1 (2013): 1–32.

Harder, J.Y., 'L'incommensurable', in *Kant et les Mathématiques, Les Cahiers Philosophiques de Strasbourg* 26 (2009): 57–80.

Harper, W., 'Kant's empirical realism and the Second Analogy of experience', *Synthese* 47 (1981): 465–480.

——, 'Kant on space, empirical realism and the foundations of geometry', *Topoi* 3 (1984): 143–161.

Hatfield, G., 'Empirical, rational and transcendental psychology: psychology as science and as philosophy', in P. Guyer (ed.) (1992), pp. 200–227.

——, 'What were Kant's aims in the deduction?', *Philosophical Topics* 31 (2003): 165–198.

Heathwood, C., 'The relevance of Kant's objection to Anselm's ontological argument', *Religious Studies* 47,3 (2011): 345–357.

Heidegger, M., *Kant and the Problem of Metaphysics* (Bloomington: Indiana University Press, 1991 [1929]).

——, *Phenomenological Critique of Kant's 'Critique of Pure Reason'* (Bloomington: Indiana University Press, 1995 [1977]).

Heis, J., 'Ernst Cassirer's neo-Kantian philosophy of geometry', *British Journal for the History of Philosophy* 19,4 (2011): 759–794.

Henrich, D., 'The proof-structure of Kant's Transcendental Deduction', *Review of Metaphysics* 22 (1969): 640–659.

——, 'Kant's notion of a deduction and the methodological background of the first *Critique*', in Förster (ed.)(1989), pp. 29–46.

——, *The Unity of Reason: Essays on Kant's Philosophy* (Cambridge, MA: Harvard University Press, 1994).

Herman, D. J., 'The incoherence of Kant's Transcendental Dialectic', *Dialectica* 45 (1991): 3–29.

Hinske, N., 'Die Rolle des Methodenproblems im Denken Kants', in N. Fischer (ed.), *Kants Grundlegung einer kritischen Metaphysik. Einführung in die 'Kritik der reinen Vernunft'* (Hamburg: Meiner, 2010), pp. 343–354.

Hintikka, J., 'Kant's "new method of thought" and his theory of mathematics', *Ajatus* 27,3 (1965): 37–47.

——, 'Are mathematical truths synthetic a priori?', *Journal of Philosophy* 65 (1968): 640–651.

——, 'Kantian intuitions', *Inquiry* 15 (1972): 341–345.

——, *Logic, Language-Games and Information: Kantian Themes in the Philosophy of Logic* (Oxford: Clarendon Press, 1973).

——, 'Kant on existence, predication, and the ontological argument', *Dialectica* 35 (1981): 127–146.

——, 'Kant's theory of mathematics revisited', *Philosophical Topics* 12,2 (1981): 201–215.

——, 'Kant's transcendental method and his theory of mathematics', *Topoi* 3,2 (1984): 99–108.

Hoagland, J., 'The thing in itself in English interpretations of Kant', *American Philosophical Quarterly* 10 (1973): 1–14.

Hoefer, C., 'Kant's hands and Earman's pions', *International Studies in the Philosophy of Science* 14 (2000): 237–256.

Hogan, D., 'How to know unknowable things in themselves', *Noûs* 43,1 (2009): 49–63.

——, 'Noumenal affection', *The Philosophical Review* 118,4 (2009): 501–532.

——, 'Three kinds of rationalism and the non-spatiality of things in themselves', *Journal of the History of Philosophy* 47,3 (2009): 355–382.

——, 'Kant's Copernican turn and the rationalist tradition', in P. Guyer (ed.) (2010), pp. 21–40.

——, 'Metaphysical motives of Kant's analytic-synthetic distinction', *Journal of the History of Philosophy* 51,2 (2013): 267–307.

Horstmann, R. P., 'Space as intuition and geometry', *Ratio* 28 (1976): 17–30.

——, 'The metaphysical deduction in Kant's *Critique of Pure Reason*', *The Philosophical Forum* 13 (1981): 32–47.

——, 'Der Anhang zur transzendentalen Dialektik (A642/B670–A704/B732). Die Idee der systematischen Einheit', in G. Mohr & M. Willaschek (eds), *Immanuel Kant. Kritik der reinen Vernunft*, in the series *Klassiker Auslegen* (Berlin: Akademie Verlag, 1998), pp. 525–545.

Hossenfelder, M., 'Allison's defense of Kant's transcendental idealism', *Inquiry* 33 (1990): 467–479.

Howell, R., 'Intuition, synthesis, and individuation in the *Critique of Pure Reason*', *Noûs* 7 (1973): 207–232.

——, *Kant's Transcendental Deduction: An Analysis of Main Themes in the Critical Philosophy* (Dordrecht: Kluwer, 1992).

——, 'The conundrum of the object and other problems from Kant', *Kantian Review* 8 (2004): 115–136.

Hudson, H., *Kant's Compatibilism* (Ithaca, NY: Cornell University Press, 1994).

Hughes, R. I. G., 'Kant's Third Paralogism', *Kant-Studien* 74,4 (1983): 405–411.

——, 'Kant's Analogies and the structure of objective time', *Pacific Philosophical Quarterly* 71 (1990): 141–163.

Humphrey, T., 'The historical and conceptual relations between Kant's metaphysics of space and philosophy of geometry', *Journal of the History of Philosophy* 11 (1973): 483–512.

Hurley, S., 'Kant on spontaneity and the myth of the giving', *Proceedings of the Aristotelian Society* XCIV (1994): 137–164.

——, 'Myth upon myth', *Proceedings of the Aristotelian Society* XCVI (1996): 253–260.

Hymers, M., 'The role of Kant's Refutation of Idealism', *Southern Journal of Philosophy* (1991): 51–67.

——, 'Kant's private-clock argument', *Kant-Studien* 88 (1997): 442–461.

Insole, C., 'Intellectualism, relational properties and the divine mind in Kant's pre-Critical philosophy', *Kantian Review* 16,3 (2011): 399–427.

Jacquette, D., 'Kant's Second Antinomy and Hume's theory of extensionless indivisibles', *Kant-Studien* 84 (1993): 38–50.

Janiak, A., 'Kant as philosopher of science', *Perspectives on Science* 12,3 (2004): 339–363.

Jankowiak, T., 'Kant's argument for the principle of intensive magnitudes', *Kantian Review* 18,3 (2013): 387–412.

Jardine, N., 'Hermeneutic strategies in Gerd Buchdahl's Kantian philosophy of science', *Studies in the History and Philosophy of Science* 34 (2003): 183–208.

Jong, W. de, 'How is metaphysics as a science possible?', *Review of Metaphysics* 49,2 (1995): 235–274.

——, 'Kant's analytic judgments and the traditional theory of concepts', *Journal of the History of Philosophy* 33,4 (1995): 613–641.

——, 'The analytic-synthetic distinction and the classical model of science: Kant, Bolzano and Frege', *Synthese* 174 (2010): 237–261.

Justin, G., 'On Kant's analysis of Berkeley', *Kant-Studien* 65 (1974): 20–32

——, 'Re-relating Kant and Berkeley', *Kant-Studien* 68 (1977): 77–89.

Kanterian, E., 'The ideality of space and time: Trendelenburg versus Kant, Fischer and Bird', *Kantian Review* 18,2 (2013): 263–288.

——, 'Bodies in *Prolegomena* §13: Noumena or phenomena?', *Hegel Bulletin* 34,2 (2013): 181–202.

Keller, P., *Kant and the Demands of Self-Consciousness* (Cambridge: Cambridge University Press, 2001).

Kemp Smith, N. A., *Commentary to Kant's 'Critique of Pure Reason'*, second edition (London/New York: Macmillan, 1923).

Kerr, G., 'Kant's transcendental idealism: A hypothesis?', *International Philosophical Quarterly* 51,2 (2011): 195–222.

Kielkopf, C. F., 'Kant's deontic logic', *International Logic Review* 7 (1976): 66–75.

Kim, J., 'Concepts and intuitions in Kant's philosophy of geometry', *Kant-Studien* 97,2 (2006): 138–162.

Kitchener, R. F., 'Is transcendental psychology possible?', *New Ideas in Psychology* 17 (1999): 195–203.

Kitcher, P., 'Kant on self-identity', *Philosophical Review* 91 (1982): 41–72.

——, 'Kant's Paralogisms', *Philosophical Review* 91,4 (1982): 515–547.

——, 'Connecting concepts and intuitions at B160n', *Southern Journal of Philosophy* XXV (supplement) (1986): 137–150.

——, 'Kant's patchy epistemology', *Pacific Philosophical Quarterly* 68, 3–4 (1987): 306–316.

——, 'Discovering the forms of intuition', *The Philosophical Review* 96,2 (1987): 205–248.

——, *Kant's Transcendental Psychology* (New York: Oxford University Press, 1990).

——, 'Changing the name of the game', *Philosophical Topics* 19 (1991): 201–236.

——, 'Revisiting Kant's epistemology', *Noûs* 29 (1995): 285–315.

——, 'Kant on self-consciousness', *The Philosophical Review* 108,3 (1999): 345–386.

——, 'Kant's epistemological problem and its coherent solution', *Philosophical Perspectives* 13 (1999): 415–441.

——, 'On interpreting Kant's thinker as Wittgenstein's "I"', *Philosophy and Phenomenological Research* 61 (2000): 33–63.

——, *Kant's Thinker* (New York: Oxford University Press, 2011).

Kitcher, Ph., 'Kant and the foundations of mathematics', *The Philosophical Review* 84,1 (1975): 23–50.

——, 'A priori', in P. Guyer (ed.) (2006), pp. 28–60.

Kjosavik, F., 'Kant on geometrical intuition and the foundations of mathematics', *Kant-Studien* 100 (2009): 1–27.

Klass, G. M., 'A framework for reading Kant on apperception: seven interpretive questions', *Kant-Studien* 94,1 (2003): 80–94.

Klemme, H., *Kants Philosophie des Subjekts* (Hamburg: Meiner, 1996).

——, 'Die Axiome der Anschauung und die Antizipationen der Wahrnehmung', in G. Mohr & M. Willaschek (eds), *Immanuel Kant. Kritik der reinen Vernunft*, in the series *Klassiker Auslegen* (Berlin: Akademie Verlag, 1998), pp. 247–266.

Klimmek, N., *Kants System der transzendentalen Ideen* (Berlin/New York: Walter de Gruyter, 2005).

Kneller, J., *Kant and the Power of Imagination* (Cambridge: Cambridge University Press, 2007).

Koistinen, O., 'Descartes in Kant's Transcendental Deduction', *Midwest Studies in Philosophy* 35 (2011): 149–163.

Krauser, P., 'The operational conception of 'reine Anschauung' in Kant's theory of experience and science', *Studies in the History and Philosophy of Science* Part A 3 (1972–73): 81–87.

——, '"Form of intuition" and "formal intuition" in Kant's theory of experience and science', *Studies in the History and Philosophy of Science* Part A 4 (1973–74): 279–287.

——, 'Kant's schematism of the categories and the problem of pattern recognition', *Synthese* 33 (1976): 175–192.

Kreines, J., 'Kant on the laws of nature: Laws, necessitation, and the limitation of our knowledge', *European Journal of Philosophy* 17,4 (2009): 527–558.

Kroon, F. & R. Nola, 'Kant, Kripke, and gold', *Kant-Studien* 78 (1987): 442–458.

Kuehn, M., 'How, or why, do we come to think of a world of things in themselves?', *Kantian Review* 16,2 (2011): 221–233.

Kwang-Sae, L., 'Kant on empirical concepts, empirical laws and scientific theories', *Kant-Studien* 72,4 (1981): 398–414.

Landy, D., 'Inferentialism and the Transcendental Deduction', *Kantian Review* 14,1 (2009): 1–30.

Langsam, H., 'Kant, Hume and our ordinary conception of causation', *Philosophy and Phenomenological Research* 54,3 (1994): 625–647.

——, 'Kant's compatibilism and his two conceptions of truth', *Pacific Philosophical Quarterly* 81 (2000): 164–188.

Langston, D., 'The supposed incompatibility between Kant's refutations of idealism', *Southern Journal of Philosophy* 17 (1979): 359–369.

Langton, R., *Kantian Humility: Our Ignorance of Things in Themselves* (Oxford: Oxford University Press, 1998).

——, 'Reply to Lorne Falkenstein', *Kantian Review* 5 (2001): 64–72.

——, '*Problems from Kant* by James Van Cleve', *Philosophy and Phenomenological Research* LXVI,1 (2003): 211–218.

——, 'Elusive knowledge of things in themselves', *Australasian Journal of Philosophy* 82 (2004): 129–136.

——, 'Kant's phenomena: extrinsic or relational properties? A reply to Allais', *Philosophy and Phenomenological Research* LXXIII,1 (2006): 170–185.

La Rocca, C., 'Methode und System in Kants Philosophieauffassung', in S. Bacin et al. (eds), *Kant und die Philosophie in weltbürgerlicher Absicht. Akten des XI. Internationalen Kant-Kongresses*, Band 1 (Berlin/New York: de Gruyter, 2013), pp. 277–297.

Lau, C.-F., 'Kant's epistemological reorientiation of ontology', *Kant Yearbook* 2 (2010): 123–146.

Laywine, A., 'Problems and postulates: Kant on reason and understanding', *Journal of the History of Philosophy* 36,2 (1998): 279–309.

——, 'Kant on the self as model of experience', *Kantian Review* 9,1 (2005): 1–29.

Leavitt, F. J., 'Kant's schematism and his philosophy of geometry', *Studies in History and Philosophy of Science* Part A 22 (1991): 647–659.

Leech, J., 'Kant's modalities of judgment', *European Journal of Philosophy* 20,2 (2012): 260–284.

Leppäkoski, M., *The Transcendental How: Kant's Transcendental Deduction of Objective Cognition* (Stockholm: Almqvuist & Wiksell, 1993).

——, 'The two steps of the B-Deduction', *Kantian Review* 2 (1998): 107–116.

Lipson, M., 'On Kant on space', *Pacific Philosophical Quarterly* 73 (1992): 73–99.

Longuenesse, B. *Kant and the Capacity to Judge* (Princeton: Princeton University Press, 1998).

——, 'Kant's categories and the capacity of judge: responses to Henry Allison and Sally Sedgwick', *Inquiry* 43 (2000): 91–110.

——, 'Kant's deconstruction of the principle of sufficient reason', in Longuenesse (2005), pp. 117–142.

——, *Kant on the Human Standpoint* (Cambridge: Cambridge University Press, 2005).

——, 'Kant on a priori concepts. The metaphysical deduction of the categories', in P. Guyer (ed.) (2006), pp. 129–168.

——, 'Kant on the identity of persons', *Proceedings of the Aristotelian Society* CVII (2007): 149–167.

Loparic, Z., 'The logical structure of the First Antinomy', *Kant-Studien* 81,3 (1990): 280–303.

Macbeth, D., 'Empirical knowledge: Kantian themes and Sellarsian variations', *Philosophical Studies* 101 (2000): 113–142.

Macann, C. E., *Kant and the Foundations of Metaphysics* (Heidelberg: Winter, 1981).

Marshall, C., 'Kant's appearances and things in themselves as qua-objects', *Philosophical Quarterly* 63, 252 (2013): 520–545.

——, 'Kant's one self and the appearance/thing-in-itself distinction', *Kant-Studien* 104,4 (2013): 421–441.

Matherne, S., 'Kant and the art of schematism', *Kantian Review* 19,2 (2014): 181–205.

Martin, G., *Kant's Metaphysics and Theory of Science* (Manchester: Manchester University Press, 1955).

Mattey, G. J., 'Kant's conception of Berkeley's idealism', *Kant-Studien* 74 (1983): 161–175.

——, 'Kant's theory of propositional attitudes', *Kant-Studien* 77,4 (1986): 423–440.

McCall, J. L., 'A response to Burkhard Tuschling's critique of Kant's physics', *Kant-Studien* 79 (1988): 57–79.

——, 'Metaphysical foundations and ponderomotive nature', *Kant-Studien* 96 (2005): 269–311.

McCann, E., 'Skepticism and Kant's B Deduction', *History of Philosophy Quarterly* 2 (1985): 71–89.

McDowell, J., *Mind and World*, second edition (Cambridge, MA: Harvard University Press, ²1996).

——, *Having the World in View: Essays on Kant, Hegel, and Sellars* (Cambridge, MA: Harvard University Press, 2009).

McLear, C., 'Kant on animal consciousness', *Philosophers' Imprint* 11,15 (2011).

Meerbote, R., 'Apperception and objectivity', *Southern Journal of Philosophy* 25 (S1) (1986): 115–130.

——, 'Systematicity and realism in Kant's transcendental idealism', *Southern*

Journal of Philosophy 30 (S1) (1991): 129–137.

Mensch, J. *Kant's Organicism. Epigenesis and the Development of Critical Philosophy* (Chicago: University of Chicago Press, 2013).

Melnick, A., *Kant's Analogies of Experience* (Chicago: University of Chicago Press, 1973).

——, 'The geometry of a form of intuition', *Topoi* 3,2 (1984): 163–168.

——, *Space, Time and Thought in Kant* (Dordrecht: D. Reidel, 1989).

——, 'Kant's proofs of substance and causation', in P. Guyer (ed.) (2006), pp. 203–237.

——, *Kant's Theory of the Self* (London/ New York: Routledge, 2009).

——, 'Two charges of intellectualism against Kant', *Kantian Review* 18,2 (2013): 197–219.

Merritt, M. M., 'Analysis in the *Critique of Pure Reason*', *Kantian Review* 12,1 (2007): 61–89.

——, 'Reflection, enlightenment, and the significance of spontaneity in Kant', *British Journal for the History of Philosophy* 17,5 (2009): 981–1010.

——, 'Kant on the transcendental deduction of space and time', *Kantian Review* 14,2 (2010): 1–37.

——, 'Kant's argument for the apperception principle', *European Journal of Philosophy* 19,1 (2011): 59–84.

Messina, J., 'Kant on the unity of space and the synthetic unity of apperception', *Kant-Studien* 105,1 (2014): 5–40.

Meyer, M., 'Why did Kant write two versions of the Transcendental Deduction of the categories?', *Synthese* 47,3 (1981): 357–383.

Mijuskovic, B., 'The premise of the Transcendental Analytic', *The Philosophical Quarterly* 23 (1973): 156–161.

——, *The Achilles of Rationalist Arguments* (The Hague: Nijhoff, 1974).

Miles, M., 'Kant's "Copernican Revolution": toward rehabilitation of a concept and provision of a framework for the interpretation of the *Critique of Pure Reason*', *Kant-Studien* 97 (2006): 1–32.

Miller, G. W., 'Kant's first edition refutation of dogmatic idealism', *Kant-Studien* 62 (1971): 298–318.

——, 'Kant and Berkeley', *Kant-Studien* 64 (1973): 315–335.

Miller, L. W., 'Kant's philosophy of mathematics', *Kant-Studien* 66,3 (1975): 297–308.

Mischel, T., 'Kant and the possibility of a science of psychology', *The Monist* 51 (1967): 599–622.

Mitscherling, J., 'Kant's notion of intuition', *Kant-Studien* 72,2 (1981): 186–194.

Moore, A. W., 'Aspects of the infinite in Kant', *Mind*, new series vol. 97 (1988): 205–223.

——, 'The Transcendental Doctrine of Method', in P. Guyer (ed.) (2010), pp. 310–326.

——, 'Bird on Kant's mathematical antinomies', *Kantian Review* 16,2 (2011): 235–243.

Moretto, A., 'Philosophie transcendantale et géométrie non-euclidienne', *Kant et les Mathématiques, Les Cahiers Philosophiques de Strasbourg* 26 (2009): 117–140.

Morrison, M. C., 'Community and coexistence: Kant's Third Analogy of experience', *Kant-Studien* 89 (1998): 257–277.

Mosser, K. *Necessity and Possibility: The Logical Strategy of Kant's Critique of Pure Reason* (Washington, DC: Catholic University of America Press, 2008).

Motta, G., *Kants Philosophie der Notwendigkeit* (Frankfurt a/M: Peter Lang, 2007).

——, 'Five meanings of "contingency" in Kant's *Critique of Pure Reason*', *Pli: The Warwick Journal of Philosophy* 22 (2011): 110–123.

——, *Die Postulate des empirischen Denkens überhaupt* (Berlin/New York: de Gruyter, 2012).

Mueller, A., 'Does Kantian mental content externalism help metaphysical realists?' *Synthese* 182,3 (2011): 449–473.

Nagel, G., *The Structure of Experience: Kant's System of Principles* (Chicago: University of Chicago Press, 1983).

Nolan, J., 'Kant on meaning: two studies', *Kant-Studien* 70 (1979): 113–130.

Norris, C., 'McDowell on Kant', *Metaphilosophy* 31,4 (2000): 382–411.

Nussbaum, C., 'Concepts, judgments, and unity in Kant's metaphysical deduction of the relational categories', *Journal of the History of Philosophy* 28,1 (1990): 89–103.

——, 'Critical and pre–Critical phases in Kant's philosophy of logic', *Kant-Studien* 83,3 (1992): 280–293.

Nuyen, A. T., 'On interpreting Kant's architectonic in terms of the hermeneutical model', *Kant-Studien* 84 (1993): 154–166.

Nuzzo, A. *Ideal Embodiment: Kant's Theory of Sensibility* (Bloomington: Indiana University Press, 2008).

Onof, C., 'Kant's conception of the self as subject and its embodiment', *Kant Yearbook* 2 (2010): 147–174.

——, 'Thinking the in–itself and its relation to appearances', in D. Schulting & J. Verburgt (eds) (2011), pp. 211–236.

Onof, C. & D. Schulting, 'Kant, Kästner, and the distinction between metaphysical and geometric space', *Kantian Review* 19,2 (2014): 285–304.

Osborne, G., 'Two major recent approaches to Kant's Second Analogy', *Kant-Studien* 97 (2006): 409–429.

O'Shea, J. R., 'The needs of understanding: Kant on empirical laws and regulative ideals', *International Journal of Philosophical Studies* 5,2 (1997): 216–254.

Palmquist, S. R., 'Kant on Euclid: geometry in perspective', *Philosophy of Mathematics* 5 (1990): 88–113.

——, *Kant's System of Perspectives* (New York: University Press of America, 1993).

Parsons, C., 'Infinity and Kant's conception of the "possibility of experience"', *The Philosophical Review* 73 (1964): 183–197.

——, 'Kant's philosophy of arithmetic', in C. Posy (ed.) (1992), pp. 43–79.

——, 'On some difficulties concerning intuition and intuitive knowledge', *Mind* 102 (1993): 233–246.

Pasternack, L., 'Kant on opinion: Assent, hypothesis, and the norms of general applied logic', *Kant-Studien* 105,1 (2014): 41–82.

Paton, H. J., *Kant's Metaphysics of Experience*, 2 vols. (London: Allen & Unwin, 1936).

Patton, L. 'The paradox of infinite given magnitude: Why Kantian epistemology needs metaphysical space', *Kant-Studien* 102,3 (2011): 273–289.

Pereboom, D., 'Kant on intentionality', *Synthese* 77 (1988): 321–352.

——, 'Kant on justification in transcendental philosophy', *Synthese* 85 (1990): 25–54.

——, 'Is Kant's transcendental philosophy inconsistent?', *History of Philosophy Quarterly* 8 (1991): 357–372.

——, 'Self-understanding in Kant's Transcendental Deduction', *Synthese* 103,1 (1995): 1–42.

——, 'Assessing Kant's master argument', *Kantian Review* 5 (2001): 90–102.

——, 'Kant's metaphysical and transcendental deductions', in G. Bird (ed.)(2010), pp. 154–168.

Pippin, R. B., *Kant's Theory of Form* (New Haven: Yale University Press, 1982).

——, 'Kant on the spontaneity of mind', in R. B. Pippin, *Idealism as Modernism. Hegelian Variations* (Cambridge: Cambridge University Press, 1997), pp. 29–55.

Plantinga, A., 'Kant's objection to the ontological argument', *Journal of Philosophy* 63 (1966): 537–546.

Pollok, K. '"An almost single inference" – Kant's deduction of the categories reconsidered', *Archiv für Geschichte der Philosophie* 90,3 (2008): 323–345.

Porter, L., 'Does the Transcendental Deduction contain a refutation of idealism?', *Kant-Studien* 74,4 (1983): 487–499.

Posy, C., 'The language of appearances and things in themselves', *Synthese* 47 (1981): 313–352.

——, 'Dancing to the antinomy: a proposal for transcendental idealism', *American Philosophical Quarterly* 20 (1983): 81–94.

——, 'Kant's mathematical realism', in C. Posy (ed.) (1992), pp. 293–313.

Powell, C. T., 'Kant, elanguescence and degrees of reality', *Philosophy and Phenomenological Research* 46,2 (1985): 199–217.

——, *Kant's Theory of Self-Consciousness* (Oxford: Clarendon Press, 1990).

Proops, I., 'Kant's legal metaphor and the nature of a deduction', *Journal of the History of Philosophy* 41,2 (2003): 209–229.

——, 'Kant's conception of analytic judgment', *Philosophy and Phenomenological Research* 70,3 (2005): 588–612.

——, 'Kant's First Paralogism', *The Philosophical Review* 119,4 (2010): 449–495.

Quarfood, M., *Transcendental Idealism and the Organism. Essays on Kant* (Stockholm: Almqvist & Wiksell, 2004).

Radner, M. & D. Radner, 'Kantian space and the ontological alternatives', *Kant-Studien* 78 (1987): 385–402.

Rand, S., 'Apriority, metaphysics, and empirical content in Kant's theory of matter', *Kantian Review* 17,1 (2012): 109–134.

Rauscher, F., 'The appendix to the Dialectic and the Canon of Reason: the positive role of reason', in P. Guyer (ed.) (2010), pp. 290–309.

Reich, K., *The Completeness of Kant's Table of Judgments* (Stanford: Stanford University Press, 1992).

Rescher, N., 'On the status of "things in themselves" in Kant', *Synthese* 47 (1981): 289–299.

——, *Kant and the Reach of Reason* (Cambridge: Cambridge University Press, 2000).

——, 'Kant's neo-Platonism: Kant and Plato on mathematical and philosophical method', *Metaphilosophy* 44,1–2 (2013): 69–78.

Robinson, H., 'Incongruent counterparts and the Refutation of Idealism', *Kant-Studien* 72 (1981): 391–397.

——, 'Intuition and manifold in the Transcendental Deduction', *Southern Journal of Philosophy* 22 (1984): 403–412.

——, 'The priority of inner sense', *Kant-Studien* 79 (1988): 165–182.

——, 'Two perspectives on Kant's appearances and things in themselves', *Journal of the History of Philosophy* 32,3 (1994): 411–441.

Roche, A., 'Kant's principle of sense', *British Journal for the History of Philosophy* 18,4 (2010): 663–692.

——, 'Allais on transcendental idealism', *Kantian Review* 16,3 (2011): 351–374.

——, 'Transcendental idealism: A proposal', *Journal of the History of Philosophy* 51,4 (2013): 589–615.

Rödl, S., *Kategorien des Zeitlichen* (Frankfurt a/M: Suhrkamp, 2005).

Rogerson, K. F., 'Kantian ontology', *Kant-Studien* 84,1 (1993): 3–24.

Rohlf, M., 'The ideas of pure reason', in P. Guyer (ed.) (2010), pp. 190–209.

Rohloff, W., 'From ordinary language to definition in Kant and Bolzano', *Grazer Philosophische Studien* 85,1 (2012): 131–149.

Rosefeldt, T., 'Frege, Pünjer and Kant on existence', *Grazer Philosophische Studien* 82,1 (2011): 329–351.

Rosenberg, J., '"I think": some reflections on Kant's Paralogisms', *Midwest Studies in Philosophy* 10 (1986): 503–530.

Rosenkoetter, T., 'Kant on apperception and the unity of judgment', *Inquiry* 49,5 (2006): 469–489.

——, 'Truth criteria and the very project of a transcendental logic', *Archiv für Geschichte der Philosophie* 91,2 (2009): 193–236.

——, 'Absolute positing, the Frege anticipation thesis, and Kant's definitions of judgment', *European Journal of Philosophy* 18,4 (2010): 539–566.

——, 'Kant and Bolzano on the singularity of intuitions', *Grazer Philosophische Studien* 85,1 (2012): 89–129.

Rosenthal, J., 'A Transcendental Deduction of the categories without the categories', *International Philosophical Quarterly* 33 (1993): 449–464.

Rubenstein, E. M., 'Rethinking Kant on individuation', *Kantian Review* 5 (2001): 73–89.

Rukgaber, M., 'Time and metaphysics: Kant and McTaggart on the reality of time', *Kant Yearbook* 2 (2010): 175–194.

Schaper, E., 'Kant's schematism reconsidered', *Review of Metaphysics* 18 (1964): 267–282.

——, 'The Kantian thing-in-itself as a philosophical fiction', *The Philosophical Quarterly* 16 (1966): 233–243.

Schmiege, O., 'What is Kant's Second Antinomy about?', *Kant-Studien* 97 (2006): 272–300.

Schrader, G., 'The thing in itself in Kantian philosophy', *Review of Metaphysics* 2 (1949): 30–44.

——, 'The transcendental ideality and empirical reality of Kant's space and time', *Review of Metaphysics* 4 (1951): 507–536.

——, 'Kant's theory of concepts', *Kant-Studien* 49 (1958): 264–278.

Schulting, D., 'On Strawson on Kantian apperception', *South African Journal of Philosophy* 27,3 (2008): 257–271.

——, 'Kant's Copernican analogy: beyond the non-specific reading', *Studi Kantiani* XXII (2009): 39–65.

——, 'Kant's idealism: the current debate', in D. Schulting & J. Verburgt (eds) (2011), pp. 1–28.

——, 'Limitation and idealism: Kant's "long" argument from the categories', in D. Schulting & J. Verburgt (eds) (2011), pp. 159–191.

——, *Kant's Deduction and Apperception. Explaining the Categories* (Basingstoke/New York: Palgrave Macmillan, 2012).

——, 'Non-apperceptive consciousness', in R. Pozzo, P. Giordanetti & M. Sgarbi (eds), *Kant's Philosophy of the Unconscious* (Berlin/New York: Walter de Gruyter, 2012).

——, 'Kant, non-conceptual content and the 'second step' of the B-deduction', *Kant Studies Online* (2012): 51–92.

Schwyzer, H., *The Unity of Understanding: A Study in Kantian Problems* (Oxford: Clarendon Press, 1990).

Sellars, W., *Science and Metaphysics: Variations on Kantian Themes* (London: Routledge & Kegan Paul, 1968).

——, '". . . this I or he or it (the thing) which thinks . . ."', *Proceedings of the American Philosophical Association* 44 (1972): 5–31.

——, *Kant's Transcendental Metaphysics* (Atascadero: Ridgeview, 2002).

——, *Kant and Pre-Kantian Themes* (Atascadero: Ridgeview, 2002).

Senderowicz, Y. M., 'Figurative synthesis and synthetic a priori knowledge', *Review of Metaphysics* LVII,4 (2004): 755–785.

——, *The Coherence of Kant's Transcendental Idealism* (Dordrecht: Springer, 2005).

Sgarbi, M., *Kant on Spontaneity* (London/New York: Continuum, 2012).

Shabel, L., 'Kant on the "symbolic construction" of mathematical concepts', *Studies in History and Philosophy of Science* Part A 29,4 (1998): 589–621.

——, *Mathematics in Kant's Critical Philosophy* (London/New York: Routledge, 2003).

——, 'Reflections on Kant's concept (and intuition) of space', *Studies in the History and Philosophy of Science* Part A 34,1 (2003): 45–57.

——, 'Kant's "argument from geometry"', *Journal of the History of Philosophy* 42,2 (2004): 195–215.

——, 'Kant's philosophy of mathematics', in P. Guyer (ed.) (2006), pp. 94–128.

——, 'The Transcendental Aesthetic', in P. Guyer (ed.) (2010), pp. 93–117.

Skorpen, E., 'Kant's Refutation of Idealism', *Journal of the History of Philosophy* 6 (1962): 23–34.

Smit, H., 'The role of reflection in Kant's *Critique of Pure Reason*', *Pacific Philosophical Quarterly* 80,2 (1999): 203–223.

——, 'Kant on marks and the immediacy of intuition', *The Philosophical Review* 109 (2000): 235–266.

Smith, S., 'Kant's picture of monads in the *Physical Monadology*', *Studies in History and Philosophy of Science* Part A, 44,1 (2013): 102–111.

Smith, W., 'Kant and the general law of causality', *Philosophical Studies* 32,2 (1977): 113–128.

Stang, N., 'Kant's possibility proof', *History of Philosophy Quarterly* 27,3 (2010): 275–299.

——, 'Did Kant conflate the necessary and the 'a priori'?', *Noûs* 45,3 (2011): 443–471.

——, 'Kant on complete determination and infinite judgement', *British Journal for* the History of Philosophy 20,6 (2012): 1117–1139.

——, 'Freedom, knowledge and affection: A reply to Hogan', Kantian Review 18,1 (2013): 99–106.

——, 'The non-identity of appearances and things in themselves', Noûs 48,1 (2014): 106–136.

Stapleford, S., Kant's Transcendental Arguments: Disciplining Pure Reason (London: Continuum, 2008).

Stephenson, A., 'Kant on non-veridical experience', Kant Yearbook 3 (2011): 1–22.

Stern, R., 'Metaphysical dogmatism, Humean scepticism, Kantian criticism', Kantian Review 11 (2006): 102–116.

Stevenson, L., Inspirations from Kant (New York: Oxford University Press, 2011).

Stine, W., 'Self-consciousness in Kant's Critique of Pure Reason', Philosophical Studies 28 (1975): 189–197.

Sturm, T., 'How not to investigate the human mind: Kant on the impossibility of empirical psychology', in E. Watkins (ed.) (2001), pp. 163–184.

——, 'Freedom and the human sciences: Hume's science of man versus Kant's pragmatic anthropology', Kant Yearbook 3 (2011): 23–42.

——, 'What's philosophical about Kant's philosophy of the human sciences?', Studies in History and Philosophy of Science Part A 43,1 (2012): 203–207.

Strawson, P. F., The Bounds of Sense: An Essay on Kant's Critique of Pure Reason (London: Methuen, 1966).

——, 'Imagination and perception', in Freedom and Resentment and Other Essays (London: Methuen, 1974), pp. 45–65.

——, 'Kant on substance', in Entity and Identity (Oxford: Clarendon Press, 1997), pp. 268–279.

Stuart, J. D., 'Kant's two refutations of idealism', Southwestern Journal of Philosophy 6 (1975): 29–46.

Suchting, W. A., 'Kant's Second Analogy of experience', Kant-Studien 58 (1967): 355–369.

Sutherland, D., 'The role of magnitude in Kant's critical philosophy', Canadian Journal of Philosophy 34,3 (2004): 411–442.

——, 'Kant's philosophy of mathematics and the Greek mathematical tradition', The Philosophical Review 113,2 (2004): 157–201.

——, 'Kant on fundamental geometrical relations', Archiv für Geschichte der Philosophie 87,2 (2005): 117–158.

——, 'The point of Kant's axioms of intuition', Pacific Philosophical Quarterly 86 (2005): 135–159.

——, 'Kant on arithmetic, algebra and the theory of proportions', Journal of the History of Philosophy 44,4 (2006): 533–558.

Thielke, P., 'Discursivity and causality: Maimon's challenge to the Second Analogy', Kant-Studien 92 (2001): 440–463.

——, 'Fate and the fortune of the categories: Kant on the usurpation and schematization of concepts', Inquiry 49,5 (2006): 438–468.

Thomas, A., 'Kant, McDowell, and the theory of consciousness', European Journal of Philosophy 5,3 (1997): 283–305.

Thompson, M., 'Singular terms and intuitions in Kant's epistemology', Review of Metaphysics 26 (1972): 314–343.

——, 'Things in themselves', Proceedings and Addresses of the American

Philosophical Association 57 (1983): 33–49.

Tolley, C., 'Bolzano and Kant on the nature of logic', *History and Philosophy of Logic* 33,4 (2012): 307–327.

——, 'The generality of Kant's transcendental logic', *Journal of the History of Philosophy* 50,3 (2012): 417–446.

——, 'The non-conceptuality of the content of intuitions: A new approach', *Kantian Review* 18,1 (2013): 107–136.

Turbayne, C., 'Kant's refutation of dogmatic idealism', *The Philosophical Quarterly* 5 (1955): 225–244.

Van Cleve, J., 'Four recent interpretations of Kant's Second Analogy', *Kant-Studien* 64 (1973): 71–87.

——, 'Substance, matter and the First Analogy', *Kant-Studien* 70 (1979): 149–161.

——, 'Putnam, Kant, and secondary qualities', *Philosophical Papers* 24 (1995): 83–109.

——, *Problems From Kant* (New York: Oxford University Press, 1999).

Vanzo, A., 'Kant on the nominal definition of truth', *Kant-Studien* 101 (2010): 147–166.

——, 'Kant on truth-aptness', *History and Philosophy of Logic* 33,2 (2012): 109–126.

——, *Kant e la formazione dei concetti* (Trento: Verifiche, 2012).

——, 'Kant on empiricism and rationalism', *History of Philosophy Quarterly* 30 (2013): 53–74.

——, 'Kant on existential import', *Kantian Review* 19,2 (2014): 207–232.

Verburgt, J., 'How to account for reason's interest in an ultimate prototype? A note on Kant's doctrine of the transcendental

Ideal', in D. Schulting & J. Verburgt (eds) (2011), pp. 237–254.

Vogel, J., 'The problem of self-knowledge in Kant's "Refutation of Idealism": two recent views', *Philosophy and Phenomenological Research* 53 (1993): 875–887.

Walker, R. C. S., *Kant* (London: Routledge & Kegan Paul, 1978).

——, 'Synthesis and transcendental idealism', *Kant-Studien* 76 (1985): 14–27.

——, 'Kant's conception of empirical law', *Proceedings of the Aristotelian Society*, supplementary volume 64 (1990): 243–258.

——, 'Kant on the number of worlds', *British Journal for the History of Philosophy* 18,5 (2010): 821–843.

Walsh, S., 'Incongruent counterparts and causality', *Kant-Studien* 98 (2007): 418–430.

Walsh, W. H., 'Philosophy and psychology in Kant's *Critique*', *Kant-Studien* 57 (1966): 186–198.

——, *Kant's Criticism of Metaphysics* (Edinburgh: Edinburgh University Press, 1975).

Ward, A., 'On Kant's Second Analogy and his reply to Hume', *Kant-Studien* 77 (1986): 409–422.

——, 'Kant's First Analogy of experience', *Kant-Studien* 92 (2001): 387–406.

Warren, D., 'Kant and the apriority of space', *The Philosophical Review* 107,2 (1998): 179–224.

——, *Reality and Impenetrability in Kant's Philosophy of Nature* (New York: Routledge, 2001).

——, 'Kant on attractive and repulsive force: the balancing argument', in M. Friedman, M. Domski & M. Dickson (eds), *Discourse on a New Method*.

Reinvigorating the Marriage of History and Philosophy of Science (Chicago, La Salle, IL: Open Court, 2009), pp. 193–241.

Wartenberg, T., 'Order through reason', *Kant-Studien* 70 (1979): 409–424.

Washburn, M., 'The second edition of the *Critique*; towards an understanding of its nature and genesis', *Kant-Studien* 66 (1975): 277–290.

——, 'Did Kant have a theory of self-knowledge?', *Archiv für Geschichte der Philosophie* 58 (1976): 40–56.

Watkins, E., 'Kant's theory of physical influx', *Archiv für Geschichte der Philosophie* 77,3 (1995): 285–324.

——, 'Kant's Third Analogy of experience', *Kant-Studien* 88 (1997): 406–441.

——, 'The argumentative structure of Kant's *Metaphysical Foundations of Natural Science*', *Journal of the History of Philosophy* 36 (1998): 567–593.

——, 'Kant's justification of the laws of mechanics', *Studies in History and Philosophy of Science* Part A 29 (1998): 539–560.

——, 'Kant on rational cosmology', in E. Watkins (ed.) (2001): pp. 70–89.

——, 'Kant's transcendental idealism and the categories', *History of Philosophy Quarterly* 19 (2002): 191–215.

——, 'Forces and causes in Kant's early pre-Critical writings', *Studies in History and Philosophy of Science* Part A 34 (2003): 5–27.

——, 'Kant's model of causality: causal powers, laws, and Kant's reply to Hume', *Journal of the History of Philosophy* 42 (2004): 449–488.

——, *Kant and the Metaphysics of Causality* (Cambridge: Cambridge University Press, 2005).

——, 'Kant and the myth of givenness', *Inquiry* 51,5 (2008): 512–531.

——, 'Kant on the hiddenness of God', *Kantian Review* 14,1 (2009): 81–122.

——, 'The System of Principles', in P. Guyer (ed.) (2010), pp. 151–167.

——, 'Kant, Sellars, and the myth of the given', *The Philosophical Forum* 43,3 (2012): 311–326.

Watkins, E. & M. Fisher, 'Kant on the material ground of possibility: from *The Only Possible Argument* to the *Critique of Pure Reason*', *Review of Metaphysics* 52 (1998): 369–395.

Waxman, W., *Kant's Model of the Mind: A New Interpretation of Transcendental Idealism* (Oxford: Oxford University Press, 1991).

——, *Kant's Anatomy of the Intelligent Mind* (Oxford: Oxford University Press, 2013).

Weizsäcker, C. F., von, 'Kant's "First Analogy of experience" and conservation principles of physics', *Synthese* 23 (1971): 75–95.

Werkmeister, W., 'Kant's Refutation of Idealism', *Southern Journal of Philosophy* 15 (1977): 551–565.

——, *Kant's Silent Decade* (Tallahasee, FL: University Presses of Florida, 1979).

——, *Kant: The Architectonic and Development of his Philosophy* (Chicago, La Salle, IL: Open Court, 1980).

Westphal, K. R., 'Kant's dynamic constructions', *Journal of Philosophical Research* 20 (1995): 381–429.

——, 'Kant, Hegel, and the transcendental material conditions of possible experience', *Bulletin of the Hegel Society of Great Britain* 33 (1996): 23–41.

——, 'Affinity, idealism and naturalism: the stability of cinnabar and the possibility of experience', *Kant-Studien* 88 (1997): 139–189.

——, 'Noumenal causality reconsidered', *Canadian Journal of Philosophy* 27 (1997): 209–245.

——, 'Freedom and the distinction between phenomena and noumena', *Journal of Philosophical Research* 26 (2001): 593–622.

——, *Kant's Transcendental Proof of Realism* (Cambridge: Cambridge University Press, 2004).

——, 'Comments on Graham Bird's *The Revolutionary Kant*', *Kantian Review* 16,2 (2011): 245–255.

——, 'Kant's cognitive semantics, Newton's rule four of philosophy and scientific realism', *Bulletin of the Hegel Society of Great Britain* 63/64 (2011): 27–49.

Westphal, M., 'In defense of the thing in itself', *Kant-Studien* 59 (1968): 118–141.

Williams, J., 'How conceptually guided are Kantian intuitions?', *History of Philosophy Quarterly* 29,1 (2012): 57–78.

Wilson, E., 'On the nature of judgment in Kant's Transcendental Logic', *Idealistic Studies* 40 (2010): 43–63.

Wilson, M., 'Kant and "the dogmatic idealism of Berkeley"', *Journal of the History of Philosophy* 9 (1971): 459–475.

Wike, V. S., *Kant's Antinomies of Reason* (Washington, DC: University Press of America, 1982).

Wolff, R. P., *Kant's Theory of Mental Activity* (Gloucester, MA: Peter Smith, 1973).

Wood, A., 'Kant's Dialectic', *Canadian Journal of Philosophy* 5,4 (1975): 595–614.

——, *Kant's Rational Theology* (Ithaca, NY: Cornell University Press, 2009 [1978]).

——, 'The Antinomies of pure reason', in P. Guyer (ed.) (2010), pp. 245–265.

Wuerth, J., 'Kant's immediatism, pre-Critique', *Journal of the History of Philosophy* 44,4 (2006): 489–532.

——, 'The Paralogisms of pure reason', in P. Guyer (ed.) (2010), pp. 210–244.

Yong, P., 'God, totality and possibility in Kant's *Only Possible Argument*', *Kantian Review* 19,1 (2014): 27–51.

Young, J. M., 'Kant on existence', *Ratio* 18 (1976): 91–106.

——, 'Kant on the construction of arithmetical concepts', *Kant-Studien* 73 (1982): 17–46.

——, 'Kant's view of the imagination', *Kant-Studien* 79 (1988): 140–164.

Zinkin, M., 'Kant on negative magnitudes', *Kant-Studien* 103,4 (2012): 397–414.

Zinkstok, J., 'Anthropology, empirical psychology, and applied logic', *Kant Yearbook* 3 (2011): 107–130.

8. KANT'S PRACTICAL PHILOSOPHY (INCLUDING RELIGION)

Acton, H. B., *Kant's Moral Philosophy* (London: Macmillan, 1970).

Allison, H. E., 'The concept of freedom in Kant's "semi-critical" ethics', *Archiv für Geschichte der Philosophie* 68 (1986): 96–115.

——, 'Morality and freedom: Kant's reciprocity thesis', *The Philosophical Review* 95 (1986): 393–425.

——, *Kant's Theory of Freedom* (Cambridge: Cambridge University Press, 1990).

——, 'Kant's doctrine of obligatory ends', *Jahrbuch für Recht und Ethik* 1 (1993): 7–23.

——, 'Kant on freedom: A reply to my critics', in Allison (1996), pp. 109–128.

——, 'Autonomy and spontaneity in Kant's conception of the self', in Allison (1996), pp. 129–142.

——, *Idealism and Freedom: Essays on Kant's Theoretical and Practical Philosophy* (Cambridge: Cambridge University Press, 1996).

——, 'Ethics, evil and anthropology in Kant', *Ethics* 111,3 (2001): 594–613.

——, 'Kant on freedom of the will', in P. Guyer (ed.) (2006), pp. 381–415.

——, *Kant's Groundwork for the Metaphysics of Morals: A Commentary* (Oxford: Oxford University Press, 2011).

Altman, M., 'Kant on sex and marriage', *Kant-Studien* 101 (2010): 309–330.

——, *Kant and Applied Ethics: The Uses and Limits of Kant's Practical Philosophy* (Malden/Oxford: Wiley Blackwell, 2012).

Ameriks, K. 'Kant's deduction of freedom and morality', *Journal of the History of Philosophy* 19 (1981): 53–79.

——, 'On Schneewind and Kant's method in ethics', *Ideas y Valores* 102 (1996): 28–53.

——, *Interpreting Kant's Critiques* (Oxford: Clarendon Press, 2003).

——, *Kant's Elliptical Path* (Oxford: Clarendon Press, 2012).

——, 'Kant, miracles, and *Religion*, parts one and two', in G. Michalson (ed.), *Kant's Religion Within the Boundaries of Mere Reason* (Cambridge: Cambridge University Press, 2014), pp. 137–155.

Anderson, P., 'The philosophical significance of Kant's *Religion*', *Faith and Philosophy* 29,2 (2012): 151–162.

Anderson–Gold, S., 'Kant's rejection of devilishness: the limits of human volition', *Idealistic Studies* 14 (1984): 35–48.

——, 'Kant's ethical commonwealth: the highest good as a social goal', *International Philosophical Quarterly* 26 (1986): 23–32.

——, 'War and resistance', *Journal of Social Philosophy* 19 (1988): 37–50.

——, *Cosmopolitanism and Human Rights* (Cardiff: University of Wales Press, 2001).

——, 'Privacy, respect and the virtues of reticence in Kant', *Kantian Review* 15,2 (2010): 28–42.

——, *Unnecessary Evil. History and Moral Development in the Philosophy of Immanuel Kant* (Albany, NY: SUNY Press, 2001).

Annas, J., 'Personal love and Kantian ethics in Effi Briest', *Philosophy and Literature* 8 (1984): 15–31.

Ansbro, J. J., 'Kant's limitations on individual freedom', *The New Scholasticism* 47 (1973): 88–99.

Archibugi, D., 'Immanuel Kant, cosmopolitan law and peace', *European Journal of International Relations* 1,4 (1995): 429–456.

Arntzen, S., 'Kant's denial of absolute sovereignty', *Pacific Philosophical Quarterly* 76 (1995): 1–16.

——, 'Kant on duty to oneself and resistance to political authority', *Journal of the History of Philosophy* 34 (1996): 409–424.

Arroyo, C., 'Freedom and the source of value: Korsgaard and Wood on Kant's formula of humanity', *Metaphilosophy* 42,4 (2011): 353–359.

Atwell, J. E., 'Objective ends in Kant's ethics', *Archiv für Geschichte der Philosophie* 56 (1974): 156–171.

——, 'Kant's moral model and moral universe', *History of Philosophy Quarterly* 3 (1986): 423–436.

——, *Ends and Principles in Kant's Moral Thought* (Dordrecht: Martinus Nijhoff, 1986).

Audi. R., *The Good in the Right. A Theory of Intuition and Intrinsic Value* (Princeton: Princeton University Press, 2004).

Aune, B., *Kant's Theory of Morals* (Princeton: Princeton University Press, 1979).

Auxter, T. *Kant's Moral Teleology* (Macon: Mercer University Press, 1982).

Bader, R., 'Kant and the categories of freedom', *British Journal for the History of Philosophy* 17,4 (2009): 799–820.

Baiasu, S., *Kant and Sartre* (Basingstoke/ New York: Palgrave Macmillan, 2011).

Bailey, T., 'Analysing the good will', *British Journal for the History of Philosophy* 18,4 (2010): 635–662.

Baker, J., 'Counting categorical imperatives', *Kant-Studien* 79 (1988): 389–406.

Banham, G., 'Kant's critique of right', *Kantian Review* 6 (2002): 35–59.

——, *Kant's Practical Philosophy* (Basingstoke/New York: Palgrave Macmillan, 2003).

——, 'Publicity and provisional right', *Politics and Ethics Review* 3,1 (2007): 73–89.

——, 'New work on Kant's Doctrine of Right', *British Journal for the History of Philosophy* 16,3 (2011): 549–560.

Barnes, G., 'In defence of Kant's doctrine of the highest good', *The Philosophical Forum* 2 (1971): 446–458.

Baron, M., 'Remorse and agent regret', *Midwest Studies in Philosophy* 13 (1988): 259–281.

——, 'Was Effi Briest a victim of Kantian morality?', *Philosophy and Literature* 12 (1988): 95–113.

——, *Kantian Ethics Almost Without Apology* (Ithaca, NY: Cornell University Press, 1995).

Barron, A., 'Kant, copyright and communicative freedom', *Law and Philosophy* 31,1 (2012): 1–48.

Baxley, A. M., 'Does Kantian virtue amount to more than continence?', *Review of Metaphysics* 56 (2003): 559–586.

——, 'Pleasure, freedom and grace: Schiller's "completion" of Kant's ethics', *Inquiry* 51,1 (2008): 1–15.

——, *Kant's Theory of Virtue* (Cambridge: Cambridge University Press, 2010).

——, 'The Problem of obligation, the finite rational will, and Kantian value realism', *Inquiry* 55,6 (2012): 567–583.

Baynes, K., 'Kant on property rights and the social contract', *The Monist* 72 (1989): 433–453.

Beck, L. W., 'Sir David Ross on duty and purpose in Kant', *Philosophy and Phenomenological Research* 16 (1955): 98–107.

——, 'Apodictic imperatives', *Kant-Studien* 49 (1957): 7–24.

——, *A Commentary on Kant's Critique of Practical Reason* (Chicago: University of Chicago Press, 1960).

——, 'Kant and the right of revolution', *Journal of the History of Ideas* 32 (1971): 411–422.

——, 'Five concepts of freedom in Kant', in J. T. J. Szrednicki (ed.), *Philosophical*

Analysis and Reconstruction (The Hague: Martinus Nijhoff, 1987), pp. 35–51.

——, 'Kant's two conceptions of the will in their political context', in R. Beiner & J. W. Booth (eds) (1993), pp. 38–49.

Beever, A., 'Kant on the law of marriage', *Kantian Review* 18,3 (2013): 339–362.

Benson, P., 'External freedom according to Kant', *Columbia Law Review* 87 (1987): 559–579.

——, 'Moral worth', *Philosophical Studies* 51 (1987): 365–382.

Benton, R. J., *Kant's Second Critique and the Problem of Transcendental Arguments* (The Hague: Martinus Nijhoff, 1977).

——, 'The transcendental argument in Kant's *Groundwork of the Metaphysics of Morals*', *Journal of Value Inquiry* 12 (1978): 225–237.

——, 'Kant's categories of practical reason as such', *Kant-Studien* 71 (1980): 181–201.

Bielefeldt, H., 'Autonomy and republicanism: Immanuel Kant's philosophy of freedom', *Political Theory* 25 (1997): 524–558.

——, 'Towards a cosmopolitan framework of freedom', *Jahrbuch für Recht und Ethik* 5 (1997): 349–362.

——, *Symbolic Representation in Kant's Practical Philosophy* (Cambridge: Cambridge University Press, 2003).

Bjerre, H., *Kantian Deeds* (London/New York: Continuum, 2010).

Bojanowski, J., 'Is Kant a moral realist?', *Kant Yearbook* 4 (2012): 1–22.

Booth, W. J., *Interpreting the World: Kant's Philosophy of History and Politics* (Toronto: University of Toronto Press, 1986).

Borges, M., 'Physiology and the controlling of affects in Kant's philosophy', *Kantian Review* 13,2 (2008): 46–66.

Bowie, N. E., 'Aspects of Kant's philosophy of law', *The Philosophical Forum* 2 (1971): 469–478.

Buchanan, A., 'Categorical imperatives and moral principles', *Philosophical Studies* 31 (1977): 249–260.

Byrd, S., 'Kant's theory of punishment: deterrence in its threat, retribution in its execution', *Law and Philosophy* 8 (1989): 151–200.

——, 'Two models of justice', *Jahrbuch für Recht und Ethik* 1 (1993): 45–68.

——, 'Kant's theory of contract', *The Southern Journal of Philosophy* XXXVI (supplement) (1997): 131–153.

Byrd, S. & J. Hruschka, *Kant's Doctrine of Right: A Commentary* (Cambridge: Cambridge University Press, 2010).

Campbell, J., 'Kantian conceptions of moral goodness', *Canadian Journal of Philosophy* 13 (1983): 527–550.

Carnois, B., *The Coherence of Kant's Doctrine of Freedom* (Chicago: University of Chicago Press, 1987).

Carson, T., '*Perpetual Peace*: what Kant should have said', *Social Theory and Practice* 14 (1988): 173–214.

Cavallar, G., 'Kant's society of nations: free federation or world republic?', *Journal of the History of Philosophy* 32 (1994): 461–482.

——, *Kant and the Theory and Practice of International Right* (Cardiff: University of Wales Press, 1999).

——, 'Kantian perspectives on democratic peace: alternatives to Doyle', *Review of International Studies* 27 (2001): 229–248.

——, 'Cosmopolitanisms in Kant's philosophy', *Ethics and Global Politics* 5,2 (2012): 95–118.

Chadwick, R. R., 'The market for bodily parts', *Journal of Applied Philosophy* 6 (1989): 129–140.

Chignell, A., 'Belief in Kant', *The Philosophical Review* 116,3 (2007): 323–360.

——, *Kant's Questions: What May I Hope?* (London/New York: Routledge, 2015).

Cholbi, M. J., 'Kant and the irrationality of suicide', *History of Philosophy Quarterly* 17 (2000): 159–176.

——, 'A Kantian defense of prudential suicide', *Journal of Moral Philosophy* 7 (2010): 489–515.

Coble, K., 'Kant's dynamic theory of character', *Kantian Review* 7 (2003): 38–71.

Cohen, A., *Kant and the Human Sciences* (Basingstoke/New York: Palgrave Macmillan, 2009).

——, 'Kant on doxastic voluntarism and its implications for epistemic responsibility', *Kant Yearbook* 5 (2013): 33–50.

Copp, D., 'The "possibility of a categorical imperative": Kant's Groundwork, part III', *Philosophical Perspectives* 6 (1992): 261–284.

Corlett, J. A., 'Foundations of a Kantian theory of punishment', *Southern Journal of Philosophy* 31 (1993): 263–283.

Covell, C., *Kant and the Law of Peace* (Basingstoke: Palgrave Macmillan, 1998).

Cummiskey, D., 'Kantian consequentialism', *Ethics* 100 (1990): 586–615.

——, *Kantian Consequentialism* (New York: Oxford University Press, 1996).

——, 'Korsgaard's rejection of consequentialism', *Metaphilosophy* 42,4 (2011): 360–367.

Cureton, A., 'A contractualist reading of Kant's proof of the Formula of Humanity', *Kantian Review* 18,3 (2013): 363–386.

Custor, O., 'Angling for a stranglehold on the death penalty', *Southern Journal of Philosophy* 50 (2012): 160–173.

Dahlstrom, D. O., 'The natural right of equal opportunity in Kant's civil union', *Southern Journal of Philosophy* 23 (1985): 295–303.

Darwall, S., 'Two kinds of respect', *Ethics* 88 (1977): 36–49.

——, 'Kantian practical reason defended', *Ethics* 96 (1985): 89–99.

——, 'The value of autonomy and autonomy of the will', *Ethics* 116,2 (2006): 263–284.

Davidovich, A., 'How to read *Religion within the Limits of Reason Alone*', *Kant-Studien* 85 (1994): 1–14.

Davis, K. R., 'Kantian "publicity" and political justice', *History of Philosophy Quarterly* 8 (1991): 409–421.

——, 'Kant's different "publics" and the justice of publicity', *Kant-Studien* 83 (1992): 170–184.

Dean, R., *The Value of Humanity in Kant's Moral Theory* (Oxford: Oxford University Press, 2006).

——, 'Humanity as an idea, as an ideal, and as an end in itself', *Kantian Review* 18,2 (2013): 171–195.

Deligiorgi, K., *Kant and the Culture of Enlightenment* (Albany, NY: SUNY Press, 2006).

——, *The Scope of Autonomy: Kant and the Morality of Freedom* (Oxford: Oxford University Press, 2012).

Denis, L., 'Kant on the wrongness of "unnatural" sex', *History of Philosophy Quarterly* 16 (1999): 225–248.

——, 'Kant on the perfection of others', *Southern Journal of Philosophy* 37 (1999): 21–41.

——, *Moral Self-Regard: Duties to Oneself in Kant's Moral Theory* (London: Routledge, 2001).

——, 'Kant's conception of virtues', in P. Guyer (ed.) (2006), pp. 505–537.

——, 'Humanity, obligation and the good will', *Kantian Review* 15,1 (2010): 118–141.

DiCenso, J., *Kant, Religion, and Politics* (Cambridge: Cambridge University Press, 2011).

——, *Kant's Religion within the Boundaries of Mere Reason: A Commentary* (Cambridge: Cambridge University Press, 2012).

Dillon, R. S., 'Kant on arrogance and self-respect', in C. Calhoun (ed.), *Setting the Compass: Essays by Women Philosophers* (Oxford: Oxford University Press, 2003), pp. 191–217.

Dodson, K. E., 'Kant's *Perpetual Peace*: universal civil society or league of states?', *Southwest Philosophical Studies* 15 (1993): 1–9.

——, 'Autonomy and authority in Kant's "Rechtslehre"', *Political Theory* 25 (1997): 93–111.

Dogan, A., 'On the priority of the right to the good', *Kant-Studien* 102,3 (2011): 316–334.

Donagan, A., 'The structure of Kant's *Metaphysics of Morals*', *Topoi* 4 (1985): 61–72.

Doore, G., 'Contradiction in the will', *Kant-Studien* 76 (1985): 138–151.

Doyle, M.W., 'Liberalism and international relations', in R. Beiner & J. W. Booth (eds) (1993), pp. 173–204.

Duncan, A. R. C., *Practical Reason and Morality* (London: Thomas Nelson & Sons, 1957).

Duncan, S., '"There is none righteous": Kant on the *Hang zum Böse* and the universal evil of humanity', *Southern Journal of Philosophy* 49,2 (2011): 137–163.

——, 'Moral evil, freedom and the goodness of God: Why Kant abandoned theodicy', *British Journal for the History of Philosophy* 20,5 (2012): 973–991.

Easley, E. S., *The War Over Perpetual Peace* (Basingstoke: Palgrave Macmillan, 2004).

Edwards, J., 'Egoism and formalism in the development of Kant's moral philosophy', *Kant-Studien* 91 (2000): 411–432.

Eisenberg, P., 'Basic ethical categories of Kant's *Tugendlehre*', *American Philosophical Quarterly* 3 (1966): 255–269.

Ellis, E., *Kant's Politics* (New Haven: Yale University Press, 2005).

Engstrom, S., 'Herman on mutual aid', *Ethics* 96 (1986): 346–349.

——, *The Form of Practical Knowledge* (Cambridge, MA: Harvard University Press, 2009).

——, 'Herman on moral literacy', *Kantian Review* 16,1 (2011): 17–31.

Engstrom, S. & J. Whiting (eds), *Aristotle, Kant and the Stoics: Rethinking Happiness and Duty* (Cambridge: Cambridge University Press, 1996).

Ertl, W., 'Persons as causes in Kant', in S. Palmquist (ed.) *Cultivating Personhood: Kant and Asian Philosophy* (Berlin/New York: de Gruyter 2010), pp. 217–230.

Fackenheim, E., 'Kant and radical evil', *University of Toronto Quarterly* 23 (1954): 439–453.

——, 'Kant's concept of history', *Kant-Studien* 48 (1956–7): 381–398.

Fahmy, M. S., 'Active sympathetic participation: reconsidering Kant's duty of sympathy', *Kantian Review* 14,1 (2009): 31–52.

Fenves, P. D., *A Peculiar Fate* (Ithaca, NY: Cornell University Press, 1991).

——, *Late Kant* (London: Routledge, 2003).

Filippaki, E., 'Kant on love, respect, and friendship', *Kant Yearbook* 4 (2012): 23–48.

Firestone, C., *Kant and Theology at the Boundaries of Reason* (Farnham/ Burlington, VT: Ashgate, 2009).

Fleischacker, S., 'Kant's theory of punishment', *Kant-Studien* 79 (1988): 434–449.

——, *Kant's Questions: What is Enlightenment?* (Abingdon/New York: Routledge 2013).

Flikschuh, K., 'On Kant's "Rechtslehre"', *European Journal of Philosophy* 5 (1997): 50–73.

——, 'Freedom and constraint in Kant's Metaphysical Elements of Justice', *History of Political Thought* 20 (1999): 250–271.

——, *Kant and Modern Political Philosophy* (Cambridge: Cambridge University Press, 2000).

——, 'Reason, right and revolution: Kant and Locke', *Philosophy and Public Affairs* 36,4 (2008): 375–404.

——, 'Kant's kingdom of ends: metaphysical, not political', in J. Timmermann (ed.) (2009), pp. 119–139.

——, 'Kant's sovereignty dilemma: a contemporary analysis', *Journal of Political Philosophy* 18,4 (2010): 469–493.

Flynn, J. R., 'The logic of Kant's derivation of freedom from reason', *Kant-Studien* 77 (1986): 441–446.

Forman, D., 'Principled and unprincipled maxims', *Kant-Studien* 103,3 (2012): 318–336.

——, 'Kant on moral freedom and moral slavery', *Kantian Review* 17,1 (2012): 1–32.

Formosa, P., 'Kant on the highest moral–physical good', *Kantian Review* 15,1 (2010): 1–36.

——, 'Is Kant a moral constructivist or a moral realist?, *European Journal of Philosophy* 21,2 (2013): 170–196.

——, 'Kant's conception of personal autonomy', *Journal of Social Philosophy* 44,3 (2013): 193–212.

——, 'Dignity and respect: How to apply Kant's formula of humanity', *The Philosophical Forum* 45,1 (2014): 49–68.

Forschler, S., 'From supervenience to "universal law": How Kantian ethics becomes heteronomous', *Kant Yearbook* 4 (2012): 49–68.

——, 'Kantian and consequentialist ethics: The gap can be bridged', *Metaphilosophy* 44,1–2 (2013): 88–104.

Forschner, M., 'Über die verschiedenen Bedeutungen des "Hangs zum Bösen"', in O. Höffe (ed.), *Immanuel Kant. Die Religion innerhalb der Grenzen der bloßen Vernunft*, in the series *Klassiker Auslegen* (Berlin: Akademie Verlag, 2011), pp. 71–90.

Franceschet, A., *Kant and Liberal Internationalism* (New York: Palgrave Macmillan, 2002).

——, 'Kant, international law, and the problem of humanitarian intervention', *Journal of International Political Theory* 6 (2010): 1–22.

Franke, M. F. N., *Global Limits: Immanuel Kant, International Relations, and Critique of World Politics* (Albany, NY: SUNY Press, 2002).

Fremstedal, R., 'Original sin and radical evil: Kierkegaard and Kant', *Kantian Review* 17,2 (2012): 197–225.

Freydberg, B., *Imagination in Kant's Critique of Practical Reason* (Bloomington, IN: Indiana University Press, 2005).

Freyenhagen, F., 'Empty, useless, and dangerous? Recent Kantian replies to the empty formalism objection', *Bulletin of the Hegel Society of Great Britain* 63/64 (2011): 163–186.

Friedman, R. Z., 'The importance and function of Kant's highest good', *Journal of the History of Philosophy* 22 (1984): 325–342.

Frierson, P., *Freedom and Anthropology in Kant's Moral Philosophy* (Cambridge: Cambridge University Press, 2003).

——, 'Providence and divine mercy in Kant's ethical cosmopolitanism', *Faith and Philosophy* 24,2 (2007): 144–164.

——, *Kant's Questions: What is the Human Being?* (Abingdon/New York: Routledge, 2013).

——, *Kant's Empirical Psychology* (Cambridge: Cambridge University Press, 2014).

Gahringer, R. E., 'The metaphysical aspect of Kant's moral philosophy', *Ethics* 64 (1954): 277–291.

Galston, W. A., 'What is living and what is dead in Kant's practical philosophy', in R. Beiner & J. W. Booth (eds) (1993), pp. 207–223.

Galvin, R. F., 'Does Kant's psychology of morality need basic revision?', *Mind* 100 (1991): 221–236.

——, 'Ethical Formalism: The contradiction in conception test', *History of Philosophy Quarterly* 8,4 (1991): 387–408.

——, 'Rounding up the usual suspects: varieties of Kantian constructivism in ethics', *The Philosophical Quarterly* 61 (2011): 16–36.

Garcia, E., 'A new look at Kantian respect for persons', *Kant Yearbook* 4 (2012): 69–90.

Gardner, S., 'Kant's practical postulates and the limits of the Critical system', *Bulletin of the Hegel Society of Great Britain* 63 (2011): 187–215.

Gass, M., 'Kant's causal conception of autonomy', *History of Philosophy Quarterly* 11 (1994): 53–70.

Geiger, I., *The Founding Act of Modern Ethical Life. Hegel's Critique of Kant's Moral and Political Philosophy* (Stanford: Stanford University Press, 2007).

——, 'What is the use of the universal law formula of the categorical imperative?', *British Journal of the History of Philosophy* 18,2 (2010): 271–295.

——, 'Rational feelings and moral agency', *Kantian Review* 16,2 (2011): 283–308.

Gelfert, A., 'Kant on testimony', *British Journal for the History of Philosophy* 14,4 (2006): 627–652.

Genova, A. C., 'Kant's transcendental deduction of the moral law', *Kant-Studien* 69 (1978): 299–313.

Gerrand, N., 'The misuse of Kant in the debate about a market for human body parts', *Journal of Applied Philosophy* 16 (1999): 59–67.

Giesinger, J., 'Kant's account of moral education', *Educational Philosophy and Theory* 44,7 (2011): 775–786.

——, 'Kant on dignity and education', *Educational Theory* 62,6 (2012): 609–620.

Gilabert, P., 'Kant and the claims of the poor', *Philosophy and Phenomenological Research* 81 (2010): 382–418.

Gillroy, J. M., 'Making public choices', *Kant-Studien* 91 (2000): 44–72.

Godlove, T. Jr., 'Moral actions, moral lives', *Southern Journal of Philosophy* 25 (1987): 49–64.

Gorner, P., 'The place of punishment in Kant's *Rechtslehre*', *Kantian Review* 4 (2000): 121–130.

Green, M. K., 'Kant and moral self-deception', *Kant-Studien* 83 (1992): 149–169.

Green, R. M., 'The first formulation of the categorical imperative as literally a "legislative" metaphor', *History of Philosophy Quarterly* 8 (1991): 163–179.

Greenberg, R., 'On a presumed omission in Kant's derivation of the categorical imperative', *Kantian Review* 16,3 (2011): 449–459.

Gregor, M., *Laws of Freedom: A Study of Kant's Method of Applying the Categorical Imperative in the 'Metaphysik der Sitten'* (Oxford: Blackwell, 1963).

——, 'Kant on welfare legislation', *Logos* 6 (1985): 49–59.

——, 'Kant's theory of property', *Review of Metaphysics* 41 (1988): 757–787.

——, 'Kant's approach to constitutionalism', in A. S. Rosenbaum (ed.), *Constitutionalism* (New York: Greenwood Press, 1988), pp. 69–87.

——, '"Natural rights" in Kant's Doctrine of Right', in T. O'Hagan (ed.), *Revolution and Enlightenment in Europe* (Aberdeen: University of Aberdeen Press, 1991): 23–29.

——, 'Kant on obligation, rights and virtue', *Jahrbuch für Recht und Ethik/ Annual Review of Law and Ethics* 1 (1993): 69–102.

——, 'Leslie Mulholland on Kant's Rechtslehre', *Dialogue* 33 (1994): 693–700.

Grenberg, J. M., 'Feeling, desire and interest in Kant's theory of action', *Kant-Studien* 92 (2001): 153–179.

——, *Kant and the Ethics of Humility: A Story of Dependence, Corruption and Virtue* (Cambridge: Cambridge University Press, 2005).

——, 'Making sense of the relationship of reason and sensibility in Kant's ethics', *Kantian Review* 16,3 (2011): 461–472.

——, *Kant's Defense of Common Moral Experience* (Cambridge: Cambridge University Press, 2013).

Grey, T. C., 'Serpents and doves: a note on Kantian legal theory', *Columbia Law Review* 87 (1987): 580–591.

Guevara, D., 'The impossibility of supererogation in Kant's moral theory', *Philosophy and Phenomenological Research* 59 (1999): 593–624.

——, *Kant's Theory of Moral Motivation* (Boulder, CO: Westview Press, 2000).

Guyer, P., *Kant and the Experience of Freedom* (Cambridge: Cambridge University Press, 1993).

——, 'The possibility of the categorical imperative', *The Philosophical Review* 104 (1995): 353–385.

——, 'The value of agency', *Ethics* 106 (1996): 404–423.

——, 'The possibility of the categorical imperative', in P. Guyer (ed.) (1998), pp. 215–248.

——, 'Life, liberty and property', in D. Hüning & B. Tuschling (eds), *Recht, Staat und Völkerrecht* (Berlin: Duncker & Humboldt, 1998), pp. 273–292.

——, 'Morality of law and morality of freedom', in P. Guyer (2000), pp. 129–171.

——, *Kant on Freedom, Law and Happiness* (Cambridge: Cambridge University Press, 2000).

——, 'Ends of reason and ends of nature: The place of teleology in Kant's ethics', *Journal of Value Inquiry* 36 (2002): 161–186.

——, 'The derivation of the categorical imperative', *Harvard Review of Philosophy* 10 (2002): 64–80.

——, 'Kant on the theory and practice of autonomy', in *Kant's System of Nature and Freedom: Selected Essays* (Oxford: Oxford University Press, 2005), pp. 115–145.

——, *Kant's Groundwork for the Metaphysics of Morals: A Reader's Guide* (London: Continuum, 2007).

——, 'Naturalistic and transcendental moments in Kant's moral philosophy', *Inquiry* 50,5 (2007): 444–464.

——, 'The obligation to be virtuous: Kant's conception of the *Tugendverpflichtung*', *Social Philosophy and Policy* 27,2 (2010): 206–232.

Harbison, W. G., 'The good will', *Kant-Studien* 71 (1980): 47–59.

Hare, J. E., *The Moral Gap. Kantian Ethics, Human Limits and God's Assistance* (Oxford: Clarendon Press, 1997).

——, 'Ethics and religion: Two Kantian arguments', *Philosophical Investigations* 34,2 (2011): 151–168.

——, 'Kant, the passions, and the structure of moral motivation', *Faith and Philosophy* 28,1 (2011): 54–70.

Hare, R. M., 'Could Kant have been a utilitarian?', *Utilitas* 5 (1993): 1–16.

Harris, C. E., Jr., 'Kant, Nozick and the minimal state', *Southwestern Journal of Philosophy* 10 (1979): 179–187.

Harris, N., 'Kantian duties and immoral agents', *Kant-Studien* 83 (1992): 336–343.

Harter, T., 'Reconsidering Kant on suicide', *The Philosophical Forum* 42,2 (2011): 167–185.

Heller, A., 'Freedom and happiness in Kant's political philosophy', *Graduate Faculty Philosophy Journal* 13 (1990): 115–131.

Henrich, D., 'The deduction of the moral law: the reasons for the obscurity of the final section of Kant's *Groundwork of the Metaphysics of Morals*', in P. Guyer (ed.) (1998), pp. 303–342.

Henson, R., 'What Kant might have said: moral worth and overdetermination of dutiful action', *The Philosophical Review* 88 (1979): 39–54.

Herman, B., 'Leaving deontology behind', in B. Herman (1993), pp. 208–240.

——, *The Practice of Moral Judgment* (Cambridge, MA: Harvard University Press, 1993).

——, *Moral Literacy* (Cambridge, MA: Harvard University Press, 2007).

——, 'Embracing Kant's formalism', *Kantian Review* 16,1 (2011): 49–66.

Herrera, L., 'Kant on the moral *Triebfeder*', *Kant-Studien* 91 (2000): 395–410.

Heyd, D., 'Beyond the call of duty in Kant's ethics', *Kant-Studien* 71 (1980): 308–324.

——, 'Moral and legal luck: Kant's reconciliation with practical contingency', *Jahrbuch für Recht und Ethik* 5 (1997): 27–42.

Hill, T. E. Jr., 'Darwall on practical reason', *Ethics* 96 (1986): 604–619.

——, *Autonomy and Self Respect* (Cambridge: Cambridge University Press, 1991).

——, *Dignity and Practical Reason in Kant's Moral Theory* (Ithaca, NY: Cornell University Press, 1992).

——, 'Beneficence and self-love', *Social Philosophy and Policy* 10 (1993): 1–23.

——, 'Donagan's Kant', *Ethics* 104 (1993): 22–52.

——, 'Kant on punishment', *Jahrbuch für Recht und Ethik* 5 (1997): 291–314.

——, 'Kant on wrong-doing, desert, and punishment', *Law and Philosophy* 18 (1999): 407–441.

——, *Respect, Pluralism and Justice: Kantian Perspectives* (Oxford: Clarendon Press, 2000).

——, 'Hypothetical consent in Kantian constructivism', *Social Philosophy and Policy* 18,2 (2001): 300–329.

——, *Human Welfare and Moral Worth: Kantian Perspectives* (Oxford: Clarendon Press, 2002).

——, 'Kant and humanitarian intervention', *Philosophical Perspectives* 23,1 (2009): 221–240.

——, *Virtue, Rules, and Justice: Kantian Aspirations* (Oxford: Oxford University Press, 2012).

Hinman, L. M., 'On the purity of our moral motives', *Monist* 66 (1983): 251–267.

Hoche, H.-U. & M. Knoop, 'Logical relations between Kant's categorical imperative and the two golden rules', *Jahrbuch für Recht und Ethik / Annual Review of Law and Ethics* 18 (2010): 483–518.

Hodgson, L.-P., 'Kant on property rights and the state', *Kantian Review* 15,1 (2010): 57–87.

——, 'Kant on the right to freedom: A defense', *Ethics* 120 (2010): 791–819.

Höffe, O., 'Retaliatory punishment as a categorical imperative', *Rivista Internazionale di Filosofia del Diritto* 66 (1989): 633–658.

——, *Kant's Cosmopolitan Theory of Law and Peace* (Cambridge: Cambridge University Press, 2006 [2001]).

Höffe, O. (ed.), *Immanuel Kant: Metaphysische Anfangsgründe der Rechtslehre*, in the series *Klassiker Auslegen* (Berlin: Akademie Verlag, 1999).

Hopton, T., 'Kant's two theories of law', *History of Political Thought* 3 (1982): 51–76.

Holtman, S. W., 'A Kantian approach to prison reform', *Jahrbuch für Recht und Ethik* 5 (1997): 315–331.

——, 'Toward social reform', *Utilitas* 9 (1997): 3–21.

——, 'Kant, ideal theory and the justice of exclusionary zoning', *Ethics* 110 (1999): 32–58.

——, 'Kantian justice and poverty relief', *Kant-Studien* 95 (2004): 86–106.

——, 'Autonomy and the kingdom of ends', in T. E. Hill (ed.) (2009), pp. 102–118.

Hudson, H., 'Wille, Willkür, and the imputability of immoral actions', *Kant-Studien* 82 (1991): 179–196.

Hunter, I., 'Kant's regional cosmopolitanism', *Journal of the History of International Law* 12 (2010): 165–188.

Hutchings, K., *Kant, Critique and Politics* (London: Routledge, 1996).

Hutchings, P., *Kant on Absolute Value* (London: George Allen & Unwin, 1972).

Insole, C., *Kant and the Creation of Freedom: A Theological Problem* (Oxford: Oxford University Press, 2013).

Ion, D., *Kant and International Relations Theory* (Abingdon/New York: Routledge, 2012).

James, D. 'The role of evil in Kant's liberalism', *Inquiry* 55,3 (2012): 238–261.

James, D. N., 'Suicide and stoic ethics in the Doctrine of Virtue', *Kant-Studien* 90 (1999): 40–58.

Janaway, C., 'Necessity, responsibility and character: Schopenhauer on freedom of the will', *Kantian Review* 17,3 (2012): 431–457.

Jensen, D., 'Kant and a problem of motivation', *Journal of Value Inquiry* 46,1 (2012): 83–96.

Jensen, H., 'Kant and moral integrity', *Philosophical Studies* 57 (1989): 193–205.

Jeske, D., 'Perfection, happiness, and duties to self', *American Philosophical Quarterly* 33 (1996): 263–276.

Johnson, G., 'The tree of melancholy: Kant on philosophy and enthusiasm', in C. Firestone & S. Palmquist (eds) (2006), pp. 43–61.

Johnson, R., 'Kant's conception of merit', *Pacific Philosophical Quarterly* 77 (1996): 310–334.

——, 'Kant's conception of virtue', *Jahrbuch für Recht und Ethik* 5 (1997): 365–387.

——, 'Weakness incorporated', *History of Philosophy Quarterly* 15,3 (1998): 349–367.

Jones, H. E., *Kant's Principle of Personality* (Madison: University of Wisconsin Press, 1971).

Jones, W. T., *Morality and Freedom in the Philosophy of Kant* (Oxford: Oxford University Press, 1940).

Kahn, S., 'Can positive duties be derived from Kant's formula of universal law?, *Kantian Review* 19,1 (2014): 93–108.

Kain, P., 'Interpreting Kant's theory of divine commands', *Kantian Review* 9 (2005): 128–149.

Karatani, K., *Transcritique: On Kant and Marx* (Cambridge, MA: MIT Press, 2003).

Kaufman, A., *Welfare in the Kantian State* (Oxford: Clarendon Press, 1999).

——, 'Rawls and Kantian constructivism', *Kantian Review* 17,2 (2012): 227–256.

Keller, P., 'Ideas, freedom, and the ends of architectonic', *International Yearbook of German Idealism* 9 (2011): 51–78.

Kerstein, S. J., *Kant's Search for the Supreme Principle of Morality* (Cambridge: Cambridge University Press, 2002).

——, 'Treating others merely as means', *Utilitas* 21,2 (2009): 163–180.

Kersting, W., *Wohlgeordnete Freiheit. Immanuel Kants Rechts- und Staatsphilosophie*, third expanded edition (Paderborn: mentis, 2007).

Kitcher, P., 'Kant's argument for the categorical imperative', *Noûs* 38,4 (2004): 555–584.

Kleingeld, P., 'Kantian patriotism', *Philosophy and Public Affairs* 29,4 (2000): 313–341.

——, 'Approaching perpetual peace: Kant's defence of a league of states and his ideal of a world federation', *European Journal of Philosophy* 12,3 (2004): 304–325.

——, 'Kant's second thoughts on race', *The Philosophical Quarterly* 57, 229 (2007): 573–593.

——, 'Kant on historiography and the use of regulative ideas', *Studies in History and Philosophy of Science* Part A 39 (2008): 523–528.

——, *Kant and Cosmopolitanism* (Cambridge: Cambridge University Press, 2011).

Klimchuk, D., 'Three accounts of respect for persons in Kant's ethics', *Kantian Review* 8 (2004): 38–61.

Kong, C., 'The normative source of Kantian hypothetical imperatives', *International Journal of Philosophical Studies* 20,5 (2012): 661–690.

Korsgaard, C. M., 'Kant's formula of universal law', *Pacific Philosophical Quarterly* 66 (1985): 24–47.

——, *Creating the Kingdom of Ends* (Cambridge: Cambridge University Press, 1996).

——, *The Sources of Normativity*, ed. O. O'Neill (Cambridge: Cambridge University Press, 1996).

——, *Self-Constitution: Agency, Identity and Integrity* (Oxford: Oxford University Press, 2009).

Kotkas, T., 'Kant on the right of pardon: A necessity and ruler's personal forgiveness', *Kant-Studien* 102,4 (2011): 413–421.

Kuehn, M., 'Kant's transcendental deduction of God's existence as a postulate of pure practical reason', *Kant-Studien* 76,2 (1985): 152–169.

Lang, A. F., 'Kant and the supreme proprietor: a response', *Kantian Review* 15,2 (2010): 78–89.

Larmore, C., 'Kant and the meanings of autonomy', *International Yearbook of German Idealism* 9 (2011): 3–21.

La Rocca, C., 'Kant on self-knowledge and conscience', in D. Hüning et al. (eds) *Das Leben der Vernunft* (Berlin/New York: de Gruyter, 2013), pp. 364–385.

LeBar, M., 'Kant on welfare', *Canadian Journal of Philosophy* 29 (1999): 225–250.

Lee, S.-K., 'Self-determination and the categories of freedom in Kant's moral philosophy', *Kant-Studien* 103,3 (2012): 337–350.

Lind, D., 'Kant on capital punishment', *Journal of Philosophical Research* 19 (1994): 61–74.

Linden, H. v. d., *Kantian Ethics and Socialism* (Indianapolis: Hackett, 1988).

Lloyd, T. D., 'Kantian and utilitarian democracy', *Canadian Journal of Philosophy* 10 (1980): 395–413.

Lo, P. C., *Treating Persons as Ends* (Lanham, MD/New York: University Press of America, 1987).

Louden, R. B., 'Kant's virtue ethics', *Philosophy* 61 (1986): 473–489.

——, *Kant's Impure Ethics* (Oxford: Clarendon Press, 2000).

——, *Kant's Human Being* (New York: Oxford University Press, 2011).

Lowe, C.-Y., 'Kant's social contract: A new transcendental principle in political philosophy', *Kant Yearbook* 4 (2012): 91–112.

Lukow, P., 'The fact of reason', *Kant-Studien* 84 (1993): 204–221.

MacBeath, A. M., 'Kant on moral feeling', *Kant-Studien* 64 (1973): 283–314.

Madore, J., *Difficult Freedom and Radical Evil in Kant* (London/New York: Continuum, 2011).

Mahon, J. E., 'Kant and the perfect duty to others not to lie', *British Journal for the History of Philosophy* 14,4 (2006): 653–685.

Maliks, R., 'Revolutionary epigones: Kant and his radical followers', *History of Political Thought* 33,4 (2012): 647–671.

——, 'Kant, the state, and revolution', *Kantian Review* 18,1 (2013): 29–47.

——, *Kant's Politics in Context* (Oxford: Oxford University Press, 2014).

Marina, J., 'Making sense of Kant's highest good', *Kant-Studien* 91,3 (2000): 329–355.

Martin, C., 'Emotion in Kant's moral philosophy', *Philosophical Studies* 27 (1980): 16–28.

——, 'Education without moral worth? Kantian moral theory and the obligation to educate others', *Journal of Philosophy of Education* 45,3 (2011): 475–492.

Massey, S. J., 'Kant on self-respect', *Journal of the History of Philosophy* 21 (1983): 57–73.

May, T. G., 'Kant the liberal, Kant the anarchist', *Southern Journal of Philosophy* 28 (1990): 525–538.

McCarthy, M., 'Kant's application of the analytic/synthetic distinction to imperatives', *Dialogue* 18 (1979): 373–391.

——, 'Kant's rejection of the argument of Groundwork III', *Kant-Studien* 73,2 (1982): 169–190.

——, 'The objection of circularity in Groundwork III', *Kant-Studien* 76 (1985): 28–42.

McCarty, R., 'The limits of Kantian duty, and beyond', *American Philosophical Quarterly* 26 (1989): 43–52.

——, 'Moral conflicts in Kantian ethics', *History of Philosophy Quarterly* 8 (1991): 65–79.

——, 'Kantian moral motivation and the feeling of respect', *Journal of the History of Philosophy* 31 (1993): 421–435.

——, 'Motivation and moral choice in Kant's theory of rational agency', *Kant-Studien* 85 (1994): 15–31.

——, *Kant's Theory of Action* (Oxford: Clarendon Press, 2009).

——, 'Kant's derivation of the formula of universal law', *Dialogue* 49 (2010): 113–133.

McKenzie, N., 'The primacy of practical reason in Kant's system', *Idealistic Studies* 15 (1985): 199–217.

McMullin, I., 'Kant on radical evil and the origin of moral responsibility', *Kantian Review* 18,1 (2013): 49–72.

Merle, J. C., 'A Kantian critique of Kant's theory of punishment', *Law and Philosophy* 19 (2000): 311–338.

——, 'A Kantian argument for a duty to donate one's own organs: a reply to Nicole Gerrand', *Journal of Applied Philosophy* 17 (2000): 93–101.

Merritt, M., 'Kant on enlightened moral pedagogy', *Southern Journal of Philosophy* 49,3 (2011): 227–253.

Meyer, M., 'Kant's concept of dignity and modern political thought', *History of European Ideas* 8 (1987): 319–332.

Michalson, G. E., Jr., 'Moral regeneration and divine aid in Kant', *Religious Studies* 25 (1989): 259–270.

——, *Fallen Freedom: Kant on Radical Evil and Moral Regeneration* (Cambridge: Cambridge University Press, 1990).

——, *Kant and the Problem of God* (Oxford/Malden, MA: Blackwell, 1999).

Mikalsen, K., 'Testimony and Kant's idea of public reason', *Res Publica* 16 (2010): 23–40.

——, 'In defense of Kant's league of states', *Law and Philosophy* 30,3 (2011): 291–317.

——, 'Kant and Habermas on international law', *Ratio Juris* 26,2 (2013): 302–324.

Mikkola, M., 'Kant on moral agency and women's nature', *Kantian Review* 16,1 (2011): 89–111.

Miller, D., 'Property and territory: Locke, Kant, and Steiner', *Journal of Political Philosophy* 19,1 (2011): 90–109.

Milstein, B., 'Kantian cosmopolitanism beyond "Perpetual Peace": Commercium, critique, and the cosmopolitan problematic', *European Journal of Philosophy* 21,1 (2013): 118–143.

Minogue, K., 'Locke, Kant, and the foundations of liberalism', in M. P. Thompson (ed.), *John Locke und Immanuel Kant* (Berlin: Duncker & Humboldt, 1991), pp. 269–283.

Moore, A. W., *Noble in Reason, Infinite in Faculty: Themes and Variations in Kant's Moral and Religious Philosophy* (London: Routledge, 2003).

Moran, K. 'Can Kant have an account of moral education?', *Journal of Philosophy of Education* 43,4 (2009): 471–484.

——, *Community and Progress in Kant's Moral Philosophy* (Washington DC: Catholic University of America Press, 2012).

Morgan, D. & G. Banham (eds), *Cosmopolitics and the Emergence of a Future* (Basingstoke/New York: Palgrave Macmillan, 2007).

Muchnik, P., *Kant's Theory of Evil* (Lanham, MD: Lexington, 2009).

Mulholland, L., 'Kant: on willing maxims to become laws of nature', *Dialogue* 17 (1978): 92–105.

——, 'Kant on war and international justice', *Kant-Studien* 78 (1987): 25–41.

——, *Kant's System of Rights* (New York: Columbia University Press, 1990).

——, 'The difference between private and public law', *Jahrbuch für Recht und Ethik* 1 (1993): 113–158.

Munzel, G. F., *Kant's Conception of Moral Character* (Chicago: University of Chicago Press, 1999).

——, *Kant's Conception of Pedagogy: Toward Education for Freedom* (Evanston, IL: Northwestern University Press, 2012).

Munzer, S. R., 'Kant and property rights in body parts', *Canadian Journal of Law and Jurisprudence* 6 (1993): 319–341.

Murphy, J. G., 'The highest good as content for Kant's ethical formalism: Beck versus Silber', *Kant-Studien* 56 (1965): 102–110.

——, *Kant: The Philosophy of Right* (London: Macmillan, 1970).

——, 'Moral death: a Kantian essay on psychopathy', *Ethics* 82 (1972): 284–298.

——, 'Hume and Kant on the social contract', *Philosophical Studies* 33 (1978): 65–79.

——, 'Does Kant have a theory of punishment?', *Columbia Law Review* 87 (1987): 509–532.

Nakhnikian, G., 'Kantian universalizability and the objectivity of moral judgments', in N. Potter & M. Timmons (eds), *Morality and Universality* (Dordrecht: D. Reidel, 1985), pp. 187–233.

——, 'Kant's theory of hypothetical imperatives', *Kant-Studien* 83 (1992): 21–49.

Neculau, R., 'Does Kant's rejection of the right to resist make him a legal rigorist?', *Kantian Review* 13,2 (2008): 107–140.

Negretto, G. L., 'Kant and the illusion of collective security', *Journal of International Affairs* 46,2 (1993): 501–523.

Nell, O., *Acting on Principle: An Essay on Kantian Ethics* (New York: Columbia University Press, 1975).

Niesen, P., *Kants Theorie der Redefreiheit* (Baden-Baden: Nomos, 2008).

Noggle, R., 'Kantian respect and particular persons', *Canadian Journal of Philosophy* 29 (1999): 449–477.

Nuyen, A. T., 'Sense, passions and morals in Hume and Kant', *Kant-Studien* 82 (1991): 29–41.

——, 'Counting the formulas of the categorical imperative', *History of Philosophy Quarterly* 10 (1993): 37–48.

——, 'The heart of the Kantian moral agent', *American Catholic Philosophical Quarterly* 69 (1995): 51–62.

O'Connell, E., 'Happiness proportioned to virtue: Kant and the highest good', *Kantian Review* 17,2 (2012): 257–279.

O'Neill, O., *Constructions of Reason: Explorations of Kant's Practical Philosophy* (Cambridge: Cambridge University Press, 1990).

——, 'Vindicating reason', in P. Guyer (ed.) (1992), pp. 280–308.

——, 'Kant's virtues', in R. Crisp (ed.), *How Should One Live? Essays on the Virtues* (Oxford: Clarendon Press, 1996), pp. 77–97.

——, 'Political liberalism and public reason', *The Philosophical Review* 106 (1997): 411–428.

——, *Bounds of Justice* (Cambridge: Cambridge University Press, 2000).

——, 'Instituting principles: between duty and action', in M. Timmons (ed.) (2002), pp. 331–348.

——, 'Constructivism in Rawls and Kant', in S. Freeman (ed.), *The Cambridge Companion to Rawls* (Cambridge: Cambridge University Press, 2003), pp. 347–367.

Onof, C., 'A framework for the derivation and reconstruction of the categorical imperative', *Kant-Studien* 89 (1998): 410–427.

——, 'Moral worth and inclinations in Kantian ethics', *Kant Studies Online* (2011): 1–46.

Orend, B., 'Kant's just war theory', *Journal of the History of Philosophy* 37 (1999): 323–353.

Packer, M., 'The highest good in Kant's psychology of motivation', *Idealistic Studies* 13 (1983): 110–119.

——, 'Kant on desire and moral pleasure', *Journal of the History of Ideas* 50,3 (1989): 429–442.

Palmquist, S., 'Does Kant reduce religion to morality?', *Kant-Studien* 83 (1992): 129–148.

Palmquist, S. & S. Otterman, 'The implied standpoint of Kant's *Religion*', *Kantian Review* 18,1 (2013): 73–97.

Papish, L., 'The cultivation of sensibility in Kant's moral philosophy', *Kantian Review* 12,2 (2007): 128–146.

Pasternack, L. 'The development and scope of Kantian belief: The highest good, the practical postulates and the fact of reason', *Kant-Studien* 102,3 (2011): 290–315.

——, 'Kant on the debt of sin', *Faith and Philosophy* 29,1 (2012): 30–52.

——, *Kant's Religion within the Boundaries of Mere Reason* (London/ New York: Routledge, 2013).

Paton, H. J., *The Categorical Imperative* (Philadelphia: University of Pennsylvania Press, 1947).

——, 'Kant on friendship', *Proceedings of the British Academy* 42 (1956): 45–66.

——, 'Conscience and Kant', *Kant-Studien* 70 (1979): 239–251.

Penner, J., 'The state duty to support the poor in Kant's Doctrine of Right', *British*

Journal of Politics & International Relations 12 (2010): 88–110.

Pereboom, D., 'Kant on transcendental freedom', Philosophy and Phenomenological Research 73,3 (2006): 537–567.

Pinheiro Walla, A., 'Human nature and the right to coerce in Kant's Doctrine of Right', Archiv für Geschichte der Philosophie 96,1 (2014): 126–139.

Piper, A., 'Kant's self-legislation procedure reconsidered', Kant Studies Online 2012: 203–277.

——, 'Kant's two solutions to the free rider problem', Kant Yearbook 4 (2012): 113–142.

Pippin, R. B., 'On the moral foundations of Kant's Rechtslehre', in R. Pippin, Idealism as Modernism (Cambridge: Cambridge University Press, 1997), pp. 56–91.

——, 'Mine and thine? The Kantian state', in P. Guyer (ed.) (2006), pp. 416–446.

Pogge, T. W., 'The Kantian interpretation of justice as fairness', Zeitschrift für philosophische Forschung 35 (1981): 47–65.

——, 'Kant's theory of justice', Kant-Studien 79 (1988): 407–433.

——, 'Is Kant's Rechtslehre comprehensive?', Southern Journal of Philosophy XXXVI, Supplement (1997): 161–187.

Potter, N., 'How to apply the categorical imperative', Philosophia 5 (1975): 395–416.

——, 'Kant on ends that are at the same time duties', Pacific Philosophical Quarterly 66 (1985): 78–92.

——, 'What is wrong with Kant's four examples?', Journal of Philosophical Research 18 (1993): 213–229.

——, 'Kant on obligation and motivation in law and ethics', Jahrbuch für Recht und Ethik 2 (1994): 95–112.

——, 'Kant and the moral worth of actions', Southern Journal of Philosophy 34 (1996): 225–241.

Rauscher, F., 'Kant's moral anti-realism', Journal of the History of Philosophy 40,4 (2002): 477–499.

Rawls, J., A Theory of Justice (Oxford: Oxford University Press, 1971).

——, 'Kantian constructivism in moral theory', The Journal of Philosophy 77 (1980): 515–572.

Reardon, B., Kant as Philosophical Theologian (Basingstoke: Macmillan, 1988).

Reath, A., 'The categorical imperative and Kant's conception of practical rationality', Monist 72 (1989): 384–410.

——, 'Kant's theory of moral sensibility. Respect for the moral law and the influence of inclination', Kant-Studien 80 (1989): 284–302.

——, 'Agency and the imputation of consequences in Kant's ethics', Jahrbuch für Recht und Ethik 2 (1994): 213–229.

——, 'Value and law in Kant's moral theory', Ethics 114 (2003): 127–155.

——, Agency and Autonomy in Kant's Moral Theory: Selected Essays (Oxford: Clarendon Press, 2006).

——, 'Will, obligatory ends and the completion of practical reason: comments on Barbara Herman's Moral Literacy', Kantian Review 16,1 (2011): 1–15.

Reid, J., 'Morality and sensibility in Kant', Kantian Review 8 (2004): 89–114.

Richards, D. A., Jr., 'Kantian ethics and the harm principle', Columbia Law Review 87 (1987): 457–471.

Riley, P., *Kant's Political Philosophy* (Totona: Rowman & Littlefield, 1983).

Ripstein, A., 'Authority and coercion', *Philosophy and Public Affairs* 32 (2004): 2–35.

——, *Force and Freedom: Kant's Legal and Political Philosophy* (Cambridge, MA: Harvard University Press, 2009).

——, 'Form and matter in Kantian political philosophy: A reply', *European Journal of Philosophy* 20,3 (2012): 487–496.

Rollin, B., 'There is only one categorical imperative', *Kant-Studien* 67 (1976): 60–72.

Rosen, A. D., *Kant's Theory of Justice* (Ithaca, NY: Cornell University Press, 1993).

Rosenkoetter, T., 'Kant on construction, apriority, and the moral relevance of universalization', *British Journal for the History of Philosophy* 19,6 (2011): 1143–1174.

Ross, D., *Kant's Ethical Theory* (Oxford: Clarendon Press, 1954).

Rossi, P., *The Social Authority of Reason. Kant's Critique, Radical Evil, and the Destiny of Humankind* (Albany, NY: SUNY Press, 2005).

Rossvaer, V., *Kant's Moral Philosophy* (Oslo: Universitetsforlaget, 1979).

Rumsey, J. P., 'The development of character in Kantian moral theory', *Journal of the History of Philosophy* 27 (1989): 247–265.

——, 'Agency, human nature, and character in Kantian theory', *Journal of Value Inquiry* 24 (1990): 109–121.

Sadler, B., 'Marriage: A matter of right or of virtue? Kant and the contemporary debate', *Journal of Social Philosophy* 44,3 (2013): 213–232.

Samet, I., 'The form of evil', *Kantian Review* 14,2 (2010): 93–117.

Sargentis, K., 'Moral motivation in Kant', *Kant Studies Online* (2012): 93–121.

Schaller, W. E., 'Kant on virtue and moral worth', *Southern Journal of Philosophy* 25 (1987): 559–573.

——, 'Kant's architectonic of duties', *Philosophy and Phenomenological Research* 48 (1987): 299–314.

——, 'Should Kantians care about moral worth?', *Dialogue* 32 (1993): 25–40.

——, 'From the *Groundwork* to the *Metaphysics of Morals*', *History of Philosophy Quarterly* 12 (1995): 333–345.

——, 'Kant on right and moral rights', *Southern Journal of Philosophy* 38 (2000): 321–342.

Schapiro, T., 'Kantian rigorism and mitigating circumstances', *Ethics* 117,1 (2006): 32–57.

——, 'Foregrounding desire: A defense of Kant's incorporation thesis', *Journal of Ethics* 15,3 (2011): 147–167.

Scheid, D., 'Kant's retributivism', *Ethics* 93 (1983): 262–282.

——, 'Kant's retributivism again', *Archiv für Rechts- und Sozialphilosophie* 72 (1986): 224–230.

Sherline, E., 'Heteronomy and spurious principles of morality in Kant's *Groundwork*', *Pacific Philosophical Quarterly* 76 (1995): 32–46.

Schönecker, D., 'Once again: What is the 'first proposition' in Kant's *Groundwork*? Some refinements, a new proposal, and a reply to Henry Allison', *Kantian Review* 17,2 (2012): 281–296.

——, 'Kant's moral intuitionism: the fact of reason and moral predispositions', *Kant Studies Online* (2013): 1–38.

Schwarzchild, S. S., 'Kantianism on the death penalty (and related social problems)', *Archiv für Rechts- und Sozialphilosophie* 71 (1985): 343–372.

Scutt, M. Z., 'Kant's moral theology', *British Journal for the History of Philosophy* 18,4 (2010): 611–634.

Seckar, B. 'The appearance of deontology in contemporary Kantianism', *Journal of Medicine and Philosophy* 24 (1999): 43–66.

Sedgwick, S., 'On the relation of pure reason to content: a reply to Hegel's critique of formalism in Kant's ethics', *Philosophy and Phenomenological Research* 49 (1988): 59–80.

——, 'On lying and the role of content in Kant's ethics', *Kant-Studien* 82 (1991): 42–62.

——, '"Letting the phenomena in": on how Herman's Kantianism does and does not answer the empty formalism critique', *Kantian Review* 16,1 (2011): 33–47.

Seel, G., 'How does Kant justify the universal objective validity of the law of right?', *International Journal of Philosophical Studies* 17,1 (2009): 71–94.

Sensen, O., 'Kant's conception of human dignity', *Kant-Studien* 100,3 (2009): 309–331.

——, 'Kant's conception of inner value', *European Journal of Philosophy* 19,2 (2011): 262–280.

——, *Kant on Human Dignity* (Berlin/New York: de Gruyter, 2011).

——, 'The role of feelings in Kant's moral philosophy', *Studi kantiani* XXV (2012): 45–58.

Shell, S. M., *The Rights of Reason* (Toronto: University of Toronto Press, 1980).

——, *The Embodiment of Reason: Kant on Spirit, Generation, and Community* (Chicago: University of Chicago Press, 1996).

——, 'Kant on punishment', *Kantian Review* 1 (1997): 115–135.

——, *Kant and the Limits of Autonomy* (Cambridge, MA: Harvard University Press, 2009).

——, '"Nachschrift eines Freundes"': Kant on language, friendship and the concept of a people', *Kantian Review* 15,1 (2010): 88–117.

Sherman, N., 'Reasons and feelings in Kantian morality', *Philosophy and Phenomenological Research* 55 (1995): 369–377.

——, *Making A Necessity of Virtue: Aristotle and Kant on Virtue* (Cambridge: Cambridge University Press, 1997).

——, 'Concrete Kantian respect', *Social Philosophy and Policy* 15 (1998): 119–148.

Silber J. R., 'The Copernican revolution in ethics: the good reexamined', *Kant-Studien* 51 (1959): 85–101.

——, 'Kant's conception of the highest good as immanent and transcendent', *The Philosophical Review* 68 (1959): 469–492.

——, 'The metaphysical importance of the highest good as the canon of pure reason in Kant's moral philosophy', *Texas Studies in Language and Literature* 1 (1959): 233–244.

——, 'The importance of the highest good in Kant's ethics', *Ethics* 73 (1962–3): 179–197.

——, 'Procedural formalism in Kant's ethics', *Review of Metaphysics* 28 (1974): 197–236.

——, 'The moral good and the natural good in Kant's ethics', *Review of Metaphysics* 36 (1982): 397–437.

———, *Kant's Ethics: The Good, Freedom and the Will* (Berlin/New York: de Gruyter, 2012).

Simmons, K., 'Kant on moral worth', *History of Philosophy Quarterly* 6 (1989): 85–100.

Singer, M. G., 'The categorical imperative', *The Philosophical Review* 63 (1954): 577–591.

———, *Generalization in Ethics* (New York: Alfred A. Knopf, 1961).

———, 'Reconstructing the Groundwork', *Ethics* 93 (1983): 566–578.

Siyar, J., 'The conditionality of hypothetical imperatives', *Kantian Review* 18,3 (2013): 439–460.

Skorpen, E., 'Making sense of Kant's third example', *Kant-Studien* 72 (1981): 415–429.

Smit, H. & M. Timmons, 'The moral significance of gratitude in Kant's ethics', *Southern Journal of Philosophy* 49,4 (2011): 295–320.

Sneddon, A., 'A new Kantian response to maxim-fiddling', *Kantian Review* 16,1 (2011): 67–88.

Sorensen, K., 'Kant's taxonomy of the emotions', *Kantian Review* 6 (2002): 109–128.

Stark, C. A., 'The rationality of valuing oneself', *Journal of the History of Philosophy* 35 (1997): 65–82.

Stern, D. S., 'Autonomy and political obligation in Kant', *Southern Journal of Philosophy* 29 (1991): 127–148.

Stern, P., 'The problem of history and temporality in Kantian ethics', *Review of Metaphysics* 39 (1986): 504–545.

Stern, R. 'Moral scepticism and agency: Kant and Korsgaard', *Ratio* 23 (2010): 453–474.

Stevens, R., *Kant on Moral Practice* (Macon, GA: Mercer University Press, 1981).

Stohr, K., 'Kantian beneficence and the problem of obligatory aid', *Journal of Moral Philosophy* 8 (2011): 45–67.

Stratton–Lake, P., 'Formulating categorical imperatives', *Kant-Studien* 84 (1993): 317–340.

———, *Kant, Duty and Moral Worth* (London: Routledge, 2000).

Sullivan, R. J., *Immanuel Kant's Moral Theory* (Cambridge: Cambridge University Press, 1989).

———, 'The positive role of prudence in the virtuous life', *Jahrbuch für Recht und Ethik* 5 (1997): 461–470.

———, 'How Bernard Williams constructed his critique of Kant's moral theory', *Kantian Review* 3 (1999): 106–113.

Surprenant, C. W., 'Cultivating virtue: moral progress and the Kantian state', *Kantian Review* 12 (2007): 90–112.

———, 'Kant's postulate of the immortality of the soul', *International Philosophical Quarterly* 48 (2008): 85–98.

———, 'Liberty, autonomy, and Kant's civil society', *History of Philosophy Quarterly* 27 (2010): 79–94.

———, *Kant and the Cultivation of Virtue* (Abingdon/New York: Routledge, 2014).

Sussman, D., *The Idea of Humanity. Anthropology and Anthroponomy in Kant's Ethics* (London/New York: Routledge, 2001).

———, 'Kantian forgiveness', *Kant-Studien* 96,1 (2005): 85–107.

———, 'Shame and punishment in Kant's Doctrine of Right', *Philosophical Quarterly* 58,231 (2008): 299–317.

Sutch, P., 'Kantians and cosmopolitans', *Kantian Review* 4 (2000): 98–120.

Svoboda, T., 'Duties regarding nature: A Kantian approach to environmental ethics', *Kant Yearbook* 4 (2012): 143–164.

Sweet, K., *Kant on Practical Life: From Duty to History* (Cambridge: Cambridge University Press, 2013).

Swoyer, C., 'Kantian derivations', *Canadian Journal of Philosophy* 13 (1983): 409–431.

Taylor, C., 'Kant's theory of freedom', in J. N. Gray & Z. Pelczynski (eds), *Conceptions of Liberty in Political Philosophy* (New York: St Martin's Press, 1984), pp. 100–121.

Tenenbaum, S., 'The idea of freedom and moral cognition in *Groundwork* III', *Philosophy and Phenomenological Research* 84,3 (2012): 555–589.

Téson, F., 'The Kantian theory of international law', *Columbia Law Review* 92 (1992): 53–102.

Thomason, K., 'Shame and contempt in Kant's moral theory', *Kantian Review* 18,2 (2013): 221–240.

Timmermann, J., 'When the tail wags the dog: Animal welfare and indirect duty in Kantian ethics', *Kantian Review* 10,1 (2005): 128–149.

——, 'Value without regress: Kant's "formula of humanity" revisited', *European Journal of Philosophy* 14 (2006): 69–93.

——, 'Kant on conscience, "indirect" duty and moral error', *International Philosophical Quarterly* 46 (2006): 293–308.

——, *Kant's Groundwork of the Metaphysics of Morals: A Commentary* (Cambridge: Cambridge University Press, 2007).

——, 'Acting from duty: inclination, reason and moral worth', in J. Timmermann (ed.) (2009), pp. 45–62.

——, 'Kantian dilemmas? Moral conflict in Kant's ethical theory', *Archiv für*

Geschichte der Philosophie 95,1 (2013): 36–64.

Timmons, M., 'Contradictions and the categorical imperative', *Archiv für Geschichte der Philosophie* 66 (1984): 294–312.

——, 'Kant and the possibility of moral motivation', *Southern Journal of Philosophy* 23 (1985): 377–398.

——, 'Necessitation and justification in Kant's ethics', *Canadian Journal of Philosophy* 22 (1992): 223–261.

——, 'Decision procedures, moral criteria, and the problem of relevant descriptions in Kant's ethics', *Jahrbuch für Recht und Ethik* 5 (1997): 389–417.

Tunick, M., 'Is Kant a retributivist?', *History of Political Thought* 17 (1996): 60–78.

Uleman, J., 'On Kant, infanticide, and finding oneself in a state of nature', *Zeitschrift für philosophische Forschung* 54 (2000): 173–195.

Vandenauweele, D., 'The Lutheran influence on Kant's depraved will', *International Journal for Philosophy of Religion* 73,2 (2013): 117–134.

Varden, H., 'Kant and dependency relations: Kant on the state's right to redistribute resources to protect the rights of dependents', *Dialogue* 45,2 (2006): 257–284.

——, 'Kant's non-voluntarist conception of political obligations: why justice is impossible in the state of nature', *Kantian Review* 13,2 (2008): 1–45.

——, 'Kant and lying to the murderer at the door . . . One more time: Kant's legal philosophy and lies to murderers and nazis', *Journal of Social Philosophy* 41,4 (2010): 403–421.

——, 'Kant's non-absolutist conception of political legitimacy: how public right "concludes" private right in the Doctrine of Right', *Kant-Studien* 101,3 (2010): 331–351.

——, 'A Kantian critique of the care tradition: family law and systemic justice', *Kantian Review* 17,2 (2012): 327–356.

Velkley, R. L., *Freedom and the End of Reason* (Chicago: University of Chicago Press, 1989).

Verhaegh, M., 'Property by agreement: interpreting Kant's account of right', *British Journal for the History of Philosophy* 14,4 (2006): 687–717.

Vilhauer, B., 'The scope of responsibility in Kant's theory of free will', *British Journal for the History of Philosophy* 18 (2010): 45–71.

Voeller, C., *The Metaphysics of the Moral Law: Kant's Deduction of Freedom* (New York: Routledge, 2001).

Ward, A., 'On Kant's defence of moral freedom', *History of Philosophy Quarterly* 8 (1991): 373–386.

Ware, O., 'The duty of self-knowledge', *Philosophy and Phenomenological Research* 79,3 (2009): 671–698.

Watson, S. H., 'Kant on autonomy, the ends of humanity, and the possibility of morality', *Kant-Studien* 77 (1986): 165–182.

Weinrib, E. J., 'Law as a Kantian idea of reason', *Columbia Law Review* 87,3 (1987): 472–508.

Weinstock, D. M., 'Natural law and public reason in Kant's political philosophy', *Canadian Journal of Philosophy* 26 (1996): 389–411.

Westphal, K. R., 'Kant on the state, law, and obedience to authority in the alleged "anti-revolutionary" writings', *Journal of Philosophical Research* 17 (1992): 383–426.

——, 'Republicanism, despotism, and obedience to the state', *Jahrbuch für*

Recht und Ethik/Annual Review of Law and Ethics 1 (1993): 263–281.

——, 'How "full" is Kant's categorical imperative?', *Jahrbuch für Recht und Ethik/Annual Review of Law and Ethics* 3 (1995): 465–509.

—— 'Do Kant's principles justify property or usufruct?', *Jahrbuch für Recht und Ethik/Annual Review of Law and Ethics* 5 (1997): 141–194.

White, M., 'Adam Smith and Immanuel Kant: On markets, duties, and moral sentiments', *Forum for Social Economics* 39 (2010): 53–60.

——, *Kantian Ethics and Economics* (Stanford: Stanford University Press, 2011).

Wiggins, D., 'Categorical requirements: Kant and Hume on the idea of duty', *Monist* 74 (1991): 83–106.

Wike, V. S., 'Metaphysical foundations of morality in Kant', *Journal of Value Inquiry* 17 (1983): 225–233.

——, 'Does Kant's ethics require that the moral law be the sole determining ground of the will?', *Journal of Value Inquiry* 27 (1993): 85–92.

——, *Kant on Happiness in Ethics* (Albany, NY: SUNY Press, 1994).

——, 'Defending Kant against Noddings' care ethics critique', *Kant Studies Online* (2011): 1–26.

Wike, V. & R. Showler, 'Kant's concept of the highest good and the archetype-ectype distinction', *Journal of Value Inquiry* 44 (2010): 521–533.

Willaschek, M., 'Why the Doctrine of Right does not belong in the *Metaphysics of Morals*', *Jahrbuch für Recht und Ethik/Annual Review of Law and Ethics* 5 (1997): 205–227.

——, 'Right and coercion. Can Kant's conception of right be derived from his moral theory?', *International Journal of Philosophical Studies* 17,1 (2009): 49–70.

——, 'The non-derivability of Kantian right from the categorical imperative: A response to Nance', *International Journal of Philosophical Studies* 20,4 (2012): 557–564.

Williams, G., 'Between ethics and right: Kantian politics and democratic purposes', *European Journal of Philosophy* 20,3 (2012): 479–486.

Williams, H., *Kant's Political Philosophy* (Oxford: Blackwell, 1983).

——, 'Kant, Rawls, Habermas and the metaphysics of justice', *Kantian Review* 3 (1999): 1–17.

——, *Kant's Critique of Hobbes* (Cardiff: University of Wales Press, 2003).

——, 'Towards a Kantian theory of international distributive justice', *Kantian Review* 15,2 (2010): 43–77.

——, *Kant and the End of War: A Critique of Just War Theory* (Basingstoke/New York: Palgrave Macmillan, 2012).

Williams, T. C., *The Concept of the Categorical Imperative* (Oxford: Clarendon Press, 1968).

Wilson, E. E., 'Kant on autonomy and the value of persons', *Kantian Review* 18,2 (2013): 241–262.

Wilson, H., *Kant's Pragmatic Anthropology: Its Origin, Meaning and Critical Significance* (Albany, NY: SUNY Press, 2006).

Wolterstorff, N., 'Is it possible and desirable for theologians to recover from Kant?', in N. Wolterstorff, *Inquiring about God. Selected Essays, volume 1* (Cambridge: Cambridge University Press, 2010), pp. 35–55.

——, 'Conundrums in Kant's rational religion', in N. Wolterstorff, *Inquiring about God. Selected Essays, volume 1*

(Cambridge: Cambridge University Press, 2010), pp. 56–67.

Wood, A., *Kant's Moral Religion* (Ithaca, NY: Cornell University Press, 1970).

——, 'The emptiness of the moral will', *The Monist* 72 (1989): 454–483.

——, 'Unsocial sociability: the anthropological basis of Kantian ethics', *Philosophical Topics* 19 (1991): 325–351.

——, *Kant's Ethical Thought* (Cambridge: Cambridge University Press, 1999).

——, 'The supreme principle of morality', in P. Guyer (ed.) (2006), pp. 342–380.

——, *Kantian Ethics* (Cambridge: Cambridge University Press, 2008).

Wolff, R. W., *The Autonomy of Reason* (New York: Harper & Row, 1973).

Wuerth, J., 'Sense and sensibility in Kant's practical agent: Against the intellectualism of Korsgaard and Sidgwick', *European Journal of Philosophy* 21,1 (2013): 1–36.

——, *Kant on Mind, Action, and Ethics* (Oxford: Oxford University Press, 2014).

Wunsch, M., 'The activity of sensibility in Kant's anthropology', *Kant Yearbook* 3 (2011): 67–90.

Wyrwich, T., 'From gratification to justice. The tension between anthropology and pure practical reason in Kant's conception(s) of the highest good', *Kant Yearbook* 3 (2011): 91–106.

Yost, B. S., 'Kant's justification of the death penalty reconsidered', *Kantian Review* 15,2 (2010): 1–27.

Yovel, Y., *Kant and the Philosophy of History* (Princeton: Princeton University Press, 1980).

Ypi, L., '*Natura Daedala Rerum?* On the justification of historical progress in Kant's guarantee of perpetual peace', *Kantian Review* 14,2 (2010): 118–148.

Zinkin, M., 'Respect for the law and the use of dynamical terms in Kant's theory of moral motivation', *Archiv für Geschichte der Philosophie* 88,1 (2006): 31–53.

Zinkstok, J., 'Anthropology, empirical psychology, and applied logic', *Kant Yearbook* 3 (2011): 107–130.

Zöller, G., 'Kant's political anthropology', *Kant Yearbook* 3 (2011): 131–161.

9. KANT'S THIRD *CRITIQUE*, AESTHETICS AND TELEOLOGY

Allison, H. E., *Kant's Theory of Taste* (Cambridge: Cambridge University Press, 2001).

——, 'Kant's antinomy of teleological judgment', *Southern Journal of Philosophy* 30 (supplement) (1992): 25–42.

——, 'Reflective judgment and the application of logic to nature', in H. J. Glock (ed.) (2003), pp. 169–184.

Ameriks, K., 'Kant and the objectivity of taste', *British Journal of Aesthetics* 23 (1983): 3–17.

Auxter, T., *Kant's Moral Teleology* (Macon, GA: Mercer University Press, 1982).

Banham, G., *Kant and the Ends of Aesthetics* (London: Macmillan, 2000).

Baxley, A. M., 'The practical significance of taste in Kant's *Critique of Judgment*', *The Journal of Aesthetics and Art Criticism* 63,1 (2005): 33–45.

Beisbart, C., 'Kant's characterization of natural ends', *Kant Yearbook* 1 (2009): 1–30.

Breitenbach, A., 'Two views on nature: A solution to Kant's antinomy of mechanism and teleology', *British Journal for the History of Philosophy* 16 (2008): 351–369.

——, 'Mechanical explanation of nature and its limits in Kant's *Critique of Judgment*', *Studies in History and Philosophy of Biological and Biomedical Science* 37 (2006): 694–711.

——, 'Teleology in biology: a Kantian perspective', *Kant Yearbook* 1 (2009): 31–56.

——, 'Aesthetics in science: A Kantian proposal', *Proceedings of the Aristotelian Society* 113 (2013): 83–100.

——, 'Biological purposiveness and analogical reflection', in I. Goy & E. Watkins (eds), *Kant's Theory of Biology* (Berlin/New York: de Gruyter, 2014), pp. 131–148.

Brittan, G., Jr., 'Systematicity and objectivity in the third *Critique*', *Southern Journal of Philosophy* 30 (1990): 167–186.

Bruno, P., *Kant's Concept of Genius. Its Origin and Function in the Third Critique* (London/New York: Continuum, 2010).

Burnham, D., *An Introduction to Kant's Critique of Judgment* (Edinburgh: University of Edinburgh Press, 2000).

Butts, R. E., 'Teleology and scientific method in Kant's *Critique of Judgment*', *Noûs* 24 (1990): 1–16.

——, 'Kant's theory of musical sound', *Dialogue* 32 (1993): 3–24.

Cannon, J., 'The moral value of artistic beauty in Kant', *Kantian Review* 16,1 (2011): 113–126.

——, 'Reply to Paul Guyer', *Kantian Review* 16,1 (2011): 135–139.

Caranti, L., 'Logical purposiveness and the principle of taste', *Kant-Studien* 96,3 (2005): 364–374.

Cassirer, H. W., *A Commentary on Kant's Critique of Judgment* (London: Methuen, 1938).

Cheetham, M. A., *Kant, Art, and Art History* (Cambridge: Cambridge University Press, 2001).

Chignell, A., 'Beauty as a symbol of natural systematicity', *British Journal of Aesthetics* 46,4 (2006): 406–415.

——, 'Kant on the normativity of taste: The role of aesthetic ideas', *Australasian Journal of Philosophy* 85,3 (2007): 415–433.

Clewis, R., *The Kantian Sublime and the Revelation of Freedom* (Cambridge: Cambridge University Press, 2009).

Cohen, A., 'Kant on the possibility of ugliness', *British Journal of Aesthetics* 53,2 (2013): 199–209.

Cohen, T., 'Three problems in Kant's aesthetics', *British Journal of Aesthetics* 42 (2002): 1–12.

Costello, D., 'Kant and the problem of strong non-perceptual art', *British Journal of Aesthetics* 53,3 (2013): 277–298.

Crawford, D. W., *Kant's Aesthetic Theory* (Madison: University of Wisconsin Press, 1974).

Crowther, P., 'Fundamental ontology and transcendent beauty: an approach to Kant's aesthetics', *Kant-Studien* 76 (1985): 55–71.

——, 'The Claims of Perfection', *International Philosophical Quarterly* 26 (1986): 61–74.

——, *The Kantian Sublime: From Morality to Art* (Oxford: Clarendon Press, 1989).

——, *The Kantian Aesthetic: From Knowledge to the Avant-Garde* (Oxford: Clarendon Press, 2010).

DeBord, C., 'Geist and communication in Kant's theory of aesthetic ideas', *Kantian Review* 17,2 (2012): 177–190.

Deligiorgi, K. 'The pleasures of contra-purposiveness: Kant, the sublime, and being human', *The Journal of Aesthetics and Art Criticism* 72,1 (2014): 25–35.

Dobe, J. K. 'Kant's common sense and the strategy for a deduction', *Journal of Aesthetics and Art Criticism* 68 (2010): 47–60.

Dowling, C., 'Zangwill, moderate formalism and another look at Kant's aesthetic', *Kantian Review* 15,2 (2010): 90–117.

Düsing, K., 'Beauty as the transition from nature to freedom in Kant's *Critique of Judgment*', *Noûs* 24 (1990): 79–92.

Duve, T. D., *Kant after Duchamp* (Cambridge MA: MIT Press, 1996).

Fisher, J. & J. Maitland, 'The subjectivist turn in aesthetics', *Review of Metaphysics* 27 (1974): 726–751.

Fricke, C., 'Explaining the inexplicable: the hypotheses of the faculty of reflective judgment in Kant's third *Critique*', *Noûs* 24 (1990): 45–62.

Friedlander, E., *Expressions of Judgment: An Essay on Kant's Aesthetics* (Cambridge, MA: Harvard University Press, 2015).

Gammon, M., '"Parerga" and "Pulchritudo adhaerens". A reading of the third moment of the "Analytic of the Beautiful"', *Kant-Studien* 90 (1999): 148–167.

Geiger, I., 'Is teleological judgment (still) necessary?', *British Journal for the History of Philosophy* 17,3 (2009): 533–566.

——, 'Transcendental idealism in the third *Critique*', in D. Schulting & J. Verburgt (eds) (2011), pp. 71–89.

Genova, A. C., 'Kant's complex problem of reflective judgment', *Review of Metaphysics* 23,3 (1970): 452–480.

——, 'Kant's transcendental deduction of aesthetical judgments', *Journal of Aesthetics and Art Criticism* 30,4 (1972): 459–475.

Gibbons, S., *Kant's Theory of Imagination* (Oxford: Clarendon Press, 1994).

Ginsborg, H., *The Role of Taste in Kant's Theory of Cognition* (New York: Garland, 1990).

——, 'Reflective judgment and taste', *Noûs* 24,1 (1990): 63–78.

——, 'On the key to Kant's critique of taste', *Pacific Philosophical Quarterly* 72,4 (1991): 290–313.

——, 'Lawfulness without a law: Kant on the free play of imagination and understanding', *Philosophical Studies* 25 (1997): 37–81.

——, 'Kant on understanding organisms as natural purposes', in E. Watkins (ed.) (2001), p. 231–258.

——, 'Aesthetic judging and the intentionality of pleasure', *Inquiry* 46,2 (2003): 164–181.

——, 'Two kinds of mechanical inexplicability in Kant and Aristotle', *Journal of the History of Philosophy* 42 (2004): 33–65.

——, 'Aesthetic judgment and perceptual normativity', *Inquiry* 49,5 (2006): 403–437.

——, *The Normativity of Nature: Essays on Kant's Critique of Judgment* (Oxford: Oxford University Press, 2014).

Gorodeisky, K., 'A new look at Kant's view of aesthetic testimony', *British Journal of Aesthetics* 50 (2010): 53–70.

Goy, I., 'Kant's theory of biology and the argument from design', in I. Goy & E. Watkins (eds), *Kant's Theory of Biology* (Berlin/New York: de Gruyter, 2014), pp. 203–220.

Gracyk, T. A., 'Sublimity, ugliness and formlessness in Kant's aesthetic theory', *The Journal of Aesthetics and Art Criticism* 45,1 (1986): 49–56.

Guyer, P., 'Formalism and the theory of expression in Kant's aesthetics', *Kant-Studien* 68 (1977): 46–70.

——, 'Disinterestedness and desire in Kant's aesthetics', *The Journal of Aesthetics and Art Criticism* 36 (1978): 449–460.

——, *Kant and the Claims of Taste*, second edition (Cambridge: Cambridge University Press, (1997 [1979]).

——, 'Kant's distinction between the beautiful and the sublime', *Review of Metaphysics* 35 (1982): 753–783.

——, 'Autonomy and integrity in Kant's aesthetics', *The Monist* 66 (1983): 67–88.

——, 'Feeling and freedom: Kant on aesthetics and morality', *The Journal of Aesthetics and Art Criticism* 48 (1990): 137–146.

——, 'Kant's conception of fine art', *The Journal of Aesthetics and Art Criticism* 52 (1994): 275–285.

——, 'Free and adherent beauty: a modest proposal', *British Journal of Aesthetics* 42 (2002): 357–366.

——, 'Beauty, systematicity, and the highest good', *Inquiry* 46 (2003): 195–214.

——, *Values of Beauty* (Cambridge: Cambridge University Press, 2005).

——, 'Kant's ambitions in the third Critique', in P. Guyer (ed.) (2006), pp. 538–587.

——, 'The psychology of Kant's aesthetics', *Studies in History and Philosophy of Science* Part A 39,4 (2008): 483–494.

——, 'Kant's teleological conception of philosophy and its development', *Kant Yearbook* 1 (2009): 57–98.

——, 'Kant and the philosophy of architecture', *Journal of Aesthetics and Art Criticism* 69,1 (2011): 7–19.

——, 'Genius and taste: a response to Joseph Cannon', *Kantian Review* 16,1 (2011): 127–134.

Hanna, R., 'Freedom, teleology, and rational causation', *Kant Yearbook* 1 (2009): 99–142.

Henrich, D., *Aesthetic Judgment and the Moral Image of the World* (Stanford: Stanford University Press, 1992).

Hughes, F., *Kant's Aesthetic Epistemology* (Edinburgh: Edinburgh University Press, 2007).

Hund, W. B., 'The sublime and God in Kant's *Critique of Judgment*', *New Scholasticism* 57 (1983): 42–70.

John, E., 'Beauty, interest, and autonomy', *Journal of Aesthetics and Art Criticism* 70,2 (2012): 193–202.

Johnson, M. L., 'Kant's unified theory of beauty', *Journal of Aesthetics and Art Criticism* 38 (1978): 167–178.

Kemal, S., 'Aesthetic necessity, culture and epistemology', *Kant-Studien* 74 (1983): 176–205.

——, *Kant and Fine Art* (Oxford: Clarendon Press, 1986).

——, *Kant's Aesthetic Theory: An Introduction* (New York: St. Martin's Press, 1992).

Kirwan, J., *The Aesthetic in Kant* (London: Continuum, 2004).

Kolb, D., 'Kant, teleology, and evolution', *Synthese* 91 (1992): 9–28.

Kraft, M., 'Kant's theory of teleology', *International Philosophical Quarterly* 22 (1982): 42–49.

Kreines, J., 'The inexplicability of Kant's Naturzweck', *Archiv für Geschichte der Philosophie* 87,3 (2005): 270–311.

Kulenkampff, J., 'The objectivity of taste: Hume and Kant', *Noûs* 24 (1990): 93–110.

Lazaroff, A., 'The Kantian sublime: aesthetic judgment and religious feeling', *Kant-Studien* 71 (1980): 202–220.

Longuenesse, B., 'Kant's theory of judgment and judgments of taste', *Inquiry* 46,2 (2003): 143–163.

Lyotard, J. F., *Lessons on the Analytic of the Sublime* (Stanford: Stanford University Press, 1994 [1991]).

MacMillan, C., 'Kant's deduction of pure aesthetic judgments', *Kant-Studien* 76 (1985): 43–54.

Maitland, J., 'Two senses of necessity in Kant's aesthetic theory', *British Journal of Aesthetics* 16,4 (1976): 347–353.

Makkreel, R. A., 'Imagination and temporality in Kant's theory of the sublime', *Journal of Aesthetics and Art Criticism* 42 (1984): 303–315.

——, *Imagination and Interpretation in Kant* (Chicago: University of Chicago Press, 1990).

——, 'Regulative and reflective uses of purposiveness in Kant', *Southern Journal of Philosophy* 30 (supplement) (1991): 49–63.

Mallaband, P., 'Understanding Kant's distinction between free and dependent beauty', *The Philosophical Quarterly* 52 (2002): 66–81.

Matherne, S., 'The inclusive interpretation of Kant's aesthetic ideas', *British Journal of Aesthetics* 53,1 (2013): 21–39.

Matthews, P., 'Kant's sublime: a form of pure aesthetic reflective judgment', *The Journal of Aesthetics and Art Criticism* 54 (1996): 165–180.

——, *The Significance of Beauty. Kant on Feeling and the System of the Mind* (Dordrecht: Kluwer, 1997).

McCloskey, M., *Kant's Aesthetic* (Albany, NY: SUNY Press, 1987).

McFarland, J. D., *Kant's Concept of Teleology* (Edinburgh: University of Edinburgh Press, 1970).

McLaughlin, P., *Kant's Critique of Teleology in Biological Explanation* (Lewiston: Edwin Mellen Press, 1990).

———, 'Mechanical explanation in the "Critique of the teleological power of judgment"', I. Goy & E. Watkins (eds), *Kant's Theory of Biology* (Berlin/New York: de Gruyter, 2014), pp. 149–166.

Meerbote, R., 'Hughes on Kant's aesthetic epistemology', *Kant-Studien* 102,2 (2011): 202–212.

Moran, R., 'Kant, Proust, and the appeal of beauty', *Inquiry* 38,2 (2012): 298–329.

Nuzzo, A., *Kant and the Unity of Reason* (West Lafayette: Purdue University Press, 2005).

———, '*Kritik der Urteilskraft* §§76–77: Reflective judgment and the limits of transcendental philosophy', *Kant Yearbook* 1 (2009): 143–172.

Ostaric, L., 'Works of genius as sensible exhibitions of the idea of the highest good', *Kant-Studien* 101,1 (2010): 22–39.

———, 'Kant on the normativity of creative production', *Kantian Review* 17,1 (2012): 75–107.

Palmer, L., 'On the necessity of beauty', *Kant-Studien* 102,3 (2011): 350–366.

Phillips, J., 'Placing ugliness in Kant's third *Critique*: A reply to Paul Guyer', *Kant-Studien* 102,3 (2011): 385–395.

Pillow, K., *Sublime Understanding: Aesthetic Reflection in Kant and Hegel* (Cambridge MA: MIT Press, 2000).

Pippin, R. B., 'The significance of taste: Kant, aesthetic and reflective judgment', *Journal of the History of Philosophy* 34 (1996): 549–569.

Proulx, J., 'Nature, judgment and art: Kant and the problem of genius', *Kant Studies Online* (2011): 27–53.

Quarfood, M., 'The antinomy of teleological judgment', in M. Quarfood, *Transcendental Idealism and the Organism. Essays on Kant* (Stockholm: Almqvist & Wiksell, 2004), pp. 160–208.

———, 'The antinomy of teleological judgment: What it is and how it is solved', in I. Goy & E. Watkins (eds), *Kant's Theory of Biology* (Berlin/New York: de Gruyter, 2014), pp. 167–184.

Rajiva, S., 'Safely satisfying reason: The metaphysics of design in Kant's teleology', *Kant Yearbook* 1 (2009): 173–196.

Reed, A., 'The debt of disinterest: Kant's critique of music', *Modern Language Notes* 95 (1980): 563–584.

Rind, M., 'What is claimed in a Kantian judgment of taste?', *Journal of the History of Philosophy* 38,1 (2000): 63–85.

———, 'Can Kant's deduction of judgments of taste be saved?', *Archiv für Geschichte der Philosophie* 84 (2002): 20–45.

———, 'Kant's beautiful roses: a response to Cohen's "second problem"', *British Journal of Aesthetics* 43 (2003): 65–74.

Rogerson, K. F., *Kant's Aesthetics* (Lanham, MD: University Press of America, 1986).

———, 'Kant on beauty and morality', *Kant-Studien* 95,3 (2004): 338–354.

Rueger, A., 'Kant and the aesthetics of nature', *British Journal of Aesthetics* 47,2 (2007): 138–155.

———, 'The free play of the faculties and the status of natural beauty in Kant's theory of taste', *Archiv für Geschichte der Philosophie* 90,3 (2008): 298–322.

——, 'Systematicity and symbolisation in Kant's deduction of judgements of taste', *Bulletin of the Hegel Society of Great Britain* 63/64 (2011): 232–251.

Rueger, A. & S. Evren, 'The role of symbolic presentation in Kant's theory of taste', *British Journal of Aesthetics* 45 (2005): 229–247.

Rush, F., 'The harmony of the faculties', *Kant-Studien* 92 (2001): 38–61.

Savile, A., 'Objectivity in aesthetic judgment: Eva Schaper on Kant', *British Journal of Aesthetics* 21 (1981): 363–369.

——, *Kantian Aesthetics Pursued* (Edinburgh: Edinburgh University Press, 1993).

Scarre, G., 'Kant on free and dependent beauty', *British Journal of Aesthetics* 21 (1981): 351–362.

Schaper, E., 'The Kantian "as-if" and its relevance for aesthetics', *Proceedings of the Aristotelian Society* 65 (1964–5): 219–234.

——, 'Kant on imagination', *The Philosophical Forum* 2 (1971): 430–445.

——, *Studies in Kant's Aesthetics* (Edinburgh: University of Edinburgh Press, 1979).

Seide, A., 'Kant on empirical knowledge and induction in the two introductions to the *Critique of the Power of Judgment*', *Kant Yearbook* 5 (2013): 79–106.

Shapshay, S., 'Schopenhauer's transformation of the Kantian sublime', *Kantian Review* 17,3 (2012): 479–511.

Shier, D., 'Why Kant finds nothing ugly', *British Journal of Aesthetics* 38 (1988): 412–418.

Schrader, G., 'The status of teleological judgment in the critical philosophy', *Kant-Studien* 45 (1953–4): 204–235.

Sloan, P., 'Preforming the categories: Eighteenth-century generation theory and the biological roots of Kant's a priori', *Journal of the History of Philosophy* 40 (2002): 229–253.

Steigerwald, J., 'Kant's concept of natural purpose and the reflecting power of judgment', *Studies in History and Philosophy of Biology and Biomedical Sciences* 37,4 (2006): 712–734.

Sweet, K., 'Reflection: its structure and meaning in Kant's judgments of taste', *Kantian Review* 14,1 (2009): 53–80.

Teufel, T., 'Kant's sensationist conception of particularity in the Critique of the (reflecting) Power of Judgment', *Kant Studies Online* (2011): 1–51.

——, 'Kant's non-teleological conception of purposiveness', *Kant-Studien* 102,2 (2011): 232–252.

——, 'What is the problem of teleology in Kant's "Critique of the Teleological Power of Judgment"?', *SATS: Northern European Journal of Philosophy* 12,2 (2011): 198–236.

——, 'Wholes that cause their parts: Organic 'self'-reproduction and the reality of biological teleology', *Studies in History and Philosophy of Biological and Biomedical Sciences* 42,2 (2011): 252–260.

——, 'What does Kant mean by "Power of Judgment" in his *Critique of the Power of Judgment*?', *Kantian Review* 17,2 (2012): 297–326.

Thomson, G., 'Kant's problem with ugliness', *Journal of Aesthetics and Art Criticism* 50 (1992): 107–115.

Tinguely, J., 'Kantian meta-aesthetics and the neglected alternative', *British Journal of Aesthetics* 53,2 (2013): 211–235 .

Tonelli, G., 'Kant's early theory of genius', *Journal of the History of Philosophy* 4 (1966), Pt. 1: 109–132; Pt. 2: 209–224.

Tuschling, B., 'The system of transcendental idealism: questions raised and left open in the *Kritik der Urteilskraft*', *Southern Journal of Philosophy* 30 (supplement) (1992): 109–128.

Uehling, T.E., Jr., *The Notion of Form in Kant's Critique of Aesthetic Judgment* (The Hague: Mouton, 1971).

Vandenabeele, B., 'Beauty, disinterested pleasure, and universal communicability: Kant's response to Burke', *Kant-Studien* 103,2 (2012): 207–233.

Vanhaute, L., 'How biological is human history? Kant's use of biological concepts and its implications for history as moral anthropology', *Bulletin of the Hegel Society of Great Britain* 63/64 (2011): 252–268.

Verhaegh, M., 'The truth of the beautiful in the *Critique of Judgment*', *British Journal of Aesthetics* 41,4 (2001): 371–394.

Watkins, B., 'The subjective basis of Kant's judgment of taste', *Inquiry* 54,4 (2011): 315–336.

Watkins, E., 'The antinomy of teleological judgment', *Kant Yearbook* 1 (2009): 197–222.

——, 'Nature in general as a system of ends', in I. Goy & E. Watkins (eds), *Kant's Theory of Biology* (Berlin/New York: de Gruyter, 2014), pp. 117–130.

Wenzel, C., 'Kant finds nothing ugly?', *British Journal of Aesthetics* 39,4 (1999): 416–422.

——, 'Do negative judgments of taste have a priori grounds in Kant?', *Kant-Studien* 103,4 (2012): 472–493.

White, D. A., 'The metaphysics of disinterestedness: Shaftesbury and Kant', *The Journal of Aesthetics and Art Criticism* 32 (1973–4): 239–248.

——, 'On bridging the gulf between nature and morality in the *Critique of Judgment*', *The Journal of Aesthetics and Art Criticism* 38 (1979): 179–188.

Wicks, R., 'Dependent beauty as the appreciation of teleological style', *The Journal of Aesthetics and Art Criticism* 55,4 (1997): 387–400.

——, 'Kant on beautifying the human body', *British Journal of Aesthetics* 39,2 (1999): 163–178.

——, *Kant on Judgment* (London/New York: Routledge, 2007).

Wunsch, M., 'The activity of sensibility in Kant's anthropology. A developmental history of the concept of the formative faculty', *Kant Yearbook* 3 (2011): 67–90.

Zammito, J., '"This inscrutable principle of an original organization": epigenesis and 'looseness of fit' in Kant's philosophy of science', *Studies in History and Philosophy of Science* Part A 34 (2003): 73–109.

——, 'Teleology then and now: the question of Kant's relevance for contemporary controversies over function in biology', *Studies in History and Philosophy of Biological and Biomedical Sciences* 37,4 (2006): 748–770.

——, 'Kant's notion of intrinsic purposiveness in the *Critique of Judgment*: A Review Essay (and an inversion) of Zuckert's *Kant on Beauty and Biology*', *Kant Yearbook* 1 (2009): 223–247.

Zangwill, N., 'Kant on pleasure in the agreeable', *Journal of Aesthetics and Art Criticism* 53 (1995): 167–176.

Zeldin, M. B., 'Formal purposiveness and the continuity of Kant's argument in the *Critique of Judgment*', *Kant-Studien* 74 (1983): 45–55.

Zinkin, M., 'The unity of a theme: The subject of judgements of taste', *British Journal for the History of Philosophy* 14,3 (2006): 469–488.

——, 'Kant and the pleasure of "mere reflection"', *Inquiry* 55,5 (2012): 433–453.

Zuckert, R., 'Awe or envy: Herder contra Kant on the sublime', *Journal of Aesthetics and Art Criticism* 61,3 (2003): 217–232.

——, 'Boring beauty and universal morality: Kant on the ideal of beauty', *Inquiry* 48,2 (2005): 107–130.

——, *Kant on Beauty and Biology: An Interpretation of the Critique of Judgment* (Cambridge: Cambridge University Press, 2007).

——, 'History, biology, and philosophical anthropology in Kant and Herder', *International Yearbook of German Idealism* 8 (2010): 38–59.

Zumbach, C., *The Transcendent Science: Kant's Conception of Biological Methodology* (The Hague: Martinus Nijhoff, 1984).

INDEX

italics in entries indicate that these pages are devoted to analysis of the term or person in question.

421